The Economics of the Good Society

The Economics of the Good Society

The Variety of Economic Arrangements

Joseph S. Berliner

BLACKWELL *Publishers*

First published 1999

2 4 6 8 10 9 7 5 3 1

Blackwell Publishers Inc.
350 Main Street
Malden, Massachusetts 02148
USA

Blackwell Publishers Ltd
108 Cowley Road
Oxford OX4 1JF
UK

Library of Congress Cataloging-in-Publication Data

Berliner, Joseph S.
    The economics of the good society: the variety of economic
arrangements / Joseph S. Berliner.
        p.   cm.
    Includes bibliographical references and index.
    ISBN 0-631-20828-3 (hbk : alk. paper)
    ISBN 0-631-20829-1 (pbk : alk. paper)
    1. Comparative economics—Case studies.   2. Income
distribution—Case studies.   3. Welfare economics—Case studies.   I.
Title.
    HB90.B47   1999
    330—dc21
                                                98-52530
                                                CIP

British Library Cataloguing in Publication Data

A CIP catalogue record for this book is available from the British Library.

Typeset in Ehrhardt 10/11 pt
by Graphicraft Limited, Hong Kong
Printed in Great Britain by MPG Books, Bodmin, Cornwall

This book is printed on acid-free paper.

Contents

Preface

Valentin was a young Soviet economist spending a semester of study in the United States under the sponsorship of his government. He was a patriotic citizen who, I suspected, was somewhat disenchanted with his country's economic and political systems and was privately attracted by the idea of capitalism "with a human face."

One evening, when my wife and I appeared at his home for dinner, a red-faced Valentin came to the door in what was clearly great agitation. "Joseph," he blurted out before we had a chance to sit down, "how can you tolerate such a madhouse?" It turned out that he had spent the afternoon poking around Boston and had come upon a sign reading "Adult Book Shop." No Soviet intellectual could fail to be drawn into a book shop, to say nothing of an "adult" one. I regret to say that the long evening's exposition of the virtues of civil liberties and private enterprise did little to relieve his shock. He had been prepared to see evidence of unemployment, homelessness, and other economic pathologies, but he was unprepared for open, thriving pornography. His evaluation of much of what he saw in the following months was colored by that, and similar, experiences.

Valentin was in some ways a mirror image of various friends, colleagues, and students, with whom I exchange views on social issues from time to time. Like him, they are distressed by what they see as grave social iniquities, from poverty to pornography, in their own countries. Unlike him, however, they see no other country that embodies their aspirations in the way that the United States embodied Valentin's. They support efforts to improve matters through political action, sometimes with small successes but often with none. The post-mortems often trail off with the disheartened remark, "What can you expect? It's the system."

That remark is usually no more than an expression of exasperation at the incompetence or venality of the people who write the laws and run the government. I have learned, however, that behind the refrain "It's the system," there often lurks a vague vision of a different and better system that would be free of the deficiencies that bedevil the societies of the day. It is not a Utopia that these people have in mind, for they recognize that every society will contain, if not Adult Book Shops, then something else that offends. Like Valentin, however, they have an abiding interest in finding better ways to organize a society's economic life.

It is for people who like to ruminate about the economic arrangements of a Good Society that I wrote this book.

One way of imagining how one's own country would operate under a different system is to consult the experience of other countries whose economies differ in various ways from one's own. The twentieth century is singular in the wide variety of economic arrangements under which large numbers of people lived for varying periods of time. They are broadly classified as socialist or capitalist, but within each of those conventional categories there have been widely diverse forms of economic organization: Mao's China differed as greatly from Brezhnev's USSR as welfare-state Sweden differed from Thatcher's Britain. Whatever idea you may cherish about how an economy should be run in a Good Society, the chances are that somebody thought of it before and actually tried to put it into practice sometime during the century. The book invites the reader to consider which of them best embodies the values she seeks in her own vision of a better society.

Many of the economic arrangements examined in this book, both capitalist and socialist, have since been modified or abandoned, and almost all of the former Communist countries are in the process of transition to various forms of capitalism. Their history is therefore of little interest to persons absorbed by the issues of the day. To confine the quest for a Good Society to economic arrangements that happen to be in operation today, however, would be to miss out on an invaluable body of human experience.

Because the subject matter relates to economies at different periods in their history, the text shifts between past tense and present in ways that may seem puzzling. The key is that I use the past tense in discussing specifically historical events, but the present tense in discussing processes and procedures. Thus, centralized economic planning as it was conducted in the USSR is discussed in the past tense, but I use the present tense to deal with such matters as the general problems of planning and the behavior of people under a planning regime.

No one can be objective in an inquiry of this sort. I claim only to have tried. Toward that end I present various ideas that I do not endorse, but I have sought to present them in a way that would be regarded as fair by people who do endorse them. I also present my analysis of various economic arrangements as dispassionately as I can, although I am sure I have been less successful there. In the discussion sections with which many of the chapters conclude I relieve the strain of the effort at objectivity by offering my own views on the matters presented in the text. The objective is not only to share my views with the reader, but to provide an illustration of how someone with a certain set of values – in this case mine – comes out after considering the evidence. People who seek different qualities in their Good Society than I do in mine should draw different conclusions from those I offer in the discussions, but I hope they will nevertheless find the main text instructive for formulating positions that are consistent with their values.

The book is written not for economists but for people generally who like to muse about making a better world. It presumes no more knowledge of economics than that which one acquires in the process of keeping informed about public affairs. A serious engagement with the issues of the Good Society, however, requires more than that; in particular, it requires an understanding of the precise sense in which economic analysis claims to show one arrangement to be "better" than another. I have therefore undertaken to present the rudiments of relevant portions of economic theory in ways that should be intuitively accessible to the reader, using illustrative numerical examples but not the graphical and algebraic argumentation in which the academic discussion of these topics is normally conducted.

I owe a great debt to many people who read and commented on portions of the manuscript at various times. Of particular benefit to me were the comments of Paul Banner, Gertrude Schroeder Greenslade, Gregory Grossman, Nadav Halevi, Holland Hunter, Mark Kramer, Robert Morris, Gur Ofer, and George Rosen. I am grateful to Jenny Tyler for the diligence and imagination with which she shepherded me through the copy-editing process. My greatest debt by far is to my wife, Ann, whose encouragement and patience carried us both through the too-many years it took to write this book.

Joseph S. Berliner
Brandeis University, and
Davis Center for Russian Studies,
Harvard University

Lexington, Massachusetts
September 1998

Acknowledgments

The authors and publishers gratefully acknowledge the following for permission to reproduce copyright material:

Excerpt from "To Posterity" in *Selected Poems* by Bertolt Brecht, translated by H. R. Hays, © 1947 by Bertolt Brecht and H. R. Hays and renewed 1975 by Stefan S. Brecht and H. R. Hays, reprinted by permission of Harcourt Brace & Company. Reprinted by permission of H. R. Hays/Ann Elmo Agency. From the book *Selected Poems* by Bertolt Brecht © 1975 H. R. Hays.

Excerpt from *A Bowl of Bishop* by Morris Bishop. © 1954 by Morris Bishop. Used by permission of Doubleday, a division of Bantam Doubleday Dell Publishing Group, Inc.

Excerpt from "The Laws of God, The Laws of Man" in *Last Poems* by A. E. Housman. US: copyright 1922 by Holt, Rinehart & Winston. Copyright 1950 by Barclay's Bank, Ltd. Reprinted by permission of Henry Holt and Company, LLC. Outside US: reprinted by permission of The Society of Authors as the literary representatives of the Estate of A. E. Housman.

Excerpts from *Man and Superman* and from *Major Barbara* by George Bernard Shaw. Reprinted by permission of The Society of Authors, on behalf of the Bernard Shaw Estate.

The publishers apologize for any errors or omissions in the above list and would be grateful to be notified of any corrections that should be incorporated in the next edition or reprint of this book.

Part I

Introduction

Chapter 1

The Variety of Economic Experience

I, a stranger and afraid,
In a world I never made.
 — *A. E. Housman*

To produce a mighty book, you
must choose a mighty theme.
 — *Herman Melville*

CONTENTS

Throughout the ages the economic lives of working people differed little from those of their grandparents. Toward the end of the eighteenth century, that ancient pattern of generational continuity began to come to an end. In the growing number of countries touched by the Industrial Revolution, productive capacity began to grow perceptibly from year to year, and increasing numbers of working people enjoyed consumption levels well beyond those of their grandparents. In the year 1900 the average worker in the industrialized countries produced more than twice as much as the average worker in 1800.[1]

The economic system under which that unprecedented explosion in productive capability occurred became known as capitalism. No one appreciated that historic contribution of capitalism more than its most bitter critic, Karl Marx. "The bourgeoisie," he wrote in the *Communist Manifesto*, "during its rule of scarce one hundred years, has created more massive and more colossal productive forces than have all preceding generations together."[2]

It is the rare revolution that has no victims, however, and the Industrial Revolution produced its share. While growing numbers of people lived better than their grandparents, many did not, particularly tenant farmers, hand-weavers, and others whose traditional sources of livelihood vanished under the force of the competition from dynamic new industries. As the nineteenth century progressed, the poverty, the inhumane conditions of factory labor, the inequality, and the cycles of depression that accompanied industrial expansion pressed on the conscience of more and more people.

Not everyone. In all societies there are people whose horizons are bounded by their own private concerns. They are to be found not only among the wealthy but among the under-privileged as well; to both, poverty is a personal fate to be avoided, not a social condition to be combatted. Their purpose is to get the most for themselves out of a world they never made and for which they bear no responsibility. That way of coping enabled many people to manage their lives through the tumultuous century.

Growing numbers, however, could not walk away from the misery they saw around them and felt obliged to confront it. People of all classes, including the most privileged, responded to the coexistence of Progress and Poverty – the title of Henry George's influential book – in very different ways, which persist to this day, though sometimes with different names. Each had its own vision of what Walter Lippman called the Good Society.

The center was occupied by people who might be called reformers. They were a diverse group, motivated by religion, morality, and in the case of some who bore titles of rank, *noblesse oblige*. They included some members of the upper classes, sometimes from titled families, who were critical of the vulgar new industrialists who ground the faces of the poor, and some gave large contributions of their own wealth to such public purposes as charity, free educa-tion, libraries, and hospitals. Most, however, were members of the rising professional and middle classes who were genuinely concerned about poverty, unemployment, child labor, and factory working conditions. The former would now be called conservatives and the lat-ter liberals (in the United States; in Europe they would be called social democrats). They saw in the new capitalism the potential for a large improvement in the material conditions of mankind, but they believed that government should serve as an instrument of reform in "the amelioration of the condition of the people,"[3] although the conservatives were more reluct-ant than the liberals to invoke the power of government. Seen from the trenches of politics in the capitalist countries today, conservatives and liberals seem to be poles apart, but on a broader spectrum of visions of the Good Society they constitute the reformist center.

Among the earliest successes of the reform movement were the British Factory Acts, which required factory owners to maintain certain minimally humane working conditions. A his-toric step in the same direction was the introduction of a broad program of social insurance for working people and others, pioneered by the great German chancellor Bismarck, who in most respects was a thoroughgoing conservative. As the century progressed, the reform move-ment succeeded in legislating such actions as a limit on the length of the workweek, regu-lations on the use of female and child labor, and restrictions on the oppressive use of monopoly power.

To the left of the center stood the socialists. In their view, the social ills of the time were so deeply rooted in the capitalist system that they could never be eliminated by reformist measures as long as that system prevailed. Socialists like Karl Marx gave the devil his due and credited capitalism with having been a historically necessary condition for starting the process of industrialization that in the long run would eliminate poverty. His quarrel with capitalism was that it had outlived its productive period; it was no longer a progressive force in history but had become a fetter on the productive capability of society. Other socialists were less forgiving of capitalism, and charged it with having done little more than despoil the land and bring misery upon the people. All socialists agreed, however, that the task was not to ameliorate the evils of capitalism but to replace it by a different economic system that would not generate those evils in the first place. All agreed also that the source of those evils lay in the institution of private property, and that only a society based on social ownership of the productive property could reap the benefits of industrialization without suffering the capitalist costs. It was above all the hostility to private property and the commitment to social ownership that characterized people who thought of themselves as socialists.

To the right of the reformist center and the socialists stood people who resisted virtually all governmental interference in the economy. They would now be called libertarians. In their view, unfettered markets were the sole path to the economic betterment of all mankind, including the poor, in the long run, and unrestricted property rights were the sole guarantee of individual personal liberty. In the modern version of that stance, when government intrudes into economic affairs it is not the underprivileged who benefit most but the middle and upper classes who are best able to turn government power to their own advantage.

As the twentieth century dawned, however, both the reformist and socialist movements had become increasingly effective political forces. The outcome was an unprecedented diversity in the ways in which societies around the world managed their economic affairs. The most dramatic event was the Russian Revolution in 1917 where one group of socialists, Lenin's Bolshevik faction of the Communist Party, seized power and introduced the world's first large socialist economy. By mid-century that system had expanded to encompass much of the world's population. The contest between two missionary economic systems – socialism and capitalism – became the century's dominating fact of political life.

Less dramatic but no less consequential was the progress of reform within the capitalist world. Greatly spurred by the Great Depression of the 1930s, the voting public in the capitalist democracies directed their governments to assume ever larger powers of control over economic life. Unemployment insurance, income maintenance for the elderly and others in need, bank deposit insurance, minimum-wage laws, protection of labor unions, and other programs of the sort expanded greatly. By the century's end the reform movement had engineered a radical transformation of capitalism from its nineteenth-century laissez-faire ideal.

The introduction of socialism and the reform of capitalism were the main contributors to the enormous diversity of the forms of economic organization that prevailed during the twentieth century. The diversity was greatly multiplied, however, by the vast differences in economic organization within each of the two great systems.

I Varieties of Socialism

The form of socialism that the Bolsheviks established in the Soviet Union was later imposed on those countries of Eastern Europe where the Soviet army remained in force after World War II. Its central features were state ownership of the country's factories and other productive property, and the central planning of economic activity. In the course of time each of those countries developed its own variant of the Soviet system. The first radical departure from the Soviet model was introduced by Yugoslavia after the country freed itself from Soviet domination in 1948. Yugoslavia rejected the Soviet principles of state ownership and central planning, which they came to see as the source of the concentrated state power that had turned Soviet socialism into political tyranny. The principle of "worker self-management" replaced the Soviet form of state ownership and management; and instead of central planning, the enterprises bought from and sold to each other under market-like arrangements. Hungary moved in a similar direction after recovering from the suppression of its 1956 revolution, replacing centralized planning by market-like arrangements. The two countries provide the principal empirical experience for judging how a socialist economy would fare if it forgoes Soviet-type central planning in favor of markets.

The most massive expansion of socialism occurred in 1949, however, when the victory of the Chinese Communists brought the world's most populous country into the socialist fold. The Chinese flirted briefly with the Soviet type of economy, but soon became critical of what they saw as the consumerism, individualism, and inequality into which that system had degenerated. With the "Great Leap Forward" in 1957, Party Chairman Mao Zedong launched a new form of socialism in which labor would be motivated by service to the people rather than by the payment of higher wages to more productive workers. Maoist socialism swept the socialist world and inspired revolutionaries in many countries, most notably Fidel Castro and Che Guevara in Cuba.

Most of the socialist economic life of the century unfolded in countries under the domination of political organizations that called themselves variously Communist or Marxist-Leninist. I shall use the term "socialist" to refer generally to societies in which the productive property is socially owned, and the term "Communist" to refer specifically to those socialist societies governed by Communist parties of the Soviet type. There were other non-Communist forms of socialism, however, that developed within democratic countries alongside capitalist economic arrangements. One such form was the Israeli kibbutz, which was committed to communal socialism of an intensely egalitarian and democratic kind. There were also a variety of worker-owned cooperatives, the most prominent of which are the Mondragon cooperatives that flourish in the Basque region of Spain. The numbers of people working in these forms of "micro-socialism" are relatively small, but those organizational forms are an invaluable supplement to the limited human experience with socialism under democratic conditions.

FROM VISIONS TO REALITY

The variety of twentieth-century economic experience provides an opportunity to confront the issues of the Good Society in a way that has not been feasible earlier. In the nineteenth century only reformers and libertarians could debate the issues in terms that related to the real world: whether, for example, the limitation of the workday to ten hours would improve or worsen the condition of the laboring class. Socialists, however, could express their own vision of the Good Society only by inviting the imagination to consider a world that did not exist: how an economy would operate if it were based on cooperation rather than competition. The absence of actual cases of socialism frustrated both critics and supporters of socialism – critics, because the glaring imperfections of capitalism-in-practice were often juxtaposed against the idealized outcomes of socialism-in-theory, supporters, because they constantly faced the irritating and unanswerable charge that "it wouldn't work."

The Russian Revolution evened the terms of the debate. The socialist version of the Good Society needed no longer to be thought of as a Utopian "republic in the clouds." The experience of the various socialist countries makes it possible to study how people actually do behave under the two different sets of economic and social arrangements. The objective of this book is to mine the variety of economic experience of the twentieth century for what it has to teach about the relative merits of the two grand visions of the Good Society and their various real-world variations.

2 Varieties of Capitalism

The capitalist countries also developed diverse forms of economic organization, reflecting, among other things, differences in historical and cultural traditions. Sweden and the other Nordic "welfare states" are distinctive in the degree of income equality that they have achieved and in the extent of social provision for the underprivileged and for the citizenry generally. For that reason they are often thought of as "socialist." The most common, and most useful, definition of a socialist economy, however, is one in which the productive property is socially owned; and except for some of the social services, Swedish production is carried out overwhelmingly in private enterprises operating in a market economy.[4] In material production, for example, only 6 percent of the Swedish labor force worked in government-owned enterprises in 1960, even less than in West Germany (7 percent), which is normally the model of conservative capitalism.[5] Sweden thus expresses its concern for social welfare by redistributing the income earned in the predominantly private-enterprise economy, rather than seeking to produce that income in state-owned enterprises.

A rather different variety of capitalism has evolved in Germany. Over a century ago the country pioneered in the establishment of a national health program that is government financed but operated by private hospitals and physicians. Industrial relations are based on extensive cooperation between employers and workers, and the law mandates that workers have representation on corporate boards of directors. The German form of capitalism, much of which has been adopted by Austria and Switzerland, is sufficiently distinctive that it is sometimes designated by the special name of "social-market" capitalism.

If one were interested in the experience of state-owned enterprises in a capitalist country, one would look not to Sweden but to postwar Great Britain, where the Labour government conducted an extensive nationalization program, reflecting the traditions of British Fabian socialism; but even there as late as 1975 only 8 percent of the labor force was working in state-owned enterprises.[6] Like Sweden, British enterprise at the time was predominantly private, the concern for social welfare being expressed primarily in the redistribution of income among the population.

The role that government can play in a market economy can be studied in the experience of France, which introduced a form of national economic planning designed for use in a capitalist economy. Based on the voluntary cooperation of privately owned enterprises, it was called "indicative" planning to distinguish it from Soviet-type planning under which the government issues mandatory directives to its enterprises. In Japan and the other countries of the Pacific Rim, governments have also been deeply involved in directing the economy and in the investment and production decisions of the enterprises. At the other end of that spectrum, Great Britain under Margaret Thatcher and the United States under Ronald Reagan went as far as any recent society has managed to go in shrinking the role of government in economic affairs.

There is a particularly wide range of experience in dealing with unemployment. Sweden has maintained a high level of employment by fairly conservative methods: they have developed a notable program over the years that combines job retraining with relocation grants, to enable unemployed workers to take up jobs in other parts of the country. Japan has attracted particular attention because of the practice of providing a lifetime-employment guarantee to workers in its large corporations, as well as the apparent relative equality in its income distribution. Great Britain was long the sole holdout against introducing a minimum wage, but the present Labour government has announced its intention to propose such a law.[7]

3   Retreat from Diversity

The diversity of forms of economic organization peaked around mid-century, after which it began to narrow. In 1970 Fidel Castro declared to the Cuban people that the country's economic performance had been a failure, and offered to resign as Chairman of the Communist Party.[8] He didn't in fact resign, but soon afterward the Cuban economy abandoned most of its Maoist arrangements and turned to the orthodox planning system of the USSR. Following the death of Mao Zedong in 1976, the Chinese peasantry, without prior government authorization, spontaneously abandoned the communal organizational arrangements that had been imposed upon them and returned to their traditional form of individual household farming. The dramatic increase in output that ensued impelled the government to sanction the radical economic transformation that is continuing to this day. Markets have replaced economic planning as the fundamental arrangement for coordinating economic life, and the state-owned enterprises of the Communist past are declining in importance as non-state enterprises of various kinds, including strictly privately owned enterprises, increasingly dominate the economy.

The most dramatic events, however, occurred a decade later, with the ascent of Mikhail Gorbachev to the post of General Secretary of the Soviet Communist Party. Gorbachev launched an initially modest program of economic and political reform that rapidly burst out of control and led to the collapse of the Soviet Union as a state and the widespread abandonment of socialism in Europe. Toward the century's end only North Korea and Cuba continued to cling to their Soviet-style socialism. Throughout the whole period of the Israeli kibbutz many of the communal and egalitarian features of the kibbutz gradually eroded. The socialist alternative had shrunk to the smallest of niches among the forms of economic organization still in existence.

The diversity of forms of liberal capitalism also contracted from its mid-century peak. As the postwar recovery proceeded, in Sweden and other countries that had pushed furthest in the development of the welfare state the voters elected governments committed to scaling back the most expansive social policies of the past. Prominent among the motives was the high level of taxation required to finance their extensive social programs. The positive response of American and British voters to the conservative appeal of Ronald Reagan and Margaret Thatcher precipitated a movement to greatly scale back the role of government in those countries. On the other side of the world, as the Japanese economy matured and its growth rate decelerated, industry's capacity to maintain its commitment to lifetime employment began to weaken.

Both reformers and democratic socialists have reason to regard themselves as vindicated by the rejection of Communism in virtually all the lands that had practiced it. However, while the scaling back of the welfare state is a retreat for the reformers, it is not entirely a victory for libertarian conservatives. It demonstrated that there are limits to the extent of the social programs that capitalism can sustain, which liberal reformers had been reluctant to concede in the past. While the social programs have been scaled back, however, the welfare state has by no means been dismantled and is likely to endure for a long time on a reduced scale. On the other hand, no capitalist country has responded to the call for a laissez-faire economy in which the role of government is reduced to the minimum – not even Thatcher's Britain or Reagan's America. The conservative center is still repelled by the "tooth-and-claw free-marketeer" and the libertarian "indifference to social responsibility," and while it still rejects government meddling in the details of economic life, it holds that the state must provide "everybody with protection in the face of life's costs and disasters."[9] The capitalism of the future is therefore likely to operate too few government social programs to satisfy the reformers but too many to satisfy the libertarians.

The consequence of these developments in both the socialist and capitalist worlds is that by the century's end the range of forms of economic organization has greatly diminished. Socialism has all but vanished as a living economic system, and virtually all capitalist countries have converged upon the program of the more conservative reformers. The twentieth century therefore passes into history as a treasure trove of the human experience in the search for better ways of managing economic affairs. The story of this remarkable century's search for the best way to organize a society's economic life is one of the mighty themes of modern history.

HEROIC AGES

Many of the economic arrangements of the twentieth century enjoyed, during their early years, what their champions saw as a Heroic Age. In those years the new arrangements operated in their purest form and the enthusiasm of their proponents was at its peak. That was the case in such societies as Mao's China during the Cultural Revolution, Sweden in mid-century, the kibbutz in the early years of the State of Israel, Japan in the 1960s, and Yugoslavia after the break with Stalin. In these and other cases, for various reasons the arrangements celebrated during that period of high idealism as the wave of a golden future were eventually modified; and in some cases, like Maoist China, they were totally abandoned by new political leaders who regarded the whole thing as having been a tragic mistake.

It might seem that there is little to be gained by revisiting the mistakes of the past. However, the understanding of all complex systems – biological, technological, and social – advances not only by the experience of things that work well but also by things that do not. For the politically engaged, why and in what respects an arrangement may be said not to have worked is a matter of great importance. For one thing, what may have worked badly in some societies in the past may yet work well in a different society in the future. Moreover, an attractive arrangement that worked poorly at one time may be redesigned to eliminate some of the deficiencies, so that it may work better in the future. For example, had Soviet scientists and engineers been as free as the Japanese to travel among the world's best laboratories and factories, the gap between the technological attainment of the two countries would surely have been much smaller. If a future socialist society, mindful of that fact, accords its citizens the freedom to travel available in a democratic society, its would not suffer from that particular deficiency in Soviet technological performance.

Hence the Heroic Age of the various economic experiments is the primary subject matter of this book. It is the analysis of the successes, the deficiencies, and the eventual modification or abandonment of their institutional arrangements that has the most to contribute to those who muse about making a better world.

4 A Future for Diversity?

History often moves in cycles on these matters, and it is unlikely that the world has seen the last of the arrangements that are now on the wane. The Japanese type of permanent employment reflects a deep longing for job security that crosses cultural lines, and if their effort to provide it should be attenuated or abandoned, it may well pop up in a different form in some other economy some day. There are times when the welfare-state vision of the Good Society wins the day, and others when a more libertarian version of the Good Society seizes the electorate.

For the citizens of the future will be no less concerned than those of the past about the deficiencies of the economies of their time. They will confront a different social, technological, and resource environment, which will generate different problems; but every generation reevaluates its institutions in terms of its own values, and there will always be people who are dissatisfied with their economy and seek a better set of economic arrangements. Even today, many of the sources of dissatisfaction are similar to those that drove the protest movements of the nineteenth century. To be sure, economic conditions in the industrialized countries are vastly improved. Nothing in the modern factory, for example, calls to mind the conditions described two hundred years ago by the British factory inspectors. Yet the protesters of the present generation view the conditions of labor in rural poultry-processing plants and on insecticide-soaked farmland with no less horror than their forebears viewed the Dickensian factory.

People of social conscience will therefore no doubt divide in much the same ways as those of an earlier time – libertarians, reformers, and – perhaps – socialists.

I say "perhaps" because strong doubts have been raised about whether socialism has any future at all. A great deal of attention was attracted by Francis Fukuyama's declaration that the collapse of Communism marked the "end of history."[10] In his view, the great debate between socialism and capitalism that dominated the history of the last two centuries has been decisively resolved in favor of capitalism, implying that the socialist ideal will never in the future command the loyalty of more than a few scattered souls. If that is so, then the socialist wing of the museum of economic history will have no more than antiquarian value. Few will visit it for enlightenment on ways of organizing a future socialist economy.

The social forces that drove the protest movements in past centuries have not been expunged, however, and may well experience a resurgence in the future. As long as such conditions as unemployment, poverty, inequality, and environmental degradation persist, the impulses that motivated the nineteenth-century reformers and socialists will resonate in their twenty-first-century descendants.

I believe the evidence is now clear that the socialist spark is far from extinguished. The Communist world has been a trap for forecasters. No one expected it to collapse when it did, or as suddenly as it did. And after the collapse no one would have anticipated that less than a decade after a Moscow crowd cheered the removal of a statue of the man who founded the Soviet secret police, a democratically elected parliament would vote to reinstall it.[11] Nor would many have guessed that two decades after the repudiation of Maoist communism, there would still be a thriving Chinese village where all the farms and factories were be collectively owned and where all families received the necessities of life free, including identical housing, TV sets, flour, a daily bottle of beer per person, and busts of Chairman Mao.[12] The nostalgia for the past that pervades much of the post-Communist world, particularly among older and poorer groups, no doubt reflects to a large degree the severe growing pains of a tumultuous young capitalism, but it also reveals the powerful appeal that some features of the old system hold for many people – such as freedom from the fear of unemployment, and relative social and economic equality. The power of that appeal will wax and wane with the success of the new capitalism, but it will always be there, ready to be marshalled in support of socialism.

Socialism has taken a beating in the capitalist world as well. Democratic socialists, for example, have always been militantly anti-Communist and regard themselves as vindicated rather than defeated by the collapse of Communism. But they have nevertheless been affected by the massive rejection of Communist-imposed socialism by the people who lived under it, and their major political organizations have moved a long way from the traditional socialist program. In particular, the German socialists earlier and the British Labour socialists recently have abandoned that most fundamental of socialist institutions – general social ownership of productive property. They maintain their commitment to advancing social and economic equality, but that hardly distinguishes them from liberal reformers. In my view, they have resigned from the socialist family, although sentiment obliges them to retain the family name.

However, there are still certain democratic socialist movements committed to social ownership, some of which – like worker ownership – appear to be growing. The notion of "market socialism" – an economy of socially owned enterprises that operates on the basis of market relations rather than central planning – retains a small but devoted following.[13] And while Communist parties are comatose in most of the capitalist world, they are far from dead. In Italy, a decade after the fall of the USSR, a former Communist leader was called upon to form a government for the first time in history.

Therefore, to see the present-day retreat from socialism as the end of the story reveals a truncated sense of history. The socialist dream is of such long standing that it is unlikely to disappear merely because the twentieth century botched the job. It should come as no great surprise if some societies restore it some day in one form or another, either in the former socialist countries or elsewhere. In my view, that would be a mistake, for reasons that will become clear in this book. However, any society that turns to it once again would do well to visit the twentieth-century socialist wing of the museum of economic history, in order to understand why it was so decisively rejected by the people who lived under it, and perhaps to design better ways of building a socialist economy than those that followed Russia's revolution.

Notes

1 Per capita GNP in the United Kingdom in 1900 is estimated to have been 2.2 times that of 1830 at constant 1900 prices. Mitchell, *European Historical Statistics*, pp. 24, 782, 797.
2 Marx, "Communist manifesto," p. 12.
3 Benjamin Disraeli, quoted by Sir Charles Petri in the *Encyclopedia Britannica* article on conservatism.
4 Some democratic socialists would like to deny the term "socialism" to authoritarian societies like those dominated by Leninist Communist parties. I find it more useful to confine the term to social ownership of capital because that makes it possible to distinguish democratic from authoritarian forms of socialism. By this definition, Sweden is best thought of not as a socialist society but as a democratic capitalist society in which the people have voted for extensive programs of social welfare and income distribution.
5 Pryor, *Property and Industrial Organization in Communist and Capitalist Nations*, pp. 14–15.
6 Redwood, *Public Enterprise in Crisis*, p. 17.
7 *The New York Times*, June 19, 1998, p. A16.
8 Quirk, *Fidel Castro*, p. 644.
9 *The Economist*, March 21, 1992, p. 98. Review of David Willetts, *Modern Conservatism*.
10 Fukuyama, *The End of History*.
11 *The Washington Post*, December 13, 1998, p. C7.
12 *The New York Times*, January 7, 1999, p. A1.
13 Bardhan and Roemer (eds), *Market Socialism*. In *A Future for Socialism* John Roemer asserts that socialists have made a "fetish of public ownership" (p. 20). In his pragmatic view, the socialist goal should be equality, and any form of ownership that advances that goal, including private ownership, should be acceptable in a market-socialist society.

Chapter 2

Economics and the Good Society

Even the hatred of squalor
Makes the brow grow stern.
Even the anger against injustice
Makes the voice grow harsh. Alas, we
Who wished to lay the foundations of kindness
Could not ourselves be kind.
— Bertolt Brecht

Concerning this point, the
dialectical theologians committed a
great, repulsive error. . . . They thought,
or made people fancy, that everything
that can be imagined is possible.
— Maimonides

CONTENTS

This book is not about the Good Society as a whole but only about one important component of it – the organization of its economic activity. It does not deal with the many other vital institutions through which a society's activities are conducted – such as those of government and politics, of the law, of the family, of the arts, and of religion. Hence, though I often use the expression "Good Society" as shorthand, it should be understood to refer only to the society's economic institutions.

There are two reasons for emphasizing the obvious point that there is more to a society than its economy. The first is that it may not be the most important part. A well-functioning economy surely contributes substantially to the quality of social life, but its contribution cannot be said to be larger than that of other institutions – most notably, the family. If one had to choose between a society with a well-functioning economy but with family life in disarray, and another society with that order reversed, other things being equal I would be inclined to choose the latter.

A society is like a mansion consisting of many parts. Its quality depends on the beauty of its design and the scale of its rooms, but it also depends on its plumbing. Economics is the plumbing of society's mansion: it is not the part one shows off to the guests and its contribution is often unappreciated – until the sewer backs up. The human purpose of a well-functioning economy is to enable the more important things in life to be carried on.

The second reason for stressing the status of the economy as one component of a larger society is that the performance of each social institution affects and is affected by the performance of the others. For example, many people are concerned with economic organization not only because it affects economic welfare but also because it affects the political life of the society. That point of view unites people with otherwise conflicting views about how an economy should be organized. Some hold that only an economy based on private property can maintain political freedom.[1] Others hold that only social ownership of property can "extend traditional freedoms to all its citizens."[2] These radically different views are in full agreement, however, that in assessing the goodness of an economy one should be concerned not only with its purely economic performance but also with the political consequences of opting for one or another kind of economic system. Yet another ominous concern is that the economic system in which we live may, over time, influence the very people we are, the values that we hold, and the quality of the community in which we live. A lot more than economic matters therefore rides on the kind of economic system to which a person becomes committed or which a society adopts.

No one should commit themselves to an economic system without first exploring its influence on the other departments of social life. Some of those influences are noted below, but a full exploration is beyond the scope of this book.

1   The Good and the Ideal

The idea of a Good Society must be distinguished from that of an Ideal Society. The latter has been the preoccupation of many social critics and philosophers throughout the ages. Since the time of Karl Marx, however, the term "Utopian" has acquired a pejorative meaning.[3] The design of ideal societies continues to serve as a useful exercise, but it can be the cause of great social mischief when the line between reality and illusion is blurred. It can become the father of disillusionment, which can turn charity into bitterness. "We who wished to lay the foundations of kindness could not ourselves be kind," wrote a saddened Bertolt Brecht.

To avoid disillusionment one should take care to eschew illusion. There are two ways in which one can pursue the study of the economy of Good Society without wandering off into illusionary speculation – the empirical way, and the theoretical way.

THE TEST OF PRACTICE

Before the Russian Revolution, socialism was the future tense, while capitalism was the present tense. After 1917 that asymmetry disappeared. There is now a large body of experience on how socialism has actually worked out in practice, in a variety of forms and in different countries. It is now possible to evaluate the socialist vision of the Good Society in the same way that the capitalist vision has always been evaluated – by examining things as they are rather than things as they might be.

The great variety of both capitalist and socialist economic arrangements that developed in the twentieth century, as described in the Preface, provides the empirical material upon which this book draws. If you have a favorite idea on how the economy of your Good Society should be run, the chances are that someone has thought of it before and that it, or a close relative, has actually been used at some time in some country in the last century.

That does not mean that ideas that may not have worked out well should be automatically rejected, for they might work better in different times and circumstances. Nor does it mean that all ideas yet untried are Utopian. Confronting the reality of how all sorts of economic arrangements have worked out in practice, however, offers some protection against the "repulsive error" of fancying that everything that can be imagined is possible.

THE USES OF THEORY

The second line of defense against Utopian extravagance is by application of the economic theory by means of which scholars have sought to understand the behavior of modern economic systems. An economic system is exceeding complex, and the performance of the total system depends on the intricate relationships among the parts. The function of theory – any theory – is to try to explain those relationships. It is theory that enables an analyst to predict the outcomes that may be expected from the use of a particular arrangement – such as the free distribution of bread, or worker ownership of production enterprises. It also helps to identify the conditions that must be present in order to achieve certain desired outcomes, such as full employment or wage equality. Not "everything that can be imagined is possible," but many things are, and theory is an invaluable aid in distinguishing the possible from the impossible. Hence many of the arrangements examined in this book are put through the mill of theoretical analysis.

The elements of economic theory employed here may be found, more elaborately developed, in any standard introductory textbook in economics. The branch of it that I have found most useful in illuminating the issues of the Good Society is called "welfare economics,"[4] but I also draw on other strands of contemporary economic theory that shed light on the nature of economic institutions.

A century ago it was widely thought that the dominant body of modern economic theory applied only to capitalist economic institutions.[5] That view was shattered by the pioneering work of Enrico Barone that opened a new branch of modern economics that came to be known as "socialist economics."[6] There is now an abundant literature applying modern economic analysis to a variety of socialist institutions such as central planning mechanisms and cooperative production enterprises. It constitutes a rich body of theory on which the economics of the Good Society can draw.

Much of it is the same theory that has been taught in recent years in advanced courses in such socialist countries as China and the former USSR. That has not always been the case. A few decades ago that body of "bourgeois" theory – as it was called in socialist circles – was held to be ideologically distorted as it applies to capitalist economies, and irrelevant for socialist economies. Only Marxian theory was studied and employed in analysis and in practice. In the later years of the socialist countries, however, the importance of modern economic theory for their own economies was generally acknowledged by informed economists and by many of their political leaders as well. To be sure, Marxian economics continued to be taught, but it lost the monopoly over economic thought that it had earlier enjoyed.

2   Structure and Policy

If a car performs badly – say it consumes too much gas – there may be something wrong with the car, or there may be something wrong with the driver. An economy may perform badly for the same two reasons: there may be something wrong with its institutional arrangements, or it may be badly run. In the first case, the problem is said to be lodged in the structure of the economy. In the second case, it is said to be a matter of bad economic policy.

Policies may be thought of as the ways of carrying out the purpose of a certain institutional arrangement. At the most general level, one economy may adopt central planning for coordinating economic activity, while another may adopt markets. Each arrangement, however, can be implemented in various ways. When markets are the coordinating arrangement, market prices can be entirely free, or some of them can be controlled by the government. Whether to employ free or controlled prices is a policy decision, relative to markets as the structure. Further down the line, if the decision is for partial price controls, that too can be implemented in various ways: which prices to control and what the controlled prices should be are then policy decisions relative to price-controlled markets as the structure.

Policy is the stuff of the day-to-day political economy of a society. It may take the form of microeconomic policy designed to influence the behavior of individual units of economic activity – whether to legislate a minimum wage in labor markets, for example, or whether to permit state-owned enterprises to retain some of their profit. Or it may take the form of macroeconomic policy designed to influence overall activity – like raising the interest rate in order to reduce the upward pressure on prices by slowing the rate of overall economic growth.

Specific policies like these are relatively easy to change if they are found to be unsatisfactory. Economic structure at any level, on the other hand, is more difficult to change, and changes in fundamental institutional arrangements – private or social ownership, for example – are tantamount to revolutions. Hence they rarely come to the fore in public debate or occupy the nightly news.

Since the performance of an economy depends on both its structure and its policies, both should occupy a place in the economics of the Good Society. Since each structural arrangement – central planning or markets, for example – generates its own set of policy issues, the number of such issues that would have to be analyzed would be very large. The economics of the Good Society as laid out in this book is therefore primarily about structure and only incidentally about policy. Policy issues are introduced only selectively, notably, when badly designed policies might cause the economic arrangement to be at fault. For example, it was Soviet policy to set the price of bread and other food products at very low subsidized prices. Bread was so cheap that collective farmers bought up large quantities of it to feed their pigs, which earned them a considerable supplementary income. That ludicrous state of affairs is sometimes interpreted as evidence of the deficiency of the central planning arrangement. Central planning would have worked perfectly well in this case, however, had the government adopted a more sensible pricing policy. Similar stories can be told about the market arrangements that work out badly because of the policies that are applied.

Disputes about policy are family quarrels: the partisans accept the basic economic arrangements of their society but differ on the best way to run them. Disputes about structure are quarrels between families: they are about which is the better family, regardless of how well each one is run. This book is about structure: it deals with issues of microeconomic and macroeconomic policy only insofar as they shed light on the performance of the economy's basic structural arrangements.

3 Institutions and Economic Systems

The economics of the Good Society draws upon the experience of many countries, but it is not about countries or about their economies. It is about economic *systems*.

An economy is a social network of persons and organizations that participate in the production and distribution of goods and services. That is the meaning of the term in such statements as "The British economy is more vigorous than it was a decade ago," or "The Chinese economy produced a record output of rice last year."

The term "economic system" refers to the set of institutions, rules, and practices – which I call institutional arrangements – under which an economy operates.[7] That is the sense in which one might say that Russia has adopted a new economic system, or that the American economic system is based on private enterprise. It is also the sense in which different countries may be said to operate with the same type of economic system.

HISTORY AND CULTURE

To assert that two economies as different as the Swedish and the Japanese employ the same economic system is to imply that they are similar in certain significant ways. The elements of similarity – for example, the predominance of private ownership of the productive property – are significant because they help explain some features of how both economies work.

They do not explain everything, however. The socialist economic system worked out differently in the Soviet Union than in East Germany or North Korea, and the capitalist system produces different results in the United States than in Japan or Sweden. Among the reasons for the differences in performance are differences in policy: one capitalist society may vote higher taxes than another in order to redistribute more of the income of the rich to the poor. Same system, but different policies, and therefore different outcomes.

Apart from policies, the performance of an economic system also depends on the historical and cultural traditions of the society in which it is embedded. Capitalism in the United States that celebrates its spirit of individualism operates differently from capitalism in Japan where people are most comfortable working on the basis of consensus, and the orderly East Germans produced a very different socialism from that of the Russians, with their "love of anarchy and their terror of chaos."[8] Yet history and culture do not fully dictate economic destiny. North and South Korea share a common history and culture, yet their economic performance is radically different, much like the difference between East and West Germany, and mainland China and Hong Kong. It was the economic system that accounts for most of the difference in their economic performance.

There is no analytic perspective so powerful as to explain the full range of a society's economic performance. Each can at best illuminate some of its features. This book investigates those features that can be accounted for by the economic system that the society employs. The influence of historical and cultural circumstances will be introduced from time to time when they help to explain variations in outcomes under similar economic arrangements.

The central question of this book is how best to organize the economy of a society that has already achieved a relatively high level of income or is in the process of achieving it. It does not directly address the question of how a poor country can transform itself into a modern high-income country – surely one of the most pressing questions in the economics of the Good Society. The reason for that exclusion is that their historical and cultural circumstances, as well as their economic conditions, are so different from those of the developed world that they could not be addressed within the scope of this book. I trust, however, that thoughtful citizens in the poor countries would find it rewarding to consider the kind of economy they would like someday to live in, as a prelude to thinking about how to get there.

THE CORE OF THE ECONOMY

"Consumption is the sole end and purpose of production," wrote Adam Smith. In the spirit of that perspective, the core of every economic system may be envisioned as a vast and ever-changing reservoir of consumer goods – I shall use the term "goods" hereafter to include both goods and services. Goods flow continuously into the reservoir from the enterprises that produce them with the physical capital and human labor at their disposal. And goods flow continuously out of the reservoir into the households that supply the labor for their production.

The flows of goods into and out of that metaphorical reservoir are organized by the institutional arrangements that constitute the economic system. The full set of arrangements that affect the reservoir is extremely large and a general introduction to the operation of a modern economy requires some attention to all of them – hence the massiveness of introductory economics textbooks. However, a small number of those arrangements generate most of the issues that are of primary importance to people concerned specifically with the best way to organize an economic system. The four sets of arrangements that I have selected for examination constitute the principal subject matter of this book.

First, the consumer goods that flow out of the reservoir end up being distributed somehow among the citizens; the arrangements for determining who should get what goods are the subject of Part II. Second, the citizens-as-workers must somehow be allocated among the jobs in the enterprises that produce those goods; the arrangements for determining who gets what jobs are the subject of Part III. Third, keeping the goods flowing into the reservoir requires an enormous amount of coordination among the activities of vast numbers of diverse enterprises, and of millions of consumers and workers. The arrangements for coordinating the activities of an entire economic system are the subject of Part IV. Finally, someone has to own the capital – the machines and equipment – with which the labor force works in the enterprises. The various private and social ownership arrangements are the subject of Part V.

Those four sets of arrangements constitute what may be regarded as the core of an economic system. In confining itself to that core, this book is unable to deal with a variety of other functions to which a full economy must attend. For example, most countries' reservoir of goods is supplemented by an inflow of consumer goods imported from other countries. How a country should manage its international economic relations – and indeed whether it should participate in such transactions at all – is a question that must be asked about a Good Society. Another question, of very ancient vintage, is what kinds of taxes should be levied to raise the revenues and acquire the goods required for the conduct of the government, and who should pay how much of the tax. Yet another is the arrangements for generating economic growth, for the citizens of all modern economies regard growth as an important criterion of goodness.

The issues involved in those matters, however, are very similar to those that arise in the analysis of the four basic arrangements with which the book deals. In working through the analysis of those core arrangements, one becomes familiar with certain common principles that underlie the analysis of all structural components of an economy, and can be readily applied to portions of the economy that supplement the core. It is rather like learning a new language by working your way through a few well-selected texts: once you have learned the language, all the other texts are accessible.

4   The Atoms of Economic Life

It is customary to think of economic systems as composed of large species such as market economies and centrally planned economies. Those species are indeed the subject of Part IV. Those large systems, however, are built up out of a great many smaller elements, some of which are common to both and some of which can be found in one but not the other. Many of the central issues of the Good Society surround these elementary components of economic systems. It is well to confront them before taking on the larger matter of the relative merits of markets and planning.

Many of an economy's institutional arrangements involve the distribution of economic objects. For example, the consumer goods that flow out of the reservoir have to be distributed somehow among the citizens. Most people judge the goodness of the economy in part by who gets how much of what goods, and that depends on the arrangement employed for distributing the goods. Similarly, in order that new goods flow into the reservoir, the citizens-as-workers must be distributed among the jobs that need to be filled. Who ends up working in what kind of job depends on the arrangement for allocating workers among jobs, a matter that greatly affects the quality of the citizens' working lives.

All distributional arrangements, some of which are quite complicated in practice, boil down to one or the other of two methods, or sometimes a combination of the two. To illustrate, the jobs that must be filled in an economy range very widely, and include physicians, ball players, accountants, lawyers, carpenters, waiters, and dishwashers. With respect to the latter, one of the oldest of the questions that have concerned social philosophers has been: in a Good Society, who should do the "dirty work" – the jobs that most people would prefer not to do?

PRICES

The most familiar arrangement consists of applying different price tags – called wage rates in this case – to the various jobs. The workers are expected to find their own jobs from among those that are to be filled and for which they are qualified. In the simplest case, if more people apply for a certain type of employment than there are jobs available, the wage rate declines; and if too few apply, the wage rate rises. Wage differentiation among jobs thus serves to attract more workers where they are needed and to discourage workers from applying where the need is limited. The price method handles the dirty-work problem by establishing a wage rate for those jobs that is sufficiently high to induce enough people to accept them. In practice, the wage premium for the less-desirable jobs is often swamped by other considerations that affect the wage rate, such as the skill required or the danger involved, but the wage is still larger than it would be in the absence of that premium.

ASSIGNMENT

The use of wage-prices inevitably generates some inequality in income, which is unacceptable in some versions of the Good Society. The alternative is the assignment of workers to jobs. Under the assignment method, an agency of society – usually the government – is responsible for knowing the kinds and numbers of jobs that have to be filled, and the qualifications of all the workers seeking jobs. The agency then assigns individual workers to individual jobs, presumably taking into account such factors as their skills, and perhaps their job preferences as well. The assignment method makes it possible to allocate the workers among the jobs while paying everyone the same wage.

The two methods are omnipresent in economic life. Every time you shop for food, or visit the dentist, or look for a job, or park the car, or call the fire department, chances are that either prices or assignment have been invoked in the process. Much as all physical objects are composed of the same set of atoms combined in different ways, so the world's economies may be thought of as built up from the same two distributional methods combined in different ways. The centrally planned economies make use of prices for some purposes and assignment for others. The market economies rely mostly on prices but resort to assignment for some purposes at some times.

Most citizens lead their lives unaware of the allocational methods underlying the day-to-day economic actions in which they engage, much as they have no occasion to take notice of the invisible chemistry of the chair they sit on or the bread they eat. One cannot look very deeply into the economics of a Good Society, however, without quickly coming face-to-face with its atoms. The reason is that most people care deeply about how the elementary actions of their economic lives are conducted. Whether you choose your own job or are assigned to it, whether you pick your own physician or are assigned to one, are matters of great importance in people's assessments of the goodness of their society's economic arrangements.

The two methods will be discussed in detail in Part II, and will figure prominently in the rest of the book.

5 The Comparative Temperament

William Saroyan tells an Armenian folk tale about an old man who brought home a cello that he had bought in the market and that had only one string. He played endlessly on that string until his distraught wife expostulated, "Husband, most men play many notes. Why do you play only one note over and over again?" "Old woman," he replied, "you do not understand such things. Most men play many notes because they are looking for the best one. I play only one note because I have found it."

I expect that the issues discussed in this book will be of interest primarily to people who are still looking for the best note. They are likely to be people who have not gone over these matters so often that they have lost their freshness.

People who have found the best note are of two kinds. Some are so aggressively committed to their version of the Good Society that other views can be understood only as the product of lunacy or of idiocy. No political position has a monopoly on that kind of disposition. They include people to whom such ideas as perfect equality or public ownership are simply too absurd to merit discussion. They also include people who could not imagine that arrangements based on profits or markets or private property could possibly form part of any serious version of a Good Society.

There are others, however, who have found their best note but still enjoy the exposure to others. They have settled upon their own version of a Good Society, but welcome the opportunity to review the arguments from time to time and perhaps to encounter a wrinkle that they had not thought of before. They have the comparative temperament.

Devout comparativists can be bores. Their ingrained response to an impassioned recitation of the evils of "the system" is to ask whether the complainant perhaps has some better system in mind. A true comparativist never judges a person by what she is against – he insists on knowing also what she is for. The comparativist is therefore never drawn into a debate on whether some economic arrangement is good or bad. He somehow always turns the conversation to whether it is better or worse than some other arrangement.

Comparative studies are a part of every humanistic and social discipline: comparative literature, comparative religion, comparative kinship systems, comparative politics, comparative economic systems, and so forth. The attraction of comparative study is that the engagement with social arrangements different from one's own opens a new avenue of understanding of one's own society as well as others. Like all education, it may be dangerous to your health. People of good sense, however, can deal with subversive ideas without themselves being subverted.

This book should therefore be congenial to readers who are fully committed to their version of a Good Society, but, having the comparative temperament, are open to a rehearsal of other ideas on the subject.

There remains one major matter that demands discussion before the substantive presentation begins in Part II. I have referred often to the assessment of the "goodness" of economic arrangements. To assert that one arrangement is better than another is to offer a value judgment. The role of values in assessing economic arrangements therefore demands elaboration. The next chapter completes this introduction with an essay on the place of values in the economics of the Good Society.

Notes

1 Friedman, *Capitalism and Freedom*, ch. 1.
2 Sweezy, *Socialism*, p. 252.
3 Marx had little use for such socialist writers as Fourier, Saint Simon, and others who devoted themselves to designing ideal societies. In contrast to those "Utopians," he regarded his own work as scientific in the sense that he sought to understand the actual "laws of motion" of society, and not merely to spin dreams about a better world. Socialism in his view was a form of society that would come about because of the inevitable forces of historical development that he had discovered, and not because some impractical idealist had shown the world a better way to live.
4 The term "welfare" does not refer here to policies in support of the poor. It has the meaning intended in the expression "the general welfare."
5 What I call "modern" economic theory is sometimes called "Western" economic theory, to distinguish it from the Marxian theory that was taught in the Communist countries of the "east." In those countries it was called by the Marxian term, "bourgeois" economics. I shall refer to Marxism by that name when the subject appears in the text.
6 Barone, "The Ministry of Production in the collectivist state."
7 The term "institution" is used here in the abstract sense that marriage is said to be a social institution, not in the concrete sense that a university is an educational institution. The expression "institutional arrangements" is adapted from Abram Bergson's study of what he called the "working arrangements for resource use" in the USSR (Bergson, *The Economics of Soviet Planning*, p. 7).
8 Le Carre, *The Russia House*, p. 120.

Chapter 3

The Question of Values

Know Thyself
> *— The Delphic Oracle*

The master said, a gentleman takes
as much trouble to discover what
is right as lesser men take to
discover what will pay.
> *— Confucius*

CONTENTS

A book that presumes to offer instruction about the Good Society must begin with the question: "Who is to say what is good?"

Assessing the goodness of different types of economic arrangements is not unlike many types of assessments that people are accustomed to making in the normal course of life, such as selecting a mate, deciding upon the city in which to live, or buying a house. No one can tell you which is the best: you have to decide that for yourself.

Houses differ, for example, in the combination of features they offer, and buyers differ in the value they place on the various features. It is of vital importance that the buyer "know herself" – in particular, that she know what features of a house she values most, for if she is mistaken about her own true values she may bear a costly burden. It is all a question of values.

If you have not thought much about houses before, it would be prudent to consult a book or two by someone experienced in the business. No matter that different advisers may offer contradictory advice. What one gets from such reading is an understanding of the kinds of things that people generally have found to be important in houses: a check-list, perhaps, of the criteria that ought to be considered in assessing various prospective purchases. That enterprise may assist you in clarifying your own values – in sorting out those housing features that are important to you and those that are not – but it may do more than that. If you are not an experienced house buyer, you will very likely discover things that you had not thought much about before, and you may find that the structure of your values has changed. After studying the advantages of a southern exposure or the disadvantages of a shed roof, the eventual purchase is likely to be more satisfactory than it would have been had it been made in the absence of that exploration of values.

The housing expert, however, can do no more than inform his readers about things that should be taken into account, and about what is known to work well under what circumstances. In the end the buyer must consult his own values in making the momentous decision.

In the general scale of things that matter, assessing the quality of houses is of small significance compared with the assessment of economic systems. The commitment to a new house can be undone with no more than a few financial and psychic bruises. The commitment to an economic system is a decision of Faustian proportions. Some who made that choice found the better world they hoped for. Others lived to regret it. It is the stuff of which grand triumphs and great tragedies are made.

People of philosophic inclination devote a great deal of thought to justifying the values they hold, drawing on scripture, religion, natural law, common sense, and other sources. For this limited inquiry into the economics of the Good Society, however, it is sufficient simply to know what you believe to be good. What you *should* believe to be good, and *why* you believe what you believe, are questions for another day.

This book will be occupied throughout with the assessment of the goodness of various economic arrangements on the basis of certain criteria, or standards, that are generally employed in economic analysis. Each criterion represents an aspect of an economic system that many people who have been through this business before regard as a thing of value; that is to say, other things being equal, the better an economic system performs by that criterion, the better that system may be said to be.

The five criteria I make use of in this book are in no sense definitive. Other analysts ignore some that are on my list and include others that are not on my list. People who have thought about these questions will find mine a familiar list, however, though perhaps packaged somewhat differently from their own.

Readers will differ in the value they place on these criteria. Some will assign much more importance than others to individual freedom of choice, or to income inequality, in assessing the goodness of an economic system. Few people, however, will be completely indifferent to freedom of choice or to inequality, or to the other criteria presented here. Some readers may also find that this list omits some matters that rank high among the values that underlie their assessment of the goodness of a society. They may wish to add economic growth, for example; for poor countries in particular would place a high value on the capacity of an economic system to generate a high rate of growth. Readers who wish to consider additional criteria of goodness that reflect their own values should nevertheless find this book helpful, for the method of reasoning is sufficiently general to be applied to any set of criteria.

1　Justice

Justice is the most ancient requirement of goodness: the thunder of the Old Testament prophets still resonates in both religious and secular denunciations of economic injustice. To many people justice is *the* criterion of an economy's goodness. Of the many meanings that fall under the category of "justice," two are of particular interest in regard to economic matters. One focusses on the procedures or rules that govern economic activity. I shall call that meaning "fairness," for it corresponds to what people usually have in mind when they declare some arrangement to be fair – as in the assertion that it is only fair that the rich pay higher taxes than the poor, or that people are entitled to keep what they earn. The second meaning focusses on the outcomes of economic activity, chiefly the distribution among the people of some economic entity like income, wealth, or security. Distributive justice is often referred to as "equity," which is term I shall use here.

FAIRNESS

If you think of economic justice as fairness, you judge the goodness of a society by the procedural "rules of the game" that underlie its economic arrangements. In one influential formulation, "whether a distribution is just depends on how it came about."[1] A prominent instance concerns income received in the form of interest payments. In virtually all modern economies, socialist as well as capitalist, some people earn interest – on their savings accounts, or on the government bonds they have purchased. There is an ancient tradition that regards it as not only sinful but also unfair that some people are able to derive an income from the seemingly non-productive activity of simply keeping money in the bank or lending it out, while most people have to work for their income. The issues of fairness involved in the earning of income in the form of interest enters into the discussion of saving in chapter 7.

Fairness figures most prominently in regard to sources of income, but it also arises in a variety of other contexts. For example, one arrangement for getting a society's unpleasant work done is rotation. That arrangement has a claim to being fair because everybody takes a turn cleaning the toilets or washing the dishes. However, if that work is more repugnant to some people than to others, there is a sense in which the burden is heavier on them than on the others. A Good Society concerned about fairness might prefer a different arrangement that permits such people to avoid the unpleasant jobs if they compensate by doing extra work elsewhere (chapter 9).

EQUITY

People who judge the goodness of the society by the standard of distributive justice are concerned not with rules but with outcomes – usually the degree of equality with which income, security, political influence, social status, opportunity, and other benefits are distributed among the people. The discussion here will focus on the distribution of income, which is what most people think about, but the distribution of other outcomes like security (chapters 19–20) and wealth (chapter 27) will be considered at appropriate places in the text.

There is a wide range of views on what constitutes a just distribution of income in a Good Society, but most people subscribe to one of three standards.

Fairness again   The first is the aforementioned standard of justice as fairness: if you regard the rules as fair, then you are entirely agnostic about the distribution of income. You are bound to regard any distribution that emerges from the operation of those rules as equitable, no matter how unequal it may be. In assessing the huge incomes earned by top basketball players, for example, you would look only at the hiring and bargaining procedures that lead to those incomes. If those procedures are fair, then you must regard those incomes as justly earned; if they are unfair, then the incomes are unjustly earned – but only because of the unfairness of the rules, not because of their large size.

The rules of the game sometimes include a "level playing field," or equality of opportunity. From this standpoint, inequality of income derived from accidents of birth, ranging from parental qualities to inherited wealth, would be considered unfair. If you share that sentiment, you would regard the income distribution as unjust, not because it was too unequal, but because some of the incomes were unfairly earned. Under this standard, the notion that income inequality may be excessive has no meaning apart from the fairness of the rules under which that inequality was generated.

Equality   Under the second and more familiar standard of distributive justice, one judges the equity of an arrangement by the degree of inequality in the income distribution to which it gives rise.

The extreme proponent of this standard is the pure egalitarian, who judges any departure from absolute equality, for whatever reason, to be inequitable. The egalitarian standard judges the rules by the outcome – any rules that lead to an unequal distribution are unfair, contrary to the fairness standard, under which the outcomes are judged by the rules – any distribution is equitable, however unequal, if the rules are fair.

While the notion of equality sounds fairly unambiguous, people who regard themselves as egalitarians can differ widely on whether a particular distribution is truly equal. To give but one example, if a disabled citizen is to have equal access to all the society's opportunities, more of the society's resources must be devoted to his activities than to those of other citizens. Hence a distribution that is equal in the per-capita sense would not be regarded as equal by someone whose standard of equality takes differences in needs into account.

Most people who subscribe to the equity standard of distributive justice are not pure egalitarians, however. They regard some degree of inequality as entirely equitable if it follows from fair rules and if it serves some socially acceptable purpose such as supporting work incentives. Other things equal, however, large differences in income, in their view, detract from the goodness of the society, and very large differences, though vaguely defined, are seen as a threat to political and social stability.

Poverty   Distributive justice has traditionally been thought of as the relation between the incomes of the rich and the poor. A more recent view is that in judging how justly a society distributes its income, one should look only at the condition of the poorest citizens and ignore the condition of rich. The concern is less that too many are too rich than that too many are too poor. In the past quarter-century, poverty has displaced inequality as the primary criterion of distributive justice in the minds of many people, perhaps even most. There are many formulations of this standard, one of the most prominent of which is that inequalities are just "only if they result in compensating benefits for everyone, and in particular for the least advantaged members of society."[2]

The relation of poverty to income distribution is complex. Poverty is sometimes thought of, somewhat mechanically, as the condition of the people at the lower end of the income distribution – perhaps the lowest tenth, or the lowest quarter. The trouble with that definition is that in a rich and relatively equal society, the statistical poor would not regard themselves, nor would others regard them, as living "in poverty." For that reason poverty is usually defined by some admittedly fuzzy "poverty line" – the level of income or consumption that the society considers to be the boundary between merely low income and poverty. By that definition it is at least possible for a rich Good Society to eliminate what is thought of as poverty.

The extent of income inequality depends largely on the society's economic arrangements: on whether property is privately or publicly owned, for example, or how wages are determined. The extent of poverty, however, depends on much more than the economic arrangements. There will be less poverty in a rich economy than in a poor one with the same economic arrangements. Societies also differ in their cultural traditions regarding the obligations of the state and the richer citizens towards the poor. Two societies may be identical in their basic structural arrangements, but the citizens of one may choose to transfer more income from the rich to the poor than the citizens of the other. The extent of poverty will then differ in the two societies, although their economic arrangements are the same in all other respects.

Hence, if you observe a society with a great deal of poverty, that should not be taken as reason for rejecting its economic system: the same system in another society might generate less poverty, or perhaps even more.

2   Security

In ancient times justice was thought to be within the reach of civilized societies. Not so security. Drought, plague, and disease were the natural lot of mankind. In the colder climates, how many members of the family would live to see the spring depended on how bitter the winter was and how long it lasted. With divine revelation a society could use the seven fat years to prepare for the seven lean, but God was sparing in his interventions.

Today we no longer regard natural conditions as an inevitable source of insecurity. The reason is the high level of productivity made possible in large part by the social division of labor. That very interdependence among people and societies, however, is the source of a new type of insecurity. The jobs that people hold depend on many conditions that tend to change: customers switch from older products to newer ones and new technology renders old skills obsolete.

Economic security is regarded as a thing of value in all modern economies. Economic systems differ greatly, however, in the degree and in the kind of security that they provide, and in its distribution among the citizens.

The security of the flow of income is the major concern of most people. Loss of income may be due to such causes as physical disability, aging, or the death of the family's major earner. However, since most people derive their income primarily from their jobs, the fear of and the experience of losing a job are the most widespread sources of insecurity. In addition to the loss of income, the psychic pain of being fired leaves a scar that never fully heals, particularly in those who prided themselves on their reliability and competence as workers and who came to regard their jobs as permanent. "Downsizing" and plant closing therefore play a major role in electoral politics in democratic countries; the fear of plant closing is indeed a major obstacle in the path of the transformation of former socialist countries to market-based systems.

If a worker who has lost a job has a reasonable prospect of finding a new one soon, the personal impact is relatively slight. The probability of finding a new job depends on such personal factors as age, experience, and skills, but it also depends on the general level of unemployment. When the economy is prosperous, it is not unrealistic to expect to find another one soon, but the loss of a job in a period of economic depression, when many other workers are also unemployed, is a devastating experience.

In virtually all modern economies there are some forms of government assistance designed to ease the insecurity due to unemployment and other causes. As in the relief of poverty, however, there is enormous variation in the nature and extent of such programs. One reason is that countries differ in the size of the taxes they are prepared to pay to finance the social programs. Another, however, is that the economic arrangements required to provide job- and income security sometimes have undesired side-effects. The larger the size and the duration of unemployment benefits, for example, the greater the incentive for some people to remain unemployed, in some cases illegally earning additional income in the "underground economy." That seems to be the experience of the European Community, where the relatively high unemployment rate is very likely caused in part by the relatively generous unemployment benefits.

Security as a criterion of goodness should be thought of as relative rather than absolute. It is possible to imagine an arrangement that would provide for absolute security of job and income, such as lifetime tenure for all workers in their first job. Such an arrangement, however, would have certain disadvantages, one of which is the neglect of risk-taking.

There are certain economic activities that are so attractive to some people that they would risk a great deal in order to engage in them. The prospect of becoming a celebrated screen actor, or a top ball player, or a "master of the universe" of bond-trading, induces many young people to exert enormous effort in their own training, in full knowledge that the proportion of aspirants who succeed is very small. A society that regards competition as a bad thing might figure out a way to eliminate it from such activities, but if it also values the peaks of human performance in the arts and elsewhere, competition of that sort is likely to be permitted. The success of some must therefore mean the failure of many others. A Good Society is likely to strive for arrangements in which security can somehow be combined with the insecurity of risk-taking in certain activities. For example, economic activities might be graded by degree of security, so that the citizen could take account of the riskiness of an employment in her calculus of the merits of different jobs. Then risk-averse people for whom security is a dominating personal value would find the protection they seek, while those who seek the glory road would be free to take the risk.

Security, like income, also has a distributive dimension. Under some arrangements, some people enjoy a great deal of security and some very little. Japanese lifetime-employment practices, for example, have provided a high level of security for a certain proportion of the labor force, but the rest experience considerable insecurity. In the USSR, on the other hand, security of employment was distributed quite equally among the working population.

3 Sovereignty over Production

Every country produces an annual statistical abstract that reports the year's production of all major goods and services. In 1985, the year that Mikhail Gorbachev came to office, the USSR produced 585,000 tractors, 164,000 metal-cutting machine tools, and 113 million square meters of housing. In that same year the United States produced 38,000 tractors, 35,000 metal-cutting machine tools, and 208 million square meters of housing.[3] The United States also reports that in 1987 Americans spent about $5 billion on pets and pet products, the same as they spent on photographic equipment; but there are no corresponding data in the Soviet statistical abstract.[4]

PRODUCTION SCENARIOS

The combination of goods that a country produces in the course of a year reflects the particular way in which a country's resources have been used. It may be thought of as that year's production scenario, but it is not the only scenario that the economy was capable of producing. If more labor and other resources had been put into housing instead of other industries, it could have produced a different scenario consisting of more housing but less of other things. In principle, there is a very large number of different scenarios that can be produced by varying the quantities of resources devoted to each production activity.

The combinations of goods that an economy is capable of producing are not unlimited. Some combinations are impossible because the resources available in any year are finite, and there is just so much that the most productive of economies can squeeze out of the resources available to it. The number of possible combinations is nevertheless large enough to offer the society a wide range of scenarios from which to choose.

The combination of goods that a society chooses to produce – the so-called "product mix" – is a matter of great consequence in the assessment of the goodness of an economic system. For many people it has the urgency of a moral issue. The contemplation of a nation that devotes so much of its resources to the maintenance of its suburban lawns and the feeding of its cats and dogs while millions live homeless in the streets raises legitimate questions about the moral basis of the society: not for cat-and-dog people, to be sure, but for many others. The Soviet government did not publish as much detailed production data as the United States, and it is therefore difficult to assess the goodness of its product mix. It is known, however, that a substantial proportion of its population lived in poverty, as defined by Soviet analysts.[5] The same moral question can therefore be raised about the production of such luxuries as the Bolshoi Ballet, color television sets, and high-fidelity music systems, in a country in which many citizens still lived in poverty.

Everyone is entitled to his own view on how much cat food a Good Society should produce. Economic science has nothing to contribute directly on the value aspect of that question; that is to say, it offers no basis for declaring housing to be morally superior to cat food. It does, however, offer a useful way of thinking about the various arrangements by which a Good Society might select the combination of goods and services to be produced.

The choice of the product mix is an important issue because some combinations of goods are thought to be "better" than others, and one of them many be the "best" of all. A society that aspires to goodness should therefore seek those arrangements that would produce the combination it judges to be the best.

But people are likely to differ in their views on which of many combinations of goods is the best. You might rule out all product mixes that include large quantities of whiskey, while I may downgrade the ones that devote too much to cats. Therefore the society must first settle the matter of whose judgment of goodness should prevail.

WHO SHOULD DECIDE?

There are two clashing views on the best way for a society to decide what goods should be produced, each reflecting a certain value. The issue emerges most clearly in the case of consumer goods.

In the individualist view, the Good Society should produce whatever goods the citizens as individuals wish to consume. If I want to spend my money on my cats and my lawn, a good economy should be responsive to my wishes, regardless of the dim view that you or "society" may take of my preferences.

The societal view is that the society as a whole has an interest in seeing that the best combination of things is produced. That interest would not be served if the product mix were the chance result of whatever each of us happens to prefer when consulting only our purely personal preferences. What is best for the society is not merely the sum of what each of us thinks is best for ourselves. In the Good Society the final product mix should constitute a societal decision rather than the mechanical sum of individual choices, although some account may be taken of what the citizens as individuals wish to consume.

In the language of economics, the question is whether it is better that the locus of "sovereignty" over production be lodged in the citizens individually, or in the society collectively. If you hold the individualist value, you would give high marks to the economic arrangements of market economies, in which "consumer sovereignty" is said to prevail. If you subscribe to the societal value, your Good Society would be better served by the arrangements of the centrally planned economies, in which "planner sovereignty" is said to prevail.

Consumer sovereignty and planner sovereignty are rarely employed in their pure form. In most countries one of them predominates, but some of the other is introduced from time to time. In the capitalist economies consumer sovereignty predominates, but there are various deviations from it. Some deviations are the consequence of the political process: the government may take action to reduce the production of some things that people are prepared to buy, like narcotic drugs or pornographic publications; or it may subsidize housing construction in order that more of it will be produced than otherwise. Other deviations are the consequence of various economic arrangements: in industries in which monopoly prevails the quantities of output produced are less than the population would wish to consume (chapter 17). In the planned economies planner sovereignty predominated, but for a wide range of consumer goods the planners sought to direct production into those goods for which consumers showed their preference in their spending behavior. The expansion of the production of consumer durables like automobiles, refrigerators, and hi-fi equipment in the later decades was the Soviet planners' response to consumer preferences for these items.[6]

The nature of the two values will be explored in greater depth in the comparison of markets and planning in Part IV, where sovereignty over production serves as the major criterion of goodness.

4 Choice: Goods and Jobs

The issue of sovereignty concerns the process that determines the kinds and quantities of goods that the economy will produce. It therefore also determines the kinds of jobs at which the citizens will work, since the decision to produce housing, for example, means that some citizens will have to work on construction projects, in lumber mills, in glass factories, and in other jobs required to produce the housing. Thus, in a society that values individual sovereignty over production, the citizens will consume different goods and work at different jobs than in a society that values societal sovereignty.

Once the consumer goods have been produced, however, they have to be distributed among the citizens; and once the set of required jobs is determined, the workers have to be distributed among those jobs. The distribution of goods among consumers and of workers among jobs is the second stage of the economic process.

The locus of "choice" is the name of the criterion of goodness with respect to the second stage. The values involved in this stage are similar to those in the first: your assessment of the goodness of an economic arrangement depends on whether you believe it to be better that the decisions be made individually or in some societal fashion.

The locus of sovereignty is not something that people experience directly. You may live out your entire economic life without having noticed or cared whether the goods you find in the shops are the consequence of individual or societal sovereignty over production. The locus of choice is a very different matter. Your life as consumer and worker under a regime of individual choice would be drastically different under a regime of societal choice. Most people regard the locus of choice as more important than the locus of sovereignty as a criterion of the goodness of the society.

CONSUMPTION CHOICE

A collection of goods can be distributed among consumers in many different ways. Under one arrangement, for example, all consumers would be given exactly the same basket of goods, which would produce a uniform distribution of the goods. A more familiar arrangement is one in which the consumers use their income to buy the goods they want. That arrangement would produce a very different distribution of the same goods among the consumers – even if all consumers had the same income. Yet other arrangements would yield different distributions. How to decide which of all possible distributions is the best for your Good Society?

The answer depends on whether you value societal or individual choice in the distribution of consumer goods. If the former, your criterion of goodness is said to be "planners' choice" and you would prefer the arrangement in which the society decides who gets what goods. If the latter, your criterion of goodness is said to be "consumer choice," and you would prefer the arrangement in which consumers buy their own goods.

Most modern societies, both capitalist and Communist, favor consumer choice. The Communist countries are particularly interesting in this respect because on the question of what goods the society should produce, they prefer planner sovereignty over consumer sovereignty, but on the matter of the distribution of those goods among the people, they prefer consumer choice over planner choice. That is to say, the society, through its planners, decides what goods will be produced, but once they are produced, the matter of who gets which of the goods is left to the citizens as individuals.

Some socialist societies, however, ranging from the Israeli kibbutz to Maoist China, have regarded consumer choice as a pernicious principle of distribution. As they see it, consumer choice both reflects and fortifies the egoistic individualism that predominates in capitalist societies and undermines the solidarity toward which a Good Society should aspire. To people who share that societal view, the criterion of the goodness of distribution arrangements is planner choice, rather than consumer choice.

The locus of consumption choice is discussed further in Part II, where it is employed as an important criterion of the goodness of alternative arrangements for distributing consumer goods.

JOB CHOICE

Coordinate with the question of which consumers should get which goods is the question of which workers should hold which jobs. There are many conceivable arrangements for channeling the workers among the jobs that need to be filled. They can be randomly assigned to the jobs, or the jobs can be rotated among them, or they can choose their own jobs under certain restrictions. Each arrangement would produce a different distribution, or "allocation," of workers among jobs. Under one arrangement I might work as a manager of a food shop and you as a field hand. Under a different arrangement, other workers would hold these jobs and we would hold other jobs. Again, the question is, which is the best of all the possible distributions?

The rhythm of the argument should now be fairly clear. If you hold that the individual citizen should be the arbiter of which allocation is the best, then your criterion of the goodness of the society is whether it provides for "worker choice." If you hold by societal decision-making on such matters, then the "best" distribution is what some responsible agency of the society regards as "best," and your criterion of goodness is "planner choice."

Worker choice is the accepted value in most modern economies and is the most widely used job-allocation arrangement. That includes most of the Communist countries as well, where planner sovereignty over the sphere of production is combined with worker choice of their own jobs. The societies that demur from that arrangement are the same ones that reject consumer choice, and for similar reasons – under worker choice the citizen asks himself, "Which job is best for me?" They hold that it would be a better society if young people aspired to "serve the people" – the slogan of Maoist China – rather that to satisfy their individual preferences. To people who share that value, the allocation of workers among jobs should be determined by planner choice rather than by the choice of individual workers.

The locus of job choice is a major criterion of goodness in the analysis of labor in Part III.

5 Efficiency

Selection of the loci of sovereignty and of choice settles the question of who in the society will make what decisions. It does not yet settle the question of the basis on which the decisions should be made. Under planner sovereignty, for example, a planning board has the authority to decide what next year's product mix should be, but that still leaves open the question of what criterion they should employ for deciding which of many feasible combinations of goods is the best. The criterion that is most widely used for that purpose is efficiency.

Efficiency is an idea over which battle lines are often drawn. To some people it is what the Good Society is all about – whatever is efficient is good. To others an obsession with efficiency is exactly what a Good Society should avoid. In the end each person must make up her own mind about the place that efficiency should occupy in her Good Society. First, however, it is important to appreciate the precise meaning of that highly charged term as it is used in economic analysis.

The broad context in which the concept of efficiency is employed is one in which there are several ways of achieving an objective, some of which are "better" than others, and one of which is the "best" of all. The specific context that is most often encountered, however, is one in which there are several economic arrangements that may be used for distributing economic objects of various sorts. In the prototypical example, central economic planning and markets are two arrangements for allocating the country's labor and other resources among the various lines of production. Each will result in the production of one combination of goods out of the many combinations that could be produced. An arrangement is said to be efficient if the combination of goods that it causes to be produced is the best – or the "optimal," as it is often called – of all the combinations that could have been produced.

Efficiency in the context of a distributional task of that sort is called "allocative efficiency." That is the most widely used meaning of efficiency – so widely, indeed, that when writers use the term efficiency without a qualifying adjective, they are usually referring to allocative efficiency.[7] I shall follow that practice in what follows: efficiency will mean allocative efficiency unless otherwise stated.

An economic arrangement can be efficient in some respects and inefficient in others, much as a mechanical system like an automobile can be efficient in some respects (say fuel economy) and inefficient in others (acceleration). Three such respects are of particular interest from the perspective of a Good Society.

EFFICIENCY AND PRODUCTION

A typical application of the concept of efficiency is a variant of the example given above, in which a number of workers must be allocated among enterprises that produce the same good. Imagine that there are ten coal mines in a certain region, and 10,000 miners to fill the jobs.

The number of ways in which the miners can be allocated among the mines is exceedingly large. In one allocation, 1,000 miners may be assigned to each mine; suppose that with that allocation the ten mines produce a total output of 100,000 tons a month. In another allocation, 800 miners may be assigned to the first two mines and the others parcelled out equally among the eight other mines, yielding a total coal output of 150,000 tons. And so on. How should one decide which of all possible allocations is best of all?

The answer in this example appears to be self-evident – the second is the better allocation because total coal production is larger. That answer presumes that the society's objective is to produce as much coal as possible with the available resources. And, indeed, it is the rare society that does not regard a larger volume of production – of most things – to be better than a smaller volume. Allocative efficiency in that respect may be called "production efficiency." Given that the objective of the activity is to produce coal, that allocation of workers among jobs under which the largest quantity of coal is produced is the optimal allocation, and an economic arrangement that leads to that optimum is said to be productively efficient.

What holds for coal holds for shoes, for air transportation, and for every product in the economy. In a productively efficient economy, the output of every product is as large as possible with the labor and other resources allocated to that product. The citizens of that society will have available more goods and services than they would have if production were carried out less efficiently.

Some problems are best addressed by asking whether a certain arrangement is efficient or not. In the case of others it is more useful to ask whether one arrangement is more efficient than another. Whether the absolute or the relative meaning of efficiency is used in the text depends upon the context.

CONSUMPTION PREFERENCES

"All That Meat and No Potatoes" is the title of a popular song that amused audiences some time ago. Like all good art, it touched a nerve. People have strong preferences about consumer goods, and some collections of goods provide more satisfaction than others.

A productively efficient economy produces the largest quantities of meat and of potatoes possible with the resources allocated to the two activities. It may nevertheless be a very bad economy if it produces too much meat and no potatoes. That is to say, it should attend not only to the output of each good but to the proportions in which the various goods are produced. It should not be content with any combination of goods but should strive for the optimal combination. The optimal "product mix" – as it is called – is said to be that combination of goods which "maximizes" something variously called "utility," or "satisfaction," or "well-being," or "consumer welfare."[8]

The goodness of an economic arrangement should therefore be assessed not only by the standard of productive efficiency, but also by the standard of efficiency in terms of consumption preferences. Attending to consumption preferences may rank very high, or very low, on your overall scale of values, but in choosing the economic arrangements for your Good Society, you should know how those arrangements perform by that criterion.

JOB PREFERENCES

Imagine now an economy that is efficient in both of the foregoing respects: it produces the largest possible quantity of each good, and also produces that combination of goods that best satisfies the consumption preferences of the citizens. The achievement of those happy outcomes requires that certain jobs have to be performed. However, just as the citizens-as-consumers have their preferences among goods, the same citizens-as-workers also have their preferences among jobs. Some jobs are regarded as highly desirable, and others are so unpleasant that some people would give up a great deal rather than have to perform them; and like consumption preferences, job preferences differ from person to person.

The fact that people prefer some jobs over others introduces yet another dimension of allocative efficiency with which a Good Society should be concerned. An arrangement may be said to be efficient with respect to job preferences if the set of jobs that the citizens-as-workers have to perform is the best of all possible sets of jobs in terms of the citizens' job preferences. The optimal set of jobs is said to maximize the "utility," or the "job satisfaction," of the citizens-as-workers.

The ability of a Good Society to create the jobs that its people find most desirable is strongly constrained, however, by the dependence of production on jobs: if certain goods are desired, certain jobs have to be done by somebody. If one ignored consumption preferences, the optimal set of jobs would include only those jobs that each citizen-as-worker would most like to perform. The society would then have to make do with a bizarre set of consumer goods and services. A great many ball games and paintings would be produced, but little coal would be mined and few fast-food meals would be served. The welfare of the citizens-as-workers would be very high, but their welfare as consumers would be very low.

The Good Society must therefore strike some balance between the consumption preferences and the job preferences of the citizens. How well that trick is performed by the two major economic arrangements – markets and planning – is discussed in Part IV.

IN PRAISE OF EFFICIENCY

What starts out as a good conversation about a better way to run the world often degenerates into recrimination about the other person's values. It is often the term "efficiency" that ignites the match.

The notion of efficiency is held in low regard by many people who regard themselves as aficionados of the Good Society. To be concerned with efficiency is the surest mark of the philistine: it is conclusive evidence of an incapacity to appreciate the finer things in life. Admit the purveyors of efficiency into your midst, and out go art, philosophy, and everything else that makes for a Good Society.

I have found, however, that it is usually not the concept itself that is objectionable but rather an excessive concern with efficiency to the exclusion of all other values. If that is the objection, then I share it with the critics, as the rest of this book will show. It will be stressed throughout this book that an economic arrangement should not be adopted by a Good Society on grounds of its efficiency alone, for it may do great violence to other social values.

I part company, however, with people who hold that it is inappropriate even to include economic efficiency among the criteria for evaluating the goodness of a society. That view is often accompanied by a disdain for material things – a rather unseemly stance in people who live comfortable lives themselves. To banish efficiency from the agenda of a Good Society is to hold that income doesn't matter – that people would be no better off if they consumed more, and no worse off if they consumed less, than they presently do. Seen in that light, few people would be indifferent to the efficiency with which the economy operates. The economy may not be part of the grand architecture of a society, but it is an important part of its plumbing, and efficiency is one of the economic plumber's principal tools.

There is no modern society that rejects the value that, other things equal, the people are better off with more rather than fewer of most ordinary goods. To be sure, there have been substantial differences in the ways in which the goodness of various kinds of goods has been regarded. In some socialist countries a preoccupation with consumer goods was regarded with disdain, as evidence of a "bourgeois" disposition, and was greatly discouraged by the prevailing social norms, or at least by the official norms. Even in those cases, however, the object of disdain was not production in general but only the production of and excessive preoccupation with consumer goods. The effort devoted to the production process overall, and particularly the production of such industrial products as steel, machinery, and equipment, was no smaller than that in the most materialistic of capitalist countries.

The person who has the right to be genuinely indifferent to efficiency is someone who would decline an increase in her income if it were offered to her, on the grounds that there is nothing more that she would wish to buy. I believe there are such saintly souls, though they are rarely clamorous about their saintliness.[9] There are also some ascetic cultures, usually with deep religious commitments, in which very little value is placed on material goods. All that may be required of the economy of that kind of Good Society is that it provide some minimal quantities of the goods required to enable the people to devote themselves to their more important religious and social activities.

It might seem that in a society of that kind, efficiency would be an inappropriate criterion for judging the goodness of economic arrangements. However, the social benefits of efficiency can be reaped in many ways, depending on the society's values. In a materialistic society they are used to increase the consumption of goods, but in a spiritual society they can be used to produce the same minimal quantities of goods with less labor. More time could then be devoted to religious or social activities, or, more generally, to leisure. The goods could also be produced with less violence to the country's forests and fisheries and other natural resources of the land. A society of that sort should therefore also regard efficiency as a proper criterion for judging the goodness of an economy.

6 The Structure of Values

Specifying the things that matter – the criteria of assessment – in evaluating the goodness of an economic system constitutes half the job. The other half consists of deciding which economic arrangements perform best according to those criteria.

You and I may be in perfect agreement on the criteria by which we judge the goodness of an economy, yet we may disagree on the institutional arrangements that should be incorporated in that economy. There are two reasons for that disagreement.

THE WEIGHING OF EVIDENCE

One reason is that we may have different views on the outcomes to be expected from various economic arrangements. Will worker ownership be more efficient than private ownership because the workers have a personal investment in the enterprise's performance? Or will worker ownership be less efficient because of the "free-rider" problem – that some members may hold back on their effort because all members share equally in the enterprise's earnings?

Questions of this sort are the stuff of scholarly controversy. They occupy a large part of this book, in which I present both the theory and the empirical evidence regarding the outcomes to be expected from alternative institutional arrangements. Even in the natural sciences, dispassionate observers studying the same evidence often come to different conclusions. In the softer social sciences it is all the rarer to encounter evidence so compelling that only one conclusion can reasonably be drawn. Hence you and I may weigh the evidence on ownership forms and other arrangements differently, and come to different conclusions regarding their relative efficiency.

THE WEIGHTING OF VALUES

The second reason that you and I may prefer different institutional arrangements is that we may assign different weights to the various criteria. It is that difference that often accounts for the surprise, and sometimes the dismay, at discovering that a good friend who always seemed to share your values takes a very different position on some important issue of public affairs. The call for Liberty, Equality, and Fraternity rallied millions in support of the French Revolution. On the day after the Revolution, however, it turned out that people packaged those three values in very different proportions, corresponding to very different conceptions of the Good Society.

An ideal world would contain a large set of institutional arrangements varied enough to fit every possible combination of values. If you and I wished for an economic system in which consumer sovereignty prevailed, one that was perfectly efficient, where income was equally distributed, and so on down the list of our criteria of goodness, a set of institutional arrangements would exist that would achieve precisely those outcomes. The economy of your Good Society would be the same as mine.

Unfortunately mankind has not been so ingenious as to have invented so wide a range of institutional arrangements. Rarely is one way of carrying out an economic function – rewarding work effort, for example – better in every respect than all other ways of carrying out that same function. Normally the economic arrangement that scores higher by one criterion of goodness is not the best by other criteria: the most just may not be the most efficient.

Hence you and I may value both efficiency and justice in our visions of the Good Society, but the limited set of known institutional arrangements compels us to choose among them. After weighing the goods and bads of two sets of economic arrangements, I may choose the economic system that is more efficient but less just than the system you choose. I am more willing than you to "trade off" some justice for efficiency. We differ in our assessments of the Good Society because, although we both value efficiency and equity, we differ in the weights we assign to those criteria of goodness.

Tomorrow's Good Society, however, may be better than today's. New institutional arrangements are invented from time to time that make it possible for an economy to improve its performance by one or more criteria in such a way as to make for a better society. The "negative income tax," for example, is an invention designed to make it possible to improve the income distribution in capitalist countries with a smaller loss of efficiency than other income-maintenance arrangements entail. Yugoslav socialists invented the institution of worker self-management that had certain advantages as an alternative to state ownership as practiced under Soviet socialism.

It is unlikely, however, that the repertory of economic arrangements will ever be so large as to make it possible to satisfy any combination of values that a person or a society may hold. Much as one house may have the better view but another the larger rooms, so one set of economic arrangements may be more efficient and another offer more security or justice. In the end one must simply plunge in and choose the house or the system that attains the highest overall score in one's mental calculus of values.

7   The Public and the Private

What is best for me need not be the best for my society. If there were no difference between the two there would be no difference between private interest and the public interest.

There are people who seek to understand how economic systems work in order to equip themselves to derive the greatest benefit their system can provide for themselves and their families. That is a perfectly respectable use of knowledge. It is important, however, to

distinguish the place of the private from that of the public. One can support a piece of legislation, for example, because it will improve one's personal position, or because it will improve
the quality of the society. One would like to believe that it will do both, but it is difficult to
be confident about one's judgment of the public interest when personal interest is also involved.

The politics of the Good Society reserves an honorable place for private interest, but there
are places in which it is inappropriate. A public official, for example, must not consult his
private interest in deciding how to vote on a piece of legislation. Nor should the citizen consult only his private interest in such public acts as voting for a representative.

The economics of the Good Society is concerned with the public interest. Yet the choice
of the best economic system, I have argued, must be based on what one personally values
in an economic system. That appears to say, in effect, that the best economic arrangement
is that which best serves one's private interest. How, one might ask, should one distinguish
the private from the public interest in this matter?

THE VEIL OF IGNORANCE

The best guidance I have found on this question is the work of John Rawls.[10] To come to a
disinterested opinion about what makes for a just society, he proposes, you should regard
yourself as "situated behind a veil of ignorance" regarding the position you yourself will occupy
in that society. As applied to the economics of a Good Society, that rule recommends that
you think about each economic arrangement as if you did not know whether you would be
a worker or a manager or a farmer, or rich or poor, or male or female. The reasoning is that
if you knew in advance what social position you would occupy, self-interest might induce
you to select a different economic system from that which you would otherwise select. On
the question of whether the right of private ownership should extend to the ownership of
other people, for example, as in slave societies of the past, your view about the goodness
of that arrangement might well be colored by the foreknowledge of whether you would be
master or slave. A society in which early birds catch the worms would be very appealing to
birds, but less so to worms.

The rule does not at all assure that no one would designate slavery as a desirable arrangement in her Good Society. There are people who would be willing, or say they would be
willing, to risk being a slave for the sake of a chance to be a master. Nevertheless the rule is
a reasonable way of excluding self-interested choices and focussing attention on the values
that one holds regarding a Good Society in general, as distinct from what one might hold
from the vantage point of one's own personal stake in it. It is a commendable rule for anyone to follow when he is disposed to ask whether the values underlying his assessments of
social matters are simply a reflection of his private interest or whether they express a more
disinterested concern with the general interest.

No one can tell whether someone else is violating that rule. I may pretend that my public support of higher wages for more productive people, rather than an equal-wage arrangement, is a position taken behind the veil of ignorance; when in fact I privately expect that I
would do very well under the first arrangement since I fancy myself to be a highly productive person. The rule is not designed to expose frauds, however, but to counsel an honest
person on how to think about the public interest. Like statistics and other techniques, it can
be used to deceive, but it can also help in finding the truth if one is seeking it.

AN OBJECTIVELY GOOD SOCIETY

Reasoning under the veil of ignorance, one can develop a vision of a Good Society that means
something more than simply what is good for oneself. Yet it remains a highly subjective

concept, in the sense that it is defined by the structure of each person's values. The best economic system, as presented in this book, turns out to be nothing more than what you or I or anyone else happens to think it is.

Some people find that disquieting. They would like a more objective criterion by which the goodness of an economic system can be defined.[11] Happily, no authority has yet succeeded in identifying the economy of the Good Society in a way that transcends the values of its citizens.

This book therefore stops at that water's edge. I have pushed the analysis as far it can go in answer to the question of how a citizen might develop and sharpen his own vision of the economy of a Good Society. Differences in such visions contribute to the vitality of a society and to the public debate on how the economy should be governed. Citizens who have thought their way through to their own informed conception how the economy of a Good Society should be organized have something to contribute to that debate.

Notes

1   Nozick, *Anarchy, State, and Utopia*, p. 15.
2   Rawls, *A Theory of Justice*, p. 14.
3   US Directorate of Intelligence, *Handbook of Economic Statistics, 1990*, table 41.
4   US Bureau of the Census, *Statistical Abstract of the United States, 1997*, table 1065.
5   Matthews, *Poverty in the Soviet Union*.
6   When Nikita Khrushchev was head of the Soviet Union, after having witnessed the extent of highway congestion and the vast expenditures on private automobiles in capitalist countries, he announced that the Soviet automobile economy would evolve in a more sensible direction. Instead of imitating the Western pattern, the USSR would develop a large fleet of automobiles for rent, instead of for private purchase – rather like the rental-car system which is in fact widely employed in the West. That policy, in his view, would enable Soviet consumers to enjoy the use of automobiles in a way that would permit the society to produce fewer automobiles and therefore more of other things. In Mr Khrushchev's scale of values, planner sovereignty was preferable to consumer sovereignty as a way of deciding on the product mix in this case. If consumer sovereignty had been permitted to prevail in the case of automobiles, the purchasing behavior of Soviet citizens left little doubt that they, as individual consumers, would prefer to purchase their automobiles rather than rent them.
    In the event, Khrushchev's proposal was never put into practice. Soviet consumers did indeed prefer to own their own automobiles, precisely as in capitalist countries.
7   Efficiency in other contexts goes by different names, such as "technical efficiency," "informational efficiency," "X-efficiency," and so on.
8   Who decides which product mix is optimal depends on the locus of sovereignty to which the society is committed. Where societal sovereignty prevails, the optimal product mix is the one that best satisfies the consumption preferences of the planners. Where individual sovereignty prevails, the optimal product mix is that which best satisfies the consumption preferences of the consumers. The same considerations apply to the optimal combination of jobs, as discussed below.
9   Even such saints, however, should agree to accept the additional income because they could distribute it to the poor. More generally, as long as some members of the society have less than they need, the larger the output the more that is available for distribution to the least advantaged. Therefore the more efficient economy should be regarded as the better economy even by people who have no desire for additional income for themselves.
10 Rawls, *A Theory of Justice*, pp. 137–42.
11 An influential effort to provide an objective conception of well-being is that of Amartya Sen, *Inequality Reexamined* (Cambridge, MA: Harvard University Press, 1992). Rejecting the notion that whatever an individual chooses should automatically be presumed to be good for him, the alternative he proposes is that equality should be defined in terms of "functioning"; that is, people in wheelchairs need more resources in order to be able to function equally with others. As Robert Sugden has argued, in "Welfare, resources, and capabilities," however, it is difficult to see how equality of functioning can be objectively established.

Part II

Citizens as Consumers

Chapter 4

Who Should Get What Goods?

And the Lord Created a Garden
East of Eden ... And He filled it with
every kind of Tree, each after its
Kind.

> — *Genesis*

It is the nature of desire not to be
satisfied, and most men live only
for the gratification of it.

> — *Aristotle*

CONTENTS

Economic systems are organized for the purpose of producing goods and distributing them among the people. The production arrangements determine the kinds and quantities of goods that are produced, and the distribution arrangements determine who gets how much of each good.

Production is the more important of the two in the sense that differences in the economic levels of different countries reflect primarily their relative productive capabilities. Most of this book therefore deals with production arrangements. Production, however, is merely a means to an end and not the end itself. Its purpose is to support the consumption requirements of a society. Therefore, before turning to the production process, it is useful to consider how the consumer goods ought to be distributed among the citizens after they have been produced. Many of the central issues in the economics of the Good Society emerge most sharply in the context of the question of who should get how much of what goods.

Although economic well-being depends more on the ability to produce things than on the ways in which they are distributed, the distribution process is not at all unimportant in a society's sense of economic well-being. A great deal of inconvenience and discontent can result from bad distribution arrangements: endless waiting in queues, for example, or the bribery of officials responsible for the distribution of housing. Governmental efforts to end a hemorrhage of budget subsidies have provoked tumultuous riots, as occurred in Poland in 1976 following an increase in the price of meat. Aware of the potential for violent response, other governments like that of the USSR remained prisoners of a long history of such subsidies, which made it impossible to proceed with reforms that would have greatly eased the economic conditions of consumers. On the other side of the world, the mayor of New York City had to respond to angry protests over inequities in the distribution of public housing: it seems that some small families occupied large apartments while large families were crammed into small ones.

Surely, one would think, there are better ways of managing economic arrangements than those. The Good Society – as well as the not-so-good – has an interest in employing the best possible arrangements for distributing the meat, housing, ball games, and other consumer goods that the society produces.

In order to separate the problems of distribution from those of production, it will be assumed in Part II that the society has a satisfactory way of arranging for the production of the goods the people desire. For the present, we may imagine that a certain set of goods pours out of the production enterprises each day, reserving for later consideration what goods should be produced. That abstraction is rather like seeing the economy through a lens that conveniently filters out the production process, thus permitting full concentration on the flow of consumer goods. The question is, how should those goods be distributed among the citizens of a Good Society?

I Abundance and Scarcity

In a world of abundance the natural arrangement would be some form of free distribution. The sales persons, for example, might be instructed to deliver to each citizen whatever goods she requested, without charge. Something close to such an arrangement has in fact been long enjoyed by a few people in many countries. In the past it was only kings and nobles who enjoyed the power of unlimited consumption. Today it is also enjoyed by the untitled families of the very rich. In the USSR, curiously, some highly popular artists and writers were said to have enjoyed a similar status. Their royalty incomes accumulated to such large sums that they were unable to spend all they had earned.[1] After a point the bank simply stopped counting and gave these special depositors an unlimited line of credit that never needed to be repaid.

Mankind as a whole, however, experienced that degree of abundance but once, at the very beginning of human history, and then only for a short time. The Creator sought to focus the attention of his noblest creatures on the moral choice alone, and therefore relieved them of the need to make economic choices as well. The Garden of Eden provided an abundance of all the consumer goods they could want, including some very attractive apples. They flunked the moral test, however, and their race thereafter could satisfy their consumer wants only by toil and sweat.

In the modern world abundance might be said to prevail if the available productive resources are capable of supporting a free-distribution arrangement. The shops could then be continuously restocked as the shoppers took without charge all those goods that they desired. In the absence of abundance so-defined, however, the free-distribution arrangement could not be sustained. The shops would be depleted shortly after each shipment arrived from the factories, and they would remain empty for varying periods until the next shipment arrived. The term "scarcity" is used to describe a condition of that sort.

Most economists, of all stripes, regard the human condition, now and for the indefinite future, as one of scarcity rather than abundance. Indeed, the subject matter of economics is commonly defined as the analysis of the use of resources that are scarce relative to people's wants.[2] Scarcity is to economics as illness is to medicine. Medical science does not prohibit smoking; it merely says that if you smoke too much, you have a high chance of dying from lung cancer. Similarly, economics does not say that a society cannot provide all citizens with housing of the very best quality; it merely says that the more housing that is produced, the less of other good things can be produced. Most of what economics has to teach would be useless if scarcity gave way to abundance, much as most medical advice would be pointless if the human body were immune to illness.

The assumption that scarcity is the normal and inevitable condition of mankind is sometimes regarded with suspicion by people concerned with social issues. Surely, runs the criticism, the most productive societies in history are capable of providing more than enough for every citizen. That they do not do so demonstrates not that scarcity is in the nature of things, but that modern economies are very badly run. From that perspective, the scarcity assumption appears to reflect a very narrow preoccupation with the economies of our time, both capitalist and socialist, to the exclusion of more rational ways in which a modern economic system might be organized. If that criticism is valid, the assumption of scarcity may be appropriate for the analysis of existing societies but may be too restrictive to support a study of how an economy should be organized in a genuinely Good Society, as this book proposes to undertake.

That criticism strikes at the cornerstone of modern economics. Why worry about how best to use a country's resources under conditions of scarcity if scarcity could be eliminated by the proper economic arrangements? The best-crafted travel guide on seeing Europe on $10 a day has little useful advice for the traveller whose budget is unlimited. The criticism must be confronted directly, for economics has no wisdom to offer on how economic affairs might be managed in a world of abundance.

2 Scarcity and Wants

The term "abundance" connotes a state of plenty, and in normal discourse its meaning is not ambiguous. In some contexts, however, account must be taken of the fact that prince and pauper have rather different ideas about how large a collection of goods must be in order to be regarded as abundant. Economics is precisely such a context, and the term "abundance" has therefore taken on a technical meaning that involves not simply quantities of things but the relationship of those quantities to people's desires for them. It is a relative, rather than an absolute concept. However large a collection of goods may be, if people would willingly consume even more of them if they were available, that collection is regarded in economic analysis as scarce, relative to wants.

There would be less misunderstanding if the terms "scarcity" and "abundance" were replaced in economic discourse by the terms "insufficiency" and "sufficiency." Few people would be put off by the proposition that a most abundant collection of goods may nevertheless be insufficient to support a free-distribution arrangement in which everyone was entitled to take as much of everything as he wished. It is precisely that kind of condition that is described as one of scarcity in economic analysis.

Critics of the assumption of scarcity sometimes miss the point that it is intended as a relative rather than an absolute concept. Inequality of income, for example, is sometimes held to be the culprit responsible for what economists call scarcity. Where inequality is very large, the rich consume so much of what is produced that goods appear to be scarce to the rest of the population. It would seem to follow that with an equal distribution of income, scarcity would disappear, at least in rich countries. Scarcity, from that perspective, is not a universal fact of social life but the consequence of a bad social arrangement.

Suppose, however, that income were equally distributed. In the United States in 1996, the average American purchased about $19,000 worth of consumer goods and services.[3] That would certainly be regarded as a princely living by most of the people in the world, and a very good living by most of the people in the richer countries. The United States could therefore be said to have achieved abundance in that popular sense of the word. Even under such conditions of absolute abundance, however, it would be the rare person who would not consume much more than $19,000 worth of goods a year if he could freely walk out of any shop with any goods he desired.

The popular notion of abundance therefore finds no place in the economics of the Good Society. None of the important questions could be addressed if one knew only that the society enjoyed abundance in some absolute sense. One would have to know, in addition, whether the people would or would not consume more goods if they were freely available. If they would, scarcity in the economic sense still prevails, even in a world of absolute abundance, and the Good Society must employ some arrangement other than free distribution.

3   Wants and Needs

The assumption of scarcity, even in relation to wants, is sometimes said to be unnecessarily gloomy from the perspective of a Good Society. There is an important distinction to be drawn between wants and needs, runs the argument, and while wants may be virtually unlimited, it should not be beyond the production capability of a modern economy to satisfy all the people's needs.

While there are many different meanings to the notion of "need," they all imply a certain social consensus on what constitutes a decent, or normal, level of consumption. In practical terms that level may be established in various ways: by a survey of opinion, by a commission of experts, or by a voting procedure. It may be thought to embody the society's notion of the borderline between the comfortable and the excessive.

The distinction between wants and needs is often implicit, for example, in the characterization of certain wants as frivolous ("more elegant automobiles, more exotic food, more erotic clothing, more elaborate entertainment"[4]) compared to the wants of the poor for decent food, clothing, and shelter. In the socialist literature, however, the concept of need is explicit, notably in the Marxian slogan, "from each according to his ability, to each according to his needs."[5] Marx regarded that principle of distributive justice as appropriate to the distant future when abundance is finally achieved and a Good Society could be organized on fully communist lines. Since a communist society would be less materialistic and acquisitive than preceding societies, both capitalist and socialist, needs and wants would coincide. People would not want grander houses, or more foreign travel, or larger collections of books or CDs than the social norm.

Until that time, however, distributive justice would have to be restricted to paying each citizen "according to his work," rather than according to his need. The workers would then use their (unequal) pay to satisfy their wants. Marx therefore assumed that the post-revolutionary socialist society would continue to be characterized by scarcity relative to wants – the standard economic assumption. Only in the unspecified communist future would abundance be finally attained, making it possible to distribute consumer goods according to need, regardless of how large that might be.

Taking their cue from Marx, the Soviet Union devoted considerable effort to the calculation of consumption needs. The social need for housing space, for example, was established in 1926 as nine square meters per person. At that time the actual average housing space in the country was about half of that. It was therefore not intended as a poverty minimum but as the societal judgment of what a decent housing arrangement for a Soviet citizen ought to be.

Hence the focus on needs rather than wants, in these and other instances, does not invalidate the assumption of scarcity. Even if people want no more than they need, however need is defined, productive capability will fall far short of that level long into the future.

4   The Limitation of Wants

Since scarcity is a relative concept in the technical economic sense, the degree of scarcity can be changed in two ways. On the one hand, it can be diminished by an increase in the productive capability of the economy. That, indeed, is a major economic objective of most countries and of virtually all versions of the Good Society. On the other hand, scarcity may also be diminished, and perhaps even converted to abundance, by a large scaling-down of the people's desire for material goods and services. That alternative is rarely addressed in conventional economic analysis, but it is often considered as a proper objective of a Good Society, and in some instances has been put into practice.

SELF-RESTRAINT

When the meat is passed around the family table, the portion that each member takes for herself is tempered by an awareness of the amount of meat on the serving plate and the number of other diners. Children are taught to restrain themselves in that way, and in that small version of a Good Society, the method of free distribution can prevail. Reasoning from that form of social behavior, some people argue that in a genuinely Good Society, consumption behavior in general would be conducted in that socially responsible way. People would not take such large portions from the common store that some of their fellow citizens would be deprived. Hence a supply of goods that is scarce under an individualistic form of social organization would be abundant under a better form of social organization.

Voluntary self-restraint in consumption does indeed prevail in many small societies of various kinds, so that the method of free distribution can operate quite satisfactorily. The larger and more diverse the society, however, the less can one count on self-restraint. In a Good Society consisting of millions of people, many would no doubt behave in that exemplary way, but many would also take what they desire from the common store, with no regard to, and indeed with little knowledge of, the deprivation that their behavior imposes on others.

No modern society has ventured to employ a distribution arrangement whose success depends on people voluntarily consuming less than they want to consume. Nor does voluntary self-restraint command much attention in discussions of consumption in a Good Society. Societies that emphasize self-restraint focus attention not upon consumers' behavior, but on consumers' wants: their objective is not to induce people to consume less than they want to consume, but to induce them to want less.

The curtailment of wants has been justified on two grounds. One is that wants may be distorted or inflated by defective social arrangements that would be eliminated in a Good Society. The other makes a moral case for the limitation of wants.

THE SOCIAL CASE

If individual wants were autonomous – in the sense of being determined solely by physical or cultural factors – the goodness of the society might properly be judged by the extent to which the economic arrangements satisfy those wants. If wants are also influenced by those very social arrangements, however, the assessment of goodness of those arrangements is more complicated.

Under capitalism, for example, production is supposed to be guided by the consumption desires of the population. The economic arrangements are such, however, that producers are motivated to take actions designed to influence individual wants. Among them are advertising and new-product innovation.

Advertising   The incessant and uninvited bombardment of the senses by advertising strikes many people as one of the most obnoxious features of capitalism. In additional to that aesthetic objection, it is a staple of social criticism that advertising serves only to distort the size and structure of the people's wants. Any social arrangement that does no more than satisfy the very wants that it has artificially created cannot be said to contribute to the society's well-being. Arrangements that include commercial advertising should therefore be rejected by a Good Society, although it might be desirable to provide strictly informational advertising.

Advertising, however, is not a basic structural feature of the capitalist, or of any other, economy. In a democratic society it can be regulated lightly or heavily by public policy. In fact most capitalist economies do regulate it to some degree: by outlawing fraudulent advertising, by forbidding advertising in some public places, and in other ways. It could in principle be regulated out of existence if enough people were sufficiently hostile to it, though not without a variety of consequences for the performance of the economy. The question at hand, however, is not whether advertising detracts from or contributes to the goodness of the economy. It is whether advertising is partly or fully responsible for the continued prevalence of scarcity in societies that are prodigiously productive.

There is no doubt that advertising increases the demand for a great many things. Huge advertising budgets account for much of the sudden skyrocketing of prices and sales of a new Christmas-present doll, or of the immense financial success of a new blockbuster movie or deodorant. One should not judge the power of advertising by such success stories alone, however, for while those achievements make headlines, there are dozens of other heavily advertised products that never make the grade and quietly fade away, with no public awareness of their demise. Advertising may be powerful but it is not all-powerful.

Advertising may be particularly effective with certain classes of goods, such as addictive substances like tobacco and alcoholic beverages. Even with normal goods like automobiles, a company that discontinued its advertising would surely lose substantial sales to its competitors. And if every automobile company stopped advertising, total automobile sales would also very likely decline, although the decline in industry sales would probably be smaller than if only one company stopped advertising.

In both of those cases, however, the decline in automobile sales would leave more disposable income in people's pockets, at least some of which would very likely be spent on the purchase of other goods. The question is, if all advertising stopped, should one expect scarcity to vanish?; that is, would the overall demand for consumer goods fall so low that they could be freely distributed without charge?

Economists have long studied the statistical evidence on the relation between advertising and the sales of various products and product groups. Their primary interest has not been in the issue of scarcity but in such questions as whether advertising gives a company so much market power that it is protected from competition.[6] However, the research has produced a great deal of evidence on the overall effect of advertising on consumption. The general conclusion, as expressed by one prominent analyst, is that "overall, advertising does not emerge from the empirical literature on consumer demand as an important determinant of consumer behavior."[7] It is possible that there is a connection between advertising and consumption but that the data are too faulty or the econometric methods are too weak to detect it. The connection, if there is one, must be very small, however, because those same econometric methods were powerful enough to pick up important changes in consumer behavior such as the drop in cigarette consumption following the publication of the 1964 Surgeon General's Report.[8] It therefore appears that advertising clearly affects the distribution of sales among brands, and to some extent among classes of goods, but is not a major determinant of how much of their income people spend on consumption overall.

That conclusion is consistent with the consumption practices of earlier ages, which suggest that people whose incomes enable them to enjoy much more than the necessities of life do enjoy them to the limit of their incomes. The consumption of many princes and barons, indeed, often exceeded the incomes they were able to squeeze out of their subjects or tenants, which put them in perpetual debt to moneylenders. The term "conspicuous consumption" was later coined by Thorstein Veblen well before modern advertising was invented, and many people everywhere are likely to strive to "keep up with the Joneses" to some degree as long as there are Joneses who consume more than they do.

I have found no studies of the effects of international differences in rates of advertising, but it is not evident that variations in advertising account for the fact that in some countries people spend more of their income on consumption than in others. Nor is advertising so powerful as to persuade people generally to work more hours for the sake of more income and consumption; on the contrary, workers in Germany and elsewhere continually push for increased leisure, defying advertisings' enticement to earn more and consume more. In the Communist countries, on the other hand, there was virtually no advertising, but the people were notoriously driven to acquire consumer goods. That might be explained by their relatively low standard of living, but the acquisitive urge was no less keen in the highest-income families. Perhaps they were infected by the consumerism of the capitalist world, but no country is ever likely to succeed in cutting its people off entirely from knowledge of consumption practices elsewhere.

Many people, though certainly not all, would prefer a world in which there was limited or no advertising. It should not therefore be expected, however, that even the total elimination of advertising would finally conquer scarcity and enable the society to distribute all of its consumer goods freely. Scarcity will continue to require some form of controlled distribution of goods for the foreseeable future.

Innovation   The desirability of curtailing wants is also implicit in the critique of the process of innovating new consumer products in capitalist economies. Capitalist firms are motivated not only to produce goods that people want, but also to develop new goods in the hope that people will want them enough to pay for them. An economy in which production is motivated by private profit therefore continually expands the people's wants by continuously providing tempting new goods.

John Kenneth Galbraith has forcefully raised the question of whether a society's economic welfare can be said to be improving when its citizens, having satisfied one want, are forever confronted with new ones to be satisfied. He likens such a society to a squirrel in a cage, forever striving to "keep abreast of the wheel that is propelled by his own efforts."[9] Unlike advertising, however, this interesting philosophical question has not become an issue in public policy. No capitalist country has undertaken to eliminate the artificial component of consumption introduced by new-product innovation, nor have the Communist countries been any less enthusiastic in their efforts to encourage innovation. On the contrary, the rapid innovation of new products is everywhere regarded as a mark of the goodness of economic arrangements, and is likely to be so in any Good Society in the future.

THE MORAL CASE

Unlike the social case for the limitation of wants, the moral case has had a powerful impact. The basis of the argument is that a preoccupation with the acquisition of goods is morally degrading, particularly in the extreme form that it sometimes takes in capitalist societies. "Consumerism" deflects people's energies and thoughts from spiritual and cultural activities that contribute more to the moral quality of life.

Moral disapprobation of excessive consumption has been expressed in both capitalist and socialist societies. In capitalist societies, however, moral suasion on this matter has been the province of religious institutions and not of the state; indeed Max Weber's classic theory of the origin of capitalism assigns the critical role to the frugality of the consumption practices of the early Protestant sects, combined with a strong motivation to work and save. In Communist countries, however, it has been regarded as the duty of the state to inculcate socially oriented attitudes and to discourage individualistic attitudes, notably in the USSR, China, and Cuba. Socialist societies that rejected that message were criticized by others: "goulash communism" is the derisive epithet that was directed at Hungary when it abandoned centralized planning for a more market-based, consumer-oriented form of socialism.

The USSR   The socialist rejection of capitalist-style preoccupation with consumption colored Soviet life in the first decades after the revolution, when frugality was an important element of the Communist ideology. Party members were expected to set the tone and to teach by example: they received very low wages, dressed in simple workers' clothing, and lived a modest lifestyle. Their time and energies were singlemindedly devoted to the building of socialism. A concern with material things was the mark of a bourgeois temperament and was strongly criticized in Party circles and in the intelligentsia generally.

By the time of Josef Stalin's death in 1953, however, the ethic of frugality had greatly eroded. The crucial event was the introduction of material incentives for workers and managers at the inception of the intense industrialization drive of the 1930s. It became increasingly acceptable to strive to acquire more of those material goods that the society had to offer, such as larger apartments, furniture, clothing, and household appliances. By the end of Leonid Brezhnev's long tenure of office in 1982, the acquisition and display of consumer goods had become as conspicuous as in the capitalist world, although the level of consumption was markedly lower.

China   Revulsion at the consumerism of the USSR was, indeed, one of the factors contributing to the political break between China and the Soviet Union around 1960. To Mao Zedong and his colleagues the preoccupation with material consumption was among the more disgusting manifestations of what they regarded as the Soviet betrayal of socialism. The political break was followed by an effort to inculcate the virtues of socialist frugality that went far beyond what the Soviets had ever tried to do. The Chinese Communist Party used all of its power of example and indoctrination to propagate the virtues of frugality and modesty of lifestyle. Local and national Party members dressed in simple clothing and directed the substantial social pressures at their command to discouraging the show of stylish clothing, hair coiffeurs, makeup, jewelry, or other items of luxury. Young people were taught to interpret the desire for such frivolous things as evidence of a deficiency of character, and of unsuitability for an honorable career in the new society.

With the launching of the Cultural Revolution in 1966 the drive against bourgeois values escalated and people could get into serious trouble if they were known to hold such values, to say nothing of exhibiting them. The Chinese, indeed, were more explicitly concerned with people's values than the Soviets were. Millions of people were put through the rigorous discipline of "reeducation," in prisons or in exile to distant farms, with the purpose of changing their values, rather than merely changing their behavior. Prominent among those approved values was simplicity of material life.

That policy endured for a quarter of a century, from the time of the revolution in 1949 to the downfall of the "Gang of Four" after the death of Mao in 1976. Shortly afterward the policy was completely rejected by the new Party leadership. Within a remarkably short time, the uniform blouses and pants of the past gave way to skirts and colorful dresses, and the Mao jackets gave way to blue jeans, T-shirts and Western-type men's suits. Hairdressing shops opened up and cosmetics reappeared. Farmers whose incomes had increased began building new houses, with the two-story house emerging as the symbol of the new prosperity.

The experience of most other socialist societies has been similar. In none of them did the effort to infuse a frugal consumer ethic survive the first generation after the revolution.

The kibbutz Frugality has been an ideal not only in socialist societies but also in communities of various sorts. By communities I mean social groups that are parts of larger societies, like the Amish in the United States and the Israeli kibbutz. The latter is of particular interest because of its strong socialist orientation.

The kibbutz experience differs from the Soviet and Chinese in many ways. Before the establishment of the State of Israel in 1948, the average kibbutz consisted of only about a hundred families. It was a democratic community: all officials were elected and most jobs that carried authority were rotated, in order to prevent the formation of class differences or the accretion of power. It was a voluntary association, and members were free to leave for another kibbutz or for the city if they were discontent. What is crucial for our purposes, however, is that the socialist kibbutz[10] shared with Communist China a deeply held commitment to frugality and modesty of lifestyle. Accordingly, both work clothes and dress clothes were simple and inexpensive, and the members had very few items of clothing. Cosmetics and jewelry were frowned upon, and houses were small and spare.

In the course of time, however, as the income of the kibbutz increased, frugality gave way to greater liberality in consumer expenditure. More stylish clothing was bought by the kibbutz for its members. Houses were expanded, more elaborate furnishings were bought, and many kibbutzim built their own community swimming pools. There is little to distinguish the material lifestyle of kibbutz members today from that of urban people of equivalent incomes.

The evidence points to the conclusion that the prospects for a secular society to maintain a frugal tradition beyond the generation of the founders are very dim. That is not to say that it is impossible; no evidence based on the experience of societies of the past can exclude the possibility that some society in the future may succeed at it. That possibility exerts a powerful influence on the leaders of new revolutions. Fresh from having achieved what many had declared impossible in the past – the revolution – they have a powerful inclination to believe that they can achieve the impossible in peace as well as in war. They are determined not to follow the retreat from socialism of the corrupt societies of the past – notably the USSR. They feel deeply that "we revolutionary Chinese" – or Cubans or Vietnamese – will show the world the road to true socialism.

It is therefore entirely possible that some future revolutionary society will again strive to create its own version of the "new socialist man," undaunted by the failures of those efforts in socialist societies of the past. Some may succeed at first, but the weight of the evidence is that they will not succeed in the long run. The children and grandchildren of the founders tend to lose the revolutionary *élan* and to desire more of what they come to regard as the material good things of life.

We can only speculate on why that happens. Clearly, knowledge of the consumer goods available in the richer countries exerts a powerful influence on the wants of people in poorer countries – the so-called "demonstration effect." It is conceivable that if a frugality-minded society could insulate itself from contact with the richer capitalist societies, it might be able to preserve the austere ideals of the revolutionary period. There were indeed periods in which the USSR and China sought to do precisely that, in order to prevent the infection of their people by foreign bourgeois ideas. Both eventually gave up that effort, in part no doubt because of the heavy cost that policy entails in technological and economic progress. As long as new consumer goods continue to be developed abroad, the knowledge of their existence will tend to create new wants in countries that do not yet have them.

Economic experience therefore gives reason to doubt that any society other than a small religious community can succeed in eliminating scarcity by scaling back on people's wants. Hence, no nation is likely to have the capability of producing all the consumer goods that the people would desire if the goods were freely available. If the economics of the Good Society is to deal with the world of fact rather than of fancy, it must assume that goods are scarce relative to wants, and that scarcity will prevail for a long time into the future.

The fact of scarcity means that in all societies most people will have to be content with far fewer goods than they would like to consume. The Good Society must therefore strive to arrange that the goods that are available are distributed among the people in the best possible way, that is, in a way that is most consistent with its values.

Notes

1 Since productive property could not be privately owned, the high-income Soviet citizen could not invest in land or in securities like stocks and bonds (except for government savings bonds). The income that was not spent for consumer goods therefore simply accumulated in a bank account.

2 The term "scarcity" may refer either to the limited quantity of resources, which is the standard formulation, or to the limited quantity of goods that can be produced with those resources, which is the formulation used in Part II of this book.

3 US Bureau of the Census, *Statistical Abstract of the United States, 1997*, table 699.

4 Galbraith, *The Affluent Society*, p. 140.

5 Marx, "Critique of the Gotha Programme," p. 277.

6 Comanor and Wilson, "The effect of advertising on competition."

7 Schmalensee, "Advertising," p. 35.

8 Schmalensee, *The Economics of Advertising*, p. 207.

9 Galbraith, *The Affluent Society*, p. 156.

10 Not all the kibbutzim were committed to socialism. Some were primarily Zionist and some religious. The non-socialist kibbutzim did not share the anti-consumption ethic of the socialist kibbutzim, although they shared many of the same problems.

Chapter 5

Distributing Goods by Assignment

In the higher phase of communist
society, after ... all the springs
of cooperative wealth flow more
abundantly – only then can society
inscribe on its banners: from each
according to his ability, to each
according to his needs!
– Karl Marx

Now there arose up a new king
over Egypt, which knew
not Joseph.
– Exodus

CONTENTS

Since the fact of scarcity precludes the free distribution of consumer goods, the society must have some arrangement for regulating the distribution of the available consumer goods among the people. Most societies use the price method, which permits the citizens to choose the goods they wish to buy, within the limits of their income. Some societies, however, regard that method as inconsistent with their values. They are more attracted to an arrangement in which the society decides which goods should be assigned to which members, rather than each member deciding that for herself. That viewpoint reflects a certain conception of the Good Society with which most citizens of modern economies are not familiar.

Imagine a community in which there are no visible signs of class distinctions. There are no large differences in the members' dress or their house furnishings, and in any case, they have little interest in material things. No one has any possessions that the others do not have. An elected committee administers the distribution system, which provides the members with most consumer items, including educational and health services, all of which are delivered without charge. The members take their meals together in community dining halls, rather than in their separate homes, which strengthens the bond of fellowship. They have no need for money, there is no advertising, no merchants competing for their favor, no shopping and haggling over prices, no "keeping up with the Joneses." They have no experience with unemployment, and they live with the confidence that if they are unable to work, their family will fare no worse than if they could. All their material needs are provided for, within the limit of the community's resources, which leaves them free to devote most of their time to non-material pursuits and to activities that promote the society's goals, to which they are deeply committed.

That imaginary community encapsulates the vision of the Good Society held by the proponents of the assignment method of distributing consumer goods. No actual community conforms to it in all respects, although many of its features are embodied in such organizations as monastic orders and military establishments.[1] One can readily understand the appeal of distribution by assignment in those organizations, which have a particular kind of personnel and a fairly specific mission. It has also been adopted, however, by some societies of a more conventional sort where it was thought to provide the best environment for working, marrying, raising children, and living a good life. By what values, one may ask, does assignment qualify as a proper distribution arrangement for a Good Society?

I Assignment and Uniformity

A strong commitment to equality is surely an important part of the answer, but it cannot be the whole answer. Equality could also be achieved by the use of prices, simply by giving each person the same quantity of money. The citizens would then buy different things, depending on their personal preferences; but if all have the same income, the results should satisfy the most ardent egalitarian. And indeed most societies devoted to the principle of equality have found the price method perfectly serviceable.

The societies that chose the assignment method therefore had other purposes in mind than equality in consumption. One of them was uniformity. This may be seen in the experience of three societies that used the assignment method at various times in their history – the Israeli kibbutz, Maoist China, and the USSR.

THE KIBBUTZ

The kibbutz (the term connotes a community bound by a common purpose) is a voluntary democratic socialist community that derives its living from its farming and other production operations. There are about 120,000 people living in 260 kibbutzim (plural of "kibbutz") in Israel, each with 250–500 adult members.[2] Although they account for only 3–4 percent of the country's population, they have had an enormous impact on its political and social history.

Equality, interpreted as distribution according to need, is one of the cardinal values, and all members enjoy the same access to consumer goods, which is entirely unrelated to the work they do. The members provide the labor and share the responsibilities of management. In their transactions with the market economy surrounding them, they operate much like an ordinary enterprise: they derive their money revenues from the sale of their products in the Israeli and world markets, and they buy production inputs and consumer goods in those markets. Their consumption consists both of market-purchased goods and of the products of their own labor, such as food grown on their farm, and clothing and furniture made in their own workshops.

The purest form of the distribution of consumer goods by the assignment method was practiced in the early Israeli kibbutzim. While they were rich in communal spirit, they were exceedingly poor in material things, and virtually all goods were distributed freely among the members. Nobody "owned" anything: each member took the garments she needed from the communal laundry. Size and style were regarded as trivialities to which little attention was paid. By and large the goods consumed by any one member were virtually indistinguishable from those consumed by the others.

In the course of time, however, as the volume and variety of consumer goods increased, a more complex system of distribution evolved, driven largely by the members' growing desire to satisfy their personal preferences. By the 1950s, which may be considered the Classical Age of the kibbutz movement, four different variants of the assignment method had emerged, each dealing with a different category of consumption.[3] The members would vote each year on how much should be spent on each category.

Items in the first category, which included food, children's education, health, and welfare services, were supplied free of charge and were consumed on the basis of need. Meals were prepared and served in the communal mess hall by the members who worked in that facility, and each member would take what he wished. Thus people had equal access to these services and those who needed more consumed more, of both food and medical services.

The second category – called the personal allocation – consisted of clothing, footwear, and items of personal care which the members received in equal quantities. These items were now owned personally, in contrast to the common ownership of the past, but items in one group might not be substituted for those in another – a music lover could not acquire more CDs by surrendering part of his ration of clothing or books. Housing and furniture were distributed in a similar way, but with provision for differences in need: larger families, for example, had access to larger housing units.

The third category was the "personal budget" – a small cash allowance of "holiday money" that was distributed equally among the members. The money could be used for purchases in the kibbutz store or in the shops in the market economy. The personal budget, in effect, replaced the assignment by the price method, for the member used the money to buy whatever goods he desired and the community had no say in what he acquired.

The fourth category consisted of appropriations to meet the special needs of individual members. Since the members had no money except the small personal budget, they had to turn to the kibbutz for large expenditures such as travel funds to visit a sick parent or the financing of higher education. The member did not have a "right" to funds for such purposes but had to make a case for his request before the General Meeting, which then debated the case and voted on whether to appropriate the funds.

Under this complex goods-distribution arrangement, the individual members possessed very few things that all the other members did not also possess. Recently-built housing units were somewhat better than older ones, but the furnishings were virtually identical. There was some slight variation in clothing styles, but they were all purchased by the administrator or made by the resident tailor or dressmaker. The distribution was therefore not only equal but highly uniform.

SOVIET WAR COMMUNISM

Shortly after the Russian Revolution, the USSR stumbled into the use of the assignment method through the pressure of circumstances rather than through deliberate policy. The new government issued huge quantities of paper money which quickly destroyed the old monetary system. As the value of the ruble plunged, barter increasingly took the place of monetary exchange, and rationing was introduced to control the distribution of necessities like food and fuel.

If that were the whole story, the period would be quite unremarkable, and not unlike the wartime experience of a great many countries during the century. In the revolutionary fervor of the time, however, the more enthusiastic socialists saw the disappearance of money and the resort to distribution by assignment as the fulfilment of the Communist dream. Measures were therefore taken to accelerate the process of the "withering away" of money. Many nationalized enterprises were ordered to deliver goods to each other without payment, and they increasingly paid their workers in rations of goods rather than worthless money: "wage payments in kind [came] to be substituted for payment in depreciating paper rubles."[4] The availability of consumer goods contracted sharply during the period, but in the course of time a substantial portion of the goods still being produced were distributed by the authorities without charge. By 1920 they included postal and telephone services, water and electricity, housing, transportation, and basic food rations.[5] Had the civil war not brought production to a point of virtual collapse, the distribution of consumer goods by assignment might well have encompassed the whole economy. It would have been a world of uniform equality in which no one possessed what his neighbor did not possess.

In 1921, the dire economic situation compelled the abandonment of the economic system of War Communism. Private markets were legalized once again, monetary stability was restored, and the price method governed the distribution of goods for most of the rest of Soviet history.

MAOIST CHINA

Long after the Soviets abandoned their brief experiment with distribution by assignment, the Chinese decided to try their hand at it, and to do it right this time. Shortly after coming to power in 1949, the Chinese Communist leadership fashioned the country's economic institutions on the Soviet model of that time. In the course of a few years, however, relations between the two countries soured, and were all but severed after the Soviets turned up the heat by suddenly terminating their massive program of economic assistance to the struggling young Communist country. The break in relations freed the Chinese to express openly their view that the USSR had long since betrayed the goals of socialism by adopting all the trappings of capitalism that promoted individualism, consumerism, and inequality. They saw the "goulash communism" of the USSR not as a form of genuine socialism but as "state capitalism." In Chairman Mao Zedong's view, the powerful revolutionary energies of the Chinese people had been stifled, rather than released, by the Soviet institutions that they had adopted, such as incentive-based wage differentiation, and the vast centralized bureaucracy. In 1958, in a rebuff to their Soviet mentors, that model was dramatically rejected and replaced by the set of policies known as the Great Leap Forward.

Prominent among those policies was the organization of the entire rural population into 26,000 communes, averaging about 4,000–5,000 families.[6] The commune was to be managed by officials elected by the members, but in practice it was the Communist Party that filled the management positions. The new policy incorporated a massive drive for equality, the major effect of which was to reduce wage inequality (chapter 10). It also extended, however, to the arrangements whereby consumer goods were distributed within the communes.

Consumer goods were divided into two categories. The smaller proportion was put on sale for purchase with wage earnings, in the normal manner of the price method. The larger proportion, however, was distributed in kind, by the assignment method. The combination of direct distribution and money wages was known as the "supply-and-wage" system.

The goods and services that were provided by assignment were distributed uniformly among the peasants, with every family receiving the same allotments.[7] Food was provided without charge in commune mess halls, which were organized in order to free women for work in the communal economy. Education and medical services were also provided free in commune schools and clinics,[8] and the plans called for the eventual enrollment of all children in boarding kindergartens and primary schools.[9] The proportion of consumption distributed by assignment varied among communes, reaching an extreme of 70 percent in those with the most enthusiastic Communist leadership.[10]

The commune program originally called for the assignment of housing as well. The people were to move out of their individual homes into large communal dormitories in which husbands, wives, and children would live separately from each other. Except for a few instances, however, that part of the program was never put into practice because of its high cost, so that commune families continued to dwell in their individual cottages as in the past.[11]

The commune system was confined to the countryside. The urban population continued to work for wages and to buy their own consumer goods in the traditional fashion. Assignment made its appearance, however, in the form of extensive rationing. Many goods were in such short supply that they could be purchased only with ration coupons, the distribution of which was the province of the administrators. Hence, while the distribution of consumer goods by assignment made large strides during the Great Leap Forward, money and the price method continued to be used for many goods in most of the country. Uniformity in consumption nevertheless proceeded quite far – at least among the masses, for the political elite rapidly found ways of augmenting the quantity and variety of their own families' consumption.

Uniformity was furthered by the high degree of equality in the distribution of income. While the large regional income differences of the past continued to prevail, within regions China came closer to achieving income equality than any of the Communist countries; and when incomes are equal, people's consumption patterns tend to be more similar than when incomes are unequal. Uniformity in consumption was also promoted by the state's control over the production process: the variety and diversity of the consumer goods that were produced was greatly restricted. One thinks of the China of those days as the land of the uniform blue padded jacket, worn by both men and women on all occasions. The price method of distribution enabled the people to buy some of the available goods for money, but the government saw to it that the range of goods available for purchase was narrowly restricted.

2 The Ethics of Uniformity

Distribution by prices gives the maximum expression to individual preferences, and the near-universal use of the price method in modern societies signifies that consumer choice is widely held to be the proper criterion for judging the goodness of a distribution arrangement.

The adoption of the assignment method, however, reflects a commitment to societal choice rather than consumer choice as the appropriate criterion of what makes for a Good Society. What sort of value system undergirds the preference for societal choice?

Two ethical principles appear to drive that preference.

THE COMMUNAL ETHIC

In the three societies described above, the devotion to societal choice derives from what may be called the communal ethic. In that conception of a Good Society, the quality of the citizen's life should depend heavily, perhaps even primarily, on his participation in the life of his society. The mental world of the people should be occupied with their communities and their neighbors and not with their individual selves. "The goal of the people," wrote Mao, "is not 'one spouse, one country house, one automobile, one piano, one television.'"[12] The contrasting ethic of individualism, in the sense of the preoccupation with oneself, is regarded as a lower order of existence, widely practiced in the rest of the world from which they have withdrawn, in a sense, in order to live by higher principles of social consciousness.[13] People who live under a regime of consumer choice spend a good deal of their time thinking about that most individual of matters – what "I" want, instead of what would be best for all of us to have. A child growing up in such a world is socialized to think mostly about herself and not about the community. The assignment method, in contrast, broadens the scope of the choices that the society makes with the general interest in mind, and narrows that of the choices that each citizen makes with his personal concerns in mind.

One can understand how people strongly committed to a communal ethic, and perhaps in profound rebellion against a former society dominated by an individualist ethic, might find their way to the assignment method of distributing goods. That does not yet explain, however, why the societies that adopted that method also used it to achieve uniformity in consumption.

The assignment method does not require that goods be distributed uniformly among the citizens. The distribution might be decided upon in some societal arrangement, such as a community meeting or a governmental distribution agency; but the policy might be to distribute the goods in a way that takes account of different people's preferences. The society may decide that Smith should have a sailboat, that Jones should have a woodworking shop, that Brown should have a piano, and so on in accordance with individual consumption preferences. As practiced in the kibbutz and China, however, the assignment method was not implemented in that way. On the contrary, insofar as possible each citizen was assigned the same collection of goods.

Among the reasons for the preference for uniformity was the benefit derived from economies of scale in production, notably in China: more jackets can be produced if they are all of the same style than if there are many styles. That consideration could be expected to weigh heavily in a poor country. To some degree the preference for uniformity was a matter of making a virtue out of necessity, but there is no reason to doubt that uniformity was genuinely regarded by the people as making for a better socialist society.

Apart from that practical reason, however, uniformity is attractive because it eases the task of assuring equality when different people prefer to consume different goods. A distribution in which everybody gets the same things is unquestionably equal, but when people get collections of *different* things, it is not at all evident that they are equal. Despite the best efforts of an administrator to preserve equality, if the citizens receive different collections of goods, each one may feel that the collection assigned to him is of lesser value than that assigned to others. Uniformity may therefore have been adopted because it is the distribution that would best contribute to solidarity by avoiding conflict and resentment.

Perhaps something of this sort is in the minds of the people who use the assignment method to achieve a uniform distribution of consumer goods. The literature suggests, however, that there is more to it than that. Uniformity is not merely a device for minimizing conflict but also serves the positive purpose of promoting another principle, which may be called the spiritual ethic.

THE SPIRITUAL ETHIC

The notion is that a preoccupation with spiritual matters, whether secular or religious, is morally superior to an obsession with material things. All socialist societies profess a disdain for the "consumerism" that pervades the bourgeois world. To raise your child in that kind of world, bombarded by advertising and conspicuous consumption, is to ensure that his head will be excessively occupied with things to buy. The better society is one in which spiritual concerns dominate and material things are held in low regard. The people are involved in music and the arts, or in sports, or in politics, or in the social services, or in virtually anything but the acquisition of more goods.

Where consumer choice prevails, people inevitably spend much of their time and thought choosing among different goods. Children who grow up under such conditions become consumption-oriented adults, to the detriment of their devotion to higher things. In some families and societies the preoccupation with shopping for material things may be very slight, but in others it may be very large, with a corrupting effect on others.

A society that places a very high value on the spiritual ethic will therefore be attracted to an arrangement in which everybody wears the same clothes, has the same furniture, and eats the same foods. The citizen has neither the need, nor the opportunity, to invest time and thought in what elsewhere can become an endless quest for more and better material goods. Uniformity of consumption thus consigns material goods to that small corner of the good life that is all they deserve, and opens the way to a life rich in spiritual concerns.

3   Retreat from Uniformity

In the course of time the practice of uniform distribution has gradually eroded in the kibbutz, and was completely abandoned in China.

The kibbutz   In the kibbutz, dissatisfaction with uniformity took the form of a gradual increase in pressure for a wider range of choice among goods. It was stimulated by incidents like the gift of a teapot to a young member from her non-member parents. She began to brew tea in her own room, and to invite some friends to join her. The purists regarded the possession of a private teapot not only as a breach of equality but also as an egregious violation of the principle of communal eating and an unacceptable rejection of communality in favor of personal privacy. It symbolized the erosion of the society by a gradual accommodation to the baser human drives, and the "teapot scandal," as it became known, was debated endlessly in the General Meetings throughout the kibbutz movement.[14] The traditionalists eventually caved in and the problem was dealt with by buying private teapots for all members. Since the kibbutz is a democratic association, changes in people's values on such matters as uniformity and choice are eventually reflected in changes in institutional arrangements.

One line of reform was the replacement of the restrictive "personal allocation" by a new distribution arrangement called the "comprehensive budget."[15] Under this technique the members would receive an equal allotment of money tokens, which could be used for any of the items previously distributed in physical form as a personal allocation. The member could then acquire whatever combination of shirts, CDs, art books, and other items he wished within the limit of his allotment of tokens. The tokens could be used in the kibbutz store, or converted into cash for off-kibbutz purchases. The advantages claimed for the comprehensive budget are that it would enable the members to acquire the goods they most wanted instead of what the community thought they should all have, and that it would eliminate the red tape and the inevitable frictions involved in administrative allocation.

The proponents of the comprehensive budget had, in effect, rediscovered money and the price method, though in the slightly disguised form of money tokens. More radical reformers proposed to drop the disguise by distributing not money tokens but actual money, which would then take the place of both the personal allocation and the cash allowance. This measure would, in effect, replace the assignment method by the price method for all goods except those directly distributed without charge like food and elementary education.

These reforms do not violate the rule of equality since each member receives the same value of tokens or money. They do, however, violate the rule of uniformity, since their express purpose is to provide a larger domain of choice in which purely individual consumption desires could be indulged – and it is that which drew the fire of the conservatives. If anyone doubts the passions that can be evoked by the innocent-sounding issue of the distribution of consumer goods, let him read the accounts of those heated debates in the meeting halls of the kibbutzim.

Almost all kibbutzim now distribute a substantial proportion of their earnings in the form of either money tokens or money. In a similar vein, many have voted to permit members to take some of their meals in their own apartments, and funds have been appropriated to supply all apartments with refrigerators and stoves. The principle of income equality has been unbreached, but the sphere of uniform consumption has greatly contracted. Visitors note that the material conditions of life on the kibbutz no longer differ radically from the "bourgeois" life of the country at large that the founders had sought to escape. The best bet is that the sphere of distribution by assignment will continue to shrink, although vestiges of it may well endure for a long time.

China   In the kibbutz, uniformity of consumption was originally instituted because the members believed that it contributed to the goodness of the society. As the dominant values gradually changed, the democratic process made it possible to change over gradually to a distribution arrangement that permitted a wider range of consumer choice. In China, in contrast, uniformity of consumption was introduced not because it reflected the popular view of how people wished to live, but because it reflected the views of Mao and his supporters of how the people ought to live. Dissatisfaction with uniform distribution by assignment could not be expressed openly, but there appears to have been very little popular support for the practice, which may be judged from the enthusiasm with which the people embraced the new "consumerism" that materialized soon after the death of Mao.

The Great Leap Forward led, after a few years, to a catastrophic decline in production. Unfavorable weather conditions contributed greatly to the disaster, but "peasant and worker resistance to the extreme emphasis on the psychic element"[16] were a major factor as well. The production crisis precipitated a bitter dispute within the Party, followed by a remarkable reversal in policy in which the drive for equality embodied in the Great Leap Forward was all but abandoned. The new slogan was "Egalitarianism is neither socialism nor Communism . . . [but] is reactionary, backward, and retrogressive."[17] With respect to consumer goods distribution, the proportion of goods distributed by assignment was drastically cut back and assignment was restricted to providing a guaranteed minimum subsistence for commune families.[18] Since most of the workers' consumption depended once again on how much they could buy with their wages and not on free distribution by an administrator, the motivating power of wage earnings was restored.

The Great Leap Forward embodied the egalitarian vision of Chairman Mao, and the disaster weakened his authority in the Party. He managed to regain power in 1966 and pursued that vision once again in the tumultuous Cultural Revolution, but after his death in 1976, the new leadership under Deng Xiaoping rejected the assignment method wholesale. Urban shops now feature a great variety of clothing and the city crowds are dressed as variously as in any capitalist country. The expansion of beauty parlors and hairdressing salons for women is a conspicuous manifestation of the attenuation of the spiritual ethic and the dominance of individual consumption preferences. As a one-party state China's way has been different from that of the kibbutz but the direction of change has been the same.

UNIFORMITY AND EFFICIENCY

If equity and societal choice are among your criteria of goodness, then the assignment method is an appropriate arrangement for your Good Society. If efficiency is also one of your criteria of goodness, how does the assignment method score by that criterion?

An arrangement for distributing consumer goods among the people may be said to be efficient if it results in the best of all possible distributions of those goods. In the Maoist and kibbutz visions of the Good Society a uniform distribution is defined as the best. Hence the assignment method is more efficient than the price method, for only under the former can the best distribution be achieved.

Uniformity in consumption, however, is not the only distribution that can be achieved by the assignment method. One can imagine a society that adopts the assignment method but has no particular devotion to uniformity. They believe that it makes more sense for people to get the goods that they desire rather than the same goods as everybody else. They might then instruct the administrator to distribute the goods in a way that would take account of individual preferences. Music lovers would receive better hi-fi equipment and more CDs, for example, but fewer clothes and no personal teapot. How would the assignment method perform by the criterion of efficiency in such a case, when it was not burdened by the commitment to uniformity?

There happens to have been a society-in-microcosm that found itself in just such a circumstance. It employed the assignment method for distributing consumer goods, but unlike Maoist China and the kibbutz, it regarded consumer choice as an entirely desirable and natural basis for distributing its goods. An examination of that case provides a useful introduction to the meaning of efficiency in a society that values consumer choice.

4 A Prisoner-of-War Camp

During World War II the internees in German prisoner-of-war camps had two sources of supply of food and other consumer goods. One was the rations supplied by the German military authorities. The other consisted of packages of supplies delivered by the International Red Cross. To the good fortune of economic science, a prisoner in a British officers' camp was an economist, R. A. Radford, who undertook to observe, record, and analyze the economic arrangements that developed in the camp community.[19] One such arrangement dealt with the distribution of the goods supplied in the rations and in the Red Cross packages.

The Red Cross packages contained identical sets of goods: cans of tinned beef, diced carrots, condensed milk, toilet articles, chocolates, packs of cigarettes, and so forth. Since the production of the goods was not under the control of the community, work incentives were not an issue and equality was the natural principle of "income" distribution. Each prisoner accordingly received one package. The German rations of food and clothing were also distributed equally. The camp thus found itself operating, under the force of circumstances, with an arrangement characterized by equality of income and uniform distribution of consumer goods. It was a pure form of distribution by assignment.

Unlike the kibbutz and China, however, the assignment method was adopted in the camp for strictly practical reasons of convenience and not in order to support some other value like uniformity. The response of the prisoners to the assignment method under that condition is a rare historical case of the spontaneous development of barter trade, culminating finally in an arrangement that was a rudimentary form of the price method.

The distribution system evolved through a series of stages. When the camp was first formed and the Red Cross packages began to arrive, the goods were rather casually redistributed among the prisoners. For instance, most non-smokers simply gave their ration of cigarettes to friends who smoked. Others traded some of their less-desired goods for more-desired goods. After several appearances of the packages, however, it became increasingly clear that this form of goods distribution was likely to endure for some time, and people began to deal less casually with the disposition of their periodic goods-income.

In the second stage a bulletin board materialized, on which some people posted their offers to trade. The bulletin board greatly improved the quality of the information available to the prisoners. Gradually the growing number of offers converged upon a very small range, and the posted offers to trade became fairly uniform: the "cigarette-price of beef" might settle down to 12 cigarettes per can of beef. People were less likely to experience the disappointments of the first stage, when one might have traded a tin of beef for 10 cigarettes only to learn later that other people would have paid 15 cigarettes for it.

The third stage consisted of the gradual shift to cigarettes as the primary good in which trading offers were expressed. People would trade their meat or chocolates for cigarettes even if they were non-smokers, in the expectation that the cigarettes could later be traded for other desired goods. Cigarettes thus gradually took on some of the properties of money. They served as the "medium of exchange," in the sense that one would both "sell" and "buy" things with cigarettes. They also served as a "store of value," in the sense that one could accept cigarettes today in exchange for unwanted goods, in the confidence that the cigarettes could be used to buy more desired goods sometime in the future.

The final stage was the establishment, with the agreement of the camp commander, of a store that issued money tokens in exchange for goods. One could sell one's beef or chocolates to the store in exchange for a specified number of Bully Marks, which were pieces of paper issued by the store. The Bully Marks could then be used at any time to buy tea or coffee or other things that were served at the store, or to buy other goods that had been traded to the store by other POWs. The prices in Bully Marks at which the goods or services could be purchased at or sold to the store were established by the POWs who volunteered to manage it.

By the time the war ended and the camp closed, a full-blown money system had developed. There was not yet, however, a fully developed price method for distributing the goods. The goods continued to be delivered to the camp in the form of Red Cross packages and camp rations, and then assigned to the prisoners in equal amounts. However, the store and the money system made it possible for a substantial portion of the goods to be easily converted into money and then redistributed in a manner in which the individual preferences of the prisoners could be served.

5   Barter

Even when supported by a strong moral conviction, the assignment method has tended to erode in the course of time. When there is no such moral force behind it, however, it erodes at once. That was the experience of the POW camp. Each new delivery of Red Cross packages was followed at once by a burst of bartering.

The POW camp was a most unusual society, but the economic processes that emerged there reflect in microcosm certain arrangements, like barter, that have appeared throughout history. In modern societies in particular, barter tends to appear when some consumer goods are distributed directly by the assignment method. For example, in the USSR and most Communist countries, housing was directly distributed by an agency of government and the rent charge was negligibly small. Most people were delighted at the low rent, but in the course of time some found that their housing did not match their desires. One person would get a new job in another part of town and seek an apartment closer to her work, or a family would grow and the old apartment would be too small. There were other apartments inhabited by older couples or widows with more rooms than they needed. Similar mismatches occur in cities in capitalist countries in which rents are controlled at low levels. In all such cases, people tend to seek out others with whom a trade can be made. If the law permits, the barter is done legally, but if not, it is often done illegally. In Soviet cities, for example, there were bulletin boards on which people posted notices of apartment exchanges that they wished to make, sometimes supplementing the offer with a sum of money or other scarce goods to consummate the exchange.

Barter trade is surely one of the oldest of human institutions. It was practiced in societies that predated by millennia such present-day systems as capitalism and socialism. A practice that durable must reflect some human wisdom that should be taken account of in the design of a Good Society, else the outcome may prove to be very different from the design.

Historical experience can serve as a guide only to what is likely to happen. The Good Society should be concerned not only with what is likely to happen but also with the normative question of whether it ought to be permitted to happen. In this case, the question is whether barter makes for a better or worse society than one without barter.

6   Barter and Efficiency

The spontaneous evolution of the POW camp's distribution system suggests that the prisoners found each successive stage of barter exchange to be better than the preceding one; for if it were not, it would not have been accepted. The reasons for that particular institutional evolution contain an important lesson about the meaning of an assertion that one arrangement is "better" than another.

The initial distribution of the Red Cross packages fully satisfied the society's sense of equity, but it left something to be desired. Some people have a sweeter tooth than others, and some have a strong fancy for tinned beef. It would seem that a better distribution would be one in which the one would get more sweets and the other more beef. Equity is still important, but one would think that the goods could be distributed in some other way that would be no less equitable but would also take account of differences in preferences.

Bartering was the response of the POWs to just that sentiment. The non-smokers traded their cigarettes for bully beef or other things they preferred, and those with a strong urge for chocolates traded other things for more chocolates. In the course of time, the original uniform distribution was thoroughly transformed into a non-uniform distribution through barter trading.

Intuitively one feels that the second is a better distribution than the original one, for two reasons. First, everyone who bartered must have been better off, since bartering was voluntary and no one was under compulsion to barter away any of his goods unless he regarded it as worth his while. Second, nobody can have been hurt by the bartering: at the worst those people who did not barter at all ended up with the same goods as they received initially, and were therefore no worse off than they would have been in the absence of barter. That widely shared intuition implies a certain test of goodness: one distribution is better than another if there are some winners and no losers.

THE PARETO CRITERION

The rule of "some-winners-no-losers" was formalized a century ago by the Italian scholar, Vilfredo Pareto, and serves to this day as the basis of much of what economists mean by the assertion that some distributions are "better" than others, or that a certain distribution is the "best" of all, or the "optimum."

Pareto's criterion of the goodness of a certain distribution of goods requires that an initial distribution be compared with all other ways in which the same collection of goods could be distributed among the same people. One then asks whether there are any among those other distributions in which one or more people are better off and no one is worse off than under the initial distribution. If any such other distributions exist, they are better than – or "Pareto-superior" to – the initial distribution. If no such other distributions exist, then the given distribution is the best, or a "Pareto-optimal" distribution. An economic arrangement that leads to an optimal distribution of goods is said to be "efficient," or "Pareto-efficient." It is also said to yield the highest level of "satisfaction," or of "consumer welfare." The common-sense meaning is that a collection of goods provides more satisfaction if the right goods go to the right people than if the same collection of goods were badly distributed among them.

Applying the Pareto criterion to the POW camp, it is evident that the initial uniform distribution of the goods was not optimal. The burst of barter trading following the delivery of the Red Cross packages demonstrated that there were many ways of redistributing the goods that were Pareto-superior to the initial distribution because some people were better off and none was worse off. What is not readily apparent, however, is that the effect of barter trading was to reshuffle the goods among the prisoners in such a way that the distribution after the completion of bartering was not merely better than the original distribution but was also Pareto-optimal. That must be so, however, because the bartering process does not come to an end until no POW can find anyone else with whom he can make another mutually beneficial trade. The cessation of trading therefore signifies that the goods are now so distributed that no one could find a way of improving his own position without worsening that of another – without stealing someone else's chocolates, for example.

That is a remarkable conclusion, of very large significance for the economics of a Good Society. It signifies, first, that there exists at least one known arrangement – barter trading – that is efficient, in the sense that it causes the available consumer goods to be distributed optimally among the people. Secondly, it signifies that an optimal distribution can be attained by the voluntary activity of the people themselves, without the participation of any central administrative agent or government. That should be comforting to all whose vision of a Good Society assigns a minimal role to government, from anarchists at one end of the spectrum to libertarians at the other.

The conclusion is that in a society that values consumer choice over societal choice, the uniform distribution of goods by the assignment method is an inefficient arrangement. Barter trading, on the other hand, is efficient because it effects a redistribution of the goods among the people in a way that leads to an optimal distribution. It remains true, however, that assignment is the better method if the criterion of goodness is societal choice.

Unfortunately, the theoretical virtue of barter trading is compromised by its practical difficulties. It is a very clumsy way of working toward an optimal distribution. Even in the POW camp, after a few months' experience with barter trade it began to give way to a rudimentary form of the price method of distributing the goods. The establishment of the store, and then the issuance of money in the form of Bully Mark coupons, were steps in that direction. It was not yet a full-blown price method, for the goods were still distributed initially in kind – in the Red Cross packages and camp rations. Had the war not ended when it did, it is likely that a full price arrangement would have been adopted. The goods would have been delivered to the store instead of being delivered initially to the prisoners. The store would have issued money coupons to the prisoners, who would then have used the money to buy the goods they wanted from the store. The goods would then have been distributed by a full-blown price method.

7 Equity and Barter

The Pareto criterion has been criticized as a biased and misleading standard for judging the goodness of economic arrangements. The criticism is levelled primarily at the "no-losers" condition. To require that no one be worse off in order that one distribution be pronounced as better than another is to rule out all but the most inconsequential ways of improving a society, runs the argument. For example, it rules out even the smallest redistribution of food or housing from the rich to the poor, because the rich would be "worse off" by that action. The no-losers restriction is thus extremely conservative, for it encases the status quo in concrete.[20] A criterion of that sort, it would seem, offers no useful guidance in the search for a Good Society. Since this book relies heavily on the Pareto criterion, that criticism must be addressed.

It is correct to say that by the Pareto criterion, a redistributive income tax – which taxes the rich to increase the income and consumption of the poor – does not qualify as "efficient" because the rich are worse off. On the other hand, it cannot be pronounced as *inefficient* either. The Pareto criterion simply does not apply to cases in which equity is affected because some people are worse off.

It does not follow, therefore, that a redistributive income tax diminishes the goodness of the society as a whole, for efficiency is not the only criterion of goodness. It would be a much better society by the equity standard of distributive justice, for example, because after the tax is in operation, the poor consume more and the rich less. The new distribution, moreover, may be scrupulously optimal by the Pareto criterion. In that case, the society can be said to be more equitable and no less efficient than before the tax.

It is rather like an imaginary "Pareto IQ Test," the instructions for which clearly state that the test is valid only for students whose native language is English. Hence if Helen, Steve, and Chang receive scores of 120, 105, and 60 on the test, Helen can be said to have a higher Pareto IQ than Steve; but Chang, who lives in Shanghai, cannot be said to have a lower IQ than either. The test is simply not defined for non-speakers of English. Similarly the Pareto criterion of efficiency is simply not defined for assessing the goodness of a distribution in which somebody is worse off than under the initial distribution.

The no-losers condition greatly restricts the sphere of application of the Pareto criterion. A great deal of clarity is gained by that restriction, however. The merit of the no-losers condition is precisely that it makes it possible to draw a clear distinction between issues of equity and efficiency.

Consider, for example, a divorce settlement in which the family property had previously been divided between the spouses on the basis of considerations that had been agreeable to both of them at a happier time. The divorced parties could agree to accept the pre-divorce distribution of the assets, or they could redistribute the assets between themselves in a great many different ways. Among all those possible redistributions, there are some to which one spouse or the other would not agree because they would regard themselves as worse off. The question of whether any of those "non-Pareto" distributions are better than the pre-divorce distribution must be decided on grounds of equity. For instance, if most of the assets had been registered in the husband's name, a court might decide that it would be equitable to reassign some of the assets to the wife. In that case a redistribution under which the husband is worse off but the wife better off is held by the court to be more equitable.

There may be another subset of "Pareto-type" redistributions, however, under which both parties would be better off. A specialist in efficiency, for instance, might propose a transfer of ownership of the beach cottage and the power boat to the husband in return for a transfer of full ownership of the main house to the wife. If both parties agree to that redistribution, then that new distribution is better than the original one by the criterion of efficiency.

In separating considerations of equity from those of efficiency, the Pareto criterion gives a certain priority to equity. It says, in effect, that when any redistribution hurts somebody, the question of whether it makes for a better society should first be decided on grounds of equity. Once that determination is made, however, the efficiency expert can be called in, as it were, to determine whether the second distribution is optimal in the Pareto sense. If it is not, he may devise yet other ways of redistributing the goods that are more efficient but no less equitable than the second.

Winners and losers under bartering   Applying the foregoing to the POW camp, to assert that barter trading is an efficient arrangement in the Pareto sense implies that the post-barter distribution is no less equitable than the original uniform distribution, since no one needs to trade anything if it would make him worse off. A closer look at the experience of the internees, however, gives reason to question whether there are indeed no losers under trading.

One source of creeping inequality, for example, is that people differ in their trading skills, ranging from those who are clearly befuddled or regard the whole business with distaste, to those who are extremely shrewd at it or obsessed by it. In the POW camp "stories circulated of a padre who started off round the camp with a tin of cheese and five cigarettes and returned to his bed with a complete parcel in addition to his original cheese and cigarettes."[21] In that case it is clear that the redistributed collections of goods are unequal: if the padre ended up with what everyone had originally but with some additional cheese and cigarettes, the rest of the camp must have ended up collectively with less than they had originally.[22]

Such barter-induced inequality can be evaluated in two ways. First, the degree of inequality of this sort can be regarded as acceptably small. As long as people start initially from an equal position, if they freely give up some items for others they prefer, they should be regarded as substantially, if not completely, equal after the trade.[23]

A second interpretation is that bartering takes time and effort, which people would not put forth except in the expectation of some personal gain. It is therefore analytically equivalent to applying labor in a production process, which adds to the value of the initial resources. People such as the energetic padre do end up with a more valuable collection of goods than some others, the excess serving as the "wage" of the labor he expended. If one's criterion of equity is sufficiently flexible to justify some degree of inequality if it is derived from the application of labor, then the post-barter distribution can be regarded as entirely equitable if not precisely equal.

By the criterion of equity, therefore, there should be no serious objection to barter in a Good Society that values consumer choice, even though it leads to a non-uniform distribution.

8 Ethics and Barter

The experience of the POW camp suggests that consumer choice exerts a powerful appeal as a criterion for assessing the goodness of economic arrangements. It is not without its disadvantages, however, from the broader perspective of what makes for a Good Society. Barter trade is consistent with the value of consumer choice, but it also introduces certain moral issues that are of very ancient vintage.

One casualty of the barter process in the POW camp was altruism. Non-smokers originally simply gave their cigarettes to friends who smoked; after bartering developed, however, they traded their cigarettes for other goods. If the cultivation of altruism ranks high on one's scale of values (one must recall that all this was before the Surgeon General's warning on the dangers of smoking), then the introduction of trading must be judged to have diminished the goodness of the society. That view of the matter is part of the ethical basis of the Maoist and kibbutz positions. From their perspective, to give things to one's neighbor without demanding something in return is both to express and to strengthen the solidarity of the community; to give only in return for what one can get is to treat one's neighbor as an object rather than as an a communal part of oneself.

That view is not confined to political radicals. It occupies a place in many ethical systems, both secular and religious. It is often derived from the notion that the Good Society is one in which people relate to each other like members of a family. The distributive arrangements within a family are based on love and altruism, and it is repulsive to contemplate the parent giving to the child only with an eye to what can be gained in return. By extension, relations among members of a Good Society should be based on love and altruism rather than personal benefit.[24] That view of the matter underlies the hostility expressed in much of the world toward people engaged in trade and commerce.

To people who regard the family as the ideal model of what all human relationships should be, the introduction of trading in the POW camp will seem to have diminished the goodness of that society. They would be inclined to suppress barter trade, but they should be aware that the consequence is a less efficient distribution of the goods. If much of the population does not share their values, it would be virtually impossible to prevent them from trying to get more of the goods they want by trading away some of the goods for which they have little use.

9   Discussion

My purpose in this chapter was to present the views of the proponents of distribution by assignment and of uniform consumption in a reasonably dispassionate way – in a way that people who cleave to those ideas would regard as a fair statement of what they believe and why they believe it. No one can be fully dispassionate on such matters, and I can only hope that my presentation will be regarded as passably objective on the highly charged subject of what makes for a Good Society. In the discussion section of this and later chapters, however, I take the liberty of expanding on my personal views.

The notion that consumer goods should be equally distributed in a Good Society is entirely reasonable, even if it does not correspond to one's own idea of what makes for such a society. The additional notion that uniformity of consumption also contributes to goodness, however, will strike most people as quite absurd. That notion, however, has exerted a profound influence on the lives of millions of people at various times and places, which is reason enough to try to understand why so many people have held it.

By what line of reasoning can the yearning for a Good Society lead to so strange a notion as uniform consumption? I proposed above that the link between the two is the commitment to the ethical principles of spirituality and communality. Many people share those values in some sense, however, but do not find uniformity of consumption at the end of that logical road. There must be some additional considerations in the reasoning that leads from those values to uniformity.

The communal ethic   The communal ethic holds that the best society is one in which most decisions are made by the society in the interest of the society, rather than by each member in his own interest. The criterion of goodness of the distribution arrangements is therefore societal choice, rather than consumer choice.

The preference for societal choice leads to the assignment method of goods distribution. It is not evident, however, that it must also lead to uniformity. It is possible to distribute the goods non-uniformly, so as to take account of individual needs and preferences where these are regarded as legitimate. The family is an institution that does precisely that. The kibbutz also does that at times. A young person who has a talent for music and a strong desire to cultivate it may be given outside music lessons at the expense of the entire community, much as in a family. The decision is made in a community meeting, however, and the majority of members have to be persuaded that the decision is in the interest of the community and not merely the indulgence of a purely personal preference.

In a small community of face-to-face relationships, such differentiation can be accomplished. There are bound to be hard feelings from time to time when one petition is turned down and another accepted. By discussion and patient negotiation, however, the common goods can be distributed non-uniformly among the members in such ways that the members would regard themselves as having been treated equally over time.

The larger the society, however, the harder it is to pull that off. The trust that is built up over years in a face-to-face community cannot be extended to the distribution agent of even a benevolent government, who cannot know all the members of the society personally. The surest way to satisfy the sense of equality under those conditions is through uniform distribution. That, indeed, was the motivation even in the relatively small community of the POW camp. By that line of reasoning, if you subscribe to the communal ethic you are bound to prefer the assignment method of distributing consumer goods, and then to accept uniformity as the proper form of distribution in all but the smallest of societies.

The flaw in that argument, in my opinion, consists of a misapplication of the notion of a communal ethic. There is a germ of truth in the notion that it would be a better society if people considered not only their individual interest when they made their decisions but also the interest of their neighbors and of the society; only the purest egoist would protest that proposition. Like all germs, however, it can cause disease. The disease in this case is the extension of that innocent proposition to a preference for societal over consumer choice in the distribution of consumer goods generally.

The case for the virtue of the communal ethic is often based on the family as the ideal model of the relationships that should prevail in a Good Society. I introduced that metaphor in the discussion of the ethics of trading in the POW camp. There, it will be recalled, as trading developed non-smokers ceased to give their cigarettes freely to their friends but began to require something in exchange. Something was surely lost when attention to one's own preferences crowded out attention to one's comrade's preferences. In my own view, however, that criticism of barter trading makes impossible demands upon people, and is in fact subversive of true family relationships. I suspect that people who imagine themselves capable of relating to all others like brothers are in fact incapable of relating to their brothers as brothers, much like the old saw about people who love mankind but hate people.

I hold the more pluralistic view that people should relate to others in diverse ways, according to the substance of the relationship. On matters relating to one's family, kin, and friends, one should be constantly concerned about others' needs and desires, and should give of one's own out of love, although if the others do not uphold their own obligations, one is entitled to be more restrained. And on matters relating to people in need generally, and to larger issues of the goodness of the society, one should give of one's own without expectation of direct benefit.

There is a large sphere of social affairs, however, in which the proper relationship between people is that each gives something to the other in recognition of the mutual benefit of the exchange – a relationship of contract, as it were. Much of what Alfred Marshall called the "ordinary business of life" is of that sort, including the bartering of consumer goods as it was practiced in the POW camp. Since no responsible person enters freely into an exchange unless he perceives himself to benefit in some way, a contractual relationship is beneficial to both. That kind of relationship is at the heart of that most momentous of ancient social innovations – the division of labor.

The ideal citizen of the Good Society, in that alternative view, is discriminating in his relationships. He provides selflessly for his family and kin first, is generous to his neighbors and to the needy, and strives to make the most of the lawful opportunities for material improvement that the society affords. Contractual relationships occupy an honorable place in social life, along with family-like relationships.

It should be noted that the rise of the barter process in the POW camp did not mark the end of social responsibility. When the Medical Officer became concerned because some heavy smokers were exchanging their food rations for cigarettes to an extent that began to affect their health, the camp commander ordered that basic foods be excluded thereafter from the barter system. The prisoners would also surely have responded if one of them had fallen ill and required extra rations. Individualism should not be confused with an extreme egoism that leaves no room for love and altruism.

It is entirely proper for moral authorities, both clerical and secular, to call upon all people to live as if they were brothers and sisters. Perhaps in an Ideal Society in this or another world they could do so. In a merely Good Society, however, the best economic arrangements are those that recognize the distinct virtues of both family and contractual relationships. To accept the merit of the communal ethic in principle does not bind one to prefer societal over individual choice as the criterion of goodness with respect to any or all economic arrangements.

My own Good Society therefore leaves ample space for relationships based on love as well as relationships based on contract. Great mischief can come of a commitment to build a society on one or the other alone.

The spiritual ethic   The profound revulsion against consumerism, it seems to me, derives from the experience of having lived in a society with extreme inequality of income. To people who grow up as moral or political rebels in a world with extreme inequality, the consumption of the rich takes on the aspect of obscenity and becomes the focus of their outrage. Conspicuous disdain for consumption is a way of distancing oneself from the conspicuous consumption of the rich. Spartan living becomes the symbol of one's commitment to building a better society.

The spartan way of life is further encouraged and enforced by the conditions under which revolutionary activity takes place. People committed to total struggle against oppression are not normally engaged in regular gainful employment, and much of what they do earn they contribute to the struggle. It is a hard life, and the less one's concern with material comforts, the better prepared one is for the rigors of that life. Spartan living thus comes to symbolize the difference between the radical and the ruling class.

The trouble is that the values born in the conditions of an oppressive society tend to be carried over into the new society in which they are no longer appropriate. In a world with extreme differences in income, the sharp contrasts between the consumption of the rich and the poor are mostly due to the differences in their income, and not to differences in their preferences. That is, the major reason the poor do not drive BMWs is that they can't afford them, not that their taste in cars is so different from the rich. When income is equitably distributed in a Good Society, however, differences in consumption reflect primarily differences in personal preferences, not differences in income. If the price method were then used to distribute consumer goods under those conditions, the only differences in consumption would be those due to differences in personal preferences; and in a relatively homogeneous society, they would be small indeed. Hence, in a society with an equitable distribution of income, the spiritual ethic degenerates into a fetish if it continues to take the form in which it was originally conceived in the unjust past.

The case for the assignment method therefore makes little sense when equalization of incomes has already eliminated the main cause of differences in consumption. The people will rally round an arrangement that restricts their individual choice if its consequence is to eliminate extremes of consumption. They will see little point to it, however, if its only effect is to prevent any citizen from consuming strawberries and cream unless all citizens consume strawberries and cream.

The place of material things relative to spiritual pursuits is a proper moral concern in a Good Society. In my own view, the citizens of such a society should strive to create an environment in which children are sheltered from the incessant enticement of new things to buy, and they should seek to live in communities that share that value. However, the primary responsibility for the cultivation of spiritual values should be lodged not in the society or the government but in individual citizens and their institutions of family, religion, education, and the arts. I applaud the efforts of school and church and Scouts and the arts council to propagate those values and to counteract the pressures for preoccupation with material goods. My own Good Society would enable the citizens to do these things, but it would not enlist its economic arrangements in the mission of constraining its citizens' consumption excesses.

Some day a new society may appear in which the people and their leaders are so committed to spiritual and communal ethics and to their expression in uniformity of consumption, that the assignment method would survive for generations. The experience of societies like China and the kibbutz suggest, however, that it is not very likely.

It is difficult to imagine conditions more favorable to the assignment method than the kibbutz – smallness of size, democratic institutions, a strong egalitarian ideology, and so on. Yet even under those conditions, in the course of time dissatisfaction with the uniformity that accompanies the administrative method grew, and along with it an increasing pressure for the expression of consumer choice.

The prospects for the administrative method in a full society are even dimmer. Conditions in China were also as close to ideal for the success of the assignment method as any large revolutionary society is likely to be – with a charismatic leader like Mao, a victorious peasant army, and a Communist Party with long experience in the countryside. Yet there too the attempt to distribute goods by assignment in a communal context met with failure. As for a full society under democratic conditions, it is highly unlikely that a large and diverse population would opt for societal choice over consumer choice as the foundation of their distribution arrangements.

This conclusion applies only to the use of assignment as the dominant method for distributing goods. All modern countries, capitalist and socialist, make use of assignment in special cases, particularly in the case of "non-ordinary" services like health, education, and, increasingly, child-care services. Public schooling, for example, is distributed uniformly in most countries in much the same manner as clothing is distributed in the kibbutz: each child is supposed to receive the same educational services as all others. What has been largely abandoned is the use of assignment as the basic mode of distribution for goods and services generally.

There are two other forces that contributed to the eventual abandonment of the assignment method in those instances, and they are likely to have the same effect on future societies that adopted that method.

Generational change   I read the evidence to demonstrate that when a society chooses the assignment method, it is motivated by a powerful commitment to uniformity of consumption. That commitment, however, is peculiar to the generation of the founders of the new society, and what follows is a familiar Fathers and Sons story. The founders are people who had been disaffected by the previous form of social organization, and feel the weight of a sacred obligation to build a truly Good Society, of a kind in which they had never lived. Their own lives were spent in difficult material circumstances, in civil or military struggle or both, and they now enjoy the enormous prestige of having been part of the heroic years. Material things had been of little importance to them; on the contrary, the best of their stories recount the material deprivation they suffered for the cause. They had also experienced through much of their lives the true solidarity of embattled communities, and had witnessed and participated in grand acts of self-sacrifice for the sake of the group and the cause.

It is not difficult to understand that the first generation's view of their new Good Society should incorporate some features of both, the best of their lives and the best of their dreams. Hence the committed effort to build a society based on a disdain for material things and the ethic of communality.

In voluntary communities like the kibbutz, those values are widely shared, for those who do not share them can and do eventually leave. The values can therefore endure for a long period of time. In national states like China and Cuba, however, much of the population had not participated in the revolutionary movement, and many of them did not share their leaders' dedication to material austerity and communality.

In the course of time the founding generation moves on and is replaced by their children and grandchildren "which knew not Joseph." Their life experiences are radically different from those of their forebears because they were brought up in the new society, and they have no personal recollection of the inequities and tyrannies that impelled their forebears to pioneer in the creation of a new and better society. The inconveniences of the present that their parents took lightly are regarded less charitably by them. To the founding generation the Good Society was a promise for the future, but for their children and grandchildren it is high time that the promise be redeemed. In the absence of large inequities in income, it makes little sense indefinitely to deny citizens the pleasure of pursuing their own consumption preferences.

International communication   The spread of knowledge of consumption practices in more individualistic societies is a powerful counter-force to the official celebration of austerity and uniformity. If that knowledge could be kept from the population, as authoritarian governments often seek to do, the appeal of foreign consumption practices might be muted. It has proven to be impossible, however, to close off large countries from all information about the rest of the world, and if neither Stalin's USSR nor Mao's China could do it, it is doubtful that others are likely to succeed. Even if they could, they are likely to be unwilling to pay the accompanying technological and economic price of restricting intercourse with the advanced countries of the world.

There is very little prospect, therefore, that the assignment method of distributing consumer goods can endure beyond the founding generation of a new society in an entire country. However, all is not lost for people who are committed to uniformity and to the ethics of spirituality and communality. The lesson is rather that they should devote their efforts to the establishment of small voluntary communities of like-minded persons in countries that permit that sort of organization. It is possible to live under a system of distribution by assignment with others of similar disposition, but it is unlikely that an entire country will long tolerate that arrangement.

Distribution by assignment will therefore receive little attention in the rest of this book. The variants of the Good Society to be explored below are those that use prices and money to distribute consumer goods among the people.

Notes

1   In the Naval Academy, for example, the cadets eat together in the common dining hall and housing is provided by the organization, along with educational, health, sports, and entertainment services. They are issued identical quantities of uniform clothing, room furniture, and other items, all without charge. The cost of providing all these items is borne by the military "society," as it were. The distribution arrangement is managed by an administrative officer, who decides what kinds and quantities of goods are provided, within a certain overall budget.

   This system of distribution by assignment helps to produce a community that comes close to complete equality. It is shorn of the most visible signs of class difference that pervade the larger society. For cadets who come from underprivileged backgrounds, it is often the first environment in their lives in which they are spared what has been called the "hidden injuries of class" (Sennett and Cobb, *The Hidden Injuries of Class*). There is only one dominating basis of differentiation – ability and performance in the furtherance of the common military goals.

2   Ben Rafael, *Status, Power, and Conflict in the Kibbutz*, p. 2.

3   The classification is based on Barkai, somewhat modified. *Growth Patterns of the Kibbutz Economy*, ch. 2.

4   Dobb, *Soviet Economic Development*, pp. 107, 120.

5   Nove, *An Economic History of the USSR*, p. 664.

6   Perkins, *Market Control and Planning in Communist China*, pp. 83–4.

7   Eckstein, *China's Economic Revolution*, p. 83.

8   Perkins, *Market Control and Planning in Communist China*, p. 8.

9   Macfarquhar, *The Origins of the Cultural Revolution*, p. 105.

10 Hoffman, *Work Incentive Practices and Policies in the People's Republic of China*, p. 46.

11 Eckstein, *China's Economic Revolution*, p. 82.

12 Quoted in Macfarquhar, *The Origins of the Cultural Revolution*, p. 297.

13 The disdain for individualism applies to material things but need not extend to matters of the spirit. In the kibbutz, individual talents are zealously cultivated: children who are especially gifted in the arts are encouraged to develop their abilities with the support of community funds. People are fiercely independent and outspoken in their opinions, although as in any small community someone who rejected its basic values would have a hard time of it.

14 Blasi, *The Communal Experience of the Kibbutz*, p. 28.

15 Barkai, *Growth Patterns of the Kibbutz Economy*, pp. 17–18. The money tokens provided for in the comprehensive budget could be used only within the kibbutz, unlike the "holiday money" that was paid in the national currency, which could be spent off the kibbutz.

16 Hoffman, *Work Incentive Practices and Policies in the People's Republic of China*, p. 120.

17 Hoffman, *Work Incentive Practices and Policies in the People's Republic of China*, p. 109.

18 Hoffman, *Work Incentive Practices and Policies in the People's Republic of China*, p. 110.

19 Radford, "The economic organization of a P.O.W. camp."

20 Pareto was a supporter of Italian fascism, which strengthens the case that his criterion was designed to serve the political interests of the ruling class, rather than to provide an objective criterion of goodness. An idea may be useful, however, even if one is not inclined to invite its inventor to dinner.

21 Radford, "The economic organization of a P.O.W. camp," p. 191.

22 The others may still regard themselves as better off individually if each ended up with a collection of goods that he preferred to his initial collection.

23 The purest of egalitarians might reject the Paretian proposition that if some gain and none loses, the degree of equity has not been disturbed. One could make the case, for example, that if the rich get richer while the poor are no less poor, inequality has increased because the spread between rich and poor has widened. Equity in that case might demand that the rich share some of their gains with the poor.

24　Family and kinship relationships do, of course, also involve reciprocal obligations. In traditional societies there are powerful social pressures that enforce the children's obligation to support the parents in their old age, and powerful sanctions against persons who fail to meet those obligations. That actions are taken by individuals out of love does not preclude the relationship involving an implicit exchange. The implicit-exchange aspect of family relations is sometimes ignored in discussions in which the family is taken as the model of the economics of a Good Society.

Chapter 6

Distributing Goods by Prices

> What is a cynic? A man who knows
> the price of everything, and the
> value of nothing.
>
> — *Oscar Wilde*

> Her feeling toward the rich was a
> sort of religious hatred; they had
> probably made all their money out
> of high retail prices ... and Mrs.
> Cadwallader detested high
> prices ....
>
> — *George Eliot*

CONTENTS

Consumer goods are distributed by the price method in virtually all the countries of the world, both socialist and capitalist, and both past and present. That in itself, however, should not commend the price method to people concerned with the Good Society. To say about anything that everybody does it is rarely a testimonial to its goodness. It is more often the prelude to an embarrassed confession of having committed some abomination. Yet the near-universality of the price method is a compelling reason for seeking to understand what it is about that method that has led to its general approval. Unless your own values are wildly different from those of most people around the world, the chances are that after having evaluated it by your criteria of goodness, it will qualify for your own Good Society as well.

The price method should not be confused with what is usually called the "price system," or the "market mechanism." It finds its widest use, to be sure, in the markets of capitalist economies, but it should not be thought of as a creature of capitalism. It is used, in fact, for a variety of purposes in non-market socialist economies as well. It is also widely used by non-market organizations like universities and libraries to distribute parking space among users, local governments to distribute water and sewage among the citizens, and so forth. Like the assignment method, it is best thought of as a technical arrangement that may be used for distributing goods or resources in a variety of different contexts.

Continuing with the abstraction of a consumption-only economy, the consumer goods that flow continuously into the economy must be distributed among the citizens. Under the price method each citizen receives a certain money income each month and spends it all on the purchase of the consumer goods he desires. At the end of the month some people will have bought more books than others, some will have attended more ball games, some will have had more dinners out. In that fashion the price method effects a certain distribution of the flow of goods among the people.

The question is, is the price method a better arrangement than the assignment method for distributing consumer goods in a Good Society? Three criteria of goodness are most germane on this issue: the locus of choice, efficiency, and justice.

1   Prices and Choice

Consumer choice and societal choice are not exactly household words, even in households in which family talk sometimes touches on the Good Society. Most people around the world, however, regard it as entirely natural that money should be required in order to acquire goods, and that those who have the money should be able to spend it on the goods they want. It would come as a surprise to learn that there is another possible arrangement in which money is not used, and in which the society as a whole decides what each household may consume. Few people, however, are likely to regard that method of distributing goods as "better" than the price method that they know well. That judgment of relative goodness implies that the locus of choice is indeed one criterion by which they assess the goodness of economic arrangements, and that it is of some importance to them that consumer rather than societal choice prevails in the distribution of most consumer goods.

It is evident that when the criterion of goodness is consumer choice, the price method is a better arrangement than the assignment method, for under the price method each consumer chooses his own collection of goods.

2   Efficiency in Consumption

For many people, to be able to acquire the goods they want instead of those that their neighbors think they should have is the powerful attraction of the price method. Perhaps the greater attraction, however, is the claim that it also satisfies the criterion of efficiency.

The concept of economic efficiency was adapted from classical mechanics, where the "mechanical efficiency" of one machine is said to be higher than that of another if it produces a larger "useful output" of work with the same "total input" of work. The notions of "output" and "input" are readily transferable to a production operation, and in economics one production process is said to be more efficient than another if it yields a larger output (say, of shoes) with the same total input (labor, leather, fuel, and so forth).

In the context of consumption, the mechanical analogy is not quite so apparent. With a small dose of poetic imagination, however, one can readily think of consumer goods as "inputs" in a consumption process that yields an "output" called consumer "satisfaction," or consumer "welfare."[1] The assertion that one arrangement for distributing goods is more efficient than another can then be taken to mean that with the same "input" of consumer goods, a larger "output" of consumer welfare is attained.

"Consumer welfare" is a rather amorphous concept, however. One cannot simply "add up" the output of consumer satisfaction enjoyed by different people, as one can add up the output of coal from different mines. If the notion of efficiency in consumption is to serve as more than an appealing metaphor, there must be some way of actually determining whether the level of consumer welfare generated by one distribution of goods is higher, or lower, or the same, as the level of welfare generated by a different distribution of the same collection of goods. The great contribution of Pareto was to supply a way of doing just that. To apply his criterion, you ask about one distribution "Is there any way of redistributing the same collection of goods among the same people which would leave some people better off and no one worse off?" If the answer is no, then that distribution may be said to yield the highest level of consumer welfare possible with that collection of goods, and the arrangement that gave rise to that distribution is said to be efficient in Pareto's sense.

In all that follows, whenever the term efficiency is used in the context of consumption, it is the Pareto criterion of efficiency that is intended.

Applying the Pareto criterion to the POW camp in the last chapter, it was shown that barter trading is an efficient arrangement for distributing a collection of goods. Bartering absorbs time and effort, however, even in a small community, and is inconceivable as a general method of distributing goods in a large and modern society. The price method is simpler and infinitely more convenient. Fine as they are, however, simplicity and convenience are not yet enough to commend the price method for a Good Society. It must also be shown that it is efficient.

To relieve the suspense, let it be said at the outset that the price method is an efficient arrangement provided that it is properly managed. I say "properly managed" to forewarn that the price method will not produce an optimal distribution under all circumstances. Certain conditions must be present if that happy result is to be attained, two of which are examined below. They are not very restrictive conditions, for they usually prevail by and large when the price method is used in practice.

3   Efficiency of the Price Method

The proof that the price method is efficient is one of the jewels in the crown of modern economic theory. It goes a long way to explaining why virtually all economists, in both capitalist and socialist countries, regard that arrangement as the only sensible way of distributing most consumer goods. The proof is laid out in every college textbook, often in mathematical language and in elaborate detail. The following is an intuitive explanation of the gist of the argument, taking the experience of the POW camp as a point of departure.

Bartering, it was shown, led in the end to an optimal distribution of the goods delivered in the Red Cross packages. It is relatively easy to visualize the process that led up to the final optimal distribution. Barter exchange is therefore an "iterative" process, in which each trade, being voluntary, satisfies the "some-winners-no-losers" condition of efficiency. With each successive trade the level of consumer satisfaction must increase, and it keeps increasing until there are no longer any trades to be made that would increase it any further.

One can virtually "see" the operation of the social process that guarantees that the final distribution will be optimal.

No such transparent process operates in the case of the price method. Each consumer goes about spending his income in ways he considers sensible, and yet somehow, it is claimed, in the end the available goods turn out to be distributed in the best possible way. Why should that be? There is no assignment agent trying to match up the right goods with the right people. The consumers do not announce to each other which goods they want to trade for which, as they do in barter trading. By what magic does it turn out that the final distribution is better for everybody than any other possible distribution?

PREFERENCES AND EFFICIENCY

The key to the efficiency of the price method may be found in the condition under which POW bartering comes to an end. When a new delivery arrives, you and I receive the same numbers of chocolates, cigarettes, and other goods. I am a heavier smoker than you and would be willing to give up one of my chocolates for 7 (or more) of your cigarettes. You would be willing to give 12 (or fewer) of your cigarettes for one of my chocolates. Those numbers – 7-to-1 and 12-to-1 – are indicators of the magnitude of our preferences between cigarettes and chocolate. They are more properly called "marginal" preference indicators, because they refer to small increases or decreases in quantities of cigarettes and chocolates, rather than the total number of those goods that the consumer has acquired.

When two people's preference indicators differ in magnitude, both would gain by bartering. In the example, if we settled on an exchange of – say – 9 of your cigarettes for 1 of my chocolates, we would both regard ourselves as better off.

That exchange, however, alters our preference indicators. Like a small boy exchanging baseball cards, the more cards of his favorite player that he acquires, the smaller the number of other-player cards he would offer for yet another card of his favorite. Similarly, having now acquired more cigarettes than I had originally, my preference indicator changes. Now I would give up an additional chocolate only if I received 9 (or more) cigarettes in exchange; and you would give only 11 (or fewer) cigarettes for yet another chocolate. Our new preference indicators – 9-to-1 and 11-to-1 – are now closer to each other but since they still differ, we can continue to barter to our mutual benefit.

It may now be evident where the argument is going. With each additional exchange, the parties' marginal preference indicators converge until they eventually become equal – at say 10-to-1. When the goods have been distributed in such a way that everybody's preference indicator between any two goods is the same as everybody else's, there is no other possible distribution in which someone would be better off without someone else being worse off. That distribution is therefore optimal by the Pareto criterion.

Hence, the general test of whether a distribution is Pareto-optimal is that all preference indicators are equal.

PRICES AND PREFERENCES

Bartering, it has been said, is a primitive way of arriving at an optimal distribution. It can now be shown that the price method also leads to an optimal distribution, but in a much less cumbersome way.

Suppose that in a typical market a pack of cigarettes sells for $2 and a chocolate bar for $0.20. In the course of a month I could buy many different combinations of the two goods, but I settle on the one combination that best satisfies my consumption. That combination, whatever it is, reveals something important about my preferences between the two goods.

For at those prices, with the same expenditure I could have had an additional pack of cigarettes by buying 10 fewer chocolate bars, or 10 additional chocolate bars for 1 less pack of cigarettes. The fact that I did not choose those possible combinations reveals that the combination I chose was such that my preference indicator between cigarettes and chocolate was 10-to-1 – the same as the price ratio of cigarettes to chocolate.

Other consumers purchase different combinations of the two goods, depending on their incomes and their preferences for the goods. In all cases, however, when they settle upon the combination they find most satisfying, their individual preference indicators must also be equal to the price ratio of 10-to-1.

But since all preference indicators are equal to the same price ratio of 10-to-1, they are equal to each other. Therefore the distribution of cigarettes and chocolate is Pareto-optimal because it passes the general test of equal-preference-indicators.

The trick is that under the price method all consumers align their combinations of purchases to the same prices. It is as if the citizens of London all set their watches by the Westminster clock. All their watches would then show the same time, without any communication among the people and with no administrative agent striving for that result. Similarly, when all consumers align their purchases to the same prices, their preference indicators turn out to be the same, which signifies that the distribution of the goods is optimal. Hence the price method is efficient because the consumers, consulting only their personal preferences, end up choosing those combinations of goods that cause the final distribution to be optimal.

EFFICIENCY IN PRACTICE

Bully for that abstract argument, the skeptic might say, but what about the real world? Skepticism is indeed a healthy response to claims about goodness derived from abstract exercises, like the "model" of how consumers behave that was sketched out above. That the price method can be shown to be efficient in a model does not at all signify that it would also be efficient when operating in an actual economy.

The credibility of a model depends, among other things, on whether its central features correspond reasonably well to those in the world.[2] The skeptic has reason to doubt that people do in fact spend their money with the deliberate care that the model assumes. Many are rather casual and spontaneous in their purchases, especially on small items like cigarettes and chocolates, and some people insist, sometimes ostentatiously, on ignoring the right-hand column of the menu.

Yet most people make some effort to spend their money sensibly, or at least not to fritter it away; everyone from time to time has said, in effect, "I would like to have more of that, but it costs too much." Anyone who pauses to watch the shoppers in the supermarket or the mall cannot fail to be impressed at the intensity of their interest in prices, and the merchants are all too keenly aware that the higher the price of an item, the less of it they are likely to sell. Perhaps the prudent conclusion is that while people differ in the extent to which they seek to squeeze the most satisfaction out of their expenditures, the mass of consumers by and large do seek to get the most for their money.

Hence, if a society adopts the price method, the distribution of consumer goods among the citizens may not be the absolute best of all possible distributions. Other distributions may be possible in which there would be gainers and no losers, so that with the same quantities of goods, the society's consumption welfare would be higher. The trouble is that there are no known economic arrangements that are so efficient that they can be expected to detect and bring about one of those better distributions. The major alternative, the assignment method, is defended by its proponents on grounds other than its efficiency. The price method therefore has a strong claim to being the best arrangement, if not a perfect one, for a Good Society by the criterion of efficiency.

THE IMPORTANCE OF BEING EFFICIENT

One of the lessons of the POW camp is that the efficiency of a distribution arrangement can have a major impact on the economic welfare of a society. The arrival of the Red Cross packages, to be sure, enhanced the welfare of all the prisoners, despite the inefficiency of the initial uniform distribution. If barter had been prohibited, however, each prisoner's consumption would have been confined to the goods originally distributed, and the level of consumer welfare would have been relatively low. The redistribution of the goods through barter trading greatly increased the level of consumer welfare derived from the same collection of Red Cross goods. It is in that sense that efficiency makes it possible to derive the greatest possible consumption welfare from a given collection of goods.

4 Getting Prices Right

The claim that the price method is an efficient way of distributing consumer goods does not mean that it is efficient under all conditions. One of the principal conditions for efficiency is that the prices must be right. Getting prices right means a great many things in different contexts. Some of those meanings are developed in Part IV, where the relations between prices and efficiency are considered in both planned and market economies. There is one condition, however, which is particularly important in the case of consumer goods, and which in practice is often violated. This condition is that prices should be "clearing" prices.

Prices should be high enough that the shelves are not empty of goods most of the time because they are sold out soon after delivery. They should also be low enough so that goods do not pile up unsold on the shelves. In market economies such prices are called "market-clearing" prices. I use the simpler expression "clearing prices" so that it can apply either to markets or to non-market arrangements, such as the setting of the price of meat by a central planning bureau, or the administration of water distribution by a municipal water department. The clearing level in the latter case would be the price at which the quantity of water bought by the people every week or month is equal to the amount that the department supplies every week or month.

The reason that prices should be at clearing levels is that if they are not, the price method is no longer efficient and the goods are not optimally distributed among the people. That rather antiseptic assertion may not strike terror into the reader's heart, but the annals of modern economic systems are filled with instances in which inefficiency of that sort has brought enormous inconvenience, and sometimes misery, to masses of people. It has also caused governments to fall. The pity of it is that much of that inefficiency was unnecessary and should be avoided in a Good Society.

To see why efficiency requires clearing prices, imagine that the clearing level for the price of a movie ticket in a 5,000-seat theater is $12. If the price is set at that level, everyone to whom the movie is worth $12 or more is able to see it, and only those to whom it is worth less than $12 are excluded.

If the manager sets the price at $8, however, perhaps 6,000 people will turn up to see the movie. The tickets are sold until the house is full, and week after week a thousand or so would-be moviegoers are turned away. Among those who are turned away, there are some who want to see the movie badly enough that they would gladly pay $12 or more for a ticket if they could get one. On the other hand, among those who manage to buy a ticket are some for whom the movie is worth barely $8, but no more. We are therefore back in the POW camp, where the wrong goods initially went to the wrong people.

As in the case of the camp, all parties would be better off if the goods were properly redistributed among them. In this case, someone who managed to get an $8 ticket would be glad to surrender it for $9 or more to one of the excluded people who wants it badly enough. If both agreed to the exchange, the new distribution must be better that the original one. That, in fact, is precisely what "speculators" do when goods are badly enough underpriced.

Despite the inefficiency introduced by non-clearing prices, virtually every country that uses the price method violates the clearing-price rule in some respects. Such departures from efficient pricing are usually justified by the claim that they make for an increase in distributive justice which more than compensates for the decrease in distributive efficiency.

5 Justice

A distribution of goods that is best in terms of Pareto efficiency is not necessarily the best by all criteria of goodness. It merely means that there is no way of improving the welfare of Alpha without reducing the welfare of Beta. But Alpha may be very poor and Beta very rich. A society that valued both efficiency and equity would be entirely justified in redistributing some goods from Beta to Alpha in the interest of greater distributive justice.

Once the redistribution has been carried out, however, the Good Society should require that the new distribution be optimal. It would be foolish, for example, to achieve equality – if that were the standard of equity – by simply giving Alpha and Beta identical collections of goods, in the manner of the assignment method. That distribution might be regarded as equitable but it would not be optimal. The efficiency argument is that, whatever the distribution that the society regards as equitable, both Alpha and Beta could be better off if the goods were distributed by the price method; that is, if incomes were distributed equitably, the same total quantity of goods would then be distributed both equitably and efficiently.

However, in virtually all societies the distribution of income is unequal. When the goods are distributed by the price method under that condition, the disparity between the consumption of the poor and the rich may be so large as to be widely regarded as unjust. In such cases the price method is often regarded as the villain of the piece.

The price method does not warrant the hostility that emanates from that line of criticism. The source of the inequity in consumption in those cases is to be found in the inequality of the income distribution, and not in the price method of distributing the goods. The price method as an economic arrangement is doing its job well – the people acquire what they most want to consume instead of what the society wants them to consume. Inequity in consumption is the fault not of the price method of distributing goods, but of the initial distribution of the income that enables the rich to acquire so much more than the poor.

The Good Society should therefore not automatically reject the price method if the distribution of consumer goods proves to be inequitable. The first-order task should be to modify the income distribution so that it conforms to the society's sense of distributive justice. There are many instruments of economic policy for attaining that result; they are the standard fare of economic policy – such as the taxing the rich in order to transfer income to the poor.

The redistribution of income that emerges from the play of democratic politics is always a compromise. Hence, there are substantial numbers of citizens who regard the distribution of income as unjustly unequal, even after it has been redistributed through the political process. In response to their concerns, societies often turn to policies that help to augment the consumption of the poor in ways that do not involve a direct assault on the distribution of money incomes, and which are therefore more acceptable politically. This is often done by underpricing – that is, setting prices that are lower than clearing-price levels.

The consequence of underpricing is that the quantity of the good that people wish to buy exceeds the quantity that is available for purchase. How that consequence plays out may be explored in three cases where goods are underpriced for the sake of greater distributive justice.

RENT CONTROLS

Urban housing is often the object of such legislation. The argument is that among all consumer goods and services, urban housing merits special consideration. Rising clothing and food prices force the poor to consume less of them, but rising apartment rents impose the more onerous burden of having to leave home and community to find cheaper housing. Nor is it the poor alone who are the object of concern. People who regard the maintenance of stable communities as important for the goodness of the society are also concerned that rising rents promote the process of "gentrification" that drives long-term residents out and brings newer and more affluent residents in.

Rent controls enable the original residents to remain in their apartments without having to reduce their consumption of other goods. The distribution of goods is no longer optimal, however, for the reason adduced in the theater example given above. Suppose the market clearing rent is $1,000 but the controlled rent is $500. Then some people to whom the apartment is worth $1,000 or more of their income are turned away, while the original renters to whom it may be barely worth $500 of their income continue to occupy it. The price method is therefore inefficient in this case, for the prices are not at market-clearing levels. The society may be said to have "traded off" some efficiency in consumption for what it sees as greater distributive justice.

Rent control, moreover, is a very crude instrument of policy to deal with the narrow issue of the housing conditions of the poor. For one thing, the policy is unfair, for many of the people who live in rent-controlled apartments are in fact quite well off. They enjoy the unmerited benefit of paying lower rents than people of equal income, and they occupy apartments that could go to people for whom they have more value, including some of the poor. They simply benefit from the implicit transfer of income from their landlord's pockets to their own, which are sometimes much deeper than their landlord's.

An alternative policy would be to apply a means test, under which only people certified as poor would pay rents that are below clearing levels. Yet another alternative would be to let all rents settle at their clearing levels, but to provide rent vouchers to the poor to enable them to pay those rents, as is done in many cities. The vouchers would be equivalent to a transfer of income to the poor through the tax system. That alternative would also be fairer because the burden of improving the housing conditions of the poor would be borne by all taxpayers, and not by the rental landlords alone. Rental vouchers permit the price method to do what it does well – distribute goods in the best possible way among consumers – while at the same time providing the poor with the housing conditions that the society considers just. They are also fairer because the cost of the social program is borne by the entire society instead of those who happen to own the rental housing.

NATIONAL EMERGENCY

All societies that employ the price method override it in times of national emergency such as wars or natural disasters. At such times the supply of many consumer goods is drastically reduced. Were the price method to continue serving to distribute the reduced supply of goods, the clearing prices of many goods would rise to extremely high levels. Almost all the goods would be bought up by the rich, with little or nothing left for the lower-income population.

No society is willing to accept a distribution of goods, including the necessities of life, which is so unequal, particularly in times when the survival of the society depends on the solidarity of its citizens. All resort to some sort of rationing, under which the price method of distributing goods is replaced by a form of the assignment method. There are many forms of rationing, but all entail a societal decision to assure that every citizen is able to consume some minimal quantity of the goods regardless of her income. The citizen may be required to pay a certain price for her ration of meat or bread, but the price is far lower than it would be if the price method were in full charge of the distribution.

Rationing has a number of attractive features. It appeals to a certain sense of justice: everyone gets the same amount of the good. "No one gets two houses until everybody gets one," reads a populist Cape Cod bumper sticker. It is that element of equity that commends it in such stressful periods as wartime. As a permanent feature of a Good Society, however, it fails the test of efficiency. As in the POW camp, it tends to lead to a certain amount of bartering, so that the initial uniform distribution is transformed into one in which the citizens end up with more satisfying collections of goods. Unlike in the POW camp, however, the initial distribution of income is unequal, so that the rich are able to consume more than their allotted rations by buying up some of the ration coupons of the poor, even when that is illegal.

The replacement of the price method by rationing makes for a better society under emergency conditions. Rationing is a very bad arrangement under normal conditions, however, so that every society abandons it for the price method as soon as possible after the emergency has passed and the supply of goods returns to its normal level.

GENERAL UNDERPRICING

The strongest justification for the underpricing of consumer goods is that under certain conditions it can help to compensate for an inequitable distribution of income. That justification is strongest in capitalist economies, where the distribution of income is determined by such factors as the distribution of property ownership and the play of market forces. Citizens might therefore look upon that income distribution and pronounce it inequitable. In the Communist countries, however, incomes were determined directly by the central planning bureau, which had the power to decide the wages or salaries of every occupation. It may therefore be assumed that the income distribution was equitable in the judgment of the planners and the government they served.

To be sure, there were groups who received incomes that many regarded as undeservedly large – high-ranking Party members and black-market operators, for example – and there were also large groups that were classified as poor. Inequality, however, "did not seem to be the basis of a deep resentment or burning antagonism."[3] To regard the income distribution of the most egalitarian countries in the world as inequitable would be to set a standard for a Utopian, and not a merely Good, Society. Few countries are ever likely to do better than they did.

Since there were no significant income-distribution inequities to be compensated for, one would expect consumer goods prices to be set at clearing levels. Yet few policies have had as negative an impact on the economic life of the citizens of the Communist countries as the deliberate and extensive violation of the clearing-price rule, particularly in the USSR which had the longest experience in this matter.

QUEUING

Nothing used to strike the visitor to the USSR more vividly than the endless hours that Soviet citizens spent patiently waiting in lines. And not always so patiently: the sudden appearance of a meat delivery would sometimes cause a crush of shoppers rushing to the meat counter, with the harried sales clerk shouting "*Na ochered, grazhdanka!*" (Get on line, citizeness!). When a shipment of Czech shoes or Italian dresses was put up for sale in a department store, people would rush to that counter and form a new queue. Year in and year out the queues remained, consuming millions of the non-working hours – and sometimes the working hours – of Soviet citizens.

Perhaps the most underpriced consumer item was housing. Soviet families spent only about 3 percent of their income on rent and utilities, compared to 20–25 percent in capitalist countries. The inevitable queue in that case took the form of large waits for new housing. A young growing family that needed more room would sign up for a larger apartment, and would then have to wait years until one became available. The length of the queue was longer than it need have been because people with satisfactory housing found the rent to be so low that they had no incentive to leave. Hence elderly families often lived in apartments with more rooms than they needed, while younger families had to double up with their parents until an apartment came along.[4]

The purpose of non-clearing prices cannot have been to help the poor, for they affected rich and poor alike. Automobiles, which were thought to be expensive and were bought largely by the well-to-do, were actually extensively underpriced; had they been priced so high that there was no queue for the limited number of automobiles on sale, that price would have been several times higher than it actually was. Used cars generally sold unofficially for more than the official price of newer models of the same cars. It took as many as five years or more from the date an order was placed to when the automobile was finally delivered.[5] Nor does queuing assure that the goods will be bought by the poor and not the rich. They simply go to the first in line. If the goods are of some importance to the rich, one can be sure that they or their agents will be at the head of the line. In the USSR people of means used to hire others to queue up for them. The richer are also more likely to have a family member who is not in the labor force, and in the USSR an important economic function of those members, often an older person, was to attend to the queuing. Hence again, if the purpose is equity, it is better to secure it by transferring income to the poor rather than by pricing practices that turn the whole society into a perpetual queue.

The use of the price method for distributing goods, but with prices that are generally too low, leads to a distribution something like that in the POW camp. Some of the excluded persons at the end of the meat queue are willing to offer more than the official price to those who acquire the goods, and some of the latter find it worth their while to accept the two or three rubles and return home with perhaps one less kilo of meat but with a bottle of wine that they had not intended to buy. And as in the POW camp, the patent maldistribution of the goods creates a powerful incentive for people to undertake the redistribution of the goods in a more sensible way. The pity of it is that since the income distribution was relatively equitable – in both the USSR and the POW camp – there was less justification for underpricing than there might be in a market economy. That is to say, there is no reason to keep prices low for the poor if there are no poor.

Extensive underpricing was the source of a number of other deficiencies in the Communist economies which are discussed in chapter 18.

PRICES AND IDEOLOGY

The desire for greater equity is not therefore a convincing explanation of the widespread use of non-clearing prices in the Communist countries. The explanation is more likely to be found in certain primitive ideas about the nature of the price method of distributing consumer goods. The notion that the right prices are clearing prices conflicts with some widely held popular sentiments of what the prices ought to be in a Good Society. To the man in the street, not only in socialist but in capitalist countries as well, the best prices are low prices. The idea that some prices might be *too* low does not come naturally: it is like saying that someone is too healthy, or too rich. Hence the assertion that the price of meat in the USSR was too low or that the price of gasoline in the US should be raised sounds perverse; at the least it does not sound like a prescription for a Good Society.

Some acute misunderstandings and political tensions derive from that difference between the popular notion that the best prices are the lowest prices, and the economic notion that the best prices are clearing prices. Political leaders often cave in to the popular view, or share it themselves, to the detriment of the economic welfare of the people.

6 Discussion

There are two polar conceptions of the nature of the Good Society that are embodied in the stereotypes of the cowboy and the communalist. The legendary rugged, self-reliant cowboy rides into town to sell his cattle, transact some business, right some wrongs, and taste briefly of some of the frivolities that society affords. He then rides off alone into the setting sun to pursue his personal destiny.

The ideal communalist is intoxicated with love of the people. He seeks a world in which the people share equally in their common successes and failures. His personal destiny cannot be separated from that of the people. Like the cowboy, he has little taste for luxury, but unlike the cowboy, when he rides off, he is part of a like-minded company setting out on a challenging project to improve the welfare of all. Both have little interest in the acquisition or consumption of material goods. Each has his own conception of how he would like the world to be, and neither is greatly concerned with the pure economics of his Good Society.

Both conceptions place a high value on the locus of choice as a criterion of the goodness of a society. They are poles apart, however, on the best form of choice. The cowboy seeks the society that offers the broadest range of individual choice, while the communalist seeks the broadest range of societal choice. In the interest of equity, the cowboy might accept some small restrictions on his right to choose, and the communalist might accept some limited scope for individual choice. They would make no concessions, however, if the purpose were mere efficiency.

The difference between the two types emerges in their contrasting attitudes toward many institutions of economic life, such as the arrangements for distributing consumer goods. The cowboy could not abide the notion that an agency of the society – presumably the government – might tell him what he can or cannot buy and what the price must be; his commitment to individual choice inclines him naturally to the price method. To the communalist, the idea that every good should have a price, which may be so high as to exclude some people from consuming it, reeks of the very worst of societies: social solidarity requires some sort of societal administration of the distribution of goods in which the different needs of one's friends and neighbors are taken into account.

Some of my best friends over the years have been pure cowboys or pure communalists at heart. They are rarely friends of each other. Each finds the other's conception of a Good Society incomprehensible at best and loathsome at worst. The Lord High Executioner seeking a punishment to fit the worst of crimes would sentence the cowboy to live his life out in the togetherness of a commune, and the communalist to wander forever on the lone prairie.

I am happy to report, however, that most people are neither purely one or the other; they combine some of both and are ranged across the entire political spectrum. Those near the conservative right and the socialist left retain a soft spot for the cowboy and the communalist respectively, but the closer they are to the center, the less their personal identification with the extremes. They have a certain broad preference for individual or societal choice, but they are open to persuasion that under some circumstances the other form of choice may make sense.

The difference between cowboys and communalists is most evident in the arrangements for the production of goods rather than for their distribution. As will be developed in Part IV, capitalist economies, dominated by cowboys, rely primarily on the price method for organizing the production system, whereas the socialist economies, dominated by communalists, rely primarily on the assignment method. With respect to distribution, however, apart from a few romantic dalliances with the assignment method described in the preceding chapter, the socialists surrendered to the price method.

Both capitalist and socialist economies have sinned by setting some prices in ways that detract from the efficiency that the price method is capable of delivering. Some of those ways have been elaborated in this chapter. The violations of the efficiency-pricing rules that are found in capitalist countries, however, are not so extensive as to significantly diminish the goodness of the distribution arrangements. Clearing prices are virtually universal, so that there is little loss of efficiency on that account. With regard to such exceptions as rent controls, there may be more efficient ways of accomplishing the equity objectives, such as vouchers or direct income transfers, but they are often not feasible politically. That efficiency loss is accompanied by some gain in equity, however, so that the net effect may be an improvement in the goodness of the economy when all the criteria of goodness are reckoned up in the balance.

It is rather a different matter in the socialist countries. Although the Communist leadership accepted the price method of distributing consumer goods, as communalists their heart seems always to have yearned for the assignment method. The price method was rather like a concession made under protest, and they seem never to have been comfortable with it, or to have fully appreciated its virtues with respect to both efficiency and equity. The notion that the larger the number of people who desire a good the higher its price should be never penetrated into the consciousness of the leadership. Having accepted the price method begrudgingly in the first place, they seem to have set about emasculating it so that it could never perform the functions for which it is best suited.

The effects of extensive underpricing were conspicuously evident in such forms as queuing and corruption, which detract substantially from the quality of the citizen's life as a consumer – not only material life, but moral life as well. I once asked a friend who had recently emigrated from the USSR what he found to be the most striking difference between life there and in his new country. "I still cannot get used to it," he said, "but a whole year has passed and I have not once had to pay anyone a bribe."

The Hungarian economist Janos Kornai captured that ethos of the Communist countries in the term "shortage economy."[6] In the case of consumer goods the endemic shortage was a direct consequence of the government's pricing policy and was therefore entirely self-inflicted. There was no shortage in an absolute sense; it was not, for example, like the shortage of food or medicine that might follow a natural disaster. Imagine an "efficiency scenario" in which the USSR produced exactly the same quantities of consumer goods in the past 50 years as it actually did, but the government set all prices at clearing levels. The people would have paid more of their income for such items as meat, automobiles, and apartment rents, but prices would have been lower on other goods such as furniture, clothing, and refrigerators. Under this efficiency scenario the people would have consumed exactly the same quantities of consumer goods over the years as they consumed in fact, but without having had to suffer the inconvenience of the years of queuing and the indignity of having to bribe black-marketeers.[7]

When Mikhail Gorbachev launched the process of post-Communist transformation, the mood of the time was best captured in the often-expressed hope of finally becoming a "normal" country. "Normal" meant many things political, social, and economic, but one of its meanings was the ability to supply one's family with food and other goods by entering a shop, finding the goods available for sale, paying the price, and bringing them home.

I do not claim that inefficiency in the distribution of consumer goods was the major cause of the historic transformation initiated by Gorbachev. Inefficiency in the production system and in the management of technological advance no doubt carried much more weight. But the mismanagement of the price method and the consequent inefficiency in the distribution of consumer goods was a significant part of the package of dissatisfactions that generated the nostalgia for a "normal" life.

Notes

1   The term "satisfaction," like the older term "utility," refers to the subjective experience of the consumer. The term "welfare" is intended to connote an objective condition that may be inferred from some observable act like the purchase of a good.
2   It also depends on how successful the model is in explaining or predicting events in the real world. This model does quite well in that respect. For example, it explains such important economic regularities as the tendency for the sales of a good to decline when its price rises, and for the sales of goods that people spend a lot of their income on to be more responsive to price changes than goods on which they spend very little.
3   Inkeles and Bauer, *The Soviet Citizen*, p. 319.
4   Morton, "The Soviet quest for better housing."
5   Welihozkiy, "Automobiles and the Soviet consumer," p. 822.
6   Kornai, *Economics of Shortage*.
7   The cost of distributional inefficiency may be gauged by imagining that a representative Soviet citizen were presented with the following choice: he could consume 10,000 rubles worth of goods a year under Soviet conditions, or 9,000 rubles worth of goods a year under the conditions of the efficiency scenario. If he choses the second option, then the welfare loss due to the abnormality of Soviet consumer life would be at least 10 percent. The consumer goods produced in the USSR would have yielded at least 10 percent more consumer satisfaction if they had been sensibly priced.

Chapter 7

Money and the Payment of Interest

> The love of money is the root of all Evil.
> *— I Timothy*
>
> Lack of money is the root of all evil.
> *— G. B. Shaw*

CONTENTS

A society that adopts the price method must also adopt a number of complementary institutional arrangements, some of which do not enjoy a good reputation in some versions of the Good Society. First, the price method requires the use of money, and the management of money by both the people and the government becomes a significant element in how they conduct their economic affairs. Second, whenever money is used, some people tend to accumulate money savings, which require safekeeping, so that banks and bankers materialize.

Third, the accumulation of savings in banks makes it possible for some people to borrow those savings in order to make large purchases like houses, repaying the loan gradually over a number of years. Fourth, borrowers are often prepared to repay a larger sum than they borrowed, so that the paying of interest emerges as a normal feature of economic activity.

The price method is therefore like your daughter's prospective bridegroom: you had better look carefully into his pedigree or you may be shocked at who turns up at the wedding. This chapter explores some of those other arrangements that accompany the adoption of the price method and offers some assessments from the perspective of the Good Society.

I   A Medium of Exchange

In many theological versions of the Good Society, money is the source of sin. That sin can be escaped by the use of assignment instead of prices for distributing goods, but no modern society is likely to use the assignment method for any length of time. The Good Society must therefore learn to live with money and to control it so that it serves the social good.

The history of the POW camp provides a classic instance of the spontaneous development of money. In a relatively short time, the internees began trading their tinned beef and other goods for cigarettes, and soon, without anyone planning or organizing it, cigarettes became "money."

The use of a material good like cigarettes as a society's money is a modern version of the ancient story. Shells, cattle, precious metals, and many other goods have served as money at various times and places. In such cases the money-good is valued for its own sake as well as for its "moneyness," that is, its general exchangeability for other goods. In the last few centuries, however, many new forms of money have been invented, the most prominent of which is paper money – a thing that has no value in itself but which other people generally accept in exchange for goods. Paper money, along with metal coins for small purchases, together constitute most countries' "currency." Until quite recently most day-to-day consumer-goods purchases in modern economies have been made with currency. The use of personal checks and credit cards is of more recent vintage.

When money is used as the instrument by means of which goods are distributed under the price method, it is said to serve as a "medium of exchange." The citizens of modern societies do not normally think of themselves as engaged in "exchange." That is because the term "exchange" often connotes barter, and barter is rare in modern economies. People are accustomed to thinking of themselves as "having a job" that produces a certain money income, which is then used for purchasing consumer goods. There is no evident "exchange" in those arrangements, but those transactions can be viewed as the exchange of a week's labor for a sum of money, followed by the exchange of that money for goods. So great is the convenience of money and so common its use that many people would be surprised to be told that these effortless activities are in fact a fairly complex form of exchange.

There are times when the veil that conceals the exchanges that take place through the use of money is pierced, and the exchange relationships come to the fore. That happens during periods of hyperinflation, when prices escalate wildly day after day. People rapidly lose confidence in the value of the country's money and eventually refuse to accept it in payment for their labor or other services. That was the case, for example, in the period of War Communism (chapter 5), when the revolutionary Soviet government printed new money in such profusion that the workers were increasingly reluctant to accept their wages in rubles and began to demand real goods instead. To retain their labor force, enterprises resorted to paying their workers in goods instead of money. Street bazaars then sprang up, where people sought to exchange one of the goods they had received in exchange for other goods they needed more badly. It is in such periods of economic pathology that the implicit exchange-basis of a modern economy becomes unhappily apparent.

A society that uses money gains a great deal in the quality of economic life. It should be aware, however, that it is giving a hostage to fortune, for it must forever thereafter attend to the proper management of its monetary system, else the whole economy can suddenly find itself on the verge of collapse.

The primary function of money is to serve as the medium of exchange when prices are used for distributing resources and goods. Wherever money is employed for that purpose, however, it tends to perform other functions as well, one of which is to serve as a "store of value."

2   A Store of Value

In the modern economy, the typical citizen somehow receives a money income – say $3,000 a month – which she uses to make her purchases. She normally spends all of her income in the course of the month, and then receives a new sum of $3,000 with which to begin the next monthly cycle. On the first day of the month she holds a balance of $3,000, which declines gradually as the end of the month nears. Therefore, on average over the month she holds a money balance of $1,500. If there are 1,000 citizens, the quantity of "money in circulation" is $1,500,000 on average.

There are occasions, however, when a citizen wishes to time her purchases differently from that standard pattern. She may wish, for example, to save some of her income in order to make a large purchase at some future date, perhaps an automobile or new bedroom furniture. Money is then said to serve as a "store of value," in the sense that money income does not have to be converted into consumption as soon as it is earned, but can be stored up for the purpose of future consumption.

Saving of this sort – for the purpose of satisfying personal consumption preferences – might be objectionable in a society that values societal choice in consumption, especially in the extreme form of uniformity. In a society that values individual consumer choice, however, there can be no objection to saving. Choosing between consumption today and consumption tomorrow differs in no essential way from choosing between shoes today and shirts today.

The practice of saving can be highly beneficial to an economy. One of its major benefits is that resources that would otherwise have gone into the production of consumer goods become available for use in investment – that is, in building new factories and machines that increase the country's future production. Savings, however, also create certain massive problems. One of them that afflicts market economies is the fluctuations in output and employment that are called recessions or depressions. These matters relate to the country's production system, however, the discussion of which will not be taken up until Part IV. There is another problem, however, that does not involve the production system directly and can therefore be examined in the context of our present concern with consumption only.

If money were used only as a medium of exchange, the average citizen's money balance over the month might amount to $1,500; but when people also use money for saving, their average balances are larger than that. They may indeed run into the thousands of dollars or more. That poses a certain problem, for the larger the money balances that citizens hold as savings, the greater the temptation for thieves.

3   Banks and Bankers

Theft is no doubt more ancient than money. Stealing a spear or a wife or a horse, however, is more difficult to pull off than stealing money. With the widening use of the price method, and therefore of money, it became increasingly urgent to find ways of protecting people's money from theft. Hence the rise of banks, and the emergence of bankers to run them.

It may come as a shock to some devotees of the Good Society that once it decides to distribute its consumer goods by the price method, there is no escaping banks and bankers. Banking shares in the disrepute in which money itself is sometimes held; it is an institution one expects to flourish in an egoistic and exploitative society, but not in one that lays claim to goodness. If that attitude predominates, a society may indeed choose to outlaw banking. The price method could still be used for distributing consumer goods, but the society would then run the risk of an unacceptable amount of theft.

You may hold that if it is a Good Society in all other respects, the members will have no motivation to steal from each other, and there would therefore be no need for banks and bankers. It is not unreasonable to expect that under some social arrangements the disposition toward thievery would be lower than in others. To design social institutions for a world in which there would be no scoundrels at all, however, crosses the line that separates the Good Society from Utopia. In the spirit of this book, we must assume that the scoundrels are forever with us, and that all but the most intimate of communities will be compelled to make provision for the protection of the innocent.

Banks must therefore be established for the minimal purpose of safeguarding the money savings of the citizens. The "savings bank," as it is called, accepts money presented to it for safekeeping, creates a deposit account in the name of the saver, and stores the money in a safe place that is inaccessible to all but the most accomplished of thieves. The money is then said to be "withdrawn from circulation," in the sense that it is not intended to be spent on the purchase of goods in the immediate future.

All modern societies, whether they call themselves capitalist or socialist, have established savings banks.[1] They differ primarily in the form of ownership. In the Communist countries the citizens held virtually all of their savings in saving banks, all of which were owned by the state; the bankers were public employees, like everyone else. In capitalist countries the banks are generally privately owned, although there is a smattering of cooperatively owned banks and some other ownership forms.

The form of ownership need therefore be no bar to the acceptance of banks and banking in a Good Society. Some people are more comfortable with the idea that if we must have banks, they should at least be people's banks, owned and run by the society. Others, fearful of the nastier sides of governmental bureaucracy, would prefer a system of competing privately owned banks. In the discussion to follow, I shall assume that the banks are publicly owned, but the argument applies equally to private banks.

4 Borrowing

Saving is a way in which citizens can increase their future consumption by reducing their current consumption. There are circumstances, however, in which people prefer to do the opposite – to consume more today than their income would permit and to compensate by consuming less tomorrow. That is the normal case with young families with children. The family would like to spend more than its current income of $3,000 per month in view of their current pressing family needs, and would be glad to make up for it by consuming less than $3,000 per month in the years after the children have left the home. Over the cycle of a lifetime, however, their total consumption would be about the same as if they consumed the same amount in each period.

That inter-temporal redistribution of consumption could be accomplished without banks. The would-be borrowers could seek out savers and arrange to borrow the saved funds for a specified number of years, after which the money would be repaid according to a mutually agreeable schedule. The saver thus becomes a lender as well. Had the POW camp lasted for a longer period of time, the prisoners would no doubt have developed a way of temporarily lending to and borrowing from each other. Such an arrangement may be thought of as a primitive form of barter-over-time. When banks are in operation, however, borrowers need no longer search for those citizens who happen to be savers. They can simply go to the bank and apply for a loan of some of the money that had been deposited in the bank by anonymous (to the borrowers) savers.

If the world followed Polonius' view of the Good Society, neither borrowing nor lending would be permitted. Prudent people would be expected to save in anticipation of large future expenditures, but their savings would not be lent to others who wished to consume more of their income today. Many people of moral disposition no doubt share Polonius' sentiment that borrowing reflects self-indulgence and imprudence; but no society has built such prohibition into its economic arrangements.

Borrowing for consumption purposes is most highly developed in capitalist countries, where the people's desire for consumer goods coincides with the interest of private industry in encouraging expenditures on consumption. In such countries the largest loan that most people ever take out in their lifetime is a mortgage-secured loan for the purchase of a dwelling. If borrowing were not possible, it would take many years before a family could save enough out of each $3,000 monthly income payment to buy a $200,000 house. The opportunity to borrow makes it possible to buy the house many years earlier, while the family can make the greatest use of it. This is the classic form of borrowing – to consume more (housing services) today than one's income can pay for, and to repay by consuming less in the future than one's income could pay for. Borrowing for the purchase of an automobile is the second largest loan that most people take out. It is evident that the consumption of the citizens of those countries would be significantly different, and less satisfactory, in the absence of arrangements for borrowing for consumption purposes.

The governments of most Communist countries sought to encourage saving by their citizens, but they did not seek to stimulate consumption by acts of policy.[2] Consequently there were virtually no facilities for consumer borrowing. By and large, a family's present consumption was limited to what could be bought with its current income and accumulated savings; there were few arrangements for shifting some of one's future consumption to the present.

The relative weakness of consumer borrowing in Communist countries was more a consequence of historical circumstances than of the imperative of socialism. The countries that adopted socialism in the past century were relatively poor and their governments discouraged consumption in order to devote more resources to investment in new industrial plant and equipment so as to be able to consume more in the future. Moreover, the leaders of new revolutionary societies tend to promote their own ascetic values and to discourage manifestations of the "consumerism" of the corrupt pre-revolutionary past. There is no inherent reason, however, why a good socialist society should regard consumer borrowing differently from a good capitalist society. Judging from the popular hunger for consumer goods in the last decades of the Communist countries, a socialist society that was responsive to the people's consumption wishes would be as hospitable to consumer borrowing as any capitalist country.

5   The Taking of Interest

There are a great many decisions that bankers have to make, regardless of whether the banks are publicly or privately owned. Many of those decisions derive from the risk that borrowers may not repay their loans, either for reasons beyond their control or out of pure mendacity. Rules must therefore be developed for assessing risk and for discouraging non-repayment. The rules are likely to differ in some respects in socialist and capitalist societies, but in such matters as embezzlement and absconding they are likely to be similar.

There is a second type of risk against which the banks must guard. Depositors normally have the right to redeem their deposits at any time, and if a great many of them happen to want their money back on the same day, the bank must be able to provide them with the funds. If it has lent out too much of the deposited funds, however, it may not have enough money left in its vault to pay them all back. Banks are therefore required to keep a certain proportion of the funds deposited with them as a reserve. If the required reserve ratio is 25 percent, they are authorized to lend out no more than 75 percent of their deposits.

When the quantity of money that the bank is authorized to lend is larger than the quantity that people wish to borrow, the bankers' task is relatively simple. They need only transfer to creditworthy borrowers some of the deposited funds that they are authorized to lend. If banking did no more than facilitate that kind of monetary "intermediation," as it is called, it would be churlish to deny it a place in a Good Society. The interesting problem arises in the case in which the quantity of money that citizens seek to borrow happens to exceed the quantity that the bank is authorized to lend: or in the language of economics, in which the quantity of loanable funds demanded exceeds the quantity supplied. All the borrowers cannot then be satisfied. Savings in this circumstance are "scarce," and have therefore to be allocated somehow among the borrowers. The question is, by what method should the bank distribute the scarce savings among the creditworthy borrowers?

Wherever a society confronts an allocation problem – whether in the distribution of goods among consumers, or of savings among borrowers, or of anything else – it must choose between the same two fundamental arrangements: the assignment method, or the price method.

ASSIGNMENT

Under the assignment method the manager of the people's bank would decide how much of the savings available for borrowing should be allocated to each of borrowers. There are various rules that the society might adopt to guide that decision. One such rule might be equal proportions: if the available savings amounted to only 70 percent of the total borrowing requested, then each borrower would receive a loan of 70 percent of the amount he requested. That, of course, would be a foolish rule indeed.[3] An alternative rule might be relative need: the banker, perhaps assisted by a committee of fellow citizens, would judge the merits of each borrowing request and allocate the savings to those borrowers whose need is judged to be greatest. A loan of funds to pay for a Caribbean cruise might be judged less worthy than a loan to visit an aged mother. Other, and perhaps better (in terms of the values of a Good Society) decision-rules might be promulgated, but the main point is that some administrative agent of the society makes the decision on who gets how much of the scarce good – savings in this case.

PRICES

Under the price method, borrowers are required to pay a price in exchange for the privilege of borrowing. The price is usually expressed as a percentage of the amount borrowed per month or per year. If the price were 5 percent per year, for example, then someone borrowing $10,000 would pay a price of $500 for a one-year loan (or $250 for a six-month loan). He would receive the one-year loan of $10,000 on, say, May 1, and would have to repay the bank $10,500 on the following May 1.

Under the price method the manager of the people's bank exercises no discretion in the distribution of the loans, except perhaps with regard to the applicants' creditworthiness. Her function is not evaluative but technical – to estimate the interest rate at which the amount of borrowing applied for is equal to the amount available for lending. When that interest rate prevails, every citizen who is prepared to pay that price receives a loan from the bank for the amount he wishes to borrow.

The rationale of the price method is that the higher the price, the smaller the amount the borrowers would wish to borrow. Raising the price of a loan would cause some would-be borrowers to scale back the amount they seek to borrow, and others perhaps to postpone or cancel entirely their plans to borrow. At some price the amount that people wish to borrow would be just equal to the amount of savings available for lending. Then every borrower willing to pay the price could receive the loan he requests. That is the "clearing price" defined earlier – the price at which the quantity demanded just "clears out" the quantity available for distribution.

The price, in this case, has a name that carries a great load of historical and emotional baggage. It is, of course, "interest." The choice between assignment and prices is therefore dominated by the question of whether the charging of interest is an appropriate activity in a Good Society.

THE USES OF INTEREST

The answer should be influenced in part by what happens to the money that is collected by the people's bank in the form of the interest paid by the borrowers. One possibility is to use the money for various beneficent public purposes, such as purchasing books for school children or tidying the public parks. The usual arrangement, however, is to hand the interest over to the savers as a supplement to their incomes. Thus, if the clearing price – called the "interest rate" in this case – happened to be 6 percent, a citizen who maintained a deposit of $10,000 for a year would find his balance raised to $10,600 at the end of the year.

The payment of interest to the savers would have another effect on the allocation of savings. Some savers might be inclined to save more if the bank paid interest, and some non-savers might start saving a bit. Therefore, the higher the interest rate, the larger the quantity of savings likely to be supplied, which would satisfy more of the would-be borrowers' desire for funds.

Hence if interest is both charged to borrowers and paid to savers, the rate of interest would provide the people's bank with a very flexible device for dealing with the allocation problem. By increasing the interest rate, the bank would simultaneously increase the quantity of money citizens wish to save and decrease the quantity others wish to borrow, and the opposite would occur when the interest rate is reduced.

It should be noted again that the price method is not tied to "markets." It can be used by publicly owned banks in socialist economies that have no markets and do not operate under the "price system." In the socialist planned economies the banker is still a government administrator, but when the price method is used for distributing loans, her discretionary power is severely limited. A borrower need not come hat in hand having to cajole or bribe the banker into granting him the loan. In principle, the banker must lend any amount requested by any qualified applicant who agrees to pay the established interest rate.

6   Interest and Efficiency

The distribution of savings among borrowers would be different under the assignment and price methods. Some people who would be able to borrow to buy a car or finance a wedding under one method would not be able to do so under the other: they would have to settle for a smaller wedding, or forgo consumption for a number of years until they had saved enough to buy a car. The Nation's Fate may not hang on such matters, but any family that owns its home thanks to a mortgage loan should recognize that the goodness of the society depends in some measure on how well its savings are distributed among those of its citizens who wish to consume more today than their income allows.

A variety of criteria come into play in assessing the merits of the two methods from the perspective of a Good Society, one of which is efficiency.

GOODS TODAY OR GOODS TOMORROW?

If people had identical consumption preferences, finding the best distribution of a given collection of goods would be a trivial matter. Everybody simply would get the same things as everybody else. It is only because people want different things that a society must worry about the efficiency of its distribution arrangements.

The differences in preferences that come most readily to mind are those examined in the last chapter: with the same income, you and I buy different collections of goods. The fact that some people save and others borrow, however, indicates that consumption preferences differ in another way: you may prefer to consume more today and less tomorrow, while I may prefer the opposite. It is because of the difference in preferences regarding the timing of consumption – or "time preference" – that saving and borrowing occur.

If you were offered a choice between a Mercedes today and a Mercedes five years from now, under ordinary circumstances you are likely to choose the Mercedes today. Most people would make the same choice, reflecting a fairly general preference for consumption today over consumption in the future, but that preference is not absolute. Offered a sufficiently large increase in future consumption, most people would be willing to reduce their present consumption by some amount.

Most important for efficiency, however, is that people differ in the intensity of their preference for consumption today relative to tomorrow. I might be willing to give up $1,000 worth of consumption today for as little as $1,100 more consumption next year. My "time preference ratio" may then be said to be 10 percent. You, however, would not give up $1,000 of present consumption for less than $1,500 of additional consumption next year. Your time preference ratio is then 50 percent. Your preference for present consumption is therefore much stronger than mine, since it would take more future consumption to induce you to part with some of your present consumption.

Differences in preferences between consumption today and consumption tomorrow are analogous to differences in preferences between CDs today and Reebok sport shoes today. Hence the reasoning that was developed in the last chapter regarding efficiency in the distribution of two goods at one point of time applies fully to efficiency of the distribution of consumption between two periods of time.

THE ASSIGNMENT METHOD

Suppose the people's bank is authorized to lend out $1,000,000 of the citizens' current savings, to be distributed by the assignment method. Prospective borrowers submit their requests for loans, accompanied by explanations of the uses they would make of the borrowed funds. The sum of all the requests amounts to $1,200,000. A loans committee consisting of the bank officer and a number of respected citizens evaluates the applications and distributes the available funds in accordance with the instructions set by the society. Some applicants get all the funds they applied for, some get less, and perhaps some get nothing. Is that the best possible distribution of the available funds?

Societal choice The assignment method is most attractive to a society that values societal choice over individual consumer choice. The loans committee would be expected to distribute the loans in the way that makes sense from the society's perspective, rather than from that of the individual members alone. That might mean, for example, considering the needs of the loan applicants rather than their wants, or evaluating the social merits of the purposes for which the applicants seek to borrow.

Operating on the guidelines approved by the society, the loans committee distributes the available funds in the way that they think best. The assignment method may therefore be said to be efficient, in the trivial sense that whatever distribution the loans committee decides upon is best by definition.[4]

Under a regime of societal choice, the citizens agree to ignore or suppress their individual time preferences, in the interest of the common good. In a small and intimate society like a kibbutz, that personal discipline may indeed prevail, perhaps for a long time. In a large and diverse society like China or the USSR, however, there will surely be some or many citizens who insist on expressing their individual time preferences. I, for example, may have received a much smaller loan than I had applied for and am so greatly distressed that I continue to seek the funds I need, and am prepared to offer a large sum of money in order to be able to borrow more. The distribution is therefore much like that in the POW camp, and will produce the same incentives for bartering – present and future consumption in this case, rather than dry socks and tinned beef. My request to borrow $6,000 having been denied, I may offer to pay as much as $7,000 next year to anyone who would lend me $6,000 out of the large loan she had managed to obtain. If someone accepts my offer, then the distribution carefully worked out by the citizens' loans committee fails the barter test of efficiency. Hence assignment may prove to be efficient in a small community that abides by the value of societal choice, but it is likely to be inefficient in a society in which many citizens seek to express their individual time preferences.

THE PRICE METHOD

Under the price method, the banker, relying on past experience, would announce an interest rate high enough to reduce the volume of loan applications to the $1,000,000 he is authorized to lend – perhaps 8 percent per year. My desire for the loan is strong enough that I would still ask for the full $6,000; I am fully prepared to pay the $480 a year in interest, and even more if I had to, to borrow that sum. You, who would have borrowed $10,000 if there were no interest charge, may now regard a loan of that size as "not worth it" if you have to pay $800 a year in interest. You may decide on a cheaper car, or a smaller wedding, and therefore apply for a loan of only $5,000, with an annual interest charge of only $400. In that fashion, if the banker has set the interest rate at the right "clearing" level, the sum of the loan applications will be just about the $1,000,000 he is authorized to lend.

It is evident that the price method is highly attractive to a society that values individual choice, for the distribution that emerges reflects only the time preferences of the individuals. There is no authority charged with asking whether the distribution is the best from the societal perspective. More significant, however, is that the distribution is also optimal. That may be seen by applying the barter test of efficiency.

Under the distribution that emerges from the operation of the price method, no one would pay more than 8 percent interest to borrow additional funds from someone else, for he could borrow as much as he wants from the bank at that rate. And no one would re-lend any of his borrowed funds for less than 8 percent, because it costs him that amount to borrow the funds from the bank. Hence the distribution passes the barter test, for there is no way of redistributing the borrowed funds by a voluntary exchange in which both parties would regard themselves as better off.

What is remarkable about the price method in this case, as in the case of consumer goods generally, is that efficiency comes about automatically, as it were, without the intervention of any human agents like a loans committee. The source of that efficiency in the case of differences in time preferences is the same as that which operates in the case of preferences among goods. Differences in marginal preference ratios between two goods correspond to differences in marginal time-preference ratios between two periods of time. Citizens adjust their purchases of goods to the same prices, so that when each one spends his income on what he regards as the best collection of goods, his marginal preference ratios are the same as everyone else's and there is no basis for any further barter exchange (chapter 6). In the present case, it is the interest rate that serves as the Westminster clock to which all citizens adjust their borrowing so that their marginal time-preference ratios are equal. Since a distribution with that property passes the barter test of optimality, the price/interest method must be efficient in distributing the savings among the borrowers.

7   Equity and Other Values

Leaving interest aside for the moment, there ought to be no equity concerns about saving and borrowing *per se* in a Good Society. Since the borrowed amounts are eventually repaid, each citizen's lifetime distribution of income is largely unchanged. Saving and borrowing merely permit them to arrange the time-stream of their consumption differently from the time-stream of their incomes: borrowers consume more today and less tomorrow than their current income would permit, and savers do the opposite.

Issues of equity and other criteria of goodness arise only if the total amount that people wish to borrow exceeds the available savings, which must then be allocated somehow among the borrowers. The question is, which of the two allocation methods is more appropriate for a Good Society insofar as criteria other than efficiency are concerned?

ASSIGNMENT

Insofar as the locus of choice is a criterion of goodness, if you place a high value on societal choice in your Good Society, you will regard it as entirely proper that citizens submit their loan applications to a jury of their peers, and provide the information needed in order for them to decide which applications are the more meritorious. In a pure commune like the kibbutz a great many economic decisions affecting the members are made in that way.

If you value individual choice, on the other hand, you would regard it as an insufferable invasion of your privacy that such matters should be the subject of community discussion and decision. You would much prefer an arm's-length negotiation with a banker who will pry into your affairs only to the extent that he needs to judge your creditworthiness. The assignment method would therefore get high marks in a society that values societal choice, but not in one that values individual choice.

Distributive justice   The assignment method of allocating savings ought to be acceptable in a Good Society by the criterion of distributive justice. All that happens is that in any one month or year, there may be greater inequality in the distribution of consumption than in the distribution of income, because savers are consuming less than their income and borrowers more. That inequality is reversed, however, when the loans are repaid: borrowers then consume less than their current income and savers more. In the course of time, therefore, the distribution of consumption follows the distribution of income, and since the latter should be equitable in a Good Society, so should the former.

Fairness   With respect to justice as fairness, the assignment method relies upon the decisions of the manager of the people's bank, supplemented perhaps by a consultative committee of citizens. They can take account of differences in income, or of relative need, or of any other considerations that in their judgment are relevant to a fair distribution of the loans among the borrowers. Since each application is assessed by a panel of reasonably objective citizens, it is difficult to quarrel with the fairness of such an arrangement.

The power to make such decisions does, unfortunately, open the door to corruption. A would-be borrower may be tempted to bribe a public official, which must be a concern wherever public officials serve as agents of the society. In large and heterogeneous societies, indeed, the prospect of corruption may create a general disposition against the use of the assignment method, because of the power it places in the hands of public officials.[5] If adequate safeguards are in place, however, the grosser forms of corruption may be contained, although the more subtle forms are virtually impossible to eliminate, even in the smallest and most solidary of societies.

Corruption aside, however, in a Good Society citizens wishing to borrow should expect to receive a fair hearing for their applications, relative to those of others, before an appropriate public agency. The decision of that agency can be taken as representing the values of the society regarding the relative merits of different uses of borrowed savings.

PRICES

There is no price method without a price, which in the case of savings is called interest. An assessment of the price method must come fully to grips with the passionate hostility evoked by the idea of interest.

There are few matters in the entire domain of economics that have aroused as much ire as the taking of interest. The full moral authority of both the Catholic Church and of Islam were brought to bear against the taking of interest in the Middle Ages, and it was not until relatively modern times that it has been permitted, though it is still not everywhere regarded as the noblest of occupations. The powerful image of Shylock, the vile usurer, symbolizes the moral opprobrium associated with money lending. How a society deals with interest on loans must surely be a major indication of its goodness.

Distributive justice   People who might appreciate the efficiency case for interest may nevertheless regard it as unthinkable that the taking of interest might be consistent with the other criteria of the goodness of a society. Distributive justice is likely to be the source of the first alarm, for the introduction of interest changes the distribution of income and consumption. Some income and consumption are shifted from borrowers to savers: savers are able to consume a larger proportion of the available goods because of the interest they earn, and borrowers a smaller proportion because of the interest they have to pay.

It may seem to follow that the charging of interest must result not only in a different distribution of income, but also in a more unequal distribution of income between rich and poor. That would indeed be the case if the savers are predominantly the rich and the borrowers are predominantly the poor. In a world in which income is equitably distributed, however, it is not evident that interest payments would generally flow from lower- to higher-income citizens. Savers would differ from borrowers not primarily by differences in their incomes but by differences in their individual time preferences: the borrowers would tend to be citizens who have a much stronger preference than savers for living it up today, relative to future consumption. In any event, if the initial distribution of income is equitable, the introduction of interest on savings is unlikely to change it radically.[6]

I suspect, however, that the foregoing argument, by assuming an equitable pre-interest distribution of income, misses the point regarding the source of hostility to the idea of interest. This hostility no doubt derives from the role of interest in societies with a highly inequitable distribution of income. In a modern society that is divided into rich and poor, and even more when it is divided into the very rich and the very poor, it is often the poor – people who are down on their luck – who resort to borrowing for consumption purposes, and the savers are generally the richer.[7] In that case the payment of interest is indeed one of the ways in which the rich grind the faces of poor people like the widow who can no longer make the payments on the mortgage.

It would be an error, however, to transfer to a Good Society attitudes acquired from having lived in and learned about societies that were very bad in various respects. In a Good Society, where there are neither rich nor poor but only income differences that are regarded as entirely legitimate, people would apply for loans not out of distress or extreme need but for the sake of personal convenience in the timing of their consumption. Under such conditions the gain in consumption efficiency is likely to outweigh such changes in income distribution as may occur.

Fairness   Distributive justice, however, is probably not the principal source of the hostility to interest. Closer to the mark is the sentiment that the introduction of interest on money implants an element of unfairness in a Good Society. To assess the fairness of an interest charge it is important to distinguish the *payment* of interest by borrowers from the *earning* of interest by savers.

The payment of interest on loans may be regarded simply as the payment of a price in order to buy a "good" that other citizens also wish to buy. If it is not held to be unjust that a "high" price be paid for a ticket to the World Series or a flight on the Concorde, then it should not be regarded as unjust that a "high" price be set on a loan of savings that many other people also wish to borrow. That is, the charging of interest to borrowers should be regarded as unjust only by people who regard the use of money and prices as unjust *per se*.

The issue of fairness is rather different in the matter of the payment of interest to savers. In paying interest on their loans, borrowers consume less over their lifetime than they otherwise would; they choose to do so for the sake of being able to consume more of that smaller total today rather than tomorrow. The payment of that interest to the savers enables the latter to consume those goods that the borrowers agreed to forgo. Is it fair that by the act of merely maintaining a savings account in the bank, savers can consume more than non-savers?

We have not yet considered the sources of the citizens' incomes, which are related to the way in which the society organizes the process of production, but in a Good Society we may assume that those sources are regarded as entirely fair. The cab driver who takes you to the airport and the surgeon who treats your tumor both provide labor services that are everywhere thought to justify a payment in return. One may question the fairness of the *size* of the cab fare or of the surgeon's fee, but no one would hold it to be unfair that they earn incomes for those activities.

The implicit basis of that notion of fairness is that if I provide a service that is valued by other people, I am entitled to remuneration for it. The question here is whether putting some of my income in the bank constitutes "providing a service."

Of the many arguments that have been offered in justification of the earning of interest on savings, the one that is most relevant to the present case is that savers provide a service by deferring their consumption. Perhaps they will take one week of vacation this year instead of two, or forgo the purchase of a new car for another year or two. The consequent savings are transferred to some grateful borrowers who otherwise would not have been able to satisfy their desire to consume more than their current incomes would permit. The evidence that this service is valued by the borrowers is their willingness to pay the interest charge to obtain the loan. By this line of argument, saving is indistinguishable from the provision of any other type of legitimate service, like the driving of a taxi or the removal of a tumor.

There ought therefore to be no prohibition against the earning of interest on savings in a Good Society on grounds of fairness.

LABOR VALUES AND AESTHETIC VALUES

Opposition to the payment of interest derives from a variety of values, two of which predominate in discussions of the Good Society. I shall call them – for want of better terms – labor values and aesthetic values.

The labor argument concedes that the act of saving can be regarded as a service of sort, but of a very peculiar sort. It consists of the passive process of "making money on money," which is not at all like the active process of driving a cab or treating a tumor. One doesn't need to spend time or effort doing it: one simply waits and the money piles up. It piles up, indeed, during the very same hours that the cab is cruising and the surgeon operating. Implicit in that criticism is the view that the only legitimate reason that some people should be able to consume more than others in a Good Society is that their labor has contributed more to the quantity of goods available for consumption. Since the act of saving involves no labor, the saver has no legitimate claim to a larger share of the available goods on account of his savings.

The aesthetic argument singles out a group of economic activities that are regarded with distaste. The most egregious among them are banking, finance, commerce, and advertising – especially when carried out on a large scale. These activities are described in such pejorative terms as "speculation," "buying cheap and selling dear," "clipping coupons," "huckstering." They are viewed as the domain of parasites, who contrive to extract for themselves a large share of the goods that should be consumed by the people who actually produce them in such genuine economic activities as farming, manufacturing, or trucking. Income from lending is thought to be particularly odious because the borrowers are often people in distress – a Venetian merchant whose ships have sunk, or a widow whose home mortgage is about to be foreclosed.

The sentiments embodied in these labor and aesthetic values are widely held, in various combinations, in virtually all modern economies. In capitalist societies they are part of the set of ideas known as "populism," which finds true virtue only in the occupations of the hardworking farmer, the dedicated craftsman, and other people who devote their labor to small-scale business pursuits. Some of those values, particularly the aesthetic, are also widely held in upper-class families of inherited wealth and among people engaged in intellectual pursuits; and they are manifest in the disdain felt for people who spend their lives making money, trading government bonds, manufacturing plastics, or selling just about anything.

These sentiments were also alive and well in the Communist societies, and were indeed embodied in some of their economic institutions. The Communist countries called themselves "workers' states," and labor was highly glorified in the official ideology. It was not uncommon to see a delegation of coal miners feasting in one of the best restaurants in Moscow, highly visible by the proletarian cut of their suits and dresses and by the boisterousness of their comportment. For most of the Soviet period, jobs in banks, financial agencies, and retail trade carried little prestige and small salaries.

It is significant, however, that despite the prevalence of these sentiments, no modern society has carried them to the point of debarring the payment of interest on savings. In capitalist countries the only concrete expression of the second-class status of interest is that some governments tax earnings from interest at a higher rate than earnings from wages and salaries, reflecting the sentiment that income from labor is somehow more legitimate than non-labor income like interest. In the Communist societies, the state savings banks paid interest on savings accounts, although the rate was relatively low – generally about 2–4 percent per year. The governments also sold interest-paying bonds to the people. And while activities like finance and trade carried little prestige, their contribution to the economy was sufficiently recognized that no serious attempt was ever made to abolish them on the grounds of their unsuitability in the socialist version of the Good Society. Indeed, their status grew over time, so that in the last decades of the Soviet regime, senior officials in those occupations were fully entrenched in the upper echelons of the Communist establishment known as the "nomenklatura."[8] The spoiled children of bankers and trade officials were heavily represented among the "golden youth," who were a staple of social criticism in Soviet films.

Everyone must form his own judgment about whether saving is a service meriting compensation, or whether the entire cluster of activities associated with interest and moneymaking should find no home in a Good Society. That society should reflect the values of its citizens, and if aesthetic and labor values predominate, they should find expression in the economic institutions. In particular, if the abhorrence of "making money on money" is widely and strongly held, it should be debarred, even at some cost of efficiency. It should be done, however, only after full consideration of the experience of other countries, particularly Communist countries where the same sentiments prevailed, but where, in the end, it was thought that the loss in efficiency was too large to justify the gain in other values. A society so committed to such other values, however, should be prepared to find that other economies surpass it in efficiency.

CHOICE

In deciding to adopt the price method, a society signals its wish that the individual rather than the society serve as the locus of choice. The critic would point out, however, that something valuable in human relationships is lost by that decision. The substance of that critique should be understood, whether or not one agrees with it.

The point may be made by considering the case of a direct loan between two friends. Suppose Pierre's car has broken down and he needs to buy a new one now. Gaston has been setting money aside for his daughter's future wedding. Should Gaston charge Pierre interest for the loan of his savings?

In a society that regards familial relationships as morally superior to contractual relationships, the payment of interest in this case will be deplored. The more pragmatic citizens might concede that it would not be improper for interest to be paid if Gaston's savings were on deposit in the public bank where it was earning interest; in that case, it would not be a breach of the spirit of friendship if Pierre paid Gaston at least the amount of interest he would lose if he withdrew his savings to make the loan to Pierre. In some circles, however, and indeed in some whole cultures, payment for a loan of that kind would be regarded with disgust.[9] Those who hold such views believe that deep relationships of friendship, which are sustained by such social practices as gift exchange and interest-free lending, could not survive in an economy devoted to individual choice and therefore to arrangements like the price method.

That objection to the charging of interest merits more discussion than can be offered here. A few conjectural points may be made, however. First, it is indeed possible that the admittance into a society of the price method and of the payment of interest may, in the course of time, contribute to the "commercialization" of interpersonal relations: people may become accustomed to accomplish by impersonal contracts what in the past had been accomplished by personal gifts and loans. Second, however, the nature of friendship or kinship relations in a society probably says more about the culture of the people than about their economic arrangements: the tendency of Russians to reach for the dinner check and of Americans to split it among the diners predates Communism and will no doubt persist long into the future. And third, changes in such elements of culture as friendship and kinship are driven primarily by massive social forces like urbanization and modernization; the impact of economic arrangements on these matters is comparatively minor.[10] Therefore, the critique of the price method on the grounds of its subversion of traditional values may be valid in some small measure, but it more often constitutes a nostalgic longing for a simpler and purer past than a weighty factor to be taken account of in the assessment of economic arrangements.

8 Discussion

I have never understood the passionate animosity toward money that is shared by many socialists, Utopians, and theologians. It has always seemed evident to me that if evil has a root, it lies elsewhere than in the mere use of money. The hostility toward money is so deeply held and widely dispersed, however, that the dream of a moneyless economy will probably recur forever in loose discourse about a Good Society. It may even be attempted from time to time in the fervor of revolutionary change, and may endure for longer periods in small groups devoted to communal ideals. But I doubt that any society would continue for very long without rediscovering the virtue of that most ancient of inventions.

My own version of a Good Society therefore makes place for a monetary system, both because it is an absolute precondition for a level of consumption that I would find acceptable, and because I absolve it of all guilt for the evils that have been charged to it in other societies. If the rich grind the faces of the poor, it is not the use of money that is the culprit but the economic arrangements that endow the rich with too much money and power and the poor with too little.

I see only social benefit from the desire of some citizens to save some of their money income and of others to borrow the savings. Both contribute to efficiency and are consistent with individual choice, upon which I place a great value in this case.

With regard to the method of allocating the savings, the matter may be put this way. Suppose there were two societies, alike in all respects except that one provided interest-free loans under the assignment method and the other provided interest-bearing loans under the price method. In which would I rather live?

I have no direct experience with the use of the assignment method for allocating savings, but I am familiar with its operation in a closely related matter. A young member of an Israeli kibbutz wished to study at an institution of higher education. Since at that time kibbutz members received very little of their income in the form of money, the cost of higher education had to be paid out of the income of the kibbutz itself. This young man's request came in due course before the General Meeting of all members. Among the questions raised in the lengthy discussion were whether the subject he wished to study would be of use to the kibbutz, how well prepared he was relative to other aspirants, whether he was likely to remain a member of the kibbutz after he had graduated, how much of the kibbutz income should be spent on the higher education of its members relative to other meritorious expenditures, and so forth. In the end the meeting voted to allocate the funds for his higher education. Significantly, one of the deciding reasons was the concern that if the young people's aspirations for higher education were not satisfied, too many of them would leave the kibbutz.

That is not the way in which I would wish any important decisions of my life to be made. I recognize that the kibbutz is in many ways an extended family, and the membership meeting is like a family gathering for making decisions in which the whole family has a stake. With a slight stretch of my imagination I can even see that as a tolerable state of affairs, but not as one that I would freely choose. Perhaps the reason is that I have spent many years learning, visiting, and musing about societies in which various forms of assignment have been used, and I have a good sense of what life is like under that arrangement. The more I learned about life under a regime of societal choice, the greater the value I placed on individual choice, and I would not willingly surrender it on matters of this kind.

All of that applies to a voluntary, democratic community within a larger society. On the level of the full society, I would regard the assignment method as intolerable on such matters as saving and borrowing. It would be most unpleasant to have to make my case for a loan to a public official, who must inevitably be a "bureaucrat," and who has the authority to decide which of all the applicants will receive their loans. Matters would not be improved if the decision were made by an elected town committee: I am not sure I would want them all poring over the personal information I would have to supply in order for them to be able to compare the social merit of the use that I would make of the loan with that of the other applicants.

As a borrower, I would find it very nice not to have to pay interest, which is not charged at all under the assignment method. But with the weight that I place upon individual choice, that would not compensate at all for loss of privacy that accompanies that method. A further disadvantage is that in the absence of an interest payment to savers, the volume of savings will be smaller, and my chances of receiving a loan when I want it would be correspondingly reduced.

I would therefore much prefer to pay an interest charge and to be eligible for the loan if I qualify on strictly financial grounds. Not that I find it pleasant to have to make my case for a mortgage loan before an official of my local savings bank, and to wait upon his decision. But that decision is likely to be made on the basis of my creditworthiness alone and not because he finds no social merit in the use I intend to make of the loan, or because someone else has a greater need for a loan than I. Moreover, if he turns me down there are other banks that are eager for my business. In capsule, on such matters as the borrowing of money, I prefer to pay for a contractual relationship with a bank rather than to enter into a familial relationship with my fellow citizens.

The issues of justice on this matter strike me more as interesting intellectual games than as substantial considerations regarding the goodness of the society. There is merit in the argument that savers perform a service by "deferring gratification," but no great injustice would follow if people whose income had been justly earned received no further interest income for having deposited some of it in a bank. On the other hand, the issues that are raised by the labor and aesthetic values discussed in the text are substantial. I personally find the scorn for commerce, finance, and management to be distasteful, particularly in people with relatively high incomes who are unaware of the extent to which their affluence derives from the activities of the very people they disdain. Apart from my personal view on this matter, however, an economy that incorporated those values in its design would be so unproductive that even people who hold those values would reject it. The economics of the Good Society should not be about the kind of people you would like to share a beer or a cocktail with, but about how to produce and distribute the goods and services that support social life.

All in all, I could live quite adequately in an economy that forbade the use of interest on consumption loans. My own Good Society, however, would make a place for interest. By the criterion of justice I would judge it to be neither much better nor much worse than one that rejected interest, but by the criteria of choice and efficiency, it would be decidedly better. I would rather pay interest to the bank for my loan than have to plead my case before a community meeting or an assignment agent, and I see no miscarriage of justice in the transfer of my interest payment to a citizen whose savings made my loan possible. The rationing of the available savings by an interest charge also distributes the savings among borrowers more efficiently than the assignment method would. All in all, the use of interest would make for a better society in terms of my own criteria of goodness.

These conclusions apply to the simplified consumption-only economy with which Part II of this book has been concerned. In such an artificial world, the only contribution of saving is to enable the citizens to alter the time-stream of their consumption. In a real economy, however, in which goods have to be produced before they can be consumed, saving makes a vastly more important contribution. It permits the society to increase the size of its capital stock – its factories and machines – so that the total volume of consumer goods available can increase in the course of time. Under such circumstances, the efficiency with which an economy manages money and savings can have a huge impact on its performance. Issues of justice would also loom much larger, because money would be borrowed not only for consumption purposes but also to finance investment in new capital. Interest can therefore have a larger impact on income distribution. The discussion of saving and interest in this chapter should therefore be regarded as a dress rehearsal for the analysis of the justice of "property income" in chapter 27.

Notes

1   Savings banks are to be distinguished from commercial banks, which are found only in capitalist countries. Commercial banks make loans to enterprises for such purposes as laying up a stock of consumer goods before the Christmas buying period. After the holiday the merchants repay the loans from the proceeds of their sales. In socialist countries the state-owned shops also need to stock up on goods before holiday periods, but their short-term need for money is met by the government's state bank, rather than by capitalist-type commercial banks.

2   The people's savings were not borrowed by other citizens, but they were borrowed by their governments. If personal savings had been smaller, the Communist governments would have had to tax the population more heavily in order to finance their commitments to provide for such activities as free education, national defense, and investment.

3   It is foolish because it ignores the obvious response of borrowers to that kind of rule. Once it became known that the bank is lending only 70 percent of the amount applied for, some would-be borrowers, perhaps many, would simply apply for about 30 percent more than they needed. That response would defeat the purpose of the 70-percent allocation rule.

  This is an instance of the general problem of "moral hazard," which was endemic in the Communist countries, where the assignment method was widely practiced. In industry, for example, when bonuses were awarded to enterprises that overfulfilled their output plan quotas, many of them responded by underreporting their production capacity, so they would be assigned lower quotas.

  One might hope that moral hazard would disappear in a Good Society, for the citizens would not subvert the intent of the established rules by that sort of self-oriented behavior. The matter will be discussed later in the text, but to anticipate my own conclusion, no one has yet figured out how to organize a large society in which self-interest would not become very widespread in the course of time. The exception is small communities with strong ideological or religious commitments.

4   The citizens must be aware, however, that a loans committee consisting of different members would probably decide upon a different distribution. Therefore, while they may accept the result because they approve of the procedure, they are unlikely to be greatly impressed with the argument that whatever distribution a committee decides on is optimal.

5   This is not to say that corruption is absent in private economic activity. Particularly in very large private corporations, for example, many officials are in a position to profit personally at the expense of the corporation with a reasonable prospect of not being detected, and a certain number of them succumb to the temptation. The difference is that in private enterprise there are more likely to be other persons whose own pocketbooks are at stake and who are directly motivated to prevent the misappropriation of what they regard as their own property. I believe the evidence to be overwhelming that, taking the culture as given, the larger the proportion of all transactions in which a public official has the power to decide who will receive a government favor, the larger the extent of corruption.

6   This conclusion applies only to the world-without-production under consideration here, where citizens borrow only for consumption purposes. When citizens borrow for production purposes – to finance the building of a new factory, for example – the total volume of borrowing is very large, and the income earned from savings makes a significant difference in the income distribution.

7   In earlier times, the major borrowers were kings and princes, who turned to moneylenders to finance their wars or their high consumption levels. Many banking fortunes were made by loans of these sorts. Only in modern times have people of lesser means been able to borrow to augment present consumption levels.

8   The term refers to the list of positions in government and the economy for which special clearance procedures were required. Before a candidate could be appointed to a position on the "nomenklatura," his entire ideological and political history was scrutinized by a special Party commission and by the secret police organization, the KGB.

9   In societies in which gift exchange is standard practice and serves to promote social solidarity, it is very often the case that strict rules of reciprocity have been developed. If the example described in the text occurred in such a society, Gaston would make a gift of $100 to Pierre, and Pierre would very likely reciprocate after a decent interval with a gift to Gaston, perhaps of a bit more than $100. The exchange would be regarded as a normal manifestation of friendship, of a higher moral order than would be found in commercial societies. Devices of this sort have often been used in commercial societies also, to circumvent ecclesiastical prohibitions against usury.

10 For example, whatever the nature of its economic arrangements, as an economy develops, people turn increasingly to financial intermediaries like savings banks and cooperative credit unions for consumer loans, and less often to family and friends. In economic matters, a familial relationship like that between Gaston and Pierre eventually becomes an anachronism.

Part III

Citizens as Workers

Chapter 8

Who Should Get What Jobs?

Ship carpentering, flagging of sidewalks
by flaggers . . . dockbuilding, fishcuring,
ferrying; . . .
— Walt Whitman

Octopus fishers, catch octopus;
And fingerwavers, wave your fingers;
Bus boys, bus girls, buss, buss.
— Morris Bishop

CONTENTS

How a citizen fares in the role of consumer is a major test of the goodness of an economic system. No less palpable, however, is the citizen's experience in the role of worker.

There were 126.7 million people in the civilian labor force of the United States in 1996. Among them were 18.2 million laborers and operators, 15.2 million in sales occupations, 4.5 million mechanics and repairers, and 850,000 athletes.[1] The numbers are different in other countries, but everywhere the kinds of jobs at which the people work are the consequence of a complex process that includes the training of labor, determining the number and kinds of jobs that need to be filled, and parcelling the workers out among those jobs.

There are two sides to the process that produces the society's job structure. The supply-of-labor side determines which workers will hold which of the available jobs. It consists of fitting the worker-pegs into a set of job-holes. The demand-for-labor side determines what those job-holes are: how many jobs there will for bookkeepers, for coal miners, and for all other occupations. Part III of this book deals only with the supply side, for it is there that many of the issues that are of particular concern in the Good Society tend to arise. The question asked here deals with the allocation of the workers among the available jobs, whatever those jobs happen to be. Part IV takes up the demand side and plunges directly into the matter of how the two sides combine to determine which citizens end up holding what kinds of jobs.

To focus on the way that citizens-as-workers come to hold their jobs, it is useful to assume that the enterprise's output depends only on the number and types of workers it employs. In practice, output and the job structure also depend on the nature of the enterprise's capital stock – if there were no trucks, there would be no jobs for truck drivers. They also depend on the flow of supplies – materials, fuels, and so forth. To maintain the focus on the issues of labor allocation, however, it is convenient to abstract away from those factors, assuming simply that each enterprise possesses a certain stock of machinery, equipment, and other items of capital, and that the flow of supplies is sufficient to maintain any desired level of output. In that labor-only economy, where output depends only on changes in employment, labor is said to be the only variable factor of production.

1   Wages or Assignment

The arrangements that modern economies have used for allocating workers among jobs are variations of the same fundamental methods that are used for the distribution of goods among consumers – prices and assignment. Under the price method – which may be called the wage method when applied to labor – each job pays a wage that the workers receive for supplying their labor for a week or some other specified period of time. The workers are expected to find their own jobs from among those for which they are qualified. To the extent that they have a choice among jobs, they take the one that they find most satisfactory on the basis of the wage rate and other considerations.

Under the wage method the workers sort themselves out among jobs on the basis of self-interest: they seek the jobs that they regard as the best for themselves personally. That appeal to self-interest is repugnant in certain versions of the Good Society. In that view the citizens-as-workers should be allocated among the jobs in the way that best serves the interest of all the people, rather than of themselves as individuals. The assignment method is designed for that purpose. Under that method, some members are designated to assign the workers to the jobs in which they can best contribute to the society, and the workers take the jobs to which they are assigned.

2   Differences among Workers

In a world of clones, the task of allocating the workers among jobs would be trivial. If every worker could remove an inflamed appendix or fill a tank of gas as well as any other, it would make no difference which worker performed which job – the outcome would be the same. It is because workers are not homogeneous that the labor-allocation task is complex and interesting, for in that case it makes a great deal of difference whether the right workers occupy the right jobs. Of the many ways in which workers differ from each other, three have been of particular prominence in the literature on what makes for a Good Society.

Workers differ, first, in their attitudes toward various kinds of job. Some prefer work outdoors while others prefer an office or shop environment. Some prefer to work with their hands; some like jobs that involve contact with other people; some enjoy working out production problems on paper. Some prefer making things and others selling things. Chapter 9 considers whether and how the citizens' job preferences are taken account of in societies that have employed one or the other of the two allocation methods.

A second difference is that some workers exert more effort on the job than others. I refer here not to differences in skill, but to the effort exerted by workers of the same skill. Everyone knows that most people work at a normal pace, some tend to goof off when they can, and some simply work harder than most. It is evident that no society can be completely indifferent to the effort put forth by its citizens-as-workers. How the wage and assignment methods have served to motivate work effort in societies that have used them is the subject of chapter 10.

Third, some workers are more productive than others because of the skills they possess. The operator of a computer-controlled machine tool, for example, contributes more to production than an assembly-line worker. Insofar as the Good Society wishes to produce as much as it can for the benefit of the people, it is vital that labor be allocated among jobs in the way that makes the best possible use of the productivity of its workers. The term "productivity" is not unambiguous, however, and chapter 11 explores various meanings of the assertion that one worker is "more productive" than another.

In taking account of differences in productivity among workers, however, it is no longer sufficient to ask only how well the worker-pegs are fitted into the given job-holes, which is the subject of Part III. One must also ask whether that set of job-holes makes the best use of their productivity. That is to say, the society must be concerned not only with the supply side, with assuring that the best plumbers fill the plumbing jobs and the best cooks do the cooking. It must also attend to the demand side as well, for the number of plumbing and cooking jobs to be established depends on the goods and services that the society wishes to consume. A full assessment of how well the two labor-allocation arrangements take account of differences in productivity must therefore be deferred to Part IV, which considers the grand arrangements for coordinating the supply of labor – and of other things – with the society's demand for them.

Note

1   US Bureau of the Census, *Statistical Abstract of the United States, 1997*, table 645.

Chapter 9

![Chapter divider bar]

Who Should Do the Dirty Work?

Which of us is to do the hard and dirty work for the rest — and for what pay?
Who is to do the pleasant and clean work, and for what pay?

— John Ruskin

Shirley: I wouldn't have your conscience, not for all your income.
Undershaft: I wouldn't have your income, not for all your conscience, Mr. Shirley.

— G. B. Shaw

CONTENTS

A teenager agreed to sweep in front of two small houses in Greenwich Village twice a week. It was a good deal for a 15-year-old: $15 for a half-hour's work. At the end of the first day's work, however, he was furious. "'I have dust in my nose and mouth, my clothes are filthy and I'm all sweaty', he complained, his handsome face contorted with anger. 'I'm quitting.'"[1]

Nor is street sweeping the most unpleasant of the jobs at which millions of people work. A *Wall Street Journal* reporter, after a tour of poultry-processing plants, recycling plants, and others, found himself in a "Dickensian time warp" of dehumanizing and dangerous working conditions.[2]

Perhaps if the workers who hold such jobs were better educated, they would have found more satisfactory work. It turns out, however, that education does not guarantee that. Even many college graduates have to settle "for jobs with modest salaries and no future while hoping for better work or saving for graduate school."[3]

There are many reasons why many workers are not able to find satisfactory jobs under the employment arrangements of a capitalist economy. The socialist countries, however, also had their share of jobs that workers regarded as unsatisfactory, and they appear not to have done much better in that regard. An official of the Food Service Workers Union in the USSR once complained that too few students were enrolling in training schools that prepared young people for jobs in public catering. Public catering, he wrote, is an honorable occupation that provides an absolutely essential service for the people, but it has a bad reputation. The reason, in his opinion, was that screenwriters and authors tended to portray it as of very low status. The solution he proposed was for the Writers' Union to order its members to depict food service jobs in a more favorable light in their books and films.[4]

No society has yet found an arrangement for allocating its members among jobs in such a way that nobody ends up with a job he finds unsatisfactory. Among the reasons is that people have different notions about which jobs are satisfactory. If people were asked to list the jobs they would like to hold in order of their preference – without regard to such considerations as income – there would be a considerable diversity in their rankings. The rankings would not be random, however. There are some jobs that would be high on most people's lists, and others that would be low. The rankings would vary from society to society, and among social classes and other groups within societies. In most modern societies, however, there are certain jobs that would appear near the bottom of everybody's list. They are the jobs that are associated with the dirty work of the society – sweeping streets, cleaning toilets, washing dishes, doing bedpan duty in hospitals and nursing homes. Most of them are thought of as "dead-end jobs," offering no prospects for a genuine career. The question of who should do that work has long engaged the minds of people concerned with the goodness of a society.

1 Eliminating the Dirty Work

One response is to deny that the question needs to be addressed at all, on the grounds that a truly Good Society would bend its efforts toward finding ways of eliminating such jobs. There is some merit in that view. The case can be made on moral grounds that a society ought not to permit itself to consume goods and services the production of which requires that some of its members engage in demeaning work. Technological progress has indeed made it possible to keep the streets cleaned in wealthier countries without the brooms and shovels of the past, and automatic dishwashers and clothes washers have replaced much of the human labor that was formerly expended on those activities. Even in a poor country like India, technological means have been introduced for the removal of human feces, a task that had traditionally been the occupation of very low-caste Untouchables.[5] A Good Society would very likely provide strong support for research and development in those directions, which would accelerate the process of replacing such jobs by machines.

It is unlikely, however, that any society in the foreseeable future will completely eliminate all the dirty jobs that it will wish to be performed. To cling to the notion of a technological fix as a way of not having to deal with the dirty-jobs problem is like insisting that the elimination of scarcity will solve the problem of allocating consumer goods. The economics of the Good Society must confront the question of dirty jobs if it is not to be another Utopian exercise.

Indeed, even the Utopian philosophers accepted the challenge of the problem, sometimes with surprising solutions. Charles Fourier, celebrated for reasons other than his psychological acuity, anticipated that in his ideal community the joy of labor would motivate people to do the work that needed to be done. As for the dirty work, Fourier, who happened to be a bachelor, observed that there is a segment of the population that possesses a natural "madness for dirt" – namely, children. He thus closed the circle by providing that, in his Good Society, it is the children who collect the garbage and "take over the field of unclean work, a charity of high statesmanship" because it saves the lowest classes from the contempt of the rest of society.[6]

No society has yet obliged by providing an actual instance of the Fourier solution. All societies, however, have had to employ some arrangements for allocating workers among jobs, and these provide the experiences that may be drawn upon for judging how a Good Society might set about that task.

The dirty-work problem may be viewed as a special case of the more general problem of how to deal with differences in workers' job preferences. There are some jobs that some people would wish to work at even if they were under no economic compulsion to work at all: writing books, healing the sick, playing professional baseball, riding herd on cattle perhaps. Most people, however, hold jobs that they would not gladly work at if they were free to work at no job at all. In the language of economics, the "disutility of labor" in a particular job is said to vary among workers. From this general perspective, the dirty-work problem signifies only that some jobs are associated with an extreme degree of disutility in the preferences of most workers. Therefore, whatever arrangement the Good Society selects as appropriate for taking account of workers' preferences in general should also serve as the best solution to the dirty-work problem.

2 Volunteering

In one of his most celebrated passages, Karl Marx set forth his vision of how work would be done in a communist society, in which the citizen was no longer alienated from his own labor. He would "do one thing today and another tomorrow, . . . hunt in the morning, fish in the afternoon, rear cattle in the evening . . . without ever becoming a hunter, fisherman, shepherd . . . ."[7] That commonwealth of free men spending their time in whatever employments they wish continues to represent a widely held view of how life would be lived in a Good Society. It is particularly attractive to people who are passionate about the things they do for a living, or that they wish they could do for a living – like writing poems or playing basketball.

Marx implicitly had in mind a world in which scarcity had been largely eliminated, but that qualification is sometimes ignored in popular ruminations on how things might be better run. The Good Society with which this book is concerned, however, must still deal with the fact of scarcity. Goods must still be produced by human labor, and any labor-allocation arrangement must be assessed by how well it serves in directing the workers into the jobs that must be filled if the society is to succeed in producing the goods it desires.

One can envision a society in which the right of the people to perform whatever labor they wish was so highly valued that all jobs would be filled only by volunteers. Everyone would be expected to work at some job, but for no reward other than the satisfaction of performing it. Some citizens with a strong social conscience, particularly in a small and intimate community, would no doubt choose to work at some things that the society needed, even if their purely personal preference lay elsewhere. Some of their time would be spent in hunting, fishing, and cattle-rearing not only out of their purely personal preferences but also because they understood that their society required the products of those activities.

A certain volume of consumer goods would therefore be produced under that arrangement, but its quantity and composition would diverge widely from what the people would wish to consume. Some things would be available in great abundance – fish and game, poems, and ball games. But the production of even those things would encounter certain difficulties. Performance activities like rock concerts and ball games need audiences, and if a great many people volunteered to produce these services, the number of "consumers" might be disappointingly small. Moreover, the writing of poems requires that some people work at producing the pens and paper, and concert halls and sports stadiums have to be built, heated, and cleaned – activities for which there are unlikely to be enough volunteers.

In principle, a society might be so committed to free choice of jobs that the people-as-consumers were prepared to live with the consumption of whatever things the same people-as-producers wished to produce. In practice, however, it is doubtful that such a society could survive. The people also need food to eat and fuel to heat their homes. Some persons with highly developed social consciences, particularly in smaller communities, would no doubt volunteer to grow the food, work in the cannery, and mine the coal. Some might even volunteer to do the dirty work. There are people who believe that the spirit of a truly Good Society would be such that all the jobs would be filled by volunteers. It would nevertheless be wise to prepare for the likelihood that the number volunteering for the less popular jobs would be far short of that required to produce what the society would regard as desirable or necessary. Few would judge that economy to be very good overall, even though everybody worked only at the job she liked.

When too few people volunteer for too many jobs, the responsible authorities are strongly tempted to twist some arms in order to increase the number of volunteers. A number of socialist countries succumbed to that temptation at various times, and a variety of social pressures and administrative inducements were marshalled toward that end. When volunteering is no longer strictly voluntary, however, it is better considered as an instrument of the assignment method of allocating labor that is discussed in section 5 below.

While pure volunteering cannot serve as a general method of labor allocation, it can and has been used as a supplement to other methods. In many countries large numbers of people volunteer their labor for charitable causes like helping the poor and weak, and staffing the wards of hospitals, and they turn out in great numbers to assist in national emergencies like floods and fires. And in some societies like Cuba (see below), volunteering has served to supplement the basic labor-allocation arrangements. No country, however, has yet attempted to employ volunteering as its basic arrangement for allocating labor among jobs, nor is it a realistic prospect for the future.

3 Job Rotation

An alternative way of dealing with job preferences that do not fit the society's needs is to rotate certain of the jobs among the members. Rotation has been used to deal with the dirty-work problem by requiring all citizens to take their turn at them, as in the kibbutz (see section 5 below). It has also been used at the other end of the job-preference scale to limit the time that certain jobs may be held by the same citizens. Such time limitations have usually been set on administrative and political jobs, out of the concern that if those jobs are held for long periods of time by the same citizens, certain undesirable social consequences may follow: they may acquire more power and higher social status than others, and they lose touch with the sentiments of the ordinary citizens. To forestall such consequences, those jobs are rotated to other citizens from time to time.

Like volunteering, however, rotation has never served as the basic labor-allocation arrangement in any society. It has been used only as supplementary method of dealing with certain jobs; for example, in Yugoslavia (see section 5 below) and in the Northwest Plywood Cooperatives (chapter 26). The basic arrangements are the same two methods – prices and assignment.

4   Different Wages for Different Jobs

The price method is by far the most widely used institutional arrangement for labor allocation in modern societies, both socialist and capitalist. There are some differences in the way in which it is implemented in the two types of society, but its basic features are the same in both.

The price method operates by affixing a wage rate (or salary) to each job. The worker then decides which job to take – of those for which he qualifies – on the basis of the wage rate and other considerations associated with each job. The wage rate is the "price" of labor; like the price of a consumer good, it is the amount of money that must be paid by the purchaser – the employing enterprise in this case – to secure the use of an hour or a month of a worker's labor service.

Under the price method the worker has the responsibility for finding his own job, and the employing enterprise has the responsibility for finding its workers. In the United States the process of matching workers and jobs is facilitated by the use of newspaper advertising by enterprises and job seekers, by governmental and private employment agencies, and by union hiring halls. In the USSR the traditional method was the posting of notices of job openings at the factory gate, which the workers would learn about by word of mouth or by making the rounds of the factories. In the last years of the Soviet state, however, governmental employment agencies were introduced.

A central feature of the price method is that wage rates vary among jobs. Societies that use the price method differ, however, in the specific arrangements by which wage rates are determined. The major difference is that in capitalist countries wage rates are set by the employing enterprises under various constraints set by market conditions, whereas in the centrally planned socialist countries an agency of government decides upon the wage rates that employing enterprises must pay. The details of wage-determination procedures are set forth in Part IV.

The logic of the price method is that wage differences should serve to allocate the workers among the jobs to be filled. If the number of qualified people seeking a particular kind of job is less than the number of such jobs that are to be filled, the wage should rise in order to attract more workers; and in the opposite case it should decline in order to reduce the number seeking that type of job. The actual wage-setting procedures may not lead fully to that result, however, or they may greatly slow the process by which wage rates rise or decline. In the long run, however, since workers are free to leave their jobs and seek others under the wage method, there is a tendency for employers in both capitalist and socialist countries to contrive to offer higher wage rates for the kinds of workers they badly need.

It bears repeating that the price method must not be confused with markets. One may hate the market, yet love the price method for some purposes. The Communist countries decisively rejected the market in favor of central planning for the core of their production system, but they clung to the price method for distributing goods among consumers and workers among jobs.

5 Assigning Workers to Jobs

There are two reasons why the price method clashes with some socialist versions of a Good Society. The first is that it necessarily generates inequality in income and consumption: it cannot do its job of allocating workers among jobs except by introducing inequality in wages. The second is that it operates by appealing to people's self-interest rather than to the common interest. The worker is encouraged to ask "What's in it for me?" rather than to ask how he can best contribute to the society's needs. For these and other reasons, the assignment of workers to jobs by an agency of the society has always had a certain appeal as a labor-allocation device.

How the assignment method works is best set forth by describing its operation in some of the societies that have employed it.

THE KIBBUTZ

The price method stops at the enterprise's gate. *Within* the boundary of every enterprise – in every modern economy – the assignment method rules. Once the worker is employed, she is assigned to her production tasks by whoever has that authority – whether a capitalist boss, or a socialist manager. In both cases the workers accept the employer's right to assign them to any of a certain range of production tasks.

The Israeli kibbutz is, among other things, a production enterprise, rather like a worker-owned cooperative, and the members are assigned to their jobs as in any enterprise. It has two distinctive qualities, however. One is a passionate commitment to equality among the members – not only with respect to income and consumption but also to social status. The other is that the work is done by coequal "members," rather then by hired workers who could be fired if they refused assignment. Those two conditions provide an unusual setting for the assignment of workers to their jobs.

Rotation The jobs that need to be carried out each day are derived from the kibbutz production plan, which is voted by the membership. In the early years most production jobs were rotated in order to broaden the members' skills as workers and to give them an understanding of all branches of the kibbutz economy. Rotation, however, makes no allowance for job preferences – everybody takes his turn at every job. Eventually the view prevailed that "an unhappy worker is an unhappy kibbutz member." Rotation gave way to an effort to satisfy the members' job preferences, and members were increasingly permitted to work permanently in the branch they preferred – poultry farming, the tailor shop, or whatever. The move to permanent jobs was accelerated by the gradual increase in education, in technology, and in non-farming production activities; there was too much to be lost by rotating a young worker who had learned to repair a tractor into some other branch like cattle-rearing.

The principle of rotation remained the permanent practice in the case of certain jobs like guard duty and – most notably – kitchen work. Food preparation, serving, and cleaning up the common dining room are carried out almost exclusively by members who work at it for a specified period of time. Originally a practical measure to deal with a labor-allocation problem, it became a major instance of the "ideologization of the improvised."[8] Kibbutz boosters like to point to it as evidence of the commitment to true social equality – no one is of such high status as to be absolved of the necessary but undesirable task of washing the dishes. The first prime minister of the country made a practice of taking his turn at kitchen work when he vacationed on his kibbutz from time to time.

Job rotation supplies an answer not only to the specific problem of the dirty work, but also to the general problem of inequality in social status. Even in the robustly egalitarian ethos of the kibbutz, some jobs are more esteemed than others, despite the fact that they confer no more income than other jobs. The concern was that if some members occupied the high-prestige jobs permanently, they would attain a higher social status in the course of time, and those who do the dirty work would come to occupy a low status. In the long run such social differentiation would very likely be transmitted to the children.

To forestall the corroding influence of that process of social differentiation, all administrators are elected by the general membership for stated periods, in the range of one to perhaps five years, so that many members have a crack at administration and very few exercise the power of office for very long. A large number of committees are required to administer the affairs of the kibbutz, and every member except the most inept bears some responsibility for administration at some time.

The labor coordinator   With the change to permanent status for most ordinary jobs, the more popular branches tend to be oversubscribed. Some members, usually the younger ones, must therefore wait their turn to become permanent workers in their preferred branches. They are the source of the labor for the less popular branches. The allocation of these workers among the jobs that need to be filled is the task of the labor coordinator who, like all officials, is elected for a term. The coordinator must also deal with seasonal peaks, which require the transfer of some workers from their permanent branches to others where they are temporarily needed.

The problem is to induce members to take jobs that are not their first choice when they cannot be offered higher wages and when they cannot be fired if they refuse. That the kibbutz has succeeded in that allocational task for so many years is testimony to the members' commitment to the shared goals. People go where they are assigned because they accept the legitimacy of the assignment process, to which they implicitly agree when they join the kibbutz. A powerful supporting factor is the opinion of the other members, with whom they work and live side-by-side all their lives in their "collective village."

Yet there are bound to be conflicts in this loose set of arrangements. If ten people are needed for a week's work in the canning shed, the labor coordinator has the responsibility of deciding who should be assigned to those jobs, and of obtaining their agreement to accept them. His power is so limited, however, that he "does not tell the individual member to move from his permanent branch; he begs him to do so."[9] He must persuade the member that it is a reasonable request, that he has not been unfairly picked out for that particular assignment, that there are not other people who should make the move, and so forth. A "difficult" member who repeatedly refuses assignment may be brought before the General Meeting, where both sides argue their case before their fellows. While the labor coordinator is usually supported, there are times when the assembly takes the member's side.

The role of labor coordinator is regarded as one of the most difficult of the many elected offices, and also one of the most time-consuming. She works at her own job all day, and then spends the evening arranging the job assignments for the next day and finding the people to fill them. It is not surprising that members have become reluctant to accept that job, that those who do accept it hold it for no more than a year, and that it is increasingly turned over to younger members.

Winds of change   Originally engaged almost exclusively in agricultural pursuits, the kibbutzim have been forced by economic necessity to diversify into other production activities.

A further reason for diversification was that the young people, whose educational level had risen, found agricultural pursuits unsatisfying. The new manufacturing enterprises are designed in part to keep the youth from leaving for the cities, for in revolutionary societies generally, the children of the founders are more concerned with their own job preferences and less with the original social goals of the movement. Since many of the new manufacturing operations are fairly high-tech, they require so specialized a knowledge of both business and technology that rotation among less-experienced personnel is increasingly costly. A growing number of such jobs are therefore held more or less permanently by specialized members of the kibbutz, much like an American or Soviet enterprise.

Unlike the distribution of consumer goods by assignment, however, there has been no retreat from the assignment method of directing workers into most of the jobs. There is no groundswell of support for the use of wage differences to get the dirty work done. Nor is there likely to be, for income equality is virtually synonymous with the idea of the kibbutz. If wage incentives were introduced, there would be no reason for people to continue with that difficult way of life in preference to leaving for the fleshpots of the outside world.

YUGOSLAVIA

Following their break with the Soviet Union in 1948, the Yugoslavs rejected the Soviet practice of permanent government-appointed chief executive officers – called "directors." In its place they instituted the practice of "worker self-management" under which the workers elected one of their number to serve as director. Directors, however, tended to be repeatedly reelected, raising the concern that they would become a "new class" of citizens that would threaten to replicate the class nature of Soviet society, as the Yugoslav socialists saw it. Their solution was to introduce a rotation system, which was hailed as a step toward the "democratization of our cadre policy." Under that system, directors were required to step down after a specified term, and others elected in their place.[10] The Yugoslavs, however, did not adopt rotation as a way of filling the unpopular jobs; nor did any society other than the kibbutz.

THE USSR

In the Communist world, the assignment of labor was first forcefully advocated by Leon Trotsky in the early years of the Russian Revolution when the new socialist society was feeling its way toward the best arrangements for operating the economy.[11] Fresh from his triumph as the organizer of the victorious Red Army, he proposed to apply to the people's economy the methods that had succeeded so well in the people's army. Labor would be assigned to the jobs that needed to be done in the same way that soldiers are assigned to their jobs in the army. The divisive forces of capitalist society having been smashed, there seemed no reason to reintroduce the individualistic wage methods of the past and the wage inequality that they entail.

Trotsky's vision found little favor among his fellow Bolshevik leaders, who recoiled at what they regarded as the "militarization of labor." After that brief flirtation with the assignment of labor, the Soviets turned to the wage method of allocating labor. With the exception of the period around World War II, Soviet workers were generally free to leave their jobs and to seek new ones if they wished, and the movement of workers among enterprises was in fact substantial. The authorities relied primarily on the wage method for allocating the workers among jobs, much as in capitalist countries, although with certain differences that reflected the socialist context (chapter 14).

Managed volunteering   The wage method was supplemented, however, by the practice of volunteering, which remained a permanent, though small, part of the Soviet labor landscape. The practice of *ad hoc* volunteering for special projects originated in the early years after the revolution, when it served as the expression of a genuine wish by many people, particularly young enthusiasts, to supply extra time and effort, with no material reward, to support the common goal of building socialism. They were known as "Saturday volunteers" (*subbotniks*). As revolutionary ardor gradually faded in the course of time, certain of those programs were taken up by the Party and became a permanent part of the repertory of organized activities in which the population was mobilized to demonstrate their political loyalty. Foreign visitors would from time to time come upon a group of men and women sweeping a section of the city streets and removing the debris from the lots, while dressed in conspicuously middle-class clothes. They were latter-day *subbotniks* – office workers and others mobilized by the Party to volunteer an occasional day's work for that social purpose. Technically one could refuse, but to do so would be a conspicuous act of political dissent. Few did. Moreover, many bored workers looked upon it as a bit of holiday from their jobs.

From time to time the Party resorted to managed volunteering to provide a labor force for large-scale special projects. One of the most famous was a spectacular program in 1954 to increase the food supply by bringing 13 million hectares of virgin land under cultivation. It was declared to be "an important patriotic duty," and the Young Communist League was mobilized to encourage young people to volunteer for the campaign. Some went for a few months, some for longer periods, and some 300,000 people moved to the new farmlands permanently.[12]

Managed volunteering of these sorts is not quite the same as the pure assignment of workers to jobs, but to the extent that people were under some pressure to volunteer, it is a close cousin. However, it was resorted to only for special projects. In the normal course of events, workers found their way to their jobs without any exceptional administrative direction. It was only in some of the latter-day Communist countries that the assignment method was revived.

GUEVARIST CUBA

All the postwar Communist countries started out by adopting the wage practices of the "older brother" – the USSR. Two of them eventually discarded the Soviet model, however, and struck out on a radically different path. China under the leadership of Mao Zedong and Cuba under the strong influence of Che Guevara vehemently rejected the use of wage incentives and undertook to run their economies on the basis of "moral" incentives rather than "material" incentives, in the language of the time. These new institutional arrangements for allocating labor, which were similar in the two countries, are best discussed in the case of Cuba, which was more accessible for study.

It was a time when the influence of Mao Zedong and the Chinese Revolution was particularly strong in the socialist world, and Che Guevara, who shared that world view, was the most prominent ideological and organizational leader of the Cuban economy. It was unseemly, he urged, for a socialist society to pander to the worst side of people by offering them personal material incentives, rather than cultivating their better, collectivist side by offering them the opportunity to do that work which was most needed by the people. That point of view was a scarcely concealed criticism of the Soviet Union, which many in the socialist world regarded as having betrayed socialism because of the longstanding use made there of the price method and the associated money-wage incentives.

The "revolutionary offensive" to unseat Soviet-type wage incentives began in the late 1960s. Its spirit is captured in a resolution of the Ministry of Labor declaring that the advances made by the revolution "clearly demonstrated that man is capable of realizing truly productive feats without requiring the application of wage forms in which the increase in productivity carries with it a higher wage."[13] Accordingly, an assault on wage incentives began, in the course of which wage differences were greatly narrowed and monetary bonuses for productivity were eliminated. Equality was further advanced by distributing increasing quantities of consumer goods and services without charge, which further reduced the dependence of workers' consumption on their wage earnings. Social incentives of the Soviet variety had been in place from the beginning, including awards, honors, titles, and various forms of public recognition, but with the attenuation of wage incentives, much more Party effort went into publicizing them and organizing their distribution. At the same time a massive program of political education was undertaken to strengthen the motivating power of the social incentives. A Commission on Revolutionary Orientation enlisted writers, sociologists, and others to help motivate the people to value the many titles and other claims to social rank for which workers could compete.[14]

Thus committed to greater equality, the governors of the Cuban economy had to devise some way – one that did not require wage differentiation – of parcelling out the labor force among the jobs that had to be done if the national production plan was to be fulfilled. Without actually having been intended, the assignment method came into being.

Under that arrangement, all workers were obliged to register their qualifications with the local employment office of the Ministry of Labor in order to obtain jobs. They also carried a 14-page identity booklet that contained records of their places of employment, type of jobs held, attendance and punctuality, volunteered labor, work speed, and political attitudes. The local employment office had two main functions. As in most economies, most workers would go to the same job day after day, so that the employment office was involved only in the placement of people who were without jobs. Its second function was to recruit workers for enterprises and projects, both local and elsewhere, that needed more labor in order to fulfill their plans.

How labor was allocated by the employment office may be illustrated by the administration of a ruling of the Ministry of Labor that certain jobs could be held only by women. The men who had held those jobs had to be reassigned to agricultural and more arduous tasks. They were interviewed first by the Cuban Women's Federation and then by the Ministry of Labor. Then, wrote the national newspaper, the worker "chooses a new job according to his vocation, education, trade, etc., and the need for manpower in various areas throughout the country." The report stated that the majority of those interviewed expressed satisfaction with the measure.[15] Evidently an effort was made to satisfy the workers' preferences where possible, which many workers found to be satisfactory, but some had to be assigned to jobs in occupations or locations which were not to their liking but for which there was a national need. By procedures of this sort the local administrative agencies contributed to the allocation of the country's labor among the set of jobs needed to meet the production plan, without having to offer wage incentives to induce workers to take jobs where they were needed.

Managed volunteering   The allocative machinery of the Ministry of Labor operated too gradually to keep up with the manpower needs generated by the planners' ambitious investment and production goals. It was therefore supplemented by a program of managed volunteering that was much more elaborate than that pioneered in the USSR. The highly organized campaigns managed to bring out millions of man-hours of labor for special projects, particularly in agriculture. In one month in 1967, for example, 250,000 people volunteered for six days per week for two, three, or four weeks. At another time 150,000 people were reported to have volunteered for a coffee-planting program in the Escambray mountains. According to one estimate, the volume of labor volunteered in 1967 amounted to around 250,000 man-years, or about 10 percent of the regular labor force.[16]

Since the rejection of wage incentives was a fundamental tenet of the new version of social-ism, the organizations responsible for mobilizing the volunteers drew heavily upon the afore-mentioned structure of social incentives that had been elaborately built up, including "pennants, medals, buttons of all varieties, honorable mentions in the work center's book of honor and its bulletin board." At the same time, however, when an enterprise was mobilized for a volunteering campaign, and the full force of Party, trade union, and government author-ity was calling on workers to perform their patriotic duty, to refuse to volunteer was inevitably taken as a political statement. Even some friends of the revolution were concerned at what they saw as the "semi-militarization of agriculture."[17]

In 1970 the government put its confidence in social incentives to the test by announcing the goal of producing 10 million tons of sugar cane, which was larger than the country had ever produced before. The hope was that the 10-million-ton harvest, which became a battle cry, would serve as dramatic proof of the power of social incentives to perform feats of pro-duction unimaginable with mere wage incentives. The administrative recruitment of workers to help out with the harvest was so intense that in that frenetic year more than a third of the entire labor force worked at least part-time in agriculture.[18] The Cuban experience is one of very few that history has provided of a country that committed itself so fully to the management of its labor force by the assignment method instead of by wage incentives.

The retreat from social incentives   In the end, the massive mobilization of labor did not suc-ceed in producing the targeted 10 million tons, and the campaign was widely considered a failure. The harvest did in fact set a historic record, but the campaign absorbed so much of the country's labor and other resources that industrial output went into a decline. The government was also confronted with evidence of declining productivity and of growing worker fatigue and hostility because of the pressures for unpaid volunteering and overtime, all of which led to the first strikes in the fall of 1970.[19] The alarming economic situation precipitated a political crisis that culminated in a sharp change in economic organization amounting to the rejection of the Maoist vision that had been embraced by Che Guevara. The government stated publicly that it had gravely erred in its view that a socialist economy could thrive on the basis of social incentives also. Its more sober judgment, as expressed by Fidel Castro, was that the two types of incentives – social and economic – must be combined, but in such a way that "economic incentives do not become the exclusive motivation of man and so that moral incentives do not become a pretext for some to live off others."[20]

What followed was a wholesale replacement of the assignment method by the price method of allocating labor. The wage spread was increased to provide a stronger incentive for workers to improve their skills. Wages were more closely linked to the quantity and quality of work performed, and production bonuses were readmitted. Wage supplements were restored for the less attractive jobs in workplaces with abnormal conditions. The economy was reorgan-ized along the lines of the conservative wage-based Soviet model that had prevailed before Che Guevara's revolutionary offensive.

CHANGING JOBS

The pure assignment method as envisioned by Leon Trotsky requires that once a worker was assigned to a job, she could not leave it without permission. The requirement made sense since few workers would stick to the unpopular jobs – and particularly the dirty jobs – to which they had been assigned if they could leave with impunity whenever they wished.

The USSR bound workers to their jobs for only one period in its history – from 1940 to 1956.[21] That practice was introduced by Stalin in order to put an end to the unacceptable degree of "flitting" by workers from one enterprise to another in search of the "long ruble."

During World War II the people accepted the restrictions on job mobility as justified by the war effort, but as the postwar years moved on, dissatisfaction grew. It is significant that among the first acts of the post-Stalin government was the relaxation of the severe wartime restrictions on labor, including the law that made it a crime to leave one's job without permission. Since that time the price method remained the principal arrangement for the allocation of workers among jobs, with a few exceptions such as the obligation of higher-education graduates to accept assignment to their first jobs. Workers, accordingly, changed jobs about as often as in capitalist countries.[22]

In the countries that relied on the assignment method at various times, there was no mass defection from unpopular jobs, even though workers were free to quit their jobs. A major reason is that in the Communist countries there were very large benefits to having a job, in addition to the wage. Most workers lived in enterprise-owned apartments at highly subsidized rents, and in view of the prevailing housing shortage they were disinclined to risk losing that important benefit. The enterprise also provided day-care facilities and summer camps for employees' children, health and recreation services, subsidized vacation opportunities, and so forth. A worker's job was therefore much more a part of this social and emotional life than in capitalist countries.

China offered certain additional benefits to state-enterprise workers. The enterprise accepted the obligation of providing jobs for its workers' children. It was also a major supplier of rationed and other consumer goods, which were sold to its workers at reduced prices. A job in a state enterprise was therefore highly valued by the workers, and few would give it up voluntarily for another job. Seeking a job in a different location was particularly difficult because one had to be registered for permission to live there, because housing was very tight, and because one had to obtain food and other rations from the local agencies.

For these reasons, there were virtually no resignations from state enterprises in China, even in periods when job assignment was widely practiced. Most resignations were from small state enterprises or local "collective" enterprises that did not offer the full range of supplementary benefits. There were also resignations by workers who had been reassigned to other enterprises, particularly in cases of family separation and reassignment to distant regions. Hence, the formal right of workers to leave their jobs did not, as one might have guessed, interfere with the operation of administrative job assignment.[23]

6 The Locus of Choice

Turning now to an assessment of the two allocation arrangements, if workers in a capitalist country were asked to evaluate the labor practices of another country, they would very likely ask first of all, "Are there enough jobs for everybody?" In their final assessment, job security might well top the list of criteria of goodness. The capacity of a system to maintain full employment, however, touches upon virtually all elements of the economic system, and the discussion of that topic must be deferred until chapters 19 and 20. For the present, therefore, the question of job security must be passed by. In the assessments to follow, I shall assume that the society has found a method of assuring a reasonable level of employment and job security, and proceed to other criteria of assessment. With regard to arrangements for the allocation of workers among jobs, the pertinent criteria are locus of choice, justice, and efficiency.

The question of who should decide who gets what jobs does not ordinarily occupy a large place in discussions of economic organization. Yet how that question is answered is of enormous consequence in determining the quality of the citizens' working lives.

The position one takes on the question boils down to a matter of values. In this case, the choice is between individualist and societal values. If you are committed to individualist values, you would prefer the worker to be the locus of choice – in your Good Society each worker should have the right to choose his own job insofar as that is practical. If you hold by societal values, you would prefer that the society make the choice – your Good Society is one in which citizens accept the jobs that "serve the people," as in the Maoist formulation, rather than seek the jobs they personally prefer.

In a society that takes worker choice as the criterion of goodness, the price method is the better of the two arrangements. The worker's choice cannot be entirely free, of course, but is constrained in a variety of ways. For most workers in both socialist and capitalist countries, for example, wages are the only source of income, so that they can scarcely be said to be free not to work; the Constitution of the USSR, indeed, declares the holding of a job to be an obligation of a citizen, and a person without a job faces prosecution under the "anti-parasite" laws. One might also contend that when a very low wage is attached to some jobs, it makes a mockery of the notion that the people who hold those jobs actually "prefer" them and are exercising free choice. Those objections, however, relate to justice, and not to choice, as the criterion of the goodness of economic arrangements; if the concern is that some workers earn wages that are unjustly low, one should seek ways of remedying that particular deficiency, rather than rejecting the wage method generally.

As for the dirty work, in the abstract world under consideration here where all workers are equally productive, those jobs might have to offer a very high wage in order to attract the number of workers required by the job structure. The unpopular jobs would then be freely chosen by those workers who are most attracted by the high wage and least distressed by the conditions of the work. Hence, the price method should be fully acceptable to someone for whom worker choice is an important value. In real societies, of course, whether capitalist or Communist, workers are not equally productive, and the productivity – as the society defines it – of those with little education and few skills tends to be low. They therefore face a very restricted range of jobs for which they qualify, and the wage rates tend to be very low. Among that group of jobs, however, those that involve the dirty work tend to be better paid than others that are regarded as more pleasant.

If the dominating value is societal rather than worker choice, the assignment method is the better one. In a society that is good in all other respects as well, the workers would have sufficient trust in their agents to accept the assignments willingly. As in the ideal of Maoist China, if they are sent to remote parts of the country to perform difficult labor, they do so as part of the shared sense of contributing to a social goal. They undoubtedly have their own (perhaps secret) preferences among jobs, but they agree that all personal preferences should be submerged in the pursuit of a common social objective.

The dirty work is therefore done, under this method, by people who are assigned to it, which should be perfectly acceptable in societies devoted to the value of societal choice. One might be concerned about the fairness with which the assignments to such jobs are made, but that is a matter of justice rather than of choice; that is, if the assignments are unfairly made, the proper recourse is to find ways of ensuring fair assignments, rather than to reject the assignment method itself.

7 Can Unequal Wages Be Just?

Turning from locus of choice to justice, the price method is fair with respect to job preferences in the sense that all workers are treated equally. No one is given an opportunity that is not available to all the others. The incumbents of the dirty job cannot complain on grounds of fairness, for they are free to move to other jobs on the same terms as anyone else if they are willing to accept the lower wage.

At the other end of the preference scale, the more popular a particular kind of job, the lower the wage will be. Workers are therefore penalized in their wages if they happen to prefer the jobs that most other people also wish to have. Some people may regard that as inequitable: why should I be penalized, they may ask, merely because many other people happen to want the same job that I do?

If one accepts the fairness of paying higher wages for the less popular jobs, however, one must also accept the fairness of lower pay for more popular jobs – unless one is prepared to settle for a slogan like "higher wages for all jobs." The society must have some way of deciding who, of all the qualified people who would like those jobs, should be privileged to hold them. Under the price method the most popular jobs go to the highest bidders, so to speak – those who are willing to give up the most in wages in order to have that job. The jobs therefore go to those whose preferences for them are the strongest. That seems like a fair way to "ration" the limited number of such jobs. The alternative is to adopt some variant of the assignment method, but that involves abandoning the commitment to worker choice.[24]

Non-wage benefits

The price method provides justice in treatment, but it does so by legitimizing inequality in wages. If a high social value is placed on wage equality, however, it might appear that the price method can still be rescued by providing some non-wage benefit to attract people into the less desired jobs. That benefit may take the form of leisure: the duration of the work day or the length of the annual vacation may be varied, so that those who accept the least desired jobs have the benefit of working fewer hours. That variant of the price method might be highly attractive to some people: to artists or sport fishermen, for instance, who would greatly value the opportunity to have more time for painting or fishing. The benefit might also take the form of a supplement to consumption, like a larger apartment or free tickets to the ball game. In this benefit-variant of the wage method, every worker receives the same money wage, but those who accept the less desirable jobs, including the dirty work, are enabled to consume more – more leisure or more housing or whatever the benefit. The supplementary benefit is the compensation for the greater disutility of labor in the least attractive jobs.

The problem with that solution is that it preserves equality in appearance but not in fact. The benefit-variant of the price method introduces what may be called a "full wage," consisting of the conventional money wage plus some other thing of value like leisure or a larger apartment.[25] Equality in the money wage is thus preserved by introducing inequality in the full wage. Thus, while it may appear that workers in all jobs get the same wage, the total "consumption" of the dirty-job worker is larger by the amount of the larger apartment or the greater leisure.

On grounds of justice, therefore, the pure price method should not be judged as less worthy than the non-wage-benefit variant. There is no getting around the fact that any society that has certain jobs to be filled and that bases its job-allocation arrangements on the price method must live with wage inequality – if not in the money wage then in the full wage.

Equity and equality

Whether wage inequality must be regarded as inequitable, however, is another matter. One may hold the value that only the strictest equality is acceptable in a Good Society; but it can also be argued that the inequality generated by the price method is entirely consistent with a reasonable standard of equity. People who earn more because they are willing to do the work that others regard as too disagreeable should not be regarded as unfairly enjoying a special privilege.

Economic theory distinguishes two types of wage differences: compensating and non-compensating. Compensating differences are those that are required to provide equity to people working under different circumstances. If a higher wage is offered in dangerous employments than that in safe ones, for example, that wage difference should be regarded as legitimate compensation for the risk.[26] Indeed, it would be inequitable if workers in dangerous employments received no more compensation than those in the safer jobs. Similarly, the higher wage that the price method offers to those who do the society's dirty work should count as a compensating difference, and would be judged as entirely equitable by all except the purest egalitarian.[27]

The principle of compensating wage differences works best in large labor markets where labor is mobile and many workers have a genuine choice among jobs. It carries very little force in a small rural town where the only jobs available to many people are in the poultry-processing plant. It would bring no joy to those low-wage workers to learn that they are actually getting a premium because of the unpleasantness of their work. However, to the extent that some people, or their children, are motivated to move elsewhere in search of less odious work, the wages of those who remain behind are indeed higher than they would otherwise be.

8 Assignment and Justice

If a society is committed to strict wage equality as its criterion of equity, the assignment method is the only practical way of channeling the workers into a given structure of jobs. If the workers had no preferences at all for one job over another, any allocation of the workers among the jobs would be as good as any other. However, if they are not indifferent to their job assignments, wage equality cannot be the sole standard of equity but must be supplemented by other considerations.

Who, for example, should be assigned to the dirty work? One method would be random assignment. There is a rough sort of justice in that way of administering the assignment method, but it seems unreasonably arbitrary that the luck of the draw should determine so important a part of a person's fate as her job. There is no prominent example of that method having actually been employed.

ROTATION

The rotation variant of the assignment method has a certain element of fairness in the sense that it spreads the pain – everyone contributes her share of the unpleasant work. In the informal environment of a small community like the kibbutz that method can indeed add to the spirit of social solidarity. The informal nature of that society also makes it possible to tolerate the occasional delinquency of those members who find the work particularly disagreeable, as long as it is acceptably occasional and the person compensates by the extra effort she puts into her other assignments.[28] In extreme cases the members can vote to exempt someone entirely from that job in exchange for other duties he would perform.

While job rotation appears, on the face of it, to achieve a certain kind of fairness with regard to unpopular jobs, it does so by ignoring differences in the *intensity* of job preferences: kitchen duty must be done by every member, some of whom may find it exceedingly disagreeable while a few may even prefer it to other jobs. It may indeed be argued that it is inequitable, in the sense that it imposes a much larger burden on some members of the society than on others. While there is no objective measure of such things, everyone understands that if two people are required to spend a month's rotation in the kitchen – or in a coal mine, or in a cannery, or in a classroom for that matter – what may be a merely unpleasant experience to one may be a month of torture to the other. From this perspective, the price method may be regarded as more equitable because no worker needs to suffer an exceedingly unpleasant job if he is prepared to accept a sufficiently smaller share of the consumption pie instead.

SOCIAL INCENTIVES

When applied on a countrywide basis, as in Cuba and China, the assignment method is always accompanied by an official structure of non-monetary rewards such as prizes, banners, and honorific titles like Hero of Socialist Labor. Rewards of those sorts tend to create a social hierarchy, with those who regularly win the most honored awards at the top, and those who never win anything at the bottom. The effect is that while wage inequality is banished, social inequality sneaks back in. Everybody and their children know who's on top and who's on the bottom. People who subscribe to individualist values are more likely to be repelled by inequality derived from social incentives, while those who subscribe to societal values are more likely to be hostile to inequality that derives from wage incentives.

ATTENDING TO JOB PREFERENCES

The commitment to wage equality and societal choice in channeling workers into jobs does not at all require that preferences be entirely ignored; it requires only that they do not dominate in the allocation of jobs. In a Good Society that employs the assignment method, the assignment agents are likely to try to take preferences into account to the extent that it is possible. That could be done by making liberal use of volunteering. If the number of workers who volunteer for a particular job happens to be fewer than the number of such jobs that need to be filled, it would be entirely reasonable to assign people to those jobs. That could be done with the dirty work, for example, and with other jobs that are low on the list of worker preferences. Then only the remaining unfilled jobs would have to be filled by assignment or rotation. It is only those workers who happen to prefer the more popular jobs whose preferences cannot all be satisfied by the volunteer variant. Some of them would have to be assigned to the dirty work and the other unpopular jobs, contrary to their preferences.

Another way to take workers' preferences into account is by the use of a supplementary non-wage benefit. As argued above, however, the benefit variant cannot honestly be regarded as consistent with equality: the workers who accept the dirty jobs do enjoy a higher level of consumption, all things considered, than the others. While it may be more acceptable socially and symbolically to offer longer vacations or larger apartments rather than higher wages for the dirty jobs, it must be realized that this alternative involves some sacrifice of equality, though of an equitably compensating kind.

9 Efficiency

The meaning of efficiency always depends on the context. In the context of consumption as elaborated in Part II, where citizens differ primarily in their consumption preferences, efficiency means achieving that distribution of consumer goods among the citizens which best satisfies their consumption preferences. In the present context of work and jobs, where citizens differ primarily in their job preferences, efficiency means achieving that allocation of workers among jobs which best satisfies their job preferences. In view of the similarity of the contexts, it should not be surprising that the analysis of job preferences turns out to be formally similar to the analysis of consumption preferences.

THE PRICE METHOD

The source of the problem is that workers regard some of the jobs for which they are qualified to be less attractive than others. Under the price method, the reason any worker would accept a disagreeable job is that the additional consumption he would enjoy because of the higher wage more than compensates him for the disagreeableness of the work. Moreover, workers differ in the intensity of their preferences in this respect. Some workers so dislike certain jobs that a very large increase in consumption would be required to induce them freely to accept those jobs. Others feel less intensely about it: a smaller increase in consumption would be sufficient to induce them to accept those jobs. Workers span a wide range of attitudes regarding the amount of additional consumption that would induce them to take the less agreeable jobs.

In the distribution of consumer goods the standard criterion of efficiency is that formulated by Pareto: a distribution is optimal if there is no other possible distribution of the same goods in which there would be winners but no losers. Adapting that criterion to the problem at hand, a particular allocation of workers among jobs may be said to be optimal when no other allocation can be found in which some workers would be better off and none worse off.

Suppose now that the workers are initially allocated among jobs in some arbitrary manner and the wage rates are the same for all jobs. If the workers are free to exchange jobs for money, some worker holding a dirty job would be willing to give up some of his wages in exchange for a more agreeable job. Some other worker holding the better job may find the offer attractive: in her scale of job preferences the disutility of the dirty work is more than compensated for by the additional consumption. Both would therefore regard themselves as better off if they exchanged jobs, along with an agreed-upon transfer of some money to the worker who accepts the dirty job. Since no one else is affected by the exchange, that exchange of jobs for money produces a better allocation of workers – in the Pareto sense – than the original allocation.

Such an exchange is rather like that in the POW camp, where the price method would produce the best distribution of consumer goods without the inconvenience of barter trade. In the problem at hand, the price method accomplishes a similar result. If the "right" wage rates prevail, the workers would voluntarily sort themselves among jobs in such fashion that all the jobs would be filled, including the dirty work. The price method therefore passes the "barter test" of efficiency: no worker could find another offering so large a payment that she would be willing to exchange jobs with him.

It follows that a society that places a high value on the workers' right to choose their own jobs according to their preferences should adopt the price method, because it produces the best possible allocation of workers among jobs in terms of their own preferences.

That does not at all mean that everyone could hold the job he desires – that could happen only in Ideal Society, not a merely Good one. The best that can be said is that every qualified worker could hold the job he desires *if* he were willing to accept the consumption level that goes along with the job's wage.

THE ASSIGNMENT METHOD

When citizens differ in their job preferences, the assignment method is inefficient with respect to those preferences. The worker is rather like the POW who receives his ration of cigarettes and tinned beef – he is better off with them than he would be without them, but he would be much better off if he exchanged some of them for things he would rather have. Similarly, a worker who receives a wage plus an undesirable job is likely to wish to trade some of his wage in exchange for a different job. Some holder of another job may be glad to exchange jobs with him in return for the additional money. The assignment method therefore fails the barter test of efficiency. If the degree of inefficiency is large enough, it will require the exercise of tight control to prevent the rise of a sub-rosa exchange of jobs for money.

The supplementary-benefit variant of the assignment method is no less inefficient. The worker who receives the longer vacation to compensate for his dirty job may prefer the additional income he might secure by giving his vacation time to someone else who would be happy to offer part of his wage for it. If such trading were permitted, the jobs, wages, and vacation time would eventually be reshuffled among the workers until the optimal distribution of all three valued things would emerge.

The aseptic tone of the term "inefficiency" should not obscure the human cost of a bad job-allocation arrangement. Those workers with the most intense aversion to working in the mines or cleaning the toilets suffer a great deal from assignment to those jobs. They would be prepared to give up a large share of their wages if only they were allowed to take some less objectionable job. The Good Society may nevertheless decide that other values like societal choice or equity should take precedence, but that decision should be taken in full awareness of the personal suffering that it may entail.

For the same reasons, job rotation does not diminish the inefficiency of the assignment method. A worker rotated for a month into a job he regards as painful would gladly exchange some of his consumption with another worker, who would gladly substitute for him in that job in return for the additional consumption. Such an exchange would achieve a better allocation of the two workers between the jobs in the Pareto sense. It would be truer to the spirit of the assignment method, however, if people substituted for others in a job rotation for love of their friends or neighbors, rather than for the love of their own money and consumption.

10 Discussion

I could once imagine myself living quite cheerfully in a Good Society in which jobs are assigned, particularly if the dirty jobs were rotated. Rotation satisfied my sense of equity, and I rather liked the idea of everyone taking a turn at cleaning the toilets and washing the dishes. I still think I could manage a working life in a small democratic cooperative enterprise like a kibbutz, though it would not be my first choice. I would miss the opportunity to do the kind of work I like best, but the social value of egalitarian and cooperative living might well provide adequate compensation. Many of my friends – probably most – would regard the prospect with horror, but I think they would still regard it as a nice place to visit.

In a large society, however, I now have no doubt that I would find job assignment intolerable. That view first began to form in my mind when, as a graduate student, I had the opportunity to interview former Soviet citizens living in Western Europe after World War II. The lack of freedom to leave an oppressive job was, to many informants, one of the most difficult burdens to bear in Stalin's USSR. The testimony of my informants about what it was like to live under that restriction made a deep impression on me, and contributed to the modification of my views about my own Good Society.

I have since read accounts of working life in China and Cuba in their periods of revolutionary zeal when assignment was widely employed, and the experiences were similar to that of my informants. Reading between the lines of the accounts, I can envision the misery that must entail: certainly not for all workers, but enough to convince me that the assignment method must have some very strong justification – like war – to qualify for adoption in a Good Society.

The justification for that method under normal conditions is the commitment to the value of societal choice as a morally superior way of allocating jobs in a Good Society. I can imagine that justification may have considerable force, even in a large society, if the population overwhelmingly shared that value. There was indeed an admirable quality in the response of the young Chinese man whom I asked what career he wanted to follow: "Whatever the people need," he replied – though I could not guess how sincere that response was. Americans will recognize the kinship of that message to one of their own inspirational evocations: "Ask not what your country can do for you, but what you can do for your country."

In the early years following a successful revolution, societal values are in fact often widely held: during the first Soviet Five-Year Plan, Stalin and the Party did kindle a genuine enthusiasm among both workers and professionals, who volunteered in great numbers for assignment to the great new construction projects of the socialist Good Society soon to be ushered in. The same was very likely the case in Maoist China and in Cuba. The trouble is that those sentiments tend not to endure. In the light of subsequent history it is now clear that many Chinese who voiced their wish to take whatever jobs would "serve the people" did so not out of conviction but out of a judicious concern for their personal safety; and many others who may have genuinely held that commitment at the height of the Cultural Revolution changed their minds after having had the experience of job assignment. A society cannot long retain its claim to goodness if significant numbers of the people wither in assigned jobs when they desperately wish for others.

The assignment method is sometimes justified not because the people are committed to the value of societal choice but because job assignment will help to inculcate that value in them, rather like the justification for distribution of consumer goods by assignment. From that perspective, a proper objective of a Good Society is to cultivate the nobler rather than the baser sentiments of its people: the people may not be happy with the assignment method today, but if it endures for a period of time, the appropriate societal values will eventually be nurtured. By contrast, the price method serves only to strengthen the individualistic values inherited from the bourgeois past.

That paternalistic view of the people is not uncommon in new revolutionary governments. The leadership's message to the people is, in effect, "Because you grew up in a rotten society, you are naturally pretty rotten yourselves – no offense meant – but in the course of time the good institutions under which you will now live and work will transform you into decent socialist men and women." I did not always see the notion of creating a "New Soviet Man," or a "New Cuban Man" in that light, but that is how I see it now.

The assignment method is sometimes justified by people whose main commitment is to wage equality but who do not particularly favor societal choice. In a society that holds those views, some of the more objectionable qualities of that method are likely to be mitigated. The worker need not be regarded as somehow morally defective if he has no great urge to serve the people but wishes only to work at a job he likes. Such individual preferences can be honored to some degree – by such devices as volunteering and rotation. That society is also more likely to take family needs into account in issuing job assignments. Such relaxed implementation of the assignment method, however, is more likely to be found in small communities than in large societies where the administration of the job-assignment process cannot fail to be bureaucratized to a large degree.

A major concern about the assignment method is that it places a great deal of power over people's lives in the hands of the agents responsible for the assignments. Wherever such power is introduced in the organization of social institutions, one must be concerned about the possibility of abuse and corruption. It would be difficult for the administrative agent to resist family pressures to assign his kin to the better jobs, or to decline bribes offered by people seeking good assignments. That danger is of considerable consequence not only in the allocation of jobs, but in all cases in which some members of the society hold discretionary power over the distribution of things that are greatly desired – good apartments, or fresh meat, or rationed gasoline. In small communities like the Israeli kibbutzim there are substantial social defenses against such corruption, but in large societies it remains a continuous danger, particularly in post-revolutionary generations when the societal values begin to give way to more individualistic values. The issue is no respecter of economic system but applies to capitalist and socialist economies alike when those societies undertake the assignment of desired things. Price controls, for example, place a great deal of power in the hands of administrators of goods in both types of system, and in both they tend toward abuse. The assignment method of job allocation would invite corruption in capitalist systems no less than in socialist. In opting for the assignment method, therefore, a society must anticipate having to deal with corruption.

Under the price method, by contrast, no administrators stand between the employer and the worker. The wage rates are sometimes set by administrators – for the whole economy in a Soviet-type economy, and for the individual enterprise in a capitalist economy. The setting of wage rates in these cases involves the assignment of things rather than of people, which I find much less objectionable. The actual arrangements for implementing the price method do also sometimes leave opportunities for corruption: criminal elements can demand payoffs from employers or workers, and nepotism can certainly play a role in job placement. Most workers are unlikely to encounter such activities under the price method, however, while every worker must pass through the administration bureaucracy under the assignment method. Every popular job gives the administrator the power to make major decisions in the lives of the workers who come before him wishing to be assigned to it.

The assignment method has no strong partisans in any large societies, either socialist or capitalist, at this time. Cuba abandoned it in 1970 after the failure of the critical 10-million-ton harvest campaign, as did China after the death of Mao in 1976. Labor controls in China now focus mainly on keeping the rural population from pouring into the cities in response to the wage prospects that they offer.

Only in the small community of the kibbutz is the assignment method still used, though not as extensively as in the Heroic Age. For a long time the method served well. The combination of assignment and rotation, in administrative as well as laboring jobs, produced a population of people particularly well schooled in exercising authority, which accounted to some degree for the disproportionately large contribution that kibbutz members made to the political leadership and military defense of the country. The method is undergoing modification, however, as a consequence of the more diversified production activities. The rising level of technology has made it necessary to hire some specialists who are not members of the kibbutz and who are paid a wage for their services. Some kibbutzim also now hire outside manual labor – much of it Arab labor – a practice unimaginable in the early years when that would have been rejected as exploitation. Assignment continues to be practiced in those activities in which it is reasonably efficient, but it is no longer as central to the labor-allocation process as it once was.

I conclude that the assignment method is unlikely to endure in any large society beyond the generation that made the revolution. That there are no major instances of societies employing it at present only reflects the fact that there have been no major revolutions in recent years. It is quite conceivable that some future revolutionary society will try the assignment method again, undeterred by the history of earlier efforts, for the very idea of prices and wages will always be regarded with hostility in certain conceptions of how a Good Society should manage things. It is a fair prediction, however, that the assignment method will not long endure in such future efforts, as it has not in the past.

Whatever the notions I once held about the merits of societal values in such matters as job choice, on the basis of all I have read and seen I now regard the right of the worker to choose his job as a value of very high importance in my Good Society. I recognize that the consequence is a society with wage inequality, but that is not inconsistent with my notion of justice. On the contrary, in the world of equally productive workers under discussion here, I would regard it as inequitable if those who took on the unpleasant jobs earned no more than the others. In that abstract world, the price method provides an excellent solution to the dirty-jobs problem. It would not trouble me if the person who washed my dishes in the restaurant earned higher wages than I earned as a teacher of his children. It is not only an equitable but also an efficient arrangement, for I would not do his job for all his wages nor would he do mine for mine.

Perhaps this is as far as the abstraction should be pushed without snapping the link to reality. In no country where the price method is used are the most unpleasant jobs highly paid. The reason is that the influence of job preferences is but one of many other considerations that influence wage levels, such as differences in effort and productivity, which we have not yet considered. Yet if you have an eye for that sort of thing, you can see the dirty-work problem forever playing its role in the big picture. When a strike broke out at the staid Harvard Club of New York City, one of the issues was reported to be management's proposal for dealing with the "throwing-up" problem. Their proposal "would have ended a $10 bonus paid for doing what are termed dirty jobs. Those are defined by management as 'cleaning vomit, blood, excrement, etc.'"[29] The workers evidently found the price method entirely acceptable: they were prepared to clean up the mess, but they thought it only right that they be paid extra to do it. The dirty-work problem will always be with us.

Notes

1   *The New York Times*, April 30, 1994, p. 23.
2   *The Wall Street Journal*, December 1, 1994, p. 1.
3   *The New York Times*, May 1, 1994, p. 1.
4   The article made a deep impression on me when I read it in the *Current Digest of the Soviet Press* years ago. Unfortunately I have not been able to find the reference.
5   *The New York Times*, November 13, 1989, p. A7.
6   Quoted in Gray, *The Socialist Tradition*, p. 189.
7   *The German Ideology*, quoted in Freedman (ed.), *Marx on Economics*, p. 271.
8   Near, *The Kibbutz Movement*, p. 396.
9   Shepher, *The Kibbutz*, p. 71.
10   Farkas, *Yugoslav Economic Development*, pp. 94, 68.
11   Nove, *An Economic History of the USSR*, pp. 72–3.
12   Nove, *An Economic History of the USSR*, pp. 330–1.
13   Jimenez, "Worker incentives in Cuba," p. 133.
14   Bernardo, *The Theory of Moral Incentives in Cuba*, p. 54.
15   Bernardo, *The Theory of Moral Incentives in Cuba*, p. 65.
16   Bernardo, *The Theory of Moral Incentives in Cuba*, p. 77.
17   Huberman and Sweezy, *Socialism in Cuba*, pp. 147–9.
18   Zimbalist and Eckstein, "Patterns of Cuban development," p. 10.
19   Dominguez, *Cuba*, p. 274.
20   Quoted in Jimenez, "Worker incentives in Cuba," p. 129.
21   Nove, *An Economic History of the USSR*, pp. 261, 346.
22   Granick, *Job Rights in the Soviet Union*, p. 101, reports that over-40 Soviet workers quit more often than over-40 American workers, but quitting rates among younger workers were about the same.
23   Walder, *Communist Neo-traditionalism*, pp. 69–71.
24   There are always people who would like wage equality and the assignment method, provided they were assured of being assigned to the jobs they prefer. That self-interested stance violates Rawls' rule on the veil of ignorance – that the goodness of an arrangement should be judged on the assumption that the judge has no knowledge of the position he might occupy in the society (see chapter 3).

People who cannot accept the discipline of that restriction will find the subject of economics useful, but not the subject of the economics of the Good Society.

25 If the benefit takes the form of fewer hours worked for the same wage, it amounts to an increase in the wage rate, that is, in the wage per hour of work. It is only in the most superficial sense that such a benefit can be regarded as maintaining wage equality. Nevertheless, most people do regard leisure as different from normal consumption. A world in which everybody's consumption was the same but the people who did the dirty work had more hours off from work would be widely regarded as quite acceptably egalitarian. Only economists are likely to demur, but they often dwell in a thought-world of their own.

26 The differences are substantial. In the United States the number of work-related deaths per 100,000 workers per year ranges from 297 for stone cutters and carvers to 0.11 for elementary-school teachers. Leigh, *Causes of Death*, pp. 44, 91.

27 An example of a non-compensating difference is a non-job-related restriction on the ability of some workers to enter a particular occupation or job. If employers refuse to hire workers who are black, or female, or the children of capitalists, for jobs for which they are qualified, the wages of the other workers in those jobs are higher than they would be in the absence of that discrimination.

28 Blasi, *The Communal Experience of the Kibbutz*, p. 84.

29 *The New York Times*, April 23, 1994, p. B27.

Chapter 10

Should Work Effort Be Rewarded?

Octavius [earnestly] ... I believe most intensely in the dignity of labor.
Straker [unimpressed]. That's because you never done any, Mr Robinson.
                                                                    – G. B. Shaw

CONTENTS

Guiding the flow of workers into their jobs is a major part of the task of managing a country's labor resources. Like leading a horse to water, however, the task doesn't end there. The workers must be motivated to work diligently at their jobs. That requires another set of economic arrangements – for eliciting an appropriate level of work effort.

A popular anecdote among development economists is about a farmer going off to the Grange to hear the County Agent talk about a new strain of hybrid corn. On his way to the meeting he sees his friend rocking in his chair on the front porch, watching the setting sun. "Not coming to hear the county agent?" he asks. "Nope," answers his friend, "I already know how to farm better than I do."

In all societies there are people who know how to farm better than they do. In some societies, however, their number is much larger than in others. Culture no doubt explains much of the difference. It is a commonplace that German and Chinese attitudes toward work are different, shall we say, from those of Russians and Latin Americans. Yet there are considerable variations within a culture-area. The Chinese population of Hong Kong and other parts of the Chinese diaspora are famously industrious, while work habits on the Communist mainland were notoriously lax. Similar differences have been observed in North and South Korea, and in East and West Germany before their union.

Much of those differences in work effort is the consequence of differences in economic arrangements. At one extreme, one can imagine policies so poorly designed that workers tend to "goldbrick": to exhibit very little initiative and to care little about the quantity or quality of output they are able to produce. At the other extreme are arrangements that would motivate the same workers to exert a high level of effort. The enormous effect of economic arrangements on effort has been dramatized by the experience of the people of the former Communist countries. Tatyana Savkina, who had been an engineer in a Soviet state enterprise, Union, now earns her living buying consumer goods in Turkey and selling them back in Russia. Recalling her job in the old days, "I could drink tea with colleagues, talk, and leave early and see a play," she said. "Now there is no time for anything except work."[1] Same person, same country, but vastly different economic arrangements.

That is not to say that the best arrangement is invariably that which generates the highest level of effort. A society may well choose deliberately to accept a low level of consumption in return for a low level of effort, rather than a high level of consumption at the cost of a high level of effort. Effort may be thought of broadly as the opposite of leisure which, like consumption, is one of the good things that a society can provide. The Good Society ought to seek not the maximum of consumption, but the optimum – the best balance between leisure and consumption.

Where that balance is struck depends on the economic arrangements. Under some arrangements the level of effort may turn out to be lower than the society collectively or its members individually regard as appropriate. That unfortunate outcome is captured in an expression, local variations of which appeared in all Communist countries: "They pretend to pay us, and we pretend to work." Under better arrangements, the same people would have exerted a level of effort that they would have regarded as more sensible. Even under the best of arrangements, however, there are some people who will go out of their way to attend the Grange meeting, and others who will prefer to watch the setting sun.

How the Good Society should deal with the fact that people differ in the effort they put into their work is the concern of this chapter. Work effort may be thought of as the combined effect of the number of hours worked and the intensity of work during those hours. The distinction between time and intensity will be alluded to occasionally below, but for the most part effort will be thought of as the combination of the two elements.

The alternative methods for dealing with work effort are the same as those used for the allocation of labor among jobs – prices and assignment. Wage incentives are an application of the price method: they motivate effort by appealing to the worker's desire for personal material benefit. The worker who exerts more effort that results in more output receives a larger income. Since wage differentiation is precluded under the assignment method, social incentives take its place. They motivate effort by appealing to the worker's desire to serve her society. All workers receive the same money wage, but those who exert more effort derive a benefit from their sense of having contributed to the common good and from the public appreciation of that contribution.

I Wage Incentives

There is a great variety of ways of tying the workers' wages to the output they produce. The purest form of wage incentive is the use of piece-rates. This method of wage payment is widely used for large portions of the labor force in both capitalist and socialist countries.

The most common form of piece-rate wage payment is one in which workers performing a certain task are assigned a quota specifying the quantity of work that is to be produced under normal conditions in a given period of time. A factory operative, for example, is assigned a quota of 40 garments to be sewn in a day. If he produces exactly the specified quantity of output, he receives the standard wage for the job. If he produces more than the quota, he receives a supplement to his basic wage: so many additional rubles or dollars for each unit of production over the quota. Practice varies in the case of failure to produce the quota: the worker may receive less than his basic wage, or he may eventually be dismissed from that job, and perhaps reassigned to a lower-wage job. Shirking is thus punished by a reduction in wage earnings, and diligent effort is rewarded by an increase in wage earnings.

Piece-rates are most widely used in production operations in which effort is closely related to the quantity of output that the worker produces, as in many forms of manual work. In most jobs, however, output is the result of so many different factors that the contribution of each worker's effort cannot be readily distinguished. In such cases effort may be rewarded by an increase in the basic wage, or by the payment of periodic bonuses, the size of which depends in part on the supervisor's assessment of the worker's effort. In addition to these specific wage incentives, the prospect of promotion and the accompanying wage increase serve as a general incentive for effort in many workplaces.

2 Social Incentives

Those versions of the Good Society that place a high value on equality find it unthinkable that wage incentives should be used to motivate effort. The principal alternative in such cases is the establishment of social incentives. The use of social incentives for eliciting effort is similar to their use for allocating workers among jobs, as set forth in the last chapter, but in some countries they are used somewhat differently in the case of effort.

THE KIBBUTZ

In the original kibbutz ideology, labor was held to be a mode of self-expression and personal liberation, and not of "disutility." One worked not only out of the necessity of earning an income but because it was part of being a whole person. Therefore as the socialist society of the kibbutz was conceived, there would be no "problem" of eliciting work effort: people would put no less effort into their work than an artist into his painting or an athlete into her training.

That "messianic" view of work no longer prevails.[2] Most members would be quite prepared to work very little and to enjoy a great deal more leisure if that could be done without a reduction in the community's consumption level. But it cannot, and the economic affairs of the kibbutz are discussed in sufficient detail in the General Meetings that the dependence of consumption on work effort is generally understood.

However, while the link between total consumption and total effort is evident to all, there is no link at all between individual consumption and individual effort. That disjunction creates an environment in which a "free-rider" problem might arise. Since members who put in less than the normal time and effort do not suffer a relative decline in consumption, as they would under the wage method, they all have a certain incentive to shirk. If that incentive were actually acted upon by the members, it could be quite destructive in a cooperative production operation, a concern that has led at times to dire predictions of disaster.[3]

Yet the universal assessment by observers is that the level of individual effort has been reasonably high. The reason is to be found in the close relationships that prevail among members of a small voluntary society devoted to communal living. Shirking at work is not easy to get away with in the intimate kibbutz economy, where everyone is a position to monitor his neighbor's work. Moreover, because of the rotation of offices, most people have served as a foreman at some time or other and have had the responsibility of seeing that the group's work gets done. And since all are aware of the potentially destructive impact of shirking, few would court the public disapproval that it would bring. Unlike the world outside, where one walks away from one's job at the end of the day, the disapproval of the people you live with year after year can be devastating. The small and intimate kibbutz is an ideal environment for purely social incentives to flourish.

To be sure, instances of shirking have arisen from time to time, but they have usually been dealt with adequately by social pressures, or in extreme cases by expulsion. There are signs, however, that the traditional methods of social control may be weakening. It has been reported that some kibbutzim have taken to paying members in proportion to the number of work hours they put in – a clear move to penalize shirking. That measure strikes at the heart of the basic principle that individual consumption should be dissociated from individual production. Other kibbutz labor institutions have also been modified in the course of time; as mentioned earlier, some kibbutzim have begun to hire outside labor, in the face of the early militant hostility to capitalist-type "exploitation" of labor. If these trends continue, the kibbutz will look more and more like a conventional production enterprise.

The experience of the kibbutzim, and of producer cooperatives that share some of their characteristics (chapter 26) does not validate the high hopes of Mao Zedong that social incentives properly managed would greatly outperform wage incentives in unleashing the energies of the people. But supporters of social incentives can take some comfort in the knowledge that in individual communities and enterprises, under certain conditions, that arrangement can be no less productive than wage incentives. Those conditions, however, may be difficult to reproduce on the scale of a large and heterogeneous society and to maintain over the course of generations.

THE USSR

The Russian Revolution, inspired by both Marxian and Russian socialist traditions, held the promise of replacing the capitalist system of "wage slavery" by one in which the workers, now the owners of the country's capital, would work for the common good. The Bolshevik leaders understood that it would take time before people's attitudes toward labor and effort would change from those inherited from the capitalist past, and in the early years of the new regime some degree of wage inequality persisted. It was kept within limits, however, by the egalitarian commitment of the trade unions. With Stalin's consolidation of personal power and the beginnings of the rapid industrialization drive in 1929, the forces promoting greater wage equality were crushed, and a new policy was introduced that relied on wage incentives to accomplish a variety of objectives, such as motivating workers to acquire new skills and to strive for more responsible positions like foreman or shop chief. The Soviet Union made wage differentiation respectable in the Communist countries, all of which adopted the practice in varying degrees. Wage incentives, however, were supplemented by social incentives.

Wage incentives   The principal incentive for motivating effort was the piece-rate wage system – the classic capitalist arrangement for accomplishing that objective. It appeals to the worker's self-interest by tying wage earnings to the number of pieces produced per hour. Piece-rates were applied more extensively, it appears, than in any other country. As a further spur to effort, a variety of production-based bonuses were also made available. The total wage structure was such that the effort workers put into their jobs made a significant difference in their wage earnings.

Social incentives   While wage incentives for effort appealed to workers' self-interest, the Party sought also to tap into the socialist enthusiasm to be expected from people now living in the world's first workers' state. Unlike in the kibbutz, however, the marshalling of social incentives was not left to the informal and subtle influence exerted by the opinion of neighbors and co-workers. It was organized into a large program of formal activities run by the Party and operating both on the national level and in all the enterprises in the country.

One element of the program was the organization of contests of "socialist emulation," in which neighboring enterprises would compete to overfulfill their plans by the largest margin. During the contest, reports were posted daily in each enterprise on who was ahead and how much additional output was needed to take the lead. Individual workers or workshops would announce their intention to redouble their production efforts, and the progress of the contest was reported regularly in the press. The contest would end with a festive public celebration in which the leading workers and enterprises would receive public recognition.

A second element was the Stakhanovite movement, which gained world attention for a time. In a well-publicized event, a coal miner named Alexei Stakhanov achieved a record by cutting 14 times as much coal as the norm.[4] The Party seized upon the event to mount a national campaign urging workers everywhere to break production records, and local Party officials, seeking recognition by their superiors, organized Stakhanovite events in their factories. Reports on the progress of the Stakhanovite movement filled the press for many years.

These and related activities were represented by the Party as evidence of the workers' commitment to the building of socialism. In practice, however, they appealed not only to people possessed of a genuine socialist commitment but also to those who were motivated by personal goals. Initiative and active participation in programs of social incentives paved the way for the advancement of a Party activist up the career ladder. Ordinary workers who participated in the events saw their photographs displayed on factory bulletin boards and sometimes in the newspapers. They were seated on the platform in ceremonial occasions, and sometimes flown to Moscow for national events where they dined in the best restaurants and returned with purchases of luxuries rarely seen in the provinces. In addition to that heady stuff, money prizes were distributed to the winners of various social-incentives activities.

While many workers threw themselves into organized programs of these sorts, others regarded them with sullen cynicism. Everybody seemed to know that Stakhanov's triumph was a fraud, that he had achieved his production record not by his own efforts, but with the help of a great deal of labor and other resources put at his disposal to enable him to break the record. Like workers in capitalist enterprises, they had a keen nose for management's efforts to squeeze more work out of them, and were not unaware that the breaking of production records by Stakhanovite workers was often followed by a tightening of work norms, on the principle that "If he can do it, so can you." One could not be unaware that one's co-workers, both Party members and not, who threw themselves into social-incentives activities were generally out for themselves rather than for the building of socialism.

The combination of monetary and social incentives succeeded in generating a high level of work effort in the decades following the launching of the five-year plans in 1929. There is no way of knowing, however, how much effort was motivated by the social-incentives activities that would not have been forthcoming in their absence. In any event, in the course of time the social-incentives activities became more and more bureaucratized. Socialist emulation contests became a matter of going through the motions, and Stakhanovism vanished. By the 1970s, social incentives had atrophied and wage incentives carried virtually the full burden of motivating work effort.

At around the same time, however, wage incentives also began to lose their effectiveness in stimulating work effort. Among the reasons was the growing dissatisfaction with the quantity and quality of the consumer goods that wages could buy. Labor discipline was further undermined by a growing labor shortage and by a job-protection policy that made it virtually impossible for management to dismiss workers because of shirking (chapter 20). Consequently the incidence of shirking gradually crept upward, judging from anecdotal evidence on the increase in unauthorized absences from work and the slower pace of work within the factory. Soviet *émigrés* were struck by the work tempo in American factories compared to the indiscipline that had come to characterize the Soviet workplace.

Perhaps the best that can be said is that if there had been no organized social incentives, the level of work effort might have been somewhat smaller than it was, particularly in the early years of the Communist regime. It was wage incentives rather than social incentives, however, that bore the main burden of stimulating effort. Had the Soviet economy relied solely on social incentives, in the manner of the kibbutz, the level of effort would have been substantially, perhaps disastrously, lower.

CHINA

Mao Zedong and his followers, as has been noted, deeply believed that the people would exert vastly more effort if they were inspired by the grand idea of building socialism, rather than by the petty prospect of a few more yuan for producing a few more bushels of rice. It was that view that inspired the Cuban enthusiasm for social incentives portrayed above. The Maoist view was put to the test during the Great Leap Forward (1958–60), when social incentives reached their high point. Perhaps never in history had so concerted an effort been made to fire up the imagination of the masses in support of solidarity and equality. The conditions were uniquely favorable, with a revered revolutionary leader at the helm and a poor population earnestly striving to improve their material well-being.

China did not take the risk of abolishing monetary incentives completely. Workers still needed to hold jobs to earn the wages with which to support their families. However, the spread between the highest-paid and lowest-paid workers was greatly narrowed. Moreover, monetary incentives for effort virtually disappeared. Piece-rate wages were replaced by straight wage payments and bonuses were largely eliminated. Money prizes continued to be paid to the winners of production contests, but it was the societal rather than the personal benefit of the contests that was stressed. In the rural communes, the small household plots that the peasants had cultivated on their own time were suppressed, and the rural markets where they sold their farm animals and produce of their household plots ceased to operate.[5]

The suppression of monetary incentives was accompanied by a massive program to strengthen social incentives. As a sympathetic Western source wrote, "non-material incentives by themselves may not work effectively *unless they are accompanied by effective political indoctrination and education*" (italics in the original).[6] In that spirit, Party members were mobilized to conduct frequent education sessions designed to imbue the peasants and workers with the spirit of service to the society and to derogate self-interested concern with money and wages. The people were exhorted to volunteer their labor without pay, for days or weeks at a time, in the building of roads and dams and in irrigation and land reclamation. "Involvement in such ventures becomes a clear patriotic duty, and large numbers have felt impelled to contribute the extra exertion for the successful execution of water conservation plans. Those reluctant to join the effort have been subject to strong social pressures." Mass meetings were often held to exchange experience, make suggestions, and "rectify individual work habits and attitudes through criticism and self criticism."[7]

The launching of the Great Leap Forward did mobilize a huge volume of effort that went into the large new economic projects. In a short time, however, an exhausted population began to resist the repeated calls for the exertion of new efforts. It also became increasingly evident that the massive use of volunteer labor involved considerable hidden costs, in such forms as the time of Party members and others devoted to the campaigns, the increase in worker fatigue, and the removal of workers from their normal tasks in which they were more productive. In both urban and rural enterprises, moreover, labor discipline began to erode. A group of reporters wrote, for example, that "some [mine] workers began to think that how much they worked made no real difference and relaxed their effort gradually."[8]

The decline in work effort was one, though not the only one, of the reasons for the catastrophic decline in output that brought the Great Leap Forward to an end. In the reaction against Mao's program that followed, piece-rate wages were widely restored, peasants were permitted once again to work their private household farm plots, and rural markets reappeared. The pressures on workers and peasants to volunteer labor were reduced, and paid contract labor was used on most construction projects. Social incentives got one more lease of life during the Cultural Revolution, with the same negative effect on effort and output.[9]

Following the death of Mao in 1976, the new leadership under Deng Xiaoping radically reversed the course of the Chinese economy. Deng was no doubt committed in general to the value that society is the proper locus of choice in a Good Society; however, his experience brought him, like so many of his colleagues, to the painful conclusion that social incentives did not kindle the enthusiasm of the masses, as he had once fervently believed. "Socialism is not poverty," was his retort to those who criticized his turn to wage incentives. Prominent among the measures subsequently introduced was the abandonment of the large communal farms and the restoration of family farming in which each family's income was closely tied to the effort and ability that they brought to their farming. Measures were also introduced in the non-farm economy to provide larger wage payments for more productive workers. The result was a speedy recovery of production and exceptionally rapid economic growth throughout the post-Mao years.

The Chinese experience is a major piece of historical evidence on what a socialist society should expect from the adoption of social incentives for work effort. The best assessment I have found is that they can succeed in increasing the crude labor input in the short run in well-selected projects, but the longer they go on the less effective they become. In the best of circumstances, when they are used as a supplement to a wage-incentive system, they can increase the effort that a labor force puts into its work. But "whenever nonmaterial incentives have superseded material incentives as the main motivating force in work situations, they have been least effective and have usually generated severe cumulative negative effects."[10]

Historical evidence is never decisive in questions of this sort. There were forces other than social incentives operating in China which also contributed to the decline of production during the Great Leap Forward, such as the onset of extremely poor weather conditions. During the Cultural Revolution, when social incentives had their second chance, the antielitist tyrannizing of people with higher education and technical training introduced a great deal of turmoil in the production enterprises. The rapid recovery of farm output after the death of Mao, moreover, was due not only to the change in incentive methods but also to the change in property relations, particularly the change from large-scale communal farming to farming of small plots by family members. How much of the fluctuations in performance can be ascribed to the incentives arrangements alone is impossible to say, but it is clear that the Maoist dream of a boundless reservoir of work effort that could be released through social incentives never did materialize.

JAPAN

The socialist countries were not alone in employing social incentives alongside wage incentives. Mixtures of the two basic incentives arrangements may be found in some capitalist countries as well.

In Japan, for example, workers in large corporations are divided among various hierarchies – blue-collar, white-collar, managerial – within each of which wage rates are differentiated by skill-grade level.[11] All workers at the same grade level in the same hierarchy earn the same wage, however. That arrangement is designed to encourage workers to cooperate with each other in maintaining high levels of output and quality, and they are evaluated on the basis of their performance in that respect. The arrangement is a form of social incentive in the sense that the workers are encouraged to work for benefit of their work group, rather than for their own monthly paycheck alone.

The corporations also devote a great deal of attention to cultivating a spirit of corporate loyalty and solidarity. Company anthems are sung on many occasions; workers participate in group exercise sessions; managerial officials dine together after work hours, and so forth. Fans of the Japanese system credit the employees' personal identification with their enterprises for much of high level of work effort.

From the perspective of production, corporate social incentives have an advantage over the pure piece-rate method, which motivates workers to attend only to their own performance as individuals, without respect to the performance of their fellow workers. For example, they have no incentive to interrupt their own task in order to provide assistance to another worker. Instances in which the combined output would be higher if the workers cooperated, rather than each attending to his own task, are therefore missed.

The longer-term motivation for work effort is promotion to a higher level in the hierarchy at which the wage rate is higher. The best workers are promoted most rapidly, and they reach the top level of their hierarchy at the youngest age.[12] Shirking is discouraged by delaying or denying promotion, by reassignment to a lower-wage hierarchy, or in extreme cases by dismissal. Workers are evaluated by their supervisors, and in case of allegations of injustice the company trade union may file a claim for review. Workers therefore understand that their effort is under constant scrutiny, and that a high level of effort may not show in each month's paycheck but will show clearly in the course of their successive promotions and in the rate of increase of their wages over time.

Social incentives in Japanese industry and in the kibbutz are similar in that they focus on the enterprise: you work hard not for the benefit of the whole society, as in Cuba and China, but for the benefit of your own work group and company. The Japanese case differs from all socialist societies, however, in that it does not presuppose income or social equality. It is consistent with the assessment offered above in the case of China that as a supplement to a well-designed wage-incentive system, rather than a substitute for it, social incentives can be effective in eliciting a higher level of work effort.

The Japanese experience demonstrates that social incentives are not unique to socialist economies but can be successfully incorporated in capitalist economies as well. It is evident, however, that the Japanese form of social incentives is highly specific to the cultural traditions of that country; it is difficult to imagine American workers joining together to sing the Ford Motors anthem.

Hence, it should not be thought that capitalist countries can employ only wage incentives and that only socialist countries can employ social incentives. In fact, all modern countries employ wage incentives, whether socialist or capitalist, while some of the latter employ social incentives as well. The question for the Good Society is not which one to employ, but in what proportions and in what forms the two should be employed. That brings the discussion to the assessment of their relative merits.

The two incentives arrangements differ principally with respect to three of the criteria of goodness: locus of choice, justice, and efficiency.

3 Individual or Societal Choice?

A society that values individual choice will prefer those institutional arrangements that afford its members the maximal opportunity to exercise personal choice over their actions. Wage incentives for effort offer such an opportunity. Workers whose personal preference is for more income, even at the cost of having to work harder, are able to exercise that choice, as are those whose personal choice is for more leisure.

A society that values societal choice, on the other hand, would be hostile to wage incentives, out of the conviction that they are conducive to individualism and therefore to the attenuation of social solidarity. The citizens should be taught to think of their work as a contribution to their community and not merely to their personal benefit. For a society to offer its members more goods if they would produce more output is as repulsive as a family whose members negotiate the terms on which they contribute to each other's needs.

Two qualifications need to be made to those broad generalizations. First, under normal conditions the wage-incentive arrangement does not give workers an unlimited opportunity to choose the level of effort that suit them best. People who are self-employed – like farmers, craftsmen, and dentists – have the maximal opportunity to divide their time between work and leisure. People who work in organizations, however, have to conform to a certain time schedule, which limits their range of choice.

Within that limitation, however, there remains a substantial degree of choice. Organizations and occupations differ in the intensity of work, and in choosing their jobs workers sort themselves out according to their effort preferences. Someone with a strong preference for leisure, for example, would not seek a job in a high-pressure corporate law firm, nor would someone with a strong preference for income be attracted to a civil-service career. Over the span of a lifetime, moreover, the choice of retirement age offers a major opportunity to express one's preference for leisure or income. Even when the number of work hours is specified, there is often a considerable range of choice regarding the effort put into the work. Assembly-line jobs offer the least degree of choice, but piece-rate jobs offer a good deal of choice. Informally, most jobs provide some opportunity to select one's level of effort through coffee breaks, length of phone calls, leaning on the shovel, and other devices known to goldbricks throughout the world.

The second qualification is that the social-incentives arrangement does not deprive people entirely of a range of personal choice between work effort and leisure. Workers with a strong desire for leisure may be able to work less than the socially established norm. A pragmatic community might agree to a deal in which members of that sort would give up a share of the consumption to which they are entitled, for the sake of greater leisure; but such a side arrangement would come perilously close to the wage-incentive method that the community has presumably rejected. In the extreme, some worker may simply defy the social norm, although she must be prepared to face the strong disapproval of her fellow workers.

Workers can also choose to exert *more* effort than the norm if, in the spirit that Mao Zedong sought to cultivate, they wish to contribute more to the service of the people. One might indeed contend that is a nobler kind of choice than is available under wage incentives, for it is made altruistically, without the expectation of personal monetary reward.

Both incentives arrangements therefore provide scope for individual choice in the amount of effort that citizens put into their work. The difference is that wage incentives enable the worker to receive more income and consumption in return for more effort, while social incentives deny that particular alternative. Social incentives, however, enable the worker to acquire various kinds of status and prestige from his production effort that are not normally available in more individualistic societies, although to some extent such social rewards do follow on the coat-tails of income.

A societal decision regarding the locus of choice affects not only the general level of effort but also the distribution of effort between those with extreme preferences for either income or leisure, and those whose preferences cluster around the social norm. Under wage incentives, those who have the strongest preference for leisure relative to income can exert less effort than others, and those who have the strongest preference for income can exert more effort than others. Under social incentives, however, all are under pressure to work at the pace that the collective has designated as appropriate. If you happen to be "like everybody else" – within the normal range of preferences – there is not much difference between the two methods. But if you are "different," you would be better able to satisfy your preferences under the wage-incentive arrangement. It is not surprising, after all, that people who do not run with the herd would do better under individual choice than under societal choice.

4 Justice

If you believe that strict income equality is the only proper standard of equity for a Good Society, you would be most comfortable with social incentives, for in principle, every worker receives the same wage regardless of differences in job preferences, effort, or performance. But while social incentives preserve income equality, they promote social inequality. Even in a communal society like the kibbutz, some people are smarter, more skilled, or better organizers than others, and an informal pecking order tends to arise. Everybody knows who are the leaders and who the followers. Every effort is made, however, to keep these inevitable social distinctions to a minimum – by the rotation of offices and by the deliberate avoidance of titles and prizes.

In Communist economies, however, the organized promotion of social incentives through prizes, titles, and the other trappings of socialist production-contests greatly increases the extent of social differentiation. Honors, public praise, and deference are valued things in any society, and if some people get much more of them than others, they occupy higher positions on the social scale. At the lower end, those who exert little effort are to some degree stigmatized. Everybody knows who are the virtuous workers and who are the laggards who must be constantly lectured at. They know it, and more importantly, their children know it. A wage-egalitarian society can therefore be highly unequal in social status.

Moreover, the "society" usually means the government, and there is reason to be a bit nervous about putting the government in charge of the distribution of social status. Since Communist governments also accept some degree of wage inequality, the social differentiation that normally flows from wage differences compounds that which flows from organized social incentives.

If your standard of justice is not absolute equality but the principle that people who contribute more to the society's output should enjoy a larger share of that output, then the wage-incentive method is to be preferred. By that standard, it would indeed be *inequitable* if people who produce more for the society receive no more income than those who produce less (chapter 21). A diligent worker who found his effort unrewarded in the form of a higher wage would experience a feeling of irritation and a sense of injustice at seeing other people "getting away with murder" while he put in a full and energetic day's work.

Like organized social incentives, however, wage incentives also lead to social inequality, by familiar social processes. Therefore there is no escaping some degree of social inequality as long as the society is committed to encouraging and therefore rewarding effort. One could argue that distributive justice would be better satisfied by social-without-income inequality (social incentives) than by social-and-income inequality (wage incentives). That argument strengthens the case for social incentives, but it would not satisfy someone who holds that people who contribute more should earn more. That person is likely to accept some degree of social inequality as a price worth paying for the justice of an arrangement in which people who contribute more earn more.

If you require both social and income equality in order to satisfy your standard of justice, then neither wage incentives nor social incentives nor any other known form of incentives will be acceptable. The kibbutz community comes close to that standard, but no full society has managed it. It is conceivable that such an arrangement on a countrywide scale might succeed in eliciting a level of effort from its people sufficient to produce all the output it desired. The experience of modern societies suggests, however, that it would be Utopian to expect that happy result. At any rate, no modern society has been willing to take that risk. All have accepted the legitimacy of some form of inequality, and have differed only in whether that inequality is generated through wage incentives or social incentives.

EFFORT AND ABILITY

There is a certain problem of justice that must be confronted in the implementation of both effort-incentives arrangements. The source of the societal interest in work effort is the fact of scarcity – that the quantity of goods the economy is capable of producing is smaller than the quantity the people would like to consume. It is the value that is placed on output and consumption that explains the concern about work effort in all versions of the Good Society.

However, while each worker can produce more output if she exerts more effort, the output produced by any two workers may differ for reasons other than their respective levels of effort. One student can dash off an excellent paper with little apparent effort while another produces a mediocre paper despite a large expenditure of effort. A strong worker can cut more sugar cane in a day than a weaker worker, with no apparent difference in effort. Regardless of whether the rewards are social or monetary, if they are apportioned according to the quantity of output produced per day or per week, people will be rewarded not for effort alone but also for other qualities that are distinct from effort.

One reason that some workers are more productive than others is that they have acquired more skills through education, or through work experience, or in other ways. Whether and how a society should reward its workers differentially because of differences in acquired abilities is a question of major importance, and will be taken up in chapter 21. For the present, that question can be deferred by confining the discussion to workers who have the same acquired skills.

Even among workers with the same acquired skills, one worker may produce more than another for reasons other than differences in effort: in particular, because of differences in natural ability. It is difficult to make a case in equity for rewarding people simply because they are stronger, or more dexterous, or can jump higher, or have unnaturally strong vocal cords. Such differential rewards are likely to be regarded as unjust in some versions of a Good Society because they are unmerited, based as they are on qualities over which the citizen has no control. Differential rewards for effort, in contrast, may be considered as merited because citizens can control the level of effort they put into their work.

The problem with both incentives arrangements is that a worker's output is the result of both, effort and natural ability, and it is often extremely difficult to separate the one from the other. Hence, when output is used as measure of the amount of effort exerted, the inseparability of effort from ability is a source of inequity. Workers are differentially rewarded for the personal qualities with which they happened to be born.

The extent of that source of injustice may not be very large, however, for two reasons. First, much of what appears to be natural differences in ability is not natural at all but the result of a great deal of earlier work and effort. Some people are stronger than others because they have worked at it, in sports and in exercise of various kinds. Some people are smarter than others not (or not only) because of innate ability or social advantage, but because they have worked at the cultivation of their mental abilities: within the same cultural group some kids read books while others hang out. In these cases the higher wage is not an unmerited award for natural ability, but may be regarded as a proper reward for the effort exerted in acquiring higher levels of ability.

Second, there are ways of crudely identifying and rewarding effort separately from output. Under both incentive methods good supervisors can usually tell which workers put in a hard day's work and which take the longest coffee breaks, and the former can be differentially rewarded. Such practices are particularly prominent in workplaces where the output of a work group can be identified readily but the contribution of each member is difficult to distinguish. The judgment of the work group and of the supervisor about the effort exerted by each member can then be taken into account in the awarding of differential bonuses. Something of the sort has been done in a variety of countries such as capitalist Japan and socialist USSR.

Such pure effort-awards have to be somewhat limited in size, however. It would be rather perverse if they were so large that a worker who produced a certain output with very little effort ended up with a smaller total reward than one who had to exert a great deal of effort to produce the same output. Perhaps the most saintly of capable workers would regard that as just, but most are likely to regard themselves as having been unjustly penalized because of their natural ability.

If our concern were with an Ideal Society, deficiencies of that sort would be troublesome, for they would imply that such a society is unattainable. Since our concern is not with an Ideal but with a merely Good Society, the choice between social and wage incentives should not be impossible to make, even if neither arrangement conforms perfectly to our sentiments regarding justice.

5 Efficiency

It remains to ask which of the two arrangements is the better by the criterion of efficiency. It is not immediately apparent, however, what efficiency might mean in the context of work effort.

A citizen's time may be thought of as divided between work effort and leisure: the more the effort, the less the time and energy for leisure. Leisure, in turn, may be thought of as a good; like a consumer good, it is something one would like to have more of rather than less of. What restrain workers from devoting all of their time to leisure and none to work effort are income pressures and social pressures. If income from work effort were not required in order to obtain consumer goods, and if there were no social pressures for work effort, they would spend their time like Marx's liberated human being – hunting, fishing, and tending cattle, as the spirit moved them. In a world of scarcity, however, the Good Society must adopt some arrangement to motivate the effort required to produce the goods that the society desires.

Each incentives arrangement leads to a certain distribution of effort and income among the citizens. Some citizens exert more effort under one arrangement than the other, and some receive more income under one arrangement than the other. Accordingly, one arrangement may be said to be more efficient than the other if the distribution of effort and income to which it gives rise is "better" than the distribution resulting from the other arrangement.

Consider first a society operating under a regime of pure social incentives. The people decide collectively upon the appropriate workweek – say 50 hours; and everybody is expected to work 50 hours a week with appropriate intensity. Access to consumer goods does not depend explicitly on income, for everyone receives the same income, in money or consumer goods; and the citizens' actual work effort depends on their personal devotion to the social objectives and to social rewards and pressures.

Suppose now that the same society adopted the method of wage incentives. Instead of the people deciding collectively how many hours everybody will work, each citizen decides for herself how many hours she will work. Access to consumer goods depends on the income derived from work; hence the more the leisure, the smaller the income, and the smaller the quantity of consumer goods that can be secured.[13] Citizens with a strong preference for leisure will choose to work fewer hours than the average, while those with a strong preference for consumer goods will choose to work more hours than the average.

Thus, the distribution of work effort and consumer goods that results from social incentives is different from that which results from the use of wage incentives. The question is, which of the two distributions is the better one?

As in all such matters, the prior question is who decides which is better – the society collectively, or each citizen individually? If the commitment is to societal choice and the prevailing value is equality in income and consumption, then the social-incentives arrangement is efficient – by definition, as it were. If the society is committed to individual choice, however, then the question of which is the better arrangement is more complicated, and more interesting. Applying the Pareto criterion of efficiency, if there are two distributions of work and consumer goods among the citizens, the first distribution may be said to be better than the second if one or more citizens are better off under the first and nobody is any worse off; and the arrangement that produced the first distribution is the more efficient.

If all workers had identical preferences, the two arrangements would yield identical distributions. Under social incentives the workers would all vote for the same workweek – say 50 hours – and under wage incentives the same workers would voluntarily choose to work 50 hours. Since the distribution of work effort and consumer goods would be the same, neither arrangement could be said to be more efficient than the other.[14]

Under normal circumstances, however, some people have stronger-than-average preferences for leisure relative to consumer goods, and some have stronger-than-average preferences for consumer goods relative to leisure. The citizens-as-workers therefore differ in their consumption–leisure preferences much as the same citizens-as-consumers differ in their preferences among consumer goods. It should not be surprising, therefore, that the analysis of the efficiency of work-effort arrangements is virtually identical to that of consumer-goods distribution arrangements (chapter 6). Since the analysis has already been presented in the case of consumer goods, it can be presented more briefly here.

Suppose you and I have very different attitudes toward work effort and consumer goods. Under social incentives we would both work 50 hours a week and receive equal quantities of income or consumer goods. I, who would dearly like to spend more of my time fishing and hunting, would be willing to give up as much as $10 for the privilege of working one hour less a week. You, on the other hand, love the things that only money can buy, and would dearly like to earn more income so that you could buy more of them. You would be glad to work one extra hour a week for an additional $5 or more. Both of us would therefore regard ourselves as better off if you took my place at work for one or more hours a week, and I gave you a gift – say $7 or $8 – for each hour that you substituted for me at work.

Social incentives thus fail the "barter test" of efficiency. Much like the barter exchanges in the POW camp, the distribution of work and consumer goods between you and me after our exchange would be better than the original distribution because both of us would be better off and presumably no one would be worse off.

Wage incentives can now be shown, by the same logic, to be an efficient arrangement. If the wage rate were $10 an hour, I might decide to work 30 hours a week for an income of $300, and you might put in 50 hours of work for an income of $500. Neither of us has any reason to exchange hours of work and money, because we are able to secure directly what we regard as the best combination of the two. The wage-incentive arrangement therefore passes the barter test of efficiency, for it produces a distribution of work and consumer goods between the citizens such that there is no possible redistribution in which there would be winners but no losers.

The intuition underlying the reasoning is that social incentives are inefficient because they lock every worker into the same combination of leisure and income, regardless of their personal preferences. Wage incentives, on the other hand, permit each worker to tailor his choice to his own preferences. It stands to reason that some workers would be better off with wage incentives, and none should be worse off, because they are free to choose the same combination of leisure and consumer goods that would prevail under social incentives.[15]

6 Productivity and Efficiency

The case for the efficiency of wage incentives as presented above should impress people who place a high value on the individual as the locus of choice. For many reasons, however, it would evoke only a yawn from people who regard societal choice as their criterion of the society's goodness. It would seem to them that the argument entirely misses the point of social incentives. Among the reasons is that it assumes that the total effort forthcoming under social incentives would be about the same as under wage incentives; only the distribution of that effort among the members would differ. It is a fundamental article of faith of proponents of social incentives, however, that their arrangement will elicit a much larger volume of effort than could ever be attained under wage incentives.

Critics of social incentives, on the other hand, see the free-rider problem as a major difficulty with that arrangement. For example, if every worker farms her own piece of land, the less effort she exerts, the less output she will have available for herself. If the land is farmed in common, however, and the product is distributed equally regardless of individual effort, a certain amount of shirking is bound to occur. If shirking were not punished by material deprivation, it would be resented by others who, in the course of time, would withdraw their own effort rather than continue to be taken advantage of, and total output would fall. From this perspective, the total volume of goods produced under wage incentives will be larger because effort is rewarded and shirking is punished.

Advocates of social incentives regard that conception of "economic man" as a reasonably accurate description of workers in an individualistic and exploitative society. It is precisely because of its accuracy that they wish to organize a better society – one in which workers would not behave in that way. In their Good Society, conditions would be established such that workers would be motivated to supply their effort not on behalf of their private benefit but for the common benefit of all. Workers would be no more inclined to take a free ride on the backs of their fellow workers than the members of a family are inclined to take advantage of each other. If by chance some workers do exhibit a tendency to shirk, they would be subject to the strongest of sanctions – the disapproval of their friends and co-workers.

The question in dispute may be described as the comparative "productivity" of the two incentives arrangements, rather than their comparative efficiency. The difference between efficiency and productivity will be elaborated in the next chapter, but it may be introduced briefly here.

If a group of workers produces a larger output under one incentives arrangement than under another, that arrangement may be said to be more productive. If some workers receive a higher wage and none receives a lower wage under one incentives arrangement than under another, that arrangement may be said to be more incentive-efficient. This concept of incentive-efficiency is derived from but is not identical to Pareto's concept of efficiency.[16]

Suppose now that 1,000 workers produce $100,000 worth of goods per year under wage incentives. The average worker then receives a wage of $100. The most productive worker earns a higher wage – say $200 – while the least productive earns perhaps $50. What might happen if that society switched over to social incentives? Three possibilities may be identified.

First, social incentives are just as productive as wage incentives, so that total output is $100,000 and everybody's wage is $100. The most productive workers earn less than under wage incentives, however, while the less productive workers earn more. Since some lose while others gain, social incentives cannot be said to be more efficient.

Second, social incentives might be moderately more productive, so that output per worker rises to $150,000 and everyone's wage is $150. Workers of average and less-than-average productivity then earn more than their former wage, but the more productive workers earn less than their former $200 wage. Since some workers are still worse off, social incentives cannot be said to be more efficient, even though they are more productive.

Third is the proposition that social incentives are so much more productive than wage incentives that output rises to more than $200,000 – say $250,000. Everyone then receives a wage of $250, which is higher than the most productive workers earn under wage incentives. Since there are now winners and no losers, social incentives are both a more productive and a more efficient arrangement than wage incentives.

Two conclusions follow. First, only if the productivity difference between the two arrangements is very large will the more productive arrangement also be the more efficient. If the productivity difference is not very large, neither method may be more efficient than the other, for some workers may be better off under the one and other workers may be better off under the other.

Second, as intuition alone would suggest, the more productive workers are generally better off under wage incentives and the less productive under social incentives. The more productive workers would also be better off under social incentives, however, if that arrangement did indeed elicit as much more effort from all the workers as Mao and his followers believed it would.

EFFICIENCY AND COMPENSATION

It might therefore seem that, barring very large differences in productivity, the choice between the two incentives arrangements depends not on their relative efficiency but on questions of distributive justice. Should the Good Society choose the arrangement in which the average and above-average workers are better off but the less productive workers worse off – i.e. wage incentives, or the arrangement in which the average and above-average workers are worse off but the less productive workers are better off – i.e. social incentives?

In some versions of distributive justice, policies that favor the least privileged members are to be preferred to those that favor the more privileged. If one holds that value, social incentives are to be preferred. There is an alternative, however, which should also have some appeal in terms of other reasonable notions of justice. Some of the benefit that the more productive workers derive from the wage-incentive method could be redistributed to the less productive workers so that they would be no worse off under wage incentives. That alternative is known as the "compensation principle."

For example, suppose the common wage under social incentives is $100. Under wage incentives the weakest worker's wage is only $50 while the strongest worker's wage is $200. The strongest worker might then offer a gift of $60 to the weakest worker. The effect of that transfer is that both workers are better off under wage incentives than under social incentives. With that kind of compensating redistribution, no one need be worse off under the wage-incentive method and some – the stronger workers – are still better off. Therefore, after compensation of the losers, the wage-incentive arrangement may prove to be more incentive-efficient than social incentives even if, in the absence of compensation, it were not so much more productive as to be also more efficient.

The relative incentive-efficiency of the two methods depends, then, on their relative productivity. In the abstract one can make a plausible case for the higher productivity of either method. In the past, when socialism was all theory and no practice, socialists were inclined to regard social incentives as more powerful than wage incentives. It appeared self-evident that people motivated by equality and the common good would exert more effort than when working for the unequal wages paid by capitalist bosses. Proponents of capitalism, on the other hand, had no doubt that wage incentives were more powerful than social. Today, however, with the experience of numerous countries from which to judge, views on this matter are more varied, particularly among socialists.

My own conclusion from that experience is that well-organized social incentives can increase work effort when they serve as a supplement to a system of wage incentives, as in Japan. As an alternative to wage incentives, under the best of circumstances, such as the kibbutz, they can rival the productivity of wage incentives. But for modern societies generally, Mao's conviction regarding the greater productivity of social incentives has not been borne out. The experience of China, and of Cuba as well, suggests the opposite – that on a national scale, wage incentives are much more productive than social incentives.

Whether they are so much more productive that they can also be said to be more efficient is difficult to judge. As a rough test, one might ask whether the income earned by the least productive worker on a post-Mao family farm is larger than the equal wage earned by all peasants in a Maoist agricultural commune. I suspect that the answer is no: that there are peasants whose ability to manage their family farm is so limited that they were better off with the low but equal rice-wage of Maoist days. The commune carried them along, as it were, and provided them with a level of living that they could never manage to achieve as independent farmers. If there are such people, then family farming, productive though it is, is not more incentive-efficient than the commune, for those people are worse off than under communal farming. However, the post-Mao rise in farm output was so spectacularly large that the winners could probably compensate the losers and still be better off; in that case, family farming might be considered more incentive-efficient as well as more productive than the commune.

7 Discussion

My own Good Society would employ wage incentives for the motivation of work effort, as does every modern economy, socialist or capitalist. Among other things, since wage-incentive systems generally link wages to output, people who produce more are paid more, which I regard as entirely in accord with justice. I recognize, however, that the arrangement has certain deficiencies from the perspective of my own values. For example, people whose natural abilities are superior to others are also paid more, which may be defended on practical grounds but is hard to argue on grounds of justice. Moreover, the administration of wage incentives is rarely so effective as to preclude inequities: within the same organization some people put in a full day's work while others earning the same income make endless trips to the water cooler.

For all its deficiencies, however, the wage-incentive arrangement does by and large enable people to choose that combination of effort and consumption that they most prefer from among the combinations that are available to them. If my tastes run to a high standard of living, I can do something about it; if I prefer a working life with little pressure and long vacations, I can do something about that too. It is advantages of this sort that one has in mind in the assertion that wage incentives are an efficient arrangement.

Incentive-efficiency however, is surely not the main reason that wage incentives have replaced social incentives wherever the latter have been tried. Neither Stalin in 1929 nor Fidel Castro in 1970 would have been overwhelmed by the argument in this chapter that wage incentives are better than social incentives because they produce a better distribution of effort and consumer goods among the workers. What motivated the adoption of wage incentives was not their incentive-efficiency but their productivity, relative to social incentives. That is to say, wage incentives get a lot more work out of the people than social incentives.

The reason for the difference in productivity, in my view, is not to be found primarily in the merits of wage incentives, but in one major deficiency of social incentives: namely, if I receive the same income regardless of my work effort, there is very little incentive for me to do more than the minimum that I can get away with. That is an ancient piece of wisdom that only recently acquired the new name of the free-rider problem.

The experience of the use of social incentives suggests that the effectiveness of that arrangement depends decisively on the size and nature of the society that adopts it. In a small homogeneous community like the kibbutz, the members of which are self-selected by their deep commitment to society as the locus of choice, the free-rider problem can be dealt with reasonably well. People live and work very closely together, and there is a keen awareness of the dependency of each upon all. No member can ride for very long on the effort of the others without a backlash of community disapproval. There are no better conditions for the successful operation of social incentives.

If social incentives have a future, it lies in voluntary communities of that sort, or in the more limited form of producer cooperatives (chapter 26). It should not be surprising if the social tensions of the next century will motivate groups of people to form their own communes or production organizations based on the societal idea of a Good Society. The members of the founding generation may very well make a success of it, and may find it a more satisfactory way of organizing their working life than that in the larger society. The experience of the kibbutz suggests that successor generations may not have the same commitment to that way of life as the founders, but producer cooperatives, in which people work together but don't try to live together, may develop into more durable organizations.

It is unlikely, however, that social incentives will be adopted again on the scale of a full society. If wages were entirely unrelated to effort in a large, heterogeneous, and mobile society, it would be impossible to establish and to maintain a set of social rewards and sanctions capable of disciplining free-riders. The level of work effort and output would therefore be far less than the government or the citizens themselves would regard as acceptable. Even with the wage incentives employed by all the socialist societies in this century, the level of effort has been comparatively low. Had they employed social incentives, they would very likely not have endured as long as they did.

Therefore, unless the history of the twentieth century is entirely erased, any future society intent on implementing the socialist version of the Good Society will permit individual choice rather than societal choice to govern the organization of labor, much as individual choice will govern the distribution of consumer goods. The domain of societal choice will be restricted to the sphere of production activities.

What distinguishes the activities of working and consuming from the activity of production is that the former involve the management of people while the latter involves the management of things. Things have no preferences, but people do. Imagine how difficult production would be if one ton of coal differed from another in its preference for the kind of furnace in which it is to be burned. One worker, however, is not like another worker, and one consumer is not like another consumer. They differ in their preferences for leisure and for goods, and they cannot be easily be managed in the manner of a ton of coal.

In the Maoist ideal of the Good Society, the people would suppress their individual preferences in the common interest. The ideal citizen "serves the people" by taking whatever job she is assigned to, with no regard for her personal job preferences, and by accepting whatever goods are assigned to her, without regard to her preferences among goods. She is thus without preferences, like a ton of coal. The organization of labor and the distribution of consumer goods would in that case be no more complex than the organization of production.

What defeats the principle of societal choice is that people are different from coal. "Vive la difference!" is the cry that comes to mind.

Notes

1 *The New York Times*, November 9, 1996, p. 6.
2 Spiro, *Kibbutz*, p. 265.
3 Barkai, *Growth Patterns of the Kibbutz Economy*, p. 9.
4 Nove, *An Economic History of the USSR*, p. 233.
5 Hoffman, *Work Incentive Practices and Policies in the People's Republic of China*, pp. 97–102.
6 Wheelwright and McFarlane, *The Chinese Road to Socialism*, p. 143.
7 Hoffman, *Work Incentive Practices and Policies in the People's Republic of China*, pp. 69–71.
8 Hoffman, *Work Incentive Practices and Policies in the People's Republic of China*, p. 75. See also p. 104.
9 Walder, *Communist Neo-traditionalism*, p. 89 and *passim*.
10 Hoffman, *Work Incentive Practices and Policies in the People's Republic of China*, p. 77.
11 Aoki, "Toward an economic model of the Japanese firm," pp. 11–13.
12 OECD, *Economic Surveys*: Japan 1996, pp. 104–6.
13 In most societies there are other sources of income than work effort, such as interest on savings and other property income (chapter 27). The larger the income the citizens earn from such other sources, the less the pressure to exert effort as a worker. Other sources of income are ignored in the present discussion.
14 This may seem like a trivial conclusion, but it may shed some light on the relatively successful performance of small collectivist communities like the kibbutz. Such communities generally consist of people with a strong commitment to a certain religious or secular ideology. Members who find themselves at variance with the community values tend to leave. Under such circumstances, the members' preferences with regard to such things as work and consumer goods, while not identical, are probably much more like each other than would be the case in a large and more heterogeneous society. Therefore, if a kibbutz switched over from social to wage incentives, the work-effort decisions of the members would be likely to be very similar, at least for a time. Hence no great difference in efficiency would be experienced under the two arrangements. This result is therefore not entirely trivial.
15 One qualification should be noted. The argument assumes that the citizens' assessments of their welfare are "independent," in the sense that my assessment of my welfare depends entirely on the composition of my own package of leisure and goods, with no regard to the packages that others have chosen. Suppose, however, that your $500 lifestyle decreases the satisfaction I derive from my $300 lifestyle; I, in other words, am envious of your income and would be happier if you did not have more money than I.
   If envy is regarded as a proper sentiment that should be respected in a Good Society, then neither arrangement can be shown to be more efficient than the other. For whatever distribution happened to emerge, any redistribution that increased somebody's income would automatically cause some envious person to be worse off. A Good Society, however, is unlikely to sanction envy as a proper concern, so that the argument in the text would be valid.
16 Pareto-efficiency concerns the distribution of a given collection of goods among different persons. Incentive-efficiency as used here concerns the distribution of different collections of goods (wages in the present context) among different persons.

Chapter 11

The Meanings of Labor Productivity

By nature, men are nearly alike;
by practice they get to be wider apart.
— *Confucius*

Let us now praise famous men.
— *Ecclesiasticus*

CONTENTS

Workers differ not only in their job preferences and in the effort they put into their work, but also in their ability to perform various kinds of work. Some people can design and build complex machines; others can operate the machines but cannot design them. Of those who design machines, some are more imaginative and diligent than others, and of those who operate the machines, some run them faster and more accurately than others. In these and countless other ways, workers differ in what is broadly thought of as their productivity.

If every worker could perform in every job as well as any other worker, it wouldn't matter which citizens work at which jobs: every allocation of labor would produce the same output as any other. If the job structure provided for 50 cake-baking jobs, and if everyone could bake as well as everyone else, the same number of cakes would be baked regardless of who held those jobs. If some workers can bake more and better cakes than others, however, it makes a great deal of difference whether the right citizens are set to work at the right jobs; for if they are not, the society will have fewer cakes, clothes, and all the other things than it is capable of producing. A society that regards a higher level of material welfare as a good thing should therefore be concerned with whether and how its economic arrangements take account of the differences in productivity.

1 Productivity Differences and Values

How one feels about the fact that some workers are more productive than others depends on one's values. To some people it is cause for celebration. The richness of social life derives from the ability of some people to play the violin or tell a story – or run a farm or wield a hammer – better than others. The Good Society, from this perspective, should praise all men, famous and ordinary, and provide the fullest opportunity for them to cultivate their talents and use them in the employments they most prefer, which, it may be hoped, will be in the general interest.

There is another view, however, which holds the fact of differences in worker productivity to be the cancer of a society. The Good Society should bend its efforts toward the elimination of those differences; at the least it should reject institutional arrangements that explicitly generate and recognize such differences and thereby perpetuate them. This view is most strongly held by people for whom social equality is a dominating value.

The two points of view derive from deeper convictions on that ancient question of political and social philosophy – the content of human nature. At one extreme is the view that differences among people are innate and natural, and that the best society is one that recognizes that fact in its social and economic organization. At the other extreme is the belief that the human being is a *tabula rasa* at birth, and virtually all differences among people are the consequence of differences in childhood and later experiences. "Every shoemaker could have been a Shakespeare" is one expression of that perspective. Its modern version is an anti-elitist sentiment that sees the acclaim of exceptional performance as a blow to the self-esteem of low performers. From that perspective, a society devoted to equality should not celebrate differences in attainment but should strive to eliminate them, by designing its institutions in such a way as to provide, to the greatest extent possible, identical environments for all its citizens, particularly its children.

Most people, however, hold views that span the spectrum between those two extremes and regard the differences among people as the joint result of both nature and nurture. For example, one can subscribe to a qualified egalitarian value that supports social policy directed toward reducing inequality, but which does not regard that policy as a failure if it does not eliminate fully the productivity differences among people.

There are many ways in which a society that values equality can contrive to reduce the productivity differences among people, among them through the arrangements for the education and training of the young. That could be done by a levelling-up strategy of improving pre-school and elementary education in order to reduce the proportion of citizens with the least-developed production skills (chapter 21). It could also be done by a levelling-down strategy of curtailing opportunities and expenditures on higher education, designed to reduce the proportion of workers with extremely high skills. The latter strategy did indeed flourish for a time during the Chinese Cultural Revolution, a major element of which was a powerful anti-elitist drive. Its more gruesome manifestation was the slaughter of millions of educated citizens in Cambodia during the Pol Pot regime. The levelling-down strategy clashes so sharply with the competing value of improving economic conditions that it is likely to prevail only during brief periods of revolutionary zeal; and indeed it was sharply repudiated in China following the demise of Chairman Mao.

Despite the most determined effort to equalize productivity by education, however, there will always remain an important residual source of productivity differences based on innate differences among people. That will always be the case in the arts, in the sciences, in sports, in medicine, and in countless other occupations. I once knew a machinist about whom it was said that with his fingers alone he could detect a taper of as little as 0.003 centimeters in a one-meter rod. No reasonable society is likely to regard its goodness as diminished by such distinctive attainments on the part of its citizens, although it may take pains to protect itself from the status inequalities that sometimes flow from them.

More troublesome are differences in such natural abilities as leadership or managerial skills. To take advantage of such skills the society must empower those of its citizens who possess them to exert authority over other citizens: enterprise managers must have the power to issue orders to workers and to punish those who disobey. That kind of power has been a particularly nettlesome problem for societies that value equality and societal choice, for it is virtually impossible to retain equality of social status under such circumstances. Societies like Yugoslavia and the kibbutzim have sought to deal with it by rotating the job of production leader, but when very few people are exceptionally skilled in such matters, there is a high price to be paid if production leadership does not reside in the best hands.

Hence, to the extent that a society values material well-being, it would not be content with a labor-allocation arrangement that ignored differences in productivity. The quantity of goods that the economy could produce for its people would suffer if the workers were distributed among jobs with no regard to the differences in their skills in performing those jobs. There is no country so other-worldly – not Maoist China or Guevarist Cuba or the Israeli kibbutz – that the material well-being of the citizens is of no concern.

Since those differences will be with us for a long time, the Good Society must consider whether and how to take account of them in its arrangements for allocating its workers among the jobs that need to be filled and for distributing income among them. Whether the society opts for the wage method or the assignment method of allocating labor, it will surely wish to know how well those methods contrive to use those differences in worker productivity in the interest of the society.

2 Productivity and Efficiency

The preceding chapters assessed the efficiency of the two labor-allocation methods in terms of the workers' preferences – preferences among jobs, and preferences between consumption and leisure. There was little reason to assess their efficiency in terms of output as well, for when workers do not differ in productivity, every allocation would produce about the same output as any other. That simple world vanishes when we seek to consider how the two labor-allocation arrangements fare in a world in which workers differ in productivity. It now becomes terribly important that the right workers end up in the right jobs, for if they do not, output will be smaller than it could potentially be. Insofar as the society regards more output as better than less, the criterion of the goodness of its economic arrangements is, again, efficiency.

The preceding chapters have considered the efficiency of economic arrangements with respect to preferences – consumer preferences among goods, and worker preferences among jobs. In the present context the concern is over efficiency with respect to production. It will be referred to as "production efficiency," to distinguish it from efficiency with respect to preferences. It should be noted that, in principle, an economy may be efficient in one respect but not in another, much as an aircraft may be efficient with respect to payload, but not with respect to air speed. Similarly, an economy may be efficient with respect to production, but not with respect to consumption preferences; that is to say, it may produce the largest possible set of consumer goods, but the goods may be badly distributed among the consumers.

Part IV will undertake the assessment of the efficiency of economic arrangements with respect to both preferences and production. The concern in the rest of this chapter is with production efficiency alone.

Production efficiency requires, at the least, that cooks should be set to cooking and shoemakers to making shoes, and not the other way round. That much is evident. But it requires a great deal more than that. To begin with, it requires some clarification of the meaning of the expression "labor productivity."

3 Average Productivity

The assertion that some workers are more productive than others usually means that the quantity, or the value, of what they produce in a certain period of time is larger than that of others. One of the many sources of such differences in productivity is the variety of personal characteristics: diligence, strength, dexterity, or social or mental skills of various sorts. A second source is the variety of occupational skills that may enable one worker to produce more output, or a more valuable output, than another worker with fewer or different skills. The worker who can operate a coal cutting machine can produce more coal in a day than the miner who can only wield a pick.[1] Occupational differences in productivity would persist even if were no personal differences; that is, if all persons were equally diligent, strong, and dexterous.

Occupational differences in productivity are easy to observe when they refer to workers producing the same product, as in coal mining. They are more difficult to observe when they refer to different products. It is not evident, for example, what might be meant by the assertion that a welder is more productive than a coal miner, or that a surgeon is more productive than a shoe salesman. Usually that assertion means that the *value* of the output produced by the more productive worker is greater than the value of what the other worker produces in the same period of time. Value, in this context, refers to the physical output expressed in prices of some sort. When the product consists of ordinary things like food and clothing, and the price method is used for distributing them, the prices that consumers pay are usually taken as measure of their value (chapter 6). Thus, to say that an orchid grower is more productive than a carpenter is to mean that the dollar value of the orchids that one grower produces in a year is greater than the dollar value of the work that a carpenter produces in a year.[2]

When referring to a group of workers, the expression "labor productivity" usually refers to output per worker: if 50 miners produce 10,000 tons of coal (per week, or per month), their labor productivity is said to be 200 tons (per miner per week or per month). Labor productivity in this sense is called the "average product" of labor, or sometimes average "physical" product when the output is expressed in terms of physical units like tons or yards. When it is expressed in terms of monetary value, it is referred to as "average *value* product:" if the price of a ton of coal is $30, for example, then the productivity of mining labor, or its "average *value* product," would be $6,000 (200 tons × $30 per ton). The concept of value product is essential when the output consists of a heterogeneous collection of goods, like clothing or electrical equipment. For example, the average value product of labor in a clothing factory, where many different kinds of garments are produced, would be expressed as so many dollars worth of clothing per day.

The average product of labor is a convenient and widely used concept in judging the performance of an economy. The difference between poor and rich countries, for example, is reflected in the difference in the average product of their labor, and the annual rate of increase of the average product of labor is a useful indicator of the extent to which the people's economic welfare is rising. It is because of that close relation between economic welfare and productivity that every modern society strives to raise the average productivity of its labor force. One way in which this is done is by investment in machinery, equipment, and other forms of capital that increase the output that the work force can produce. Another is through education and job training – nowadays referred to as "investment in human capital." In the course of time such policies can contribute greatly to the increase in the average product of the country's labor and therefore in its material welfare.

That one country enjoys a higher average labor productivity than another does not signify that it has the better economic arrangements, however, any more than winning a war signifies that the victorious general is the better commander. His army may have won not because of his better generalship but because of the overwhelming force of the arms and troops at his disposal. People who know about military affairs may declare the losing general to be much the better of the two. In like fashion, one economy may enjoy a higher average product of labor than another not because of its better economic arrangements but because it is better endowed with natural resources, or it has a larger stock of capital inherited from the past, or its people work more hours per year. Winning is important, of course, but people who know about these things judge the goodness of an economy not by its output per worker but by how well it does with the resources available to it – which is to say, its efficiency.

Average productivity is therefore a good measure of the output produced by a country's labor force, but it says nothing about how efficiently that labor force is used. For an assessment of efficiency one must look not at the average product of labor but at a different measure of productivity – the marginal product of labor.

4 Marginal Productivity

Imagine two similar economies in which the size and skills of the labor force are the same and which are endowed with the same machinery and other productive resources. There is no unemployment, and the workers perform their jobs with equal diligence and effort. The economies differ only in the way in which the workers are allocated among all the jobs in the economy. An enterprise that employs 500 manual workers and three bookkeepers in one economy may employ 600 manual workers and only one bookkeeper, in the other.

To the casual eye it might seem that their labor-allocation arrangements, though different, are equally good. All the workers are employed somewhere; they perform their jobs with normal diligence; and the factories in both economies are humming along turning out large quantities of goods. There is no visible sign that something is not well in one of those economies – except that year after year one economy produces fewer goods than the other.

The reason is that in the less efficient economy the workers are not allocated among jobs in the way that takes the maximum advantage of the differences in their productivity. What is pernicious about this kind of allocational inefficiency is that it is invisible. Were there significant unemployment, one would know that the labor-allocation arrangements were not working as well as they should, but if everyone is fully and productively employed, there is no visible cue that labor has in fact been badly allocated among jobs. The people know only that they are not as well off as those in the other economy, although they work just as hard. It is only under the microscope of economic analysis that one could see that the allocation of labor has been badly managed in that economy.

In the real world, of course, there is no economy so similar to your own that it can serve as a standard for judging how well your country's labor force is allocated. It may be evident that other countries produce more than yours, but there are always dozens of reasons why that may happen. How then could one know if one of the reasons is that the wrong workers are working at the wrong jobs?

That might seem like a simple-minded question, but it turns out to involve some rather complex issues. It is therefore a question that political leaders, I am sorry to report, often find rather tedious – even leaders of societies that aspire to goodness. They are too deeply concerned about the grand architecture of their society and have no patience for the plumbing, nor for those bookkeeper-advisors who would press these tiresome matters upon them.

Chairman Mao, for one, envisioned the secret of his country's productivity to lie in the spirit that true socialism would inspire in the masses, and not in the calculus of how the workers should be allocated among jobs. The consequence is that many political leaders do not appreciate the loss of material welfare that their people may have to bear because of policies that ignore the complexities of efficiency issues. No engagement with the economics of a Good Society can be serious if it does not come to grips with the issues involved in the proper use of its resources.

The essence of the problem may be explored in its simplest form by imagining an enterprise called The Anthracite Company. Whether the enterprise is owned by a socialist Ministry of Coal Production devoted to the interest of all the people or by a capitalist corporation devoted to the interest of the stockholders doesn't matter: both want the enterprise to produce as much coal as possible.

The enterprise operates two coal mines with a labor force of 50 miners, 30 of whom are assigned to North Mine and 20 to South Mine. The question is, how can one tell whether that particular allocation of the labor force between the mines produces the largest possible combined output of coal?

An inspector from the home office might seek the answer by checking the average product of labor in the two mines, which turns out to be the same – say 500 tons per miner in both mines. It might therefore seem to him that the manager is doing his job well and should be rewarded. In fact both he and the manager should be fired. An economically literate inspector would understand that average productivity gives no cue at all about whether the workers are properly allocated between the mines. He would ask instead, by how much coal production would change if one or more workers were reassigned from one mine to the other.

Suppose, for example, that if one worker were transferred from North Mine to South Mine, North's output would drop by 100 tons, but South's output would rise by 450 tons. The combined coal output would then be 350 tons larger. It follows that the manager had not in fact figured out the best way to allocate his 50 workers between the two mines. If he had more of them working in South Mine and fewer in North Mine he could have produced more coal for the people or more profits for the stockholders.

The numbers 100 and 450 in the example are called the "marginal product" of labor. Marginal product is the amount by which the output of a production operation would change if the labor force were increased by one (or more) workers. The lesson of the example is that whenever the marginal product of labor is larger in one operation than another, the workers have not been optimally allocated between them: more output can be obtained by transferring one or more workers from the higher-marginal-product operation to the lower-marginal-product operation.

It does not follow from the example, though it may seem to, that the reassignment of a second worker to South Mine would gain another 350 tons of coal output, and the same with the reassignment of a third, and a fourth, until all 50 miners are working in South Mine and North Mine is shut down. The reason it does not follow is that most production technologies are limited by a characteristic known as the "law of diminishing returns."

Diminishing returns   Most enterprises – restaurants, assembly lines, or coal mines – can produce more if they have more labor. Beyond a certain point, however, the gain from additional workers becomes smaller and smaller.[3] In a well-run mine, the labor force is set to work on the richest seams that are closest to the minehead. If additional miners were added to the labor force, each one would then be set to work on the next best seam a bit further from the minehead, and would therefore add less coal to the mine's total output than the one before him. The marginal product of mining labor would therefore gradually decline as more workers are taken on. In South Mine, it would decline from 450 with the original labor force of 20, to perhaps 370 with 21 workers, to 250 with 22 workers, and so. In the extreme, the mine may be so overstuffed with workers that the marginal product of one additional miner might be very small or even zero.

The process works backwards as well. As the number of miners is gradually reduced, the poorest coal seams are the first to be abandoned, then the next poorest, and so on. Hence the marginal product of labor would rise as the work force shrinks. In North Mine it would rise from 100 tons with the original labor force of 30, to perhaps 150 tons with 29 workers, to 250 tons with 28 workers, and so on. When the mine is greatly understaffed, each miner is so valuable that the loss of yet another one would cause output to fall by a very large amount.

The best allocation   Because of the law of diminishing returns, as successive workers are transferred from North Mine to South Mine, the marginal product of labor tends to rise in North Mine from the original 100 tons, and to decline in South Mine from the original 450 tons. Therefore, with each successive reassignment, the size of the output-gain diminishes from the original 350 tons. It follows that after a certain point the marginal product in the two mines tends to converge to the same amount. With an allocation of 22 workers in South Mine and 28 workers in North Mine, for example, the marginal product of labor in both mines may be 250 tons. In that case there is no further gain in output to be had by any further reassignment of workers. Transferring one more worker from either mine to the other would cause output to fall in the first mine by the same amount (250 tons) as it would rise in the other.

The process is somewhat like pouring water from a largely full glass into a largely empty glass. The level declines in the first and rises in the second until the levels are equal. Unlike the pouring of water, however, the pouring of workers from the lower- to the higher-marginal-product mine increases the combined output of the mines, which reaches a maximum when the level of marginal product in both mines is the same.

The answer to the question with which this discussion began is now evident. The test of whether a certain allocation of labor among similar activities is optimal is to be found in their marginal products. If they are unequal, the allocation is not optimal and total output can be increased by reallocating some workers from the low-marginal-product activity to the high-marginal-product activity. If the marginal products are equal, the allocation is optimal and the total output is at its maximum.

The requirement of equal marginal products is said to be a "condition of efficiency," for only when that condition is fulfilled are the activities producing the largest possible output.

Any society that counts efficiency as one of the criteria for assessing the goodness of its economic arrangements will find the concept of marginal product to be an indispensable tool for that purpose. It will be greatly relied upon in Part IV.

5   A Disquieting Result

The simple mining example produces a somewhat disturbing result. People would like to think that their productivity depends entirely on their own abilities – that they are more productive because they are smarter or stronger or more skilled and experienced. It now turns out, however, that productivity depends not only on those qualities but also on the number of other workers who happen to possess them. Even if the miners are identical in their abilities, the more miners there are the lower their productivity – both average and marginal. That means that as more miners become available for employment, the lower the productivity of mining labor – and the same for teachers, surgeons, machinists, and all other occupations.

It is somewhat humbling to learn that the productivity of your labor is a matter of its "scarcity." Like the value of a sack of potatoes, it can fall or rise simply because there are more or fewer people who possess your skills. Perhaps even more disturbing, if the society decides to tie wage rates to productivity, the more workers who enter an occupation the lower the wage rate will be. It doesn't take much thought to realize that one way of keeping one's wages high is to keep the number of available workers in your occupation low. This matter will also be considered in Part IV.

The relationship between productivity and the size of the labor force applies to an entire economy as well: the more people employed in a country with a given endowment of productive resources, the smaller the increment in output that would be produced by new additions the labor force.[4] In the extreme, the quantity of labor relative to its capital and other resources may be so large that the marginal product of labor may fall to zero; that is to say, if some of the population emigrated, their labor would not be missed and the country's output would not fall at all. The notion of "overpopulation," indeed, is sometimes defined as a condition in which the population is so large relative to the resources that the marginal product of labor is zero, or even negative.

6 Occupational Differences

The test of efficiency in the allocation of labor is relatively easy to apply when there is only one type of labor, as in the simple mining example presented above: the marginal product of labor must be equal in both mines. In that example, the workers are assumed to be homogeneous, in the sense that each worker has the same ability as every other. They are said to be "perfect substitutes" for each other, meaning that one miner could replace another miner with no change in the quantity of coal mined.

Virtually all production activities, however, employ workers who differ in their productivity as individuals. Those productivity differences derive primarily from differences in occupational skills. The accountant and the cobbler each know, and are able to do, many things that the other cannot. Perhaps one should say cannot do "as well," for the accountant could make certain repairs in shoes, and the cobbler could perhaps keep some accounts after a fashion. They may therefore be said to be "imperfect substitutes," in the sense that one miner might be replaced by a certain number of accountants - perhaps five, or perhaps 20 – with no loss in coal output. It is intuitively evident, however, that the production of both shoes and tax returns would be larger if the cobbler stuck to his last and the accountant to his books.

To investigate the consequences of differences in occupational skills, suppose that there are two kinds of mining labor – say ten mining-machine operators and 50 loaders. The operators are trained to run the expensive coal-cutting equipment, and the loaders assist the operators, set up the pit props, and transport the coal. The question now is, "How can one know if labor has been properly allocated when there is more than one type of labor?"

The answer turns out to be similar to that in the simpler example. The optimal distribution is one in which the marginal product of the machine operators is the same in both mines and the marginal product of the loaders is the same in both mines. The reasoning is a simple extension of the marginal condition: if the marginal product of the operators (and the loaders) were not the same in both mines, total output could always be further increased by transferring one or more operators (and loaders) from the lower-marginal-product mine to the higher.

When that best allocation of both kinds of labor has been achieved, the marginal product of the various kinds of labor will generally differ. The marginal product of loaders, for example, may be 500 tons in both mines, while the marginal product of machine operators may be 2,000 tons. One machine operator is then said to "substitute for" five loaders in production, in the sense that the output that would be forgone if there were one less machine operator could be compensated for by five additional loaders. An hour of a machine operator's labor may also be said to be "worth" five times that of a loader's labor, in the sense that an additional machine operator would add to the output of coal five times as much as that of an additional loader.[5]

7 From Productivity to Production

Following the analytic procedure of the preceding chapters, we should now turn to an assessment of the efficiency of the price method and the assignment method in accounting for productivity differences among workers, applying the test of efficiency presented above. There is a major problem in following that procedure in this case, however.

The meaning of the proposition that marginal products should be equal in all employments is unambiguous in the case of homogeneous commodities like coal, where output can be meaningfully expressed in physical units. Its meaning is not self-evident, however, with regard to the economy as a whole, with its large and heterogeneous collection of industries.

For example, machinists with comparable skills work in a great many industries. Suppose the marginal product of machinists is 300 tons of coal in all the coal mines and 5,000 yards of cloth in all the textile mills. Machinists are then distributed optimally among coal mines, and among textile mills. But are they distributed in the best possible way between coal mines and textile mills?

Those numbers say that if one machinist were transferred from coal mining to textiles, coal production would decline by 300 tons, while textile production would increase by 5,000 yards. The optimality of that allocation of machinists then depends on the value that the society places upon more coal relative to more textiles. If 300 additional tons of coal are regarded as having about the same social value as 5,000 additional yards of textiles, then the allocation of machinists between the two industries is just right, or optimal. However, if the society would prefer to have the 5,000 additional yards of textiles, even at the cost of 300 fewer tons of coal, then the original allocation is not optimal: too many machinists are working in the coal mines and too few in textile mills.

Thus, when differences in productivity among workers are to be taken into account, efficiency is no longer a matter of fitting the worker-pegs into a given set of job-holes. One must ask whether the holes themselves – the job structure – are of the right size and shape. We must ask not only how a Good Society should distribute its workers among the jobs that are to be filled, but also how it should decide what those jobs should be.

The first of those two questions relates to the "supply of labor," referring to the conditions under which the workers supply their labor to the enterprises that employ them. The second relates to the "demand for labor," referring to the number and kinds of jobs the society wishes to have filled. The demand for labor, in turn, derives from the society's preferences among the various goods and services that could be produced: the number of window-cleaning jobs and poultry processing jobs depends on how clean the country wishes its windows to be and how much chicken it wishes to consume.

Therefore, this is as far as the inquiry into productivity differences can proceed while confining the analysis to consumption and labor. Consuming and working are the activities of the households that form the economy. The discussions in Parts II and III have been conducted as if there were an imaginary screen separating the household sector from the production sector. Consumer goods pass through that screen from enterprises to households; we considered how the goods are distributed among households, but not why that particular set of goods is produced in the first place. Labor services pass through the screen in the opposite direction, from households to enterprises; we considered how the workers are distributed among jobs, but not why one particular set of jobs comes to be created in the first place. Part IV removes the screen and plunges into the organization of the production sector where the goods are produced and the jobs created.

Notes

1   *If* a coal cutting machine is part of a mine's capital stock. A machine operator working in an enterprise that had no machines would be no more productive than one who lacked that skill. The point is a useful reminder that the productivity of labor depends not only on the workers' skills but also on the quantity and quality of the machinery and equipment with which they work. How labor productivity varies with the size and composition of the capital stock is beyond the scope of this study, however.
2   In this simplified discussion, it will be recalled, it is assumed that the good is produced by labor alone, ignoring the materials and other inputs used in actual production operations.
3   The qualification "beyond a certain point" is important, for in some technologies, when there are very few workers the marginal product of labor may *increase* as more workers are added. Two miners working together may be able to produce more than twice the output that one miner could produce when working alone. The law is properly called the "law of *eventually* diminishing returns."
4   When the population of a country is very small relative to its resources, however, the marginal product of labor may rise for a time as new immigrants arrive. That was very likely the case in America in the nineteenth century and earlier.
5   The analysis assumes that the stock of capital in each mine is given; that is, that each mine has a certain number of coal cutting machines and other equipment. If the number of operators assigned to a mine increases beyond the point at which the machines are fully employed, the marginal productivity of machine operators will fall sharply.

Part IV

**Coordinating
the Economy**

Chapter 12

The Awesome Task of Coordination

The heel bone's connected to the toe
   bone,
The toe bone's connected to the ankle
   bone ...
   — Spiritual

CONTENTS

The production system of a modern economy is an enormous network of social arrangements. From the perspective of the economics of the Good Society, however, two sets of those arrangements are fundamental. One consists of arrangements for coordinating the activities of the workers, consumers, enterprises, and other economic agents. The other consists of arrangements that govern the ownership of the enterprises and other productive property.

This Part is devoted to the coordination mechanism. Property ownership is the subject of Part V.

1   The Enterprise

The central institution in the production process is the enterprise. It is the enterprise that produces the goods and services that are distributed among the citizens-as-consumers. It is the enterprise that provides the jobs at which the citizens-as-workers are employed. How the enterprise ought to be organized is therefore a matter of vast importance in a Good Society.

The nature and the size of the enterprise vary enormously in modern economies. It may be as small as the panel truck of a solitary electrician in England who works alone or with a single assistant, or it may be as large as the Anshan Steel Works in China that employs many thousands of workers. It may occupy no more than the garage of a private home in Cincinnati or the personal household plot of a Soviet collective farmer, or it may include dozens of spatially separated establishments.

The enterprise is the gateway that separates two types of activity that together constitute the production process of the society. One is the production activity that takes place within the enterprise. It is there that thread is spun into cloth, or that iron castings are machined into engine blocks. The other is the transactions among enterprises. The cloth is shipped to a garment enterprise where it is sewn into suits, and the engine block is shipped to an automobile assembly plant. Coordinating the activities that take place within enterprises is commonly referred to as "management," while the coordination of transactions among enterprises is part of what is conventionally thought of as "economics."

The division of the society's productive activity among tens of thousands of autonomous enterprises is compatible with an arrangement in which a society's productive property is privately owned, with each enterprise representing one private group's share of the total property. After a socialist revolution, however, when all the property is owned by all the people, it is reasonable to question whether the old boundary between enterprise and economy needs to be or ought to be retained. Social ownership makes it possible to replace competition by cooperation and to let production be guided by the general welfare rather than the profitability of individual enterprises. Managers and workers would be motivated to identify with the entire economy, rather than with that tiny portion of it that provides their jobs and pay. Under these conditions, textile factories would no longer need to haggle with garment factories over the terms of sale; they could all be managed rationally as if they were departments of One Big Factory. The sphere of economics would shrivel to nothing and the sphere of management would expand to embrace the entire economy.

That idea won the day among the leaders of the Soviet Union in its first decade. The administration of all large nationalized enterprises was turned over to the Central Economic Council which "was in a very real sense acting like a single state firm." That huge administrative task was subdivided among a number of departments called "trusts [that] were in total command of 'their' factories."[1] The factories had no bank accounts of their own but operated through "budget financing"; instead of financing their expenditures out of their own revenues, they operated like a branch office of the post office – they turned all their receipts over to the state budget and received their operating funds from the state budget. The managers of these former enterprises became mere foremen, most of their functions having been taken over by their trusts. In fact they ceased to be called "enterprises" and became in effect like departments of a huge centralized corporation.

The results were highly unsatisfactory for a number of reasons. For one thing, the trusts proved to be unable to micro-manage efficiently the hundreds of their formerly independent enterprises. For another, so little authority remained with the managers of the former enterprises that they could not be held responsible for the performance of their units. Eventually, following a heated controversy, the Party gave up on the idea of One Big Factory and declared that thereafter the enterprise was to be "the basic unit of administering industry." These new socialist enterprises had their own bank accounts and financed their expenditures out of their own revenues, sometimes with government subsidies. Their managers were individually accountable for the efficiency of the organization's operation. By the time the system of national economic planning came into full operation in the 1930s, intra-enterprise production activity was once again the responsibility of enterprise managers, much as under capitalism. The task of the central planners was to coordinate the economy – the network of transactions among enterprises – in place of the market mechanism that had performed that task in the capitalist past.

One might have thought that the Soviet experience would have discouraged later social-ists from succumbing to the seductive idea of running the whole economy like One Big Factory. Yet it surfaced again in Cuba. It seems to be particularly attractive to revolutionary leaders like Che Guevara who are strong on social policy but weak on economics. Against the advice of Soviet and many non-Soviet economists, budget-financing was introduced in a large sector of the economy.[2] As in the USSR, however, that arrangement was later abandoned and the separate status of individual enterprises was restored. They maintain their own bank- and financial accounts, and they pay for their labor and other inputs out of their own revenues.

Some future version of a socialist Good Society may well try its own hand once again at running the economy like One Big Factory. The chances are, however, that the experiment will last no longer than in the past. Enterprises of the conventional type are likely to remain the basic unit of production organization in all modern societies.

2   Coordination and the Division of Labor

The productivity of an economy depends on how well both the internal and the external activities of enterprises are conducted. Intra-enterprise productivity depends on such factors as the quality of the technical knowledge of management and workers and the morale of the workplace. Extra-enterprise productivity reflects the quality of the economic system: whether the cloth and engine blocks are delivered at the right time and in the right quantities to those enterprises that can make the most productive use of them.

Coordinating the work flow within the enterprise is the task of enterprise management. The complexity of that task derives in part from the division of labor, that miracle of the Industrial Revolution described by Adam Smith in a much celebrated chapter of the *Wealth of Nations*. Smith was fascinated by a pin factory in which production had been broken down into a complex set of sequential operations, making possible a level of productivity far beyond the reach of older-type craftsmen, each of whom made one pin at a time. The modern world is so used to the division of labor that we can scarcely imagine the awe with which that great social invention was greeted by the people of Adam Smith's time.

The division of labor in a modern society, however, extends far beyond the walls of the individual enterprise. Just as each workshop is a link in a production chain within the enter-prise, so each enterprise is a link in a production chain that involves many other enterprises. The pins shipped out by the pin factory are bought by shirtmaking factories that use them for packaging their shirts, which are then sold to department stores that sell them to the consumers at the end of the chain. Just as the production operations within each enterprise have to be coordinated, so must these inter-enterprise transactions be coordinated else there will be too few or too many pins produced, or too few or too many shirts.

The set of social arrangements that performs the same coordination function between and among enterprises and households that management performs for the production operations within enterprises is called the "economic mechanism." The choice of an economic mecha-nism is one of the crucial economic decisions that a Good Society must make, for its material well-being depends in large measure upon that choice.

3   The Production Process

The heart of the economy is the process of production, which is conventionally described as the transformation of "inputs" into "outputs" which are then distributed among various users. The task of coordination is to arrange both for an orderly flow of the mass of inputs into the enterprises where they are transformed into outputs, and for an orderly flow of the mass of outputs to their users. The complexity of that task derives in the first place from the huge variety of inputs and outputs.

INPUTS

In the simple economy analyzed in Part III, labor was the only input to which attention was given. A complete economy, however, makes use of a great many inputs that are conventionally classified into three groups:

1 *Factors of production* Every enterprise employs a labor force that works with a certain quantity of capital, such as plant and equipment, which is situated on a tract of land. The services of that labor, capital, and land – the so-called primary factors of production – are the "factor inputs" into the production process.

2 *Intermediate products* In addition to the factor inputs, the enterprise's production process normally requires inputs of "intermediate products." These are such products as raw materials, fuel, semi-fabricates, components, and other supplies, which are produced in other enterprises.

3 *Imports* Every modern economy makes extensive use of goods and services produced in other countries. A resource-poor country like Japan imports almost all of the coal, lumber, and other non-labor inputs used by its producing enterprises.

OUTPUTS

In the simple economy studied in Part II, consumer goods and services were the only form of output under consideration. A complete economy, however, produces a great variety of outputs that consist of two broad types. One is the "intermediate products" referred to above, which are fed back into the economic process in the form of inputs into the production operations of other enterprises. The other is called "final products," which may be thought of as the end purpose of the economic process. Automobiles and lobster dinners, for example, are final products that are produced in order to be consumed and enjoyed, while steel sheet and lobster pots are intermediate products that are produced because they are needed in the production of automobiles and lobster dinners.

The goods and services that comprise the final product constitute in the aggregate that momentous magnitude called the GDP – or Gross Domestic Product. They consist of four major groups, defined by the economic status of the principal end user.

1 *Consumption* Consumer goods and services purchased by the population are the largest component of the final product. In 1986 consumption consisted of about 53 percent of total output in the USSR and about 65 percent of total output in the United States.[3]

2 *Investment* The second category – investment – consists of capital goods like machinery and equipment that are acquired by enterprises to be used for production purposes. Capital goods are similar to intermediate products in the sense that they too consist of things acquired by enterprises from other enterprises. The crucial difference is that they are "durable": an intermediate product like leather is "used up" in the production of a pair of shoes, but a shoemaking machine lasts for years during which it is used for the production of millions of pairs of shoes. By convention, the acquisition by an enterprise of a capital good that costs more than a specified value and that has a useful life of more than a year is classified as investment.

About 23 percent of all final products in the USSR consisted of investment and about 20 percent in United States in 1986.[4]

3 *Government* Goods purchased by agencies of government are generally the third largest component of GDP. Government purchases range from furniture for use in government offices to aircraft carriers delivered to the armed services.

4 *Exports* The fourth category consists of goods that are not acquired by the three domestic users identified above, but are exported to other countries. Exporting is the principal way in which a country pays for its imports.

The complexity of the task of coordinating that intricate web of inputs and outputs can be seen most clearly in the case of intermediate products.

4 Mechanisms of Coordination

An intermediate product like coal is produced by some enterprises and used by others: it is an output of the former, and an input of the latter. The first task of coordination is to manage the *production* of coal – to see to it that the coal mines in aggregate produce enough to supply the production needs of power plants and all other users of coal. The importance of that condition is that if it is not met, some enterprises and workers will be idle some of the time and the economy will produce less output than it potentially can.

Coordination requires more, however, than that the total output of coal be sufficient to meet the total production requirements for coal as an input. Those two totals might be correct, but unless someone is minding the store, some users may receive more than they need and others less than they need. The second task of the coordination mechanism is therefore to manage the *distribution* of the coal from the hundreds of suppliers to the thousands of users. Poor coordination with respect to the distribution of goods will also cause the economy to produce below its potential.

The coordination mechanism is therefore responsible for managing the economic relations between the enterprises that produce a good and those that use it, or between supply and demand, in the shorthand of economics. The instruments available for the coordination process are the same two fundamental economic arrangements that are now quite familiar – prices and assignment. The characteristics of those two methods were discussed in detail in Parts II and III with respect to the distribution of consumer goods and the allocation of workers among jobs. They operate in a similar, though not identical, manner with respect to intermediate products.

Supply The supply of an intermediate product like coal is the sum of all the coal that each mine manager has decided to produce. Under the price method, each mine manager makes that output decision for his own enterprise alone, on the basis of a variety of considerations, prominent among which is the price of coal. Under the assignment method, an agency of the society decides how much coal each mine should produce. Those decisions are transmitted as directives to the mine managers, who then organize their own enterprise's production operations accordingly.

Demand The demand for coal is the sum of the quantities required by all coal-using enterprises in order to produce their own output. Under the price method each enterprise decides for itself how much coal it will use, on the basis of a variety of considerations, of which the price of coal is again of major importance. Under the assignment method, an agency of government decides how much coal each enterprise is to receive. The enterprise is then given authorization to procure that amount of coal for its production activities.

With two methods of deciding upon both the supply of and the demand for each product, there are four logical combinations of coordination arrangements, each of which corresponds to a type of economic mechanism:

1   *The market mechanism*   When both the supply and the demand for an input or an output are determined by the price method, the arrangement is called a "market," and the coordination mechanism is called the "market mechanism" (or sometimes the "price system").

2   *The planning mechanism*   When both the supply and the demand for an input or output are determined by the assignment method, the arrangement is called the central planning mechanism, or simply the planning mechanism.

Those are the two fundamental economic mechanisms in what might be called their pure form. There are two other arrangements that modify the pure mechanisms by combining the price and assignment methods.

3   *The mixed-planning mechanism*   The Communist countries generally rejected the assignment method in favor of the price method in the interchanges between the household sector and the production sector, as elaborated in Part II. The demand for consumer goods by households is managed by the price method – consumers pay for the goods they choose to buy; but the supply of consumer goods is managed by the assignment method – the planners assign production targets to the enterprises. Similarly, the supply of labor by households is managed by the price method – workers find their own jobs; but the demand is managed by the assignment method – the planners assign hiring quotas to enterprises. Hence, the transactions between households and enterprises are coordinated by what may be designated as a "mixed-planning mechanism." All transactions within the production sector, however, are coordinated by the pure central planning mechanism.

Writers often refer to the labor "market" in the Communist economies. It is only on the supply side, however, that something like market-like behavior can be said to prevail. The demand for labor is derived from a national plan, a process that bears no similarity at all to what happens in markets (chapter 14). To refer to that arrangement as a market is to suggest analogies that are misleading, for there are fundamental differences between a coordination arrangement in which only supply or only demand is governed by the price method, and an arrangement in which both operate under the price method.

The confusion can be avoided by confining the term market to an arrangement in which *both* supply and demand are coordinated by the price method, and referring to the Communist arrangement as a mixed-planning mechanism.

4   *The mixed-market mechanism*   An economy that relies primarily on the price method might employ the assignment method for some purposes. Educational or medical services may be supplied not by price considerations but by direct distribution: an agency of government, for example, may decide how much of those services is to be produced and how they are to be distributed. The blackboards and bandages, however, are acquired by purchase from the enterprises of the production sector that operate under the price method. Such an arrangement may be called a "mixed-market mechanism."

5   Economic Mechanisms and Government

The fundamental difference between the two mechanisms lies in the role of government. Under the planning mechanism the government is the coordinator. It is the government's planning agency that bears the responsibility for assuring that total steel production matches total steel requirements, for assigning production quotas to each of the hundreds of steel mills, and for arranging that each of the thousands of steel users receives delivery of the steel it needs, when it needs it. Under the market mechanism, each steel mill decides for itself how much steel to produce and to whom to sell it, and each steel user must make its own arrangements for receiving delivery of the steel it needs, when it needs it. Nobody is responsible for assuring that total steel production matches total steel requirements: the market mechanism is supposed to take care of that.

In practice, no country uses its mechanism in its pure form. All are mixed economies to some degree. The planned economies rely primarily on assignment, but the distribution of consumer goods and the supply of labor are generally managed by the price method. Most of them also permit pure markets to function in the case of certain goods, in the sense that the price method prevails with respect to both supply and demand. The most prominent example is the farmers' markets, where collective-farm members are permitted to sell the products of their small household plots to urban consumers at whatever prices they can command in the market.

In the countries that use the market mechanism, on the other hand, government always plays some role in the management of economic affairs, sometimes small and sometimes quite large. That is particularly the case in times of national emergency. During World War II, a War Production Board was established in the United States with the authority to control the production and distribution of a variety of commodities that were required for war-related production. The Board employed the assignment method, issuing production quotas to copper-refining companies that they were obliged to meet, and ensuring that the copper output was shipped to the highest-priority producers of military products. Workers were not assigned to jobs in the manner of Guevarist Cuba, but enterprises were limited in the number of workers they could hire who had skills that were badly needed for military production. Even under such drastic conditions, however, the market mechanism continued to guide the bulk of the economy: most producers were not assigned production quotas, although the government continued to fix many prices. In normal times, governments intervene in less drastic ways, for such purposes as maintaining full employment and regulating the behavior of enterprises: for example, by forbidding certain production activities in the interest of environmental protection and by limiting the number of hours that employees can be required to work.

The proper mix of markets and government in economic affairs is, indeed, the preeminent issue in political-economic controversy. More than anything else it distinguishes "liberals" from "conservatives" – in the American meaning of those terms – although there is a curious inversion in the use of the terms in the Communist and capitalist countries. To be a liberal in the Communist countries was to favor the wider use of market-like arrangements in the planned economy: greater stress on profit in enterprise decision-making, for example, and an expanded scope for small-scale private enterprise. To be a conservative was to urge tighter control by the government. In the capitalist countries, in contrast, liberals call for more involvement by government in the regulation of the markets, while conservatives want to restrain government from interfering in the activities of markets or in the outcomes that emerge from market-based activities.

The contest between conservatives and liberals is often heated, but the more temperate protagonists understand that theirs is a normal "family quarrel" among people who are committed to the existing economic mechanism but have different views on the policies that might make it work better and on what "better" means.

6 Property Ownership and Economic Systems

Just as every society must arrange for the coordination of the economic activities of its citizens and enterprises, so it must establish arrangements for the ownership of the productive property of the enterprises. The ownership arrangements that have been employed in modern economies fall into two broad groups, private and social, although there are important variations within each group, which are the subject of Part V.

Each ownership form can be combined, in principle, with each economic mechanism to form an "economic system." By tradition, an economic system is referred to by its ownership form. Thus, "capitalism" is the name of an economic system in which private ownership is the predominant ownership form, and a "socialist" economic system is one in which social ownership is the predominant ownership form.

People who are aware of the grave deficiencies of both systems are sometimes inclined to damn both their houses, seeking a solution in a "third way."[5] Sweden for its income equality, Japan for the large role of government in economic life, and Yugoslavia for its worker self-management, have at various times been promoted as examples of such a third way. It is more illuminating, however, to view them not as distinct types of economic systems but as examples of the wide range of institutional variation that is possible under the traditional rubrics of capitalism and socialism. If those two words are merely spoken rather than hissed, they are still the most serviceable categories for a general evaluation of the goodness of economic arrangements.

All capitalist economic systems employ markets as their economic mechanism. The reason is partly historical, for private ownership and markets grew up together, as it were. Wherever people have been free to own land and tools, there were markets in which they sold the products of their land or of their workshops – to other people, or to merchants who then resold them to other people. Markets were major centers in the social and economic life of antiquity – in the Mediterranean civilizations, in China, in Africa, and elsewhere. The guild masters of medieval Europe were private owners of small-scale productive property who hired journeyman-workers and apprentices and sold their products in markets that were closely regulated by their guilds.

There is also a practical reason, however. Private ownership would confer on the Orbis Company, for example, the right to cut back on its production of medical books and plow part of its profit back into equipment to produce video tapes, in the expectation of a large profit. The planning mechanism, however, could not operate at all unless the planners had the right to require the Orbis Company to produce whatever the plan called for.

Socialist economic systems, however, can operate under either economic mechanism. Soviet-type socialism combined state ownership of enterprises with central planning as the coordinating mechanism. But, in principle, state-owned enterprises could operate under the market mechanism. The manager of a state-owned Orbis Company would be appointed by and responsible to a government agency, but the company would operate very much like a privately owned company, except that the profit would go into the coffers of the state treasury instead of the pockets of private owners.

To distinguish the two kinds of socialist economic systems, the Soviet-type arrangement that combines social ownership with the planning mechanism is often called "state socialism," and the arrangement that combines social ownership with the market mechanism is called "market socialism." State socialism has been virtually universal among socialist countries, but a few countries – notably Hungary and Yugoslavia – adopted arrangements at various times that contained some of the properties of market socialism. Since the demise of state socialism, there has been a turn to market socialism as the best model of a future socialism.[6]

The performance of an economy depends on both its economic mechanism and its ownership form. It is therefore not easy to tell whether some aspect of an economy's performance – for example, whether the rate of technological innovation is high or low – should be ascribed to the ownership form, or to the economic mechanism, or to the combination of the two. One might indeed argue that one ought not try to separate them at all; that is, one should regard the rate of innovation as the joint result of the particular combination of economic mechanism and ownership form, without seeking to disentangle the influence of the one from the other.

That approach would concede, however, that there is nothing worth saying about the economic mechanism itself apart from the ownership form with which it is conjoined, or about an ownership forms apart from the economic mechanism in which it is embedded. I do not think that is so. For example, both private and social ownership endow the hired managers of large enterprises with enormous power over the use of the property they control, which creates the possibility that they may use that power to promote their own interests rather than those of the "owners." That separation of ownership from control is a potential source of inefficiency in the performance of the economic mechanism. It is important to appreciate, however, that the source of that problem lies in the ownership form and not in the economic mechanism as such.

To keep the two sets of issues apart, it is convenient to study the economic mechanism in Part IV as if there were no problems of ownership to be considered. Part V then considers how the picture changes when issues of ownership are considered: for example, when the enterprises are run by hired managers rather than directly by the owners.

7 Origin of the Economic Mechanisms

Before the Russian Revolution of 1917, all the modern economies of the time employed the market mechanism for the coordination of economic activity. Conjoined with the institution of private ownership of capital, those economies were referred to as "capitalist."

Opposition to the capitalist system generated many political movements in the nineteenth century, many of which embodied the conviction that the only way to eliminate periodic crises and poverty was to organize the society's economic mechanism not on the basis of markets, but on the basis of government planning. Planning would replace what Marxists referred to as the "anarchy of the marketplace."

Before the Russian Revolution , however, the notion of a planning mechanism was only an idea. Its superiority over the market mechanism was regarded as so self-evident, however, that few socialists devoted their efforts to examining in analytic detail how it might work. Marx himself, much of whose political life was devoted to a struggle against those socialists whom he disdained as "Utopian," counselled against building dream worlds of how a socialist society should be organized. True to his word, he devoted his own effort to the critique of capitalism, and only under the press of political necessity did he offer some judgments about how things ought to be done under a socialist system.

To someone earnestly searching for an economy suitable for a Good Society, the planning mechanism looked like a very good bet indeed. But the more hard-nosed searcher should have been cautious. If you accepted the market mechanism, you pretty well knew what you were getting, for there was ample experience around the world on how it works out under a variety of conditions. But if you accepted the planning mechanism, you were buying no more than an attractive idea, with no empirical evidence on how it might work out in practice. Unfortunately many socialists gave little thought to the asymmetry between the grim reality of market-based economies and the idealized and untested idea of a planned economy.

After the Russian Revolution, however, it was no longer necessary to juxtapose a real system against an ideal one. A decade after that revolution the Soviet leadership dismantled what was left of the market mechanism in their country and replaced it almost entirely with a planning mechanism. Following World War II many countries in Eastern Europe, Asia, and elsewhere also adopted the planning mechanism. By the advent of Mikhail Gorbachev in 1985, planning had endured for many decades in a great number of countries. Hence, unlike in your grandfather's day, if you are interested in exploring the potential of the planning mechanism for your Good Society you are no longer obliged to turn only to a world of ideas. You can observe how both markets and planning have worked in practice, and then choose that which best conforms to the values by which you judge the goodness of a society.

As in all such matters, there are many variations on these two main themes. The market mechanism works differently in the US, Sweden, Japan, and the former Yugoslavia; and the central planning mechanism worked differently in the USSR, the former German Democratic Republic (East Germany), and Bulgaria. Those variations are small, however, compared to the difference between the two mechanisms. The mechanisms are rather like biological species: each has many variations, but a terrier is no less a canine than a wolfhound.

The variations are exceedingly important in the economics of the Good Society because they demonstrate that the poor performance of the economic mechanism in one economy – such as one's own, perhaps – does not imply that the mechanism should be rejected in favor of another. One must at least be informed of the performance of other countries that use the same mechanism. For example, many Americans are prepared to reject the market mechanism because the performance of the economy fails to satisfy many of their criteria of goodness. The same Americans, however, are often enchanted with the Swedish economy, which happens to employ the same market mechanism. Much as a physical mechanism like an automobile can be driven well or badly, so an economic mechanism can be managed well or badly. It would be foolish to reject a Ford car because your friend's Ford performs badly. One needs the evidence of how Fords perform with other drivers and under different conditions. The variations among countries provide that kind of evidence in the case of economic mechanisms.

The next two chapters in Part IV describe the way in which the two mechanisms operate to coordinate economic activity. The four chapters that follow then assess the performance of the two mechanisms with respect to the criterion of efficiency. The last three chapters conclude the assessment by considering how the two mechanisms perform by other criteria of goodness such as job security and justice.

Notes

1 Nove, *An Economic History of the USSR*, pp. 69, 97.
2 Bernardo, *The Theory of Moral Incentives in Cuba*, pp. 15–22.
3 US Directorate of Intelligence, *Handbook of Economic Statistics, 1990*, table II. Consumption and output are calculated in rubles for the USSR and in dollars for the US. Since ruble prices did not reflect real costs (see chapter 18), it was customary for analysts to recalculate Soviet consumption and output in US dollars. Calculated in that way, Soviet consumption came to 48 percent of total output. The usual interpretation of the difference between the two estimates is that the Soviet consumption rate lay somewhere between 48 percent and 53 percent, depending on how it is calculated.
4 US Directorate of Intelligence, *Handbook of Economic Statistics*, table II. As in the preceding note, these numbers are calculated in each country's own prices. When recalculated in dollars, Soviet investment amounted to about 30 percent of output.
5 Stiglitz, *Whither Socialism?*, pp. 253–4.
6 Bardhan and Roemer, "Market socialism."

Chapter 13

How Markets Coordinate an Economy

There are few ways in which a man can be more innocently employed than in getting money.

– Samuel Johnson

CONTENTS

The most primitive form of a market is a physical location called a marketplace. Everyone is familiar with flea markets, or fish markets, or farmers' markets. Boston's Haymarket – once a place to which farmers delivered their hay loads, to be sold to purchasers who came there for the purpose – is now a place where food merchants bring their produce on Saturdays and sell it from pushcarts to Boston residents who come to buy because of the freshness of the foods and the good prices. More elegant, but also more nerve-racking, are the securities and commodities exchanges. The New York Stock Exchange is a marketplace where the member-stockbrokers buy and sell stocks to each other, on behalf of their client stockholders. At the Chicago Board of Trade, a typical transaction is the commitment by one party to deliver, and by another party to accept delivery of, a certain quantity of grain of a certain type for a specified price on a certain future date.

Most business transactions, however, are not conducted in such physically concentrated marketplaces. Raincoats are bought and sold in a great many shops, some near each other and some fairly scattered. To a raincoat manufacturer in St Louis, the "market" in which she sells consists of many actual (and potential) wholesale and retail businesses throughout the country, and increasingly throughout the world. To a department-store owner in Atlanta, the "market" from which she buys her raincoats is equally widespread. To a shopper for a raincoat, the "market" is the set of stores in which she customarily shops, which may be concentrated in a small area, or may cover a large area if she likes to drive and has a yen for a bargain.

A market may be thought of as a set of activities in which persons or organizations buy and sell a certain range of goods or services to each other. While all markets have certain common properties, however, there are many ways in which they differ from each other. A major distinction is that between "product markets" and "factor markets." Among product markets, in turn, there are differences between those in which the product is bought by consumers (jeans, CDs), and those in which the product is bought by producing enterprises (steel castings, tanned hides, metal cutting machines). Factor markets are those in which the three factors of production are bought and sold: labor services, capital, and land.

The main actors in the market drama are the citizens-as-workers on the one side, the citizens-as-consumers on the other side, and the enterprise managers in between. All three actors contribute to the coordination of economic activity by the ways in which they respond to the prices of goods and the wage rates of labor.

The market mechanism employs the price method for managing both the demand side and the supply side of market transactions. The household part of the story was told in Parts II and III: the demand for goods by the citizens-as-consumers is determined by the prices of the various goods, among other things; and labor supplied by the citizens-as-workers is determined by the wage rates of the various jobs, among other things. To complete the story, what needs to be explored now is the production part of the story – the supply of goods by enterprises to the product markets, and the demand for labor and other inputs that enterprises require in order to produce their output.

1   Profit and Production

The goods that the citizens-as-consumers acquire and the jobs that the citizens-as-workers perform are the end result of a great many decisions taken by the managers of the country's enterprises. In a simple labor-only economy the crucial decisions are how much output to produce, and how large a labor force to hire in order to produce it.

THE PURSUIT OF PROFIT

In choosing to produce a certain quantity of output rather than some other quantity, the manager must have some objective in mind.[1] For the purpose of formal analysis of the market mechanism, economists find it convenient to assume that the manager strives to make the largest possible profit for his enterprise – to "maximize profit," in the conventional usage. Everybody understands, however, that there are many constraints – legal, ethical, and social – that inhibit enterprises from squeezing every possible dollar of profit out of the production operation. Managers, like people generally, differ in the extent to which they abide by such restrictions. Some have a strong sense of responsibility toward their workers, customers, and community. At the other extreme are those who pursue profit with as little regard for others as they can get away with. The assertion that the enterprise seeks to earn as much profit as it can should therefore be understood to acknowledge that there are many restrictions on the actions managers may take toward that end, and that many will use all practical means to evade those restrictions when they clash with profits.

Despite the restrictions that society places on profit-making, there are people who regard any mechanism in which the driving force is profit as automatically disqualified as an arrangement suitable for a Good Society. To evaluate that point of view, it is useful to distinguish the question of who should *own* the profit, from the question of whether enterprises should concentrate on *making* profit. The question of who should own the property, and therefore the profit, in a Good Society must be deferred until Part V, but it bears recalling here that markets can be employed under conditions of either private ownership or social ownership. People who reject the profit motive out of hand usually do so because of its historical association with private property, under which the profit is owned by the capitalists. However, in a socialist society that employs the market mechanism – or "market socialism" – the profit of the enterprises would belong to all the people. The larger the profit, the more the society can spend on such public uses as health care, education, the arts, better housing, and whatever else the people desire. It should not therefore be puzzling that the pursuit of profit is an acceptable objective of market-economy enterprises in socialist as well in capitalist versions of a Good Society, although some people will forever deny that a profit-oriented economic arrangement can have any claim to goodness under any economic system.

In order to detach the concept of profit from its usual association with capitalism, in the discussion to follow I shall have in mind the more neutral context of a market-socialist economy in which enterprises are predominantly socially owned. The analysis would be essentially the same in most respects for a capitalist economy in which private ownership predominated.

Economizing on Labor

The enterprise's profit depends, among other things, on the wages it pays out to its workers to produce the goods, the sales of which constitute its revenue. It therefore behooves a Hungarian socialist manager, no less than a German capitalist manager, to be concerned that every forint or mark spent on hiring labor must be justified in terms of the profit that it will produce.[2] That means that the manager will seek to economize on the use of labor: whatever the quantity of output produced, it should be produced with the smallest possible use of labor.

The notion that managers should use as little labor as possible does not offhand seem to be a prescription for a very Good Society. In countries that suffer from extensive unemployment, for example, it might be a better society if managers violated that rule by hiring unemployed workers whom they did not actually need. We shall later take up the momentous issue of unemployment, but for the present the matter of labor allocation is best discussed separately from that of unemployment. It is therefore useful to proceed with the assumption that labor is fully employed in a Good Society, and that the central task is to assure that it is distributed among jobs in such a way that the people derive the largest possible output from their labor services. From that perspective, the manager who employs workers whom he does not need is depriving the people of some goods that could be produced if those workers were more productively employed in other enterprises. The managers should regard the people's labor as a valuable resource, to be used as sparingly as possible in their enterprise's production activities.

That does not mean that in a Good Society workers should be dismissed the instant that the production need for them disappears, as might happen, for example, as a result of a labor-saving technological innovation. The citizens might well decide that their collective interests as workers outweigh their collective interests as consumers, and they might indeed be willing to give up a great deal of production for the sake of an arrangement in which no workers would ever be dismissed because of a technological change. There are other possible arrangements, however, in which workers displaced by new technology are retrained and transferred, in a humane way, to new employments, possibly in different enterprises.

The citizens would then enjoy a larger level of consumption than they would if no workers were ever dismissed.

A more precise formulation would therefore be that, in the pursuit of profit, the manager seeks to economize on labor in all ways consistent with the laws and customs of the society. The employment experience of the citizen-as-worker can therefore vary greatly from society to society in accordance with the values embodied in each society's laws and customs.

2 Output and Profit

Over the long run the size of an enterprise's profit depends on such activities as the introduction of new products, the implementation of cost-reducing production techniques, and the expansion of output through investment in new plant and equipment. The nature of the coordination process, however, can be most clearly seen in the day-to-day business of managing an enterprise that produces an established good or service with the plant and equipment that are currently in place. The critical decision in this short-run activity is choosing the quantity of output that yields the largest volume of profit. That, from the individual firm's perspective, is the optimal output.

THE PROFIT PEAK

Profit is the difference between the total revenue received from the sale of the enterprise's output, and the total cost of producing that output. Managers have different ways of figuring out what their most profitable output level is, ranging from elaborate market-research studies and cost analyses in large companies, to seat-of-the-pants judgments in small businesses. They all boil down, however, to what may be envisioned as a table listing various levels of output in the first column, and the profit that each output would yield in the second. The estimated profit for each level of output is based on the price at which the enterprise expects to sell that output, and the wage rates and other prices it expects to pay for the inputs needed to produce it. Normally there is one output level in the table at which the corresponding profit is the largest. Suppose the profit-maximizing output for a certain bakery is 1,000 loaves of bread per day. That must mean that if the company produces more than that – say 1,100 loaves – its profit will be no larger and possibly smaller, and similarly if it produces less than that. To put the case more generally, let the expression "marginal profit" refer to the amount by which profit changes when the level of output changes by a small amount. Then the test of whether an enterprise is producing the output at which its profit is at its peak level is that its marginal profit must be zero. It follows further that if the marginal profit is larger than zero, the company is not at its profit peak: it can increase its profit by increasing its output.

The analogy to a mountain peak is instructive. As a climber ascends the mountain, each step carries her a bit higher. As she nears the top, the gain in altitude from each "marginal" step gets smaller and smaller. Finally, when she reaches the area at the peak, she is on level ground. No additional "marginal step" would carry her any higher – there is no place higher to go. That, indeed, is the analytic definition of the mountain peak – the place at which a small further step is purely horizontal. In like fashion, when an enterprise's output is at the peak of its profit mountain, the marginal profit is zero (or negative) – there is no higher-profit place to go.

The discovery that marginal profit is zero when profit is at its peak is unlikely to send the reader into a seizure of analytic ecstasy. It is nevertheless a fact of vast significance in the economics of the Good Society. It is important not only because it is an integral feature of the coordination process of the market mechanism, but also because it underlies the claim for the efficiency of that mechanism, which will be put forth in chapter 15. It is important as well, however, in understanding how the market coordination process works.

3 Coordination: Consumer-goods Markets

There are two sets of actors in a goods market: consumers on the demand side, and enterprises on the supply side. Each is motivated by a particular objective: consumers wish to get the most for their money, and enterprises wish to make as much profit as they can. The attainment of each one's objective depends on a variety of factors, prominent among which are the prices of things; and when prices change, the actors adjust their economic activities in response. It is the responsiveness of prices, and of the actors to prices, that drives the coordination process of the market mechanism.

On the supply side of a consumer-goods market like bread are the bakery enterprises, each of which consults its own profit table and decides for itself what output will yield the largest profit. Each bakery's profit estimates are based, among other things, on the price at which they expect a loaf of bread to sell. The total quantity of bread delivered to the market each day reflects, among other things, the accuracy of the price- and wage-rate estimates that underlie the calculations in the profit tables.

On the demand side of the market are the consumers, each of whom divides his purchases between bread and other things like blue jeans and CDs. The total quantity of bread purchased in the market reflects the prices of bread and other things, as well as the preferences and incomes of the consumers.

Hence, the price of bread enters prominently into the decisions of both producers and consumers of bread.

Since each bakery makes its output decision in ignorance of how much the other bakeries plan to produce, in the absence of adequate coordination they might produce much more in the aggregate, or much less, than the consumers in the aggregate wish to buy. The function of the coordination mechanism is to minimize such excesses or shortages.

DISTURBANCES

The operation of the mechanism can be seen most clearly in the way in which the market responds to changes in prices. Suppose, at the outset, that the market happens to be coordinated: the quantity of bread that the producers are delivering happens to be the same as that which the consumers are purchasing. The market is said to be in "equilibrium" and the existing average price – say $2 per loaf – will prevail week after week. In long-established markets that is normally the case: the amounts produced and consumed and the price remain substantially stable.

From time to time, however, well-coordinated markets of that sort are subjected to "disturbances" of various kinds. A popular new health diet stressing the virtues of non-fat carbohydrates may cause the demand for bread to rise. On the supply side, the spread of a pest that attacks bread grains may cause world grain production to fall, with a corresponding decline in the supply of bread. In consequence of such disturbances the previously coordinated market is no longer coordinated: it is in "disequilibrium." It is in the way that the market responds to disequilibrium that one can see the coordinating process in action.

A disturbance affects the market by increasing or decreasing either the supply or the demand for a good. The adjustment process is similar in all four cases, and may be illustrated in the case of one of them – a disturbance that causes an increase in the demand for bread.

Suppose the market for bread is initially in equilibrium: the average price is $2 a loaf, and 300,000 loaves are produced and consumed per week. The effect of the disturbance is that some consumers now drop one or two more loaves of bread into their shopping basket than they did before. If sufficient bread were available, they might in aggregate consume 400,000 loaves per week instead of the 300,000 they consumed before. But the bakeries continue to supply the 300,000 loaves that had been optimal in the past.

The initial effect of the disturbance takes the form of an "excess demand" of 100,000 loaves, or what is commonly called "shortage." Some purchasers – individuals, food markets, and wholesalers – experience the advent of shortage by finding that bread is sold out before they are able to obtain the quantities they wish to buy. Some anxious consumers and wholesale distributors may come to market earlier the next day to be sure to get their supplies, but if the shortage persists, some purchasers will still be unable to buy enough to satisfy their needs or those of their customers. The bakeries experience the onset of shortage in the more rapid sellout of the output they had formerly produced and in the increase in orders from the shops and wholesalers.

In the absence of an effective coordination mechanism, that condition of shortage could continue for a very long time, to the great distress of consumers. People who have lived under such conditions for protracted periods are aware of the enormous inconvenience of not knowing whether the bread or meat that had been planned for dinner will be available that day, or of the long wait in queues to buy the goods before they are all sold out.

The market mechanism does not shield the economy entirely from such disturbances. Its virtue is rather that when the disturbances do occur, certain forces are triggered that serve to eliminate the incipient shortage and restore balance to the market. The following is a stylized account of the coordination process; in practice the forces are sometimes quite sluggish and operate somewhat differently in different markets.

Price response   The first response of a market to the experience of shortage is that the price begins to rise. The forces that generate the upward pressure on prices vary from market to market. On the supply side, under normal conditions competition limits the price each bakery would dare to charge, for fear of losing customers to the others. Under conditions of shortage, however, they have less concern about being undersold by their competitors. Some therefore take the risk of raising the price, and others promptly follow suit.

On the demand side, some purchasers of bread suffer from the shortage more than others. The livelihood of the restaurants, for example, depends on their ability to provide the fresh bread and other menu items to their diners. They are therefore likely to object less to a price increase, and may indeed offer to pay a higher price, rather than risk missing out on the limited supply.

In these and other ways, the onset of shortage sooner or later translates into an increase in the price of bread to a higher level than the initial $2 a loaf – say a 5 percent increase to $2.10. The price increase, in turn, generates responses on both the supply and the demand sides.

A price response is critical to the operation of the market mechanism. Societies sometimes decide to freeze prices so that they are unable to change in ways that would reflect the onset of shortage. When that occurs, the coordination process fails to operate. The persistence of shortage in that case should be regarded not as a deficiency of the market mechanism but of the restriction that prevents it from working.

Producers' response   The first response of the bakeries to an increase in price is to revise their profit-table calculations. Suppose the profit of the Sourdough Bakery had formerly peaked at an output of 1,000 loaves a day. The marginal profit was therefore zero at that output level; this means that if it produced one additional loaf of bread, its revenue would increase by $2, but its cost would also increase by $2. The effect of the price increase is that if it produced one additional loaf its revenue would now increase by $2.10, but its cost would be the same as before – $2. The marginal profit at the original output of 1,000 loaves is therefore no longer zero but $0.10. At the new price, profit no longer peaks at the old output of 1,000 loaves. The bakery metaphorically recalculates its profit table and finds that at the new price its profit peaks at a larger output level – say 1,100 loaves. It therefore responds to the price increase by increasing its output by 100 loaves.

Consumers' response   The price rise causes the consumers in the aggregate to moderate their demand for bread when the price is higher. To be sure, not all consumers respond in that way. Some consume the same amount of bread at the higher price as they did at $2, either because they are too affluent to notice so small an expenditure, or because they cannot imagine a meal without the two slices of bread they now regard as exceptionally healthful. At the other extreme are consumers who stop buying a good entirely if the price rises a bit – although there are unlikely to be many such people in the case of bread. Most consumers, however, belong to neither of those extremes but trim their expenditures on bread to some degree when the price is higher. They are the "marginal" consumers, and it is their response that drives the demand side of the coordination mechanism. That response is to reduce the quantity of bread that they will buy at the new higher price.[3]

The market response   The two sets of actors in the consumer-goods market therefore respond to the price increase in opposite ways. As a result of the producers' responses, the total quantity of bread delivered to the market is larger than before the disturbance: production rises from 300,000 loaves to perhaps 350,000. And as a result of consumers' responses the quantity that they will buy declines – from 400,000 loaves to perhaps 380,000. Therefore the magnitude of the shortage – the excess-demand gap – induced by the disturbance is reduced to 30,000 loaves. Since demand continues to be in excess, however, the adjustment process continues, and keeps continuing until the excess demand finally vanishes and the market is once again fully coordinated. At the new equilibrium the price is higher than before the disturbance – perhaps $2.30 a loaf – and the quantity produced and consumed is larger than before – perhaps 360,000 loaves.

The market mechanism's adjustment process takes time, so that in any particular week many markets must be expected to be in disequilibrium. The case for the market mechanism as the coordinating arrangement in a Good Society therefore is not that it keeps markets rigidly in equilibrium, but that when disturbances do occur, they trigger responses that move the markets toward a new equilibrium.

The metaphor often used is that of a constant-temperature thermostat. Under normal conditions heat is supplied to a room at the same rate per hour as it is consumed. The temperature therefore remains steady and the heating system is said to be in equilibrium. If there is a disturbance to the system – say a door has been left open – the equilibrium is upset: "demand" for heat exceeds the "supply" and the temperature begins to fall. The state of disequilibrium triggers off the thermostat, however, which signals the heating system to supply more heat until the desired temperature is restored. At the new equilibrium, more heat is supplied and consumed per hour than before the disturbance, but the rates of supply and consumption are once again the same and a constant temperature is maintained.

It is therefore no serious criticism to point out that market economies often experience under- or over-production of one thing or another, which is then followed by shortages or by surpluses that have to be disposed of at discounted prices in "sales." Under- and over-production of individual goods are the market mechanism's way of informing enterprises and consumers that they must adjust; they are as necessary to the economic adjustment process as a drop in temperature is to the thermostatic adjustment process.

It would be a valid criticism, however, if the swings were very large or if adjustment took a long time, just as a thermostat would be rejected if it required the room temperature to fall to 40 degrees before the heating system kicked in, or if it took hours before the temperature increased to normal. These are matters that will be considered in the discussion in chapter 17 of the market mechanism as it operates in practice.

4 Coordination: Labor Markets

The two actors in labor markets are the citizens-as-workers on the supply side, and the producing enterprises on the demand side. As in the case of product markets, the motivation of the enterprise is to make as much profit as possible. It is in pursuit of that profit that it establishes jobs for which it employs workers. The motivation of the workers is to get the best possible job from among those for which they qualify. A number of considerations enter into enterprise decisions on how many workers to employ and into worker decisions on which jobs to take, but both sides assign a prominent role to wage rates. It is the responsiveness of wage rates to economic conditions, and of the actors on both sides to wage rates, that drives the coordination process in labor markets – much as prices drive the process in product markets.

The coordination process is best examined as before by the way in which the market responds to a disturbance. Suppose the wage rate in the bakery labor market is $20 an hour and 4,000 workers are employed. The market is in equilibrium in the sense that the bakeries have all hired the number of workers they need at that wage rate, and no worker who seeks a bakery job at that wage rate fails to find one. Suppose now that a national military buildup creates many more defense production jobs that some bakery workers find more attractive. The number of workers in bakery jobs therefore declines – to perhaps 3,500. The initial effect of the disturbance is therefore a labor shortage in the bakery labor market.

Wage-rate response   The onset of shortage generates forces that cause the wage rate to rise. As in the case of product markets, the way in which that occurs varies greatly from market to market. Some of the bakeries, for example, may offer higher wage rates in order to pirate some workers from other companies. Other companies then match or raise the offers in order to maintain their own labor force. On the supply side, the more confident workers may press a higher wage rate on their employers as a condition of staying on the job. Because of forces of these sorts, a labor shortage cannot long endure without finding expression in an increase in the wage rate.

Producers' response   Labor markets differ from consumer-goods markets in one important respect. In all modern societies, good or bad, most labor is a means to an end, and the end is the production of final products like bread. There is a demand for the labor of bakers because people wish to consume bread. The demand for labor is therefore said to be a "derived demand": derived, that is, from the demand for the good, the production of which requires that labor.

The demand for labor originates in the same profit tables that underlie the bakeries' calculations of the bread output at which profit is at its peak. For the Sourdough Bakery, suppose that output is again 1,000 loaves per day. That output decision determines the employment decision; the production of 1,000 loaves requires a certain number of workers – say 30.

The effect of a rise in the wage rate, however, is that 1,000 loaves is no longer the profit-maximizing output because the marginal profit at that output is no longer zero. Before the disturbance, for example, the revenue from the sale of an additional 100 loaves was no larger than the cost of producing them. Now that wages have risen, however, the cost of producing an additional 100 loaves is higher than the revenue received from selling them. The bakery is therefore losing money, so to speak, on the last 100 loaves. Its profit would be larger if it reduced output from 1,000 to perhaps 900 loaves. That output, however, does not require the 30 workers needed before, and the bakery therefore reduces its employment, from 30 to perhaps 28 or 27 workers.

As all bakeries respond in this manner to the increase in the wage rate, the total number of workers they wish to hire falls below the original level of 4,000.

Workers' response   If the wage rate remained at $20, only 3,500 workers would take up the bakery jobs. The higher wage, however, serves to attract some additional workers to the bakery jobs.

Workers in one labor market differ in their responsiveness to an increase in the wage rate in other labor markets. At one extreme are some workers who would not accept a bakery job at any wage. At the other extreme are workers who are on the margin, in the sense that a relatively small increase in bakery wage rates would attract them away from their present employment into bakery work. It is the marginal workers who, like the marginal consumers, provide the mobility that makes the market mechanism work. The worker response to the rise in the wage rate is therefore an increase in the number of workers seeking jobs in the bakeries – from the low point of 3,500 in the wake of the disturbance.

Market response   The two sets of actors in the labor-market drama therefore respond to the wage-rate increase in opposite ways. The enterprises tend to reduce their demand for labor and the workers tend to supply more labor. The magnitude of the excess demand for labor caused by the disturbance therefore diminishes. As long as some degree of excess demand remains, however, the adjustment process continues until the excess vanishes. The new equilibrium wage rate at which that occurs is higher than before the disturbance – it may have risen from $20 to $25 an hour – and the number of workers employed in bakeries falls from 4,000 to a new equilibrium employment of perhaps 3,800.

5   Interdependence among Markets

The economic system is so intricate a web of interrelationships that the adjustment process in one market generates new ripples of adjustment in other markets. One set of interrelationships is that between goods markets and labor markets. In the examples given above, an increase in the demand for bread affects employment in the bakery labor market, and a decrease in the supply of bakery labor affects the production of bread.

A second set of interrelationships involves spillovers among goods markets and among labor markets. An increase in the demand for bread, for example, is likely to be accompanied by an increase in the demand for, and therefore the production of, goods like butter, margarine, and other foods that are normally "complements" to bread consumption. It would also cause the production of "substitutes" for bread to decline: potatoes, for instance. Similarly the workers who leave their bakery jobs spill over into other labor markets. The initial disturbance therefore sets off a chain of adjustments in markets other than those directly affected. A third set of interrelationships involves markets for intermediate products. An increase in the demand for bread leads to an increase in the demand for flour, sugar, packaging, energy, and all other materials used in bread production. Those markets are therefore also thrown out of equilibrium by the initial disturbance in the bread market. But flour, sugar, and packaging also require inputs from other markets, and the other markets require inputs from yet other markets, and so on. All the markets affected by the spillover from the original disturbance must undergo an adjustment process of their own, and the adjustment in each market becomes a disturbance to another market, though the magnitude of the successive disturbances fortunately diminishes with the distance from the original disturbance.

The merit of the market mechanism is not only that it restores individual markets to equilibrium when they are subjected to disturbances, but that it takes account of the exceedingly complex interdependence among markets and moves the economy toward "general equilibrium" in all markets. That alone makes it a serious candidate as the economic mechanism of a Good Society.

6   Discussion

The expression "response to disturbances" has a rather aseptic tone, but it alludes to a lively social process that I find to be quite remarkable. A recent instance that still amazes me is the explosive growth of video–cassette rental shops. Only a decade or so ago there were no such goods or shops. Then came the disturbance, in the form of the innovation of an inexpensive home video–cassette player. Immediately afterward the first video rental shops appeared, usually small, lightly stocked, and tentative. Soon afterward others opened up, increasingly in the same town in which some had come before. They became larger, brighter, and eventually as omnipresent as your favorite pizza parlor or hamburger shop. Many a barber shop and stationary store had to give up their quarters under the onslaught. Judging from the numbers of customers I see browsing and renting each evening, a lot of people are getting a great deal of consumer satisfaction from this powerful market response.

I still find it awesome that such a remarkable transformation of the economic landscape can come about without any central coordination of the millions of economic acts that must have been involved. And that is but one of the vast number of responses to disturbances that occur incessantly in a market economy.

Anyone contemplating a Good Society must be impressed with the market mechanism's powers of coordination. But that of course is only the beginning of the investigation. To say that an economic mechanism succeeds in coordinating an economy is not to say that it does it well, any more than to say that a hospital treats many patients is to say that it treats them well. A well-coordinated economy could also be a miserable place in which to live. The question of how well the economic mechanisms satisfy the criteria of goodness is the subject of the rest of Part IV.

But first, one must examine how economic activity is coordinated under the planning mechanism, to which the next chapter is devoted.

Notes

1   The analysis here assumes that there is only one way of producing a product. In practice, there are ordinarily many different techniques that could be used. Some parts can be built out of aluminum or plastic or other materials; the product can be produced with a lot of hand labor and little machinery, or with a lot of machinery and little labor; and so forth. Deciding *how* to produce a product is as important as deciding *how much* of it to produce, and a full assessment of the economic mechanism would require analysis of both types of decisions.

 The main lessons for the Good Society can be learned by concentrating on the output decision, however. Hence I have simplified the analysis by dealing only with the case of a single production technique. Any standard textbook of economics can be consulted for a more extended analysis of the choice among production techniques.

2 The same may be said about all other production inputs – materials, fuel, equipment – but in the labor-only economy with which we are concerned, variations in output are assumed to depend only on variations in labor.

3 If the marginal consumers cut their purchases of bread sharply in response to a price rise, the demand is said to be "elastic": the response to the price increase will be a large drop in purchases. If they cut their purchases by very little, the demand is "inelastic."

Chapter 14

How Planning Coordinates an Economy

Make no little plans; they have no magic
to stir the blood.
— *Daniel Hudson Burnham*

CONTENTS

Central planning as an economic mechanism must not be confused with organizational planning. Universities, sports clubs, and other organizations in every country plan for their future and take various actions to implement their plans. All governments also do some kind of planning. The 700-page Budget of the United States Government is a plan. The Japanese government has a plan in which some industries are targeted for expansion, and various governmental measures are undertaken in order to implement that plan. When a government purchases weapons or typewriters from industry in accordance with its military or regulatory planning, it might be said that the government is indirectly planning the production of those enterprises.

Unfortunately the distinction between organizational planning of these sorts and central economic planning is often missed. It is sometimes asserted, for example, that in practice, the difference between central planning and markets is merely one of degree. Business organizations in market economies engage in planning no less than the government of the USSR, it is said, and all capitalist governments are heavily involved in the regulation of industry. Therefore all modern economies are really planned economies to some degree; the USSR and China simply plan more of their economy than Japan or the United States.

In the same vein, I have heard Soviet observers assert that both the American and the Soviet economies were fundamentally planned economies; as they saw it, the essential difference was that the Americans were better planners. They concluded that the way to improve the performance of the Soviet economy was not to abandon planning for markets but to learn the tricks that the best capitalist countries use in their more successful planning. That viewpoint served for a long time as a defense of central planning against the radical minority who held that only by abandoning central planning for markets could the country hope to match the economic performance of the capitalist world.

That way of thinking reflects a dangerous confusion between organizational planning and planning as an economic mechanism. It is true that when the United States government places an order for weapons with the General Motors Corporation, it is directing the production of that company into military items, much as the Soviet government directed the Saratov Tank Factory to produce certain specified weapons. In the United States, however, once the order is placed, the responsibility for getting the weapons produced falls entirely upon General Motors. The company must contract for its labor and supplies, and it engages other companies as its own subcontractors. Its inputs are therefore supplied entirely through markets. In contrast, when the Soviet government placed its weapons order with the Saratov enterprise, it also undertook to provide that enterprise with the materials, labor, energy, and other supplies needed to produce the weapons. That is what is "central" about central economic planning: the complex flow of materials and supplies *among* all enterprises is planned and managed by the government.[1] Under the market mechanism, in contrast, enterprises buy from and sell to each other directly, through market transactions, not by instruction from government officials.

The government does play an important part in all market economies as well, which is why they are properly designated as "mixed economies" or "mixed-market economies." The role of government in a market economy, however, large though it may be, is radically different from that in a centrally planned economy, where the entire sphere of inter-enterprise transactions is organized and managed by the government. However large the extent of organizational planning, no market-economy country undertakes to manage the flow of transactions among all its enterprises in the manner of the centrally planned economies.

1   The Tasks of Central Planning

The central planning bureau is the agency that assists the government in making its decisions regarding the composition of the country's output. The focus of the government's interest is that set of final products that constitute the gross domestic product; it is the government that must decide how much of the country's output should be devoted to consumption, how much to investment, and how much to the civilian and military needs of government. When that essentially political decision is taken, it becomes the planners' responsibility to direct the country's economic activity toward the attainment of those political-economic goals.

There are three related tasks that the planners must perform. The first relates to final products. Enterprises that produce consumer goods, weapons, and the like must be assigned output plans that provide for the production of the quantities of those goods that the government wishes to have produced. Provision must also be made for the distribution of those goods to the consumers, enterprises, and government agencies that will use them.

The second task relates to intermediate products. The coal production plan, for example, must be large enough to enable all coal-using enterprises to meet their production plans. Every producing enterprise must also be told when and how much of its output to ship to each user, and each user must be told which producers are responsible for providing the inputs they require to meet their production plans.

The third relates to the primary factors of production. The country's labor, capital, and land must be allocated among all enterprises in the quantities required for the fulfillment of their production plans.

The responsibility of the central planners is to achieve consistency in carrying out those three sets of tasks. Consistency with respect to output means that sufficient labor and other inputs are available to produce the planned output. Consistency with respect to labor means that the labor requirements laid out in all the preliminary plans do not exceed the number of available workers. Consistency with respect to intermediate products requires that the total output planned by all producers of a product – like coal – is no less than the total requirements of coal of all planned users of coal.

Under the market mechanism, there is one basic coordination procedure, in which the price method operates on both the supply and the demand side of all markets. Under the planning mechanism, however, there are two fundamentally different coordination procedures. Transactions that involve households – the demand for consumer goods and the supply of labor – are coordinated by a mix of the price method and the assignment method. It is only in the case of goods like intermediate products, such as rubber and chemicals, that the pure planning mechanism operates: that is, the assignment method is used on both the supply and demand sides. An account of the coordination procedure under the planning mechanism must therefore deal not only with consumer goods and labor, but with intermediate products as well.[2]

2 Enterprise Output

The senior managerial official in a market economy is the chief executive officer. The CEO of Worldwide Shipping Inc., operating under the supervision of a board of directors, sets the policy of the company and decides what cargoes are to be carried, what rates are to be charged, what ports to call at and what sailing schedules to follow. Captains are hired to command the ships and to follow the instructions of the home office.

A senior managerial official in a planned economy is often thought to be the equivalent of a corporation CEO, but the equivalence is illusory. He is more like the captain of one of Worldwide's ships: he is in full command of the ship and its crew, but he takes his orders from the home office. In the Soviet case the "home office" is an agency of the government that is called the ministry. The minister, in turn, takes his orders from the central government and its planning bureau. There are no genuine CEOs in a planned economy, unless they be the central planning bureau, which may perhaps be regarded as a collective CEO of the entire economy viewed as a single mammoth enterprise.

The manager-captain of the planned-economy enterprise is told by the government and the planners what goods to produce, to whom to deliver his output, what prices to charge, and what wage rates to pay. He is hired to run the enterprise, and its performance depends greatly on his ability, but he does not make such major policy decisions as how much to produce and what price to charge.

Under both economic mechanisms, the major decisions are made on the basis of a body of knowledge possessed by the enterprise personnel regarding production conditions within their own enterprises. The core of that knowledge consists of the various production techniques (e.g. welding or riveting, automated or manual, etc.) with which a given level of output can be produced, and the quantities of labor and other inputs that are required under each technique. The mechanisms differ, however, in the way in which that knowledge enters into economic decisions. The market-economy manager uses that knowledge directly in deciding how much output the enterprise should produce and which technique should be used. The planned-economy manager, however, converts that knowledge into information that is then tucked into an envelope or typed into a computer and sent off to the central planners. The planners use the information for formulating the national plan, which eventually takes the form of instructions to the manager on how much he should produce and how much labor he is authorized to use for that purpose.

Proponents of planning regard the centralization of production and employment decisions as one of its great advantages over the market mechanism. The argument runs as follows.

In a market economy each enterprise makes its production and employment decisions in ignorance of what of other enterprises are intending to do. A lumber mill that decides to expand production, for example, cannot know that other mills may be about to do the same thing, or that the demand for lumber is likely to fall because some large builders are planning to cut back on construction, or that the supply of logs is likely to fall because the timber companies are having difficulty recruiting labor. It is inevitable that when individual production decisions are made with so limited a range of vision, some things will be over-produced and some will be underproduced, disproportions that the market mechanism is forever having to correct after they have occurred. They need not occur at all, however, if there is some central agent that knows in advance what all enterprises are intending to do, and can therefore prevent the disproportions from occurring in the first place. The central planners are that agent. They know the production intentions of all enterprises because they determine what those intentions are. The appeal of the planning mechanism is that it can avoid the waste of resources that is inevitable under the myopic conditions of the marketplace.

3 The Planning Mechanism

The planning mechanism can be described with greater assurance than the market mechanism. One cannot "see" the market mechanism: its properties must be distilled from the differing experiences of a variety of countries, and observers can differ in their interpretation of what it is and how it operates. The planning mechanism, on the other hand, has been committed to paper, in the form of manuals of instruction on how plans are to be made. One doesn't have to infer how the mechanism operates from observation of the actions of the participants: it is all there on paper, in the manuals.

It is rather like the difference between describing "how corporations are managed," and describing how the Superior Electronics Corporation is managed. Nobody can tell you what "corporations" do; you have to infer that from the experience of corporations generally. The people at Superior Electronics, however, can tell you exactly what they do. In that respect a centrally planned economy is rather like a mammoth single national enterprise. Like the managers at Superior, the central planners can tell you what they do, and they do indeed tell it in the planning manuals.

The planning procedures of the various planned economies, as they are set forth in the planning manuals, differed from each other in various ways, much as the market mechanism operates differently in the countries in which it is employed. The degree of variation was rather less than in market economies, however, because of the towering influence of the Soviet Union on the leaders of other Communist countries. The following account is therefore based on Soviet central planning as it was practiced in the last decade of the Soviet Union, but it may be thought of more generally as the way in which planning was conducted in virtually all of the Communist countries.

The description presented below is taken from an important planning manual that was issued by the USSR State Planning Commission in 1974, as well as from other Soviet and foreign sources.[3] The manual contains detailed instructions to all persons involved in the planning process on how to prepare their portions of the national plan. I have extracted those instructions that apply to the planning of consumer goods, intermediate products, and labor.

It should not be thought that planning was in fact conducted precisely as the manuals specify, any more than the management of a corporation is conducted precisely in accordance with its organization charts. The picture presented below should be seen as one of how planning is supposed to happen, not of how it happens in practice. Chapters 17 and 18 will consider how both mechanisms actually operate under the conditions that prevail in real economies.

4 Plan-making

The construction of an annual plan begins with the issuance of a set of so-called "control figures," which are prepared by the central planners as a way of launching the planning process.[4] The control figures are a set of output targets that represent the planners' initial estimates of what a coordinated plan for the forthcoming year – say 1981 – might look like. They rely heavily on forecasts of what the economy will have succeeded in producing in the course of the present year, 1980. The control figures for the 1981 plan make use of those forecasts, but they are modified on the basis of the country's experience under the current plan – for example, which plans are likely to be fulfilled by the end of 1980 and which are not. The planners also take account of various expected changes in the next year's economic conditions, such as newly built factories that will start operation in 1981, changes in the government's priorities on such outputs as housing, defense, and new investment, and changes in the size and composition of the labor force. The latter are of particular importance because one of the major objectives is to set the production targets in the control figures high enough to provide full employment for the labor force. For this purpose the central planners rely on the regional planning agencies' estimates of next year's labor supply.

When the control figures have been approved by the Party and government, they are disaggregated to the level of the ministries that supervise the enterprises, and are eventually broken down into individual control figures for each enterprise. The enterprise uses the control figures given by the ministry as the basis on which to construct its detailed preliminary plan.

THE PRELIMINARY PLAN

The preliminary plan is a document that covers virtually all aspects of the enterprise's activities. One section is the production plan, which specifies the quantities of each type of product that the enterprise proposes to produce during the plan year. Another is the labor plan, which specifies the quantities of each type of labor required to meet the targets of the production plan. A third is the supply plan, which lists all intermediate products such as materials and fuel that will be required in the course of the year.

The production plan is based on the output targets assigned to the enterprise in its control figures. The Kolomensk Farm Machinery Company, for example, may be assigned a control figure of 1,000 harrows. The enterprise's planning department then prepares a 1,000-harrow production plan by calculating the labor requirements and other inputs required to produce that output.

The input norm   Input requirements are calculated by means of set of "input norms," or what economists call "input coefficients." An important input norm is the "labor norm," which specifies the quantity of labor required to produce a unit of output.[5] In the Kolomensk plant, for example, the labor norm for a Class IV machinist may be 6.0 hours of labor to produce one Harrow Model H25X. If the production plan is 1,000 harrows, the labor requirement is then 6,000 hours of Class IV machinist labor – or 3 man-years when the work year is 2,000 hours. In that manner the full list of requirements for each class of labor is set forth in the preliminary labor plan.

Similarly, a materials norm specifies the quantity of materials that are required to produce a unit of output and that must be obtained from other enterprises. The Harrow Model H25X may require 1.2 tons of 20-gauge grade-3 steel sheet, 8 Standard-12.4K ball bearings, and so on. By multiplying these materials norms by the 1,000-harrow output target, the production staff develops the full list of materials requirements that are specified in its preliminary supply plan.

Balancing the plan   When the preliminary plan is completed, the enterprise transmits it to its ministry, with a copy to the regional office of the central planning bureau. The ministries consolidate the plans of all their enterprises to form their own plans, which are then transmitted to the central planning bureau. In that way the central planning bureau comes into possession of the preliminary plans of all the economic ministries, while its regional planning offices possess the preliminary plans of all the enterprises in their regions.

The planning bureau begins the coordinating process by drawing up a set of planning tables called "material balances," one for each of the major products in the economy. A material-balance table consists of two columns, one tallying up the total output of a certain product as specified in the preliminary production plans, and the other tallying up the total requirements for that product as specified in the preliminary supply plans. In the language of markets, the tables present the proposed quantity to be supplied and the proposed quantity demanded of each product. The adjective "material" means that the tables are drawn up in physical units like tons or yards, rather than value units like rubles; that is to say, it is the tons of coal and not the rubles' worth of coal with which planning is primarily concerned.

Material balances deal with total national supply and demand, and are drawn up on an economy-wide basis by the central planning bureau.[6] Similarly "balances of labor resources" are drawn up for the country as a whole. These balances list in one column an estimate of the number of workers of each kind in next year's labor force, and in the other column the number of workers of each kind requested in the enterprises' preliminary plans. However, since jobs must be filled by locally available labor, labor balances are also drawn up by all the regional planning bureaus for their own regions.

When preparing their preliminary plans, managers take account only of their own enterprise's circumstances. They are therefore ignorant of the output plans of their suppliers, of the labor requirements of other enterprises in the region, and of the labor supply in the region. It is therefore to be expected that, on the first cut, the preliminary planning tables do not balance; the aggregate quantities demanded may exceed or may fall short of the aggregate quantities supplied. It is at this point that the planners earn their salaries. Their crucial responsibility is to "balance the plan"; that is, to coordinate the enterprises' labor and materials requirements with the corresponding supply.

5   Central Planning of Labor

Early in the planning year (1980), the central planners receive from their regional offices a set of estimates of the numbers of workers expected to be available for work in the forthcoming year (1981) for which a plan is to be made. The supply of labor consists primarily of employed workers, most of whom remain with their enterprises year after year, and often for a lifetime. The supply is reduced each year by such factors as retirements and illnesses, and is augmented each year by new entrants consisting primarily of graduates of educational institutions.

Labor planning is closely integrated with education planning. There is a large network of vocational and technical schools that are operated by enterprises and ministries for the purpose of training young people for jobs in their industries. The schools are closely connected to the local enterprises, and the curriculum often includes practical work in the enterprises in which the students are likely to be employed after graduation. Thus, most students in the Kiev Farm Machinery Technical School will get their first jobs in a local farm machinery company, where they have probably done some practical work in the course of their schooling.

As part of the education-planning system, technical-school admissions are governed by forecasts of future labor requirements implicit in long-term production plan projections. The number of new openings in the technical schools of the public catering industry, for example, is based on projections of the future need for young workers in factory canteens, in town cafeterias, and so forth. There is inevitably a margin of error between such forecasts and the actual requirements several years later when the students are graduated, but education planning helps to keep the flow of new entrants roughly in line with each year's new occupational requirements. Graduates of these schools are under obligation to work for two years after graduation in the enterprises of the sponsoring industry.

General secondary schools are operated not by production organizations but by the Ministry of Education. Their purpose is to prepare students for higher education. Admissions to higher-education institutions are also based on forecasts of the future national requirements for chemical engineers, mathematicians, economists, literary scholars, and so forth, and the number of students admitted is much smaller than the number of secondary-school graduates. Many of the latter therefore proceed directly into the labor force after graduation. Graduates of higher-education institutions are under obligation to accept a three-year assignment in whatever enterprise the planning authorities designate. Most such assignments are in local enterprises, but some are in other regions, sometimes quite remote. The authority to assign engineers and other trained specialists to jobs outside their regions of residence further facilitates the balancing of the supply of labor with regional labor requirements.

On the basis of estimates of the inflow of new graduates as well as other sources of new labor, the regional planning offices estimate the number of new workers expected to be available for jobs in the forthcoming year. Their estimates are submitted to the central planners, who then aggregate the regional estimates into a national account of the labor that will be available during the plan year. Labor is classified into a number of large categories, such as unskilled, skilled, technicians, and so forth. These numbers constitute the supply side of the planning tool – the national balance of labor resources.

The demand side of the labor balance comes from the ministries' preliminary plans. Those plans specify the quantities of each kind of output that the ministries' enterprises propose to produce during the year, and the quantities of each kind of labor they require to fulfill those output targets. The sum of the requirements for each kind of labor constitutes the demand for labor implicit in the preliminary plan.

When the ministries deliver the aggregated preliminary plans of their enterprises to the central planners, the latter draw up an initial trial labor balance, juxtaposing the estimated supply against the preliminary planned demand. Because of the tautness of the control figures, the planners expect, and usually find, that the demand exceeds the supply for many kinds of labor: the preliminary national demand for unskilled labor may exceed the estimated supply by perhaps 200,000 unskilled workers. The preliminary plan is then infeasible, for lack of sufficient labor.

One way of achieving balance is to reduce the preliminary output plans of some products to levels at which the labor requirements will not exceed the supply. The crucial planning instrument for that purpose is the labor input norm.

Labor input norms   Like the enterprises, the planning organizations maintain a file of labor input norms for all products and for all kinds of labor. The national labor input norm for unskilled labor in housing construction, for example, may be 3 man-hours per square foot of new housing. Hence, a reduction in the preliminary housing construction plan by 1,000,000 square feet would reduce the demand for unskilled labor by 3,000,000 man-hours, or by 1,500 unskilled workers at a workyear of 2,000 hours.

Using the labor input norms in that way, the preliminary output targets may be gradually whittled down to a level at which the 200,000 excess demand for unskilled labor is fully eliminated. Similar adjustments are made for the other main categories of labor as well.[7] The revised set of targets constitutes a feasible plan because the labor requirements are no larger than the quantity of labor available.

That first feasible plan may not be the best of all possible feasible plans, however. The available labor could be redistributed among the industries so as to produce more housing and fewer jeans, or less housing and more bread. In consultation with the political authorities, the planners select that combination of products that is judged to represent the highest level of societal welfare. That combination is then adopted as the national plan.

It takes several months for the central planners to make all the adjustments in the preliminary plans required to produce a final plan. Ideally, when they have finished their work, the final plan represents the best combination of products that the country is capable of producing, and the quantity of labor required to produce them is no larger than the quantity that is available.

6 Regional Planning of Labor

In the case of most major outputs and inputs, plan-making takes place entirely at the national level, or in some cases at the level of the republic. In labor planning, however, the regional planners have an important function to perform that they do not perform in regard to non-human inputs. The reason for the difference is that aluminum extrusions, for example, can be produced in one part of the country and shipped to another for use there. Therefore if the national output plan is equal to the national planned use of aluminum extrusions, the plan can be considered to be coordinated, with transportation requirements properly taken into account. The citizens-as-workers, however, cannot be shipped around the country like carloads of aluminum extrusions. The labor plan for carpenters cannot therefore be coordinated by assuring that the nationwide supply of carpenters is equal to the nationwide planned use of carpenters in construction and elsewhere. Labor is essentially a local matter, and genuine coordination requires that the supply in each labor region be equal to the planned requirements in that same region. Some degree of regional imbalance can be redressed by such methods as the recruitment of temporary labor migrants, but the task of labor allocation is fundamentally regional.

Regional labor balances   Like the central planners, the regional planners draw up balances of labor resources on the basis of the preliminary plans of the enterprises located in the region. And as in the case of the center, the initial trial balances often show excesses of some types of labor, although local shortages of some types may also occur.

The regional planners, however, do not have the authority to alter the production plans of the regional enterprises, most of which take their orders from the central ministries. Their responsibility at this stage is simply to inform the central planners of the imbalances in their region. The central planners strive to take account of the most egregious regional imbalances, but it is beyond their power to produce a plan that is balanced for every major kind of labor not only at the national level but within each region as well.

When the final national plan is adopted, each regional planning bureau receives its copy of the final plans of all the enterprises within its region, which include the enterprises' authorizations to hire specified numbers of workers of each kind. The planning manual instructs the regional planners to draw up final balances of labor resources, but it is vague on the procedures to follow in the usual case in which there are local surpluses and shortages for certain types of labor.

If labor were allocated among jobs by the assignment method, the local imbalances could easily be attended to. If there are too many textile engineers and too few skilled bakery workers, some engineers could simply be assigned to bakery work. The assignment method is used in the case of certain classes of workers like recent graduates, but in the main the planned economies have rejected labor assignment. The alternative is to rely on the wage method for coordinating the local labor supply with the demand.

Wage rates and employment   The effectiveness of the wage method depends on the flexibility of wage rates. If the regional planners had the authority to raise wage rates in the case of shortages and reduce them in the case of surpluses, the workers would voluntarily sort themselves out among the authorized jobs. If the shortage were general, higher wages could also serve to bring more retirees and others into the labor force. None of the planned economies were willing to give the regional planners that authority, however. Wage rates were set centrally, on the basis of a variety of considerations that were regarded as part of the commitment to socialism. Among them were considerations of distributive justice – keeping wage differences to a minimum – and keeping wage rates stable over time.

Hence, while the wage method may be said to have prevailed in a very general sense, the planners did not possess the instrument needed to make it work the way it is supposed to – wage differentiation. It was as if the Party chose reluctantly to adopt the price method, but then couldn't bring itself to do the things needed to make it work right. The consequence of this was that regional planners, having neither the power of assignment nor the authority to alter wage rates, were unable to complete the process of matching up the workers with the jobs. The planning system surrendered, as it were, and the task of dealing with the residual local imbalances was carried out by a combination of administrative and informal methods (chapter 18).

While central control over wage rates and prices made it difficult for the planners to channel all the workers into the approved job slots, it had a certain important advantage. The central planners did not have to worry about the inflationary wage spiral that the policy of full employment might entail. The citizens-as-workers therefore benefitted from the full-employment policy, but they surrendered the right to compete for higher wages when their skills were in great demand.

Hence, the central planners coordinated the supply and demand for labor on a nation-wide basis, but in a way that left a variety of regional imbalances. The regional planners worked off the imbalances by a variety of methods, both formal and informal, so that in the end virtually all workers were employed in the enterprises located in the region.

7   Materials Planning

The planning of intermediate products like materials, fuels, and semi-manufactures of all kinds is vastly more complicated than labor planning. Among the reasons is that labor serves only as an input into the production of goods, but materials are both an input and an output. That greatly expands the number of products for which the planners are responsible.

As non-human inputs, materials are not of prime concern in the economics of the Good Society. No one cares how they are treated or whether they are abused, and their preferences on these matters are of no account. They cannot be neglected in analysis, however, because how they are managed affects the efficiency of the economy.

Materials input norms   The fundamental instrument in materials planning is the input norm, much as in labor planning. Suppose the preliminary plan reveals a shortage in the sheet steel balance: the production plan is 1.2 million tons, but the requirements by steel users such as building construction, machinery, and shipbuilding amount to 1.4 million tons. The decision is made to retain the latter target, and to make that feasible by increasing the sheet steel production plan by 200,000 tons.

An increase in steel production, however, requires increases in the production plans of all of its inputs, such as fuel oil, coke, and firebrick. Those increases are calculated by means of the input norms. Suppose the fuel oil input norm is 1.3 tons per 1,000 tons of sheet steel. The fuel oil production plan is then adjusted upward by 260 tons ($200,000 \times 1.3/1,000$), in order to supply the fuel needs for an additional 200,000 tons of steel. Similarly the norms for coke, brick, and other inputs into steel production are used to calculate the required increases in the production plans for those intermediate products.

However, an increase in the steel production plan requires not only more inputs into steel, but also more inputs into those inputs. Hence a second round of adjustments is made in the same way, on the basis of materials input norms. Suppose that fuel oil production requires rubber as an input, and the rubber input norm into fuel oil production is 1.7 pounds per ton. The production of the additional 260 tons of fuel oil for the steel industry therefore requires an increased rubber production of 442 pounds (1.7×260), to be delivered to the fuel industry. And similarly for all other inputs used in fuel oil production.

Thus the adjustment of every preliminary plan quota for the purpose of achieving balance spills over into all its inputs, and then into all the inputs' inputs, and so on. The size of the adjustments diminishes in successive rounds, however, so that after a few rounds they are generally small enough to be handled out of normal inventories. Provision must also be made at each round, of course, for the additional labor required to support each increase in production.

It is evident that the process of plan-balancing is an extremely complicated matter. The complexity increases, moreover, with the number of products, and with the number of specialized inputs required by the technology. There is a great deal of past experience upon which the planners can rely, however, and sometime before the end of the planning year (1980) they are supposed to present a final plan (for 1981) for approval by the government and the Communist Party. After approval is granted, the planners assign final plans to the ministries, which in turn assign final plans to their enterprises.

The enterprise's final plan usually differs in various ways from the preliminary plan that it had originally submitted many months before. Ideally, the materials inputs that each enterprise is authorized to acquire should be fully consistent with its final production plan, and the total quantity of each material required to enable all users of that material to fulfill their plans should be equal to the total amount of that material that will be available for use. Similarly, the labor force that each enterprise is authorized to hire should be sufficient to meet its final output quota, and the total demand for each kind of labor in each region should be equal to the number of workers of each kind available to fill those jobs.

8 Discussion

It is a tribute to human ingenuity to have developed not one but two social mechanisms that more or less succeed in coordinating the complex production activities of millions of people. Under the market mechanism the capitalist countries have produced levels of wealth unimaginable in the past, yet without any central intelligence coordinating the activities of the millions of economic agents. Under the planning mechanism a small group of technicians managed to coordinate the economic activities of a huge country that became the second largest industrial power in the world.

From one perspective, the market mechanism is the more remarkable. If you sought to explain to a Martian that the entire Soviet economy was coordinated by the work of a few thousand people sitting in the Central Planning Committee in Moscow, he would find it impressive but believable. If you then sought to explain that the United States economy produced even a larger volume of production under a mechanism in which no human organization was responsible for coordinating the whole system, the Martian would no doubt regard you with suspicion or disbelief.

The difference is rather like that between an airplane flown by a human pilot and one flown by automatic pilot. It is impressive but understandable how a human being can fly a plane, but there is something unnatural about a plane flying without a human pilot. In the same vein, planning seems like a more "natural" way than markets to run a complex operation. Understanding how the market mechanism works takes more cerebral effort than understanding how the planning mechanism works.

From another perspective, however, the planning mechanism is the more remarkable. There have never been heated debates over whether a market mechanism would "work." It was out there and working long before the philosophers and economists figured out its "laws of motion," much as the physical world existed long before Isaac Newton discovered its laws of motion. What was debated was not whether the market mechanism would work but how it worked, how well it worked, who benefitted and who lost, how it could be made to work better, how long it could endure, and so forth.

The planning mechanism, in contrast, was invented, not discovered. It never existed before it was created by Soviet officials, much as the electric light bulb didn't exist before Thomas Edison created it. Long before it was invented there was an intense debate on whether central planning could work at all. Many influential economists believed that it could not, for a variety of reasons. Some argued that in the absence of the profit motive, it would be impossible to harness the individual effort needed to energize an economy. Others believed that the interrelationships of a modern economy are so complex that they could not be managed by a single planning bureau. Defenders of planning believed, of course, that it was an eminently feasible way of running a modern economy.

In the nineteenth century those competing views on the feasibility of central planning could not be tested on any actual economic system. The twentieth-century Communist economies provided the test. It seems to me that history should judge the defenders of the feasibility of planning to have won that debate. During the Cold War the question of whether planning can work at all simply disappeared from the controversy over the merits of alternative economic systems. The subject of debate was not whether but how well the planning system worked, both absolutely and relative to the market economies.

It might seem that only students of the history of these matters would bother to notice that a great victory in an old battle has been quietly won. That victory, however, has a certain importance in the economics of the Good Society. In science and technology, the question of whether something works or not is of critical significance. To scientists committed to such ideas as high-temperature superconductivity, solar energy generation, and low-temperature nuclear fusion, the announcement that one laboratory got it to work is the great breakthrough. That the first models generally work badly does not discourage others. On the contrary, money and people rush into the field, for once the uncertainty about whether something will work at all is removed, it greatly increases the prospect that it can be made to work better, and perhaps even well.

In like fashion, the demonstration that central planning worked should be of great importance to people who regard it as the better coordination-mechanism of a Good Society. That the first models worked badly need not be a source of discouragement – they always do. Once it has been shown to have worked at all, there is a prospect of getting it to work better in the future.

The fact that planning worked is the good news that history brings to friends of planning. There is also the bad news, however, that virtually every country that adopted planning has since abandoned it in favor of markets. That does not entirely preclude the possibility that some society in the future may run a planned economy better than its twentieth-century Communist forebears did. It does suggest, however, that the reasons for the massive defection from planning need to be closely examined. The chapters that follow should be useful for that purpose.

Notes

1 Products that use local materials and are sold locally are generally planned by the local government (such as a province, or a republic), rather than by the central government. That form of regional decentralization greatly reduces the size of the planning task of the central organization. Because of its huge size, Chinese planning was particularly decentralized regionally in this respect. The regional enterprise operates in the same way as the national enterprise, however; the only difference is that it receives its instructions from the regional capital rather than the national capital.

2 Capital goods may also be thought of as a form of intermediate product, in the sense that they are also produced by enterprises for enterprises and are coordinated by the pure planning mechanism. Planning of the production and distribution of capital goods is beyond the scope of this book, but many of the issues are similar to those involving intermediate products.

3 USSR Gosplan, *Metodicheskie ukazaniia*.

4 The priorities expressed in the control figures are those of the political authorities, not of the planners. The planners are best thought of as technicians whose job is to construct a plan that incorporates the goals of the political leadership. Since the top leadership cannot be consulted on every jot and tittle of the plan, however, the planners' judgments inevitably play a considerable role in the formulation of the plan. The top officials of the planning agencies, however, are all members of the Communist Party, and therefore have a good sense of what the leadership wants.

5 The norm used in actual practice is the "output norm" (*norma vyrabotki*), which is expressed as output per unit of labor time. For purposes of exposition, it is more convenient to work here with its inverse, the "input norm," which is expressed as the labor time required per unit of output.

6 As noted above, balances of materials like cement that are produced and used locally are drawn up by the local planning department.

7 When preliminary output targets are reduced to deal with an excess demand for unskilled labor, the excess demand for other types of labor is also reduced in various amounts. In some cases it may turn into an excess supply; that is, there may not be enough jobs for all skilled workers. The details of the labor-balancing procedure on this matter have not been published.

Chapter 15

When Markets Work Perfectly

In this best of all possible
worlds . . . everything is for the
best.
— *Voltaire*

All happy families are alike but an
unhappy family is unhappy
after its own fashion.
— *Tolstoy*

CONTENTS

That an entire economy can be coordinated without the intervention of a central agency of government is so remarkable a thing that it may be churlish to inquire too closely into how well coordinated it is. The achievement should perhaps be appreciated like that of a talking horse – the fact that it talks at all is wonder enough; it detracts little from the achievement that its words make no sense.

Yet a Good Society must ask not only whether its economic mechanism succeeds in co-ordinating economic activity, but also how well it succeeds. Its performance must therefore be assessed by the same criteria of goodness that are applied to all economic arrangements. This chapter, and the next three, are devoted to the criterion of efficiency.

In Parts II and III the efficiency of various elementary economic arrangements was assessed primarily in terms of the people's preferences. That meaning of efficiency was sufficient for assessing the goodness of the goods-distribution and labor-allocation arrangements examined there. In assessing the implications of differences in productivity among workers, however, a second meaning of efficiency was introduced – productive efficiency (chapter 11). Since the society counts on its economic mechanism for both the production and distribution of goods, one must require of an economic mechanism that it be efficient not only with respect to preferences but also with respect to production.

I Markets and Efficiency

One of the most celebrated results of modern economic thought is the proof that, under certain specified conditions, the market mechanism is a perfectly efficient arrangement. That proof is the culmination of a long search that began with Adam Smith's vision of a Good Society as one in which the pursuit of self-interest guides the society toward the accumulation of wealth "as if by an invisible hand." What is remarkable about that vision is that efficiency comes about not because a government seeks to attain it, but solely because all the participants act in pursuit of their own self-interest.

The assertion that the market mechanism is efficient is often uttered like a mantra – without qualification of any sort. It is routinely expressed in that way in the popular press and in ideologically loaded writings, but no respectable economists would subscribe to it, whatever their political orientation.

The relation between markets and efficiency can be expressed in two ways. One assertion is that the market mechanism can be counted on to allocate a country's resources efficiently *when certain conditions prevail*. The other is that the market mechanism does not allocate resources efficiently, *except when certain conditions prevail*. The two formulations may seem to come to the same thing, but they reflect an important difference, particularly with regard to the role of government. The first formulation reflects the view that market economies in practice need very little fixing, and when "the politicians" try to do the fixing, they usually make things worse. The second formulation is preferred by people who believe that market economies in practice need a great deal of fixing, and that the responsibility for fixing them lies with "the government."

While economists differ on the merits of government intervention when the conditions required for efficiency do not prevail, there is broad agreement on what those conditions are. Understanding them is of obvious importance not only for informed participation in the political-economic family quarrels of countries that employ the market mechanism, but also in confronting the broader question of whether markets are the better economic mechanism for a Good Society.

Markets and ownership Most people first encounter the case for the efficiency of the market mechanism in the context of a capitalist economy, and they come away with the impression that the argument is confined to a capitalist economy. Efficiency, however, is surely one of the values desired in all but the most bizarre versions of the Good Society, and the argument that markets can produce an efficient allocation of resources should be of great interest to all people concerned with such a society. To make the point, I shall present the argument in the context of a market–socialist economy, where all the farms and factories are owned by the state but carry out their production, purchasing, and sales activities in a network of markets. Like the managers of privately owned capitalist enterprises, the managers of these state–owned socialist enterprises are expected to make as much profit as they can, and they are amply rewarded for their success in that respect. Unlike capitalist enterprises, however, the profit goes into the coffers of the Public Treasury, rather than into the bank accounts of the capitalist owners.

2 An Ideal Market Mechanism

Efficient economies, like Tolstoy's happy families, are all efficient in the same way: they all produce the largest output possible with a given set of resources. Inefficient economies, however, are inefficient after their own fashion. Some suffer from different sources of inefficiency than others and some squeeze less output than others out of their resources.

In order to distinguish among the various forms of inefficiency and to understand their diverse sources, economic science follows the method of the natural sciences, where ideal worlds are often invented for the purpose of analyzing the behavior of the real world. The physical world, for example, is idealized through such constructs as a frictionless surface, a perfect vacuum, or a temperature of absolute zero. Those conditions do not exist in nature, but the imagined world is an essential part of the process of understanding the behavior of things that do exist in nature.

Economics deals with efficiency in the same manner. The idealized world is carefully spelled out in what is now called the "standard model." The economy described in that model proves to be perfectly efficient, but only if the economy conforms to so restrictive a set of conditions that no real economy can be said even to approximate them. The full list of those conditions is too lengthy to be set forth here, but two of the most important will serve as examples. The first condition is that all markets must be characterized by "perfect competition," and the second is that there must be no "externalities."

PERFECT COMPETITION

The efficiency with which markets operate depends critically upon the state of competition among the three sets of agents – consumers, workers, and enterprises. The function of competition is to limit the price that economic agents can charge for a good or service that they wish to sell. In a product market, for example, every manager seeks to charge that price that yields the largest profit for the enterprise. If the Zenith Soap Company is a "monopolist," meaning that there are no competing soap producers, that price may be exceedingly high, with correspondingly large profits. However, if there are several other soap producers competing for the same customers, Zenith loses the power to set whatever price will yield the largest profit. The company is compelled to charge a somewhat lower price or it will lose most of its customers to the competition. Prices are therefore lower and profits smaller. If there are *many* other competing soap producers, the range of prices that any of them could charge is further restricted and profits are even smaller. In all such markets, however, where a producer can set a price higher than others without losing *all* her customers, the state of competition is said to be "imperfect."

Pursuing that line of thought to its limit, the extreme case is one in which there are so many soap producers that none of them has any control at all over the price he can charge. One price tends to prevail in the market, and any producer who tries to charge a price higher than that of the others will lose all of her customers to the others. In such a market the manager of the Zenith Soap Company would be like a wheat farmer: it would not occur to her to ask what price she should charge, for the price is whatever the market says it is. Prices in such markets are barely higher than the cost of production, and profits are regarded as of normal size.

In one vivid formulation, the small producer in a perfect market is said to be a "price-taker," while the large producer in an imperfect market is a "price-maker."

A market of this extreme form is said to be "perfectly competitive," or a "perfect market" for brevity. It enjoys a very special status in the body of economic theory for a reason that is of great importance to a Good Society – it is only in the case of that kind of market structure that the market mechanism can be said to be an efficient arrangement for allocating a country's resources.

The degree of competition is crucial to efficiency not only in product markets but in all markets. In the case of a labor market, for example, suppose that the going wage for carpenters in a certain region is $150 a day. If a very large building contractor decides to double his work force of carpenters, it will make a big impact on the market. Since he will have to pull some carpenters off of other construction jobs, or draw them from other industries or neighboring regions, he will have to offer somewhat more than the going wage. The effect will be to force up the wage that all contractors have to pay – to perhaps $160 or $200 a day. Competition for labor does prevail in that market, but it is "imperfect." If all contractors are small, however, and one of them takes on a new job and has to double the number of carpenters he employs, his action will hardly make a ripple in the market. He can get all the carpenters he needs for little more than $150 a day. Competition in that labor market is "perfect."

The concept of perfect competition is valuable not because it offers a good description of what most markets are actually like. In fact perfect markets are relatively rare; they consist mainly of markets for homogeneous goods like farm products and minerals. The value of the concept is rather that it serves as an idealized model that makes it possible to identify the conditions that must be present if markets are to allocate resources efficiently. On matters of economic policy it serves as a standard against which to evaluate tariffs, anti-trust legislation, environmental protection, and so forth. It is the basis of most of the useful things that economics has to say about what are good economic arrangements and what are bad ones. It is for that reason that it is an indispensable tool in studying the economics of the Good Society.

EXTERNALITIES

A second condition required for an efficient market economy relates to such matters as the effect of economic activity on the environment. Enterprises have to pay the cost of the coal they use in production, but they normally do not have to pay the cost of the environmental degradation due to the factory smoke released into the atmosphere. The latter cost is borne – or "paid for," one might say – by the rest of society. That production activity is said to generate "externalities," in the sense that the environmental cost is external to the enterprise. It will be shown presently (chapter 17) that when a production activity generates externalities, the market mechanism fails to allocate resources efficiently, even when all markets are perfect.

The market mechanism's claim to efficiency is limited to a world in which all markets are characterized by perfect competition, by the absence of externalities, and by a variety of other conditions, some of which will be discussed in chapter 17. I shall use the expression "ideal" hereafter to refer to an economy in which all those conditions prevail.

3　Three Tests of Efficiency

The record of a country's economic activity is published each year in the government's statistical abstract. Among the statistics is a tabulation of all the goods and services produced in the country that year, and of the size of the labor force and its allocation among industries.

The market mechanism's claim to efficiency is that in an ideal market economy, those statistics would represent the best use that the country could possibly have made of its available resources. Efficiency, like personal health, is a many-sided thing, and much as a physician performs a battery of tests to assess a person's overall health, there is a battery of tests to assess the overall efficiency of an economy. Three tests, however, tell that part of the efficiency story that is of greatest interest from the perspective of the Good Society. They are based on the three aspects of efficiency that have been developed in preceding chapters.

First is production efficiency. Does the economy produce the largest possible output of each good with the labor and other resources that are employed in the production of that good?

Second is efficiency with respect to consumption preferences. Of all the collections of goods that the economy is capable of producing, does it produce that collection which best satisfies the preferences of the citizens-as-consumers?

Third is efficiency with respect to job preferences. Do the jobs required to produce the goods best satisfy the job preferences of the citizens-as-workers?

The next three sections present the case that under ideal conditions the market mechanism passes all three tests. Their subject matter is not how people actually behave in markets but how they *would* behave under the conditions specified. Parts of the argument are fairly intricate and some people find it tiresome. It is indispensable, however, for assessing the claims of rival versions of the Good Society, for the reasoning underlies much of the material in the following chapters that inquire into the efficiency of the ideal central planning mechanism and into the sources of inefficiency under both market and planning mechanisms as they operate in the less-than-ideal conditions of the real world.

4　Production Efficiency

There are two forms of waste about which a Good Society should be concerned in selecting its economic mechanism. One is unused resources. That form of waste is highly visible – darkened factories, silent machines, and idle workers stand as stark evidence that an economic mechanism is not working right. The second form of waste is not visible to the casual eye, but it may nevertheless involve a massive loss of potential output. The source of that waste is inefficiency in the allocation of the available resources among the producing enterprises.

Allocative inefficiency is particularly insidious because of its invisibility. With all factories operating full time and all workers employed, there is no apparent reason for reproaching the people responsible for the running of the economy. The citizens may grumble because they seem not to be living as well as the people in other countries, but there are so many possible causes of differences in living standards that there is no clear reason to point to allocative inefficiency as the primary cause. Like an illness that produces no fever or other symptoms, the patient doesn't know that he is ill.

An economy that is inefficient in this sense may be said to contain a great deal of slack in the use of its resources, though they are fully employed in production. Consider two factories that produce one good – say toys. The factories are identical in all respects except that work in the first is poorly coordinated while in the second it is perfectly coordinated. The first factory produces 1,000 toys and the second produces 1,200 toys. It may then be said that there is a slack of 200 toys in the poorly coordinated factory, while there is no slack in the coordinated factory. The poorly coordinated factory could produce more toys because of its slack, but the perfectly coordinated factory could not because it is already producing as much as it can.

Extending the analogy to two goods, suppose an economy produces only food and clothing. If it is poorly coordinated it produces a certain amount of both. Better coordination would squeeze some of slack out of the economy and it could produce more food or more clothing or more of both. If an economy is perfectly coordinated, however, all of the slack would have been be squeezed out and it would be producing up to the limits of its capacity. There is then no way that economy could produce more of both food and clothes. It could produce more of one good like clothing, but only by producing less of another like food; it could do that by transferring some food workers to garment factories. An economy operating with such commendable tautness is said to have achieved "productive efficiency," or to be "on its production-possibilities frontier."

The claim for the market mechanism is that when it is entrusted with the coordination of economic activity, things will be arranged in such a way as to leave no slack in the allocation of resources. The economy will operate with full productive efficiency in the sense that there would be no way of squeezing any additional output out of the available resources by reallocating them differently among the enterprises.

EFFICIENCY AND MARGINAL PRODUCT

Of the many ways of measuring the productivity of labor, the one which is most relevant to efficiency is the notion of "marginal productivity." The case was made in chapter 11 that the condition for efficiency in the allocation of workers among jobs is that the marginal product of labor must be the same in all enterprises. The point was illustrated in the case of two coal mines, in the first of which the marginal product of labor is 100 tons a day, and in the second, 450 tons a day. The distribution of the workers between those two mines cannot be optimal, because the economy could produce 350 more tons by shifting a worker from the first mine to the second. In contrast, when the marginal product of labor is the same in all mines – say 250 tons – there is no slack left in the mining industry. Shifting a worker from any one mine to any other would increase the output of the second mine by the same amount – 250 tons – as it would decrease the output of the first.

One can readily see how an optimal allocation of that sort could come about under the planning mechanism. A clever Minister of the Coal Industry could achieve it simply by assigning the appropriate number of workers to all of the mines. Under the market mechanism, however, each mining company decides for itself how many workers to employ, with no regard to the number of workers employed in other mines or to their marginal product. It is rather mysterious that under that apparently haphazard arrangement the workers should end up being allocated among the mines in such a way that their marginal product is the same in all of them. That, however, is precisely what happens when the market mechanism operates under ideal conditions.

EFFICIENCY WITHIN INDUSTRIES

The argument assumes that the enterprises, whether privately or socially owned, are managed by competent people who are motivated to make as much profit as they can. Suppose there are 5,000 workers employed in the 50 bakeries that comprise the industry. Each manager operates his enterprise at the output at which his company's profit is at its maximum. The 50 managers may be envisioned as perched, as it were, on the peaks of 50 profit mountains. Some are very large mountains, with profits in the millions, and some are very small, with profits in the thousands. Large or small, however, they are all the same in one important respect: the marginal profit in all the bakeries is zero (chapter 13). None of them can increase their profit by producing more, or less, than the output at which their profit is at its peak.

The marginal profit refers to the effect on total profit of a small change in output. A change in output, however, generally corresponds to a certain change in employment. Hence, if marginal profit is zero when output changes by a small amount, it must also be zero when employment changes by a small amount. The latter formulation is the more useful in assessing the efficiency with which labor is allocated, which is the present concern.

Suppose a certain bakery is producing its most profitable output with the smallest possible labor force required by the production technology. If it increased employment by one hour of labor, output would increase by a certain amount – say 20 loaves. The marginal product of labor is therefore, by definition, 20 loaves per work-hour in that bakery when it is producing at its peak-profit output.

Producing goods and producing dollars   Bakery labor may be thought of as producing either loaves of bread, or dollars' worth of bread. Hence, the marginal product of the bakery's labor may be expressed either as 20 loaves of bread, or as $40 worth of sales revenue if the market price is $2 a loaf. To distinguish the two ways of expressing labor's product, the 20 loaves are called the marginal "physical product" and the $40 is called the marginal "revenue product." When the term marginal product is used without an adjective, it may refer to either meaning, depending on the context.

Consider the Sourdough Bakery that is producing the output at which its profit is at its maximum, so that marginal profit is zero. That signifies that it does not pay to increase output by hiring an additional baker, because his marginal revenue product would be no larger than the cost of hiring him. The cost of hiring additional labor in a perfectly competitive market is simply the market wage rate – perhaps $100 a day. Since marginal profit is zero, the marginal revenue product of an additional worker must also be equal to the wage rate of $100. Therefore, if the market price of bread is $2 a loaf, the marginal physical product of labor in Sourdough must be 50 loaves.

Under perfect competition, however, all enterprises have to pay the same wage rate – $100 – and they all sell their bread at the same price – $2. What is true for Sourdough must therefore be true for all the bakeries – their marginal product is 50 loaves. The marginal product of labor must therefore be the same in all enterprises. Hence, the bakery industry is productively efficient: there is no way of squeezing more output out of the enterprises by reallocating the workers among the bakeries.

DIGRESSION ON MARGINAL COST

In the standard textbook of economics, the sentence before last would read, "The marginal cost of producing bread would therefore be the same in all enterprises." That formulation in terms of "marginal cost" expresses the same relation as our formulation in terms of marginal product, but from a somewhat different perspective.

The term "marginal cost" refers to the cost (in dollars) of producing one additional unit of *output*. Marginal product refers to amount of additional output (in numbers of loaves) produced by one additional unit of *input*. The two terms are closely related. In the illustration, since the marginal product of a day's labor is 50 loaves of bread, it takes 1/50 of an additional day of labor to produce 1 additional loaf of bread. At a wage rate of $100 per day's labor, 1/50 of a day's labor costs $2. That number – $2 – is the "marginal cost" of bread production.

Since labor is the only variable input in the simplified economy under consideration here, marginal cost consists solely of labor cost. In a complete economy, however, there are other variable inputs required for production, such as fuel, materials, and so forth. In that context, marginal cost includes all the variable costs. That is, to say that the marginal cost of producing something is $2 means that it takes $2 worth of labor, fuel, and all other required inputs to produce 1 additional unit of that thing.

The marginal-cost approach is the more useful in the general case of a complete economy in which many goods are produced with many inputs. Since standard introductory economics usually studies the general case, the condition of efficiency is usually expressed as "marginal cost equals price." The marginal-product approach, however, provides a clearer exposition of the reasoning in the case of a labor-only economy. It is therefore used here and in most of what follows.

In examining the efficiency of the planning mechanism, however, much of what needs to be dealt with concerns the planning of non-labor inputs such as intermediate products – energy, raw materials, semi-fabricates, and so forth. The analysis of planning will therefore employ the marginal-cost approach from time to time. The main point, however, is that the conclusions of the one approach are identical to those of the other.

EFFICIENCY AND WAGE RATES

The labor-allocation process described above has an important implication for the wages earned by workers of different grades and occupations. Insofar as the distribution of income is something the society cares about, the wage-determination implications of the market mechanism should be of major importance in assessing the appropriateness of that mechanism for a Good Society.

If the market wage rate for bakers is $100 a day, each manager adjusts the number of bakers so as to produce that output which the profit table shows to be the most profitable. The optimal employment may be 40 workers in one bakery, 120 in another, and so on.[1] In all the bakeries, however, the marginal revenue product of labor will be $100 a day.[1] Hence the wage rate for any occupation tends to be equal to the marginal revenue product of that occupation. If marginal product is larger in one occupation than another, wage rates are correspondingly larger. Thus the degree of wage inequality is determined by the differences in the marginal productivity of the different types of jobs for which the citizens are qualified.

Efficiency is one of the strong selling points of the market mechanism. A society that adopts it, however, also adopts the wage-determination process that accompanies it. That process results in a certain distribution of wages among the citizens, and the society should be sure that that distribution, which may be quite unequal, is consistent with justice and other criteria of goodness to be discussed presently.

EXTENSIONS

The foregoing analysis has dealt with the simplest possible case, in which there is only one product and only one kind of labor. The conclusion extends to the more realistic case in which there are many industries and many different kinds of labor, but the proof is beyond the reach of words and numbers. For the purpose of the economics of the Good Society, however, it is sufficient simply to report the results, without an explanation of the rationale behind them. The interested reader can consult the economic textbooks, which devote many pages of graphs and formulae to the more complex cases.

When there is more than one kind of labor, the number of workers of each kind that the enterprise employs depends on their relative wage rates and their relative productivity. For example, if the two types of labor are skilled and unskilled, the pursuit of profit leads the enterprise to employ that number of each such that their marginal money product is equal to their wage rates. Thus, if their wage rates are $150 and $100 per day, Sourdough Bakery's profit table might lead to the employment of perhaps three skilled workers and 11 unskilled. On analysis, it would turn out that at those employment levels, the marginal product of skilled labor is $150 and the marginal product of unskilled labor is $100.

Since wage rates and prices are the same for all bakeries, the marginal product for skilled labor will be the same in all bakeries, and the marginal product for unskilled labor will be the same in all bakeries. The same conclusion would follow for any number of different kinds of labor: the marginal product of all equally qualified pastry chefs will be the same, and the same with all sales clerks, delivery van operators, countermen and others. Hence the industry will be productively efficient, for in all categories of labor, the workers will be optimally allocated among the bakeries.

What is true for the bakery industry is also true for all industries. Substitute the Acme Bluejean Company for the Sourdough Bakery in the examples given above and the story will be the same: the marginal product of each kind of labor will be equal in all blue jeans factories.

Hence the market mechanism passes the first test of efficiency: the economy produces the largest quantity of each good that can be produced with the labor allocated to its production.

5   Goods and Preferences

A productively efficient economy is better than many possible worlds, but it may not be the best of all possible worlds. In fact, it may be a most unattractive world, for it may produce a bizarre set of goods for the citizens. It may, for example, devote so much of its labor and other resources to housing production that there is little left over for food production. The population would then luxuriate in their homes but have very little to eat. That economy could still claim to have eliminated all slack in the use of the available resources, in the sense that it could not possibly produce more of both housing and food. It could produce more food, however, if it transferred some of its resources from housing to food production. After such a transfer, the economy would still be productively efficient, but the combination of goods produced would be much more satisfactory to the citizens-as-consumers.

In the short run – say in a month's time – the possibility of producing more housing by transferring some workers from food to housing production is quite limited. In the course of a year, however, a considerable amount of retraining and relocation could be done, and housing production could be increased. And in the long run – in the course of several years – the plant and equipment in the construction industry could be increased and housing could be greatly expanded. It is in that long-term framework that one may think of a productively efficient economy as capable of producing many different combinations of housing and food, as well as of other goods.

Productive efficiency is an important property of an economic mechanism, for it guarantees that there is no waste in the use of the country's resources. There still remain, however, a large number of combinations of housing and food that provide more of one and less of the other. Productive efficiency is entirely neutral on this matter: it offers no basis for declaring any one of those productively efficient combinations to be better than another.

A Good Society should therefore demand more of its economic mechanism than mere productive efficiency. It should require in addition that of all the productively efficient combinations of goods that could be produced, its economic mechanism should pick out the one combination that best satisfies the consumption preferences of the citizens. That is precisely what the market mechanism claims to be able to do.

The argument in support of that claim proceeds in three steps. The first considers the combination of goods produced by the enterprises, each of which seeks to make the largest possible profit for itself. The second considers the combination of goods bought by the consumers, each of whom buys those things that best conform to his or her consumption preferences. The third step demonstrates that the first collection of goods is the same as the second.

PRODUCTION POTENTIAL

Consider a simple economy that produces only two goods – bread and jeans; where labor is the only required input; and where all enterprises are operating at their profit peaks. The marginal product of labor in all bakeries is the same – say 2,000 loaves of bread per day; and the marginal product in all jeans factories is the same – say 100 pairs of jeans per day. Those numbers signify that by transferring labor between the two industries jeans can be "transformed" into bread – to use the economics metaphor – at the rate of 20 loaves per pair of jeans; or the other way around. That number – 20 in this case – is an indicator of the economy's production potential, in the sense that it indicates the potential increase in the availability of one good if one less unit of another good were produced.

It turns out that in an ideal market economy, when every enterprise is producing at its profit peak and the economy has settled down to its equilibrium state, its production potential is fully reflected in the market prices. In the example above, the price of a pair of jeans will have settled down to 20 times the price of a loaf of bread. What that means is that the prices of things reveal the production potential of the economy. If the price of one good is $40 (or $400) and the price of another is $2 (or $20), one can infer that 20 units of the second good could be transformed into 1 unit of the first good by a suitable reallocation of labor.[2]

SOCIETAL PREFERENCE

The production potential indicator signifies, in this case, that in addition to the market-derived product mix, the economy can potentially produce a product mix containing one additional pair of jeans but at the cost of 20 fewer loaves, or a mix with one less pair of jeans but 20 more loaves of bread. Which is the best of the three possible product mixes?

The prior question, however, is "Who should decide what is best?" Societies that have adopted the market mechanism generally prefer for sovereignty over production to be lodged with the citizens as individuals – or "consumer sovereignty" as it is called in the case of consumer goods.[3] In that case the "best" product mix is that which the citizens-as-consumers prefer.

Preferences are located in people's heads, however, and neither society nor analysts can observe their preferences among product mixes that have not been produced. Moreover, consumers differ in their preferences: some can eat no fat and others can eat no lean. It is therefore not at all self-evident what it might mean to say that "the consumers" prefer some other potential product mix to the one generated by the market mechanism.

Economic theory does in fact propose a way of identifying consumer preferences. It was introduced earlier (chapter 6) in the discussion of how consumer goods are distributed under the price method. Most consumers spend their money on what makes the most sense to them. Analytically, that comes down to buying that collection of goods such that their marginal preference ratios are equal to the corresponding price ratios. For example, if the prices of jeans and bread are $40 and $2, a price-conscious consumer selects that combination of the two goods such that, over a period of time, 20 additional loaves of bread would provide about the same consumption satisfaction as 1 additional pair of jeans; that is to say, the consumer's preference ratio ends up being 20 to 1 (i.e. 20 loaves of bread per pair of jeans). Since all consumers pay the same prices, however, when each one has selected her own best combination of jeans and bread, each one's marginal preference ratio ends up being the same as everyone else's. Hence, if one knows the prices of things, one knows the preference ratios of all consumers. Therefore, the prices of goods, which are public, reveal the private preferences of the citizens, much as the same prices reveal the economy's production potential.

Since all consumers' preference ratios have the same value, it is reasonable to regard that ratio as an indicator of the preferences of "the consumers" – or even of "the society" where consumer sovereignty prevails. It can therefore serve as the yardstick with which to judge whether the citizens-as-consumers prefer one product mix over another. Hence, if the prices of two goods are $40 and $2, one can assert that the society's marginal preference indicator is 20 to 1 for those two goods, and that the consumers would all regard 1 additional unit of the $40 good as equivalent in consumption value to 20 additional units of the $2 good.

Preference and potential

A production potential indicator of 20 loaves of bread per pair of jeans means that the economy can produce 1 more pair of jeans but only by giving up 20 loaves of bread. A societal preference indicator of 20 means that the consumers would not regard themselves as better off with a 1-pair increase in jeans production if they had to give up 20 loaves or more in order to obtain it; nor would they regard a 1-pair decrease in jeans production as worth the while for a gain of 20 or fewer loaves of bread.

Generalizing from this example, the societal preference indicator measures what the consumers *want* the economy to produce, while the production potential indicator measures what the economy *can* potentially produce. Hence, when the economy is producing a product mix such that the two measures are equal, there is no other product mix that the economy can produce and that the consumers would rather have. The equality of the societal preference indicator and the production potential indicator is therefore said to be the "efficiency condition" with respect to the product mix.[4]

When the market mechanism guides the allocation of resources, however, that condition always prevails when markets have settled down to their equilibrium levels. Hence the majestic conclusion that the market mechanism is efficient under ideal conditions because it leads the economy to produce that combination of goods that the citizens prefer to all other combinations that could be produced.

The effect of income inequality

The mix of goods that the market produces depends not only on the citizens' consumption preferences but also on their incomes. If the income distribution is extremely unequal, the market will produce a different mix of goods than if income were more equally distributed. For example, if many people earn ten times the average income, the market will produce more yachts and mansions than if few people were that rich. In either case the market is an efficient arrangement, but each product mix is optimal only with respect to the corresponding income distribution.

A society that valued only distributive justice would arrange for whatever income distribution it regarded as the most just – say it is pure equality – and the market would then produce the best product mix for that income distribution. But that best-product-mix may be highly unsatisfactory in terms of consumer satisfaction; the policy of equal income may so dull the incentive for work effort that total output may be very small – say only 10 pairs of jeans and 10 loaves of bread per person. If a small degree of inequality were permitted, however, the best product mix might increase to 12 jeans and 11 loaves per person. And with yet greater inequality the market might produce even larger product mixes.

A Good Society that valued both distributive justice and the welfare of its citizens-as-consumers would therefore accept some degree of inequality for the sake of better material conditions of life. Conceptually, it would gradually increase inequality, evaluating at each step the associated marginal gain in consumer welfare. At some point it would decide that the social loss from a further small increase in inequality would exceed the social gain in consumer welfare. That combination may be the considered the grand optimum. The society has achieved neither the optimal level of justice nor the optimal level of material welfare, but it has found the best combination of the two values.

6 Jobs and Preferences

It should not be surprising at this point in the narrative to find that the market mechanism is no less efficient in satisfying the citizens' job preferences than it is in satisfying their consumer preferences.

If the workers see no reason to prefer a job in one industry to a similar job in the other, the same wage rates will prevail for the same type of labor in all industries under perfect competition – say $20 an hour. Suppose, however, that some or all workers regard the work in one industry – say bakeries – as unpleasant, because of the heat or other working conditions. Then fewer workers will apply for bakery jobs and more will apply in other industries like jeans production. As the coordination process swings into operation, wages will rise in the bakeries and decline in the jeans factories. The size of the wage premium for bakery work will depend on the intensity of job preferences. Workers who regard the difference in work conditions as of little significance would take a bakery job if the wage were as little as $1 or $2 higher than a jeans-factory job. At the other extreme are workers who would not take a bakery job however large the margin over jeans production. When the labor market is once more fully coordinated, bakery labor might earn perhaps $23, and jeans-factory labor, $18.

Since the workers sort themselves out among jobs, if market wages settle down to a stable wage premium of $5 for bakery work, then the only citizens working in bakeries are those to whom 5 extra dollars more than compensate for the unpleasantness of the work conditions. Those who work in jeans factories are those who dislike hot work so much that it would take a premium larger than $5 to induce them to take a bakery job. It follows that the market mechanism is efficient with respect to job preferences, for the allocation of workers among jobs is optimal in Pareto's sense: there is no other way of allocating the workers between the two industries that would not cause some workers to be worse off than in the jobs they have chosen.

The wage premium can lay claim to represent "the society's" preference for one job over another. If the intensity of the distaste for a particular type of employment should decline, in the course of time the size of the wage premium will also decline, and the premium will even disappear if conditions in that type of employment should come to be regarded as no less desirable than elsewhere.

THE DIRTY WORK ONCE MORE

A wage premium of $5 an hour for bakery work signifies that a great many workers dislike that job enough to be willing to forgo that much income in order to avoid it. Does it not follow that the welfare of the citizens-as-workers would be higher if those jobs were reduced in number, or even abolished? Would it not be a better society if there were no dirty jobs, no dead-end jobs, and no jobs that most people would rather not have to do?

It would be – if the only preferences that counted were those of the citizens-as-workers. However, the citizens are also consumers, and they supply their labor as workers in order to satisfy their demand as consumers. The welfare of the citizens-as-workers cannot therefore be evaluated without concern for the welfare of the citizens-as-consumers.

How then to balance consumption preferences against job preferences? Consider first the market-derived allocation of labor in the foregoing illustration, and suppose that one worker were transferred from the unpleasant bakery to the more desirable jeans factory. One consequence is that the society is no longer efficient with respect to consumption preferences, for it is producing more jeans and less bread than the citizens-as-consumers desire. Considering the transferred worker's job preferences, however, it would seem to be a better society, because that worker is now employed in an environment he prefers, while all others are unchanged. But since the wage rate is lower in jeans production ($18 an hour) than in bread production ($23 an hour), that worker's level of consumption falls. Taking account of both his consumption preferences and his job preferences, he must be worse off, because that choice was available to him under the market mechanism and he rejected it. That is, when confronted with the choice, he revealed that he preferred hot bakery work at $23 an hour to jeans-factory work at $18 an hour. The transfer must therefore reduce his welfare as a consumer, even though it might increase his welfare as a worker.

Pursuing that line of reasoning, when a perfectly competitive market is in equilibrium, any reallocation of labor from less pleasant to more pleasant jobs increases the workers' welfare from the perspective of job preferences, but it diminishes their welfare when both job preferences and consumer preferences are taken into account. The market-derived allocation of workers is therefore optimal in Pareto's sense, because every other allocation would cause some people to be worse off.

7 Interdependence of Goods and Jobs

The responsiveness of the market mechanism to the preferences of the people both as consumers and as workers is reflected in the way it responds to a disturbance. Suppose some new development in health research or fashion-consciousness causes a great many people to cut down on their bread consumption, and therefore to spend more than before on other things, among them jeans. A chain of consequences would automatically follow in perfect markets.

First, the price of bread would fall relative to the price of jeans.

Second, because of the price changes, bakeries would find that their profit peak was now at a smaller rate of output than before, and garment manufacturers would find it profitable to increase the production of jeans.

Third, because of the changes in rates of output, the number of jobs in bakeries would decline, while the number of jobs that the garment factories wish to fill would increase.

Fourth, since fewer hot jobs in bakeries would need to be filled, the wage rate required to induce enough people to take those jobs would decline, and the wage rate in jeans production would rise. Workers with the least aversion to hot work would remain in bakery production, while those with the greatest aversion would find the wage-premium in bakeries no longer worth the unpleasantness and would transfer to jeans production.

Finally, when the system settled down after all the adjustments in consuming and working had been made, the distribution of citizens-as-workers among jobs would once again be optimal, given the change in the preferences of the citizens-as-consumers.

A similar sequence of adjustments would occur as a result of a disturbance in the labor market. Suppose that the introduction of expensive air-conditioning greatly reduced the heat level in bakeries. Some jeans workers would then seek employment in the bakeries because of the higher wage, launching a train of changes in both product markets and labor markets. After the adjustment process had been completed, the distribution of bread and jeans among the citizens-as-consumers would once again be optimal, given the improved working conditions in bakeries.

8   Discussion

Models, like psychedelic drugs, can be dangerous for your health if used to excess. The danger is that they produce so pleasant a high that you sometimes confuse illusion with reality. You may think you are talking about how things work in the real world when you are in fact talking only about how they work in an imaginary model of that world. Excessive inhalation of the perfect competition model of the market mechanism often produces that unfortunate result, because that model has the appealing property of producing perfect efficiency without any governmental intervention.

In an early design of this book I planned to devote no more than a few paragraphs to ideal models, for the economics of the Good Society is not about the merits of alternative Utopias but about economic systems as they operate in practice. It therefore seemed that the book should focus on how alternative systems actually work and not how they might work under ideal conditions. Since all human institutions are imperfect, that meant studying not only their achievements but also their deficiencies.

I discovered, however, what I am sure other writers of books like this have found before. I could readily give a solid account of all the deficiencies of both markets and planning as they are reported in abundance in the literature of social and economic criticism, and which are generally well known to the reading public. When I sought to go beyond a descriptive account into the analysis of those deficiencies, however, it quickly became evident that without a clear picture of what a good economic arrangement might look like, it was impossible to explain precisely the sense in which some arrangements are bad. For example, everybody understands intuitively that there is something bad about monopoly, which will be considered in chapter 17. Unless one has come to grips with the abstract notion of perfect competition and the specific sense in which it is a good arrangement, however, one can have only the most superficial understanding of why monopoly is a bad arrangement and therefore something to be concerned about in a Good Society that employs the market mechanism.

I trust therefore that this chapter and the next, which deal with ideal models, will not be considered a breach of faith in a book that professes not to be about Utopias.

Notes

1   Intuitively, the manager looks upon labor as a means of earning profit. He figures, "If I hire one additional worker, it will cost me $100 in wages. If the output that the worker produces brings in $120, I will make an additional $20 on his labor and it pays me to hire him. And I will keep on expanding employment until my work force gets so large that hiring one more worker would bring in less than $100. It doesn't pay me to hire any workers beyond that because I wouldn't make any additional profit on them." When all managers reckon in that way, employment in all the bakeries will expand until the marginal revenue product of bakers' labor is $100 in each one.
2   Suppose the wage rate is $200 a day. Under perfect competition every enterprise has to pay $200 for an additional day's labor. The marginal revenue money product of labor must therefore also be $200 in all enterprises, whether they produce jeans or bread or anything else.

If the marginal bakery worker is producing $200 worth of bread when the price of bread is $2 a loaf, he must be producing 100 loaves of bread a day. And if the marginal money product in jeans production is also $200 when the price of jeans is $40 a pair, the marginal physical product of labor must be 5 pairs of jeans per day. That is to say, the marginal (physical) product of labor in bread production (100) is 20 times the marginal (physical) product of labor in jeans production (5), which is exactly the ratio of the price of jeans ($40) to the price of bread ($2). It is rather as if you and I spent the same sum of money on clothing: if you buy $40 dress shirts and I buy $2 T-shirts, the number of my T-shirts has to be 20 times the number of your dress shirts.

The assertion that the marginal product of bread is 20 times that of jeans means, however, that 20 is the value of the economy's production potential for the two goods: the economy could produce at most 20 more loaves of bread by producing 1 fewer pair of jeans.

3   In planned economies sovereignty over production is generally lodged with an agency of the society. See chapter 16.

4   The standard technical formulation in economic textbooks is that the "marginal rate of substitution is equal to the marginal rate of transformation."

Chapter 16

When Planning Works Perfectly

A policeman's lot is not a happy one.
— **W. S. Gilbert**

CONTENTS

The perfect competition model is the workhorse of the economic analysis of markets. It is the standard point of departure in the study of the efficiency of economic arrangements, and students are mercilessly drilled in the analysis of its properties.

There is no model that does for central planning what perfect competition does for markets. Economists in the Communist countries did indeed study planning with the objective of developing techniques for improving its efficiency, but they worked without the benefit of a time-tested standard model that specified the conditions under which central planning works efficiently and those under which it does not.

However, a great deal of material was published in the Communist countries that enabled economists, both there and abroad, to identify and analyze the sources of inefficiency in planning. Knowledge of the causes of inefficiency in the real world makes it possible to specify the conditions that would have to be present in order that inefficiency of that kind not occur. Those conditions provide a basis for constructing a model of "perfect planning" that would do for the planning mechanism what the perfect competition model does for the market mechanism. The model presented below is presented as such an idealization. Its purpose is to provide a framework for examining the efficiency of the planning mechanism that parallels the examination of the efficiency of the market mechanism in the preceding chapter.

The model is based on four assumptions about how the economic actors behave in that idealized Good Society.

The first concerns political power: the government is elected on the basis of a program that represents its vision of a Good Society, and it makes those economic decisions that will contribute most to the implementation of that program.

The second relates to computation: the government's planners have all the computational capability available within the limits of the electronic data-processing art.

The third deals with information: managers of the state-owned enterprises accurately transmit to the planners all the technical knowledge about the production capabilities of their enterprises that the planners solicit. The planners therefore possess all the knowledge about the enterprises' production operations that they believe they need to carry out their work.

The fourth involves incentives: enterprise managers strive diligently to carry out the production plans assigned to them by the central planners. This condition corresponds to the perfect-market assumption that managers strive diligently to maximize profit.

There are other ways in which one might postulate a set of assumptions under which the planning mechanism might be expected to perform with maximum efficiency, but these four will serve the purpose.

How then does the efficiency of an idealized planning mechanism of this sort compare with that of the standard idealized market mechanism? The analysis to follow continues to deal with a simple economy in which labor is the only variable input that matters and consumer goods are the only output, but issues involving other inputs and outputs will be touched upon when necessary.

I   Efficiency and Values

Efficiency is sometimes held to be a value-free concept: to assert one arrangement more efficient than another is not supposed to imply that it is better than the other. In social-science discourse, however, there is normally a value or two lurking behind that assertion.

There is, first, the choice of the standard for measuring efficiency. There is no such thing as all-purpose efficiency. It always implies some standard of assessment, and an arrangement that is efficient with respect to one standard may not be efficient with respect to another. The designation of a particular standard usually, though not necessarily, implies that that standard is a good thing. Economics focusses on efficiency with respect to production and preferences because of the value judgments that more goods are better than fewer goods, and that it is better to produce the goods that people most prefer.

A value judgment is also involved in the question of whose preferences should count in deciding whether an arrangement is efficient or not. In the case of the market mechanism, the standard for assessing efficiency is the preferences of the individual citizens as consumers and workers. One collection of goods is held to be better than another if the citizens prefer it to the other, and an arrangement is said to be efficient if it selects the best collection of goods defined in that way. The underlying value is that sovereignty over production should be lodged in the citizens as individuals.

To many critics of the market system, that fixation on individual satisfaction epitomizes the moral degeneration of bourgeois society. In their view of the Good Society, economic activity should be guided not by each citizen striving to do what is best for herself, but by the collective striving of all the people for the good of the whole society. They envision the possibility that the society as a whole may be better off if the citizens consume less of some goods and more of others than they would individually prefer to consume. A Good Society, for example, may wish to produce less pet food and more baby food, less pornography and more poetry, fewer cigarettes and more fishing rods, than would be produced under an economic mechanism that caters only to individual preferences. It may decide that when congestion and pollution are taken into account the society would be better off producing fewer automobiles than the citizens as individuals would wish to buy.[1] It may decide that the economy should devote fewer of its resources to present consumption than the citizens as individuals would prefer; this would free up more resources for investment in new factories so that future generations could live better than the present one.

A society that holds these values will find planning more appealing than markets, for under the planning mechanism sovereignty over production resides in the society, and not in the individual citizens pursuing their self-interest. The government and its planners are given the responsibility for judging which of all combinations of consumer goods that could be produced is the best for the society. In economics terminology, under the planning mechanism "consumer preferences" are replaced by "planners' preferences" as the arbiter of what constitutes the best combination of goods.

PLANNERS' PREFERENCES

For most ordinary consumer goods, the planners are likely to be guided by the individual preferences of their fellow citizen–consumers. The planners would have no reason to prefer a different combination of blue jeans and dress pants than the citizens as individuals would prefer. In the case of such goods as automobiles and cigarettes, however, planners' preferences would be expected to differ from individual consumer preferences.

The efficiency of the planning mechanism should therefore be evaluated in different terms from those used in the case of the market mechanism. In particular, it should not be judged by how well it satisfies the citizens' individual preferences. To ask how efficient the planning mechanism is in satisfying individual preferences is to ask how well it does something that it is not designed to do. It would be like assessing a philanthropic hospital by the size of its profits.

There is a certain problem, however, in determining how well the planners succeed in the objective of promoting the welfare of the society as a whole. Each citizen has his own idea of what contributes most to the collective welfare, and in a large society those ideas are likely to differ and in some instances to clash. How then should "the society" judge whether the collective welfare would be higher if one collection of goods is produced rather than some other?

The Soviet Communist Party, which first introduced the planning mechanism, had an admirably clear view on that matter. It declared itself to be the "vanguard of the proletariat," meaning that it was the sole representative of the interests of the people. The Party assumed the responsibility for directing the country's economic activity in what it construed as the society's interest, and the planning mechanism was designed as the arrangement by means of which it could carry out that responsibility. Accordingly, the efficiency of the planning mechanism as it operated in the Communist countries is usually assessed by the extent to which it served the objectives announced by the Party.

The preferences of the citizens of the Communist countries no doubt differed greatly in many respects from those of the Party. Therefore their welfare when measured in terms of consumer preferences – what the people wished to consume – was lower than when measured in terms of planners' preferences – what the Party thought they ought to consume. Since the Party was running the show in terms of its own preferences, however, the appropriate standard of efficiency is what their preferences were. Planning may prove to be very inefficient if measured by its success in satisfying consumer preferences, but it may nevertheless be highly efficient in doing what it was intended to do – satisfy the Party's preferences.

To learn how well the planning mechanism served the Party's objectives, however, would be of little interest today to most people concerned with a Good Society. Democratic socialists, for example, have always strongly rejected the Communist claim that the Party is the proper judge of what constitutes the collective welfare. If they adopted the planning mechanism in their version of the Good Society, the collective welfare would be defined not by a single self-appointed Party but by some democratic political mechanism for translating the collective wishes of the citizens into instructions to the planners.

In a small society, that might be done in a town-meeting format, where the citizens would debate such matters as how high the rate of investment should be, whether individual or high-rise housing should be built, and whether it makes sense for every citizen to own his own automobile. In a large society, however, that Arcadian political arrangement would no doubt have to give way to an elected representative government authorized to decide, on behalf of the people, what instructions to issue to the economic planners. The people would cede to the government and the planners, as it were, the authority to decide what contributes most to the welfare of the society as a whole, subject to the periodic review at the ballot box.

Hence a society that adopts the planning mechanism should expect to consume different goods and work at different jobs than if it adopted the market mechanism. The optimal output of pet food, for example, would very likely be smaller under planning than under markets, presumably with the approval of the citizens. For a wide range of output, however, the planners are likely to produce what the citizens want: perhaps, indeed, for the great mass of ordinary consumer goods. Planners' preferences may therefore subsume individual preferences for a large range of output. Only in the case of certain types of consumption choices are the planners likely to substitute their own judgments for those of the individual citizens: for example, choices that are thought to affect not only the individuals who makes them but the society generally.

The efficiency of the ideal planning mechanism will be assessed below by the same three tests as were applied in the preceding chapter regarding the ideal market mechanism. The difference is that in judging whether an outcome is optimal or not, it is the preferences of the planners rather than those of individual citizens that will serve as the basis of judgment.

2   Productive Efficiency

Since the planners are committed to the largest possible output for the people, productive efficiency is a proper standard for assessing the performance of the planning mechanism, much as it is for the market mechanism. The condition required for productive efficiency is therefore the same – the marginal product of each kind of labor must be the same in all employments.

The productive efficiency of a market economy depends on many small decisions made by millions of economic actors – as consumers, workers, and managers. The productive efficiency of a planned economy, however, depends on many large decisions made by a few thousand planners. Therefore, to assess the efficiency of the ideal planning mechanism, one must examine the way in which the planners make their decisions. If they are made efficiently, then the marginal product of labor and other resources should turn out to be equal in all the production activities in which they are used.

BALANCED REGIONAL LABOR PLANS

Suppose the ten coal mines located in the Red River Region have received their final plans from their ministry, which provide for a total planned output of 1,000,000 tons of coal. The number of machinists the mines are authorized to hire is 5,000, which happens to be exactly the number of machinists available for work in the region. Since the plan is in balance, the regional planners have no further responsibility in this case: the machinists are simply distributed among the mines according to their employment plans. The efficiency question is whether the marginal product of machinist labor is equal in all the mines when each mine has hired the number of workers authorized in its employment plan.

The decision on how many workers each mine may employ is made in the ministry on the basis of the labor input norms described in chapter 14. The ministry officials possess a great deal of information on each mine's past production experience, and they have the mines' own preliminary-plan estimates of the labor they need to meet their output quotas. Under ideal conditions, the enterprises' output plans are fully coordinated with their labor supply.

Planning by means of labor input norms can succeed in providing each mine with sufficient labor to meet its output quota. That, however, does not guarantee that the corresponding labor-hiring authorizations constitute the best of all possible ways of allocating the 5,000 machinists among the mines. Each mine may have all the machinists it needs to fulfill its plan, but too many may be assigned to some mines and too few to others. If the 5,000 machinists are to be allocated optimally among the mines, the planning process must incorporate some procedure that contrives to distribute the hiring-authorizations among the mines in such a way that the marginal product of machinist labor is the same in all the mines.

None of the procedures used in the plan-balancing process, however, lead the planners to allocate labor in that way. If the marginal product of labor enters into the planners' decisions at all, directly or indirectly, one would expect to find evidence of it in the way in which the total output quota is distributed among the producing enterprises. The planning manuals, however, are conspicuously vague on the rules the planners are supposed to follow in deciding, for example, that Mine no. 1 should receive a coal output quota of 80,000 tons and Mine no. 2, 110,000 tons. They appear to rely primarily on such considerations as the quantity of output the mine produced last year and the quantity of new plant and equipment installed since then, but none of those considerations bear any relation to labor's marginal product. It follows that the planning mechanism is productively inefficient. The ten Red River coal mines could produce more than 1,000,000 tons of coal in the aggregate if the machinists were optimally allocated among them.

There is one consideration in the planning process that may appear to promote efficiency. A great deal of attention is given to cost of production, and larger output quotas tend to be assigned to enterprises with smaller labor input norms; that is, with higher labor productivity.[2] The labor input norm, however, measures the *average* product of labor and not its marginal product, and the mine with the higher average product of labor does not necessarily have the higher marginal product.[3] Cost considerations that are filtered through input norms therefore do not offset the inefficiency built into the planning process.

Relevance of marginal product   Concepts like marginal product are not part of the management lexicon of market-economy enterprises. The managers need have no idea of what the marginal product of labor is in their enterprises, and marginal product need not enter into their calculations of the profit that would be earned at each level of output. Yet their innocence of the concept of marginal product does not preclude the market mechanism from allocating resources efficiently. Why then should the absence of the concept of marginal product from the lexicon and the calculations of planners preclude the ideal planning mechanism from allocating resources efficiently?

Concepts like marginal product are analytic constructs, designed to explain not what people do, but how a system works when people do what they do. All that is required under the market mechanism is that managers know how to calculate the profit of their own enterprises, and strive to make as much of it as possible.[4] No other types of calculations need to be made by anyone. The concept of marginal product helps to explain why, under certain ideal conditions, the mechanism happens to allocate labor efficiently; but markets would work perfectly well if that concept had never been invented.

Not so the planned economy. The planners have to make decisions that no one has to make in a market economy, such as how much of the country's labor should be allocated to jeans production and how much to bread production. Unless those calculations are informed, directly or indirectly, by such concepts as productive efficiency and marginal product, there is no prospect that their allocations can be optimal.

Hence the irony that the "marginal calculus," as it is called, was invented to explain the market economy, which can operate efficiently without it; but it was not employed in the planned economies, which cannot operate efficiently without it.

Extensions   The productive inefficiency of the planning mechanism shows up most clearly in the simple case of one product and one type of labor, as in the foregoing coal mine illustration. It should be evident that the conclusion would be the same with multiple types of labor, of other inputs, and of products.

For example, if two types of labor are employed – say loaders and machine operators – efficiency requires that the marginal product of loaders be the same in all mines and also that the marginal product of machine operators be the same in all mines (chapter 11). Since the planning mechanism does not attain equality of marginal product in the distribution of any one type of labor among jobs, all types of mining labor are allocated inefficiently.

The central planners allocate not only labor but all inputs, including intermediate products, among industries and enterprises. The principal instrument of calculation for non-labor inputs is also the input norm – gallons of fuel oil required to mine a ton of coal, for example. Most intermediate inputs are like labor, however, in the sense that the marginal product of fuel oil, for example, varies in each mine according to the rate of coal production. Efficiency in the use of fuel oil therefore requires that the marginal product of a ton of fuel oil be the same in all mines. However, because of the neglect of marginal product in planning calculations, the fuel oil does not go to the mines that would make the most economical use of it. The same applies to all other inputs used in the mining industry.

Finally, what is true for the coal industry of the Red River Region is also true for all other industries in the region: textiles, for example. The textile industry therefore also produces less output in the aggregate than it could produce if the same labor and intermediate products were allocated optimally among the mills, and the same for all other industries throughout the country.

Thus, while every *enterprise* produces all that it can with the labor and other inputs that the planners assign to it, each *industry* produces less than it could if the inputs were optimally allocated among its enterprises. Hence the planning mechanism is not productively efficient, for it leaves a certain amount of slack in the economy, in the sense that it could produce more of both coal and textiles.

UNBALANCED REGIONAL LABOR PLANS

Although central planning does not produce an optimal allocation of labor even under ideal conditions, it does assure that on the national level the number of jobs is sufficient to employ the entire labor force. Balance on the national level, however, does not preclude imbalances in some regions, with which the regional planners are expected to deal. That gives them a certain influence on the final allocation of labor among jobs – which opens the possibility that the regional planners may repair some of the inefficiency that central planning builds into the regional labor plans.

When a regional plan authorizes the hiring of more labor than is available, some of the region's enterprises must end up with less labor than their plans authorize them to hire. In a case of an excess demand for labor of this sort, the regional planners do not have the authority to change the output plans of the enterprises, but they do have some control over the number of new workers the enterprises succeed in hiring. Thus, if they knew that under the final plans the marginal product of machinist labor would be larger in Mine no. 1 than in Mine no. 2, they could assign more of the available machinists to the former than to the latter, thus reducing, and perhaps even eliminating, the inefficiency due to the difference between marginal product in different mines. They could then do the same for textiles, and for all other enterprises in the region.

The planning procedures, however, place no such responsibility on the regional planners. One reason is technical. There are likely to be many different industries in the region, and many enterprises in each industry. Even if every enterprise manager knows the marginal product of each type of labor at various output levels in his own enterprise, the regional planners could not possibly have the technical expertise to process that information for the hundreds or thousands of heterogeneous enterprises in the region. The more important reason, however, goes to the root of the productive inefficiency of the material-balance method of planning.

3 Productive Efficiency and Coordination

That the central planning mechanism as it operated in the Communist countries does not pass the test of productive efficiency, even under idealized conditions, is, I believe, the assessment of virtually all economists, including both those who lived in those countries and those who lived abroad. The reason is implicit in the name that the originators of Soviet planning gave to their method of coordinating economic activity – the "method of material balances." The objective of the balancing method is to produce a national plan in which the planned supply of every input is equal to the planned demand for it in every enterprise. The economy would then be fully coordinated in the sense that no enterprise would fail to fulfill its output plan quota for lack of sufficient inputs of labor or intermediate products.

But a plan can be perfectly coordinated in that sense, and yet be productively inefficient if the planning process has no way of taking account of the marginal product of labor and other inputs. Ideally one would want a planning mechanism that would lead the planners to construct a plan that was not merely coordinated, but was also the best of all coordinated plans. The material-balance method of planning, however, contains no warning-light to alert the planners to the possibility that their laboriously constructed plan may not be optimal – that there may be some other feasible plan that would also be perfectly coordinated but would be a better plan because larger quantities of coal, textiles, and all other goods would be produced. Since the method of material balances is all about coordination, and not about efficiency, it is not surprising that even under idealized conditions, the planned economy is coordinated but not efficient.

THE ORIGIN OF PLANNING

The reasons for this puzzling deficiency in the planning mechanism are primarily historical. The Communist countries all adopted the planning methods used by the most experienced of them – the Soviet Union. Those methods originated in the early years of the Soviet regime. In the first decade following the Bolshevik Revolution, the Soviet leadership tolerated a certain degree of private ownership, particularly in farming, commerce, and small-scale manufacturing. The market mechanism was therefore also permitted to continue in operation, although under a variety of restrictions.

With the launching of the First Five-Year Plan in 1929, however, private ownership was replaced by state ownership virtually everywhere, and the uneasy toleration of the market mechanism came to an end.[5] Operating within the Marxian system of thought, the leadership regarded markets no less than private property as an integral part of the capitalist system of production, the abolition of which was the purpose of the revolution. One could not be a Marxist at the time and doubt that planning would outperform markets as the coordinating mechanism of their new Good Society.

The State Planning Committee (called *Gosplan*) had been established soon after the revolution, but during the years that markets were permitted to operate, the Committee's role as the coordinating agency was severely limited. The abolition of markets, however, thrust upon the Committee the responsibility for quickly establishing a new arrangement for performing the coordination function that had formerly been carried out by the market mechanism: the enterprises had to be told what to produce and where to obtain the inputs they needed to produce it. Coordination thus became the urgent mission of the State Planning Committee. It was in that environment that the balancing method of planning was born.

At least three factors account for the choice of the balancing method and its long sway. The first was ideological. The central article of Marxist faith was that the productive power of socialism was vastly greater than that of the dying capitalism. All that was needed to release that productive power was the replacement of the defunct markets by a new economic mechanism to coordinate the activities of the socialized enterprises. The workers and their factories needed only to be told what to produce and to be given the resources with which to do it; and the planners needed only to ensure that the coal mines produced enough coal for the power plants, that the power plants produced enough electricity for the manufacturing plants, and so forth. If those things were done well, there was no question but that in the course of time the creative energies of the masses would be finally released and the people's factories would pour forth larger volumes of goods than had ever before been seen. That was the world of thought that gave birth to the balancing method of planning and its singular preoccupation with coordination.

The second reason was practical. The revolutionary leadership was short of personnel who were politically trustworthy and who also had the skills to plan and manage the country's economy. They were also gravely undersupplied with the resources that such an effort required: the abacus was long the main calculational instrument in government offices. The balancing method had the virtue of simplicity, which would have been lost had the planners sought to achieve not only a coordinated plan, but also an optimal plan.

The third factor was political. The launching of the First Five-Year Plan coincided with the political ascendancy of Stalin and the ruthless suppression of all thought that fell outside the domain of Marxism – by now renamed Marxism-Leninism – as interpreted by his Communist Party. Many of the country's economists who had been trained in the traditions of non-Marxian economics either perished during the political terror or withdrew from active pursuit of their earlier scholarship.

As it happened, the analysis of economic efficiency was developing rapidly in mainstream Western economics at that time, while efficiency was a subject with which Marxian economics was little concerned. Unfortunately the total censorship cut Soviet economics off from that outside world of economic thought, and those economists who continued to work on the development of economic planning, both in the government and in the research institutes, had to work with concepts that could be defended as consistent with Marxism. The method of material balances concentrated on the ideologically neutral task of coordination and ignored the potentially explosive question of whether the plan was optimal or not. That question was ignored because it would have placed the analysts in the position of asking whether the economy was producing the right goods. Since it was the Party that decided what goods should be produced, inquiring into efficiency would have been equivalent to challenging the Party's ability to decide what was best for the people. The planners therefore stuck to the simple co-ordination method of material balances, which was untainted by such "bourgeois" economic notions as marginal product, diminishing returns, and Pareto-efficiency. Had freedom of economic thought not been suppressed, there is no doubt that the Soviet planners would have developed ways of building a concern with efficiency into the planning mechanism.[6]

One can only speculate on whether that effort would have been successful. They would have had to face enormous technical difficulties, some of which are set forth in chapter 18 below. The pity of it is that the economists were denied the opportunity to try to develop an efficient alternative to the planning methods that had received the Party's blessing.

4 Goods and Preferences

Planning scores badly by the test of productive efficiency, although it gets high marks for the achievement of full employment. What of the second test – efficiency with respect to consumer preferences? Does it produce that combination of goods that best satisfies the consumption preferences of the society? The test of efficiency in this matter is the same as that developed in the last chapter in the case of the market mechanism: the best combination of goods is that at which the society's production indicator is the same as its preference indicator. The only difference is that under planning, it is planners' preferences and not those of the individual consumers that serve as the arbiter of what is best.

PREFERENCES

Suppose the planning bureau works up a coordinated plan consisting of 1 million automobiles and 2 million units of new housing, which may be called Plan A. Since the planning mechanism employs the price method for the distribution of the goods, the prices will be set at the levels at which the quantities sold will be equal to the quantities that are scheduled for production according to the plan. The planners estimate that those prices would be $10,000 per automobile and $2,000 per housing unit. The society's preference indicator is therefore 5 (housing units per automobile), for the citizens reveal by their purchases that they would be willing to make do with 1 (or 100) fewer automobiles if they could get 6 (or 600) more housing units instead; or alternatively, they would prefer a combination that contained 1 (or 100) additional automobiles if they had to give up only 4 (or 400) units of housing or less.

If the planners regard automobiles and housing as ordinary goods, they would accept the people's preference indicator of 5 (housing units per automobile) as their own. However, if they believe that the social welfare consequences of automobile production were not sufficiently accounted for in the preferences of the consumers as individuals, they would be expected to substitute their own preference indicator for that of the citizens. After consultation with panels of experts and of representative citizens, they may decide upon a consumption preference indicator of 3. That is, they believe that society would be better off with more housing and fewer automobiles even if only 2 or 1 additional housing units could be built with the resources released by producing one less automobile.

PRODUCTION POTENTIAL

Whichever societal preference indicator the planners use – the citizens' or their own – the assessment of Plan A depends on the production potential indicator. That is, it depends on the number of additional (or fewer) housing units that would in fact be produced by the resources that would be released if one less (or more) automobile were produced.

For the reasons presented above in the analysis of production efficiency, however, the material-balance method of planning cannot give the planners the information they need in order to determine the actual size of the production potential indicator. In particular, the planning procedures do not make provision for assuring that the marginal product of labor is the same in all enterprises in every industry. The marginal product of labor may be $8,000 worth of automobile production in one automotive enterprise, $6,000 in another, $4,500 in a third, and so forth, and it may vary similarly among housing construction projects. There is therefore no unique answer to the question of how much additional housing could be built with the resources that would be freed up if automobile production were reduced by 1 or 100 units. The production potential indicator may be very high or very low, depending on which automobile enterprise's output plan is reduced and which construction project's plan is increased.

If the central planners knew the marginal product of labor in every enterprise, they could, in principle, micro-manage the planning procedure by deciding which enterprises' plans should be reduced and which increased. They could reduce by 1 unit the plan of the automobile plant with the lowest marginal productivity – say $4,500 – and transfer the released resources to a construction company with the highest marginal product of labor – say $9,000. With that particular transfer of resources, the production potential indicator is 2 units of housing per automobile. Since the planners' preference indicator is 3 units of housing per automobile, they judge that the society would be better off with a plan containing 1 less auto-mobile but 2 additional units of housing – call that Plan B – than with the initial Plan A.

In that way the planners could, by a series of calculations of that sort, eventually con-struct the best of all possible plans – that feasible combination of automobiles and housing that would yield the highest level of what they judge to be the consumption welfare of the society. Under ideal conditions, the planners would have all the capability they need to acquire and process the information required to calculate, for a large number of plan variants, the marginal product of every type of labor in the production of every product produced in every enterprise.

None of the plan-making procedures, however, direct the central planners toward mak-ing calculations of that sort, either explicitly or implicitly. The reason is the same as in the case of productive efficiency: namely, that planning is oriented entirely toward coordination, with virtually no attention to efficiency. Moreover, the concept of efficiency with respect to preferences is even more alien to Soviet Marxist economics than the concept of efficiency with respect to production. A central point of Marx's thought is that the value of commodities depends on an "objective" factor – the quantity of labor required to produce them. He was sharply critical of the line of economic thought that was developing at the time, which held that value also depends on the "subjective" factor of the "utility" or "satisfaction" that a commodity provides. The concept of consumer preference, as it has been employed here, is the lineal descendent of the earlier concepts of utility and satisfaction that Marx deplored. Economists and planners in the Communist countries therefore found it prudent to devote their time to matters other than the extent to which the government's production plan con-formed to the consumption preferences of the people – or of the planners, for that matter.

A society that adopts the planning mechanism should therefore not expect the economy to produce the right combination of consumer goods. The reason is not that under plan-ning, the planners' preferences substitute for individual consumer preferences: in the ideal planned economy the citizens intend their planners to attend to the welfare of the society as a whole, and not simply produce what they as individuals wish to purchase. The reason again is that the planning mechanism is designed solely to produce a coordinated plan, and not to pick out the most efficient of all possible coordinated plans.

What determines the final product mix is a very general sense of what would be acceptable to the people. The planners know that the people want and need housing and automobiles and a wide range of other consumer goods, and they plan a product mix that contains those goods in what they regard as reasonable proportions. But the question of efficiency with respect to preferences – would 10 percent more housing at the cost of 20 percent fewer automobiles increase the level of consumer welfare? – does not occupy center stage in the planning mechanism.

5 Jobs and Preferences

The Communist countries referred to themselves as "workers' states," never as "consumers' states." One would expect, therefore, that the citizens' welfare as workers would be a major concern, above their welfare as consumers. That is the third test of efficiency: does the planning mechanism provide the citizens with the work that best satisfies their job preferences?

As in the case of the market mechanism, there are two parts to that question. The first is, given the jobs that the plan has authorized, are the workers allocated among them in the best possible way? The second is whether the jobs that the plan has authorized represent the best possible collection of jobs. As in the case of consumer preferences, it is the planners' judgment that counts, and not that of the individual workers, in the assessment of which jobs are to be preferred to others.

ALLOCATING WORKERS AMONG JOBS

Since the price method is used to allocate the workers among jobs, the citizens-as-workers allocate themselves among the jobs in the same way as under the market mechanism. Each worker assesses the jobs for which she qualifies in terms of her own preference indicator – the wage premium that would induce her to accept what she regards as the less desirable job (chapter 15). The allocation of workers among jobs is therefore optimal – every other allocation would cause some workers to be worse off than in the jobs they have chosen.

THE STRUCTURE OF JOBS

While the supply of labor is managed by the wage method, the demand for labor is managed by the assignment method. Hence the efficiency of the planning mechanism with respect to job preferences depends on the way in which the planners go about deciding how many of each kind of job there will be.

Suppose the planners were presented with two collections of jobs – one with a great many dirty jobs and few pleasant ones, and the other with few or no dirty jobs and many pleasant ones. If they relied solely on their judgment of which collection would provide the highest level of welfare of the citizens-as-workers, the choice would be clear. The second is a more appealing prospect for a Good Society.

To make the decision in that way, however, would clearly be an error. In choosing among collections of consumer goods one can consider only consumer preferences, but in choosing among collections of jobs, one cannot consider only job preferences. One must also consider the goods that would be produced with each of those job structures. Under planning no less than under markets, the demand for labor is a "derived demand" – the jobs that the citizens have to perform are derived from the goods they wish to consume.

Therefore, in deciding which of many sets of jobs is the best, the planners have to consider also the goods that would be produced with each set of jobs. They must balance the welfare of the citizens-as-consumers against the welfare of the citizens-as-workers.

As an example of a typical job-preference decision, suppose that the planners regard the conditions of work in underground coal mining to be socially unacceptable, and decide that all mines should be required to install air filters. The larger the number of air filters installed, the better the conditions of work; but the production of filters requires labor and other resources that could otherwise be used to produce consumer goods. Hence, while the job structure after filter installation is preferred on job-preference grounds, the consumption level before filter installation is preferred on consumer-preference grounds.

In order to decide how large a volume of resources should be devoted to filter production, the planners must have a way of evaluating, for each level of filter production, the gain in the welfare of the citizens-as-workers and the loss in the welfare of the citizens-as-consumers. They might find, for example, that the production and installation of 10,000 filters would improve mine air quality by 10 percent while consumption would decline by 1 percent, that 20,000 filters would improve air quality by 15 percent and reduce consumption by 5 percent, and so on for various rates of filter output. They would then select that rate of filter production which, in their judgment, would provide the optimal combination of job quality and consumption, and that rate of filter production would be included in the plan. In practice, decisions of that sort are no doubt very difficult to make, but in principle they can be made.

In order to make such decisions, however, the planners must be able to calculate the amount by which consumption would decline if resources were transferred from consumer goods production to the production of filters. And there's the rub. The planning mechanism does not provide the information required for that kind of calculation, even under ideal conditions. The problem is the same as that encountered above in the case of production efficiency. Since the marginal physical product of labor differs among enterprises in the same industry, and since the marginal revenue product of labor also differs among industries, there is no unique answer to the question of how much output would be lost if a certain quantity of labor were transferred from one line of production to another. The withdrawal of a hundred workers from one electronics enterprise might cause output to fall by 10 TV sets a month, while in another enterprise it might fall by 40 sets a month. A similar withdrawal of labor from one textile enterprise might cause output to fall by 1,000 yards, from another by 5,000 yards, and so on.

Nor is there a unique answer to the question of how large a volume of resources is needed to produce a given number of filters. Since the marginal cost of production is not the same in all filter-production plants, the answer depends on how the production orders are distributed among those plants.

The government and its planners are hired to make decisions, and they do eventually decide to produce a certain number of filters for installation in the mines. Hence the welfare of the citizens-as-workers is somewhat higher than it was before, and the welfare of the citizens-as-consumers is somewhat lower than it was before. There is no way of excluding the possibility, however, that a different decision – a larger, or a smaller, investment in mine air filtering – would yield a higher level of welfare when both job preferences and consumer preferences are weighed in the balance. Which is another way of saying that the planning mechanism obliges the planners to make a great many choices affecting the job structure, but nothing in the procedures guides them toward the optimal choice. Hence the planning mechanism is inefficient in creating a job structure that best reflects the society's job preferences.

Inefficiency with respect to job preferences is therefore another fallout of the preoccupation of the planning mechanism with coordination, to the neglect of efficiency.

6 Discussion

In an efficiency contest between the two idealized coordination mechanisms, the market mechanism wins hands down. I can't imagine an economist in the world today who would contest that assertion.

A friend of planning could properly point out, however, that I have defined an ideal planning mechanism rather narrowly. The particular planning procedures that I have presented are those that were used in the Communist countries. Those procedures are tainted by the tyrannical history of the USSR. They were established under Stalin's dictatorship when free critical debate was impossible, and they were never subject to open challenge throughout Soviet history. During all those decades in which Soviet economic thought was largely cut off from the rest of the world, there developed in the West a variety of mathematical techniques that could have provided a firmer theoretical foundation for centralized economic planning.

Two such techniques that aroused the greatest interest are "input-output analysis," and "linear programming." The input-output technique was invented in the 1930s by Nobel Laureate Wassily Leontieff, a Harvard professor of Russian origin whose early economics training had been acquired in the Soviet Union shortly after the revolution. The technique was widely employed in the West for a variety of purposes after World War II. The power of the technique for economic planning is that it supplies a much more reliable method than material balancing for constructing a balanced plan. It is based on certain mathematical and statistical techniques that make it possible to construct a balanced plan fairly quickly; and if some parts of the plan need to be altered later, the full set of related changes that would have to be made in all other parts of the plan can be rapidly calculated. The speed and accuracy of the technique would make it possible, in principle, to construct several different balanced plans. The benefit is that, in a Good Society, the representatives of the people could then select the best of all those balanced plans. Planning would then be efficient with respect to both production and preferences.

Linear programming, invented around the period of World War II, is an even more powerful technique that produces not only a balanced plan but the best of all possible balanced plans. In order to achieve that remarkable result the representatives of the society must initially specify what the preferences of the society are: the social "objectives function," as it is called. They must announce their judgments of what I have called the societal preference indicators for all goods: for example, for every combination of housing and automobiles, how many square feet of housing would be worth giving up for one additional automobile, and so on for all goods. Once the values of goods are specified in that way, a variety of production data are fed into the computer which then grinds out an optimal plan – a plan that provides for the largest possible output of goods as measured by the previously specified societal preferences.

In the light of such alternative planning methods, one could argue that to take the flawed Stalinist planning mechanism, however idealized, as the counterpart of the market mechanism is to stack the cards against planning. The proper counterpart ought to be the kind of planning mechanism that a future society is likely to consider, which would surely make use of such mathematical techniques as input-output or linear programming. An idealized "perfect-computation" model of the planning mechanism would then be no less efficient than the idealized perfect-competition model of the market mechanism.[7] Looked at in that way, one would conclude that under the best of conditions, economic planning properly done need be no less efficient than the market mechanism.

There is merit in that argument, but such a comparison would stack the cards in the opposite direction. Both the market economy and Soviet-type central planning have actually been employed in a variety of countries for a considerable length of time. Mathematical planning, however, has rarely been employed in any economy anywhere, and there is no empirical evidence on whether it is feasible in practice, or how it would actually work out in practice. Its status is still that of an idea. Had this chapter been written as an idealization of that form of planning, it would have been an idealization of an idea and not of anything real.

Still, it is something to hold the allegiance of friends of central planning. Some future society may well reject the market mechanism in favor of central planning, resolving to "do it right this time" in the form of mathematical planning. It may then turn out that a super-idealized version of that type of planning would be no less efficient than the perfect-competition version of the market mechanism. The comparative efficiency of plans and markets would then have to be reassessed. Until that time, the proper comparison must be based on planning as we know it and the market as we know it.

The analysis of idealized models is a much maligned occupation. It appeals to the satirical temperament to poke fun at economists who occupy themselves with "perfect" worlds that exist nowhere on earth. In my view, however, they are an indispensable tool for probing deeply into the economics of a Good Society. It is the only way of asking, of any system, whether the problem is the jockey or the horse.

That being said, it is important not to confuse models with reality. Much nonsense about economic systems derives from confusion of that sort. The most deceptive form of argument, and of self-delusion, is to compare an idealized model of one mechanism with a real instance of the other mechanism. The deception can be either conservative or radical. Conservatives in Communist countries juxtaposed idealized planning with real markets, while conservatives in market economies juxtapose idealized markets with the messy world of real planning. On the other hand, radicals in the Communist countries juxtaposed perfect markets with real planning, while radicals in market economies juxtapose idealized planning with the grubby world of real markets.

The ultimate test of goodness, however, is not to be found in ideal models but in the way in which the mechanisms operate under the less-than-ideal conditions of the real world. The next two chapters discuss the operation of the two economic mechanisms in practice, on the basis of the experience of the countries that have actually employed them.

Notes

1 Collective judgments of these kinds are also made in societies that employ the market mechanism: liquor and cigarettes may be heavily taxed in order to discourage consumption. Under planning, however, such judgments are incorporated directly into the economy through the plan, whereas under the market mechanism they are imposed on the economy by the external power of government. Societal concerns are "internalized" in the economy under planning, so to speak, whereas under the market mechanism they are expressed by the external intervention of government in the economy.

2 If a labor input norm is 3 hours of labor per ton of output, then labor productivity is the inverse of that – one-third ton of output per hour of labor.

3 The mine with the higher average product – perhaps 100 tons per worker – may be working at full capacity, with very little place for additional labor. Squeezing another worker in may add only 40 tons to production. The marginal product in this case (40 tons) is very small relative to the average product (100 tons).

4 The analogy often drawn upon is the billiards player. An analyst would "explain" his shots by noting that the angle of reflection equals the angle of incidence, but one can be an excellent player without ever having heard those terms. Similarly, the economist "explains" the implications of profit maximization in such terms as "marginal profit" and "marginal product," but the enterprise manager and his staff go about their business of making money without reference to those analytic terms.

5 The idea of market socialism – state-owned enterprises operating under a market mechanism – had not yet been invented; it was first presented in a published paper by Oskar Lange in 1936. Even if the concept had been known at the time, however, it is doubtful that the Communist leadership would have found it an attractive alternative to central planning.

6 This political prohibition gradually disappeared after Stalin's death, and a growing number of Soviet economists came to embrace marginal analysis, urging that it be incorporated into planning and pricing. They remained a minority up to the time of Gorbachev, however.

7 Wiles, *The Political Economy of Communism*, ch. 10.

Chapter 17

Markets in an Imperfect World

Each individual ... is led by an invisible
hand to promote [the interest] of the
society more effectually than when he
really intends to promote it.
                              – Adam Smith

And with thy bloody and invisible
hand ...
                              – Shakespeare

CONTENTS

Some enthusiasts of the market mechanism regard it as so virtuous as to be suitable even
for an Ideal Society. The more measured proponents, however, regard markets as Winston
Churchill regarded democracy – a rather creaky system but much better than all the others.
In the spirit of that more moderate appreciation, an assessment of the merits of markets for

the Good Society should be founded on an understanding of the things that the market does badly as well as those that it does well. For the present, of course, good and bad refer only to the criterion of efficiency.

It is not to be expected that the market mechanism will operate in practice as efficiently as in an idealized model. Unlike Utopia, however, it is a system with which many countries have had long experience. That experience provides a basis for judging how the market mechanism is likely to perform in a Good Society that decides to adopt it, and where and why it falls short of the aims of that society.

In virtually all countries that have employed the market mechanism, the productive property has been privately owned. There is therefore little evidence on how markets would operate in practice in a regime of social ownership. The experience of private-property economies should nevertheless be of interest to partisans of social ownership, for it may suggest ways of modifying the market mechanism to make it more consistent with social ownership.

The first source of inefficiency is that markets in practice rarely conform to the prime requirement for efficiency – perfect competition. The consequences of that fact of life are spelled out in the first half of this chapter.

While perfect competition is a necessary condition for efficiency, it is not a sufficient one. A great many other conditions must also be present, for if they are not, the most perfect of markets fails to allocate the country's resources efficiently. Unfortunately, most markets in practice do not operate under those benign conditions, which is the source of the various kinds of "market failure" that are assiduously studied in economics textbooks. That literature supplies a great many reasons why a society that adopts the market mechanism should not expect it to operate as efficiently as the idealized model of that mechanism. Three of the most prominent causes of market failure provide the gist of the reasoning: externalities, public goods, and imperfect knowledge. They are the subject of the second half of the chapter.

I Imperfect Competition

Perfect competition resembles the irresistible travel brochures of Caribbean cruise lines. The cruise may well be worth taking, but it generally turns out that the cabins are not in fact that luxurious, the beaches are not that pristine, and the seas sometimes run high.

Some markets do resemble the brochure. Markets for the primary products of the earth, such as foods, raw materials, metals, and so forth, are generally perfectly competitive. Among the most prominent are those whose market prices are listed daily on the world's commodity exchanges: soybeans, pork bellies, crude oil, platinum. On the local level, when the lobsterman ties up at the Provincetown fish pier, he has to sell his catch at the going price or he can sell nothing at all.

In earlier and simpler times a large proportion of all output was produced under conditions of perfect competition. In the modern economy, however, the products of each enterprise are physically different from those of the others, in varying degrees. The computer produced by one enterprise is different from that produced by another, and the same for breakfast cereals, fork-lift trucks, and other manufactured products. Indeed, companies spend a great deal of money promoting their brand names and reminding the public that their products are different, and better, than the others. In such industries enterprises do have the power to set the prices of their products; indeed, a central preoccupation of management is "price policy" – that is, deciding how much to charge for the product. Producers in such markets are "price-makers," in contrast to the "price-takers" of competitive markets. The Ford Motor Company must decide how much to charge for its Taurus; the captain of the Sissy-K lobster boat has no choice but to take whatever the market price happens to be. Competition in markets like automobiles, in which the actors have the power to set prices, is said to be "imperfect."

Labor markets also vary in the degree of competition. Unskilled labor is fairly homogeneous, so that the individual worker has to accept whatever the going wage happens to be. At the other extreme are people with rare talents and skills like celebrated surgeons, ball players, and pop singers. Like the Ford Motor Company, they can decide how much to charge for their services.

Market imperfections can take many possible forms. There may be only one producer, or two, or several, or many. The imperfection may occur on the seller's side of the market: when there is one large producer of a consumer good, for example, but many consumers. Or it may occur on the buyer's side, as in a "company town" with one dominant employer and many workers seeking jobs. Economic actors behave differently under each of these market forms, and students of economics are routinely drilled in the analysis of those behavioral variations. The flavor of the analysis can be conveyed, however, by two examples of imperfect competition, one dealing with markets for goods and services, and the other with markets for labor services.

2   Imperfect Product Markets

The argument takes off from the familiar proposition that all enterprises adjust their output to the level at which profit is at its peak. When they do that in perfectly competitive markets, it turns out that the marginal revenue product of labor in their enterprises is equal to the market price of the product (chapter 15). The distribution of labor and output among enterprises is therefore optimal: there is no possible transfer of workers from enterprise to another that would yield a larger total output.

BRAND NAMES

Suppose that the market for potatoes is perfectly competitive and the market price is $6 a bag. The owners of Idaho Farms, however, conceive the idea of packaging their potatoes in attractive bags bearing the legend "Mother Brown's Select Potatoes," and set a price of $9 a bag on them. If all consumers decide that those potatoes are really no different from everyone else's, the company will sell nothing; competition is so perfect that no producer can charge more than the market price. Idaho Farms must scurry back to the market price.

But if some consumers believe that Mother Brown's potatoes are really better than the others, they will buy some of them, even at the higher price. Once that occurs, innocence has ended. The producer has succeeded in "differentiating" their potatoes from the others in the minds of some consumers. That gives the company a grip on those consumers which it does not have on consumers who regard Mother Brown's potatoes as no different from the others.

By partially shielding itself from the force of competition and charging a higher price for its product, Idaho Farms are able to earn more profit that they could when the competition was perfect. It is true that at the higher price of $9, they sell fewer potatoes than they sold at the market price of $6. But since they produce fewer potatoes, their total production costs are also lower. Hence, as a result of the risky but successful venture, the company's profit may be higher than it was before.[1]

With the success of Mother Brown's Select Potatoes, the state of competition is no longer perfect. The market is still competitive in the sense that the availability of other potatoes places a limit on the price that Idaho Farms can charge for theirs, but the competition is now of the imperfect sort. One might say, indeed, that there are now two distinct but related markets, in one of which there is only one producer, Idaho Farms.

The innovative company is clearly better off if its profit has increased. Whether one regards the purchasers of Mother Brown's potatoes as better off depends on one's values. You and I may have some objective standard of potato goodness that tells us that Mother Brown's are no different from the others. We would then view the "innovation" as a hoax for tricking gullible consumers into believing that those potatoes are sufficiently tastier or healthier to be worth the higher price. By our standard there is then no increase in well-being, but merely a siphoning of some dollars from consumers' pockets into those of Idaho Farms. A Good Society that adopts the market mechanism, however, generally values consumer sovereignty, rather than the opinion of experts like you and me. The standard of goodness is then the consumers' preferences. If one or more consumers choose to buy 1 bag of Mother Brown's when they could have bought 1.2 bags of ordinary potatoes, the society should regard itself as better off on that account.

Farewell to perfect competition   Better off, perhaps, but not as well off as it could be, because, alas, the economy is no longer efficient. Since competition is no longer perfect, the distribution of the country's labor resources among farms is no longer optimal.

The reasoning derives from the test of efficiency with respect to consumer preferences that was developed in chapter 15: the society's production potential must correspond to its preferences. Consumer preferences are revealed by the prices that people are willing to pay: $9 for Mother Brown's and $6 for generic potatoes. The consumption preference indicator is therefore 1.5 – consumers regard 1 additional bag of Mother Brown's as having the same consumption value as 1.5 additional bags of ordinary potatoes. That signifies that the citizens-as-consumers would regard themselves as better off with 1.5 fewer bags of ordinary potatoes if they could get more than 1 bag of Mother Brown's in exchange; or alternatively, they would be willing to give up 1 bag of Mother Brown's in exchange for more than 1.5 bags of ordinaries. The economy's potential for producing more of the two goods is revealed by the marginal product of labor in the two activities. Marginal product is unchanged on the ordinary farms – say 2.5 bags of potatoes for the marginal worker. But it is now higher than that on Idaho Farms, because they have cut back on production – say 3 bags of potatoes. The production potential indicator is now 1.2 (3.0/2.5); that is, if 1 less bag of potatoes were produced on an ordinary farm, the released labor could produce 1.2 bags on a Mother Brown's farm.

It follows that the allocation of labor among farms is no longer optimal. The preference indicator says that the people would prefer another bag of Mother Brown's even if they had to give up 1.5 bags of ordinary potatoes. The production indicator says that only 1.2 bags of ordinary potatoes would have to be given up to produce 1 more bag of Mother Brown's. The people want more Mother Brown's and the economy can produce more, but it does not do so because of the imperfection of the market.

Generalizing from the example, when competition is perfect, the producers have no "power" over the customers, so that if one of them tries to charge a higher price, he will sell nothing at all. When competition is imperfect, however, the producer enjoys a certain power over its customers so that even if the price is raised, some of them will continue to buy the product, although others will shop elsewhere. The producer is able to take advantage of that power by holding back its production in order to be able to charge more than it could if competition were perfect, and it will earn more profit by that action than it could earn if the competition from other enterprises were perfect. Or otherwise put, the profit-maximizing output of an enterprise in an imperfectly competitive market is smaller, and the price is higher, than that of an equivalent enterprise in a perfectly competitive market.

It follows that where competition is imperfect, the market mechanism is an inefficient arrangement for allocating a country's resources. In every modern economy, however, markets are overwhelmingly imperfect. The shelves of every supermarket testify to the efforts of producers who, like Idaho Farms, seek to persuade the public that their breakfast cereal or laundry soap is better than the others. Hence, insofar as allocative efficiency is a criterion for assessing the goodness of an economy, the omnipresence of imperfect competition means that the market mechanism generally fails that test in practice.

Imperfect competition is competition nonetheless, and it is fierce in many markets, ranging from fashion goods like clothing to consumer durables like automobiles and TV sets. Consumers lose some and win some from that competition. They lose when it generates large social costs such as massive advertising expenditures and product misrepresentation, and they lose from the allocative inefficiency of imperfect competition. They gain from imperfect competition, however, when it drives producers to introduce genuinely new and improved products and in other ways to attend to their preferences. The wide range of new products available to this generation that were unknown to its grandparents offers dramatic testimony to the size of the gains. Few would argue that the suppression of imperfect competition would make for a better society in the long run.

Competition, perfect or not, disciplines producers by confronting them with the prospect of the loss of profit if they raise prices too high or let the quality of the products decline. The disciplinarians are the consumers on the one hand and the producers of similar products on the other. The fewer the number of other producers, however, the smaller the disciplinary power of the consumers. The extreme case is one in which there is only one producer of the product. That type of market goes by the name of "monopoly."

MONOPOLY

The power of a monopolist is not absolute. He does not have to worry about competing producers, but he still has to be concerned about consumer–customers. If a monopolist is the sole producer of something that few people want to buy, there may be little profit to be had from the monopoly. Best of all is to hold a monopoly over a product that many people regard as indispensable, and for which there are no close substitutes, such as a new pharmaceutical drug. With a product of that sort, the number of customers would not drop very much if the price were set very high. When demand is that "inelastic," the most profitable price may be extremely high – so high that the manufacturer may decide to charge less than that in order to avoid provoking a hostile public reaction.

That hostility is often personalized. Monopolists loom as persons of evil character intent on exploiting the defenseless public, in contrast to ordinary businessmen who want no more than to earn an honest dollar. Properly viewed, however, the problem is not in the people but in the market structure. Take any manager and place him in a competitive market and he will charge what the public sees as a reasonable price. Place the same manager in a market structure in which he faces no competition and his price will seem rapacious. In both cases he is merely doing his job of making as much profit for his enterprise as he can. In general, people who are lions under one social arrangement are pussycats under another. If the outcomes are undesirable, a Good Society should try to reform the social arrangements rather than try to reform the people.

The objection to monopoly, from the perspective of the Good Society, is that it is inefficient with respect to consumption preferences. As in all imperfect markets, monopolists restrict the rate of output of their products in order to be able to charge the price that earns their company the most profit. Hence the economy produces less of the monopolized good, and more of other goods, than should be produced in a society that wishes to best satisfy the consumption preferences of the people.

There are some respects in which monopoly does serve the public interest. As long as monopolists pursue the objective of earning as much profit as possible, they will make every effort to sell as much as they can at the high price they have set. They will therefore be no less concerned to satisfy the consumer than a producer faced with strong competition. They will be technologically progressive, they will strive to maintain and improve the quality of their products, and they will be open to the innovation of new products that promise a handsome profit.

The trouble is that the monopolists' devotion to the pursuit of profit tends to erode in the absence of the spur of competition. If people cannot do without their products, they lose very little if the quality of their products deteriorates. A glimpse of that effect can be had under conditions of general shortage, such as often occurs in wartime. When customers come flocking to a seller who knows that they have no other place to turn, it is remarkable how the quality of both goods and services – particularly the latter – deteriorates. Monopoly thus detracts from the goodness of a society not only because of its allocative inefficiency, but because of the decline in the quality of its goods and services.

The full effect on quality of the absence of competition is rarely felt, however, for several reasons. The estimated loss to the economy of monopolistic restrictions on output is not very large. Moreover, pure monopoly is rare in modern economies because there are few products for which there are no substitutes at all. Large profits also attract the attention of other companies that are eager to challenge the monopolist for a share of those profits by entering the market with their own brand of the product; that consideration sometimes restrains companies from fully exploiting their monopoly power. Hence, pure monopolies are usually confined to industries where, for technical reasons, it would be wasteful for competition to prevail. The cost of building railroads or electric-power transmission lines is so large, for example, that in many circumstances it would be wasteful for more than one company to provide those services between the same cities. In the case of such so-called "natural monopolies," governments either provide the service themselves, or authorize private companies to provide it, but under public regulation.[2]

COLLUSION

Over 200 years ago Adam Smith warned that a tendency toward conspiracies by businessmen against the public is inherent under capitalism. "People of the same trade," he wrote, "seldom meet together, even for merriment and diversion, but the conversation ends in a conspiracy against the public, or in some contrivance to raise prices."[3] Every generation of managers produces new instances of the danger that he foresaw.

As if acting on the script written by Adam Smith, in 1993 three top executives of the giant food company, Archer Daniels Midland, dined secretly in a hotel room with two Japanese businessmen. For several hours they haggled over the terms of an agreement to fix prices on a valuable feed additive. They were unaware that the entire meeting was videotaped by government officials. On the basis of this and other evidence, the three executives, one of whom was the son of the company's president, were convicted of engaging in a conspiracy to fix prices. They face penalties of up to three years in jail plus fines of at least $350,000. This was one of eight criminal cases that the US government had brought against nine corporations in the food and feed industry and 11 of their executives, almost all of whom pleaded guilty.[4]

The persistence of this sort of "white-collar crime" signifies that while the business community professes a deep devotion to competition, that devotion is in fact ambivalent. Producers love competition among the suppliers of the things they buy because it holds down the prices they have to pay. But they deplore competition from producers of goods that are identical or similar to their own because it limits the prices they can charge and therefore the profits they can earn.

When the number of enterprises is very large, there is little that the managers can do to restrain the competition among them. The smaller the number of competitors, however, the greater the possibility of coming to an agreement to restrain the "cutthroat" competition among them. It takes no great imagination to recognize the benefits that all of them could gain if they could agree to charge a common price and to refrain from undercutting it. That price could be set at a higher level than could be sustained under conditions of competition. All producers could therefore earn a larger profit, perhaps much larger, than they could earn by competing with each other.

Sometimes those conspiracies are informal and often covert, as in the Archer Daniels Midland case, but in other cases they are formalized in agreements among enterprises known as "cartels," in which the producers agree to abide by a common price or to limit their production in order not to undermine the price. The famous OPEC oil cartel thrived for some time but eventually lost its effectiveness; the much older DeBeers cartel, however, continues to maintain the price of diamonds far above the level that would prevail under competitive conditions.

Countries differ in their attitude toward such restrictions on competition. Many governments, like that of pre-war Germany, have been friendly to cartels, in the belief that they provide the country's industry with an advantage *vis-à-vis* foreign producers. At the other extreme is the United States, which outlawed "combinations and conspiracies in restraint of trade" in the landmark Sherman Anti-Trust Act of 1890. In the same spirit, the American occupation government prohibited cartels in West Germany and Japan after World War II, but subsequent national governments in those countries have permitted certain kinds of cartel arrangements. Most postwar industrial countries adopted some sort of anti-cartel laws, but none has gone as far as the United States and all permit a variety of exceptions.

A Good Society that adopts the market mechanism should therefore expect, on the basis of the experience of those economies that have been there before, that very few of its product markets will operate under the condition of perfect competition. Hence, it should not expect to reap the full benefit of the efficiency promised by the ideal model. Nor should it expect to be freed of governmental involvement in the affairs of enterprises unless it is prepared to accept the consequences of monopoly and collusion.

It is conceivable that if market-economy enterprises were socially owned, the managers would not take advantage of the profit-making opportunities of imperfectly competitive markets. The limited experience of such enterprises suggests, however, that when pressed by the public for such favors as lower prices for their customers and higher wages for their workers, they are unlikely to take kindly to strong competition from other public or private enterprises that cuts into their profits. Moreover, while owners of capitalist firms know exactly what they are doing when they conspire to control prices and markets, the managers of public enterprises are likely to paint such actions as the benevolent protection of the public from "destructive competition." However, collusion would be more difficult to conceal because they would not have the protection of commercial secrecy and their books would be open to public scrutiny.

3 Imperfect Labor Markets: Management

In every modern economy a large proportion of the labor force works in large enterprises. There is no absolute need for that to be so. A Good Society might decide that its social values would be better served if no production unit exceeded a certain size. That view did indeed have a substantial following in the early years of the Industrial Revolution, when the social and ecological upheavals of nascent capitalism kindled a nostalgia for pre-capitalist days, before the coal mines replaced the green valleys. A modern version of that view of a better society was that of Mahatma Gandhi, who preached the virtues of cottage industry and the village economy. One still finds strains of that theme among environmentalists who urge that "small is beautiful."

Perhaps technological advance will some day make it possible to run a modern economy on the basis of small production units, and at the same time to achieve a level of production and consumption that would satisfy the members of the society. That prospect is hardly on the horizon, however. The best that a Good Society might do, in this respect, is to make it possible for those of its members who value smallness in their production lives to "opt out" of the mainstream of economic life and yet lead a productive life without excessive penalty in consumption. It should indeed be counted as one of the benefits of living in a wealthy market economy that a relatively large number of people can earn a modest but apparently adequate livelihood as artisans, craftsmen, and proprietors or chefs in small restaurants. One also reads striking accounts of business executives abandoning the fast track for quieter occupations as Vermont innkeepers and Cape Cod antique dealers.

Nevertheless the technology of the foreseeable future is likely to concentrate much of the production activity of the modern economy in fairly large enterprises. A Good Society that adopts the market mechanism should therefore confront the prospect that the managers might use their market power as purchasers of materials and employers of labor in ways that would lead to an inefficient allocation of the country's resources.

A SINGLE EMPLOYER

Imperfection in labor markets mirrors that in product markets. The extreme case is one in which a single large enterprise is virtually the sole employer in the area. That kind of labor market – known as "monopsony" – is the twin of monopoly in a product market. It frequently occurs in place-centered economic activities such as lumbering and minerals extraction, where the workers live in "company towns." The neat packs of chicken breasts found in food markets often originate in a poultry-processing plant that is the sole employer of unskilled labor in a poor rural community. Many small and even mid-sized industrial cities are dominated by a single large employer.

Such enterprises have learned from experience that they do have the power to influence the wage rate that they have to pay. If changes in economic conditions make it profitable to reduce the wage by 5 percent, some of the workers might quit, but most would stay on, having little prospect of finding another job elsewhere. By contrast, if a small building contractor in a large labor market decided to pay 5 percent less than the market wage to his carpenters, virtually all of them would start looking for jobs with other employers, and most or all would quit sooner or later. It is in that sense that small enterprises have no "market power" over the wage: they either pay the market wage or they go out of business. Enterprises in a perfectly competitive labor market may be said to be "wage-takers," while monopsonists are "wage-makers."

The consequence of monopsonists' power to set the wage is that the labor market is inefficient in allocating the country's labor resources. The argument parallels that relating to monopoly. Imagine a community in which there are a great many small coal mines that compete as wage-takers for the labor services of mine workers. If the market wage is $20 an hour, each enterprise settles on the output and employment level at which the marginal revenue product of its labor is $20. Each enterprise is then earning the largest possible profit, the total of which may be $1 million for the whole industry.

Suppose now that one company buys up all the others and the whole industry then operates as one large enterprise that earns the $1 million profit formerly shared by the small mines.

That company is now the only employer of coal miners in the region. As a monopsonist it is now a wage-maker, and it can reduce its total labor costs by cutting the wage rate, to perhaps $18. Some workers would quit coal mining at that wage rate and seek employment in other industries or towns, so that the company's coal output would decline. Because of the reduced wage cost, however, total profit would rise, from $1 million to perhaps $1.1 million. With the reduced labor force, the marginal product of coal mining labor would now be higher than before – perhaps $22.

Further wage reduction might increase the profit even more. At some wage rate, however, profit will reach its peak, at perhaps $1.3 million.[5] That wage rate might be $16, and the marginal product might be as high as $25; compared to the original competitive labor market in which both the wage and the marginal product of labor were $20.

Hence, monopsony fails the test of efficiency with respect to consumer preferences, for the same reason that monopoly fails that test. The monopsonist finds it profitable to employ fewer workers at a lower wage, much as the monopolist finds it more profitable to produce fewer goods so that they can be sold at a higher price. The curtailment of output drives the production potential indicator out of alignment with the consumer-preference indicator. The consumers would prefer a redistribution of labor that would produce more coal and less of other things, but the monopsonist's profit would fall if she expanded coal output.

Hence, in a monopsonized market the profit motive works against efficiency, because too few workers are employed there and too many in industries with competitive labor markets.

Several employers

Some wage rates are set under monopsonistic conditions in modern economies, but a very large proportion of workers hold jobs in industries in which there are two or more dominant employers.[6] In such markets each enterprise has some degree of market power over the wage, but it is constrained by the wage policy of the other enterprises. If Acme Dynamic decides to cut wage rates, the effect will depend on how the other employers respond. One of many possibilities, for example, is that the others do not respond at all. In that case, Acme can simply operate like a wage-maker with respect to its own labor force, in the manner of a pure monopsonist, and a certain allocation of workers among jobs will result. If the others match Acme's wage cut, the resulting allocation of labor may be the same as before the wage cut, but all companies may be earning larger profits because of the lower wage.

The variety of possible relations among oligopsonists is so large that it is difficult to generalize about the efficiency of this form of labor-market structure. Since there is no competition of the pure wage-taking sort driving the marginal product to equality with a common wage rate, however, there is nothing to guide the allocation distribution of labor toward the optimum. Hence, since modern economies are likely to contain many markets with a small number of large employers, labor markets are unlikely to operate in practice with the efficiency of the ideal model.

4 Imperfect Labor Markets: Unions

Self-interest drives not only employers but also workers under the market mechanism. Much as employers prefer to escape from competition with each other by joining together to keep wages down, so do workers prefer to escape competition with other workers, and to combine together to keep wages up. Unlike combinations of employers, combinations of workers – trade unions – were generally illegal in past centuries. In modern economies, however, that relation has been reversed. Combinations by employers to fix wages are illegal in the US and many other countries, while labor unions are almost everywhere lawful.

Monopsony and collusion violate the conditions of perfect competition on the demand side of labor markets. Labor unions violate the conditions of perfect competition on the supply side. They do this through their efforts to maintain a higher wage level than that which would result under conditions of perfect competition. Unions represent many other interests of their members, such as the conditions of work and of the workplace, but the following discussion will concentrate on wage rates.

WAGE RATES

The extent to which unions have actually succeeded in raising their members' wage rates has been the subject of extensive research, the consensus of which is that union members earn between 10 percent and 20 percent more than non-union members with the same attributes – skills, location, and so forth.[7] A wage differential of that size is not massive, but it can have a significant effect on the performance of the economy.

When unions succeed in doing what they are supposed to do – raising their members' wage rates – the consequence is a change in the number of jobs and the allocation of workers among them. The effect of such wage increases on efficiency depends on the state of competition on the demand side of the market – that is, whether the employers are powerless to influence the wage (perfect competition) or whether they possess market power over the wage (imperfect competition).

Perfect competition among employers   Suppose the equilibrium wage rate for carpenters were $200 for a day's labor. If competition were perfect, all managers would then hire that number of carpenters at which the marginal product of carpenters in their enterprise was $200 a day. Suppose now that the carpenters form a union that succeeds in raising the wage rate to $220. Employers would then recalculate their profit tables, and would find that some of the jobs on which their carpenters are working are no longer profitable at the higher wage rate. In the course of time, as contracts run out, they will shed those business activities in which a marginal day of carpenter's labor brings in less than $220 a day. Eventually, when all enterprises have adjusted to the new wage rate, construction work will have contracted to the point at which the marginal product of carpenter labor in all enterprises has risen to the new level of $220.

The consequence is that there are fewer jobs for carpenters than there were before – say 1,800 instead of 2,000. The other 200 carpenters must then seek the best alternative jobs that they can find, perhaps in other occupations or industries, or in more remote towns in which construction workers are not unionized, or as unskilled labor. The effect is to increase the number of workers seeking jobs in those other labor markets. When it becomes known that there are now more workers available for unskilled jobs, for example, the wage for unskilled labor will begin to decline, from perhaps $150 initially to $145. Some employers, in construction and elsewhere, will then find that since unskilled help can now be hired at $145 a day, it pays to take on certain jobs that can be done by unskilled workers but that were unprofitable at a labor cost of $150. Jobs for unskilled workers will thus expand as the wage rate declines until the carpenters released from the construction industry have all found jobs somewhere else. Eventually perhaps 100 of the displaced carpenters will have found jobs as unskilled workers, and the wage rate will stabilize once more, at perhaps $142. The marginal product of unskilled labor will then settle down to $142 in all enterprises in the area.

Thus, the success of the carpenters' union has two major consequences from the perspective of the Good Society. One is distributional: the earnings of the union carpenters who retain their jobs increase, but earnings decline for those carpenters whose jobs disappeared, as well as for the other workers in the enterprises and occupations where the released carpenters found new jobs.

What if all jobs were unionized, so that there would be no non-union jobs to which displaced workers could turn for employment? The unions could then drive the wage rate up for all employed workers. But while market-economy enterprises can be compelled to pay the higher wage, they cannot be compelled to hire more workers than they find profitable; and the higher the wage, the fewer workers they would find it profitable to hire. It is evident that if that union wage were set extremely high – say equal to two or ten times the original market level or more – a great many employers, unable to make any profit at any level of output, would have to close down their business and dismiss all their workers. With a modest increase in the wage, most companies would remain in business but their profit would now peak at a lower level of output and they would hire fewer workers than before. While the final outcome will depend on the government's economic policies, the likely result is that the wage rate of employed workers will be very high but the number of unemployed workers will also be high.

The second consequence bears directly on efficiency. Initially, the carpenter's wage was $200 a day while the unskilled laborer's wage was $150. At those wage rates the country's labor was allocated among jobs in the best possible way. After the unionization of carpenters, however, with the new wage rates at $220 and $142, that Arcadian state of efficiency no longer prevails. If one former carpenter were transferred from his new unskilled job in paper products back to his former occupation in house construction, the country would have $142 less of paper products per day, but $220 more housing would be produced per day. The reallocation of one worker-day would therefore increase the value of the country's output by $78, and output would increase further with every additional such redistribution until wage rates returned to their initial relative levels.

All the citizens-as-consumers therefore suffer from the gains achieved by one group of citizens-as-workers – unionized workers. The society might consent to being somewhat poorer if the unionized workers are particularly meritorious by some accepted social standard: for example, if they are the lowest-wage workers. There are better ways to remedy low incomes, however, than forcing market wage rates out of alignment: for example, by the use of direct income transfers, which will be discussed in chapter 21.

The market mechanism, it must be remembered, is based on the price method of allocating things – and the wage rate is the "price" of labor. If a society adopts the market mechanism because of its estimable results, it should be careful not to undermine it by distorting the very prices that enable it to produce those results. The worst of societies would be one that adopts the market mechanism and then does everything it can to prevent it from working well. Such a society is like a patient who reluctantly seeks the help of a physician, and then does the opposite of what the physician prescribes.

Imperfect competition among employers   Efficiency is best served where perfect competition prevails on both the demand and the supply sides of the market. But if competition is imperfect on either side of the market, the economy may be better served if it is also imperfect on the other side. That kind of market is sometimes referred to as a "second-best" arrangement; it is best that neither side possesses market power, but if one side does have such power, it may be offset, so to speak, by market power on the other side. With regard to wage rates, this means that when employers have market power over the wage, the power of unions to force a higher wage may promote efficiency rather than detract from it.

For example, in the case of the monopsonistic coal producer set out above, the company succeeded in forcing the wage rate down to from $20 to $16 and employed fewer workers than before. Suppose the workers form a union that compels the company to raise the wage rate back up to $20. The company is then transformed, as it were, from a wage-maker back to a wage-taker; as under perfect competition, if it tries to pay a lower wage rate, no miners will show up for work. The pursuit of profit in this case motivates the company to act exactly like a perfectly competitive enterprise: unable to change the wage, it adjusts its output and employment to the levels that will maximize its output under the new conditions. Output, employment, and the wage rate all return to their original levels – the efficient levels that obtained before the monopsonist bought up all the small competing mining companies.

Thus the union, in serving the interests of its members, serves the society as well in this case. The citizens-as-consumers are better off, but the monopsonist's profit falls back from $1.3 million to the original $1 million. The union compelled the enterprise to give up its ill-gotten excess monopsonistic profit of $300,000.

The union performs this felicitous service as long as it does not force the wage rate above the optimal level – $20 an hour in this case. If it compels the company to pay a higher wage rate than that, say $22 an hour, the argument of the preceding section comes into force. Inefficiency due to an enterprise's power to force the wage too low is replaced by inefficiency due to a labor union's power to force the wage too high.

COLLECTIVE BARGAINING

There are many devices by means of which labor unions seek to raise wage levels, varying from country to country, from time to time, and from union to union. The major device of that sort is collective bargaining.

In the absence of a union, in all but the most perfect markets the employer normally announces the wage for a certain job, and the individual workers either take it or leave it. Unions narrow the difference between the bargaining power of managers and workers. They give the workers collectively the ability to demand that wage rates be negotiated, and not simply imposed. What gives them the power to demand that management negotiate the wage is, ultimately, the threat of a strike. Strikes are so costly to both sides, however, that in most stable market economies they are comparatively rare.

When wage rates are determined by bargaining rather than by perfect competition, the outcome is usually a compromise between the wage that management prefers and that which the union prefers. It is highly unlikely that the wage rates that emerge from such give-and-take negotiations mirror those that would have been reached in an ideally competitive labor market. Influence, politics, fairness, and other such considerations certainly play a role. The employment decisions of enterprises, however, are responsive to those negotiated wage rates, and labor will therefore be to some degree misallocated.

Collective-bargaining procedures vary enormously among countries. At one extreme, in the large Japanese enterprise collective bargaining is kept within the family, as it were: the union typically represents only the workers in that enterprise, and it negotiates with its own managers on behalf of its members. At the other extreme, in Sweden, the bargaining is conducted on a national scale. An association representing all the unions in the country negotiates with an association representing all the employers in the country, with the government discreetly pressing for the public interest in the negotiations. The national agreement sets the main lines of the next year's wage settlements throughout the country, with the separate industry details then worked out by local unions and enterprises. American practice generally lies somewhere between those extremes: the bargaining agents typically are a national union and the management of a single enterprise, with the government taking no part.

Labor relations is an area of economic life in which the specifics of social and cultural traditions exert a powerful influence. The transferability of one country's experience to another is therefore rather limited. The Japanese record of exceptional harmony between management and labor, for example, is part of a complex cultural pattern involving fundamental values such as the legitimacy and responsibility of authority. The Swedish practice of wage bargaining between national employers' associations and national labor unions reflects many of the properties of the small and homogeneous country in which it gradually evolved. It is difficult to imagine anything like the Japanese practice in individualistic America, or the Swedish pattern in class-conscious Britain.

Unions provide a number of valuable services other than wage negotiation, which contribute to the enhancement of the welfare of the citizens, both as workers and in other roles. They compel greater attention to workplace conditions, including health, safety, work rules, and amenities. They offer protection against arbitrary dismissal, personal abuse, and other grievances that may be experienced at the hand of some oppressive company officials. The union member is spared the sense of powerlessness that the solitary worker feels in the unequal contest with the bosses. For these reasons alone, and apart from wage levels, a Good Society that employs the market mechanism is likely to be highly supportive of labor unions, particularly among lower-skilled workers.

5   Externalities

The production process under the market mechanism may be thought of as a network of contracts. Enterprises and workers contract to exchange labor for wages. Enterprises and customers contract to exchange a product for a money price. Enterprises contract with each other for the purchase and sale of their products.

Most such contracts affect only the contracting parties. Sometimes, however, contracts affect other persons. Such "third-party effects," or "externalities," may be benign. For example, a new company may turn a vacant lot into an agreeable architectural and landscaping contribution to the neighborhood. I am no party to that activity but I derive a considerable pleasure from it. Unlike many of my pleasures, however, this is one I enjoy without having to pay for it.

Most public attention, however, is focussed on harmful externalities, the dominating instance of which is environmental degradation. The new company may belch soot into the air or discharge toxic chemicals into the river. Its production therefore imposes a cost on third parties like me, in the sense that I am deprived of clean air and water I would otherwise have had. Nor do I receive any compensation for my loss, for I am not a party to a contract.

When the act of production generates externalities of that sort, resources are no longer guided to an efficient allocation by the market mechanism, even under conditions of perfect competition. The efficiency of perfect competition, it will be recalled, derives from a process in which the allocation of resources between the production of, say, hats and shoes, reflects both the benefits to those people who purchase the two products (the societal preference indicator), and the costs to the producing enterprises (the production potential indicator). Those benefits and costs are designated as "private benefits" and "private costs."

When a production process generates harmful externalities, however, the full "social cost" of production consists not only of the private cost that is borne by the producing enterprise, but also of the external cost that is the borne by third parties like you and me who receive no compensation for their loss. Similarly, in the presence of benign externalities the full "social benefit" of production consists not only of the private benefit enjoyed by those who buy and consume the product, but also of external benefits enjoyed by third parties like you and me who do not have to pay for the pleasure. Hence, in the absence of externalities, private benefits and costs are identical to the social benefits and costs; but when the production process generates externalities, the social benefits and costs of economic activities may be larger or smaller than the private benefits and costs.

A Good Society will surely wish its resources to be allocated in such a way that the marginal *social* benefits are equal to the marginal *social* costs. Perfectly competitive markets, however, guide resources toward an allocation at which marginal *private* benefits are equal to marginal *private* costs. Hence, even under perfect competition the society produces too much of those products that degrade the environment, and too few of those products that enhance the lives of people other than those who pay for their use. When markets are imperfectly competitive, the misallocation due to externalities compounds that which is due to the imperfection of competition.

Under certain special conditions, the remedy to an external effect may be found within the compass of the market mechanism. Persons or communities whose water supply is contaminated by an upstream manufacturer may offer to compensate the company if it will buy discharge-treatment equipment. In most cases, however, the government is eventually called upon by the injured parties to protect them or their property from costs externally imposed upon them.

Friends of market socialism would expect that if market-economy enterprises were socially owned, the managers would be inclined to "internalize" external costs and therefore to be more protective of the environment than private owners. Insofar as their enterprises' output and production costs enter into the society's evaluation of their performance, however, they will be under pressures similar to those that drive private-enterprise managers. Whether the pressures will be smaller is an empirical question about which one can only speculate.

6   Public Goods

If a restaurant can serve 1,000 meals a night and I enjoy the consumption of one of them, there are only 999 meals left for others to consume. The consumption of most goods and services is bound by that kind of limitation, but there are others that are not. They generally consist of services rather than material goods, such as the services of movie theaters, boxing matches, lighthouses, and armies. They are said to be non-depletable, because once the service is produced, my consumption of them does not reduce the quantity available for others to consume.

Movie shows and boxing matches, however, are like ordinary goods and services in the sense that the price method can be used to distribute them among the consumers. There are a limited number of seats in the hall or stadium, and people who wish to enjoy the spectacle are obliged to pay a price. A lighthouse is different. Once it is in operation there is no way of requiring those who benefit to pay a price for it. It provides its services to all ships that pass in the night. Similarly, once an army is functioning, its protection extends to all citizens, whether they would voluntarily pay for it or not. These goods are said to be non-excludable, meaning that once they have been produced, people cannot be compelled to pay a price as a condition of enjoying the benefit.

Goods that are both non-depletable and non-excludable are called "public goods." They play an important role in the critique of the market mechanism because they are a class of goods that would not be produced in optimal quantities under that mechanism, regardless of whether markets are perfect or imperfect. A profit-making enterprise is unlikely to build and maintain a lighthouse, because users cannot be made to pay for the services and very little sales revenue would be collected. This applies to all profit-making enterprises, whether they are privately or publicly owned.

That is not to say that none of these goods would be produced. A very large shipping company, or an association of shipping companies, might calculate that their private benefit from the protection of their own ships would be greater than their private cost of contributing to the construction and operation of a lighthouse. Similarly, many wealthy citizens might contribute voluntarily to the support of a private army to protect their persons and wealth from foreign depredation. As in the case of benign externalities, however, the scale of such activities, when based on calculations of private benefit alone, would be smaller than when the full social benefit was included in the calculation. From the perspective of a Good Society, therefore, if resources were allocated on the basis of the market mechanism alone, the provision of public goods would fall short of the social optimum.

7   Imperfect Knowledge

There was a time when most of the knowledge required to run a successful business was lodged in the heads of the owners and their associates. No company can operate that way in what is now called the Information Age. Enterprises spend a great deal of money acquiring information relevant to their operations and they maintain large staffs to process it in a form that is useful for business decisions. Indeed, how much to spend for what kinds of information is itself a business decision of considerable importance.

Yet many of the major decisions in a market economy are still made with imperfect knowledge, particularly of the intentions of other economic actors. The production decisions of a company, for example, depend crucially on estimates of the quantities of its products that its customers would buy at various prices. While the countrywide demand for a product can be forecast with reasonable accuracy, the demand for the specific products of a particular company is much more difficult to forecast. Hence, even when the economy is fully employed and purchasing power is high, some goods are produced in excess, and have either to be kept in inventory or sold off at a discounted price. Each year a certain number of companies go out of business because sales turn out to be below their expectations over an extended period of time.

Costs of these sorts entail a loss of potential output, in the broad sense that resources that have been expended on the production of goods of little or no value to the society could have been used to produce goods of higher value. They are evidence of a certain degree of failure of coordination by the market mechanism.

Imperfect knowledge may also lead to underproduction. A manufacturer of computers or of fashion blue jeans may underestimate the demand for one of their products; since it takes time to gear up for additional production, potential sales are lost. If the underproduction of some consumer goods is extensive, consumers are unable to find the goods they wish to buy and have to settle for substitutes or not buy at all. In the case of extensive underproduction of intermediate products, some users of those products discover that they are unable to obtain the inputs they had counted on obtaining, and they either find substitutes or reduce their own rate of production.

Most of the consequences of imperfect knowledge, however, consist of overproduction rather than underproduction. It is rare that enterprises are unable to obtain the materials or parts that they need, or that deliveries fail to arrive on time or in the quantities and grades that had been ordered. A supplier who developed a reputation for unreliability would have difficulty remaining in business.

Some forms of imperfect knowledge are part of the human condition, of course, and must be expected in any economy. The whims of consumers, for example, particularly with respect to fashion goods, are no more accessible to central planners than to capitalist businessmen. There are some things that are potentially knowable, however, but cannot be employed in the service of economic coordination under the market mechanism.

The total number of Christmas trees likely to be bought in the Boston area, for example, can be forecast with reasonable accuracy. Under the market mechanism, however, each seller orders trees on the basis of a rough guess about what his sales will be; there is no social arrangement to ensure that the total number of tree orders by all sellers is coordinated with the knowable total of trees that will be bought by all customers in the area. Hence the highly visible waste in the form of unsold trees on Christmas day.

With respect to intermediate products, the manager of each plastics company knows precisely what inputs he needs for his intended rate of production. But he cannot possibly know the intended production levels of all other enterprises that might be his customers, or how much of his plastic products they are likely to buy, or what the price and production intentions of competing plastics producers are. Hence he makes some decisions that he would have made differently had he known what the intentions of other managers were. The market mechanism contains no way of communicating the knowledge that each manager has of his own production intentions to other persons who could act on it in the interest of improved coordination. The deficiency is perhaps most serious in the case of investment decisions: a company that decided to build a large new factory may not have done so had it known that other companies had similar intentions, or that the product would soon be rendered obsolete by a new invention under development.

Much of the uncertainty with which decisions are made in a market economy therefore reflects a deficiency in that mechanism rather than the inherent unknowability or excessive costliness of the information. One consequence is the large stocks of inventories that firms need to maintain. In the Boston shopping area there are countless stores with mammoth displays of television sets of all brands, sizes, and prices, all tuned to the same station so that consumers can compare their qualities. Intermediate products are similarly stocked in abundance: the classified telephone book lists eight pages of companies under the category "Electrical Supplies, Wholesale."

The purpose of such large stocks is to avoid losing sales to competitors. If competition were replaced by cooperation, it would appear, such wasteful abundance would be reduced and the goods that would be produced with the released resources would provide a higher level of consumer welfare. It is such visible consequences of imperfect knowledge that have motivated many people to look to economic planning as a more efficient arrangement for a Good Society.

This source of waste would probably be smaller in a market economy in which enterprises were socially owned. The commercial secrecy that is characteristic of capitalism could then be replaced by open access to information, and every enterprise could know the production intentions of all other enterprises. As long as the enterprises were expected to maximize their profit in competition with each other, however, there would probably still be too many Christmas trees.

8   Discussion

The story of inefficiency presented above needs to be put in perspective. The effect of piling one source of inefficiency upon another gives the impression that the market mechanism is hopelessly flawed. Yet, as Mark Twain said about Wagner's music, it's not as bad as it sounds. After all, everyone knows that the most productive economies in the world are market economies. What should one make of that apparent contradiction?

Relative inefficiency   First, since all real-world systems – natural or social – are inefficient to some degree, one is accustomed to regard that degree of inefficiency as entirely normal. For example, according to both scientific and transcendental opinion, the reader of this book is presently using only one-tenth or fewer of his brain cells in the effort. That great waste of potential can be partially remedied by various techniques ranging from better dietary practices to yoga, but even then the human brain would be remarkably inefficient.

One might regard this fact as extremely disconcerting, but most people nevertheless regard themselves as reasonably productive citizens. Part of the reason, I think, is that the sense of well-being is relative, to some degree. If you had cause to feel that you were using far fewer of your brain cells than other people, you might well do something about it. But if everybody is more or less the same in that respect, a certain degree of mental inefficiency is accepted as entirely normal.

Economic inefficiency is, similarly, to a great degree relative. Unless your own country is starkly less efficient than others, a certain degree of inefficiency is acceptable as entirely normal.

The contents of this chapter should therefore not discourage someone contemplating the merits of the market mechanism for his Good Society. Nothing's perfect. Accepting the fact of the inefficiency of markets, two questions should be asked. One is how the market mechanism compares with the alternative – the planning mechanism – which is the subject of the next chapter. The other is whether there is anything that can, or should, be done to remedy the market's failures.

That indeed is the proper use of an inquiry into the sources of market failure. It should serve not to damn the market, but to identify the points at which those failures occur, so that thought might be given to remedies.

Countervailing power   Some sources of inefficiency work in opposite directions from others, and therefore cancel each other out to some extent. John Kenneth Galbraith called attention to the tendency for the growth of market power by some economic actors to generate "countervailing power" by others.[8] For example, the large profits earned by monopolists create powerful incentives for others to go after those profits by inventing close substitutes. For the same reason, high profits in new technologies like computers attract new firms, who cut into the market power and the profits of the pioneering firms. In the absence of the entry of new firms, the degree of inefficiency in product markets would be much more palpable than it is.

Similar offsetting tendencies are also found in labor markets, as has been discussed in the text. The economy would be more efficient if neither managers nor workers had any power over wage rates. In every real economy, however, both must be expected to possess some degree of power and to use it to promote their respective interests. Their interests in wage rates work in opposite directions, however. Monopsonists strive to maintain wages below the optimal level, while labor unions strive to raise them above the optimal level. Hence there is some reason to expect that there are limits to the extent to which prevailing wage rates depart from what might be their competitive market levels; and there are therefore limits to the degree of misallocation of labor.

Business failures   One highly visible form of waste generated by the market mechanism is business failure. Even in periods of high employment and general prosperity, a local drugstore goes out of business and is replaced by a branch of a national corporation, or a company whose sales have fallen to the competition may "downsize" its staff or go into bankruptcy. It is misfortunes of that sort that cause sensitive citizens to wonder whether the country would not be better off if cooperation replaced competition as the foundation of the economic mechanism.

Some business failures are the consequence of imperfect knowledge, such as investments made by a firm that it would not have made had it known of the investment plans of other firms. That waste of resources may be properly regarded as a failure of the market mechanism; it is the sort of thing that could be avoided if all investment plans are known and centrally coordinated, as under the planning mechanism. Most business failures, however, are not of that sort. They are part of the process of accommodating to change.

When a business closes down under the impact of competition, it generally means that some producer has found a way of providing better and cheaper goods and services. The rising rent that forces a local barber out of business is a signal that the premises are no longer being put to their most productive use, much as a generation earlier the rising price of land put the old farms out of business to make way for the barber and other shopkeepers. Everyone's present residence or workplace can be traced back to the displacement of some long-forgotten people who could no longer put it to its most productive use. That sort of turnover in the use of productive resources is referred to as "mobility": land and buildings move, as it were, from farming, to barbering, to video-rental shops.

The town barber, and some of his old customers, rue the closing of the shop. But the proprietor of the new flower shop or pizza parlor are now better off, as are those customers who benefit from the new conveniences. Thus some consumers and workers gain while other consumers and workers lose. A society that rewards winners in the game of competition benefits from the risk and effort that it elicits, but where there are winners there have to be losers.

A major cause of the displacement of some businesses by others is continuous innovation, both of new products and of new techniques for reducing the cost of producing them. The citizens of a Good Society are likely to encourage innovations like new pharmaceutical drugs or new toys like roller-blade skates. If new products are to be produced, however, they require resources – land and production space, machinery and equipment, and labor – that were formerly used in now-defunct lines of production. Nor is it possible to foretell when such inventions will appear. If every preceding economic activity were sacrosanct, there could be no such advances.

It is undeniable that changes of these sorts decrease the welfare of some citizens. What must be kept in mind, however, is that they increase the welfare of others. Whether you think the society as a whole is better or worse off depends on whether you agree with the proposition that, other things being equal, when one person's income increases by $100, the society should be judged to be better off by $100. If you do accept that value-laden proposition, then if a piece of property can produce a profit of $1,000 in one use and only $800 in another, the society is better off from the first use than the second. That may mean that the second user has to find a new job. But the alternative is to freeze the economy into a pattern of productive activity that makes no room for change or slows down its pace. Whatever the form of the economic mechanism – markets or planning – a society that wishes to benefit from change has to provide for mobility. Farms have to give way to new uses.

My own view is that on balance, the gains from change have been well worth the losses. I know that many old-time residents of my town of Lexington think that it was a nicer place in the old days – before I came here. I also think that it was a nicer town when I came here than it has become since the others came. But few would be glad if the town could magically revert to what it was in the old days: if it did, there would then be no place for those of us present-day residents who came here from other places.

The wreckage of failed farms and businesses should therefore not be construed as evidence of market failure. A society that accepts the market mechanism ought to start with the presumption of innocence – actions taken in the pursuit of profit should be regarded as enhancing the material welfare of most of its citizens, if not all. The presumption of innocence, however, does not at all mean that whatever the market sanctions enhances the goodness of the society. The burden of this chapter is that there are various conditions under which markets fail to achieve efficiency – one major criterion of goodness. It would be a foolish as well as a bad society that regarded profitability in the market as the sole test of the efficiency with which the country's resources are used. No society, in fact, is that foolish or that bad. All have called upon government, under some conditions or others, to correct the misallocation of resources that results from market failure.

Government   Intervention by government is the main reason that people do not feel the full brunt of the inefficiency of the market mechanism or of its more objectionable social consequences. In my view it is that more than anything that accounts for the limited damage that allocative inefficiency has inflicted on the citizens of market economies.

There is no country, for example, that permits its natural monopolies – power companies, for example – to charge whatever prices and to provide whatever quality of service they find to be most profitable for themselves. Everywhere they are either regulated by government or owned and run by government, so that they are unable to exploit their monopoly power. Hence pure monopoly does not actually inflict on market economies the damage that economic theory shows it capable of doing.

Governments also generally outlaw collusion among enterprises to limit competition by fixing prices or dividing up markets. The volume of anti-trust litigation is quite limited, which might seem to suggest that the extent of collusion is small. The very existence of anti-trust laws and enforcement agencies, however, limits the extent of actual collusion, much as the existence of an effective police force limits the volume of crime that actually occurs.

With monopoly and collusion controlled, the main arena of inefficiency is the great mass of markets in which competition prevails but of the imperfect sort – brand-name markets, for example. The allocative inefficiency of those markets could be eliminated, in principle, by governmental regulation similar to that of monopolies. Some socialist protagonists of the market mechanism have proposed ways of doing that, but they would involve the government in such tight and extensive regulation of economic activity that what would be left would be unrecognizable as the market mechanism.[9]

My own view is that the benefits of competition greatly exceed the losses due to its imperfection. The producer of Zeno Toothpaste does indeed restrict output in order to maintain a profit-maximizing price, which is inefficient, but the citizen-as-consumer gets a very valuable benefit in exchange – the intense effort by producers to please him by new products, improved products, better-packaged products, and so forth. High-minded critics of "consumerism" often deplore that intense, and often vulgar, effort to attract paying customers to one's product. The quickest antidote to that attitude would be to live for a time in an economy of the opposite kind – in the planned economies, for example, where producers and sales clerks had no interest at all in whether the customer bought the product or not. That a market be competitive is therefore far more important to me than that the competition be absolutely perfect.

Imperfect competition prevails not only in markets for goods that are very similar to each other – like toothpaste or breakfast foods – but also for genuinely new goods like pharmaceutical drugs, roller-blade skates, and cellular phones. When these innovations first appear, their producers have an initial monopoly on their production. Indeed the purpose of the patent laws is precisely to provide such a term-limited monopoly, as an incentive for people to risk the time and effort of bringing a new product to market. There can be no doubt that in the absence of that form of temporary monopoly afforded by a legal patent, the extent of the effort and funds invested in innovation would be much smaller. If a new product is not patentable, perhaps like roller-blade skates, the producer has nothing but the reputation of his brand name to justify the risk of bringing it to market; if he were forbidden to place his brand name on his product, he would think many times before taking the risk. The existence of brand names signifies that competition is imperfect, and the market is therefore inefficient, but I can't get excited about that kind of allocative inefficiency. As a consumer, I value a system that encourages so many producers to seek wealth by trying to figure out something that I might want badly enough to pay the price.

In like fashion, the failure of markets to deal efficiently with externalities and with public goods has to some degree been corrected by government action. In many countries the degradation of the environment has been slowed down and even reversed by government-enforced limitation on the emission of pollutants and on the disposal of toxic wastes. Public expenditures on a great many activities ranging from education to military defense reflect the ability of democratic polities to implement a societal judgment that if the production of these goods were left to the market alone, too little of them would be produced.

Hence, few market economies bear the full brunt of the inefficiency to which markets in practice are subject. How far government should go in fixing the market, however, is a major subject of political debate in the market economies.

Government failure   Most economists have long assumed, without much debate, that when the market fails to allocate resources efficiently, government should be called upon to set matters right. Government, in that view, is both benign and wise: benign in that it would have only the public interest in mind, and wise in that it would know how to set about remedying the inefficiency efficiently. Under the impact of conservative thought and empirical research, however, government has been put through the same kind of analytic wringer as the market mechanism, and the results have led to a much more skeptical view of its ability to correct the deficiencies of markets.

Democratic governments, in this perspective, are run by politicians whose main objective is to get elected. They therefore seek to maximize votes, much as managers seek to maximize profit. Politicians cannot be expected to pursue some notion of the public interest that might clash with the interests of important voters and powerful financial supporters. Hence when government gets involved in economic matters, the outcome is usually to the benefit of influential interest groups rather than the general public. The greater the involvement of politicians in economic activity, the greater the amount of "rent-seeking" by people who stand to benefit enormously by having a law written one way rather than another.

Elected politicians make the laws, but salaried career bureaucrats write and enforce the regulations through which they are implemented. Bureaucrats, like everyone else, seek primarily to advance their own interests, which are proportional to the size of their budgets and to the power they wield over the citizens who must come to them for approval of their projects. Hence the regulations they write are far more stringent than is required by their task, and they drown the citizens in an endless morass of forms to be filled out and licenses to be obtained. Moreover, corruption is inevitable when modestly-paid meat inspectors or issuers of liquor licenses have the power to hold up millions of dollars worth of projects.

The conclusions drawn from that line of thought are that market failure is matched by government failure, and that the effort to correct allocative inefficiency by government action generally does more harm than good. That view has had a powerful political effect in many democratic market economies, and efforts to reduce economic inefficiency by government action have been widely scaled back.

In my personal view this conservative onslaught has served as a useful antidote to what had been an overly optimistic assessment of the contribution that government can make toward increasing the efficiency of markets. The positions on both sides, however, too often reflect the extremes. There is a broad middle ground between the old extreme view that government can fix everything, and the new extreme view that government can't fix anything. Inefficiency in government is no more reason to reject the use of government in toto than inefficiency in the market mechanism is reason to reject markets in toto. Having devoted much of my life to the study of Communist economies, I am somewhat gun-shy about involving government in economic affairs. Yet I am not a pacifist in this matter, and am prepared to invoke the power of government when a convincing case can be made.

Democratic political systems permit of an enormous variety of responses to the unsatisfactory outcomes of the market mechanism. That variety reflects the differences among political institutions and cultural traditions. Germans, Swedes, Americans, and Japanese all deal in different ways with the problems of monopoly and of the losers in the game of economic competition. The trouble with democracy, however, is that if you do not share the social outlook of most of your fellow citizens, you will forever find your government's responses inadequate. Too often such dissatisfaction is misdirected against the market mechanism – the "system" – as if in the belief that things would be much better if the society adopted a different economic mechanism. A democratic Sweden or a democratic United States that operated under a planning mechanism, however, would differ from each other as widely as they now do under the market mechanism. What poses as a distaste for the "system" is often simply a distaste for the dominant cultural values of one's society.

Any society that adopts the market mechanism should expect that a major issue on the political agenda will be the proper role of government in controlling the market economy. It is one of those family quarrels, however, among people who accept the market mechanism as the best arrangement for their own society. It is an issue of economic policy, and not of fundamental economic structure. The policy question is how best to run an economy that employs the market mechanism. The structural question, which is the subject of this book, is whether to employ the market mechanism in the first place. The next chapter returns to that question by considering how the planning mechanism operates in practice.

Notes

1 At the higher price of $9, Idaho Farms sells fewer potatoes than they sold at the market price of $6, but their *revenue* from sales may actually be higher than before. It depends on how sharply sales drop off. If sales drop from 10,000 bags to only 8,000, sales revenue actually rises – from $60,000 (10,000 bags at $6 a bag) to $72,000 (8,000 bags at $9 a bag) – an increase of $12,000.

   On the cost side, however, by cutting output back to 8,000 bags, they use less hired labor, so that their cost of production falls – say by $10,000. Hence, their total profit rises by $2,000 ($12,000 more revenue and $10,000 lower costs).

   If sales drop sharply, however – say only 1,000 bags are sold at the higher price – sales revenue would drop from $60,000 to $9,000 – a decrease of $51,000. Unless the total cost of producing 1,000 bags falls by more than $51,000, total profit would be less than it was when they sold at the market price. The farm's bold business venture is then a flop, as many indeed are.

2 Even natural monopolies of these sorts often face substitutes of various kinds. A monopoly railroad faces the competition of trucks and aircraft, and a monopoly electric-power company may lose some of its business to gas companies. Moreover, technical change tends to eliminate monopolies: what was once a telephone monopoly is now a wildly competitive telecommunications industry.

3 *The Wealth of Nations*, vol. 1, ch. X, part II.

4 *The New York Times*, August 4, 1998, p. D1; and September 18, 1998, p. A1.

5 There is normally some wage rate so low that any further wage reduction would cause output and revenues to fall by more than labor cost, so that profit would decline.

6 This type of market structure is known as "oligopsony."

7 Baumol and Blinder, *Economics*, p. 812.

8 Galbraith, *American Capitalism*.

9 For example, Oskar Lange developed a rule for enterprises to follow in deciding how much output to produce, which would lead to efficiency regardless of whether competition was perfect or not. Lange, "On the economic theory of socialism."

Chapter 18

Planning in an
Imperfect World

The best laid plans of mice and men
gang aft awry.
— Robert Burns

All that meat, and no potatoes ...
— Jazz ballad

CONTENTS

Enthusiasts of central planning are hard to find these days. In the former Communist countries there is still a certain politically potent nostalgia for the old days, and among traditionally anti-Soviet socialists in the West the idea of a democratic, non-bureaucratic planning mechanism still has its advocates. At one time, however, enthusiasts of planning were a powerful force, both within and outside of the Communist world. They had little doubt that under socialist central planning a country would produce far more output than it could produce under the market mechanism.

They did recognize, however, that as planning worked out in practice, there were a great many imperfections. And within the USSR itself, as far back as the times of Lenin and Stalin, the Soviet press regularly published an abundance of materials critical of the performance of the economy. The candor with which such matters were portrayed often came as a surprise to people who were aware of the heavy political censorship of the press in those countries. The political leadership, however, had always encouraged the press to combat "bureaucratism," a rubric that covered all manner of inefficiencies in the management of economic affairs. The official view was that if the economic system were properly managed and the government's economic policies properly carried out, the operation of the economy would be fully satisfactory. Unsatisfactory outcomes must therefore be due only to the incompetence or venality of officials, which had to be perpetually exposed and corrected. Accordingly, a major function assigned to the press was to conduct such investigative reporting, taking care, however, not to criticize the system itself or the Communist Party's policies. Much of the outside world's understanding of how the planning system worked in practice is derived from published information of that sort.

Central planning, we have seen, falls short of efficiency even under the idealized conditions postulated in chapter 16. It should occasion no surprise that the extent of inefficiency was even greater in the real world, where those conditions are not present: where, for example, the planners are unlikely to have complete and perfect information on the production potential of all the country's enterprises. The purpose of this chapter is to identify the additional sources of inefficiency that emerge in the operation of the planning mechanism in practice.

I Imperfect Knowledge

When economic activity is coordinated through markets, the managers need to know only the details of their own production operations, particularly the cost of producing various quantities of the enterprise's products. They do not need to transmit that knowledge to anyone else; in fact, they strive ardently to withhold it from competitors. Under the planning mechanism, in contrast, each enterprise's business must also be the planners' business, for the government's planners are responsible for coordinating all inter-enterprise activities. The managers must therefore transmit their knowledge to the central planners, a process that the market mechanism is mercifully spared. The efficiency of central planning depends heavily on the accuracy and honesty with which managers transmit their knowledge to the central planners.

In an ideal planned economy of the kind examined in chapter 16, managers see their interests as identical with those of the society, and are motivated to submit fully and honestly all the information requested by the planners. It has long been known, however, that in practice, managers often submit information they know to be incorrect in order to protect their enterprises from the danger of underfulfilling the production plan. That practice was a response to the dominant fact of industrial life in the planned economies – the uncertainty about whether the labor and materials required to fulfill the plan would be available when needed. The enterprise might run short of labor because the local government made a practice of pressuring the managers in its region into being good citizens by detailing some of their labor force for periods of work repairing the town roads or building a new playground; or if some of the company's suppliers failed to meet their production targets, they might run short of tires or batteries or components needed to fulfill their production plans.

Operating in this environment, prudent managers tended to tailor the information they submitted to the planners in ways that would reduce the danger of being unable to fulfill the plan. The Komi Plant would report a production capacity of 27,000 tractors in its preliminary plan, hoping thereby to receive a final-plan target safely below the 30,000 it could produce if things went well. And the number of tires it reported as required to meet the plan would be comfortably in excess of the number that were actually needed. Under-reporting production capability and exaggerating requirements for materials and other inputs were two of the major devices whereby management strove to ensure that the plan would be fulfilled. Since the planners possessed highly imperfect knowledge about the number of tractors and all other products that the economy had the capacity to produce, and about the inputs required to produce them, the plans they ultimately produced were inevitably imperfect as well.

The designers of the Soviet planned economy did not anticipate at first that socialist managers of state-owned enterprises could not be trusted to provide accurate information to the planners. In the course of time, however, it was acknowledged that managers did have interests of their own which could diverge from those of the government. The principal reason for such divergence, however, is to be found not in the nature of the economic mechanism but in the nature of the ownership form – namely, state ownership of the productive property. It will therefore be discussed in Part V, which considers the consequences of various forms of ownership (chapter 24).

2   The Compression of Information

The huge magnitude of the information-flow between enterprises and planners is a second source of inefficiency, apart from that generated by management's incentives to distort the information.

The typical large enterprise in every economy produces a considerable array of related products, many of them in different models. The General Electronics Enterprise, for example, may currently produce 15 models of table radios, 10 models of television sets, 5 VCR models, and much more; if each model is regarded as a distinct "product," the number of its individual products may range into the hundreds. On the input side, considering labor alone, a good production manager knows how many assemblers, technicians, materials handlers, and so forth are needed to produce each model.

That much can be said of good managers in both planned and market economies. In a market economy, General Electronics has a hard enough time keeping track of the mass of information relating to its own production activities. In a planned economy, however, General Electronics packages all its knowledge of its own production conditions and transmits it as information to the central planners; and so must every other enterprise in the country. It is beyond the capability of any national planning organization to take account of all the shapes, sizes, models, and other characteristics, of all the products in the economy. To make the task manageable, the information submitted by the individual enterprises must be greatly compressed, and that compressed information is further consolidated by the ministries for submission to the central planning board. The process of compressing information is known as "aggregation."

The consequence of aggregation is that the labor and other input norms on which the coordination process depends are only very rough guides to the quantities of inputs actually needed in any specific production operation. For example, suppose it takes 1 hour to assemble one Moscow Radio Model 3 and 1.5 hours to assemble Moscow Radio Model 7. If the central planners could work with such detailed data, those labor norms would be quite accurate. Because of the necessity of aggregation, however, they must work with a heterogeneous group of products called "radios" that includes not only the two Moscow Radio models, but perhaps a hundred other models of radios. The labor norm would specify the number of hours required to assemble one "radio" – perhaps 2.5 hours per radio. Such a number is clearly no more than an average of the actual labor requirements for all the radio models. It is rather like a recipe derived by averaging all the ingredients of all the cakes in the cookbook. A master baker could perhaps do something with that mix of ingredients, but it would not be as fine a cake as he could bake if he could choose his own ingredients.

On the positive side, the best that one might say is that the labor norm that is used in planning is a practical approximation. It may be very close to the true norm, but then again it may be wildly off the mark. All the enterprises in the region do eventually receive their final labor hiring authorizations, which may correspond to the kinds and numbers of workers seeking jobs. There will therefore be jobs available for all the workers seeking employment. On the negative side, however, the final input plan of most enterprises does not correspond to the requirements of their final output plan. One enterprise may receive too much coal and not enough acid, or too many machinists and too few technicians; and the opposite may be true in another enterprise. Hence the country produces less output than it could produce if its labor and other resources were allocated on the basis of the detailed production knowledge of its managers, rather than on the aggregated information with which the planners have to work.

3 Prices and Costs

Central planners are no less interested than capitalist managers in minimizing the waste of labor and other resources and producing goods efficiently. It is self-evident that economy-wide efficiency requires that all enterprises produce at the lowest possible cost. In a market economy, cost-consciousness is impressed on enterprise management by the primacy of profit-making and by the pressures of competition. Under the planning mechanism, the obligation to economize on cost is impressed on management by the ministry, representing the public interest. To enforce that obligation, the ministry collects data on production cost in all of its enterprises, and the management compensation package is designed to reward the manager who cuts costs down to a minimum and to penalize the manager who is wasteful in the use of the resources entrusted in his care.

Competent managers periodically review their method of production and compare it with the cost of using other methods of producing the same output. For example, suppose the current method of producing a ton of fertilizer uses certain quantities of labor, machinery, and fuel. An alternative method of producing a ton of the same fertilizer would be to install an automatic machine that would require less labor but would use more fuel. In deciding which of the two methods to use, the cost-conscious manager would reckon up the costs of the inputs under the two methods and choose the one with the lowest costs.

This sort of periodic recalculation ensures that output is being produced at the lowest possible cost from the perspective of the enterprise. It does not necessarily ensure, however, that it is the lowest possible cost from the perspective of the economy. That depends on the prices used by the manager in figuring out his production cost. If the prices are "right," cost minimization by the manager means that the country's resources are being used efficiently. If the prices are "wrong," however, cost minimization by the manager could constitute a wasteful use of resources.

From the perspective of efficiency, the prices of inputs are right when they measure the quantity of output that could be produced with a marginal unit of each input. For example, if the price of a ton of fertilizer is 10 rubles, it should mean that any farm that uses one additional ton of fertilizer should be able to increase its output by at least 10 rubles; for if the additional output were worth only 8 rubles, the farm would be in effect depriving the economy of 2 rubles' worth of output that could be produced elsewhere. If prices are right in that sense, the cost-conscious manager ends up doing what is best for the whole society.

The standard example of how an economy can generate the right prices is the idealized model of perfect competition, where the price is set by the market and each enterprise selects its most profitable output-level in terms of that price (chapter 15). Under the planning mechanism, however, prices are set not in a market by the price method, but in the offices of the planners by the assignment method. Indeed, it is thought to be a virtue of the planning mechanism that prices are set not in the "anarchy of the marketplace," but by the conscious action of the central planners in the interest of the society. Every enterprise possesses a set of thick price catalogues issued periodically by the price department of the government. In figuring out the cost of production, it is these prices that the manager uses to calculate the cost of the inputs needed under various methods of production. Much therefore depends on how those prices are set.

PRICES AND AVERAGE COST

Following the Marxian theory of value as interpreted by the Communist Party, the Soviet price-setting officials based their calculations of the price of a certain type of fertilizer on the countrywide average cost of producing a ton of it – say 50 rubles. They then added a standard markup of about 10 percent – or 5 rubles – which was designated as profit. The price of a ton of fertilizer then entered into the price catalogue as 55 rubles. That was the price that a farm paid to the chemical company when it bought the fertilizer, and that is the price the farm used in calculating the cost of the fertilizer used in producing its grain.

It can readily be shown that when prices are based on the average cost of the inputs into production, the production decisions made by even the most conscientious manager would cause resources to be inefficiently used. To take a simple illustration, suppose an electric motor can be manufactured with either a plastic or a copper bushing, with no difference in the quality of the motor. The catalogue prices are 5 rubles for the plastic bushing and 8 rubles for the copper. Wishing to be a good citizen by producing at the lowest possible cost, the manager decides to change over to plastic bushings, figuring that the cost of production is 3 rubles less per motor than if he used copper bushings. When next year's planning time rolls around, the information he submits to the central planners includes a new requisition for plastic bushings that were not requested before, and he drops the requisition for the copper bushings ordered in the past. Accordingly, in making up the new national plan for next year, the planners increase the output plans of the plastic producers – say by 1 percent – and decrease those of the copper producers.

However, the true cost to the economy of increasing the production of plastic bushings is generally not the average industry cost of 5 rubles. For example, if the industry happens to be operating near full capacity, it is likely to cost more than 5 rubles for every additional plastic bushing produced – perhaps 10 rubles. That number – 10 rubles – is called the "marginal cost" of production (chapter 15). The marginal cost of producing copper bushings is also likely to be higher than the average cost of 8 rubles – perhaps 9 rubles. In a case of this sort, which was not atypical in the USSR, the manager's decision to substitute plastic for copper, which reduces his *own* cost of producing a motor by 3 rubles, ends up increasing *the country's* cost of production by 1 ruble.

Decisions of this sort, which are made daily by the managers of all the country's enterprises, are incorporated into the massive flow of information on the basis of which the central plans are made. The plans therefore embody millions of enterprise decisions each of which, in its small way, entails a wasteful use of resources. The consequence is that even if the plan itself were perfectly coordinated, the country's resources would be inefficiently used in the course of the year.

The dependence of prices on the average cost of production is only one of a number of reasons why prices in the Soviet Union did not reflect the true cost of production. A second is that once prices were fixed, they remained unchanged for long periods of time, during which actual production costs changed. Yet another is that the prices of many basic industrial products like fuels and minerals were deliberately set below cost and the producers had to be heavily subsidized. Products like steel that used coal were therefore underpriced, as were products like tractors that used steel, and so forth. The effects of those extensive subsidies thus spread throughout the price structure like a virus, so that the planners could not count on the prices of things to tell them very much about the real costs of producing them.

It is for such reasons that Western economists refer to Soviet-type prices as "irrational." With prices of that sort, it could indeed happen that the goods produced are worth less than the materials and other inputs used up in producing them: the production of 1,000 rubles' worth of steel may appear to use up only 600 rubles' worth of coke and other inputs, when in fact it may be using up 1,200 rubles' worth of inputs! In such bizarre cases the act of production, which under normal conditions is said to "add value" to the inputs, turns out to "subtract value." It has been estimated that in the East European Communist countries, from 4 percent (Poland) to 20 percent (Hungary) of the output of internationally traded goods was value-subtracting.[1] Hence, because of the irrationality of prices, the planners had little basis for knowing whether a bundle of resources allocated to truck production would have produced a smaller or larger value of output if they had been allocated to the production of tractors, or coal, or housing, or anything else.

4   Paper Plans

The first trial balances that the planners draw up on the basis of the enterprises' preliminary plans will generally reveal those plans to be uncoordinated. The total demand for an intermediate product like coal may exceed the planned coal production, and the total demand for semi-skilled labor may exceed the number of available semi-skilled workers. The simplest technique for achieving balanced plans is to reduce the output plans of the enterprises that use a great deal of the inputs that are not available in sufficient quantity.

In the case of a labor shortage in a certain region, for example, some of the region's textile mills might be assigned an output plan 10 percent smaller than they had proposed in their preliminary plans, with a corresponding reduction in the number of workers they are authorized to hire. By paring output plans down in that way, the gap between the estimated regional supply of labor and the enterprises' demand for labor can be reduced. In general, however, that technique was not greatly favored in the Communist countries, for a variety of reasons, chief of which is that it leaves some of the enterprises' production capacity underutilized. Moreover, the regional planners do not have the authority to adjust the plans of enterprises that are under the jurisdiction of the central government.

Since output-plan reduction can be used only sparingly, other techniques must be employed for achieving balance. The planners may arrange for the import of some workers from a neighboring region that happens to find an excess supply of labor in its preliminary plan; those workers may migrate temporarily or permanently from the region with an excess of labor to a region with a labor shortage, or they may commute if the distance is not too large. Such techniques help to reduce the size of the preliminary-labor-plan gap, but are rarely sufficient to close it. The planners are then obliged to resort to a technique referred to disparagingly as "forcing the norms." What this means is that the labor norms are arbitrarily tightened, so that the number of workers the enterprises are authorized to hire is reduced to the level of the number estimated to be available, without a corresponding reduction in output plans. They are expected to meet their production plan by drawing on "reserves," meaning that they must work more intensely, or require more overtime from their workers, or find other ways of reducing their labor input per unit of output.

The outcome is that the planners are able to report that their labor plans are balanced when in fact they are balanced in appearance only. The planning process, say its critics, produces only "paper plans": that is, enterprise plans that are balanced on paper but are unrealistically taut and unlikely to be fulfilled.

Paper planning signifies that the economic mechanism fails in its central function: the coordination of economic activity. Contrary to the exhilaration felt by the early Soviet revolutionaries at having escaped the "anarchy of the marketplace," it became evident in the course of time that coordination, far from serving as the proof of the superiority of planning over markets, had become one of its most glaring deficiencies.

Informal procedures   The effect of paper planning on enterprises is that they are often unable to hire all the workers that their plans authorize them to hire. The enterprises are supposed to pay no more than the official wage rates, so they cannot legally offer higher wages in order to attract the labor they require. Their response is to resort to various artifices for attracting workers. It often happens in planned economies that inconsistencies in the formal planning process give rise to informal procedures that help to cut through what would otherwise be an impasse. They consist, in this case, of a form of unacknowledged competition by enterprises for the available labor, on a non-wage basis: offering larger bonuses or more overtime pay, offering earnings higher than the official wage, paying for overtime that is not actually worked, declaring a semi-skilled worker to be skilled and thus permitting payment of a higher official wage, and countless other ways that have been elaborated in press accounts of such matters. These practices are in violation of the regulations, and sometimes of the laws, but they are perhaps inevitable in an economic relationship in which the demand for labor persistently exceeds the supply and where there is compelling pressure on the managers to find the labor needed to meet their production-plan assignments.

Informal activities of these sorts are market-like elements that grow like robust weeds between the cracks of the planning mechanism. They are not the consequence of venality: they would be undertaken by the most public-spirited of managers, not in order to feather their own nests, but to help fill the lacunae that are bound to occur in the best-laid plans. There are many points at which such non-regulation and illegal activities actually make the system work more efficiently than it would in their absence. Such activities, however, are unlikely to be widespread enough to compensate fully for the inefficiency of the formal planning mechanism, although they may reduce its extent.

The major consequence of the failure of coordination is pure allocative inefficiency – that invisible deficiency in which all resources are employed, but in the wrong enterprises and industries. Had that been the only deficiency, planning might have retained much of its appeal, for pure allocative inefficiency is invisible to all but the analytic eye. However, poor coordination also takes the highly visible form of production lines that are inoperative because the required fuel or materials have not arrived, of tractors delivered with parts missing, of coal piled up at the rail siding because it had not been ordered, of expensive imported equipment rusting under the open sky because the construction work on the new factory has been delayed.[2] To a political-economic leadership untutored in the subtleties of allocative efficiency, that inescapably visible effect of paper plans no doubt contributed greatly to the erosion of confidence in the superiority of the planning mechanism.

5 Bargaining

Central planning in the abstract looks like a relation among things – among inputs and outputs. In practice it is a set of relations among people. The core of the relationship is indeed outputs and inputs, but the quantities of outputs and inputs that find their way into the final plan are heavily influenced by social relationships. A major cause of the extensive influence of social relations is the fact of pervasive paper planning.

The gap between plan targets and actual production possibilities places an enormous strain on managers. Their incomes and careers depend on the fulfillment of their assigned output plans, yet the supply of the labor and other resources needed for that purpose is highly uncertain and often inconsistent with the requirements of their plans. In the course of time it became standard practice in the planned economies for managers to work outside of official channels in order to secure the labor and other inputs they needed. Alongside the formal planning system there developed a vast system of informal organization by means of which managers contrived to achieve a better record of performance than they would have if they passively accepted the plan tangets assigned to them.

Many of the methods by means of which managers saved themselves from paper plans entailed the use of personal influence. There were many sources of influence, such as holding an important position in the Party or in the government, or being a close friend of such officials. The property of the enterprise could also serve to pave the way for influence: it was a fortunate enterprise that produced scarce cherished goods that could be used as gifts, or that owned a holiday vacation resort to which ministry and planning officials could be invited to vacation free of charge.

Influential managers were those who could pick up the phone and talk directly with a senior official in his ministry or arrange a meeting with the minister himself. They might exert strong pressure to get the ministry to reduce their final output plan to a level more consistent with the labor resources allocated to them. Or they could play hardball by calling on their connections in the Party to pressure the regional planning officials into authorizing a larger labor force than that provided for in their plan. An enterprise that had underfulfilled its output plan could persuade an accommodating ministry official to reduce the original plan *ex post facto*, so that the enterprise could claim fulfillment and receive the bonuses to which it was not in fact entitled.

During plan-making months Soviet directors and their agents, travelling on expense accounts, descended on Moscow in great profusion, clogging the hallways and waiting rooms of the ministries and planning offices, working to "beat out" more favorable conditions for their enterprises. Management's influence with ministry officials went a long way in getting plan assignments and input authorizations that were favorable to the enterprise. If the enterprise ran short of inputs, either because they were not delivered or because of wasteful use, good relations with the ministry could be used to secure additional supplies.

The ministries, under pressure from the central planning board for higher output plans, were often unable to meet all the demands from the enterprises. The more of a crucial input that they promised to one enterprise, the less there was for the others. They were therefore able to extract concessions from officials of the competing enterprises. It might be a production concession, like inducing a manager to agree to introduce a complex new production process that the government's State Committee on Technology had been pressuring the reluctant ministry to adopt. Or it might be a personal concession, like an invitation to the popular hunting lodge maintained by the Party Secretary of the enterprise's region. Similar relations prevailed between ministries and the central planning board. Many of the ministers were powerful officials of the Communist Party, and when they requested special treatment from the planners, input norms would go out the window and the minister would get all or most of what he requested.

The consequence of this extensive bargaining was that enterprise output and labor plans diverged greatly from those that would emerge from the plan-balancing activities of the planners alone. Moreover, in the course of the year the output actually produced and the inputs actually employed diverged further from those that had been specified in the plans. It has been suggested that when these informal processes are taken fully into account, the economy would best be described not as a planned economy but as a "bargaining economy," or as a "managed" economy.[3] Perhaps the system is best thought of as one in which the formal planning mechanism set the broad outlines of the composition of the country's output and the allocation of its labor among those products, but in which, as a result of the bargaining process, the actual production of goods and allocation of workers diverged considerably from that which emerged from the offices of the planners.

With respect to efficiency, when the effects of paper planning and of informal bargaining are taken into account, there is no reason to expect that in the final allocation of resources, the marginal cost of production would be the same in all enterprises in each industry, or that the marginal product of labor would be equal in all enterprises and industries.

6 Externalities

Externalities like environmental degradation play no favorites. A coal-fired electric-power plant would pollute socialist air no less than capitalist air, and a cellulose plant would pollute any lake into which its effluent is discharged.

The market mechanism is incapable of dealing with externalities of this sort as long as the air and water are not privately owned. If externalities are to be controlled, restrictions have to be imposed upon the economy from the outside, normally by government action. The central planning board, however, is part of the government. In deciding how much coal-fired electric power should be produced, the planning board need not be bound by the "private" cost of power as calculated by the electric-power plant alone. It can "internalize" the full social cost of producing power, including the cost to the people of the air pollution caused by the burning of coal. The planning mechanism ought therefore to be more successful than the market mechanism in balancing the social costs and benefits of productive activity.

In practice that did not happen. On the contrary, the extent of environmental pollution in the planned economies was at least as extensive and perhaps greater than in the market economies. Large regions of the former Communist lands are polluted to a degree that would never have been countenanced in the West. The most famous case is the pollution of Lake Baikal in Siberia, the largest and once the purest freshwater lake in the world.[4] But there are many others, notably the drying up and salinization of the Caspian Sea and the virtual collapse of what was once a great sturgeon and caviar industry. The air in the industrial region of Slovakia has been characterized as the most polluted in Europe, and the heavy expenses that the West Germans bore in supporting the rapid recovery of the former East Germany was due in large part to the environmentally hazardous quality of the East German industrial plant and equipment.

Protest movements   One can gauge the extent of the damage by imagining what the West would look like today if the trajectory of environmental degradation as of a half-century ago had continued unimpeded to this day. What has made the difference is the environmental movement, the diffusion of information, and the growing public pressure that has called in the government – from outside the economy, as it were – to halt and reverse the destruction of the environment by private and public bodies. Protests by groups of citizens have been a major countervailing power to industries that impose external costs by their production activities.

Under central planning, however, there is no government that can be called in from the outside to remedy things within the economy. The government *is* the economy: the planners are part of the government bureaucracy, and the managers take their orders from that bureaucracy. To protest against pollution is therefore to protest against the government itself, something that is not tolerated by an authoritarian government. The suppressed public outrage reached such a pitch, however – initially over Lake Baikal – that some courageous Soviet citizens, particularly scientists and writers, dared openly to challenge the government's policy. Their courage, and the power of their arguments, eventually persuaded the Party to abstain from suppressing their voices. Out of that protest emerged a genuine environmental movement, the first such autonomous non-Party movement in Soviet history. The spread of political dissidence is sometimes credited to the success of the pioneers of the environmental protest.

Planning is therefore something of a gamble in an authoritarian polity. Because central planners are able to take external effects like pollution into account, less of it is likely to occur under planning than under markets. On the other hand, the planners may decide that the social cost of the pollution that a certain industry may cause is small relative to the social benefit of the goods that the industry would produce, and citizens who weigh the costs and benefits differently from the government have little recourse. In that case, these would be more pollution under planning than under markets.

Bureaucratic interests   The relative weakness of public protest movements is only part of the explanation of the failure of the planning mechanism to benefit in practice from its advantage in theory. A second reason is that industrial bureaucracies, everywhere perhaps, tend to identify their personal interests with that of the society. People whose careers are vested in the electric-power or cellulose industries tend to be committed to the growth of those industries. The closing of a factory and the shrinking of an industry means that thousands of workers' jobs and hundreds of administrators' careers are hurt. People may be relocated, but most of them will never regain the status they had achieved before. They therefore use all the tools of bureaucratic infighting to avert the shrinking of their industries for the sake of environmental protection.

Values   The effort by vested interests to head off attempts to cope with externalities is to be expected under both types of economic mechanism. The third, and perhaps the most important, reason for the failure to deal successfully with externalities is one that is specific to the planned economies. The pressure for high rates of production, emanating from the top of the Communist Party and the government, compelled decision-makers all the way down the line – even those with no vested interest in a particular industry – to suppress whatever doubts they may have had of the wisdom of undertaking economically vital production activities merely because of their environmentally destructive effects. Environmental degradation may therefore be regarded not as the unintended consequence of a poorly functioning political system but as the successful implementation by an authoritarian government of its own set of social and political values. From this perspective pollution was a price the government was willing to pay for what it judged to be the greater good of economic growth.

7   Public Goods

One deficiency of the market mechanism is that it would produce too little of such "public goods" as scientific knowledge and national defense (chapter 17). Market economies repair that deficiency by giving government the power to deflect some resources away from things that the citizens as individuals would buy for themselves to things from which they would benefit collectively but which they would not buy for themselves.

The planning mechanism has worked well in this respect. The Communist countries devoted substantial resources to education and scientific research and maintained a large defense establishment. It might indeed be argued that the planning mechanism worked too well with regard to public goods. The annual planning process would begin with a decision by the top officials of Party and government specifying how much of the country's resources were to be allocated for each of the main categories of use: consumer goods for the citizens, investment, national defense, science and technology, the arts, sports, and so forth. It was not a case of a democratic government coaxing resources away from those consumer goods that the citizens as individuals would prefer in order to remedy the neglect of public goods. It was rather a case of an authoritarian government deciding what in their judgment was best for the society, without respect to whether they were private or public goods.

From the perspective of a Good Society, however, in which the government would be responsible to the people, the planned economies probably devoted too much of their country's resources to public goods. If the citizens' preferences with respect to both private and public goods had prevailed, the planners would very likely have allocated far more of the country's resources to private consumption like housing and less to such public goods as defense, research and development, and the arts. This conclusion is a useful reminder that the outcomes of the planning mechanism, like those of the market mechanism, can vary greatly according to the nature of the political mechanism with which it is conjoined.

8 Shortage: Consumer Goods

If the impact of coordination problems were random, an economy would be characterized by excess production of some products and shortages of others. Under the market mechanism, as we have seen, the impact is biased in the direction of excess production. In planned economies, in contrast, it is biased in the direction of shortage.

The notion of "shortage" in this context does not imply absolute scarcity, such as the insufficiency of food in the wake of a drought. It is a consequence not of an inadequacy of goods but of the way in which the goods are distributed among the citizens. Since consumer goods are distributed under central planning by the price method, the culprit is usually the same: prices are too low. The prevalence of shortage is no mystery in that case. The inescapable shortage is the source of some of the most disagreeable features of life in the Communist planned economies. One of them, perpetual queuing, was discussed in chapter 5. But there were others that also greatly affected the quality of a citizen's life.

THE BLACK MARKET

If there is any universal generalization that can be made about economic behavior, it is that underpricing spawns a black market. It is a direct response to inefficiency. With a non-optimal distribution, there are always people who are willing to pay a higher price for a good than its official price. The spread between those prices creates an opportunity for enterprising persons to profit by buying the good at the low price and reselling it to people who want it badly enough to pay the high price.

There is no society so good that it can underprice goods without having eventually to face up to the black market. When the underpricing is a temporary measure, as in times of war or national emergency, the spirit of patriotism generates fierce public hostility to black marketeers, and their activity may be restrained. The United Kingdom during World War II, for example, had an extensive system of price controls and there was evidently very little profiteering. In the United States, however, postwar studies revealed a vast wartime black market in controlled commodities.[5] In both countries the black market disappeared as soon as the war ended and price controls gave way to normal peacetime clearing prices. In the Communist countries, however, since underpricing became a permanent part of normal economic life, the black market flourished to their very end.

The extent of it varied from time to time, contracting when the authorities mounted a campaign against it and packed some people off to prison, and expanding when the pressure was eased. It seems to have been particularly active in the resale of automobiles. The "specu-lators" frequented the car sales offices, and when a customer came to buy a car after years of waiting, he was bombarded with offers to buy it at many times the price he had just paid. A brisk trade also developed in the exchange of apartments. In that case the parties were not middlemen but ordinary citizens seeking to jump the housing queue or to find better hous-ing for their families. So extensive was the exchange of apartments that a "lively open air 'stock exchange' trading rooms and apartments" operated outside the offices of the govern-ment's Bureau of Housing Exchanges.[6]

CORRUPTION

The extensive queuing and reselling that occur with non-clearing pricing are transparent marks of a very bad economic arrangement that should have no place in a Good Society. More destructive to the moral quality of the society is the corruption of the officials who have the responsibility and authority to decide who will get the goods.

Given a certain supply of some good, if it is sold at its clearing price, there is always enough to go around: everybody who wants to buy it can get it. Underpricing, however, creates an artificial shortage. As a consequence the people who control the supply are often in a position to decide who will get the good. Underpricing thus introduces an element of assignment into the price method. In cases of extreme underpricing, like Soviet apartment rents which were virtually negligible, it is fair to say that assignment supplanted prices as the distribu-tional arrangement.

The power that underpricing confers on administrative agents is a breeding place for cor-ruption in any society, certainly in the long run. In the last years of the Communist regimes, payoffs to officials became a standard part of the goods-distribution system.[7] Officials in charge of meat departments were known to be particularly affluent because of the bribes they received for setting meat aside for favored customers or black marketeers. One stage further back, when a job opened up for a head of a meat department, the official responsible for making the appointment expected a huge gift from the successful candidate based on the expected illegal earnings on the job.

In the best of societies and in all cultures there are people who from time to time suc-cumb to an opportunity to capitalize on other people's confidence in their integrity. Some social arrangements, however, create more opportunities and more temptation than others. The subversion of integrity is particularly strong in a society that chooses to use prices for distributing consumer goods, but then cannot bring itself to let the price method do those things that it does well.

That problem, however, should not be ascribed to planning as such, but to bad planning. There is no good economic reason for the general practice of setting consumer-goods prices below the market-clearing levels. The planners could just as easily have set the prices at their clearing levels. If that were done, the shortage of consumer goods would vanish immediately and the black market along with it, much as they did in the capitalist countries when price controls were removed after World War II, and in the former Communist countries after the abandonment of central planning.

To be sure, the central planners are unlikely to be as successful as markets in determining the market-clearing prices of tens of thousands of consumer goods, and in keeping up with the incessant changes that would have to be made in those prices. Some will be overpriced and some underpriced, so that there will be local shortages and excesses. But on balance there should be no general shortage. That this can be done is demonstrated by the experience of Czechoslovakia, a most orthodox centrally planned economy before 1989, where consumer-goods queues were the exception rather than the rule.

9   Shortage: Producer Goods

Since intermediate products were distributed by assignment rather than by price in the Communist economies, the explanation of persistent shortage of those products is somewhat different. A number of factors contributed to it. One of them is a response to a longstanding concern, first expressed by Lenin, that in the absence of the discipline imposed by competition and unemployment under capitalism, socialist workers might simply sit on their hands, do very little work, and be wasteful of the public resources. The policy designed to combat that tendency is "taut planning," or "over-full employment planning," meaning that output plans are set high enough, and input supplies kept low enough, to compel managers and workers to economize on inputs and to elicit a high level of work effort. Taut planning may well help to maintain the level of effort, as intended, but it has a major negative consequence: a certain number of enterprises are unable to fulfill their plans with the inputs they receive, and many others operate under the threat of underfulfillment.

Because of unrealistically high output plans, managers tend to grab up whatever materials and supplies they can get hold of, as a form of "insurance" against underfulfillment of plan because of input shortages. The result is that intermediate products tend to be immediately swept up by enterprise supply agents as soon as they became available. If bricks or copper wire or lubricating oil happen to be available, they are bought up at once, just in case they happen to be needed sometime in the future.[8]

To the extent that taut planning is responsible for shortage, the fault again should be ascribed not to planning itself but to the particular way planning is done. The government could instruct the planners to set plans at such levels that they would be fulfilled by 100 percent or 95 percent of the enterprises, rather than 70 percent or 60 percent. Enterprises would then find that the intermediate products they needed were being produced in sufficient quantities, and would not feel the compulsion to over-order and to snap up such products whenever they could lay hands on them. Normal inventories would accumulate in the supply depots and shortage would vanish.

Lenin may have been right: there may be a cost to pay if taut planning is abandoned. With more slack in the plans, work may be conducted at a much more leisurely pace and less effort may be expended in economizing on inputs. The point is, however, that taut planning should not be regarded as inherent in the planning mechanism.

SOFT BUDGETS

There is a second reason why the shortage of intermediate products is likely to prevail, even if planning is not excessively taut. A number of incentives were introduced in the USSR for the purpose of motivating management to economize on costs, in the interest of efficiency. For example, if an enterprise succeeded in reducing actual cost below planned cost, management and workers were entitled to special bonuses for that achievement. This and similar measures provided a positive incentive for economizing in the production process.

Effective incentives systems, however, generally contain both carrots and sticks. The force of the invisible hand of the market is greatly magnified by the invisible foot of competition, which may force an enterprise out of business if it is too cavalier about its production costs. Central planning coordinates the economy through a conspicuously visible hand, but the problem is that there is no clearly visible foot. The positive incentives for economizing are not supported by powerful negative incentives for not economizing.

The long-run consequence of these arrangements was the erosion of management's concern for economizing on costs of production. Faced on the one hand with high production targets and substantial rewards for fulfilling them, and on the other with very weak sanctions for cost overruns, managers developed a huge appetite for accumulating supplies, maintaining surplus labor on the payroll, and undertaking prestigious but risky investment projects. Hungarian economist Janos Kornai has popularized the expression "soft budget constraint," meaning that managers were only weakly constrained by the financial losses they might incur because of their business decisions.[9]

What got the planned economies into such a bind? Perhaps the major reason was the socialist state's inability to resolve one of its central dilemmas: how to enforce financial discipline in its enterprises without resorting to that most powerful of capitalism's sanctions – bankruptcy. Tight financial discipline would compel even profitable enterprises to trim their labor force of redundant workers from time to time. If imposed on weaker enterprises, it would inevitably require that some of them be liquidated from time to time, with the attendant dismissal of substantial numbers of workers from their jobs. The prospect of a rate of job loss possibly as large as under capitalism struck at the foundation of the fundamental socialist claim to have established a workers' state. It was an unthinkable prospect for the Party, and no doubt for millions of citizens as well.

10   Discussion

The market mechanism has been around for a long time. It is over 200 years since its properties were first identified and formalized by Adam Smith, and its roots are much older than that. It has operated in a great many countries with widely differing historical and cultural traditions. The next country to choose the market mechanism for its Good Society should therefore expect no great surprises. The details of how it will perform will depend on the specific conditions of the country, but the citizens are unlikely to invent any large variations that have not been tried by some country somewhere before.

The planning mechanism is a rather different matter. The world's earliest experience with it dates only from 1929 – with the launching of the First Five-Year Plan in the USSR. It has been employed in relatively few countries, and in most of them for much shorter periods of time. Moreover, the differences have been overshadowed by one towering similarity: they all operated under authoritarian regimes dominated by Communist parties in the tradition first established by Lenin.

Historical experience is therefore less predictive of what a future planning mechanism might look like than of what a future market mechanism might look like. The conditions of a country that adopts the market mechanism are unlikely to differ widely from those in some of the other countries where it has been tried before. A country that adopts the planning mechanism, however, may well differ greatly from those that have used it in the past, for at least two reasons.

One is that it will benefit from knowledge of the sources of inefficiency that bedeviled the twentieth-century planned economies. Many of them spring not from the fundamental properties of the planning mechanism, but from specific policy decisions that could have been made differently. The system could have performed better if it had been better run by its leaders.

Second, a country that adopts central planning in the future may be committed to political democracy. That possibility admittedly strains the imagination, but stranger things have happened in the recent past. Few people imagined in 1985, when Mikhail Gorbachev came to power in the USSR, that a decade later the USSR would cease to exist, that the Communist parties would be dethroned there and in Eastern Europe, that freedom of speech and of the press would prevail, that the planning mechanism would be entirely displaced by a nascent market mechanism – and all this with a minimum of violence and bloodshed. People who have lived through those astonishing events should be chary about rejecting the possibility of a future planned economy operating in a political democracy.

Improbable though it may be, it is an interesting idea, and a useful one for exploring some implications of the inefficiency described in this chapter. The points that follow may be taken as a twentieth-century friend's advice to a future democratic society that decides to adopt the planning mechanism.

Politics and planning   The planned economy of the future is likely to have a strong socialist orientation, but if it is a political democracy, it may escape some of the sources of inefficiency of the Communist economies. In the absence of a Communist party with its monopoly of power, the planning board would be staffed with fewer Party loyalists and engineers and with more civil servants and economists. It was only the suppression of free thought that caused central planning to concentrate so singlemindedly on coordination, with no attention to the concept of allocative efficiency as it had developed in the West. Marxism in particular would lose its imposed monopoly over economic thought and would be relegated to its proper place – as a major component of nineteenth-century economic thought that, like all pioneering work, has been built upon and overtaken by changing times and subsequent research.

Under democratic politics in a Good Society, good sense is more likely to prevail, and planning would be based on the best of modern economic science. Good sense, combined with an autopsy of twentieth-century planning, could produce a planning mechanism that would be different from and better than those of the past in many ways.

Perfect computation   If central planning should ever again be adopted as the economic mechanism in some society of the future, it is unlikely to be the Soviet variety. It is much more likely to be a form of planning that incorporates a concern for efficiency through the mathematical techniques of "perfect computation" (chapter 16).

The major gain would be in productive efficiency. With mathematical planning, an effort would be made to assign production plans to coal mines, for example, in such proportions that the marginal cost of producing coal was the same in all the mines. The effort may not be entirely successful, but freed from the commitment to "material balances," the central planners of the future are likely to come closer to the mark. To the extent that they do, the available resources will yield a larger output of coal and all other goods than the earlier planners were able to attain. Similarly, resources would be more efficiently allocated among industries: not only would the right quantity of coal be produced but also the right quantities of iron, of iron beds, and of goods and services generally. A second gain would be in the quality of the prices used by economic agents throughout the economy in making production decisions; for along with an optimal production plan, mathematical planning produces a set of prices that reflect the marginal cost of production, rather than the average cost that underlies Soviet-type planning.

Mathematical planning would still suffer from those sources of inefficiency that are fundamental to central planning itself. The economy would still have to cope with the problem of managerial motivation and would still be dependent on the managers for the flow of information required for planning. The planners would still be responsible for matching buyers and sellers, so that sellers would always be assured that buyers will be found for their products, both good and bad. Because of the absence of competition, there is every reason to expect that the quality of production would suffer, much as it did under Soviet-type planning.

Consumer goods prices   The planned economies sensibly accepted the principle that consumer goods should be distributed by prices rather than by assignment. The problem was that, having opted for the price method, they were unwilling to let it work properly. The Soviet leadership in particular adopted a policy of setting the prices of many consumer goods somewhat below their clearing levels. There is nothing mysterious or pathological about the conditions to which that policy gave rise. Underpricing is the opening through which corruption creeps in because of the profit to be made by acquiring an underpriced good and selling it to another citizen willing and eager to pay a higher price.

There is no society so morally pure that it can long restrain all of its citizens from seeking that sort of profit. It requires only a few risk-takers to create a massive commerce in such "arbitrage," and since the activity is illegal and profits are high, corruption inevitably follows, in the form of payoffs to the trade officials who are legally responsible for the distribution of the goods, and to political and police officials to look the other way.

Concerns about inequality do not justify that pricing policy. Wages and pensions are set by the planners with equity concerns much in mind, and they can be set high enough so that the poorest citizens, as well as all others, could pay the full market-clearing prices for bread, apartment rent, automobiles, and other underpriced goods. The prevalence of shortage should therefore not be ascribed to the imperfection of the planning mechanism as such, but to an unrelated pricing policy that would have created consumer goods shortages under any economic mechanism that used the price method.

Hence, with no change at all in the quantity and quality of the consumer goods produced by the economy, with a proper pricing policy the citizens would find their lives as consumers to be substantially more satisfactory.

Small-scale markets   The planned economies could have lightened the coordinating burden of the planning mechanism by limiting it to large-scale activities and permitting small-scale activities to be conducted by non-state enterprises and coordinated by the market mechanism. Among the latter are kitchen gardens that produce vegetables and small livestock, retail stores, handicrafts, repair shops, and food services. Some of that was indeed done in all the Communist countries, and fairly extensively in East Germany and Poland. With some further ideological stretch it could also be extended to small-scale industrial activities like specialized repair services, consulting services, and small workshops. That would permit the central planners and the ministerial bureaucracy to concentrate on a limited range of coordination activities, instead of bearing responsibility for the entire economy. The planning of the large-scale core of the production system would be better done, and the vast sea of local and small-scale economic activity would be better carried out as well.

There are certain problems in the intermeshing of the planning and market mechanisms. For example, the planned sector would have to make intermediate products available for sale to the private sector via the market. Since some products are likely to have different prices in the two sectors, profits could be earned by the illegal diversion of intermediate products from the planned sector to the market sector. Such corruption would no doubt exist, but it is not evident that it would be larger than the corruption generated by the gaps in coordination of the planning system itself. A further benefit would be the existence of a set of market-clearing prices for those goods sold under market conditions. It would be very useful for a planning official to know that while the state-fixed price of fuel oil was – say – 1 ruble, the market was placing a value of 50 rubles on it. Yet another benefit would be the competition that market-sector enterprises would give to planning-sector enterprises in those activities in which they were both lawfully engaged. The quality of service in retail stores and food shops would no doubt be much better if the people had the opportunity to choose between state-run and non-state services.

Externalities   One of the reasons that the theoretical advantage of central planning in dealing with external effects did not carry over into practice was the suppression of freedom of assembly and of autonomous movements of protest. Had there been a place for popular protest movements, the environment would have been less severely degraded, and there would have been other benefits such as better workplace conditions and a lightening of the burdens on women.

The implication is that the poor environmental record of the planning mechanism in practice does not disqualify it from being used in a Good Society of the future. If it served an authoritarian government that placed little value on environmental costs, it could also serve a democratic society in which the people's values would dominate. In a democratic polity the citizens' own views of the social costs of externalities would find fuller expression in public policy and would be incorporated in the planners' decisions on such matters as whether to build a coal-fired electric-power plant, or a nuclear-powered plant, or no new electric-power plant.

That is not to say that environmentalists will find a democratic planned economy to be the answer to their dream. Its citizens are still likely to differ on the same issues that would divide them in a market economy. There will always be people who, having seen one redwood tree, have seen them all. In general, however, economic decisions taken at the central level are more likely to incorporate environmental concerns than those taken by enterprises under the normal conditions of a market economy.

These are some examples of ways in which the efficiency of the centrally planned economies might have been increased. There was in fact a series of efforts throughout the postwar period at what was called "economic reform," but the Party set the ground rules regarding what could be criticized and what proposals could be made. Had the political system been hospitable to the kinds of research and policy debates that are normal in democratic countries, the range of efforts at improving the coordination mechanism would no doubt have been very much wider.

It should therefore not be surprising if a future planned economy were considerably more efficient than those of the past. However, the problems set forth here in the text — aggregation, information transmission, vested bureaucratic interests, and so forth – are so central to the operation of the planning mechanism that substantial micro-coordination failures are likely to endure. Considering the deficiencies of both mechanisms, my own assessment is that under the best of circumstances planning-in-practice is unlikely to rival the efficiency of markets-in-practice.

I have presented perhaps too casually the prospect of a planning mechanism operating in a democratic political system. The mind can readily envision a Good Society of that kind, but again, things often work out differently in practice from the constructs of the mind. There are powerful reasons to question whether a democratic political system can long cohabit with a centrally planned economy. I am persuaded by the argument that a democratic polity can survive only when all or most members of the society earn their living in economic activities that are independent of the government. This requires that the mass of the productive property be owned by individuals or organizations that are independent of the government and that carry on their business in markets. The essence of the claim of central planning to superiority over markets, however, is precisely that economic activity is centrally coordinated, which means that the production enterprises do what the planners tell them to do, not what they find to be most profitable for themselves. To opt for central planning is therefore to opt for state-owned property.

I know no way of proving, either to my own satisfaction or anyone else's, my assertion that democracy could not survive in a society based solely on state-owned property. Some society may some day pull it off. It is an experiment that I would not recommend for my own Good Society, however. I shall give some of my reasons for that view in Part V, which deals with the question of property ownership in a Good Society.

This chapter completes the assessment of the efficiency of the two economic mechanisms. The remaining chapters in this Part consider how the two mechanisms perform by other criteria of goodness, beginning with security.

Notes

1 Hughes and Hare, "The international competitiveness of industries in Bulgaria, Czechoslovakia, Hungary, and Poland."
2 The idleness of resources under planning is primarily the consequence of poor micro-coordination, such as steel mills that are idle because they have not been provided with fuel. The idleness of resources under markets is primarily the consequence of poor macro-coordination, such as an increase in taxes at a time when unemployment is high and people are cutting back on their consumer-goods spending.
3 Zaleski, *Stalinist Planning for Economic Growth.*
4 Goldman, *The Spoils of Progress.*
5 Clinard, *The Black Market.*
6 Morton, "The Soviet quest for better housing," p. 806.
7 Grossman, "Notes on the illegal economy and corruption."
8 Berliner, *Factory and Manager in the USSR*, ch. 7.
9 Kornai, *The Socialist System*, pp. 140–5.

Chapter 19

Job Security and Markets

And there were seven good years,
followed by seven lean years.
— *Exodus*

CONTENTS

Inefficiency is an enemy of the Good Society because it restrains the economy from producing to its full potential. Of the many ways in which an economy can be inefficient, the last four chapters have been concerned with one – a condition in which all resources are actively employed in production, but are not allocated among their various uses in the best possible way. All factories are humming and all workers are employed in some jobs – but they are the wrong jobs, in the wrong enterprises, and in the wrong industries.

However, there is another, more pernicious, reason that an economy may produce less than its potential. That occurs when an economy fails to provide employment for a sizeable proportion of the available resources. Many factories are idle and many workers are unable to find any jobs at all.

Unemployment may be thought of as a special case of inefficiency, in which a portion of the labor force is not merely engaged in activities of relatively low productivity, but is not engaged in any production activity. The problem is not that they contribute less to output than they could under an allocatively efficient arrangement: it is that they contribute nothing at all.

The matter of full employment is important not only because of its relation to the level of output, however. It is also intimately related to one of the important criteria of the goodness of economic arrangements – security. Most people depend entirely or primarily on their job to provide the family's income. If the economic mechanism manages to provide reasonably full employment for all its workers, but in ways that create great uncertainty about how long the job will last and whether there will be another if it doesn't last, low unemployment numbers may mask a great deal of personal insecurity.

Security and justice   The introduction of the criterion of economic security at this point is a departure from the usual practice. In the standard introduction to these matters, the examination of the efficiency of an economic arrangement is customarily followed by an examination of the distributive justice of the arrangement. Efficiency versus equity is generally held to be the "big tradeoff" around which political positions are formed.[1]

That is normally the case in assessing economic policies within an economy. In my view, however, in the assessment of entire societies with different economic mechanisms, security looms as a larger issue than equity. For example, the nostalgia for the old system that still exerts political influence in the former Communist countries derives more from the security that it provided than from the equity with which income was distributed. Apart from that comparative observation, however, it has always seemed to me that in modern societies, working people are more concerned with security than equity. Perhaps if the income-spread between rich and poor were much wider than it presently is in most modern economies, concerns about distributive justice would be more salient. Under present conditions, however, in assessing the goodness of their economy, employment and job security would be at the forefront of most people's concerns.

That may be less the case with people who possess wealth or who work in occupations that tend to provide a great deal of security under normal conditions – civil servants, university professors, many corporate executives, and other highly educated professionals and intellectuals. In their musings about the Good Society, people in secure occupations are more likely to think about distributive justice, and might have to be reminded that security also merits consideration.

In the spirit of Rawls' "veil of ignorance," however, you must play the game of the Good Society not knowing whether you will end up as a doorman or a banker. You must know something, however, by direct or vicarious experience, of what an insecure life is like. The more you encounter or read about life in the less secure regions of a society, the larger the weight you are likely to assign to security in your assessment of its goodness.

There are other elements in overall economic security than those associated directly with unemployment. Price instability, for example: uncertainty about next week's value of this week's income, or the future value of a lifetime's savings, can be a source of great anxiety. The present discussion, however, will be confined to job security.

I   Transitional Unemployment

In the best of markets and the best of times a certain number of working people find themselves without jobs. Unemployment of that sort is usually the consequence of some disturbance to which the economy must adjust. A change in fashion is such a disturbance: if people stop wearing hats, a lot of unemployed hatters will be looking for new jobs. Part of the adjustment process is the movement of workers from hat-making to other jobs, usually in other enterprises, but sometimes in other industries. Moving from one job to another takes time – for searching, perhaps for retraining, and sometimes for moving to another location. Unemployment of this sort is therefore called "transitional."

Transitional unemployment occurs even in periods of high prosperity when the economy is operating at full capacity. In that case there are enough jobs for everybody, in principle; the problem is to find and place the unemployed in those jobs.

There are two major forms of transitional unemployment – frictional and structural. They are the subject of this section. The section that follows deals with the gloomier matter of unemployment in periods of depressed economic activity, when there are not enough jobs for all the unemployed.

FRICTIONAL UNEMPLOYMENT

The stark fact of life under the market mechanism is this: nobody gets a job unless some employer finds it profitable to hire him.

The demand for labor is therefore said to be "derived" from the profit that enterprises expect to earn from the sale of the goods that they produce. Hence, any change in the demand for goods by some citizens-as-consumers is translated, through the market, into a change in the jobs held by some citizens-as-workers. If, for example, you and other weight-conscious citizens decide to cut down on your consumption of bread, the market coordination process springs into action. Bread prices fall, and the bakeries find their profit falling as well. At the new price, profit peaks at a lower rate of production than before. The bakeries therefore cut back on their output and employment. You and your fellow dieters are therefore responsible in your small way for the unemployment of some poor devil of a baker.

How long your unfortunate victim remains unemployed depends, however, on what you do with the money that you no longer spend on bread. If you spend it on a variety of other goods like jeans, the producers of those other goods respond to that increase in demand by expanding their output and employment. New jobs therefore open up in those industries. After a period of transition to the new structure of consumer demand, the workers released from the bakeries find new jobs in the garment and other industries. The bakery worker therefore has no more than a minor grievance against you: the main effect of the change in your consumption practices is to oblige her to transfer from a bakery job to a job in another industry. Her spell of unemployment lasts only as long as it takes to find the new job – but the new job will always be there because of your increased demand for jeans.

Unemployment of the foregoing sort is referred to as "frictional." Some frictional unemployment is inevitable because no economy would be able to – or wish to – insulate itself fully from such disturbances as changes in consumer preferences, the discovery or depletion of natural resources, the introduction of new labor-saving production technologies, the appearance of new or improved products, the entrance of younger workers into the labor force, and so forth. Short periods of transitional unemployment are unavoidable because it takes time to find new jobs and to retrain for jobs in other industries.

The consequences for working people of successive disturbances and readjustments are never pleasant, and are extremely painful in some cases. The pains can be mitigated by various social policies that a compassionate society would surely adopt, but there is no way of eliminating entirely the periodic redistribution of some workers among jobs, short of freezing the labor force into one job structure and thereby preventing the market mechanism from accommodating to changes in consumer preferences and other disturbances through which the general economic welfare is enhanced.

The presence of frictional unemployment should not be regarded as a deficiency in the economic mechanism. In most production operations some machines remain idle some of the time – held in reserve until they are to be used. An efficient production arrangement is one in which the amount of such idle time is optimal, which is normally larger than zero. Similarly, efficiency in responding to disturbances requires that workers be transferred among jobs, which always takes time. Hence, permanent frictional unemployment does not signify inefficiency as long as it does not exceed some optimal level.

STRUCTURAL UNEMPLOYMENT

What starts as frictional unemployment sometimes endures so long that it shades off into the category known as "structural unemployment." With purely frictional unemployment, typesetters who left or lost their jobs would quickly find new ones, but if the whole industry changes over rapidly to electronic publishing, typesetters may remain unemployed for a long time because they lack the skills to fill the new jobs that are created.

The most destructive impact of structural unemployment, however, occurs in regions that are dominated by a single industry, such as the coal mines in West Virginia and the cotton mills in New England. When that industry begins to decline and enterprises close down or move out, new enterprises do not move in quickly enough to supply new jobs for the unemployed. Shops and other enterprises then lose sales and many of them also fold, adding to the initial wave of unemployment. The region sinks into a depression that may endure for a long time.

Some of the younger labor force migrate to regions where job prospects are brighter. Many of the older workers, however, retire or withdraw from the labor force, living on social insurance benefits when they can, or on public assistance when those give out, or on charitable or family support when they must. Eventually, years or decades later, some enterprises in expanding industries may be attracted to the region by the relatively low-wage labor, by proximity to a large prosperous region, or by other cost advantages. Some regions recover in this way; others never do.

Frictional and structural unemployment are similar in many ways: both are products of the transition from one structure of jobs to another, both are the fallout of benign processes like technological advances that enhance material welfare overall, and both occur even in periods of general prosperity when there are enough jobs in the country for everyone. Frictional unemployment, however, is like being caught in a storm, while structural unemployment is like being devastated by a tornado. It is so heavily concentrated in a particular region that it strikes at the heart of the social fabric. Ten thousand unemployed in a whole country is one thing, but 10,000 unemployed in one region is another. It is not a matter of some unfortunate citizens being temporarily out of work, but of a whole community decaying or disappearing.

The market economies have invented a variety of policies to contain the social damage of structural unemployment. The creation of the Tennessee Valley Authority was an effort by government to reinvigorate an entire region by providing low-cost hydroelectric power and other amenities to stimulate farming and other local business, and to attract new business from elsewhere. Sweden developed an elaborate program for encouraging out-migration from depressed areas through retraining programs and generous relocation grants. Other policies involve the nationalization of sick industries, or subsidizing companies to keep them operating, or pensioning off the older redundant workers for life.

A democratic society that uses the market mechanism should expect a healthy public debate on which policies to adopt, and how much to spend, to ease the burden of structural unemployment. The more individual-minded of Good Societies will expect its victims of structural unemployment to take more of the burden on themselves, while the more social-minded will go to great lengths to shift the burden from the minority of victims to the large majority of beneficiaries of change. Every society that adopts the market mechanism, however, must accept the risk that some of its vigorous communities will some day dry up or disappear. Insofar as security is a criterion of the goodness of economic arrangements, the market mechanism scores badly because of its vulnerability to structural unemployment.

While transitional unemployment of both sorts can be minimized by appropriate policies, it can never be eliminated in societies that employ the market mechanism. A market economy may therefore be said to enjoy "full employment" when the only forms of unemployment are frictional and structural. That is the meaning of the term in the great debate over whether the market mechanism tends to produce "full employment."

2 Full Employment

A market economy responds to technical change and other disturbances by dumping the workers who lose their jobs into the backyards, so to speak, of other industries that obligingly establish enough new jobs to reemploy them. In order that full employment may be maintained in that way, there must some benign force at work in the coordination process that somehow ensures that the number of new jobs created exactly matches the number of jobs lost. The nature of that force was a major question on the agenda of nineteenth-century economics. The answer that most economists found satisfactory was "Say's Law," named after the French economist, Jean Baptiste Say.

SAY'S LAW

When an enterprise produces and sells a product at the market price of $100, it receives a revenue of $100 from the sale. That revenue constitutes the enterprise's income, which, in a very simple economy, is paid out in the form of wages and profit: the workers might receive perhaps $80 in wages, and the owners $20 in profit. Thus, the output that a society produces generates a quantity of income that is equal to the value of that output. On an economy-wide scale, if aggregate output is $100 billion, aggregate income must also be $100 billion. Thus, the income earned in each period is sufficient to buy all the goods produced in that period, and the market mechanism sees to it that aggregate spending tends in fact to be equal to aggregate output. In the popular formulation of Say's Law, "supply creates its own demand"; which is to say that the act of producing $100 billion worth of goods creates $100 billion of income that will be used to buy all of those goods. Hence the enterprises would produce the same amount in each period, and if the labor force were initially fully employed, it would remain so indefinitely.

But what if the citizens-as-consumers decided to spend only $75 billion of their $80 billion of wages, and to increase their bank savings by $5 billion? Then $5 billion of the consumer goods that had been produced would remain unsold at the end of the period. If that "savings gap" persisted, enterprises would begin to cut back on production, and unemployment would increase. However, argued Say's Law, a savings gap of that sort could not persist when the market mechanism is permitted to perform its coordinating function. An incipient decline in aggregate spending would trigger off certain thermostat-like forces that would restore it to its previous full-employment level. In particular, with the increase in savings, competition would cause the banks and other lenders to reduce the interest rate they charge on loans. The lower interest rate induces enterprises to borrow in order to buy more investment goods – plant, equipment, machinery – to replace or modernize older capital or to expand production. The increase in investment-goods spending by business thus replaces the decrease in consumer-goods spending by consumers until aggregate spending returns to its $100 billion full-employment level. The economy now produces more investment goods and fewer consumer goods than before, in line with the consumers' preference to save more and spend less. Some workers have to change jobs from consumer-goods industries to investment-goods industries, but the only unemployment that occurs is transitional.

The implication of Say's Law is that if unsold goods begin to pile up, and workers released from employment in some enterprises are not quickly reabsorbed in others, something must be interfering with the normal operation of the mechanism. Protagonists of the market mechanism regarded the chief form of such interference to be restrictions imposed by labor unions and governments on the responsiveness of wage rates to changes in the demand for labor. Their chief prescription was to remove such restrictions so that wages would be permitted to fall to a level low enough to restore full employment.

The logic of Say's Law has a powerful appeal, and it became the prism through which most economists viewed the operation of the market mechanism. Yet to many others it seemed a very dubious explanation of the business cycle – the alternations of periods of boom and bust that long plagued the capitalist economies. In the Great Depression of the 1930s, unemployment reached unparalleled levels in the major capitalist countries, peaking at about 25 percent in the United States, with no end in sight; and it seemed increasingly implausible that it was due to "labor obstinately refusing to accept a reduction of money-wages."[2] Unlike in past depressions, moreover, this time there existed a large planned economy – the USSR – in which unemployment had not only been eradicated but to which workers from other countries were coming to help "build socialism." The contrast generated a more powerful political threat than the capitalist system had ever before faced.

Say's Law was regarded as pure apologetics by Marxists, who had long argued that unemployment was not simply an unfortunate feature of an otherwise benign adjustment process, but was a permanent and inevitable feature of the capitalist market economy. In their view, it was essential to the survival of capitalism, which could not function without a permanent "reserve army of the unemployed." In light of the extent and duration of unemployment during the Great Depression, growing numbers of people around the world came to believe that the Marxists had it right after all.

THE KEYNESIAN REVOLUTION

The devastating attack on Say's Law came not from an opponent of capitalism, however, but from a devoted supporter – the British economist, John Maynard Keynes, in his classic 1936 book, *The General Theory of Employment, Interest, and Money*. Little-understood and strongly resisted at the time, Keynes' new view eventually came to dominate economic thought. Students today are astonished to learn that before Keynes the standard textbooks of economics contained no section called "macroeconomics" – the analytic perspective that he introduced and that now occupies a good half of every economics curriculum.

The fundamental claim of the new macroeconomics was that the market mechanism cannot be counted on to automatically induce a volume of aggregate spending sufficient to buy up all the goods that the economy produces when labor is fully employed. In particular, it does not respond effectively to a savings gap, for there is no reason to expect businesses to increase their investment spending by the amount that consumer-goods spending declines. In his critique of Say's Law, Keynes argued that a business firm's decision to invest depends on a great many considerations other than current market conditions like the interest rate. It depends greatly on expectations of future business conditions, and on the sheer "animal spirits" of businessmen. It would be only by sheer accident that investment spending would increase by precisely the amount required to fill the savings gap. Aggregate spending in any period is therefore likely to be smaller, or larger, than aggregate output in the preceding period. If it happens to be significantly smaller, some enterprises find that they have not sold all of last period's output, and some of them cut back on their production and employment. They also reduce their purchases of inputs from their supplier enterprises, causing the latter in turn to reduce their output and employment. Since the suppliers also buy from other suppliers who buy from other suppliers and so on, the decline in production and employment has a "multiplier" effect, so that an initial production decline of, say, 1 percent may snowball into an eventual decline of 4 or 5 percent. The downward spiral finally comes to an end when the economy has fallen into a deep depression, which has the characteristics of an equilibrium in the sense that the pure market mechanism generates no forces tending to get the economy unstuck from that unhappy state. The world according to Keynes is therefore crucially different from the world according to Say's Law.

Keynes' analysis is bad news for the market mechanism, for it deprives its proponents of one of their most powerful claims – that it is automatically self-correcting when unemployment occurs. The good news, however, is that there are ways in which an economy that is stuck at a high level of unemployment can be stimulated to expand output until full employment is restored. The politically explosive feature of Keynes' prescription is that only the government can provide that stimulus. If private spending on consumption and investment is insufficient to maintain output at a full-employment level, then the government can adopt policies to restore total spending to a full-employment level. It could launch a large road-building program, for example, which would augment private spending by new government spending.

Keynes thus rescued the market mechanism from the charge that it tends toward protracted unemployment, but only by the device of bringing government into the economic life of capitalist countries in a more critical role than had ever been contemplated before. His work also had a powerful impact on socialist thought, for it served to weaken the conviction that capitalism was headed for a general crisis that would soon bring the system down.[3]

Since the Keynesian revolution in economic thought, capitalism appears to have learned how to protect itself from the periodic scourge that threatened to bring it crashing down. In the past half-century there have been no depressions rivalling that of the 1930s, and most observers give much of the credit for that achievement to the active use by governments of fiscal and monetary policy to maintain a high level of production and employment.

The Keynesian revolution armed the market economies with the policy instruments for stimulating the economy and escaping the ravages of deep depressions. The known instruments of macroeconomic policy, however, suffer from a number of deficiencies. For one thing, they are, in effect, medications for an ailing economy, and like medicines of all kinds, they pose the danger of undesirable side-effects. In recent years, the side-effect of greatest concern in many countries has been inflation, which threatens to invade the economy if the dose of stimulative economic policy is too large. In acknowledgement of the limitations of the present pharmacopoeia, the expression "natural rate of unemployment" has come into use to characterize the lowest rate of unemployment that an economy can attain without experiencing such unacceptable side-effects. Perhaps some day an economic medicine will be invented that will enable market economies to reduce their natural rate of unemployment to so low a level that it will consist only of transitional unemployment. Until then, any society that adopts the market mechanism must expect to suffer from what I shall call "excess unemployment," or unemployment in excess of the normal level of transitional unemployment.

Rates of unemployment vary considerably from country to country and from one recession to the next. On the basis of recent experience, an unemployment rate of about 5 percent is regarded as good performance for a capitalist country. The current rate in the United States of 4.3 percent is unusually good. However, it was as low as 1 to 1.8 percent in Japan during the 1960s, most of which was probably transitional, so that the country may be considered as having virtually eliminated excess unemployment. On the other hand, some of the countries of Western Europe are suffering from unemployment rates of 11–13 percent and more, which has become a first-order social and economic problem. The bare statistics mask a great deal of variation in the unemployment experience of individual citizens. Some may never be involuntarily unemployed in their entire lifetime, perhaps because they have found jobs that are to some degree insulated from the market – like civil servants or university professors – or because they have found jobs in an industry that happens to be stable or growing throughout their working lives. At the other extreme are workers – usually unskilled – who are in and out of jobs during their entire working lives. Of those who are unemployed at any time, some will find a new job within a few weeks, some within a few months or a year. Some are unemployed for so long that they stop looking for a job; they are then classified as "not in the labor force" or "discouraged workers," and are no longer included in the statistics of the unemployed. On average, however, a society that adopts the market mechanism should expect from two to ten or more of every hundred citizens to be unemployed on any day.

3   Living with Excess Unemployment

Unlike transitional unemployment, which is the consequence of benign processes like improving technology and increasing efficiency, excess unemployment is a pure waste of resources. To its economic cost must be added the political cost. It is the harshest charge on the socialist bill of indictment of capitalism. In democratic countries it is often the major source of political unrest, and has the potential for destabilizing governments in countries in which it has grown very large. In the economies that have abandoned planning in favor of markets, the popular dread of it has contributed greatly to the resurging political influence of former Communists. A large increase in unemployment could conceivably precipitate a rejection of democracy and of much of the apparatus of the market mechanism.

There is also the social cost. The victims are not always regarded as entirely blameless. Unemployment, for whatever reason, often carries a stigma. When some workers are dismissed and others kept on, both must wonder how the distinction was made. The survivors can easily believe that it is not a matter of pure luck but that they must possess the virtue of the elect. Those who are dismissed cannot avoid a certain loss of self-esteem. Dismissal from a job is hard enough on young people, who can often rely on some family assistance and who may not have children to support. Since they are at the beginning of their career, their next job is not likely to be much of a comedown from the last. Job loss is devastating, however, on older workers whose families have grown accustomed to a certain level of consumption that may no longer be sustainable. The social and psychological effects of insecurity are felt not only by the relatively small number of dismissed workers and their families, but also by large number of currently employed workers whose vulnerability is part of their daily mental set.

Since no one has yet figured out a way of eliminating excess unemployment, all market economies have learned to live with it in one way or another. Over the years they have produced a vast array of policies and programs designed to minimize the rate of excess unemployment and to cushion its effect upon the citizens. One set of measures consists of the aforementioned instruments of monetary and fiscal policy. The theory and practice of macroeconomic policy is one of the most hotly debated matters in modern political economy, and is a proper concern of the economics of the Good Society. That great debate is beyond the province of this book, however, which is concerned not with policy but with the way in which an economy's institutional arrangements affect the employment experience of the citizens.

There are two types of job insecurity that afflict workers in market economies – losing a job, and not having a job. The latter is no doubt the more distressing, and all countries conduct programs to help maintain workers' income-flow while they search for new jobs, to assist them in relocating to higher-employment regions, to retrain technologically displaced workers, and so forth. Since most workers have jobs, however, the insecurity associated with possible job loss is more widespread. The following discussion focusses on that matter alone.

The market mechanism has proven to be remarkably adaptable to the histories and cultures of the societies in which it is employed. Since each country has molded it to suit the values of its own citizens, widely diverse sets of arrangements have grown up for coping with job insecurity. Two countries, however, each in its own way, have tested the limits of what a market economy can do to maintain job security. They are Japan and Germany.

4 Japan: Lifetime Employment

Japan is often cited as an example of how a decent society can provide lifetime job security to its workers under the market mechanism. The basis of that achievement is the so-called "Japanese-style management system."[4] Under this arrangement the giant companies like Sony and Toyota recruit young employees directly out of school with the implicit commitment to keep them on the payroll throughout their working lives. The workers in turn agree to remain with the company until retirement, to accept transfer to affiliated companies if necessary, to perform with diligence whatever tasks are assigned to them, and to give their complete loyalty to their co-workers and to the company. Wages are paid primarily on the basis of seniority and are supplemented by semi-annual bonuses that are related to merit. Bonuses vary with the size of company profits, and may account for as much as a third of total earnings. For the country as a whole they amount to about a fifth of total employee earnings.[5]

It must be kept in mind that these enterprises operate in a fully capitalist market economy. They are privately owned, they buy and sell under market conditions, and the drive for profit is no less intense than in other countries. Governmental influence on the enterprises and the economy is more extensive than in many other countries, and many industries receive protection from foreign competition, but by and large they compete fiercely for shares of their markets, both domestic and foreign. It is therefore unlikely that lifetime employment would have developed and endured if it did not contribute to the profitability of enterprise as the owners perceived it.

The proponents of the arrangement indeed cite a great many advantages. To name just three: first, it pays the enterprise to spend a great deal on the education and training of their work force because they know that their trained workers will not run off to join another company that offers a higher wage. Second, the workers are motivated to help keep production costs down and quality high because higher company profits mean more money in their own pockets, and they welcome technological change because they have no fear of losing their jobs to new machinery. And third, when sales fall off and profits drop sharply, management reduces the size of the bonus instead of laying off workers, which helps account for the remarkably low rate of unemployment.[6]

There are some dark sides, of course. Educators and social critics worry about the effect on young people of the intense parental and social pressures to get the highest grades in school in the hope of later landing one of the coveted lifetime jobs in a top company. A second concern is that the spirit of non-competitive, consensual decision-making at all levels of the enterprise suffocates non-conformist and innovative thought. Moreover, the unemployment benefit system is designed to encourage workers to find new jobs quickly rather than to provide long-term income support. The benefit entitlement period is therefore relatively short and the size of the benefit, as a proportion of previous earnings, is among the smallest of the industrialized countries.[7]

While the lifetime employment arrangement is quite distinctive, it is not evident that the outcome is all that different from other economies at various times. Comparative studies have shown, for example, that the proportion of workers with more than 15 years employment in the same company was larger in the United States than in Japan in 1966, although it was smaller in the 1970s.[8] In 1991, the proportion of workers who had been employed in the same company for more than 20 years was 19 percent. Germany, however, was not far behind, with 17 percent in that category, while in the United States the proportion was only 9 percent.[9]

In assessing the Japanese arrangement as a model for other market economies, it must be noted that lifetime employment is practiced only in the largest and some of the middle-sized companies, and that even there it does not cover the female labor force. All in all about a third of the labor force is covered. The large companies use the smaller ones as a sort of unemployment buffer. When their sales increase, rather than take on new lifetime employees they subcontract more of their production to the small companies, who then take on more workers. When sales fall off, they reduce their subcontracts to the smaller companies, who then lay off some of their workers. The greater job security of a portion of the labor force is thus made possible by the greater insecurity of the rest. It is not therefore evident that the Japanese model can satisfy a Good Society that insists on lifetime employment for all its workers.

A second consideration is that the arrangement came into prominence at a time when Japanese production and exports were growing at a record-breaking rate of 10 percent per year, and global competition had not reached its present level. Since the mid-1970s the growth rate has declined steadily, much as in the rest of the world, and is presently in the normal range of mature economies – 2 to 4 percent. Observers have begun to question whether lifetime employment is sustainable in periods of slow growth and stiffer international competition.[10] Many leading firms have turned from promoting entirely from within the company to external recruitment of people with critically needed skills; some highly talented middle-level managers have been lured away by offers from foreign firms in Japan, and less emphasis is now placed on lifetime employment and seniority-based wages.[11] In a 1994 survey of large companies, 36 percent said that some changes were necessary, while 6 percent said fundamental revision was needed.[12]

The Japanese experience offers one vision of how a market economy can provide full job security for at least a portion of its labor force. The employment arrangements are likely to be modified as the economy approaches the normal conditions under which modern economies operate, but they will very likely continue to embody some of the distinctive features of Japanese history and culture.

5 Germany: The Social Market

The Japanese lifetime employment arrangement is a creature of the private sector; it was introduced by management, not forced upon them. The job-security arrangements in European societies, in contrast, are largely the product of pressures from labor and government, although management is often a compliant partner.

Virtually all of the European market economies have developed their own ways of combining the market mechanism with their society's sense of social responsibility. There are two rather different approaches, however, that are exemplified by Sweden and Germany. The Swedish "welfare state" will be discussed in chapter 21. The German "social market" is the subject of this section.

The postwar German economy was organized around two commitments: to the market as the country's economic mechanism, and to the society's responsibility for the outcomes of the market mechanism. The commitment to a "free market" was a way of putting an end to the cartelization, corporatism, protectionism, and connivance between big business and government that had characterized Imperial and Weimar Germany and reached a peak under the Nazis. The commitment to social responsibility reflected the view that unemployment and impoverishment need not be the inevitable consequence of an efficient economy.[13] The "social market" was the name given to that form of economy, to distance it from the toleration of social misery and the confrontational, "elbow-style" of individualism that characterized *laissez-faire* Anglo-American economic arrangements.[14]

The "market" part of the formula dominated the first years under the new arrangements. Virtually all of the price regulations, rules, and economic controls inherited from the Nazi period were precipitously abolished, and measures were taken to abolish or weaken the cartels, all with the intention of infusing the economy with vigorous "but not ruinous" competition.[15] The deeply rooted German corporatist practices were not entirely dislodged, however, and government is still actively involved in the regulation of market activity in ways that would provoke movements to "get the government off the backs of the people" in present-day America. In the interest of maintaining the quality of life, for example, the government still limits the hours during which shops may stay open.

The "social" part of the formula was initially designed with the view that all citizens who could do so were expected to make provision on their own for the normal expenses of life. The government would maintain responsibility only for those citizens who could not afford to care adequately for themselves. The deliberate purpose of that arrangement was to avoid what Chancellor Erhard called "the modern madness" of the welfare state that undermines the independence of the citizenry.[16] With the increasing prosperity that accompanied the "economic miracle" of the postwar years, however, social policy expanded from its initial restricted scope to the much broader concept of "social subsistence" – meaning that the state should provide full support for a basic, dignified standard of living, for an indefinite period, for all citizens who lack the personal resources to attain it through the labor market.[17]

Both labor and the growing middle class pressed for that expansion of the "social" part of the formula. Labor, in particular, sought continuous improvement in both the wages and the conditions of work, and a prospering management was ready to comply, which contributed to the peaceful labor relations that were one of the keys to the economy's remarkable success. By the 1990s German wage rates were among the highest in the world, and the workers enjoy an imposing set of privileges and benefits. Under the law on "co-determination," the workers elect up to half of the members of their company supervisory boards, which gives labor a strong voice in overall company policy.[18] The standard workweek is 37 hours, with six weeks of paid vacation – the shortest workyear among industrialized nations.[19] Workers are entitled to a three-month post-natal paid leave and to unpaid maternity leave for up to three years, with the right to return to their old jobs. Compensation during sick leave often fully covers the wages lost, and Germans are close to the world record in number of days of sick leave taken per year. Over half of the labor force retires before the legal age of 65, thanks in part to the generous pension arrangements.[20] Other non-wage benefits include employer contributions into a workers' vacation fund and into health and retirement programs, and an end-of-year "Christmas-money" bonus.[21] Under the lavish subsidized health schemes, workers are regularly sent on "cures" at the expense of the insurance fund.[22]

In addition to these non-wage benefits, various restrictive regulations on hiring and dismissal offer extensive job protection.[23] Workers therefore have less reason for anxiety about job loss than workers in most market economies. They do not enjoy the security offered by the Japanese-style lifetime employment arrangement; but on the other hand, the German system applies to virtually the entire labor force, unlike the Japanese arrangement that benefits only some employees of large companies. In neither country, however, is lifetime employment absolute, so that workers do face the prospect of being unemployed for some periods of their working lives. The security that the society provides for its workers therefore depends not only on the arrangements for the employed, but also on the arrangements for those periods in which they are without jobs.

In this respect Japan and Germany are poles apart. Japanese workers in trouble are expected to be cared for by their families, and there is very little public provision for that purpose. Germany, in contrast, makes extensive public provision for maintaining the income of the unemployed. Workers with children receive unemployment insurance benefits amounting to about 67 percent of their former net earnings, for a period of from six to 32 months. When the insurance period runs out, they are entitled to continued support in the form of "social assistance," which is financed by general tax revenues. Those benefits, which may reach a maximum of 57 percent of former earnings, are means-tested against wealth and other income, and recipients are required to accept a suitable job if it is available; but that restriction is interpreted so liberally that the benefits may continue indefinitely.[24]

The German social programs expanded rapidly in the prosperous postwar decades, but with the decline in the growth rate in the 1970s, attention began to focus on an ominous new development – the steady increase in the number of the unemployed and in the duration of their unemployment. Many factors influence the aggregate unemployment rate, but one of them derives from the form of the social programs that underpin the system of job security.[25]

Under the market mechanism, the number of workers that enterprises employ depends, among other things, on the cost of hiring workers. One effect of the social programs is that the cost of hiring workers is much higher than their nominal wage. There is, first, the additional monetary cost, in the form of the payments that the enterprises must make for every new worker hired. Those payments for unemployment insurance, sickness benefits, and other social programs amount to almost 80 percent of the nominal wage in manufacturing, which makes the monetary cost to an employer of hiring a production worker more than 50 percent higher than in the US and Japan.[26] A second cost of the job security programs is that they reduce the flexibility of the enterprise in responding to changing market conditions; regular workers must be kept on the payroll even in slack times when their labor is not needed.

As a consequence of these costs, German enterprises are reluctant to take on new workers who cannot be readily dismissed when business conditions turn sour. They therefore respond to changing conditions primarily by increasing or decreasing the number of hours worked by their regular employees rather than adjusting the size of their work force. Employed workers put in more overtime or are placed on short time, or part-time and temporary workers are hired when needed. Because of these responses, aggregate employment adjusts more slowly to changes in labor demand than in most comparable countries.[27]

Hence, while the high level of job security is of great benefit to those workers who have jobs – the "insiders" – it tends to increase the number of "outsiders" who are unable to find jobs.[28] Wage negotiations, for example, are more concerned with preserving the jobs of the insiders than with employment growth required to provide jobs for the outsiders.[29]

As a consequence, a capitalist country that pushes for greater job security than the market normally provides may end up with less job security overall; for example, in tightly regulated Italy, 52.3 percent of male workers hold their jobs more than five years, while in unregulated Britain 59 percent hold their jobs that long.[30] To be sure, under the social market the outsiders are relatively well provided for, as reported above. However, precisely because the benefits are so generous, the unemployed worker who takes a new job earns very little more than he would earn if he remained on the unemployment rolls: for middle-income workers the earnings from a new job may exceed the unemployment benefits by only 10 percent or less. The effect of that high "implicit marginal tax" is to increase the time that workers spend searching for a better job, and to encourage the less motivated to remain on the unemployment rolls as long as they can qualify.[31]

In fact, the level of unemployment in Germany has risen steadily over the years, and in 1998 stood at 11.2 percent of the labor force. Similarly high unemployment rates prevail in France and other market economies with similar job-security programs. Unemployment rates tend to be much lower in countries like the United States and Great Britain where job security is much weaker but the full cost of hiring workers is much closer to their nominal wage. Much attention has also been given to the fact that in the past ten years millions of new jobs have been created in the private sector in those countries, while in Germany the number of jobs has actually declined. The unemployment problem has reached a point at which the labor unions are beginning to agree to wage reductions and to surrender other job privileges that they had acquired in the past.[32]

The lesson of the German experience is that while a market economy cannot provide absolute job security for all of its workers, a society that values it can provide a high level of security for most of its workers. However, the known policies for achieving that result tend generally, though not always, to reduce the level of employment.[33] That tradeoff provides each society with the opportunity to mold the market mechanism to conform to its own values. A society that places the higher value on security should not be surprised that there are not enough jobs for all its workers. A society that places the higher value on having a job for everyone should expect that many workers will lose their jobs from time to time and most will hold several different jobs in the course of a lifetime. The market mechanism can accommodate itself to all combinations of these two values. What it cannot provide is both complete security and full employment.

6 Discussion

I dedicate this chapter to a composite Friend with whom I have had many long and frustrating conversations over the years. My Friend is a compassionate and reasonable man, like me, yet on such matters as jobs and wages we seem never to understand each other; or at least, he doesn't understand me.

My Friend regards the idea of people being fired from their jobs with such repugnance that he is prepared to renounce the "system" on that account. That ardent condemnation of the "system," however, does not imply a preference for central economic planning as it was practiced in the Communist countries, for he considers countries like Germany and Japan, and Sweden of course, as models of humane economies. Those countries, however, should be thought of as operating under the same "system" as ours in the US. They are card-carrying members of the market-economy club, and, moreover, of the capitalist branch of that club, since their productive property is overwhelmingly under private ownership.

It seems to me that what aggravates my Friend is not our market *system*, but the *outcomes* that the system happens to produce in our country. In fact, he should clasp the market system to his bosom, for it is the economic foundation on which other countries have managed to produce results of which he greatly approves.

But if he does accept the market mechanism, however grudgingly, then he must also accept its limitations, one of which is the insecurity with which the citizens-as-workers must live. It is simply peevish of him to launch into a renewed tirade against the "system" whenever he encounters some poor devil who has been "downsized" from his middle-management job and now drives a cab.

He is right, however, to point out that some market economies handle these things better than others, and to ask why we cannot do as well as they. That question opens the way to an interesting conversation: why do some countries get different results – better or worse, according to one's values – than others that employ the same market mechanism?

Culture Certainly cultural differences are part of the answer. Japanese lifetime employment is an integral part of a large package of mutual obligations. Workers identify personally with the company; executives spend a great deal of time after hours socializing together; employee groups sing company songs; workers accept the legitimacy of being reassigned wherever they are needed, and they agree to remain with the company for life. Merit is rewarded, but in a way that saves the face and dignity of those who are passed over. Perhaps if American companies offered lifetime contracts to some of their workers, they would agree to abandon all restrictive work rules and to accept all the other conditions of work in Japanese companies.

That would be of great value to management, and some American companies might indeed find it profitable to offer a limited number of lifetime contracts under those conditions. Nothing precludes American management and labor agreeing to such arrangements, but I suspect that labor would not be willing to give up all that management would require in order for them to find it profitable to offer such contracts.

Shop relations in Germany are also different from those in America. Managers usually know all the foremen and many of the workers personally, and there is a long tradition of respect for labor's skills and diligence. Workers are less likely to be dismissed for short-term gains. That cooperative relationship pays off in worker effort and loyalty, and contributes to the record of industrial peace.[34]

Hence, if everything else were the same, cultural differences of these sorts would account for some of the differences in the security enjoyed by workers under the same market mechanism.

Growth spurts   In every country there are times when many enterprises find it profitable to offer an exceptional degree of job security to their workers.[35] The companies that are most generous in that respect are generally those that are riding a wave of high profits that they expect to continue for some time, perhaps because of a long-term monopoly, or because the competition has not yet had time to eat away at their profits.

That was the case in certain American export industries in the early postwar decades. In a world that had been devastated by war the demand for American automobiles and other products was virtually unlimited. Production was running at record levels, profits were high, the demand for labor was strong, and recruiting and retaining skilled labor was a high priority for management. Skilled workers came to feel that if they landed a job in one of those industries, they were set for life; and indeed, as noted in the text, the proportion of the labor force in 1966 that worked for the same company for more than 15 years was larger in the United States than in Japan. By 1970, however, that relation was reversed as the export market returned to more normal conditions.

The Japanese lifetime-employment guarantee seized hold during the early postwar years, also largely in response to an intense need for skilled workers to maintain the momentum of what seemed like growth without limit. Offering a long-term contract is like buying capital equipment: if you expect business to be good for a long time in the future, you will find it profitable to buy a machine with a durability of 30 years, but if you are uncertain about the future, it's more profitable to rent than to buy. Similarly, long-term job contracts make more sense than "renting" labor when you are confident that you will need your workers for a long time. Now that the Japanese growth spurt has ended and the future looks more like that of the typical mature industrial country, the cost of maintaining the old practice has begun to rise and it is beginning to give way to one closer to that of other countries. These things change slowly, however, and some features of the job-security arrangements of the Golden Age are likely to endure for some time.

The expansion of job-security arrangements in Germany reflected the political consensus that, under the social-market variant of the market mechanism, no segment of the population should be left behind in the growing prosperity of the country. There, too, however, it was the remarkable postwar growth that provided the conditions under which business found it possible to acquiesce, often willingly, in the pressures from government and labor for the rapid growth of job benefits. And there too, now that the country has settled down to a normal growth rate, the economy is under great pressure to pare back those benefits.

Hence, there is no unique level of job security that the market mechanism produces. It is a fortunate generation that happens to be in the active labor force in a Golden Age when the degree of job security and other benefits is well above normal. The longer that happy period endures, however, the more it tends to be regarded as normal, so that when conditions return to what is actually normal for that economy, an angry new generation of workers feels that the politicians are mismanaging the economy and strongly resists a paring back of the benefits that its forebears enjoyed when the economy could more easily provide them. That is a recipe for political tensions and social conflict.

Jobs, security, and values   The thrust of this chapter is that job security is at its highest when production is expanding and enterprises have to compete vigorously for more labor. It follows that the highest priority of a society that values job security is to bend its efforts toward the promotion of economic growth and full employment.

Suppose, however, that the economy is operating under the best set of macroeconomic policies known to humankind and enjoys a certain level of job security. Are there not ways in which public policy could be enlisted to raise that level even higher?

The German experience demonstrates that there are ways of providing employed workers with greater job security than the market itself would provide. But as is so often the case in social matters, there is a tradeoff: taken together with the other benefits to employees, the effect is to increase the rate of unemployment. There is more security for the insiders but fewer jobs for the outsiders.

How one feels about that tradeoff depends on one's values. In my own Good Society, having a job ranks near the top – higher than security, and even wages. Barring extremes, it is better that jobs be less secure than that there be fewer jobs. It is better that more people have lower-paying jobs than that fewer people have better-paying jobs. Holding that value, I would submit every public initiative to an unemployment test: if its effect, direct or indirect, is to increase unemployment, it flunks the test. The German job-security arrangements flunk the test.

The market mechanism may be viewed as a form of reciprocal hostage-taking. The citizens-as-workers are hostage to the employers, and the employers are hostage to the citizens-as-consumers. Close attention should therefore be paid to the care and feeding of employers, for it is they who decide how many workers will be employed. If they were prepared to hire the same number of workers regardless of the cost, absolute job security could be achieved simply by a law forbidding the dismissal of any worker after he has been hired. The German approach does not go to that absurd length, but the principle is the same: if having a job is more highly valued than having a secure job, public policy should avoid measures that increase the cost of hiring labor.[36]

Ownership   The contrary view is sometimes advocated on the grounds that "business causes unemployment, so business should be forced to pay for it. Besides, business has plenty of money anyhow." That criticism reflects a certain generalized hostility toward "business," usually meaning the private ownership of enterprises. From the perspective of the Good Society, however, the question of how to deal with the insecurity generated by the market mechanism should be separated from the issue of whether the enterprises should be socially or privately owned, which is the subject of Part V. That separation may be made by the mental experiment of imagining that all enterprises are converted overnight from private to social ownership. Under that new market-socialist economy, the managers of the people's enterprises are expected to produce as economically as they can for the benefit of the whole society, so that the citizens-as-workers will get jobs only if some citizens-as-managers find it profitable to hire them, as in any market economy.

In this kind of market environment, with the hostility toward private ownership absent, it is perhaps easier to see the merits of leaving the matter of job security largely to the play of the market. The work force of enterprises in declining industries would be downsized from time to time and the released workers would quickly find new jobs in expanding enterprises, although some of the new jobs might not be as good as the old. The citizens-as-consumers would derive the maximum benefit from the efficient use of their own labor. Public policy would concentrate on easing the burden of the periods between jobs, but the cost would be shared by all the people through general taxation, rather than loaded onto the people's enterprises. That is about as much as a Good Society can expect to achieve if it hitches its cart to the market mechanism.

The message of this sermon is that a society that adopts the market mechanism should treat it like a marriage: one should do what one can to make it work as well as possible, and if that is still unsatisfactory, one should sue for divorce and get another spouse. At the least, one should avoid taking actions that are guaranteed to make the marriage worse, and then complain that the marriage is not working.

Downgrading   Producing the things that the citizens-as-consumers wish to buy today may not require all the machinists, sales managers, singers, or scientists who held those jobs yesterday. The best of societies helps to tide the worker over until he finds a new job, but what it cannot be expected to do is to assure a dismissed worker that his next job will be the equal of his last. While there may be enough jobs for all dismissed workers, there may not be enough jobs for all dismissed lawyers, or executives, or typesetters, in their former occupations. A college graduate may have to settle for a job as a cab driver, and the typesetter may have to sell shoes. For many workers, the most anguishing aspect of job insecurity is that fall in social and economic status. The older the worker and the higher his status, the greater his vulnerability to that agonizing experience. The angriest rejections of the market mechanism that I have heard describe it as a system that throws people aside like old rags after everything has been squeezed out of them.

There are ways in which a society can commute sentences of that sort. Japanese managers, particularly concerned about "loss of face," go to great lengths to maintain the appearance of status for older workers whose value to their companies has eroded. Elsewhere, managers of profitable and secure corporations often find ways of protecting their colleagues from redundancy by "kicking them upstairs"; that is, keeping them on the payroll in a respectable job that is not needed, until they retire. When faced eventually with the full force of competition, however, pressures mount for paring back the job-security arrangements to the level of countries and companies operating under more normal conditions.

In general, however, I see no way that even the best of Good Societies can entirely avoid the trauma of downgrading under the market mechanism. If you are aghast at the cruelty of an economy in which a 40-year-old account executive may be reduced to working as a sales clerk in a department store, then you would be better advised to choose the planning mechanism, rather than to press the market mechanism into providing a form of security for which it is ill adapted.

Personal traits   Finally, in assessing the employment performance of the market mechanism, notice must be taken of a small but socially significant number of workers who simply "cannot hold a job" because they lack the minimal social skills or personal characteristics for working effectively with other people. They may be unable to read or understand instructions, or they may be hooked on drugs, or they may insult other workers and get into fights, or fly into a rage when they are "bossed around," or they may steal or miss a day's work when they don't feel like coming in. After a few painful experiences with employment, they cease to look upon a job as the basis of a long-term livelihood, if they ever did. They don't expect their present job to last more than a month or two, regardless of economic conditions. When economic conditions are favorable, their spells of unemployment are relatively short, but during recessions there may be long waits between jobs.

Every society has a certain small proportion of members who are unable to play the normal social roles. The best of societies finds ways of assisting them through their lives with a minimum of insult.[37] But the unemployment of people who are unable to hold a job should not be charged against the market mechanism. It should be regarded as a social rather than an economic problem, to be dealt with by programs designed to help people with various physical or mental disabilities, such as sheltered workshops and counselling services. A Good Society should help its misfits conform to the requirements of the economic mechanism that it has chosen; but it should not redesign the economic mechanism to meet their special needs.

Notes

1 Okun, *Equality and Efficiency*.
2 Keynes, *The General Theory*, p. 9.
3 The eminent British socialist, John Strachey, reported that around 1938 he began to modify his views on the viability of capitalism on the basis of the new Keynesian thought ("Tasks and achievements of British Labour," p. 182).
4 Ozaki, *Human Capitalism*, pp. 96–111.
5 OECD, *Economic Surveys*: Japan 1996, p. 113.
6 Weitzman, *The Share Economy*, pp. 72–7.
7 OECD, *Economic Surveys*: Japan 1996, pp. 128–9.
8 Ito, *The Japanese Economy*, pp. 217–19.
9 OECD, *Economic Surveys*: Japan 1996, p. 98.
10 *JapanEcho*, Summer 1994, pp. 16–18.
11 Ozaki, *Human Capitalism*, pp. 109–11.
12 OECD, *Economic Surveys*: Japan 1996, p. 118.
13 Nicholls, *Freedom with Social Responsibility*, pp. 5–9.
14 Smyser, *The Economy of United Germany*, ch. 4.
15 Smyser, *The Economy of United Germany*, p. 68.
16 Smyser, *The Economy of United Germany*, p. 133.
17 OECD, *Economic Surveys*: Germany 1996, p. 52.
18 Smyser, *The Economy of United Germany*, p. 82.
19 *The New York Times*, November 22, 1993, p. 1.
20 OECD, *Economic Surveys*: Germany 1996, pp. 69, 123, 128.
21 *The New York Times*, December 11, 1996, p. D1.
22 Nicholls, *Freedom with Social Responsibility*, pp. 393–5.
23 OECD, *Economic Surveys*: Germany 1996, pp. 108, 120.
24 OECD, *Economic Surveys*: Germany 1996, pp. 61–2.
25 The West German economy was put under great strain by the unification with East Germany, but the rising unemployment rate affected the West as well as the East.
26 OECD, *Economic Surveys*: Germany 1996, pp. 120, 127.
27 OECD, *Economic Surveys*: Germany 1996, p. 119.
28 Lindbeck and Snower, "Reorganization of firms and labor-market inequality."
29 OECD, *Economic Surveys*: Germany 1996, p. 108.
30 *The Economist*, February 21, 1998, p. 76.
31 OECD, *Economic Surveys*: Germany 1996, p. 63.
32 *The New York Times*, June 5, 1997, p. A1.
33 There are ways in which that employment-depressing effect can be reduced. Active policies for pushing the unemployed into work tend to reduce the employment-depressing effect of even generous unemployment benefits (Nickell, "Unemployment and labor market rigidities," p. 71). The OECD recommends that financing more of the social programs through broad-based taxes rather than through wage-based contributions would be less harmful to employment and growth. Such measures can help reduce the employment-depressing effect of social programs, but they can not eliminate it (*Economic Surveys*: Germany 1996, pp. 51, 89).
34 Smyser, *The Economy of United Germany*, pp. 72–4.
35 Organizations that are peripheral to the market mechanism like universities and governments sometimes offer lifetime job tenure, but the justification in those cases is not job security for the welfare of the workers; it is the protection of academic freedom in the first case and of the civil service from political pressures in the second.

36   This position does not call for a libertarian rejection of all government intervention in the terms of employment. There are certain types of intervention for which there is strong social justification, such as child labor restrictions, limitations on hours of labor, health and safety conditions of the workplace, protection of the labor's right to organize, and prohibition of arbitrary forms of discrimination. Certain of these conditions may well have some depressing effect on job creation, but they are probably small and my guess is that the social benefits exceed the economic costs.

37   The most intriguing instance I have read of is a Native American tribe that developed a culture designed to defend the people against the devastating attacks to which they were often subject. Men were trained from birth to excel in the military arts, which demanded a degree of discipline and bravery that some of them were incapable of achieving. Rather than being expelled from the community, such men could elect to play a "female role." They lived and worked with the women, often specializing in making spears and arrow heads for the warriors. They did not share in the honors and perquisites of the warriors, but neither were they dishonored. That seems to me like a very good solution to the problem of the society's misfits.

Chapter 20

Job Security and Planning

If any would not work, neither should he
eat.
— 2 Thessalonians

Work in the USSR is a duty ... in
accordance with the principle, "He who
does not work, neither shall he eat."
— 1936 Constitution of the USSR

CONTENTS

No one is in charge of overall employment in a market economy. The economic actors – households and enterprises – devote themselves to their private pursuits, and if it turns out that there are not enough jobs for all workers, that is simply an unfortunate fact of life under an otherwise benign economic mechanism. Government may be called upon to nudge the market toward full employment, but it acts as an external force and not as part of the economic mechanism itself.

Under planning, on the other hand, someone is very definitely in charge of overall employment; indeed, a primary purpose of the planning mechanism is to assure that there is an economic actor – usually the government – who directs the activity of the economy overall. The government is a key component of the economic mechanism itself, and not an external agent who merely influences it.

The highest economic objective of the Communist governments was best expressed in the hoary political slogan of the Soviet Communist Party – "to overtake and surpass the leading capitalist countries." A corollary of that devotion to economic growth was the high priority assigned to production. Since the volume of output depends, among other things, on the quantity of labor, the government sought to employ as large a proportion of the population as possible in production activity.

The devotion to full employment was not only an economic objective, however. It was also a prime social and political objective. Unemployment was simply intolerable in what the Party had declared to be a "workers' state." News photos of the miserable unemployed masses in the capitalist countries were a staple of Communist propaganda, and the Party regarded the elimination of unemployment as a major basis of its claim to popular support. The success of the policy was reflected in the attitude often expressed by workers that, while they envied the living standards of Western workers, they were thankful for having been spared the fearful experience of unemployment.

There are few supporters of Communist doctrine in the present post-Communist world; and a Good Society of the future is likely to retain very little of that doctrine. If such a society adopted the planning mechanism, however, full employment would be as likely to rank as high among the planner's objectives as it did in the Communist period. The question, therefore, is how well the planning mechanism succeeds in achieving full employment.

I   The Intense Demand for Labor

The dominant force working toward full employment in the Communist countries originated in the central planning process itself. The central planners were guided by the Party's objective of producing as large a volume of output as possible during the forthcoming year. Since underutilized labor detracted from the objective, the central planners preferred a taut plan in which the demand for labor was somewhat larger than the estimated supply, rather than the other way around (chapter 18). Taut planning generated a constant gravitation-like force throughout the economy that tended to pull all available labor into the labor force.

The formal planning process ended when the enterprises received their final plans from their ministries. From that point on, administration took over. The enterprise labor plans specified the total amount of wages that could be spent in the forthcoming year, but within that limit, management had a great deal of latitude in deciding how many unskilled workers, machine operators, engineers, and other types of labor they wished to hire. Arrangements needed to be made to locate the required workers, to provide them with the information about what jobs were open where, and to channel them into those jobs. If that process was poorly managed, there could be substantial unemployment despite the intense demand for labor built into the taut plans.

The task was complicated by the fact that taut planning at the central level did not ensure that there was a job for every worker in every occupation in every locality. The number of skilled construction jobs in the country might be exactly equal to the number of such workers in the country, but while there might not be enough construction workers in Omsk to fulfill its housing construction plan, the housing construction plan in Tomsk might be too small to employ all the construction workers there. Regional imbalances were moderated, on the margin, by various techniques: there was some long-distance commuting and migration between neighboring regions, and labor-short regions with harsh climates were serviced by special recruiting organizations, and in some cases by penal labor. In the main, however, full employment required that the available jobs be within normal daily travel range of most of the workers.

A variety of organizations shared the responsibility for matching jobs and workers. The local Party organization kept watch over the job-placement process and was held accountable if unemployment got to be too large. There were labor exchanges that collected information on local job openings and job seekers, and helped to match the two; there were organizations that recruited workers to fill jobs in labor-short regions; and there were agencies that placed school graduates into their first jobs. School graduates were the major source of new workers in the labor force, and the process of placing them into jobs offers a good picture of how the employment administration process operated.

THE PLACEMENT OF GRADUATES

The placement of graduates of higher-education institutions posed no problem because of their obligation to serve for three years in any job to which they might be assigned. Coordination at the central level was therefore sufficient, for if there were not enough jobs for newly minted lawyers or construction engineers in their home regions, there were authorized jobs for them in other regions.

It was on the placement of the younger people – graduates of the region's vocational, technical, and secondary schools – that the job-placement process concentrated. The placement officers of the vocational and technical schools maintained close links with the enterprises and ministries that sponsored them, and they helped to negotiate the flow of the graduates into the jobs for which they were trained (chapter 14). An effort was normally made to take account of the young workers' job preferences, and the obligation of two years' service that these workers faced was not strictly enforced, so that many of them found jobs outside of the school's own placement service.

The secondary schools were designed to prepare students for further schooling, and about half of the students managed to be admitted to schools of advanced technical training or institutions of higher education. The rest entered the labor force directly. Since they had fewer production skills than the graduates of the vocational and technical schools, they were harder to place and took more time searching for a job. The officials sought to place them in jobs that corresponded to their training and their preferences, but that was not always possible. Some of the less-promising graduates who sought jobs in office work might be obliged to accept work as short-order cooks in factory canteens or as sales clerks in shoe departments.

MANAGEMENT AND JOB PLACEMENT

The regional Party and administrative authorities were strongly motivated to reinforce the center's thrust toward full employment. For one thing, in purely practical terms, to be a senior official in a region known to have too many unemployed workers was not helpful for one's career. Their task was eased by the universal acceptance of the view that finding jobs for all school graduates was the social responsibility of all Party, government, and managerial officials.

The ultimate responsibility for providing jobs, however, fell on the employers – the enterprise managers. Among their responsibilities was that of keeping production costs low and profits high; and since wage payments accounted for a large portion of production costs, they had reason to resist hiring more workers than they needed. For a variety of other reasons, however, they were inclined to acquiesce in the pressures to expand their payroll, and indeed were often welcoming of them. A few of those reasons provide a flavor of the managerial environment.

First, in the complex structure of managerial incentives, production-plan fulfillment was the most salient – far more than costs and profits. Since plan targets tended to be on the high side because of taut planning, and the flow of materials and supplies was unreliable, a labor "reserve" helped to speed up production when it had fallen behind schedule. There were also times when managers received requests from local government or Party officials that had to be honored: for example, to dispatch some of their workers to help in bringing in the harvest or building a henhouse for the local state farm. Prudent managers therefore would take care to keep as many workers on hand as they could justify, as "insurance" in case they fell behind their planned production rates.

Second, management compensation was based on a scale that provided larger salaries for managers of larger enterprises, and the size of the enterprise was defined by the number of workers. Hence, managers derived a personal benefit from having as large a labor force as they could justify to the planning authorities. And third, the total wages that an enterprise could lawfully pay out depended on the number of workers it was authorized to employ. Hiring labor was therefore virtually costless: however large the number of workers that management could persuade the ministry to authorize, its financial plan would provide sufficient funds for them to be paid.

The regional placement officials therefore encountered little reluctance by managers to employ even the least promising of graduates. Some might be hired by enterprises that had been unable to find enough workers with more ability and experience, and were willing to lower their standards of employment. The rest were placed simply by creating jobs for them – if necessary, in excess of the number of jobs formally authorized in the enterprises' plans.

These various forces, operating on the demand side, provided the jobs needed to secure full employment and the arrangements for smoothing the flow of workers into the jobs. There were a number of complementary forces on the supply side that provided a powerful motivation for people to seek jobs and to retain them once they were employed.

2   The Importance of Having a Job

The strongest incentive to hold a job is that, in the absence of private property ownership, there is virtually no source of family income other than wage earnings. For that reason alone, holding a job was more important in the Communist economies than in the capitalist.

For those who might nevertheless be inclined to manage somehow without a regular job, there was the ultimate inducement to get one – the "anti-parasite" law. The Constitution obligated the state to provide work for all citizens, but it also declared work to be a duty of the citizen. Some classes of people like pensioners were exempted from the work obligation, but others who were not employed faced the prospect of legal prosecution for vagrancy. That law was used to prosecute people who tried to support themselves in ways other than holding a normal job in a state enterprise: as artists and craftsmen, casual laborers, black marketeers, or children of the affluent. In the later years it was also used to convict people who had been dismissed from their jobs because of political dissidence. The law was administered by requiring each citizen to carry an internal passport that contained the name of the establishment in which they were employed. Failure to have such a job entry in one's passport would invite inquiry by the police. The anti-parasite law derived a certain legitimacy from the full-employment policy, for it was scarcely credible for a citizen to claim that there were no jobs, as the unemployed can often legitimately claim under the market mechanism.

The obligation to hold a job did not preclude the right to quit in search of a new job. Moreover, the intense demand for labor was a constant temptation to look for a better job because finding one was relatively easy. These considerations left open the troublesome possibility of excessive voluntary unemployment of workers in search of better jobs. The major counter-pressure was that a worker who quit a job in a Soviet-type planned economy gave up a great deal more than a similar worker in a market economy.

First, enterprises in the planned economies were responsible for a much wider range of their employees' welfare than in market economies. They provided a variety of highly subsidized non-wage benefits such as company housing, children's day-care, health benefits, vacation packages, and so forth. The worker was therefore tied fairly closely to his "collective," and did not casually give up a secure job in search of a better one.

Second, regional mobility of labor was discouraged by the housing shortage. Since housing was distributed largely by the assignment method, one had to sign up on the housing queue and wait until suitable housing was offered, which might take a long time. Third, the anti-parasite law discouraged people from taking too long to sign up for a new job. And finally, because of the full-employment policy and the anti-parasite law, there was no program of unemployment insurance. That greatly concentrated the workers' minds on keeping a job rather than seeking a better one.

3 Who Are the Unemployed?

With such powerful forces operating on enterprises to hire workers and on workers to seek and to hold onto jobs, one would expect little if any unemployment in the planned economies. That some unemployment did exist is evident, however, from the reports of it in the press, from the denunciations of it by high public officials, and from various acts of government taken from time to combat it. It is from such evidence that a picture can be pieced together of why some people were without jobs when the planning mechanism generated so strong a thrust toward full employment.

THE EXTENT OF UNEMPLOYMENT

The Soviet Five-Year Plans of the 1930s created so intense a demand for labor to build and to staff the new enterprises that the government declared unemployment to have been finally and permanently vanquished. The declaration of the end of unemployment had a powerful political impact in the capitalist world at the time, where the Great Depression had driven unemployment to record levels. Since unemployment had no official existence, the government ceased publication of unemployment statistics and the governments of the later Communist countries followed suit.

Public officials and academic researchers concerned with labor issues, however, did publish unemployment figures for particular regions or industries from time to time. These scattered data provided outside analysts with some basis for estimating overall unemployment rates. For the Soviet Union, the estimates ranged from a low of 1.1 percent to a high of 3.0 percent, at various times.[1]

Those rates are well below those in the major capitalist countries, although in their most prosperous years some of the latter experienced even lower rates of unemployment than that – notably Germany and Japan. The broad picture is that some citizens of the USSR and of the other planned economies experienced some unemployment in their lifetimes, both voluntary and involuntary, but the proportion of people affected was much smaller than in the capitalist countries over the long run.

THE CONQUEST OF EXCESS UNEMPLOYMENT

The big difference, however, was that planned economies did not experience the excess unemployment that occurs periodically under the market mechanism in times of economic distress. They did experience some fluctuations in economic activity, particularly in the volume of investment.[2] In the main, however, there were none of the periodic booms and busts that characterize economic activity under the market mechanism. Every year in the planned economy was like the peak years of the business cycle in the market economy, when the rate of production is limited only by the shortage of labor and other resources, and not by insufficient aggregate demand to purchase all the goods that the economy can produce. In one formulation, production under planning is said to be supply-driven, while production under markets is demand-driven. There were always some unemployed people in a planned economy, but this was not because of insufficient aggregate demand. It was because of frictional and structural problems that were similar to those under the market mechanism.

FRICTIONAL UNEMPLOYMENT

Since workers were free to leave their jobs for more satisfactory employment, on any day a certain number were unemployed while they were searching for new jobs. Workers quit for many reasons, among them the prospect of higher earnings, of improving one's housing, and of more satisfactory working conditions. Changing jobs was not a decision the worker would take lightly, however, for it sometimes involved a great sacrifice because of the aforementioned non-wage benefits. The loss was relatively slight for younger workers, however, and the right to quit was a valuable safety valve for older workers who found the conditions of work in their own enterprise intolerable. Public officials decried the practice of leaving a job in search of the "long ruble," but the public criticism of that practice was testimony to its prevalence.

Among the unemployed were school graduates who would often take a long time before they settled down in their first jobs. That was particularly the case with the "golden youth," the spoiled children of higher-income families who sometimes went to great lengths to avoid committing themselves to a job. There was also a mixed bag of workers who might be technically unemployed but earned a livelihood in unorthodox ways. They included, for example, construction workers who would "disappear" for a few months in the summer to sell the produce of their household plots, which brought in more income than their official jobs.[3] Others spent part or all of their time in the risky but lucrative activities of the underground economy. There was also an underclass of workers whose ambitions in life did not include settling down to a good job and raising a family. Some of them were drifters, holding a job until they had accumulated enough money to coast for a few months until it ran out. Others were workers who took advantage of the high money bonuses paid to people who signed up for limited "tour-of-duty" jobs on construction projects and in enterprises located in the harsh regions of Siberia and the Far North.[4] After a spell of such work they had earned enough to loaf for years in the hospitable temperatures of the Crimea.

The planned economies also had their share of social misfits who could not hold a regular job under any normal economic arrangement. Since the right to privacy was not among the society's priorities, workers of that sort were subject to a great many pressures to conform; they became "cases," to be dealt with by their work collective, by the enterprise Party committee and trade union, and by the law enforcement authorities. Managers, however, were under social pressures to hire and retain them, and it was difficult to dismiss them except for extreme cause. It is not evident whether misfits are better off under planning or markets. In the Communist planned economy they lived under miserable conditions and were lectured to death, but some organization or other bore the responsibility for them. In a market economy, sad to say, they can disappear without anyone noticing the difference.

Soviet figures suggested that about 20–22 percent of workers in manufacturing quit their jobs each year.[5] That number was relatively low by world standards, but it was sufficiently high to have imposed tangible recruiting and training costs on the enterprises. While workers had the right to quit, the authorities frowned upon it, particularly upon the "rolling stones." Their sentiment was that workers who were so hard to please that they could not find acceptable jobs even under conditions of full employment were not a social issue; nor would other citizens hold the planners accountable. In accord with that sentiment, the government's employment agencies were dissolved in the 1930s on the grounds that since planning had abolished unemployment forever, there was no longer any need for such services. Workers who left their jobs voluntarily should bear the full responsibility for finding others.

And so they did. Frictionally unemployed workers found new jobs by such non-planned devices as word-of-mouth, notices on bulletin boards, and making the rounds of factories. Some decades later, however, when the growth rate had begun to decline, employment agencies were reestablished, in explicit recognition of the continued existence of unemployment and of the loss of output because of it.

STRUCTURAL UNEMPLOYMENT

Planned economies need not experience such forms of structural unemployment as the decline of the New England textile cities or the rust belt of the middle-West. Investment goes where the planners decide it should go, and not where the owners of capitalist enterprises expect to make the most profit. If they plan to phase out an industry that has become inefficient because of technological change, they have the power to direct new investment there in order to provide new jobs for the existing labor force. Structural unemployment did nevertheless occur, but for reasons peculiar to the planning mechanism.

The major such instance was the urban labor force in Central Asia. There, Muslim family traditions and the relatively low educational level of women produced much higher population growth-rates than in other parts of the USSR, and the number of new entrants into the labor force each year was correspondingly large.[6] Building the factories and providing the equipment to provide jobs for that large annual inflow of workers would have diverted increasingly scarce capital from other regions where its productivity was much higher. Concerns of efficiency and growth, reinforced perhaps by political and ethnic sentiments, inclined the central government to deal with the problem by encouraging Central Asians to migrate to other regions where jobs were plentiful, rather then by providing the capital to create new jobs there. Structural unemployment in this case was the outcome of a deliberate central decision; the planners were sovereign over production, and they had the right and power to decide where production facilities were to be located.

A second form of structural unemployment occurred in regions dominated by industries in which the labor force tended to consist predominantly of the same sex: heavy concentrations of textile and garment industries, for example, where women predominated; or mining industries dominated by men. In some extreme cases, there were not enough jobs for workers of the wrong sex, who either remained unemployed for long periods, or migrated to other regions. The consequence was the socially destructive phenomenon of "cities of women and cities of men," as the problem was called. Instances of these sorts are not an expression of the planners' social policy but of imperfections of the planning process. There are thousands of economic and social factors to be considered in the location of each of the thousands of new enterprises and other investments made each year, all of which involve a great many tradeoffs. It should occasion no surprise that when a hugely complex process of that sort is centrally guided, some official would place a low value on, or perhaps simply forget, that workers are not only machine operators and assemblers but also women and men.

4 Lifetime Employment

There are two potential sources of anxiety over job security. One is not being able to find a job. The other is losing a job. By maintaining a low rate of unemployment, particularly excess unemployment, the planning mechanism succeeded in greatly relieving the workers of the first source of anxiety. Since most workers are employed, however, the prospect of losing a job is by far the more pervasive potential source of anxiety. Relieving the workers of that concern was the most impressive achievement of the planning mechanism.

JOB RIGHTS

That achievement was based on the evolution of the commitment to full employment in a way that gave the workers a set of *de facto* job rights of a special kind.[7] The right to a job came to be interpreted to mean not merely the right to employment of one sort or another, but the right to a lifetime job, and sometimes even the same job, in the same enterprise in which the worker had been employed. That feature of the "social contract," as it has been called, meant that workers were rarely dismissed from employment except for extreme malfeasance such as incorrigible drunkenness or indiscipline.

Although management's inclination was to maintain a larger labor force than their production plans required, situations occurred from time to time when they would like to pare down the labor force. For example, an eager new ministry official might seek to advance his career by a campaign to cut wage costs in the enterprises; or a labor-saving innovation might result in more redundant labor than could be concealed from even a forgiving supervisor. However, managers inclined to cut back on their labor force under these and other circumstances faced a number of obstacles. Among the reasons was that the laws enacted to protect workers from arbitrary and unreasonable dismissal obligated management to reassign redundant workers to different jobs in the same shop or department, and if that were not possible, in other parts of the same enterprise. If that were not possible either, management was responsible for placing the dismissed workers in other enterprises – in effect, begging fellow managers to take them on their payroll.

If management could demonstrate to the trade-union grievance committee that all these things had been tried and could not be done, they could then proceed with the dismissals. If they did, they might be commended and awarded bonuses by the Ministry far off in Moscow, but in their home town they were likely to face the harsh moral disapproval of the local Party, government, and trade-union officials, as well as of their own labor force. Faced with that obstacle path, management rarely found it expedient to undertake a staff reduction. Workers therefore had little fear of dismissal; most of them expected to remain employed in the same enterprise for their lifetime unless they themselves decided to quit.

A second reason for the reluctance to dismiss workers was that the socialist value system assigned a very large weight to the notion of the "work collective." The worker in a capitalist system was regarded as "alienated," in the sense that the enterprise meant no more to him than a place to which he went each workday to earn his living. The personnel of a socialist enterprise, on the other hand, as members of a "collective," produced not for the profit of capitalists but for the welfare of all the people, and they shared responsibility for the productivity of the enterprise. It was in order to reinforce that sense of collectivity that the state arranged for most workers to live in enterprise-owned housing, to go to enterprise-owned vacation resorts, and to send their children to enterprise-owned summer camps. Under such circumstances, the term "dismissal" fails to convey the full harshness of the social experience of the loss of a job.

THE IMMORTALITY OF ENTERPRISES

The most extreme expression of the concern for job security was the practice of keeping every enterprise in operation virtually forever, regardless of how old or inefficient it may have become. The law provided that such enterprises could be liquidated, but there are virtually no cases on record of it having been done. They survived on subsidies and other forms of special assistance to keep them solvent. From time to time a new management team might be brought in with a mandate to turn things around, and new equipment might be installed to increase the productivity of the enterprise's labor, but it was regarded as simply inadmissible to shut down a whole mine or factory permanently and dismiss the entire labor force from their jobs.

Apart from the devotion to job security, there was another reason that the authorities were inclined to keep unprofitable enterprises in permanent operation – profitability was not a reliable measure of the efficiency of enterprise performance. Among the reasons was that profit depended on the prices that the state set on inputs and outputs. The prices of primary products had been deliberately set low, so that most producers of coal and oil, for example, had to be subsidized because their production costs were higher than the prices they received for their products. Heavy users of energy and raw materials, on the other hand, made large profits because of the artificially low prices of their inputs. Under such circumstances, the failure of a coal mine to earn profit does not at all signify that it is inefficient or unproductive; nor do the high profits of machinery producers signify than they are efficient. An inefficient coal mine does produce coal, after all; to close it down on the hunch that the country would produce more coal if the equipment and workers were transferred elsewhere takes a leap of faith.

The reasons that enterprises were virtually never closed down are therefore perfectly understandable, but the policy contributed to the long-term deterioration of productive efficiency of the economy. Coal mines in which the best seams had long since been mined out were kept in operation in order to preserve the miners' jobs. Investment that could have been made in highly efficient new plant and equipment was diverted instead to the modernization of outdated equipment in old enterprises in order to reduce the high cost of keeping them in operation. The overall productivity of investment was therefore depressed, and in the course of time the country's capital stock was characterized by a growing number of partially refurbished old enterprises. In market economies, in contrast, when the profitability of old plant and equipment falls below a certain point, competition forces it out of operation. It is partially or totally scrapped, replaced by new modern facilities, possibly in an entirely new line of production, staffed by a different labor force.

The process of enterprise "exit" is like the weeding of a garden: flowers will grow in an untended garden, but they will not flourish unless it is regularly weeded. In the United States, for example, over an average 20-year span about 25 percent of all older large manufacturing plants are closed down – weeded out, so to speak, by the force of competition.[8] Imagine what the American economy would look like today if, as in the USSR, every company that existed in 1917 or came into existence thereafter was still in operation today. The policy of patching up inefficient enterprises in order to maintain the jobs of the workers detracted greatly from the benefit that the planned economies derived from technological advance.

Unemployment in disguise

In most market economies a certain number of enterprises are publicly owned, particularly in such industries as public utilities and transportation. Suppose a state-owned railroad introduces a new type of locomotive that makes it possible to provide the same transportation services with 1,000 fewer workers. If management were under instructions to produce at the lowest possible cost, the redundant workers would be dismissed, which would swell the unemployment statistics until they found jobs elsewhere. Politicians in power take no pleasure in rising unemployment, and in cases of this sort the railroad managers often keep the redundant workers on the payroll in order that the government not be embarrassed by a rise in unemployment.

The employment of redundant workers in that way is known as "disguised unemployment," to distinguish it from the "open unemployment" of workers who are without jobs and on no enterprise's payroll. Both types of unemployment are sources of inefficiency, in the sense that the country's labor is not employed in its most productive uses. With open unemployment, the source of inefficiency is that some workers who could produce output are producing none at all. With disguised unemployment, the workers may be producing some output but it is less than they could produce if the labor were better allocated among enterprises. The redundant workers are put to work at the best jobs that can be created for them, but if their number is very large, they may simply be idle much of the time.

The lifetime-employment arrangement in the planned economies was a way of escaping from the wastefulness of open unemployment by sweeping it under the rug of disguised unemployment. The pronouncement that unemployment under planning is much smaller than under markets does not, therefore, tell the whole story. One would also wish to know how the two mechanisms perform with regard to total unemployment, defined as the sum of open and disguised unemployment. No such estimates have been made, but if they were, markets may prove to perform at least as well, and possibly better, than planning.

In the short run, from the perspective of the Communist leadership disguised unemployment had certain advantages over open unemployment. Politically, it was less threatening to governments than the high-profile visibility of angry and idle workers. Socially, it enabled workers to retain their self-respect and social status, both of which rapidly erode under the impact of dismissal from a job. Economically, the redundant workers did continue to produce a certain quantity of output – they might be put to work on such jobs as keeping the railroad cars somewhat cleaner and the track in better repair, which would not be done if they were dismissed outright.

In the long run, however, as disguised unemployment climbed from thousands to tens or hundreds of thousands, it took a toll in the form of a lower level of material welfare than the society could otherwise enjoy. Among the reasons was that the economy would forgo the full benefit of improving technology and new products. In order to take full advantage of such welfare-augmenting innovations, some jobs had to be reduced in number and others increased, some entirely new occupations had to be added from time to time while others disappeared, and some antiquated production facilities had to be torn down and replaced by new. If these things could not be done, the planners and managers were denied the flexibility required to adjust the occupational composition of the labor force to changing methods of production. Hence, a growing proportion of the country's labor and other resources were frozen in activities that might have been efficient some time ago but were now outdated.

The second effect of lifetime job tenure on material welfare was the erosion of work effort. Positive incentives such as wage increases and promotion were used in planned and market economies alike, and accounted for much of the effort that workers put into their labor. Under the market mechanism, however, those positive incentives are bolstered by the possibility of dismissal for shirking. In providing lifetime employment, the planning mechanism forswore the use of that sanction. Perhaps the more diligent workers would work as well or better under lifetime job tenure than under the threat of dismissal, but over the long run, the knowledge that workers could not be fired was bound to lead to some relaxation of effort and discipline: taking a bit more time for lunch, calling in sick more often, or working so badly at an unpleasant job that one was eventually reassigned to a better one. Morale was further sapped as disguised unemployment became more pervasive and less invisible, with a growing number of redundant employees working at patently unnecessary jobs or simply idling the days away. The exasperation of the Soviet leadership over the "parasitic certainty of guaranteed employment"[9] surfaced in the castigation of workers who "do not have jobs, who constantly change jobs, and who do not work at the jobs they have."[10] People who have held jobs under both mechanisms are struck by the much higher pace of work under markets than under planning.

Thus, the lifetime-employment arrangement reflected a solicitous concern for workers' job security that conformed to widely held values about how a Good Society should be run, but the economy paid a price in the form of the disguised unemployment that it generated. Whether it was a good arrangement on balance depends on the values of whoever is doing the evaluating. From the perspective of the Party and its planners, who held sovereignty over production under the planning mechanism, it appeared to be a bad arrangement. One may infer from the long string of campaigns to "tighten labor discipline" and to demolish the obstacles to technological progress that Party and planners would have greatly preferred an arrangement under which the workers worked harder, even if they were less secure.

From the perspective of the people, the mass abandonment of planning at the first opportunity is compelling evidence that most of the population preferred more consumer goods even if it meant less security and more effort. It is true that many look back on the old arrangement with some nostalgia: it was a "cozy, warm, very comfortable place for people who wanted to exist with a minimum of effort," recalls a resident of East Germany.[11] Despite the nostalgia, however, very few people in the former Communist lands have voted for a return to that cozy, warm arrangement. A high level of security is a mark of a Good Society, but not if the price is too high.

5   Discussion

Once, during the Gorbachev years, I was on the way to the airport to attend a conference in Washington on Soviet labor and economic reform. The cab driver, upon learning my destination, asked why their economy was in such bad shape. I explained that one major reason was that once a worker got a job, he could never be fired. He was silent for a few moments, then replied, "I'll buy that."

It was not the response I expected. I thought I was telling a story of lamentable inefficiency. What he heard was a story of a most agreeable kind of security.

My cab driver reflected what I believe is a near-universal view about a central aspect of the Good Society. An economy that offers more job security is better than one that offers less – if there are no other differences between them. It is because of those other differences – notably efficiency – that, on balance, the less secure economy might be considered the better.

That conclusion, however, is derived from the experience of history. To be sure, the past is prologue to the future, but it is not the whole play. Future societies learn some things from the past and are not condemned to relive it in all its detail. One of the questions they are likely to ask is whether there are not ways of providing the security of the planning mechanism without paying the high cost of efficiency experienced in the past.

To people of exceeding hostility to socialism and all of its trappings, the superiority of planning over markets in the provision of job security is an irritating conclusion. It is rare that a true believer can give the devil his due, but I think the point must be conceded in any serious engagement with the economics of the Good Society.

Since that exceptional record of job security was attained by methods that introduced great deal of inefficiency in the use of labor, a society that opts for the planning mechanism on account of the security that it provides should expect that its output of consumer and other goods would be smaller than under the market mechanism. The welfare of the citizens-as-workers would be enhanced at the expense of the welfare of the same citizens-as-consumers. That, at least, is the conclusion to be drawn from the experience of the Communist planned economies.

It has always seemed to me, however, that the Communist countries were particularly unimaginative in the methods they used for achieving full job security. The commitment to a "workers' state" need not have precluded an orderly transfer of redundant workers to more productive jobs and a cautious liquidation of patently inefficient enterprises. The demagogic argument that to permit job loss of that sort is equivalent to restoring capitalism could be easily disposed of: workers would not be simply thrown out of work but transferred to jobs that produce more for the people. The transferred workers could be provided with all the income support and other compensations dictated by equity considerations. Job security would then have been achieved with a much smaller loss in output.

A planned economy of the future need not replay the game of job security in the way that it was played by the Communist countries. It might hope to provide job security in a form that entailed less inefficiency. For one thing, if it were a democratic society, the full cost to the society of absolute job security would be subjected to independent research and public debate. The citizens would then have an opportunity to weigh their welfare as consumers against their welfare as workers, and to convey their values to the planners. They might then choose a less rigid form of job security in return for a higher level of consumption – a choice that was made by the Party and not by the people under the Communist regimes.

However, in the end that choice may not differ greatly from that made in the Communist economies. Few people are entirely indifferent to the closing down of coal mines somewhere or of the abandonment of farms elsewhere. An appeal by the workers to the government to keep those enterprises in operation strikes a sympathetic chord everywhere. The Conservative government of Great Britain, for example, planned to close down a number of inefficient coal mines in preparation for the privatization of the remaining profitable mines. Most of them were quietly closed without much public notice, but in one dramatic case, the government was forced to back down in the face of strong popular revulsion, not only from members of their own party but also from the public at large.[12] The pain of such closures to their victims is extremely high, and the cost to each citizen of subsidizing such enterprises is small because it is spread over the entire population, in the form of higher prices for coal or grain, or of higher taxes to subsidize the inefficient enterprises. Elected governments are hospitable to actions that greatly benefit a few voters at a very small cost to many others, and that is likely to be the case in a planned economy as well.

Under markets, however, there is one source of opposition to government support of redundancy that is not present under planning – other workers. In a regime of competitive markets, the gains of one group of workers or enterprises often entail a loss to others. If grain farms are kept in operation by a government-supported high price for corn, livestock farmers who buy the corn find their profits eroding and some may be forced out of business. Domestic oil producers want a high tariff on imported oil, but the higher oil price cuts into the profits of plastics manufacturers. The appeal to government for job protection for some workers therefore often evokes strong opposition from others whose interests would suffer.

Under the planning mechanism, in contrast, there is no such clash of worker interests. Everyone works for the government, so to speak, so that no one loses or gains from changes in the prices of corn or oil. If the government's grain farms are kept in business by a high price for grain, the government's livestock farms do not lose jobs. Either the price of meat is raised to cover the higher cost of corn feed, or the livestock farms are subsidized to enable them to pay the higher cost of corn. Neither cattle farmers nor any other groups of workers are damaged by the support of grain-farming jobs. The full burden of that support is borne by all the citizens-as-consumers, and not by one group of citizens-as-workers.

Hence, the government in a planned economy, even if elected, will be under persistent pressure for job protection in inefficient industries, with no countervailing pressure from efficient industries. State enterprises will be increasingly diverted from the task of producing goods economically, under pressure from the government to provide jobs for unemployed citizens. Planned economies of the future are therefore likely to tilt the balance of welfare from their citizens-as-consumers to their citizens-as-workers, much as under the Communist planned economies of the past. Friends of central planning should therefore not place much hope on the possibility that under democratic conditions the same degree of job security could be attained at a smaller cost in productive inefficiency.

Notes

1   Gregory and Collier, "Unemployment in the Soviet Union," p. 626.
2   Bajt, "Investment cycles in European socialist economies."
3   Hewett, *Reforming the Soviet Economy*, pp. 40–3.
4   Goodman and Schleifer, "The Soviet labor market in the 1980s," p. 337.
5   Gregory and Stuart, *Soviet Economic Structure and Performance*, p. 261.
6   Goodman and Schleifer, "The Soviet labor market in the 1980s," pp. 332–3.
7   Granick, *Job Rights in the Soviet Union*.
8   Murrell, "Big Bang versus evolution: East European reforms in the light of recent economic history," p. 7.
9   *Current Digest of the Soviet Press*, 39(38), 1987, p. 5.
10   Goodman and Schleifer, "The Soviet labor market in the 1980s," p. 338.
11   *The New York Times*, June 4, 1997, p. A8.
12   *The New York Times*, October 22, 1992, p. D7.

Chapter 21

Justice and Other Values

What care I how fair they be
If they be not fair to me.
— *Anon.*

The evil that men do lives after them.
The good is oft interred with their
bones.
— *Shakespeare*

CONTENTS

It is the rare society that insists on absolute equality as its standard of distributive justice. Those that have tried to implement that value are interesting, indeed, precisely because they are so rare (chapter 4). The real choice is limited to the two economic mechanisms, both of which tolerate a certain degree of income inequality. The real question of equity is not whether inequality should be tolerated at all, but whether there is an equitable basis for the inequality. The discussion here will be largely confined to wage income, leaving property income for Part V.

The most widely accepted standard of equity is that workers who produce more are entitled to be paid more. People who hold to that standard may choose either the market mechanism or the Soviet-type planning mechanism for managing labor resources. Both mechanisms use the price method for allocating workers among jobs, and both provide that workers who produce more are paid more. However, they have somewhat different notions of what it means to assert that one worker is "more productive" than another.

I Markets and Wage Equity

Under the market mechanism, the measure of my productivity is the value of the additional goods that would be produced if I entered the labor force. If the difference between my working and not working is $15,000 worth of goods per year, then the value of my labor is $15,000 – the marginal productivity of my kind of labor. Because of the many imperfections in labor markets, there is generally a gap between workers' wages and their marginal productivity, but in most cases in the course of time, market forces tend to remove, or at least to narrow, that gap.

The ethical appeal of that notion of productivity is evident. Those whose labor adds more to what the society values are paid more than those whose labor adds less. There are certain implications of that form of wage differentiation, however, that are not so evident and that raise certain questions of equity that were touched on in chapter 11.

First, the value of a worker's contribution depends on the number of other workers already employed in his occupation. If there are 3,000 shirtmakers employed in the garment industry, my wage as a shirtmaker might be, say, $15,000 a year. But if a hundred more workers seek and find employment as shirtmakers, market competition will reduce my wage – to perhaps $14,000; or, if a hundred shirtmakers retire and are not replaced, my wage may rise to $16,000. There is no difference in the way that shirtmakers work in these three circumstances; all put in a good day's work, but their wages are nevertheless different. Is it fair that the wage should depend not on how well people work – on the intrinsic quality of their labor – but on how many of them happen to enter or drop out of the job market?

Second, the value of the workers' contribution depends also on the market price of the good produced by their labor. If the price of a shirt is $20, the value of the 100 shirts that an additional shirtmaker might add to total shirt production would be $2,000, which would be the shirtmaker's wage. If the price of shirts were higher or lower than that, the wage would be correspondingly higher or lower, even though the shirtmakers individually produce the same number of shirts as before. Is it fair that my wage should be lower, even though I work as diligently as before, simply because the price of shirts has fallen?

The case for the equity of these market arrangements may be explored by considering the contrary. Suppose the society decided that once a wage was established, it should not vary with the number of workers engaged in that occupation. If a shirtmaker's labor is worth $15,000 a year, then it might seem to be worth $15,000 regardless of the number of shirtmakers the society happens to employ. A fixed wage of that sort, however, would give rise to a different problem of equity. Because of the law of diminishing returns, new shirtmakers coming into the labor market would be adding less than $15,000 worth of goods to the society's production – perhaps only $14,000 or less. If the wage rate were frozen, however, they would continue to receive a wage sufficient to enable them to buy $15,000 worth of goods from the society's total production. Since the marginal shirtmakers now consume more than they produce, the consumption of the other members of the society declines. They have to consume less than they add to the total production of goods in order to enable the shirtmakers to consume more than they add to the total production of goods. That result would be patently inequitable. Coal miners' families should not be asked to reduce their consumption so that shirtmakers' families can maintain theirs.

Suppose next that the shirtmaker's wage, once established, remained the same when the price of shirts rose. The *value* that the consumers place on their output has thus increased, even though the *quantity* of their output of shirts is no greater than before. The shirtmakers would then be producing a larger value of goods for the society than the value of the goods they can buy back from the society with their unchanged wage. One might say that they are being "exploited," because the society fails to recognize the greater value of their contribution. If the price of shirts fell, on the other hand, the shirtmakers could be said to be exploiting the rest of the society, because they are producing goods of lesser value but maintaining their earlier consumption level. The fairness of the market arrangement is that the wage depends not only on your physical output, but on the value that the citizens place on what you produce. If you keep on diligently producing something that your fellow citizens desire less and less, your market reward will get smaller and smaller. At the limit, if you put a great deal of effort into producing a lot of what nobody wants to buy, you will receive no reward at all, regardless of your great effort.

There is a certain ethical appeal in a different kind of wage arrangement – one that would reflect only the "true" intrinsic worth of a day of a shirtmaker's labor, and would not change merely because there were more shirtmakers employed or because people were paying more for shirts. While such a policy might seem fair, however, it would produce unfair consequences, of the sort described above. The wage differences that the market mechanism produces therefore have a reasonable claim to be regarded as equitable, and as appropriate for a Good Society that accepts wage differences as equitable if the workers are paid according to their contribution to the material welfare.

A Good Society should therefore regard market-based wage differentiation as acceptable by at least two criteria of goodness – justice and efficiency. The criterion by which it fails is security. To accept the market mechanism is to subject the citizens-as-workers to an arrangement in which their wage rates can decline for reasons entirely unrelated to their diligence or ability.

The question of wage insecurity is similar to that asked about job insecurity in the last chapter. The difference is that wage rates can either rise or fall, for reasons unrelated to the workers' own performance, and the possibility of an unmerited increase in the wage rate compensates, to some degree, for the insecurity due to the possibility of an unmerited decline. Moreover, wage variation is a matter of somewhat lower income, unlike job loss, which may be a matter of no income at all. Wage insecurity is therefore much less threatening to the citizens-as-workers, and probably of less concern, than job insecurity.

2   Planning and Wage Equity

The ethical foundation of wage setting in the planned economies is to be found in Marx's declaration that in the period of socialism, when productive capacity is not yet sufficient to make full communism possible, workers should be paid in proportion to the labor they supply.[1] Since workers differ in natural ability, it is right that some earn more than others. That formulation leaves open the matter of the appropriate basis for determining the size of differences in the "amount of labour" that people supply.

One can be sure that in Marxism the term "labour" does *not* mean marginal productivity. Marx's major writings were published before the revolution in modern economic thought that established "marginalism" as one of its central concepts. That new body of theory, moreover, was sharply contradictory to Marxian economic theory, so that one could not accept the one without rejecting the other. The rejection of "marginalism" was long a matter of firm doctrine in all countries that described themselves as Marxist. Wage differentiation therefore had to be based on something other than marginal productivity.

Instead of seeking to measure productivity directly, the method used in Soviet-type economies was based on what the Western literature calls "job evaluation"; that is, it was the nature of the work itself, rather than the value of the output produced by that work, that determined the wage.[2]

The total wage was divided into a basic wage that was intended to measure the "quality" of the work, and a set of wage supplements designed to reflect the "quantity" of work. To determine the basic wage of each job, all occupations were classified into a number of skill grades (say Grade I to Grade VI), each of which was assigned a basic wage by the government's wage-setting authorities. The basic wage for the highest grade was roughly twice that of the lowest grade, with the other basic-wage rates set in between. With some minor variations, the basic wage for each skill grade was the same throughout the country and for all occupations.

While productivity is not measured directly in this procedure, it does enter indirectly in various ways. The major way is that productivity does usually increase with skill grade: the addition of a skilled Grade IV machinist to the labor force would very likely increase the country's output by more than the addition of a Grade I machinist. The official handbooks are rather vague, however, about the basis on which it is decided that, for example, a semi-skilled worker of Grade IV should receive a basic wage 48 percent higher than an unskilled worker of Grade I. Considerations of equity as well as productivity may enter into that judgment.

Among the wage supplements intended to take account of differences in the "quantity" of the work was one based on differences in working conditions within the factory. Workers who did hot, heavy, or dangerous work, for example, received a specified percentage more than workers of the same skill grade who worked under normal conditions. A second was a regional supplement, to compensate workers in the regions with the harshest natural conditions. Another supplement was based on the importance of the industry: it was largest in extractive industries like coal mining, smaller in some manufacturing industries like machinery, and smallest in light and consumer goods manufacturing.[3] Finally, there were various incentive supplements consisting of piece-rate bonuses, enterprise plan-fulfillment bonuses, and the like. In the Soviet Union, wage supplements accounted for about 40 percent of total wage earnings.

This approach to wage differentiation is strikingly similar to that used in many large capitalist corporations. In some ways a worker would find little to choose between the market mechanism and the planning mechanism insofar as wage determination is concerned. Under both of them her wage would depend on such factors as her skill grade, the conditions of work, and the scarcity of labor; and there would be some forms of incentive payment for high-quality work. Aside from feeling underpaid, as every normal person does, most people would regard both of these arrangements as reasonably satisfactory from the perspective of the equity requirements of a Good Society.

There is one large difference, however. In the market economy each enterprise sets wage rates only for its own workers, and it allocates its workers only among its own jobs. There are thousands of such enterprises seeking to do the same thing, however, and the efforts of each set certain constraints upon the others. One enterprise cannot change its wage rates without considering the rates that other enterprises are offering, or that they may offer in response. If it cuts the wage below what competing enterprises are offering, it may soon find its workers going elsewhere.

Under central planning, on the other hand, the government sets wage rates for all the enterprises in the country, and it plans the allocation of the total labor force among all the jobs in the country. There are no other governments competing for the same workers and thereby setting limits upon what it can do. The difference is of fundamental importance with regard to the equity of wage differentiation under the two mechanisms.

Imagine two skilled Grade VI workers, one a computer programmer and one a machinist. As Grade VI workers, they have been judged by experts to have had the same amount of training and experience, to bear the same kind of responsibility, and to be equal in the content of their work. They therefore earn the same basic wage. If they both work under hot, heavy, or unhealthy conditions, and if they live in climatically similar regions, and if they are equally diligent in their work, they will also receive identical wage supplements. The total wage of the two workers will therefore be the same. In that respect they can be said to receive equal pay for equal work.

Suppose, however, that if the computer programmer fell ill and withdrew from the labor force, the enterprise's output (and therefore the society's) would decline by $20,000. If the machinist fell ill and withdrew, however, output would decline by $30,000. The marginal productivity of the machinist's labor in that case is 50 percent higher than that of the programmer's labor. If wages are to reflect the worker's contribution to the goods available to the people, the two jobs should not receive the same pay. Equity from this perspective requires that the machinist be paid more than the programmer because of the larger contribution made by machinist labor.

The market mechanism produces a result of that sort. Enterprises may set their wage rates on the basis of job evaluation rather than productivity, but competition for labor compels them to revise their wage scales from time to time in the light of market conditions. If the company's job evaluation dictates a $20 wage rate for machinists but the market wage rate has risen to $25, the company has to pay the market wage if it is to retain its machinists. Hence competition forces enterprises to adjust relative wages in accordance with differences in productivity. The planning mechanism also sets wages on the basis of job evaluation rather than productivity, but a differential between wages and productivity can endure without end, for there is no external pressure upon the government to bring them into line.[4]

How you assess the equity of the wage system in the planned economy therefore depends on your values regarding the proper basis for wage differentiation in a Good Society. If you believe that wage differentiation should depend on job evaluation – skill, experience, working conditions, and so forth – both markets and central planning are appropriate labor-allocation mechanisms, although the market mechanism is the better of the two because it can make finer distinctions among local working conditions and skills than a centralized wage-setting bureaucracy can make. If you believe, however, that workers who are more productive – that is, whose marginal output is more highly valued by the consumers – should earn more, then the market mechanism is the better arrangement for your Good Society.

3 Limits on Wage Inequality

It might seem that if a society agrees on the fairness of a certain way of setting wages, the matter of equity is settled. Some people do indeed hold the view that if you accept the fairness of the rules by which relative wage rates are set, you must also accept the resulting spread in wage rates as just. Hence any degree of inequality should be acceptable in your Good Society as long as it is based on true differences in productivity: if one worker is 2 times or 100 times as productive as another, his wage should properly be 2 times or 100 times the other's.

There is another point of view, however, that judges the goodness of an economic arrangement not only by its rules but by its results. It holds that a certain spread of wage rates is acceptable if it is based on productivity differences, but it also holds that excessive wage inequality detracts from the goodness of the society.

The planning mechanism could accommodate both points of view. The planners could set wage rates solely on the basis of their conception of fairness and ignore the size of the resulting wage differences. But if the society wishes to set limits on wage inequality, as is likely in a planned economy, it could simply instruct the planners to incorporate that restriction into their wage-setting policy.

The market mechanism, however, cannot easily accommodate both points of view. Only when competition is perfect do relative wage rates correctly reflect marginal productivity. When competition is imperfect, as is generally the case in practice, wage rates do not reflect marginal productivity. Hence, even if you regard marginal productivity as an equitable rule for wage setting, you may hold the market-derived wage differences to be inequitable because the rule is not fairly applied. If you are concerned with the justice of the result as well as the fairness of the rule, the market is particularly troublesome because, unlike under planning, there is no central organization with the authority to set limits on wage differentiation. There are therefore no bounds to the extent of the inequality that could emerge.

If you hold the degree of inequality to be inequitable, however, you are not bound to reject the market mechanism on that account. If the dissatisfaction is insufficiently large, a democratic society can authorize its government to take steps to alter the distribution of income in the direction of greater equality. And indeed the governments of virtually all modern capitalist economies do intervene in the economy for that purpose. The nature and extent of such intervention is the source of much of the diversity in capitalist economic arrangements.

Much of the intervention is designed to reduce the spread between the rich and the poor: by progressive income taxes, for example. Other measures are directed not at inequality as such but at the conditions of the people at the bottom of the income distribution. A number of such policies are designed to increase the wages of the lowest-wage workers.

A MINIMUM WAGE

Many people hold the view that there is some minimum wage below which nobody should be obliged to work. Their concern is not with fairness of the rules; they may even concede that wage rates at both extremes are quite equitable because they are based on genuine productivity differences. They simply believe that a wage rate below a certain decent level is unacceptable in a Good Society.

Under a democratic form of central planning, a society that holds this view can communicate to the planners its wish that no worker's wage rate should be lower than that minimum. Since the planners set the wage rates for all jobs, they are in a position to carry out the society's wish. If any wage rates are subminimal in that economy, it is either because the planners wish them to be what they are, or because they have erred.

In a competitive market economy, however, wage rates can easily fall below a socially acceptable minimum in occupations in which labor productivity is very low. The fault is not that of the market mechanism, which is merely doing its job of allocating labor efficiently. The fault is rather the low level of productivity of those jobs – the people who perform that work, no matter how diligently, simply produce very little of what the rest of the society values.

"Almost nowhere in the moral-philosophic literature is it deemed just that those with only a limited kind of labor input to offer should receive only its . . . marginal product – no matter how low."[5] That assertion by the distinguished economist Edmund S. Phelps expresses the view of virtually the entire political-economics profession.

Accordingly, the market economies have developed a wide range of policies for dealing with subminimal wage rates. The best of them concentrate on improving the skills of workers who occupy the low-wage jobs. Programs that provide education and training to low-skill workers, for example, enable more of them to qualify for higher-wage jobs. As they move into the better jobs, the supply of labor to the lowest-wage jobs declines and wage rates for those jobs rise. Nothing increases the wage rates of fast-food service workers or supermarket baggers as much as a decrease in the number of people applying for those jobs.

With the best of training programs, however, a certain number of low-skilled workers may still work at jobs in which the market wage rate is regarded as subminimal. In many countries this has led to the legislation of a minimum wage.

For decades the legal minimum wage has been the darling of compassionate people because it helped to shore up the incomes of many of the poorest citizens. Economists are often of two minds about it, however, because the textbooks they read and write demonstrate that under most normal conditions, a minimum wage helps some low-wage workers, but also harms others. The logic of the argument is of great importance in the economics of the Good Society, for it concerns the limits to which the outcomes of the market mechanism can be altered by social policy.

A legal minimum wage does assure than no employed worker earns less than the minimum specified by the law. The trouble with it is that it has a number of undesirable side effects. The argument parallels that of the effects on wage rates of labor unions and monopsony (chapter 17).

Suppose the market wage for unskilled labor is $2 an hour and a law is passed forbidding enterprises to pay less than $5 an hour to any workers they hire. Since the market mechanism is built upon the price method, all enterprises that employ some workers at less than $5 an hour must respond to the change in that very important "price" – the wage rate. Before the change, for example, the Springfield Company, diligently pursuing the logic of profit maximization, hired that number of workers – perhaps 100 – at which the marginal product of its unskilled labor was $2 an hour. The impact of the new law is that the company now loses money on some of its unskilled workers. If one worker were dismissed from employment, perhaps by opening the shop one hour later in the morning or by eliminating one small finishing operation on the product, the enterprise would lose $2 of revenue from the sale of a unit of the goods produced by that marginal worker. However, it would also save the $5 that it now costs to employ him. Hence, cutting employment down from 100 to 99 workers would increase the company's profit by $3. The enterprise is not unlike the homeowner who finds it worth having the lawn cut or the house cleaned every week for $2 an hour, but would make do with bi-weekly employment of those workers if he had to pay $5 an hour.

Pursuing the same logic, more and more of the least-productive unskilled jobs would be closed out until the marginal revenue product of remaining unskilled labor in the Springfield Company rose to the level of the $5 minimum wage. Perhaps ten jobs would be closed out, leaving ten unskilled workers to find jobs elsewhere.

If the $5 wage had been introduced in the Springfield Company by the successful effort of a labor union, those ten displaced workers would seek jobs in non-union companies or in regions where the market wage was still $2 an hour; and the effect of their entry would be to depress the wage elsewhere to something below $2. When a minimum wage is imposed by government, however, there are no other companies or regions in which the wage rate is still $2. Like the Springfield Company, all enterprises are motivated by profit considerations to review their employment practices and to eliminate all jobs in which the marginal revenue product of their unskilled labor is below $5. The ten workers released by the Springfield Company are therefore joined by others released by other companies. If 10,000 workers had been employed in that labor market at the original equilibrium market wage of $2, perhaps only 9,500 are now employed at the $5 wage, leaving 500 workers unemployed, with no place to go.

It should be noted that the law does succeed in its objective of raising the wage rates of unskilled workers to $5. It therefore cannot but be applauded by friends of the poor, as well as by all the unskilled workers who retain their jobs and are now employed at wage rates much higher than before. The bad news, however, is that there are now 500 workers for whom the enterprises have no jobs that are worth filling at a wage of $5.

In the short run very few workers may actually be dismissed. Some owners, motivated by compassion or concerned about public relations, may accept a reduction in their profit rather than fire people, relying on normal attrition to pare down their labor force gradually. No new workers will be taken on to replace those who leave, however, and in the course of time unemployment will rise as the enterprises reduce their work force to the level at which their profit reaches its new peak at the wage of $5.

The link between the minimum-wage law and the level of unemployment is not transparent, however. The existence of unemployment is glaringly visible, but it takes an act of faith in the economic theory presented above to believe that one of its causes is the minimum-wage law.

A great many studies over many years have sought to verify whether the predicted relation between a minimum wage and employment can be detected in the empirical data. The consensus is that whatever effect a minimum wage has, it is not very large. A major reason is that since changes in the legal minimum have been relatively small, one should expect their effects to be small. Small effects, however, are exceedingly difficult to detect in the data, which inevitably contain a lot of "noise."[6] Most studies find a small decrease in employment, although some report a small positive effect.[7] Most analysts would probably agree, however, that in practice the larger the size of the legal minimum wage relative to the market wage, the larger the likely level of unemployment, particularly among teenage and other low-skilled workers.[8]

Monopsony again   There is an important exception to the foregoing – monopsony. Like the effect of labor unions on wages and employment, the effect of a minimum wage is different in a labor market in which there are very few employers from that in a labor market where perfect competition prevails.

Suppose a poultry-processing plant is the major employer in a poor small town, and it pays a $2 an hour. The enactment of a $5 minimum-wage law deprives the company of the power to set whatever wage it finds most profitable, much as a labor-union contract would do; it becomes a "wage-taker" rather than a "wage-maker" (chapter 17). No longer having the option of paying less than $5, the enterprise concentrates on finding that output that maximizes profit at the $5 wage rate. This will normally lead to an *increase* in both output and employment and an improvement in the efficiency of the economy. The citizens are then better off both as consumers and as workers, although the enterprise earns less profit than before the minimum-wage law.

Much of the labor force in modern economies is to be found in large labor markets, however, and the low-wage jobs are concentrated in fairly competitive industries like farming, garments, laundries, and food services. Those jobs are often the sole source of employment for workers who lack the educational, social, linguistic, and other skills required for higher-wage jobs. It is the employment opportunities of these most vulnerable workers that diminish as a consequence of a minimum-wage law.

A Good Society that adopts the market mechanism faces a hard choice on the matter of a minimum wage. The increased incomes of those low-wage workers who retain their jobs at higher wage rates after the imposition of a minimum wage must be weighed against the increased unemployment of a small but highly disadvantaged group of young people. The equity issue may be viewed as one of higher-paid jobs for some at the cost of no jobs for others.

A MINIMUM INCOME

There is a second issue of equity in regard to a minimum wage. One reason for the unacceptability of a subminimal wage is that it demeans the workers whose labor is so lightly regarded by the rest of the society. For people who place a high value on the low-wage worker's sense of personal dignity, the minimum wage has a great deal of merit. A second reason, however, which is probably more widely held, is that a very low wage condemns the worker and her family to a level of consumption that the society regards as indecently low. A minimum *wage*, however, is a poor instrument for assuring a minimum *consumption level*. The consumption level depends, among other things, upon the size of the family, and a minimum wage that would support a decent consumption level for a single worker would be crushingly low for married workers with large families.

The alternative to a minimum-wage law is a minimum family income law, which has the unusual history of having been endorsed by people with very different political-economic positions. There are many variants of such a policy, one of which was introduced into law in the United States in 1986 on the initiative of a conservative president, Ronald Reagan. The Earned Income Tax Credit (EITC) law provides a refundable tax credit for every dollar earned up to a certain limit. For a family with two or more children, the credit amounts to $3,500 when the family's income is $8,900, bringing the total family income up to $12,400. The EITC is available for families with incomes up to but not over $27,000, but the size of the credit decreases as income approaches the upper limit. Support has also been growing for a program of subsidies for qualified firms that hire low-wage workers, as a way of reducing the unemployment and increasing the pay of disadvantaged workers.[9]

Both measures are subject to the normal pitfalls of social-economic policies, whether they affect poor workers or rich corporations – from mere inefficiency to downright cheating. Of the two, however, a minimum-income policy is superior to a minimum-wage policy in several respects. It conforms to that value which holds that having a job is more important than having a better-paying job. Since it permits market wage rates to prevail, labor is allocated efficiently among jobs, the economy is producing at its full potential, and the families of all low-wage workers have an acceptable income level. Moreover, the tax burden of income supplementation is smaller than the tax burden of supporting workers who would be unemployed as a consequence of a minimum-wage law. In these respects, no one would be worse off, and many people would be better off, under a minimum-income arrangement.

4   Sweden: The Welfare State

The elimination of poverty, whether by minimum-wage or minimum-income or other policies, would fully satisfy many people's sense of distributive justice. Others of a more egalitarian bent require more. Their sights are set not on the consumption of the poor but on the spread between rich and poor. Distress over the poverty of the poor often springs from different ethical sources than distress over the wealth of the rich, but the two perspectives on justice are often found in the same political camp.

During the Great Depression poverty rather than equality dominated the social agenda of the capitalist world. The social programs developed in Sweden in particular came to be regarded as so advanced that the country was said to have pioneered a new "middle way" between capitalism and socialism.[10] In all significant respects, however, Sweden preserved "the conditions of an expansive free-market capitalist economy."[11] To be sure, some members of the socialist and labor movements advanced the goal of transforming the system gradually into market socialism, but it received little support.[12] Sweden may be thought of as an instructive case of the adaptability of democratic capitalism to the values of the people who live under that system.

The thrust of the initial social policy was the alleviation of poverty through programs of income support and free access to education and health care. The policy virtually eliminated poverty: the proportion of families with less than 50 percent of the median income fell from about 30 percent to about 5 percent.[13] It had virtually universal support: "That the age-old fear of poverty has been replaced by a new-found social security is a fundamental achievement in Sweden," writes a prominent critic of the welfare state.[14]

In the prosperous postwar years, however, the objective changed from a "residual" to a "universalistic" welfare system.[15] With poverty largely eliminated, the new objective was to extend a variety of social services to the population as a whole. It is that extension of broad public benefits to workers, to the middle class, and to the citizens generally that characterizes the "welfare state." Most capitalist countries introduced some programs of that sort, but Sweden became the prototype of the welfare state.

The Swedish variant of the welfare state embodies a number of features. Peaceful industrial relations are achieved by a procedure in which wages are set on the national level in periodic negotiations between associations of labor unions and employers. Union pressure is generally exerted in the direction of shoring up the lowest wage rates, which results in a perpetual squeeze on wage differentials in the direction of equality. The "solidaristic" wage policy is supplemented by a uniquely active labor market policy, consisting of job-training programs, grants in support of migration out of high-unemployment areas, and other measures.

A second set of programs consists of transfer payments – money payments out of tax revenues that are transferred by the government to various groups of citizens. The largest program is a generous social insurance system, but there are also unemployment and sickness benefits, family allowances, and housing subsidies that are available even to high-income families.[16] These benefits amounted to about 30 percent of the GDP in the 1980s.[17]

The most distinctive program, however, is the direct provision of various consumer services to the citizens at highly subsidized prices. Among them are such services as education and health, which are publicly provided in many capitalist countries. The Swedish program goes well beyond that, however, including day-care for children and old-age care. Government-provided consumption services rose to about 28 percent of GDP and one-third of total employment in the 1990s, higher than in any major European country. Local government has a virtual monopoly on the supply of these services, making it impossible for cooperatives or other private suppliers to compete.[18] Total government social spending, including transfer payments and public consumption services, amounted to 60–70 percent of GDP since the late 1970s, compared to 45–50 percent in other OECD countries.[19]

On the other side of the social ledger, the extent of the welfare-state programs is matched by the size of the tax revenues that the citizens pay in order to support them. In addition to an income tax that became increasingly progressive over time, there is an annual tax on wealth. Taxes climbed gradually from about 15 percent of GNP in the 1930s to about 50–60 percent of GNP in the 1980s. The marginal tax rate – the tax on each additional 1,000 kroner of the income that a person earned – reached 70–80 percent.[20] As a result of the tax system and the other welfare-state programs, the household-income distribution was among the most equal in the world: inequality in Germany was about 30 percent greater than in Sweden and in the United States was about 61 percent greater.[21]

The welfare-state programs expanded continuously in the prosperous postwar decades. Toward the end of the 1970s, however, that happy postwar time began to come to an end in much of the capitalist world, but Sweden was particularly hard hit. The growth rate declined, unemployment rose, and it suffered two depressions of a severity equal to the 1930s. More significantly, it failed to recover as rapidly as its neighbors so that it fell from the position of fourth richest country in the OECD in 1970 to sixteenth in 1995.[22]

Dissatisfaction began to mount over the costliness of the welfare state and the growing restriction of individual freedom of choice because of the expanding societal provision of consumer services. The earlier social consensus began to unravel, and in 1976 the Social Democratic Party that had presided continuously over the evolution of the welfare state since 1932 was voted out of office. In recent years there has been some retrenchment: there have been moves to privatize some of the social services, some private schools have received state support, benefit levels have been reduced, marginal tax rates have been reduced, the rules for early retirement have been tightened, and income inequality and poverty have risen a bit. The welfare state has not been dismantled, however, for public support for the social programs remains strong; public spending did not significantly decline even under conservative governments, and still amounted to about 65–70 percent of GDP in the mid-1990s.[23] Sweden remains the *première* capitalist welfare state, although it appears to have exceeded the limit of what that form of capitalism can attain, and it has lost its luster as an efficient market economy.

The Swedish experience sheds light on both the possibilities and the limitations of modifying a capitalist economy in the pursuit of greater equality. Supporters of markets can point to it as an example of the capacity of a market mechanism to respond to powerful egalitarian sentiments in a democratic society. To be sure, it remains an unequal society in many respects. However, people whose egalitarian sentiments are so strong that they would not admit Sweden into the company of Good Societies would be inclined to turn to socialism, although none of the socialist societies managed to attain pure equality either.

LIMITATIONS ON THE WELFARE STATE

The major limitation on the expansion of the welfare state is the responsiveness of the citizens to the level of taxation. If people lived their economic lives without taking any account of the taxes they have to pay, the welfare state could expand virtually without limit. For better or worse, however, people everywhere do respond to changes in taxes, much as they respond to changes in prices or wage rates. When tax rates are small, the response is also small, but the higher the level of taxation the greater the extent to which people seek out ways of acting that would reduce their tax bite.

The major concern is that the incentive to save, invest, and work for pay will erode as incomes are reduced by taxes. That is not inevitable: people might respond to an increase in taxes by working more, rather than less, in order to maintain the standard of level of living to which they have become accustomed. Most empirical studies, indeed, find no decline in effort with higher taxes; in the case of professionals and executives, effort sometimes even increases.[24] When very high levels of taxation are maintained for a long time, however, people who can afford to work less tend increasingly do so. If 70–80 percent of an extra day's wages goes to the government, as was widely the case in Sweden in the 1980s, the inclination to work that extra day is very small.[25] Hence workers hold more part-time jobs, devote less effort to acquiring new skills, and take longer leaves of absence; Swedes actually work 19 percent fewer than their contractual work hours, compared to Germans who work 25 percent more. At the same time, the volume of do-it-yourself work at home has greatly increased, for that kind of work escapes the income tax. Of particular concern is the palpable increase in cheating, abuse, and tax evasion in that traditionally law-abiding society. The nation was shocked by the melancholy declaration of Gunnar Myrdal, one of the original enthusiasts of the welfare state, that we have become "a nation of cheaters."[26]

No absolute number can be placed on the highest level of taxation that a market economy can sustain; all that can be said is that the higher the taxes the more they sap productivity and incentives. At low levels of taxation the social gains are generally worth the economic loss, but as taxes increase the balance runs the other way. Sweden's experience is that even a country with a genuine "passion for equality"[27] cannot sustain marginal tax rates as high as 70–80 percent. The limit would be even smaller in countries with less of that passion, and with a weaker tax-paying tradition, but it would always be lurking on the horizon.

A social program that is confined to the alleviation of poverty is relatively cheap and appears to be manageable at a level that is well within the sustainable tax limit of most wealthy countries. It is the potentially unlimited appetite of the middle- and upper-income groups for government benefits that could break the bank. In the United States, for example, the cost of all the entitlement programs and tax breaks in the federal budget amounted to about $1,162 billion in 1993. Of the 18 largest of those programs, such as Social Security and tax deductions for homeowners' mortgage interest, about 60 percent of the expenditures went to families whose incomes exceeded the official poverty level by 50 percent. The programs specifically targeted at the government-certified poor amounted to only $140 billion.[28] If governments were concerned only to remedy or eliminate poverty, their social budgets would be unrecognizably small.

What might project a society rapidly into the range of its taxation limit is not a concern about poverty but the taste for universal tax-supported social programs directed not only to the poor but to all income classes. It was these programs that led eventually to the retreat of the welfare state. Each of such programs may be a good thing in itself in the sense that it benefits some or all of the people; but in the aggregate they mount up in cost and may exceed the taxable limit.

Most of that story can be told in the case of the Swedish child-care program that has attracted a great deal of attention. The impetus was the promotion of gender equality by relieving mothers of the child-care responsibilities that keep many of them out of the labor force. Every municipality provides complete, subsidized, day-care for small children and long school days for older children, to enable both parents to work outside the home. There is also a generous parental leave allowance.[29]

In deciding to repair the inequality arising out of traditional family organization, Sweden exercised an option that is available in all market economies. Child-care services could be distributed in the normal manner of the price method: each family would decide whether to spend 1,000 kroner a month – let us say – on child-care services, or to spend the money for other things they desired. Alternatively, the services could be walled off from the market mechanism and distributed by assignment: all families would hand over 1,000 kroner a month in taxes to the government, which would then supply the services to all citizens free or at low prices. Why did the Swedes turn to assignment in a case of this sort?

The reason cannot be simply the pursuit of equality. Income distribution is about as equal as one can expect under capitalism. Moreover, since the program was extended to families regardless of their income, its purpose was evidently not simply to aid poor mothers. The answer appears to be the same as that which led to the adoption of the assignment method of distribution in the kibbutz and in Maoist China – the attraction of uniformity. The principle that everyone should have equal access to the service was transformed into the principle that "everyone should consume an identical quantity and quality."[30] Uniformity in the consumption of child-care services assures that differences in consumer preferences do not subvert equality; for under the price method, even with equal incomes, the cost of child-care would have motivated some mothers to care for their children at home, thus forgoing the opportunity to gain equality with men in the labor market.

The goal of assignment therefore was not to give all women an equal choice on whether to enter the labor force, but to induce as many as possible to do so. That is to say, what women would choose to do if their incomes were equal does not attain the goal of eliminating differences in the labor-force behavior of men and women. Making child-care costless to the family is thus a kind of affirmative action, offsetting the gender differences that spring from the traditional form of family organization. The ideal is a society in which men and women work uniformly on equal terms in the labor force.

The merits of universal child-care are under intense debate in Sweden. Its proponents point out that, among other benefits, it has succeeded in providing women with an unparalleled degree of equality: the proportion of Swedish women in the labor force is among the highest the world. The critics, on the other hand, noting that only 40 percent of mothers make use of the facilities despite the low subsidized price, argue that it is a self-serving program in which an interest group contrives to get the rest of population to pay for the services they alone use.[31] They note also that public child-care costs are twice the level of those in other

Nordic countries, attributing that to the monopolistic position that socialized supply gives to the public-agency providers of the service. They argue that families who are too poor to afford adequate day-care should be given special public assistance, but the mass of families should consider the cost of their child-care as a cost of living their lives in the way they prefer, much as they consider the cost of the family's food, or of a larger flat, or of an extra week's holiday abroad.

The issue is not one of basic economic structure but of economic policy, with which this book is not primarily concerned. Issues of this sort, however, offer an important lesson for the economic structure of Good Society.

The market mechanism is congenial to people who hold that the individual, rather than the society, is generally a better judge of what he ought to consume: that is, they value individual rather than societal sovereignty over production. Most people also believe, however, that there are certain "merit" goods and services the consumption of which affects not only the consumers individually but the society generally; like education and health, they generate "positive externalities." People who hold this view may be reluctant to commit their Good Society to the market mechanism because it would suffer from the neglect of those vital goods and services. The Swedish welfare state demonstrates that the market mechanism is sufficiently flexible to permit an ample space to be carved out in which societal sovereignty can replace consumer sovereignty over a range of such goods and services. Whether it *should* do so in the case of particular services like child-care is a matter for public policy, but it *can* do so if the people place sufficient value on them.

The bad news is that the tax burden that must be borne for support of such services places a limit on how large the space for societal sovereignty can be. The Swedes apparently exceeded their limit at some point and are currently retreating to a more moderate and sustainable level of taxation. Most countries do not place as high a value on equality as Sweden, and their limit is likely to be smaller. In all the wealthier market economies, however, the limit is probably far larger than would be required to deal with the matter of poverty alone. That still leaves considerable space for an equality-minded society to provide equal access to, or even uniform consumption of, a large range of consumer services.

5   Discrimination

A wage rate is attached to a job, not to a worker. An airline pilot who works as a machinist receives the pay of a machinist, not of a pilot. That raises another set of questions about equity. The economic mechanism may generate an entirely equitable wage structure but there may be something inequitable in the way in which workers are sorted among the jobs: a master plumber may earn exactly the right wage, but some kinds of people never get to be master plumbers.

In the best of societies some kinds of workers would be underrepresented in some jobs. Whether that is equitable or not depends on the basis of that underrepresentation. If it is based on job preferences, that would be entirely acceptable in a society that values individual choice over societal choice: individuals or groups that like clean hands would not choose to be plumbers. However, if the underrepresentation is based on some other social characteristic that is unrelated to the job requirements, such as sex, race, or ethnicity, it would be regarded as discrimination, and therefore inequitable.

Job discrimination may be either direct or indirect. Direct discrimination occurs when people who possess all the skills and other job requirements are denied certain jobs because of their membership in an excluded group. Indirect discrimination occurs when the members of the excluded group are denied equal access to the educational and other channels through which skills are acquired.

In capitalist market economies certain groups have traditionally been subject to both direct and indirect discrimination – notably women, and ethnic and racial minorities. It has been widely thought by people of good will that the cause is to be found in the market mechanism itself, and that it can be eliminated only by replacement of capitalist markets by socialist planning. In practice, great efforts have been made under both mechanisms in the past century to combat job discrimination, with varying degrees of success. Their experience provides another body of empirical evidence on the question of whether markets or planning is the better economic mechanism for a society that places a high value on economic justice.

The forms of job discrimination and the groups that experience it vary greatly from country to country. Two cases are particularly instructive, however: those of women in the Soviet Union, and of black people in the United States.

WOMEN IN THE SOVIET UNION

In the Soviet Marxist view of history, all forms of social oppression are rooted in the institution of private property, and they can never be eliminated, or even seriously moderated, until the property is owned by all the people and socialist planning replaces capitalist markets. Accordingly, the revolutionary leadership proceeded quickly to the task of abolishing private property and putting an end to the major forms of social inequality inherited from the Tsarist past. Prominent among the goals was the realization of women's equality.

Soviet Marxists shared with many others the conviction that the key to the goal of equality between the sexes was the liberation of women from their traditional family role in order to free them for full participation in the civic and economic life of the society on equal terms with men. Among the policies that were designed to achieve those goals were the provision of equal educational opportunities for women, and the freeing of women from child care, food preparation, and other traditional home-making activities.

One of the earliest actions of the Revolutionary government was to require that all educational institutions be thrown open equally to both sexes.[32] Women, indeed, enrolled in large numbers, and in the course of time drew abreast of men in educational attainment, although in many rural areas and in the Muslim republics differences remained. Equally significant was the enrollment of women in higher-education institutions, particularly in such traditionally male fields as science and technology. As they graduated and moved into the job market, they came increasingly to occupy jobs in fields that had been the province of men.

A variety of other measures were undertaken that increased the ability of women to play a role in the economy on the same terms as men. The legalization of abortion removed one of the traditional handicaps of women in economic competition with men. To facilitate the employment of mothers, work began on a network of infant and child-care facilities, often located in the production organizations themselves for maximum convenience. On the organizational level, the Communist Party established a special high-level Women's Department to ensure that the women's liberation movement would not be lost sight of among the many responsibilities of the leadership. In subsequent years, the original ideological commitment to women's education and labor-force participation was reinforced by the practical objective of drawing as many people as possible into the labor force in order to promote economic growth.

In the long run, the goal of women's equality was largely achieved in a number of important respects. By the mid-1970s women constituted 50 percent of all students enrolled in institutions of higher education, and 51.5 percent of the country's labor force. Of particular interest is their presence in various fields traditionally reserved almost entirely for men:

they constituted 40 percent of all engineers and 70 percent of all physicians.[33] Visitors to the USSR were often struck by the extensive presence of women workers in such fields as construction work, the merchant marine, and heavy industry.

In other respects, however, women remained subject to certain forms of discrimination similar to those in market economies. In all occupations, the higher the administrative position, the fewer the number of women; and the top jobs were almost always occupied by men. The proportion of women also varied greatly by sector, with the largest proportion of women working in the lowest-wage sectors.[34] For this and other reasons the average earnings of Soviet women were about two-thirds those of men, which is about the same proportion as in the developed market economies.[35]

On balance, the gains that Soviet women made under the planning mechanism have been of enormous magnitude, perhaps unprecedented in modern history. Proponents of planning can regard that as no small achievement. The gains have been accompanied by certain costs, however. The socialized child-care and home-making services that were to substitute for mothers' work in the home were never delivered in the abundance originally foreseen, so that the "double burden" faced by many working women everywhere was particularly heavy on Soviet women. Moreover, discrimination continued to exist right up to the end, for reasons that are eerily similar to those in the market economies: women continue to have lower aspirations than men regarding jobs and earnings, and they distinguish between "men's work" and "women's work" in terms that are very similar to those in Great Britain.[36]

Thus, Communist experience served to raise the economic status of women from the low level of the pre-revolutionary past to roughly that of the capitalist world, but in certain respects it continued to lag behind. Among the reasons is that Party control precluded the development of autonomous movements by women and other groups such as those that which evolved in the West. Had a militant, consciousness-raising women's movement been permitted, the status of women would have been higher than it turned out to be.

RACE IN THE UNITED STATES

In the century that followed the abolition of slavery, the economic and social inequality of black citizens was widely seen in the US as the country's worst evil and most intractable problem – an "American Dilemma," in the words of a sympathetic foreign observer.[37] It was a trump card in the hands of socialist critics of capitalism, who dramatized the contrast with the growing equality of women and other underprivileged groups in the Soviet Union at the time. It was presented as decisive proof, if that were needed, that social oppression could never be eradicated until capitalist markets were replaced by socialist planning.

World War II unleashed a number of social forces that compelled the country to confront the problem directly. Among them were the inception of racial integration in the armed forces and the mass migration of black rural families from the South in response to wartime job shortage in the industrialized cities of the country. There are many ways of putting together the pieces of social history that followed, but every telling of the story would include the violent social explosions in the inner cities, the rise of black liberation movements under effective and charismatic leaders, the growing active support for those movements among white youth and middle-class families, the increasingly successful resort to the courts for equal protection under the law, and the responsiveness of political parties to the growing voting power of the black community and their allies.

Under the force of the historic civil-rights revolution, the United States embarked on a massive program of "affirmative action" to narrow the racial gap in economic and other opportunities. Direct discrimination in employment, education, and other activities was proscribed by law: employers could not refuse a qualified job applicant on grounds of race. The offensive against indirect discrimination took such forms as special educational programs for children from disadvantaged families and an assault on the barriers by which black families had been excluded from residence in affluent suburbs.

In the half century that began with World War II, America experienced what may be the fastest and largest contraction of the scope of racial discrimination in modern history. As one of many indicators of the change, a 1990 international survey of the attitudes of ethnic majorities toward minorities found that in the United States 13 percent of whites held "unfavorable" attitudes toward Afro-Americans. In all the other countries the percentages of the majority that regarded the minority unfavorably were substantially larger: Russians toward Azerbaijanis, 44 percent; East Germans toward Poles, 54 percent, Spaniards toward Catalans, 22 percent.[38] Nowhere in the world, and certainly not in the planned economies, is the minority presence as prominent in the political, cultural, and economic elite. The time has not yet come to declare victory and go home, for even the members of that elite continue to be exposed to incidents of prejudice and discrimination. Moreover, the conditions of many black citizens have not improved, and in some respects have deteriorated, particularly in the inner cities. The life chances of those who are not caught in that terrible trap, however, have enormously improved.

All the credit for that remarkable development does not go to the affirmative action programs alone. Much of it, and many argue that most of it, should go to the competitive market economy and to the political-legal system – the enactment and enforcement of voting-rights and other laws that prohibit discrimination in many areas of public life where it formerly thrived.[39] Yet affirmative action programs no doubt also contributed a great deal. Like all social policies, however, they had certain negative side-effects, some of which become evident only with the passage of time. Affirmative action in the form of numerical quotas for minority groups, for example, imposes a high cost on a few members of the majority while the others pay none of the cost of that policy. The effort to equalize educational opportunity by busing pupils from predominantly minority schools to all-white schools stimulated a massive "white flight" to the suburbs, which resulted in the long run in greater racial segregation than before. It is for such reasons that many friends of racial equality, both black and white, are reconsidering the merits of some of the earlier policy instruments, though not the principle, of continued affirmative action.[40]

DISCRIMINATION AND THE ECONOMIC MECHANISM

Discrimination in employment is a classic case of the conjunction of social values and economic structure. Racism, sexism, and similar discriminatory orientations will eventually express themselves under any economic mechanism: a racist society will produce a racist economy, and a macho society will produce a macho economy, whether it is based on planning or markets.

The lesson for the Good Society is that both planning and markets are fairly neutral arrangements that reflect the social and cultural traditions of the society that adopts them. Under both mechanisms, however, the nature and extent of economic discrimination can be greatly altered through the political system. In a society with an effective authoritarian political system, the political leadership could encourage or inhibit discrimination, under both planning and markets. In a society with an effective democratic political system, job discrimination can be tolerated or restricted under both planning and markets, in response to the play of political forces. The nature and extent of job discrimination in a society therefore depends not on its economic mechanism, but on the values of the people and on the political arrangements through which those values find expression.

6 Skills and Jobs

That a citizen should be excluded from a job because of social discrimination would be regarded as inequitable in all versions of a Good Society. It would be regarded as entirely appropriate, however, to exclude workers who do not possess the skills required for the jobs for which they apply.

If all workers possessed all the skills required to qualify for all jobs, there would be no issue of equity. Most workers are excluded from most jobs, however, because they do not possess the required skills: a gastroenterologist and a machinist would not qualify for each other's job. Unless the process of skills acquisition is a fair one, however, the wage method of labor allocation cannot be regarded as equitable. Much therefore depends on how workers acquire their skills, which they do principally through education and training.

The two major sources of education are the home and the school. Pre-school home environment is perhaps the most important stage in a child's education, and greatly influences the rate at which education progresses in the subsequent years of schooling.[41] For many students, schooling ends upon completion of secondary education, but others go on to post-secondary and graduate education of various years' duration. Post-secondary schooling often includes a large component of occupational training, in the sense that the graduates are trained to enter directly into an occupation such as architecture or medicine.

Occupational training is acquired in a great many ways. Most modern countries provide it in vocational schools for pupils who do not complete the course of general secondary education. Some secondary-school graduates enter the labor force directly, while others may spend a year or more in technical-training schools before entering the labor force. A great deal of training also occurs on the job, some of it consisting of formal programs of apprenticeship or instruction, and some of it under the informal guidance of an experienced worker. Much of it consists simply of learning-by-doing and of the gradual accumulation of experience.

Because workers' productivity depends upon their skills, a society that regards productivity differences as an equitable basis of wage inequality is also likely to regard equality of access to education and training as the standard of equity. That is to say, productivity-based wage differences can be regarded as fair only if workers have an equal opportunity to acquire the skills needed to qualify for jobs that they seek. How do planning and markets perform in that respect?

The economic mechanism plays a significant part in the process whereby skills are acquired, For example, a market-economy enterprise finds it profitable to devote some of its resources to the training of its workers under certain conditions, and the opportunity for obtaining that sort of "on-the-job training" is one of the attractions that a job may offer to a worker. Some forms of training, however, provide the worker with skills that are useful only in a particular enterprise, but other forms of training generate externalities, in the sense that they increase the worker's productivity in other enterprises where they might later work. It pays a profit-oriented enterprise to finance the first form of training but not the second.

A centrally planned economy, however, would finance both forms of training because the economy as a whole benefits from both. The planners "internalize," as it were, the social benefits of training acquired in one enterprise but put to use in others. Hence the planning mechanism is more efficient than the market mechanism in the provision of on-the-job training.

The process of skills acquisition, however, involves not only the educational system and the economic mechanism but the entire social system, and most particularly, the family. The full story cannot be told within the confines of a book that deals not with the Good Society *in toto* but only with its economic system. The matter is so important in the assessment of the goodness of the economy, however, that it merits a digression into the education system and the family.

7 Education and Family

Access to elementary and secondary education under the two economic mechanisms is similar in some respects and different in others. Both suffer from one major shortcoming with regard to equality, however – differences in education, and particularly pre-school education, which are due primarily to differences in the kinds of families into which the children are born.

Income differences spring first to mind. When income is unequally distributed, higher-income parents provide their children with more things of educational value that money can buy, such as toys, travel, and tutoring. In both the planned and market economies, the children of the better-off derive benefits of these sorts from the inequality of income. The advantage of a higher family income is lesser in the planned economies, however, because in the absence of property income, income tends to be more equally distributed.

But income inequality is far from the whole story. Like consumer preferences generally, some families place relatively more value on their children's education than others. Hence, even if all families had the same income, some would choose to spend more of it than others on things that contribute to their children's education. It is therefore not only income differences but also differences in the social, cultural, and educational status of the families that influence the educational attainment of children. Because of such differences in family environment, in every society differences in children's educational attainment can be observed as early as the time they begin schooling, and increase steadily in the course of time.[42]

Generalizations of this sort do not apply to individuals, of course, but to categories of people. In every society there are youngsters who defy the prediction one would make about their educational attainment on the basis of their family background alone. Genetic factors, illness and other personal experiences, and accidents of circumstance, produce differences among children from otherwise identical family backgrounds. As a social matter, however, the cards are everywhere stacked against the child with the less-favorable family origin.

How to prevent the transmission of income- and social inequality between generations has forever been a challenge to people concerned with equality. For most Utopians it was the central problem in the design of a Good Society, but it also occupied the thought of people like Marx and Engels, who regarded themselves as anti-Utopian. Engels found his way to a solution that has long been popular in many quarters – that a Good Society dedicated to equality must transfer the work of raising children from their parents to social institutions like child-care centers and schools. Only then can every child be said to have an equal opportunity to acquire education, untainted by the differences among their parents.

No society has put that kind of policy to a full test, but some have moved a considerable way in that direction. Two cases that merit notice are the Soviet Union during its first decades, and the Israeli kibbutz.

THE USSR

In the eyes of the Bolshevik leadership, schooled in Marxism, the class-based oppression that characterizes capitalism is mirrored in all of its social institutions – among them, the family. Much as capitalists oppress workers, so husbands oppress wives and parents oppress children. The bourgeois family stood in the way of the liberation of women and the creation of the "New Soviet Man" whose loyalty would be extended to all the people rather than to his own kin.

Economic and political considerations supported that ideological hostility to the family. For example, it was estimated that food preparation in individual households in Russia took 36 million work-hours a day, while centralized food preparation would have required only

6 million hours. Releasing women from that chore would therefore not only strike a blow for gender equality but would also provide a massive injection of additional labor into social production. The political consideration was that the Bolsheviks governed a large and diverse population, huge numbers of whom were hostile to the conception of the Good Society that the Readership was resolved to bring into being. The family was a major competitor with the Party for the loyalty of the citizens, and particularly of the youth. It was the chief vehicle through which the individualism, religious superstition, anti-Communist sentiment, and other "filth of the old world is passed on to the youth."[43]

History was on their side, as the Party saw it: no one could doubt that after the socialist revolution abolished private property, the family would wither away, along with other institutions of oppression such as religion and the state itself. But not at once. Bourgeois social institutions had shaped the minds of people for a very long time, and were too tenacious to be abolished immediately. Nor were the resources yet available for replacing the traditional family functions by socialized food preparation, child-rearing, and so forth. The family would therefore endure for some time, but the society would "grow out of the family shell" by gradually taking over so many of its functions that it would soon lose its reason for being.[44]

The campaign against the family began shortly after the revolution and endured until the early 1930s. It followed a number of tracks, one of which was the weakening of the legal bonds between spouses: for example, by the introduction of "postcard divorce" – the right of either spouse to end a marriage simply by sending a postcard to the marriage registration bureau. Another major track was designed to weaken the effect of family environment on the rearing of children. Having inherited a highly class-stratified society, the first concern was to neutralize the effect of social origin on the educational attainment of children. This was done by a program of what would now be called affirmative action; that is, active discrimination in favor of previously underprivileged groups. The children of workers and poor peasants were given priority access to schools and to higher-education institutions, and children of upper-class background and of better-off peasants were admitted to schools only if there were enough spaces after the newly privileged children were enrolled.[45] The policy opened up educational opportunities for children of workers and peasants that they would not have had before the revolution. Its equalizing effect was partially neutralized, however, by the fact that they dropped out in large numbers and relatively few continued into the higher grades, while the children in families of higher education continued to receive instruction at home. The policy therefore achieved less than its promoters had hoped.

The most radical policy for diminishing family influence, however, was a campaign to deprive parents of much of the authority they traditionally exercised over their children. Legal writings of the time declared that Soviet law categorically denied the authority of the parental relationship. Children were taught in school that respect and obedience were due only to parents who supported the Party, and parents were forbidden to use physical punishment. The most chilling sign of the times was the veneration that children were expected to pay to the boy martyr, Pavlik Morozov. In 1930 Pavlik had denounced his own father as a traitor to the revolution, and was later killed by his relatives for that deed. The official idolization of Pavlik Morozov greatly restrained many parents from exercising vigorous discipline over their children.[46]

Party-directed youth organizations and schools were the chief instruments whereby the Party substituted its child-rearing doctrines for those of parents. School teachers, however, were also restrained from exercising the traditional forms of discipline over their pupils. Their authority over their pupils and the school environment was restricted; grades were eliminated and pupils' organizations were given considerable influence over curriculum. Teachers, like parents, were to be accorded respect by their pupils according to the extent of their support of the Party.[47]

Hence, children from diverse family backgrounds received a fairly uniform stream of messages from the Party and its allies about how good Soviet children should behave and what they should believe, uncomplicated by contradictory messages from religious or politically hostile parents or teachers. It was about as much as a minority government could do in reducing the impact of differing family environments on the development of children.

The anti-family campaign flourished in the 1920s when private ownership and markets were still tolerated. That toleration ended with the launching of the ambitious First Five-Year Plan in 1929. Rapid industrialization required a tightening of economic discipline, and as the young people who grew up in the 1920s began pouring into the factories and the army, reports of disciplinary problems started coming in from enterprise managers and military officers. Many of the young people refused to accept the authority of their seniors, did not readily take orders from their employers or commanders, insisted on forming committees to discuss every operational issue, and could not adapt to the requirements of tightly run organizations. For all the good that the anti-family campaign had done, it was now seen to have had one large negative effect – it had produced a generation of children too undisciplined for the great task of rapid industrialization on which the government had embarked.

The Party, now totally controlled by Stalin, responded by a radical reversal of policy. The family was declared to be a "basic cell" of Soviet society, instead of an institution slated for euthanasia as circumstances permitted. Marriages had to be registered to be legally binding, and divorce became increasingly difficult to arrange. Domesticity and parenting were lauded as prominently as they had been vilified before, and love of parents became an ethical absolute for children, without the political conditions tacked onto it in the past. Parents and teachers were exhorted to supervise the children more rigorously, and parents faced fines or even criminal prosecution for the delinquent acts of their children. In the schools, grades were restored, the activities of pupils' organizations greatly curtailed, and the authority of teachers reasserted.[48]

With the abandonment of the anti-family policy, the state gave up on its effort to eliminate the influence of parental differences on inequality in education. In the course of time family-based differences in educational attainment reemerged and endured to the end of the Communist period. The pre-revolutionary elite was replaced by a new Soviet elite – engineers, managers, artists, and political officials who had received their education in the socialist society, and many of whom were children of workers and peasants. The children of the educated Soviet elite lived in the better neighborhoods, went to the better schools, and enjoyed the services of tutors when needed. School admissions were generally based on ability, and some bright, talented children of working-class and peasant families were to be found in all the best schools. But the children of the new elite completed more years of schooling, and studied in more prestigious institutions, than working-class and peasant children. Other social differences asserted themselves as well: urban children performed better than rural, Armenian and Jewish children performed better than Russians, who performed better than Muslims, and so on. As time went on, the children of more favorable family background benefitted further from the creeping vulnerability of the system to influence and corruption in school admissions.

In the spirit of what had been declared to be a workers' state, various forms of affirmative action continued to be practiced. At the post-secondary level children of workers and peasants were often admitted even when their grades were somewhat below those of elite applicants. At the end of this long history, however, the usual factors of family background played out in educational performance: the children of low-education parents generally lagged behind those of high-education parents in educational attainment, and therefore in the acquisition of skills and access to jobs.

The Soviet experiment may be regarded as having succeeded in its primary objective: differences in family background exerted less influence on the educational attainment of children than in the society that preceded it, or that followed it. It was abandoned, however, because of the unanticipated consequence that the children were too undisciplined to suit the requirements of the modern industrial society that the leadership had set out to create.

The special conditions of that Soviet experiment were such, however, that it is unlikely to hold much appeal to people seeking enlightenment about the Good Society. Above all, it was the case of an unrepresentative and authoritarian government imposing its own values upon a largely hostile population. A very different policy for achieving many of the same objectives was that of the Israeli kibbutz, where it operated with the full consent of the population under fully democratic conditions.

THE KIBBUTZ

The pioneers of the kibbutz movement were largely young, unattached persons seeking political and personal fulfillment in the comradeship of cooperative labor and communal living. Little attention was paid to the matter of child-care until the first babies started to come along. The kibbutz then embarked on its first major transition – from "one big happy family" to a "collective village" in which the members belonged to different families.[49]

Some of the ideological considerations that dominated in the decision regarding the best arrangements for the care and rearing of the children were similar to those in the Soviet Union and in Sweden. One was the view that equality between the sexes could be maintained only if women were able to participate in the production and other activities of the society on equal terms with men; that meant that they had to be liberated from the home-centered responsibilities borne by women in the bourgeois family. The other was the firm belief that parents were a "pathogenic" factor in child-rearing; everyone would be better off if the children were reared by trained people rather than by the amateurish efforts of parents in the manner of the bourgeois family.[50] Ideological factors of these sorts were strongly supported by pressing economic considerations: it was self-evident that if the care of the babies were undertaken collectively, rather than by each family individually, there would be more time available for essential defense and farming activities and less strain on the tight housing conditions. It was out of that combination of ideological and practical considerations that the institution of collective child-rearing was born.

The children lived, ate, played, and slept, in a communal children's house, from the earliest age until they became full members of the kibbutz. Growing up together in that intimate way, they formed strong lifelong bonds, rather like a community of brothers and sisters – or at least cousins. The staff consisted of kibbutz members, for most of whom child-care was their permanent work assignment. They were usually women, who were drawn to working with children, and in whom the other members had confidence.

Several hours were set aside after work each day and on weekends for the children to visit with their parents, after which they returned to the children's house for the night. The family continued to be a major social institution in kibbutz life, and parents were involved in their own children's development as much as they wished to be. Some parents saw very little of their children, while others developed fairly close bonds with theirs.

The kibbutz children's house was about as far as a society could go in repressing the influence of family differences on children's development while maintaining the family as a basic social unit. To be sure, as the children grew up together, they developed different personalities, interests, and talents, and some performed better in school than others. But the extent to which individual differences were due to the differences among the parents was very likely smaller than among children in the larger society. Hence such inequality as developed among them in later life – which consisted of social status rather than material economic circumstances – was primarily reflective of individual endowments and experiences rather than of different family environments.

Hence, a society that places a high value on equal access to education and skills would find the kibbutz children's house to be an effective arrangement for achieving that objective. It also helped to attain some of the pioneers' other goals. It offered mothers the opportunity to participate in economic and public life on equal terms with fathers, and it helped to raise generations of children whose values were more societal and less individual than those in the outside world, and who were accustomed to living and working in close cooperation with each other.

For all those impressive achievements, however, like so many of the classic kibbutz arrangements, this one also came under assault in the course of time. The principal reason is that as the children grew to adulthood, they gradually acquired very different views from those of their parents about the value of the children's house and the kind of people it produced. The pioneers had wanted to create a "New Man," socialized from birth for the ideal communal life of the kibbutz. The children, however, wanted to live a "normal" life, like that of the friends they made in the army – more individual and less dependent on their group.[51] As they themselves became parents, many recalled the terrors of the night, away from their own parents, when the house mother was not always there to comfort them. Others regretted that they were not there to participate in such critical events in their children's lives as the taking of the first step, or to be available when the child had some frightening experience at school or some heady success. Intense debates took place in the General Meetings throughout the kibbutz movement, with the younger members urging that their children be permitted to live with them, and the older members seeing the rebellion as the betrayal of the egalitarian and societal values to which they had dedicated their lives.

In the event, a growing number of kibbutzim voted to abandon the crucial feature of the children's house – the overnight dormitory, which is now all but a piece of history. In virtually all kibbutzim, parents and children live together on a permanent basis, as in a traditional family – or, as the embittered old-timers say, a "bourgeois" family. The changeover to family living was a costly decision, for it required remodelling most of the homes in order to add bedrooms for the children. Most kibbutz children now spend their days in the community school and the rest of their time in their homes, much like children elsewhere.

The success of the classic kibbutz children's house in its time should give some comfort to people who wonder whether a Good Society with democratic institutions can suppress the inter-generational transmission of equality through family environment. The discouraging fact, however, is that it was eventually rejected by most of the people who grew up under it, even though the conditions under which it operated were close to ideal. Few societies, moreover, are sufficiently similar to the kibbutz to be able to employ that arrangement, or to expect similar results if they did – among other reasons, because the kibbutz is a self-selected, small community, whose members are very similar in social and cultural background and share a common set of values. In such a community, even with a conventional family organization, the children would begin their schooling with a family-derived endowment that is much more homogeneous than in the usual large modern society. Ironically, the equality-oriented society that has the least need for an arrangement like the children's house is the kind of society in which it is most likely to succeed.

INTER-GENERATIONAL INEQUALITY AND THE ECONOMIC MECHANISM

That some children are penalized because of the inferior economic, social, or educational status of their parents will forever distress many seekers of the Good Society. The most distressed will be tempted to strike at the roots of that evil by eliminating the traditional parent–child relationship and replacing it by socialized child-rearing. Unless they have reason to believe that they could carry it off better than the USSR and the kibbutz, however, they are unlikely to tread that path again. They will make their peace with the unhappy prospect that in the best of Good Societies some children will start off handicapped by the conditions of the family into which they were born.

The goodness of a society should therefore be judged not by whether it has eliminated all traces of family inequality in the educational attainment of children, but by the extent to which it has reduced that inequality. It might seem that a society that places a high value on reducing inter-generational inequality to a minimum should choose planning as its economic mechanism. As in the case of job discrimination, however, the economic mechanism is rather neutral on this matter. Much more important are the political system and the property-ownership arrangements.

The dominating reason for family-derived differences in educational attainment in modern economies is income inequality, which prevails in both planned and market economies, though it is much smaller in the former. Both types of economy have accepted the value of individual choice, in the sense that families are free to spend as much of their income as they wish on things relating to their children's education. Measures to "level the playing field" are normally confined to "levelling up" – that is, reducing the spread between the most and the least educationally advantaged by supplementing the resources provided to the latter. In both planned and market economies, however, there are many ways in which that is done, the most significant of which is the provision of universal free education. The children of the rich, therefore, acquire as much education as they would in the absence of government intervention, but the children of poor and middle-income families acquire much more. Some countries reduce the educational-opportunity gap more than others by such measures, but there is little prospect that any modern society will ever seek to close the gap entirely by "levelling down"; that is, by limiting the right of the rich to spend their incomes in ways that enhance their children's education.

Hence, despite measures like universal free education, urban schools are better than rural schools everywhere, and everywhere some urban schools are better than others. Richer Soviet families managed to send their children to the better schools and to buy tutorial and other educational services, much like richer American families. In these respects, it is politics and not the economic mechanism that determines how far the society will go in levelling the educational playing-field for children. A society that is militantly determined to combat the influence of family income on children's educational opportunity would find either economic mechanism sufficiently accommodating to its purpose.

Since family-income inequality is much larger in the market economies, however, the educational differences among children are much greater than in the planned economies. Again, however, the major source of the greater family-income inequality lies not in the economic mechanisms as such but in the property-ownership arrangements. Property income accounts for much of the greater income inequality in the market economies, all of which happen to be capitalist. In the absence of capitalist property income, the income distribution in the market economies would not be radically different from that in planned economies, and the educational advantage of higher-income families would be roughly the same under both mechanisms.[52]

8 Discussion

When wages are unequal a society must have a way of responding to those of its citizens who regard it as unfair that their wage is smaller than somebody else's. I have found no better way of answering that question than that which is provided by the market mechanism. The reason your wage is lower, one would explain, is that the value of what the other person produces is larger than the value of what you produce.

Since differences in productivity are heavily influenced by accident of birth, both familial and personal, this view cannot claim that it rewards only achievement or merit. My Good Society, however, would provide extensive resources for the care and education of children from deprived backgrounds, but it would not expect to eliminate all traces of the influence of early deprivation. Its claim to the loyalty of its lower-wage citizens is that it provides the fullest opportunity for economic attainment through effort and ability; but it cannot undo all the effects of the pre-employment experiences of its citizens.

That productivity-wage principle has certain odd consequences, but I find them entirely equitable. It does not seem unfair to me that my wage should rise or fall in response to changes in the supply of labor. I would be quite content if my wage as a trash collector or as a professor should increase if a "shortage" of workers with those qualifications should develop – perhaps because fewer people chose to enter those occupations. In the same vein, it should not be regarded as unfair if my wage should decline under conditions of "excess supply"; that is, when more workers are seeking jobs like mine.

Nor is it unfair that my wage should respond to changes in the demand for the things I produce. However diligently I work, if some people no longer wish to pay for the things I am good at producing, it is not unreasonable that I should earn less. I cannot expect to earn the same wage forever regardless of whether or not my fellow citizens want to consume the things I produce. I certainly think it fair that I should earn more if the demand for my goods should increase so much that people are willing to pay twice the price for them that they did before.

The same case could be made for the fairness of wage determination under the planning mechanism, for that too is based on the principle of productivity differences. Under that system, however, productivity is measured on the basis of the training required to hold the job and other elements of job-content, which have only the vaguest connection to the value of what is produced by the incumbent of the job. Wage rates are set for every occupation in the whole country, moreover, by a huge sluggish bureaucracy that cannot hope to keep up with the continuous changes in productivity wrought by the technological and other changes to which the economy is subject. Hence, a worker with certain skills will continue to receive the same wage long after people have ceased to value the goods that he produces. I would rather that my wage be set in a competitive labor market than that it be calculated by a formula applied by an official in a national bureaucratic agency.

I am aware that because of the many imperfections in competition, most people's wage rates are not in fact equal to their marginal productivity. Would it were not so! I sometimes wish the economic world were more like that travel brochure of perfect competition – that idealized world in which all workers receive their just wage based on their marginal productivity. But labor markets in fact are rarely perfectly competitive; rarely are there large numbers of workers competing for jobs and large numbers of employers competing for workers. Usually there are large numbers of workers but only a few small employers. Fortunately, labor unions help right the balance in what would otherwise be a huge preponderance of power in the hands of employers. Unions also provide indispensable protection against the insult and tyranny to which workers are sometimes subject because of the unequal distribution of market power between them and their employers. In that and other ways, countervailing forces often arise in democratic societies that limit the inequities of imperfect competition. There is very little public support for large corporations that get into trouble because of their own mismanagement, or for strikes for higher wages by workers whose wages are already far above the crowd.

It all makes for a very untidy package of arrangements. There are times when the conflict over wage rates and other work conditions is so intense and destructive that the old feeling comes on that "there must be a better way." The strike, after all, does not seem like an ideal instrument for resolving wage issues in a Good Society. It takes constant reminding about the deficiencies of the alternative – the planning mechanism – to appreciate the merits of the market mechanism as it works in practice.

In most market economies the government plays a very small role in direct wage determination. Even in Sweden, where the role of government is perhaps the largest, wage rates for individual jobs are hammered out in negotiations between individual enterprises and their labor unions within the limits of the nationwide agreements. Only in periods of national emergency like wartime do governments get into the business of detailed wage-rate determination, and that experience lends strong support to the conviction that it is a business that governments should stay out of in normal times. Particularly in a democracy, if government had the power to decide what the wage of each occupation would be, considerations of equity would dissolve entirely in the face of the pressures from politically powerful groups.

It is primarily on the matter of a minimum wage that the governments of market economies get involved in direct wage determination. In my opinion a minimum wage is bad policy. The main reason is the danger that it will lead to unemployment, particularly of young and low-skill workers for whom the availability of jobs should be a major social objective. The secondary reason is that it frustrates the ability of the market mechanism to do what it does best – use resources efficiently. When enterprises have adjusted to the prohibition against paying wages below the minimum, the wrong workers end up working at the wrong jobs, producing the wrong goods, even if the labor force is fully employed.

There are times when there is no way of achieving an important social objective without interfering with the operation of markets, but very often there are alternatives. In this case the main alternative is the minimum-income approach. As presented in the text, that policy is not without its drawbacks either, but it seems to me that the loss is less than that produced by the distortion of market wage rates and prices caused by a minimum wage. The difference between wage rates as "signals" and wage rates as "incomes" is a fundamental distinction to be drawn in the economics of the Good Society. As an alternative to a minimum wage, an income transfer leaves the wage-as-signal intact, focussing instead on that which is the real source of concern – the wage-as-income. The society decides, in effect, that it respects the power of the market mechanism to allocate labor efficiently, but it rejects one aspect of the way in which the market mechanism distributes income among the people. The effect of an income transfer is that some people – usually the underprivileged and the unskilled – consume more than their wage would permit, while all other workers agree to consume less than their wage would permit; but the wage remains what the market declares it to be.

The distinction between wages as signals and wages as incomes is often lost on people who have lived all their lives in market economies and are generously sensitive to their deficiencies – such as low incomes and unemployment – but appear not to appreciate the contribution that the market mechanism has made to the material comfort of their families and of the masses of their compatriots. The market mechanism is thought of as the enemy whose nefarious results are to be contained, rather than as a friend whose value is appreciated but some of whose actions must be modified. Like the fate of Julius Caesar, the good that the market does is rarely celebrated, while the evil is always there for all to see.

The point of this harangue is to caution against remedies that distort the signals by which markets find their way toward efficiency. There are often alternatives like income transfers that do less violence to the market mechanism, and the Good Society should prefer them to others that inject more politics and government into the determination of wages and prices.

The welfare state   The lesson of the welfare state is about possibilities and limitations. The most heartening of the possibilities is that every modern market economy has the means to virtually eliminate poverty, though it may not have the social knowledge with which to accomplish it. The limitation is that most social programs cause people to behave in ways that over time sap the vigor of the economy. If there is little or no penalty for calling in sick, or if a worker who quits a job collects 90 percent or more of his pay while unemployed, or if taxes take 80 percent or more of every extra dollar earned, you can be sure that the level of output and consumption will be lower than in similar countries with more traditional practices. Any Good Society that introduces new social initiatives without taking account of such responses is headed for a lot of trouble.

I know people who regard that assertion as a libel on the human race; they believe that if you expect good things of people, they will act accordingly. While that may well be the case in interpersonal relations, there is no better evidence than the Swedish story that that is not the case on a national scale.

My own Good Society would be modelled more on the German social-market economy than the Swedish welfare state. A full societal effort would be made to alleviate poverty and if possible to eliminate it, and to provide decent assistance to other disadvantaged citizens. The supply of such "merit goods" as education and health would not be left entirely to the market mechanism but would be extensively supported by government. For the rest, the citizens as individuals would expect to arrange such services as child-care and old-age care for themselves rather than depend on government to supply them.

Discrimination Under both economic mechanisms, discrimination in employment is in large part the consequence of discriminatory traditions in the society itself. It should not, therefore, be regarded as a deficiency of the "system," but as a deficiency of the society and of the values of some of its citizens. In a society that is free of racial, religious, or sex discrimination, the economic mechanism, whether markets or planning, would also be free of discrimination. Hence, if you want a non-discriminatory economy, find a country whose values you like and a political system that gives them expression. Don't count on the economic mechanism to do the job.

The point is important because many people who are outraged by discrimination live by the illusion that black or female workers in the American market economy would be liberated from such discrimination if America became a planned economy. What they would be liberated from is the distress of job insecurity that they share with other workers, but they should not expect to be freed from all the other ways in which social discrimination penetrates economic and other institutions. The extent of discrimination tends to decline when shortages of labor appear, as happens in periods of war or rapid growth; but that occurs under both economic mechanisms. Where discrimination is buttressed by law, as in the United States before the civil rights movement, the best hope for the elimination of discrimination lies not in the economic but the political arrangements of the society. Disadvantaged groups are rarely liberated by the good conscience of the more advantaged. It usually takes organized protest and political pressure to raise the consciousness of self-satisfied majorities enough to marshal the force of law against discrimination. Protest movements do not always succeed, and never succeed fully, but they can make headway only under democratic institutions that respect the political rights of minorities. Champions of social equality should care more about the political arrangements of their Good Society than about the relative merits of plans and markets.

Unequal access A democratic society offers a vast range of possibilities for modifying the outcomes of the market mechanism in ways that the society judges to be more equitable. There is one source of inequity, however, in which the market economies rank very low on my score-card of goodness. They are unable to provide equal access to the skills required by the job.

I trust that no democratic society will intervene in the family life of its citizens in the ways that would be required in order to insulate children fully from the effects of differences in family characteristics. The best of societies will therefore have no fully satisfactory answer to the child who asks "Why should my life chances be diminished because of the family into which I was born?"

The best that can be done in a society that aspires to justice is to adopt policies that reduce the inequality among parents and among children. I will discuss income inequality in chapter 28, but for the present purpose, I offer three observations. The first is that no society, whether planned or market, has managed to eliminate income inequality among families, however strong its dedication to equality. It would be Utopian to imagine that some Good Society of the future will finally find the formula for eliminating inequality. The prudent path is to anticipate inequality in the best of societies, and then to set about dealing with it.

The second observation is that the degree of income inequality, like that of job security, depends on much more than the economic mechanism. It varies enormously among countries with the same economic mechanism: Czechoslovakia was far more egalitarian than the USSR and the other planned economies, and Sweden and the United Kingdom are much more egalitarian than the United States and other market economies (chapter 28). The point is important because it means that both economic mechanisms can accommodate a very wide range of economic and social policies. Such policies, however, are greatly affected by cultural and historical conditions: policies that the Swedes regard as quite acceptable may be unimaginable or repugnant to the American electorate, and similarly in planned economies. That variety of economic experience suggests that the policies of an American planned economy would strongly reflect traditional American values, much as the policies of the Soviet planned economy reflected traditional Russian values. The critique of inequality in the United States is as often a critique of the values of Americans as it is a critique of the American economy.

The trouble with democracy is that if you do not share the social outlook of most of your fellow citizens, you will forever find your government's responses inadequate. Too often such dissatisfaction is misdirected against the economic mechanism – the "system" – as if things would be much better if the society adopted a different mechanism.

The third observation is that, by my values, the major problem of equal access is not inequality but poverty; that is, not the income distribution overall, but the low end of the distribution. Complete equality is beyond the reach of the best of societies, but all modern economies have the resources with which to provide their poorest families with sufficient income to provide the housing, clothing, food, schooling, and other resources required for a child's educational development. That would not eliminate family-derived inequality in access to education, but it would provide a defensible response to the child who asks whether it is fair that I be penalized because of the family into which I have been born. It would not be a bad society at all that could reply that it cannot provide each child with equal parentage, but it does assure that every child has a reasonable, if not equal, opportunity to achieve the highest level of educational attainment of which she is capable.

Notes

1   Marx, "Critique of the Gotha Programme," pp. 276–7.
2   Kirsch, *Soviet Wages*, p. 10.
3   Kirsch, *Soviet Wages*, app. A.
4   Informal competition among enterprises for particularly scarce types of labor does drive socialist managers to skirt the rules in order to offer higher wage earnings to those workers. That is done by such devices as declaring a Grade IV worker to be Grade VI, or paying for overtime that was not actually worked. However, since prices do not reflect the true social valuation of the goods produced, the value of the output produced by workers recruited in that way may bear very little relation to the padded wages that they earn.
5   Phelps, "Low-wage employment subsidies," p. 56.
6   Kennan, "The elusive effects of minimum wages," p. 1964.

7   Card and Krueger, *Myth and Measurement*. These authors have acknowledged, however, that "there was a tipping point where a great enough increase in the minimum wage would start to reduce employment." *The New York Times*, March 20, 1998, p. A14.

8   An OECD study of nine countries concluded that a 10 percent rise in the minimum wage reduces teenage employment by 2–4 percent. That rule holds where the minimum wage is high as well where it is low. *The Economist*, June 27, 1998, p. 80.

9   Phelps, "Low-wage employment subsidies."

10 Childs, *Sweden: The Middle Way*.

11 Lundberg, "The rise and fall of the Swedish model," p. 1.

12 Olsen, *The Struggle for Economic Democracy in Sweden*, p. 2.

13 OECD, *Economic Surveys*: Sweden 1993–4, p. 84.

14 Lundberg, "The rise and fall of the Swedish model," p. 34.

15 OECD, *Economic Surveys*: Sweden 1993–4, p. 78.

16 OECD, *Economic Surveys*: Sweden 1993–4, pp. 79, 86.

17 Lindbeck, "The Swedish experiment," p. 1278.

18 Lindbeck et al., *Turning Sweden Around*, pp. 94, 116; OECD *Economic Surveys*: Sweden 1993–4, pp. 79, 83.

19 Lindbeck, "The Swedish experiment," p. 1278.

20 Lundberg, "The rise and fall of the Swedish model," pp. 12, 29.

21 The Gini coefficients in the mid-1980s were .194 in Sweden, .251 in Germany, and .312 in the United States. OECD, *Economic Surveys*: Sweden 1993–4, p. 84.

22 Lindbeck, "The Swedish experiment," p. 1285.

23 Lindbeck, "The Swedish experiment," pp. 1278–82; OECD, *Economic Surveys*: Sweden 1993–4, pp. 90, 99.

24 Thurow, *Generating Inequality*, p. 49.

25 Lindbeck, "The Swedish experiment," p. 1297.

26 Lindbeck, "The Swedish experiment," p. 1301. See also pp. 1297–1300, and OECD, *Economic Surveys*: Sweden 1993–4, p. 89.

27 Lundberg, "The rise and fall of the Swedish model," p. 34.

28 The sources are the Congressional Budget Office and other government agencies, as reported in *The New York Times*, November 20, 1994, p. 5. The 60-percent figure is my estimate based on the reported data.

29 OECD, *Economic Surveys*: Sweden 1993–4, p. 88.

30 Lindbeck et al., *Turning Sweden Around*, p. 116.

31 OECD, *Economic Surveys*: Sweden 1993–4, pp. 86–8. Also Lindbeck et al., *Turning Sweden Around*, pp. 94, 118, 122.

32 Dodge, *Women in the Soviet Union*, pp. 103–5.

33 Lapidus, *Women in Soviet Society*, ch. 5.

34 Lapidus, *Women in Soviet Society*, ch. 5.

35 Ofer and Vinocur, *The Soviet Household*, ch. 7.

36 Monousova, "Gender differentiation in industrial relations"; Bowers, "Gender stereotyping and gender division of labour in Russia."

37 Myrdal, *An American Dilemma*.

38 Thernstrom and Thernstrom, *America in Black and White*, p. 531.

39 Thernstrom and Thernstrom, *America in Black and White*, pp. 531–5.

40 *The New York Times*, June 23, 1997, p. A1.

41 Hart and Risley, *Meaningful Differences in the Everyday Experience of Young American Children*, p. 210.

42 Hart and Risley, *Meaningful Differences in the Everyday Experience of Young American Children*, pp. 2–4.

43 Geiger, *The Family in Soviet Russia*, pp. 47–52.

44 Geiger, *The Family in Soviet Russia*, p. 45.

45 Widmayer, "The evolution of Soviet education policy."

46 Geiger, *The Family in Soviet Russia*, p. 54.

47 Widmayer, "The evolution of Soviet education policy."

48 Geiger, *The Family in Soviet Russia*, pp. 88–93; Widmayer, "The evolution of Soviet education policy."

49 Blasi, *The Communal Experience of the Kibbutz*, p. 124.

50 Near, *The Kibbutz Movement*, p. 365.

51 Spiro, *Kibbutz*, pp. 279–80.

52 The argument strengthens the case for market socialism. Under that arrangement the productive property is socially owned and does not generate unequal family-income flows. Income distribution would therefore be about the same as under planning, and the inter-generational transmission of educational inequality would be no greater than under planning.

Part V

Property Ownership

Chapter 22

Who Should Own
the Property?

Property is theft.
*— **Proudhon***

CONTENTS

Who should own the property in a Good Society? That question is the Continental Divide in attitudes toward economic organization. All the rivers of socioeconomic thought flow either to the Left or to the Right of that Divide. More than any other question, it has separated the streams of socialist thought from those of capitalism. All the issues that have been discussed up to this point are a side-show: interesting perhaps, and possibly important, but not yet center stage. The main act is the question of the ownership of the property of the society's production enterprises.

The issue concerns only productive property, and not personal property like household furniture and jewelry. No major society has regarded personal property as anything other than private. Small societies committed to a communal and ascetic life sometimes discourage the ownership of any personal property other than the most intimate, like toothbrushes; but among large societies, even the most communal-minded, like Maoist China, permitted private ownership of personal effects like clothing and household items. The question of what goods should be considered private – books, for example – has generated a surprising amount of heat in finely tuned ideological debate in communities like the kibbutz, but the heart of the matter is the ownership of property that is used in the society's production enterprises.

I Forms of Ownership

A society can choose from among a wide variety of forms of ownership that have been employed in modern economies. They may be divided into two main groups – private and social – but there are a great many sub-types within each group. Among the various forms of social ownership in particular, at least three need to be distinguished. Under one arrangement, the state owns the enterprises. Under a second, the enterprises are owned by public bodies of various kinds but not by the state. Under the third, each enterprise is owned by its workers. Those are the four principal ownership forms from which a Good Society must choose. They are the subjects of Part V.

In the discussion to follow, each ownership form is considered as if it were the only one in the economy. In practice, however, one form of ownership usually predominates but other forms coexist with it. In most capitalist countries at various times, post offices, railroads, naval shipyards, municipal water systems and arms factories have been government-owned. Private ownership predominates in the US today, but there are significant instances of public ownership, such as the Massachusetts Bay Transit Authority, the Port Authority of New York, the Tennessee Valley Authority, and many others. There are also enterprises that incorporate significant degrees of worker ownership, and even some that are wholly worker-owned. In the Communist countries the enterprises were predominantly state-owned, but various forms of producer cooperatives (barber shops) and private enterprises (peasant household plots) were quite substantial in some cases.

While most economies contain a variety of ownership forms, the economic tone is set by the dominant form. A British public corporation conducts most of its business with private-sector enterprises and is greatly influenced by that dominant environment. One cannot therefore infer from its performance how efficient publicly owned enterprise would be in an economy in which all enterprises were publicly owned.

Private, public, and worker ownership can operate only in combination with the market mechanism. They will therefore be examined only in a market context. State ownership, however, can operate under both planning and markets. In the Communist countries, which supply most of the empirical evidence on the subject, the economic mechanism was almost invariably planning. State ownership will therefore be examined in chapter 24 as it operates in a planned economy. From time to time, however, there will be occasion to consider how it might operate under market-based socialism.

2   The Rights of Ownership

In popular discourse the notion of ownership is fairly straightforward – one either owns something or one does not. In assessing the wide variety of ownership forms, however, it has been found useful to think of ownership as consisting of a "bundle" of different rights. That is to say, to own something is to enjoy certain rights with respect to that thing. A society is free to accord to persons and organizations certain rights of ownership but not others, according to its own criteria of goodness such as equity or efficiency. Three such rights command the most attention.

One is the right to the net income of the enterprise, which normally means the profit. Under worker ownership, for example, the workers as a group have a claim on all the net income that is left over after all other claims (supplies, interest on loans, taxes). The second is the right to sell all or part of the property and pocket the proceeds. And the third is the right to use the property for some desired end: for example, to decide on the policies of a company, including hiring and firing staff.

Ownership may consist of one, two, or all three of those rights and others, depending on the time, place, and object. The feudal landowner had only two of them: the right to the net income that could be squeezed out of his peasants, and the right to decide whether the land would be used for fox hunting or for farming; but he did not have the right to sell it. The land "belonged" to the family, past and future, and the current landowner was merely the steward of the land during his lifetime. Some of the post-Communist countries are experimenting with a similar form of land ownership, in which the farmer can work the land and keep the profit, but cannot sell it. In private-ownership economies, however, the owner normally enjoys all three rights.

In the case of state ownership, the precise identity of the "owner" is somewhat fuzzy. In Communist countries the property is said to belong to the people collectively, with the state serving as their agent; but in law as in practice, the effective owner is the state, or the government as its agent. Public corporations like the French National Railroad Association enjoy all three rights of ownership, but they do not "own" the profit in the same sense as private companies own their profit. The members of the boards of directors of public corporations are fiduciary agents of the public, bound to use the profits for the mission specified in the charter. Unlike private corporations, there are no stockholder-owners who have a claim on the profit as their personal income.

3 Restrictions on Property Rights

Every society places certain restrictions on the uses that owners may make of their property. Among the restrictions one finds in most countries at present are those that affect the environment (you cannot pollute the air without limit), public safety (you may have to construct a fence around your backyard swimming pool and remove the lead paint in a rental property), and conspiracy (you cannot conspire with others to fix prices).

The kinds of restrictions that ought to be placed on the uses that private owners may make of their property is a proper and prominent policy issue in the economics of a Good Society. It is a somewhat different topic, however, than that of the choice between private and social ownership, with which we are presently concerned.[1]

Similar restrictions are imposed under social ownership. In democratic societies, public corporations and worker-owned enterprises must abide by the same restrictions that apply to private enterprises. Matters are less clear-cut under state ownership, for the state is both restrictor and restrictee: it sets the restrictions: and also owns and operates the enterprises that are bound by the restrictions. Hence, the state may restrict the quantity of farmland that the Ministry of Electric Power takes for its hydroelectric program, but if the state's enterprises are handicapped by a shortage of electric power, the state as owner may overrule the state as restrictor. Under the other forms of social ownership, however, state and enterprise are responsible to different constituencies.

Restrictions on the uses of property are often bitterly contested by the owners or their agents, under both private and social ownership. Soviet paper producers, for example, resisted environmental restrictions on their right to dump effluent into Lake Baikal no less fiercely than Cape Cod fishermen resist restrictions on the kinds and quantities of fish they may catch. Under all forms of ownership the issue of serious debate is not whether there ought to be such restrictions, but what restrictions contribute to the goodness of the society and what restrictions do not.

The next four chapters set forth the principal features of each of the ownership forms and evaluate them by the criterion of efficiency. Issues of equity are the subject of chapter 27.

Note

1   The two are not unrelated. I may prefer social ownership to completely unrestricted private ownership, but I may also prefer suitably restricted private ownership to social ownership.

Chapter 23

Private Ownership

All men possess greater regard for
what is their own than for what
they possess in common with others.
— *Aristotle*

CONTENTS

Small companies are often owned by one or a few persons who run the business themselves. They make business decisions with the objective of earning as much profit as possible because the profit constitutes their personal income. The owners may and do forgo opportunities to earn an extra dollar of profit here or there out of ethical or social considerations, but they are aware that they are that much poorer for having made that choice.

The organization of small proprietorships does not vary greatly within or between countries. The organization of large enterprises, however, varies greatly. In most countries they are usually organized as joint-stock corporations, but they differ widely in such matters as the number and identity of the stockholders and the form of corporate governance. In Japan and Germany most of them are "closely held" by a few owners of large blocks of stocks, often banks and other companies. Some American companies are also closely held, but most large companies have huge numbers of shareholders, many of whom own minute proportions of the outstanding shares. Many people are also indirect stockholders, through their interests in pension funds, mutual funds, and other "institutional investors," who hold large blocks of stocks in many companies. Ownership of most large American corporations is therefore widely dispersed among small and large individual and institutional stockholders. Each share of stock is entitled to one vote in the election of directors, so that holders of large blocks of stocks generally have the power to elect one or more directors who represent their interests. The board of directors, in turn, hires a president and a group of senior officials to manage the enterprise. The president normally serves as the chief executive officer, although the chairman of the board sometimes assumes that role.

Management   Management receive a compensation package consisting of an annual salary and a variety of other benefits and perks the size of which vary with the enterprise's performance, in particular with its profitability. Some of the directors may own large blocks of stock, or may be the agents of large owners. Others may sit on the board because of their specialized knowledge, or because their personal relationships with government or other organizations may be of value to the company. The president and some other senior executives may also serve as directors.

The board of directors is responsible for setting major company policy. Policy initiatives normally originate in management but must be approved by the board. Prominent among such policies is the disposition of the enterprise's profit: for example, the proportions of the profit to be used for financing investment in the enterprise and for distributing to the stockholders in the form of dividends. The board is also responsible for monitoring the performance of management in the interest of the stockholders.

Labor   A major responsibility of management is to hire labor. Wage rates and conditions of labor have changed greatly over the years, and vary considerably by country, by industry, by size of enterprise, by location, and so forth. In large, unionized enterprises, management–labor relations are elaborated in contracts that are periodically renegotiated. Normally the negotiations are reasonably smooth but on occasion they are tense and hostile and may erupt in strikes.

Private ownership lends itself to a great variety of different forms of management–labor relations. In Japan all the employees of the corporation, including management, are members of a company union. Wage rates and other conditions of employment are negotiated once a year, in what has become known as the "spring offensive." Sweden has developed a system in which national organizations of labor and of management meet under the aegis of the government and work out general guidelines for wage contracts for the forthcoming period. Individual enterprises and unions then negotiate contracts within those guidelines. Germany has introduced a form of industrial democracy in which labor is given representation on corporate boards of directors. British labor relations were long characterized by bitter conflict and violent strikes, in contrast to the relative peacefulness of labor relations in Germany and Scandinavia, but have become more peaceful in recent years.

A major factor in the success of management–labor relations is the profitability of the enterprise. If the country is prosperous and the enterprise profitable, management has considerable leeway in meeting the demands of labor for wage increases, job security, and terms of employment. When those conditions are not present, management is under pressure to hold wages down and to trim the labor force, if necessary by temporary furloughs or by dismissal. Large enterprises sometimes succeed in securing government subsidies in exchange for keeping labor on the payroll, but the essence of private ownership remains the interest of the owners in the profits of their investment. If profit considerations indicate or mandate a reduction in the size of the labor force, or even the closing down of entire enterprises, this will tend to be done. The owners then lose all or part of their wealth invested in the company and the workers lose their jobs.

I   Efficiency and Enterprise Size

The case for the efficiency of private ownership derives from the ancient commonsensical notion pronounced by Aristotle that people tend to care more for the things that are their own than for things that belong to others or to a common pool. As understood by the more thoughtful exponents of that ancient wisdom, the assertion that people pursue their self-interest does not mean that they are careless or neglectful or deliberately destructive of the property of others. All it says is that, while nice people are sensitive to others, they devote more care and attention to things that are their own. On a large social scale, it says that if all the property is privately owned, the citizens will devote more attention and effort to caring for it and using it in ways that provide them with the most benefit. In the case of productive property like factories and farmland, "most benefit" translates into "most profit."[1]

In a society that employs the market mechanism, however, profit-seeking is precisely what is required for the efficient functioning of the economy. Indeed, it is only when all productive property is used for the purpose of "maximizing profit" that the market mechanism can be shown to be efficient under ideal conditions. Hence the auspicious marriage between private ownership and the market mechanism: markets need seekers after profit, and private owners can be counted on to seek the largest profit that their property can produce. No external motivation is required; self-interest alone does the trick.

The prototype of the self-interest motivation are the owners of small companies – perhaps a furniture manufacturer or a retail store – who hire and supervise the workers, watch the cash register, and generally run the business themselves. Such owners may delegate certain responsibilities to some of their employees, which requires that they monitor their employees' work, but they know the business so well that they are confident of their assessment of their workers' performance. The profit of the enterprise is the personal income of the owners, and they are aware that every excessive expenditure on labor or other purchases, and every product that fails to find a customer, cuts into that profit.

At the dawn of the Industrial Revolution virtually all capitalist enterprises were owner-managed, and there are still about 16 million non-farm proprietorships in the United States.[2] They thrive in such businesses as retail trade, repair services, food catering, handicrafts, the arts, construction, and innovative high-tech production. They continue to make a major contribution to consumer welfare and account for a disproportionately large share of inventions and innovations.

In the big picture, however, the center of gravity of the modern economy has shifted decisively to the large enterprise. The number of corporations is only one-quarter that of proprietorships, but they do 15 times as much of the country's business.[3] The dominance of large enterprises is the result of a great many technological and organizational changes, one cluster of which is referred to as "economies of scale." Suppose, for example, that the owner of a small woodworking shop is considering the purchase of new equipment to increase production of a popular coffee-table. If the shop purchases equipment designed to produce 200 tables a day, the average cost of producing a table will be $30. If the scale of production is 1,000 tables a day, however, there is a line of more automated equipment with which the tables could be produced at a unit cost of only $20. Table production in that case is said to be characterized by economies of scale over that range of output: the larger the scale of production, the lower the unit cost of production.

Technological and organizational advances have steadily generated new economies of scale in a great many lines of production, thus reducing the unit cost of production while increasing the scale of production required to produce at that low cost.[4] Wherever such economies of scale appeared, under the force of competition the new, and usually more expensive, technology gradually displaced the older. The size of the capital investment required to survive the competition increased, as did the size of the labor force needed to handle the growing volume of production. As capital requirements and managerial demands grew, it became increasingly difficult for a single person to both own and manage the business in the manner of the past. The owner-manager enterprise gradually gave way to the large corporate enterprise, where there are many stockholder-owners, none of whom participates directly in the management of the enterprise. Instead, a professional manager is hired to run the enterprise in the interest of the owners. The transfer of the managerial function to hired management was a historic step in the evolution of private ownership.

2 Principals and Agents

Some degree of discretionary authority has to be delegated to professional management, which gives them control over many parts of the business that in small companies are under the direct control of the owner. That delegation of authority to management is the source of a major challenge to the case for the efficiency of private ownership. Originally formulated in 1932 by Adolph A. Berle and Gardiner C. Means as the problem of the "separation of owner-ship and control,"[5] it has lately been studied more rigorously as the "agency problem."

The agency problem deals with a relationship in which one party – called the principal – employs another party – called the agent – to carry out a number of tasks. The principal wishes to attain certain objectives and the problem is to assure that the agent pursues those objectives and not objectives of her own. The problem is confronted in the governance of organizations of all sorts – universities, armies, and hospitals, as well as production enter-prises, and in all countries and systems.

In the context of corporate governance, the stockholder-owners are the principals and man-agement is their agent. The principals' objective is to derive as much profit as possible from the operation of the business, and they wish their agent to run the company with that object-ive in view. The nub of the problem is that agents may use the power delegated to them to pursue their own objectives, which may conflict with the principals' interest in profit.

The kind of activity that first comes to mind is ordinary embezzlement or misappropria-tion. Management is often in a position to appropriate for itself some of the property of the owners: for example, to sell a batch of the company's goods under falsified documents and have the proceeds covertly delivered in cash or deposited in a personal bank account. It is not illegal activities of these sorts that the critics of the separation of ownership from man-agement have in mind. To be sure, instances of embezzlement do occur, for there are people in every profession in every large society for whom the lure of great gain overrides both the voice of conscience and the consequences of getting caught. But instances of it are relatively rare. For one thing, corporate executives are too visible to engage in criminal activities of that sort, and the sums involved are normally too small to justify the risk. Nor is embezzle-ment a concern of large corporations only: traditional owner-managers are and always have been concerned to monitor their employees to assure that they did not walk off with their money or their goods.

What critics like Berle and Means and their followers had in mind is that corporate man-agers often implement policies that advance their personal careers but are detrimental to the interests of the stockholders. For example, they may regularly plow the enterprise's profits back into the expansion of the company rather than distribute them to the owners as divi-dends, even though the return on internal investment may be smaller than could be obtained by investing elsewhere. They may push production and sales far beyond the most profitable rate of production in order to expand the size of company. They may persuade the owners to support a merger or acquisition that may not be in the owners' best interest, but from which management benefits personally by acquiring the valuable reputation of being the team that put the company on the map. Or they may radically alter the company's finan-cial position in order to avoid a "hostile takeover" that would leave them without jobs, even if the stockholders would be better served by the takeover.

Another line of criticism is that management follows a strategy of "satisficing," rather than maximizing the profit of the company. That means that once a comfortable profit position has been achieved in a market in which competition is not intense, management finds it safer to maintain that position rather than to enter on new ventures that might be justified on profit grounds but would involve a large risk for themselves.

The matter is of great importance because the case for the efficiency of private owner-ship stands or falls on the proposition that profit drives the behavior of privately owned enterprise. It is the pursuit of profit that maintains the constant pressure to keep costs down to a minimum and to produce the right quantities of output. It is because of such pressures that private ownership leads to the happy result of overall efficiency under ideal conditions.

The issue has spawned a huge volume of research to determine whether the empirical evidence supports the view that management pursues interests of its own that conflict with the stockholders' interest in profit. Since the potential for the divergence of interests seems so large, one would expect that all analysts would find some evidence of it in the data, and the only controversy would be the magnitude of the profits lost by stockholders because of it. As it turns out, however, empirical research continues to produce mixed results.[6] Still, no one disputes any longer that management does not always strive for the maximum of profit that the enterprise is capable of earning. Corporate offices are sited in locations that management finds it pleasant to live in, mergers are undertaken for the purpose of expanding management's power and prestige, sales meetings are held at luxurious vacation resorts, directors are paid lavish sums for their service on the board, and so on.

However, while many critics comment on these sorts of backsliding from profit-making, no one proposes that there is some incentive other than profit that better explains the crucial decisions – the quantities of output to be produced, the prices to be charged, the quantities of labor and other inputs to use in production, and the investments in expansion. The pursuit of profit, if not always the maximum of profit, is still the strongest driving force in a private-ownership economy.

In view of the clear and large potential for managerial behavior that conflicts with the owners' interests in profits, one may wonder why the extent of it is so limited that it does not emerge unambiguously in the empirical evidence. A number of factors contribute to that result.

3   Incentive Contracts

The principal/agent approach stresses the importance of writing the contract between the owners and their managers in such a way that management has a personal incentive to run the enterprise in a manner that coincides with the interest of the owners. There are two problems in accomplishing that. The first is that management must be given a great deal of discretionary authority. Contracts are therefore "incomplete," in the sense that they cannot specify how management is to act in every possible contingency. The second is the problem of "asymmetric information" – the owners have much less information than management on the activities of the enterprise, such as the full list of reasons why a certain acquisition was undertaken.

The form of "incentive-compatible" contract that is thought to deal best with these difficulties is one in which the manager receives an annual bonus the size of which depends on the company's profits. Under that arrangement the manager has an incentive to make those decisions and to take those actions that most contribute to the company's profit, which is perfectly compatible with the owners' objectives.

Another widely used device is the distribution of "stock options" for successful managerial performance. A stock option is a contract in which the company gives the executive the right to buy a certain number of shares of the company's stock from the Treasurer at any time in the future, at the current market price of a share – say 1,000 shares at $50 a share. If the price of the stock rises in the future – say to $70 – the manager can earn $20,000 by exercising the option.[7] The stock option gives management a personal interest in running the company in a way that increases the attractiveness of the stock to investors, thus causing its price to be bid up, which is entirely compatible with the interest of the owners.

Clauses of these sorts in executive compensation plans powerfully concentrate the managerial mind on profits. While there are occasions when a manager's interest may be served by a decision that would reduce profits, it should not be surprising that overall profit considerations dominate in the ordinary business of running a company. Management incentive contracts therefore contribute to the efficiency of private ownership by aligning the interests of managers with those of the owners in using the productive property for the purpose of making as much profit as possible.

DO EXECUTIVES EARN TOO MUCH?

The widening use of such contracts has been accompanied by an explosive growth in managerial compensation to levels that strike the press and the public as astronomical. Michael Eisner, chief executive of the Disney Corporation, holds the record with $8.7 million received in 1996 in the form of salary and bonus, plus stock options valued at the time at $181 million.[8] The average compensation package for chief executives of the largest corporations was $1.5 million in 1995.[9] *The Economist* reports that in the 1950s "bosses earned about 40 times as much as a typical employee; now they earn over 300 times as much."[10]

The large and rapid increase in compensation has raised questions about the extent to which incentive contracts serve the interests of the stockholders and whether those large incomes are fairly earned. Suspicion is compounded by the fact that the largest proportion of managerial compensation consists not of reported salaries and other payments, but of other forms of payment like stock options, life insurance policies, and deferred compensation of various sorts, much of which is not reported to the stockholders.

No one doubts that many top executives are worth their pay to the shareholders. A celebrated case is that of the man AT&T recruited as president, Alex J. Mandl, who more than doubled the revenues of the company in three years. He was then lured away by an obscure wireless telephone company that offered him a signing bonus of $20 million. At the news of his acceptance the price of that company's shares rose by $120 million.[11] Executives of ability and reputation who can affect their shareholders' wealth by hundreds of millions do fully earn the millions they receive. They are not unlike top athletes and performers who produce staggering revenues for their employers in the age of television broadcasting. The public whistles in disbelief at the $25 million earned by the legendary basketball player, Michael Jordan, for one season's play, but few doubt that he is worth it in cold cash to the owners.

But while the best of executives merit their high remuneration, there is evidence that most get a great deal more than they merit. Graef S. Crystal, who does most of the detective work on this matter, found that in 484 of the largest American companies the link between executive compensation and company performance is very weak. The extreme case is that of the chief executive of Viacom, whose compensation was more than five times as large as would be expected on the basis of the size and profitability of his company. Most executive compensation is worked out "at the discretion of the board" rather than based on a formula or on performance.[12]

One interpretation of the large size and apparent arbitrariness of executive compensation is that private-sector managers appear to have more leeway in raising their own incomes and benefits than executives in other types of large organizations.[13] In the view of *The Economist*, the market for executives is "rigged" because the compensation committees of the boards are composed of people who are themselves top executives of other companies and have an interest in bidding up executive pay and downplaying links to performance.[14] That interpretation receives some support from Crystal's finding that where chief executives are overpaid, directors are also overpaid. In such companies the alliance of executives and directors who have appointed each other is often powerful enough to deflect or smother any stockholder protest. Such protest is also muted because, while the amounts loom large as personal incomes, they are generally extremely small in the overall profits of large companies, and the mass of stockholders scarcely feel the effect in their dividends.

An efficient incentive contract, from the owners' point of view, should do two things: it should reward profitable and punish unprofitable performance, and it should offer the manager a bonus large enough, but no larger than is necessary, to elicit the desired level and direction of managerial effort. The evidence suggests that on both counts many compensation arrangements do not serve the best interests of the stockholders. Corporate governance arrangements often enable top executives to secure highly favorable deals for themselves at the expense of the stockholders.[15] Overall, however, they have probably contributed to economic efficiency by focussing managerial effort on the profitable operation of their enterprises.

4 Monitoring

Even the proprietor of a small enterprise must monitor the work of his employees to maintain an efficient production operation. When the stockholder-owners of a large corporation employ an agent to manage their property, the task of monitoring the work of the employees is delegated to the manager, but the owners face the daunting task of monitoring the agent.

How the board conducts its monitoring function varies from country to country, along with the form of corporate governance. In Great Britain, it is often the case that most of the members of the boards of directors are themselves executives of the company, which undermines their credibility as monitoring agents on behalf of the stockholders.[16] In Germany there are two boards, one to strengthen management by providing information and counsel, and the other to monitor management; most of the members of the latter are not executives of the company. The United States is distinctive in the large number of citizens who own some corporate stock, often in small amounts: some large corporations boast of millions of stockholders on their registers. Most members of American boards are not executives of the company, and often represent interests of those stockholders who hold relatively large blocks of stock. In Japan, in contrast, the stock tends to be held by a relatively small number of owners, often by banks and other companies with which the enterprise does its business. Bank-stockholders have a particularly useful source of information about company operations by virtue of their access to banking records.

The monitoring process varies not only among countries but among enterprises in each country. In large American corporations most of the shareholders hold so few shares that it is not worth their while to spend the time and money required for independent monitoring of the activities of the enterprise in detail. They do little more than cast their votes for the board of directors, whom they hope have the same interest as theirs in the profitability of the company. Normally each share gets one vote, so that a major stockholder, who may be an individual or a pension fund or an investment bank, can often win a seat on the board. Because of the large stake in the company that these directors represent, they have a strong incentive to monitor the management closely, and constitute a formidable obstacle to a manager who departs too widely from what they regard as their best interest.[17] There are companies, however, in which resourceful chief executives can, in the course of time, pack the board with people on whose support they can count. In such cases, small stockholders find it exceedingly difficult to challenge decisions that they believe to be more in management's interest than in their own.

The legal system   Keeping watch over management is facilitated by the legal requirements in all modern economies that the company's books be audited annually by an independent auditing firm. The audited balance sheet and income statement give the board, as well as engaged stockholders, a comprehensive account of the overall financial condition and business performance of the enterprise. That makes it difficult, though not impossible, for management to conceal a record of poor performance from knowledgeable directors and stockholders. Financial reporting, to be sure, cannot provide an insight into such matters as whether management's promotion of a merger with another company is based on their faithful pursuit of the stockholders' interest, or on the benefit that would accrue to their own managerial careers. The tightness of the laws on financial disclosure, moreover, varies among countries, as does the vigor with which they are enforced.

Hence, while there are companies in which an entrenched management can control or intimidate its board of directors, in most cases the board is able to carry out its monitoring function reasonably well. Management generally knows that there are limits to how far it can depart from profit-making considerations without bringing the board down on its head.

5 Takeovers

The third restraint on management emanates from the capital market, which consists of owners of money capital seeking ways of putting it to its most profitable use. The actors in that market track the performance of managers and companies very closely and move their money about quickly on the basis of their assessments. Thus, when the chairman of Bausch & Lomb announced his resignation, the market value of the company's stock rose quickly by $150 million as investors poured funds into its shares in the expectation that a new chairman would turn the company around.[18]

It is not only by the sale and purchase of shares, however, that the capital market reveals its assessment of management, but the more active process of a "takeover" offer. An outsider group that has studied a company closely, for example, may conclude that management has been too incompetent, too venal, or too accommodating to labor's demands to generate as much profit as the enterprise is capable of producing. They believe that by firing the management, replacing it by a new one, and reorganizing the business, the profit prospects of the reorganized company would be substantially greater than at present. The outsider group may then ask the stockholders to vote for their candidates to the board of directors, or to sell their shares to the group at an attractive price, or to exchange their shares for shares in the outsider's company. If enough of the stockholders are persuaded, the outsider group can take over the majority of positions on the board of directors, oust the old management, and proceed with the proposed reorganization.[19] The threat of a "hostile takeover" is a sword over the head of a management that, whether for incompetence or for reasons of personal advantage, runs the business in a way that produces substantially less profit than other people think it can make.

In summary, profit-based compensation packages and other arrangements provide a strong incentive for management to strive for the largest profit that their companies can produce. Managers whose companies underperform must run a minefield of arrangements in which they are highly likely to be detected and eventually dismissed. There are always some who hang on for long periods of time, but in the main the pursuit of profit continues to be the principal objective of the managers of privately owned property.

6 Discussion

A society that desires its economy to produce the goods and services that best cater to the desires of the citizens-as-consumers should be strongly attracted to private ownership as its ownership form. The reason is most evident in those economic activities with which the citizens have the closest contact – small businesses that serve the public directly. You have to have lived in a society in which food markets, clothing shops, hardware stores, local transportation, repair shops, and the like are all owned and run by government in order to appreciate the joy of being served by people who value your business because of the profit they earn from it.

That does not preclude the possibility that some forms of social ownership to be discussed below, such as worker ownership, might match the diligence of private owners in catering to consumers' wishes. It would require, however, that such enterprises be driven by profit considerations in much the same manner as private owners.

The benefits of small-scale ownership are not confined to consumer goods and services but extend to productive activity generally. Small business in capitalist economies produces a large proportion of the total output under conditions in which profit considerations drive production costs down and motivate keen attention to the needs of industrial and other customers. The company that makes the nails bought by the furniture manufacturer wants very much to keep the orders for their nails coming for a long time. Small private business also offers the important quality-of-life opportunity for persons who deplore working for someone else to try to run their own show, in which they may or may not succeed.

For all the joys of small business, however, the fact of modern economic life is that any society that throws its lot in with private ownership should expect that most of its enterprises will be run not by the owners of the productive property but by hired managers. It is therefore only reasonable to question whether the dedication to profit-making that characterizes the owner-manager carries over to large enterprises. It would indeed be quite remarkable if that new class of powerful managers, who do not own the enterprises and do not directly pocket the profit, should regard profit-making with the same tender dedication as the old owner-managers.

As I read the evidence, however, it appears that, by and large, the dedication to profit-making in the modern corporation is alive and well. The principal reasons are those set forth in the text above. On the carrot side, the owners have been wise enough to offer managerial compensation plans that align the top managers' interests with their own. Profit-based bonuses and stock options open up a path to the accumulation of wealth that powerfully drives managers to run their enterprises as profitably as they can. The sticks are the arrangements that can cut the manager off from that path to wealth if profits are smaller than "the market" judges the potential to be: the imperfect but reasonably effective monitoring by the owners and their directors, and the dread prospect of the transfer of ownership to an outside group that believes the property to be capable of generating larger profits than it has in the past.

This is not to deny that there are times and places where management finds it to its interest to pursue other objectives than profits alone, as described in the text. If profits happen to be relatively high, for example, one would expect a prudent management to "satisfice" rather than "maximize" profit. The evidence suggests, however, that such practices are marginal, and are by no means the rule. The old formulation of "profit maximization" still better captures the general sense of how large enterprises are run than any other that I know of. Therefore, insofar as efficiency is one of my criteria of goodness, private ownership is quite acceptable in my Good Society, even in its managerial form.

Ownership or markets   What is not clear from the evidence, however, is the extent to which the commendable profit-seeking behavior of management is the consequence of the private-ownership form itself, rather than of the market mechanism in which it is embedded.

One of the attractive characteristics of markets is that they exert a certain disciplinary force on enterprises, whatever their ownership form. What keeps management on their toes is not only the devotion of the owners to their profits. It is also the competition of other enterprises for their customers or for their sources of finance or supply. In the absence of market competition, the keenness with which management holds down costs and develops new markets would be considerably attenuated. It is the performance of competing enterprises that provides a standard by which the owners, and outsiders as well, can assess the performance of management. Competition therefore contributes to the intensity of the pursuit of profit by management; or otherwise put, in the absence of competition, private ownership itself would not generate the same dedication to profit.

But competition is a property of the economic mechanism, and not of the ownership form.[20] Hence, what appears to be the contribution of private ownership to the efficiency of the economy – the profit drive – is in some measure the contribution of the economic mechanism. If that is so, private ownership does not guarantee efficiency; it is not a sufficient condition for the profit-seeking drive of enterprises, and therefore for economic efficiency.

The foregoing distinction between the contributions of ownership and markets is intriguing, but I don't regard it as significant in assessing the efficiency of private ownership. The reason is that private ownership is fated to be married only to the market mechanism, in the economic system called capitalism. As long as the property is devoted to its most profitable uses under that system, it doesn't matter much whether private ownership or the market mechanism should get the credit.

The distinction does acquire some significance, however, in assessing the efficiency of the market mechanism. For while private ownership needs the market mechanism, the market mechanism does not need private ownership. Markets could also operate, in principle, with any of the various forms of social ownership, under the economic system of market socialism. If socialist hired managers could be motivated to strive for profit maximization by the same devices that motivate capitalist hired managers, then the market mechanism might generate the same profit drive under market socialism. That is to say, if socially owned enterprises had to face the competition of other socially owned enterprises when all operate under the market mechanism, they would be subject to the same profit-seeking pressures that operate on privately owned enterprises under capitalism.

The most devoted proponents of private ownership would deny that. While they would concede that private ownership does not guarantee that the owners will always strive for the maximum of profit, they believe that property that is not privately owned will be used for all sorts of purposes other than the most profitable – to provide jobs for political supporters and relatives, to supply favored groups with goods at low prices, and so forth. Markets or no markets, socially owned enterprises would only play at profit-making. They would not be fired up by profit-making opportunities with the intensity generated by private ownership. Market socialism would therefore be at best a pale imitation of capitalism, and at worst an unacceptably inefficient system.

Whether market-socialist enterprises would, in practice, pursue profits with the same intensity as capitalist enterprises is an empirical question. Fortunately there are two cases in which certain limited forms of market socialism were in operation at various times – Hungary and Yugoslavia. The evidence provided by their experience will be examined in the next chapter.

In concluding this chapter I am mindful of people who are accustomed to regarding profit-making as in the same ethical category as grand theft if not genocide. They must shake their heads in disbelief at this seemingly straight-faced discussion that treats the pursuit of profit as a meritorious thing in a Good Society. It must be remembered, however, that the criterion of goodness in this chapter is efficiency and not justice. To be sure, if one holds the pursuit of profit to be entirely outside the pale of any reasonable conception of justice, capitalism has no place at all in a Good Society, no matter how efficient it may be. However, if one is at all concerned with the material welfare of the people, one should wish to know how efficient is the system that is to be rejected because of its injustice. Since the efficiency of capitalism stands or falls on the pursuit of profit, the question of the profit-making orientation of the modern corporation is of relevance to the enemies of capitalism as well as to its friends.

Notes

1 In managing the property the owner is normally concerned not simply with the profit that it will earn this year, but with the stream of annual profits extending over a span of years.

2 US Bureau of the Census, *Statistical Abstract of the United States, 1997*, table 834.

3 US Bureau of the Census, *Statistical Abstract of the United States, 1997*, table 833.

4 Some of those innovations, however, create new opportunities for small-scale business; there are many small enterprises in such activities as computer desk-top publishing, for example. The invention of "franchising" has also created a new form of small-scale quasi-ownership: owners of a McDonald's franchise invest their own money and run their business much like the prototypical shopkeeper, except that they are restricted to selling the products that McDonald's produces and advertises.

5 Berle and Means, *The Modern Corporation and Private Property*.

6 Martin and Parker, *The Impact of Privatization*.

7 In "exercising the option" in 1990, the executive buys 1,000 shares of stock from the company Treasurer at the 1985 option price of $50, paying $50,000 for the purchase. He may then sell the 1,000 shares in the stock market through his personal stockbroker for $70 a share, realizing $70,000 from the sale. Hence, the stock option that he had received as part of his 1985 compensation package earns him an income of $20,000 when exercised in 1990.

8 *The New York Times*, March 30, 1997, p. E10.

9 *Economic Report of the President*, February 1997, p. 167.

10 *The Economist*, November 28, 1998, p. 70.

11 *The New York Times*, August 25, 1996, p. E4.

12 *The New York Times*, February 22, 1996, p. D9.

13 Martin and Parker, *The Impact of Privatization*, p. 19.

14 *The Economist*, December 10, 1994, p. 18.

15 Investment, mergers, and acquisitions, undertaken by managers for reasons of ego, personal power, and prestige, may be a source of inefficiency if they divert resources away from their optimal use. Such actions do indeed occur, but they do not appear to account for a large proportion of all corporate expansion activities.

16 *The Economist*, November 25, 1995, p. 59.

17 That does not preclude the possibility that the best interests of the major stockholders may not coincide with those of the small stockholders. Small stockholders, for example, are generally in a lower income-tax bracket, and their preferred use of the company's profit may differ from that of the large stockholders. The stockholders are united, however, in their interest in the profitability of the business.

18 *The New York Times*, January 7, 1996, p. F4.

19 The potential of such contests for corporate control is socially beneficial in the sense that it weeds out management that does not use its portion of the country's productive assets in the most profitable way. The net social effect is not clear, however, for corporate takeovers do not always lead to more efficient uses of productive assets.

One kind of target for a takeover, for example, is a profitable but conservative firm that maintains a large sum of cash reserves among its assets. Corporate raiders often use that cash to retire the "junk bonds" they issued in order to raise the money used to pay the high stock price they offered to the shareholders to induce them to sell their shares to the takeover group. The result is a company stripped of the cash and other assets that provided a cushion of insurance against a temporary reversal in its business. It often happens that when the dust settles, the value of the company turns out to be less than it was before the takeover. It has been estimated that about half of all acquisitions and mergers fail to achieve the expected performance gains (Martin and Parker, *The Impact of Privatization*, p. 22).

20 The market mechanism creates the conditions for competition but doesn't assure it: large pockets of an economy may be shielded from competition by all sorts of barriers to the entry of new firms that would cut into the business of the older ones. Under central planning, however, one can be assured that there will be no competition, for that mechanism is designed explicitly to replace it by cooperation.

Chapter 24

The State as Owner

Socialists believe that it is a sin
to make a profit. Capitalists
believe it is a sin to make a loss.
— *Abba P. Lerner*

CONTENTS

State ownership was largely the province of the Communist world in the past century, but it was also to be found in some industries in many other countries. In the market economies before World War II it was generally confined to large public utilities like electric companies, railroads, water systems, and the armaments industry, but its extent increased greatly in the massive wave of nationalization that followed the war. Among the reasons was the appeal exerted in capitalist countries by the idea of introducing some elements of the planning mechanism, notably in France but also in Britain and elsewhere. State ownership was particularly attractive to enthusiasts of national economic planning: it was easier to plan an economy when responsibility for the operation of the state enterprises was lodged in various cabinet ministers and the managers were political appointees beholden to the government.

The expansion of state ownership after the war also owed much to the appeal of the Soviet economy as a model of successful economic development. In the course of time, however, with the decline and eventual collapse of the Communist bloc, state ownership lost much of its allure, and many state enterprises have since been privatized, or re-privatized. The experience of the Communist planned economies remains the most useful, however, for studying the efficiency of state ownership, and it is that experience upon which most of the following discussion draws.

I Organization of State Enterprises

State-owned enterprises in Communist countries were supervised by government agencies called ministries. All enterprises producing a certain range of products were assigned to the same ministry. Thus, the All-Union Ministry of the Automotive Industry would be in charge of that entire industry throughout the USSR, while the Ukrainian Ministry of the Coal Industry would be responsible for all the coal mines in that republic alone. All the Communist countries followed that broad administrative structure, although in a huge country like China it was more decentralized, with the provincial governments responsible for a relatively larger proportion of all enterprises.

Management   The managers of state enterprises, like those of large private enterprises, were hired officials. The chief executive was called the Director.[1] He and the chief engineer were the top managerial officials. They were appointed by the minister, and they in turn hired the rest of the managerial staff. The salaries of management were determined by the ministry, under guidelines established by other government agencies such as the Ministry of Finance. Management's earnings consisted of a basic monthly salary, plus a variety of supplements, the most important of which was usually a bonus the size of which depended on the enterprise's success in fulfilling the plan. The size of the basic salary varied with the size of the enterprise and the industry's political or military priority. Top management of large enterprises also enjoyed a variety of perks, such as full-time use of a company car, a comfortable, company-supplied apartment, and expense-account trips to Moscow and elsewhere.

Labor   Workers in state enterprises were hired by management in much the same way as in private enterprises. Soviet political theory contended that since the managers are agents of a worker's state, the workers are, in effect, hired by their own agents and cannot therefore be said to be "exploited," as are workers hired by private owners. In practice, Soviet workers did indeed recognize that their bosses did not "own" the company in the manner of capitalist bosses, but the reality did little to imbue them with the feeling that they were the real owners and the managers were their agents, as the theory would have it.

Wage rates were not negotiated but were set by a government agency. Strikes were illegal, on the rationale that since it was a workers' state, the workers would only be striking against themselves. In the same spirit, the trade unions served in effect as agencies of the state rather than as vehicles for the expression of the workers' wage demands. The trade unions did often represent the workers' interests, however, when they had genuine grievances of a non-political nature.

2 State Ownership and Efficiency

The case for the efficiency of state ownership derives from the socialist critique of capitalism. From the socialist perspective, it is perfectly understandable that workers and managers in capitalist-owned enterprises should act in their personal interest, without regard to the interest of the owners or of society as a whole. They properly regard the productive property as someone else's, and the care of it therefore merits as little effort as can be given without penalty. Of least concern is the profit earned by the enterprise, for it all belongs to the capitalist owners.

Among the deepest convictions of the socialist critics of capitalism, however, is the view that with the establishment of socialism, the corrupting influences of individualist capitalism would vanish. When the enterprises are owned by all the people, it follows as night follows day that the citizens would recognize their personal interest to be identical to that of the society. In that Good Society both managers and workers would have no motive other than to work for the common good, for the larger the country's production, the better off they and all their fellow citizens would be.

Expressed in that way, the case for the efficiency of state ownership could stand on the same premise as the case for private ownership: that people care more for what is theirs than for what is not theirs. However, under state ownership everyone can consider the property to be theirs, while under private ownership relatively few can call the property theirs. Hence, if people everywhere are motivated by self-interest, more care and effort will be devoted to the efficient use of the property under state ownership than under private ownership.

Most supporters of state ownership, however, would not be enamored of that self-interest argument in the case for socialism. The efficiency advantage of state ownership, in the more common view, is precisely that it weakens the devotion to self-interest that accompanies private ownership, cultivating in its stead a devotion to the interest of all the people. In that Good Society the citizens learn to care for the people's property with no less attentiveness and drive than private owners put into care for their private property. Various expressions of this view have been reported earlier, most notably the dictum of Mao Zedong that the promise of a few more yuan would never inspire the masses as keenly as the promise of a great socialist future.

The rejection of self-interest for social consciousness is one reason for the adoption of state ownership. Another reason is the decision to employ central planning as the coordinating mechanism. The planning mechanism can operate only if the planners have the authority to require the enterprises to accept the directions contained in the plans. That is most readily achieved if the planners and the enterprise managers work for the same boss – the state. State ownership and planning are thus as felicitous a marriage as private ownership and markets.

3   Principals and Agents Again

Proponents of social ownership would find nothing surprising in the allegation that managers of privately owned enterprises pursue their personal interests at the expense of those of capitalist owners. Yet the particular form of social ownership that the Soviets introduced – state ownership – shares many of the formal organizational characteristics of a large capitalist private enterprise. The managers are hired help, responsible for running their enterprises in the interest of the owners. Whether one thinks of the owners as all the people or as the state or government, it is evident that the owners are separated from the direct control of their enterprise in much the same manner as private owners of large enterprises are separated from the direct control of their enterprises. The potential for divergence between the interests of the social owners and their manager-agents is no less present than in the case of private owners and their manager-agents.

It was the deep conviction of Soviet socialists, however, that that formal similarity would be of little weight relative to the big difference – that ownership was not private but social. A great deal rides on the validity of that proposition – that people who live under state ownership will behave differently from those who live under private ownership. For if it turns out *not* to be so, the agency problem would be much more severe than it is under private ownership.

The problem is particularly severe if ownership is ascribed to the people collectively, for then the extent of the separation of ownership from control is much larger than under private ownership. For one thing, the very notion of ownership is somewhat fuzzy under that arrangement. Each citizen may be regarded as owning a tiny, equal share of the property of every enterprise in the country, but the Soviet citizen's ownership of some portion of – say – the Urals Machinery Plant is far less focussed than that of an American citizen's ownership of ten shares of common stock in the Ford Motor Company.

More important, however, is that there are more levels at which the interests of principals and agents may diverge. At the uppermost level, the interests of the government as agent may diverge from those of the people as principals. There are momentous issues over which that may occur; the people, for example, may have a strong preference for a high level of current consumption, while the government may believe that the country needs to devote more resources to investment in heavy industry than to current consumption. At the next lower level, the ministers as agents may have personal interests that do not coincide with those of their principal, the government; their careers may benefit by acquiring as large a volume of resources for their industries as possible – far larger than the volume of resources needed to fulfill their ministry's plan. Finally, managers as agents may have interests that diverge from those of the ministers, their principals; it may be to the managers' advantage to underreport the true productive capacity of their enterprises so that the ministries will assign them plans that are easier to fulfill. In contrast to this multiplicity of levels at which agents might pursue their personal interests at the expense of their principals, under private ownership there is only one organizational level – the board of directors – that stands between the owners and the managers. Therefore the potential for divergence between the interests of the citizen-owners at one end of the long chain and the managers at the other end is much larger under state ownership than under private ownership.

The founders of the Soviet economy did concede the possibility of instances of such self-interested behavior under state ownership, especially in the early years of the new society. Indeed, quite early in the history of the Soviet economy evidence began to appear that some managers were running their enterprises as if they were more interested in their own careers than in the interests of the society. Such deviant behavior was thought to be merely a relic of the capitalist past, like crime, religious superstition, and other forms of social pathology. Its appearance in the new society made no dent in the profound conviction that, with the abolition of private property and profit, the immorality of capitalism would eventually give way to a new morality of socialism. Managers would then have no more interest in cheating the state than a capitalist would have in cheating himself, for cheating the people's state is no different from cheating oneself.

In the Heroic Age of Soviet economic development there were indeed substantial numbers of people who embodied that socialist ideal, as there were later in the corresponding Heroic Ages of China, Cuba, and other revolutionary societies. Those dedicated revolutionaries had no personal interests that differed from those of the state – certainly no material interests, for they were often of admirably ascetic disposition. Unhappily for that socialist vision, however, in the course of time new generations of managers replaced the revolutionaries, and it became patently clear that the problem of agency had to be confronted under state enterprise no less than under private enterprise.

Why that occurred will always be a matter of dispute. Some believe it to be inevitable that when a revolutionary society turns to such mundane matters as better ways to freeze fish or how many square meters of housing a chief executive's family requires, large social concerns will give way to petty personal concerns. Others believe that the fault lay not in the stars, as it were, but with Stalin and the tyrannical, bureaucratic power through which he governed. Inevitable or not, it was eventually conceded by the Soviet leadership that self-interest had to be recognized as a factor motivating both managers and workers.

4   Incentive Contracts

Capitalist owners rely on incentive contracts, among other things, to bring their agents' interests into closer alignment with their own. Arrangements of that sort, however, fly in the face of everything that traditional socialists regard as good in their conception of a Good Society.

In the earliest days of Soviet socialism, enterprise managers who were dedicated to the revolution neither expected nor received special privileges. They were simply citizen-workers whose job was organizing things – basically no different from other workers whose jobs were shovelling coal or turning parts on a lathe. They enjoyed a certain amount of public honor and personal deference as leaders of production, but in the egalitarian spirit of the time, differences in wage rates were kept to a minimum, and managerial salaries differed little from those of workers with equivalent education and experience. Least of all was it thought necessary or proper to offer special wage incentives, either to ordinary labor or to managerial labor; for with the capitalists gone, the new citizen-owners would put no less effort into their labor than if they were working directly for themselves.

It did not take many years before that idealized perspective gave way in the face of the evidence that increasing numbers of competent workers were reluctant to take on the responsible and demanding job of management, and that those who did regarded it as unfair that they should be paid no more than their workers. The opinion grew that the commitment to wage equality was standing in the way of the country's economic development.

The decision to introduce personal incentives was preceded by a bitter controversy. It was opposed by many members of the Communist Party and of the trade unions as a betrayal of the socialist commitment to equality and to the solidarist ideal. Stalin, however, now come to full power, regarded such views as a sort of "knee-jerk" Communism, and in a historic speech in 1931 he denounced them with the epithet "equality-mongering" – a term of derogation that became famous in the Communist world. Forever after, the Communist countries felt free to employ personal incentives, including wage differentiation, in the service of economic development, though the degree varied from country to country. Some parts of the Communist world never accepted that concession to self-interest, however, and the commitment to equality and to social rather than personal incentives reasserted itself with a vengeance in the Chinese and Cuban revolutions.

The main component of the management compensation package was the supplementation of the basic salary by a bonus, the size of which depended on the performance of the enterprise. In that general respect, the incentive contract was similar to that in a capitalist corporation. The difference was the basis on which performance was evaluated. In the state-socialist economies the size of the bonus was linked to the fulfillment of the enterprise production plan, while in the capitalist enterprise it is geared to the earning of profit.[2] That difference reflects the difference in the owners' objectives. Under state socialism the objective of the owner/state is to get the plan fulfilled, while under capitalism the private owners' objective is to earn profit. Plan fulfillment and profit are therefore the natural basis for the owners to evaluate the performance of their managerial agents under the two systems.

The bonus regulations were such that the manager who consistently overfulfilled the enterprise's plan could earn a personal income substantially larger than the basic salary, which was itself considerably larger than the wage earnings of the workers. The attractiveness of a managerial position also grew over time by the accretion of aforementioned perks.

The incentive contracts did succeed in converting managerial employment into a job that competent people sought to have and to hold. Most Soviet managers worked quite intensely – certainly more than the ordinary workers – often remaining at their desks long after their workers had gone home for the day. The incentives system was therefore compatible with the planners' objective of eliciting a high level of managerial effort.

The planners require more from their managers than effort, however. They also require that the effort be directed in ways that are consistent with their own objectives. In that respect, the incentive contracts were notably unsuccessful. In a great many ways they generated managerial practices that were inconsistent with the objective of the planners. Those practices were the source of much of the inaccurate information and "paper planning" that were the cause of so much of the inefficiency of the planned economies (chapter 18).

5   Incentives and Production Decisions

The interests of the owners in a planned economy are incorporated in the plan. A good management compensation plan should therefore be such that it is in the managers' own interest to fulfill their plans. So far so good. How to measure the extent of plan fulfillment, however, turned out to be a taxing problem that was never satisfactorily solved.

At one time the incentives regulations linked the size of the monthly bonus to the volume of enterprise production expressed in terms of "gross value of output."[3] Gross value consisted of "finished products" and "goods-in-process." A tractor that had been completed during the month and delivered to the warehouse ready for shipment was a "finished product." A partially completed tractor that consisted of a chassis but no engine or transmission was reported as "goods-in-process." In the course of time, the planners noticed that toward the end of each month the volume of finished products tended to decline sharply and the volume of goods-in-process tended to rise. The reason was that finishing operations took more labor than startup operations: a worker might produce 1,000 rubles of output an hour in completing the assembly of a tractor, but 2,000 rubles an hour when starting up the production of a tractor. Hence, in months when the enterprise was running behind the output plan target, managers would reassign labor from the finishing of tractors near completion to the startup of new tractors. In that way they could fulfill the gross-output target of their plans and qualify for the month's bonus. The practice was inefficient, for the volume of the country's resources tied up wastefully in partially completed production rose far above the optimum.

That particular problem was eventually solved by changing the incentives regulations so that the bonus was linked to finished products alone; no credit was given for the volume of goods-in-process. The consequence, however, was that managers facing the prospect of underfulfilling their plan quota of finished products transferred labor from work on earlier stages of goods-in-process to the finishing of goods that could then be delivered to the warehouse. That practice was also inefficient, for production was run with a supply of partially finished goods that was too small to sustain the largest possible flow of finished goods in the long run. A second consequence was that when production was running behind schedule, managers began to deliver to the warehouse goods that were almost but not quite finished: tractors without headlight bulbs or winter coats not fully lined. By certifying that they were delivered to the warehouse, however, management qualified for the bonus. The bonus regulation thus added to the many other factors that depressed the quality of production.

Throughout Soviet history planners and managers played a cat-and-mouse game of this sort, the planners designing a new criterion for measuring plan fulfillment, and the managers figuring out ways of fulfilling it that generated some other form of inefficiency in their overall production operations. As late as the 1980s a complex new indicator was announced – "net normative output" it was called – that was expected to greatly improve the efficiency of managerial decision-making, but it generated a controversy that ended only with the ending of the planned economy itself.

Hence the incentives arrangements never did succeed in channelling the personal interests of managers in directions that were compatible with the interests of the owner – the state. The reason is that under the central planning mechanism there is no single indicator of enterprise performance so general that if managers concentrated on that alone, their decisions would be consistent with the interests of the owner-state. In contrast, under the market mechanism the owners' interest is fully expressed in a single indicator – the volume of profit; hence if an incentive contract motivates management to make as much profit as possible, the interests of owners and managers are fully compatible. That difference in the criteria for evaluating managerial performance encapsulates the difference between a co-ordinating mechanism in which production decisions are made centrally by the planners, and one in which they are made decentrally by the enterprise managers.

6 Incentives and Information

It is in the nature of the agency relationship that the agent possesses a great deal more information about the enterprise than the owners. Under the market mechanism the owners have no interest in the details of that information – that is what they pay management to worry about. They are not interested in how production decisions are made but in how much profit those decisions produce. Under the planning mechanism, on the other hand, it is the planners who make the major production decisions, and they depend on the information supplied to them by the managers in order to construct the enterprise plans.

It did not take long after the launching of the First Five-Year Plan in 1929 for Soviet managers to recognize that if they informed the central planners fully of their true production capability, they might end up with high plan assignments that were difficult or impossible to meet. In the course of time it became the general practice to doctor the information they submitted to the higher authorities on the various aspects of their enterprises' operations. Two examples will serve as illustrations, with regard to information on outputs and on inputs respectively.

THE RATCHET

Managerial performance is generally measured by the extent to which the output plan target is fulfilled. One-hundred percent fulfillment is satisfactory and entitles management to the minimum bonus; output in excess of 100 percent of plan is applauded and produces larger bonuses; less than 100 percent is unsatisfactory and normally means that no bonus is forthcoming. The manager with a reputation for fulfilling the plan regularly enjoys a good income and can look forward to promotion, perhaps eventually to the job of minister. Repeated underfulfillment of plan leads eventually to dismissal of the management.

Much therefore depends on the size of the output plan. The higher the plan target, the more difficult it is to fulfill, and the greater the possibility of underfulfilling it. Since the size of the plan depends to a considerable extent on the information submitted by the enterprise to the planners, managers would have to be saints to resist the temptation to underreport their true production capacity. Such underreporting became the standard practice of management in defending the interests of their enterprises. "Insurance" is what they called it.

The planners were aware of the tendency of management to "conceal production reserves," and responded in various ways, one of which was particularly prevalent. An enterprise might underreport its production capacity when it submitted its preliminary plan for the forthcoming year – say 1980. In the course of 1980, however, it would reveal something of its true production capacity by the output that it actually producesd. If the enterprise succeeded in producing 10,000 tons in 1980, it could not readily claim a productive capacity of less than that for 1981.

The planners seized upon that fact, and in the practice of plan-making, last year's reported production was taken as the lower limit of the enterprise's true production capacity. The practice developed of assigning the enterprise an output plan no lower than last year's actual output, and generally somewhat higher, on the assumption that there were always some "concealed reserves." Within the planned economies this practice was known as "planning from the level previously achieved," while outside analysts referred to it as the "ratchet."[4]

The ratchet principle of plan-making gave the planners a somewhat firmer basis for assessing production capacity than the enterprises' own claims. It had a certain unfortunate effect on managerial behavior, however. The manager who had only the public interest in mind would make a maximal effort to fulfill his assigned output plan, but in addition he would strive to produce as much output in excess of plan as he could. The manager who was concerned about his bonuses and his career, however, recognized that because of the ratchet principle of plan-making, the more he produced this year the higher his output plan would be next year. The normal practice of management was therefore to strive mightily to fulfill the output plan, but to refrain from overfulfilling it by more than a decent few percentage points. To produce the largest output of which the enterprise was capable would reveal its true production capacity, and that, because of the ratchet, would risk failure next year because of an excessively high plan target.

The use of the ratchet principle in planning did no doubt compensate to some extent for the underreporting of production capacity by enterprises. It nevertheless caused management to produce less than the economy was capable of producing with the available resources, which is the meaning of inefficiency.

The safety factor

The submission of information on labor and other input requirements generates the same problems as those involving information on the enterprise's output capacity. If managers give an honest estimate, they face the risk of running short of labor, for any number of reasons: the planners may not authorize the number of workers they ask for, or the local government may "request" that some of the workers be sent out to help with the harvest, or the output plan may be suddenly increased in the middle of the year without a corresponding increase in labor supply. In order to protect the enterprise from such contingencies, there developed a practice of building what was called a "safety factor" into the preliminary plan by overstating the number of workers needed. That could be done in many ways: for example, by contriving to keep the labor norms high – at ten labor hours per ton of coal instead of the six or seven that might actually be required. It became an established tradition that the good manager was the one who could "beat out" the largest authorizations for labor and other inputs from the ministry and the planners.

The consequence of management's reliance on a safety factor is that the information available to the central planners often misrepresents the true input requirements of the enterprises. Hence the plan that is finally approved appears to be coordinated but may in fact be substantially out of balance. A final national production target of 5.3 million tons of aluminum may be much larger, or much smaller, than the producing enterprises are able to deliver. It may also be short of, or in excess of, the amount actually needed by aluminum users like window manufacturers to meet the production targets assigned to them in the plan.

That state of affairs was of long standing and well understood by the central planners as well. They therefore started the balancing process by discounting the information received from the enterprises; knowing that enterprises exaggerate their input requirements, the planners felt free to provide fewer inputs than requested. Managers, in turn, aware that their input requests would be cut anyhow, tended to ask for even larger inputs; and planners, aware that managers exaggerated their needs, assigned less than was requested. The consequence was that the planners had to perform their coordination function with very imperfect knowledge of the actual production capacity and input requirements of the enterprises they were expected to coordinate, another reason for the "paper plans" that contributed to the inefficiency of the planned economies in practice (chapter 18).

7 Monitoring

Like the owners of private enterprises, the state seeks to protect its interests by monitoring the activities of its managers. Since the state enterprise does not enjoy the right of commercial secrecy that shields the private enterprise from public scrutiny, there are many more channels through which its affairs are monitored.

The chief monitoring agency in the Communist countries was the enterprise's own ministry, which received detailed reports on a regular basis from its enterprises. The regular flow of information was supplemented by ad hoc inspections on some aspect of performance with which the ministry had been dissatisfied, or on matters that might be the subject of a government "campaign" at the time – the timely maintenance of equipment, for instance. Of all outside agencies, the ministry officials responsible for an enterprise were best able to detect managerial actions that conflicted with the ministry's interests.

A variety of other government agencies were also responsible for monitoring specific areas of enterprise activity. The state bank that held the enterprise's funds was responsible for checking that its income and expenditures conformed to its financial plan, and if the enterprise's account balance fell significantly below the planned level, the bank would flag the account and monitor it with particular diligence. In the extreme it had the authority to stop payment on enterprise expenditures until the deficiency was remedied. Other agencies that monitored specific areas of enterprise activity were those responsible for planning, for tax payments, for wage and labor discipline, for the promotion of innovation, and many others.

In addition to these outside agencies, a number of groups within the enterprise served as agents of the state in monitoring management. Chief among them was the enterprise Party Secretary, who had access to all records and all personnel. His obligation was to assist the chief executive in the planning and management of the enterprise, but also to report regularly to the regional branch of the Party on the general performance of the enterprise. Similar responsibilities were borne by the secretary of the trade union, and by the secret police, who maintained an office in all large enterprises and in all enterprises of any size that engaged in classified work. Finally, all the employees were encouraged to serve as the eyes of the state, and to expose any activities that were detrimental to the interests of the state and the people.

Open to observation by all these public groups, the manager of a state–owned enterprise lived in a fish bowl compared to the manager of a privately owned enterprise. It is therefore puzzling that, despite the extensive network of monitors, the management of state enterprises was characterized by so many practices that were contrary to the intent of the government and its planners.

The explanation is to be found in the sociology of the state-owned enterprise under central planning. The successful enterprise was one that reported overfulfillment of its plan month after month and year after year. Not only was the career of the chief executive advanced by that record, but everyone associated with the enterprise benefitted as well. The Party Secretary claimed credit for it at the meetings of the regional Party organization, and all the enterprise personnel benefitted in the form of incentive supplements to their wages. The enterprise personnel therefore constituted what was called a "family circle," and had little incentive to report to the authorities that their prominent and successful chief executive cut corners here and there – as every chief executive was thought to do anyhow. Nor was the ministry particularly keen to be informed of such transgressions, for the minister himself benefitted from being able to report to his superiors in the Council of Ministers that his enterprises could be counted on to overfulfill their plans thanks to his firm hand.

Most of the formal monitoring personnel were therefore immobilized by the understanding that their personal interests were tied up with the reported success of their enterprise, and that there was nothing to be gained in bringing down a good director by exposing the darker activities by means of which he got things done.

From time to time such an exposure did occur. An enterprise might have been overreporting its production month after month, hoping to get the problem in hand the next month, or at most the following month. None of the enterprise personnel would report it. The state bank, however, which was not part of the enterprise's family circle, would notice the decline in the account balance and file a report with the ministry. Or a junior official who was "on the make" might expose the falsified reporting by disclosing it to the regional Party committee, or by publishing a letter about it in one of the government's watchdog newspapers. Matters might thus get out of hand and result in a great "skandal" in which the chief executive was fired and the enterprise Party Secretary disciplined for having participated in the coverup. Those were the chances an aggressive chief executive had to take; but in the normal course of events the common interest of the family circle prevailed.

Hence, the monitoring apparatus, extensive though it was on paper, did not succeed in discouraging managers from pursuing personal interests that conflicted with those of the state.

Monitoring the workers   Under both private and state ownership, the chief executive is the agent responsible for the protection of the enterprise property from theft and misuse for personal gain, by both insiders and outsiders. The source of the problem is the same – that many employees are in position to benefit personally at the expense of the owners. The big difference, however, is the fuzziness of the identity of the owners in the case of state ownership.

The hired manager of a private enterprise is keenly aware that looking over his shoulder are the principals – the shareholders and their board of directors who hold a personal stake in the integrity of their property. Many top managers, moreover, have become substantial owners in their own right as a consequence of the incentive contracts. For both reasons management has a strong motivation to protect the property from theft and other actions that reduce its value and its profitability.

The manager of a Soviet state enterprise, in contrast, owned no shares in his own enterprise, nor did any Soviet citizens possess such certificates of personal ownership. Managers were aware, moreover, that the ministry officials looking over their shoulder were not principal/owners but mere agents like themselves. Perhaps at the very top of the hierarchy – the Council of Ministers or the Politburo of the Party – there were a few dedicated people who treated state property as a public trust and strove to preserve it against misappropriation with all the energy of a personal owner; but between them and the managers stood a vast multilayered bureaucracy of salaried officials.

In any large system there are always persons of integrity at all levels to whom it would never occur to misappropriate public property they hold in trust. There are others, fewer in number, who are sufficiently committed to the public interest to actively oppose such acts by others. There are also others who, while committed primarily to the pursuit of their personal interest, are restrained from that pursuit by fear of getting caught with their hand in the till. In the early years of a revolution there are large numbers of people of the first sort, but with the inevitable evolution into bureaucratic organization, their number diminishes and the effectiveness of the monitoring of public officials decreases.

All the Communist countries followed that pattern, in varying degree. In the course of time, the misappropriation and theft of state property at all levels increased, including such activities as the theft of meat by food-service workers, the bribes accepted by university admissions officers, the kickbacks to officials responsible for the distribution of scarce goods, and the building of luxurious hunting lodges for the use of regional government and Party officials. In the last years of the Communist states, what to do about the growing "kleptocracy" was high on the agenda of the leadership.

In the post-mortems following the abolition of state censorship under Mikhail Gorbachev, an expression often found in the Soviet press was "that which belongs to everybody belongs to nobody." That aphorism encapsulates the sentiments of those who soon afterward led the drive to abandon state ownership in favor of private ownership.

8 Small-scale Enterprise

It would seem that private enterprises of any size would be rejected out of hand by societies whose values incline them to adopt the planning mechanism. In practice, that has not been so. While state ownership of large-scale enterprises predominated in the Communist economies, private small-scale production of certain goods and services was lawful and surprisingly widespread.

The most noteworthy instance was Poland, where almost all farm production was conducted under small-scale private ownership throughout the Communist period. In most of the other socialist countries farming was collectivized, but they all followed the Soviet institution of the private peasant household plot, an arrangement under which members of collective farms were assigned small plots of land near their houses. The members were required to devote most of their time to work on the collective-farm land, but they and their family could work their private plots on their own time. Some of the products were consumed by the household itself, but the rest could be sold directly in the specially designated "collective-farm markets," in nearby urban centers, at prices that were unregulated and were substantially above the regulated prices charged in the state shops (chapter 12).

Small-scale private enterprise was not confined to farming, however. The German Democratic Republic, generally regarded as the most rigid of the European Communist countries, took care to leave its handicraft industries in private hands when it nationalized all its large enterprises. That private sector remained one of the most productive parts of the economy. Most of the East European socialist countries also maintained a substantial sector of private small-scale non-farm private enterprises. The liberalization of small-scale private enterprise was a major component of the 1968 Hungarian economic reform known as the New Economic Mechanism, as well as of the Chinese economic reform following the death of Mao.

By the late 1980s small-scale private enterprise made an impressive contribution to the total output of certain goods and services in the Communist world. The amount of their spare time and the effort and care that the peasants lavished on their private plots was legendary. In the USSR, for example, the private plots accounted for only about 3 percent of total sown area in the USSR, but they produced over 25 percent of gross agricultural output, including about a third of all meat and milk and two-fifths of all fruits and vegetables.[5]

Since the rejection of private property is so central a feature of socialism, the broad acceptance of small-scale private enterprise in the Communist countries demands an explanation. Part of the answer lies in political history. The private-plot arrangement was a concession by Stalin to a demoralized peasantry that had suffered the ruthless collectivization of the early 1930s. A decade later, after World War II, the Polish Communist Party's grip on power was not so strong as to tempt it to launch a mass collectivization of agriculture, which would have been strongly resisted by the conservative peasantry.

Political considerations apart, however, the economic benefits of private economic activity no doubt played a strong role in its wide toleration, particularly after the rate of economic growth in the Communist world began to decline in mid-century. One of the less pleasant experiences of foreign visitors to the Communist countries was the discovery that service personnel in hotels, restaurants, and shops had no interest at all in whether or not you bought what they had to sell. Little effort was devoted to enhancing the attractiveness of the premises, and the indifference and sometimes surliness of the clerks was legendary. The citizens of those countries, of course, were not able to compare the quality of the services available to them with those in the rest of the world, but there were a number of goods and services that were produced by both state-owned and private enterprises. Various foods could be bought in both the state stores and in the collective-farm markets; and one could either report a plumbing leak to the state repair office or hire a plumber to fix it in his spare time. Invariably the quality of the goods and services provided by people who earned an income by supplying them was far superior to that provided by the wage-earners in the state shops.

The poor quality of consumer goods and services should not be ascribed entirely to the structure of the economic system. It was in part the consequence of policy – particularly the low priority the Party assigned to consumption, relative to investment and defense. Wage rates in enterprises that produced or sold consumer goods were lower than elsewhere, and the best-quality inputs went elsewhere. Had consumption enjoyed a higher place in the societal scale of values, as it might in a democratically governed state-socialist economy, the welfare of the citizens-as-consumers would very likely have been higher. It is doubtful, however, that even the most pro-consumption policy could compensate for the inattention to consumer satisfaction inherent in a regime of state ownership. Under that regime, the manager of a state food store is appointed by the local government agency responsible for the community's food supply and receives a salary and a bonus that is proportional to the extent to which the plan is fulfilled. The state expresses its concern for the consumer by requiring shops to maintain a "suggestion book" in which dissatisfied shoppers can record their grievances, and which is open for perusal by the public and by the officials of the food distribution agency.

That is the formal picture. In practice, things work out quite differently. As in the case of large enterprises, the manager has infinitely more knowledge of her shop's operations than her supervisor, who is responsible for many other shops. An experienced manager therefore has no difficulty getting a plan target that is easy to fulfill, and fudging the figures in case it is not fulfilled. Hence, in the course of time the bonus came to be paid out virtually automatically, and bore little relation to the quality of the goods and services provided so long as there was no dramatic "skandal" that could not be covered up. The suggestion book became a laughingstock. Hence, a hardworking young manager who succeeds in greatly improving the quality of service and in expanding the volume of business would find that she earns very little more for her effort than a time-server who has the right connections and had no interest in improving her shop.

The private shopkeeper in Communist countries, in contrast, has no supervisor. Her income depends entirely on her ability to keep costs down and quality high, and is not limited in size by government bonus rules. Every dissatisfied customer and every spoiled cabbage reduces her income, and the revenues from an increasing number of customers go right into her own pocket. Owner and manager are one, and no supervisor is required to monitor the care with which the enterprise conducts its business. Like the classic prototype of the capitalist owner-manager, there is no principal/agent relation to detract from the efficiency of her activity.

9 Ownership and Economic Mechanism

The evidence on the efficiency of state ownership presented above comes exclusively from the experience of countries that followed the Soviet form of state socialism combining state ownership with the planning mechanism. The problem of disentangling the effects of the economic mechanism from those of the ownership form is no less difficult in the case of state ownership than in the case of private ownership. The matter is more urgent in the case of state ownership, however. The reason is that a society that adopts private ownership has no alternative to markets as its economic mechanism. There is therefore very little practical value in the knowledge that, for example, environmental degradation is due to a deficiency in the market mechanism and not in the private-ownership form. If you adopt private ownership, you must accept the tendency toward environmental degradation that comes with the whole package.

If you adopt state ownership, however, you have a choice of economic mechanisms, for it can be combined with either markets or planning. Hence there is a practical value in asking whether some of the inefficiency that may appear to be the consequence of state ownership is actually the consequence of the planning mechanism with which it is combined, for if it is, a society that finds state ownership to be more consistent with its values than private ownership could consider adopting markets as its economic mechanism in the interest of greater efficiency.

The attraction of planning over markets derives from the conviction that cooperation is superior to competition in meeting the objectives of a Good Society. In the spirit of that conviction, the number and kinds of enterprises established by the planners are such as to satisfy the needs of the economy efficiently. In the case of large enterprises, the number and location of aluminum-extruding plants, for example, is just sufficient to supply the country's requirements for aluminum windows and related products. In the case of small enterprises like food markets, a local-government agency decides how many food shops are required to meet the needs of the community and where they would be best located. In the best of worlds those decisions would be made rationally, based on the best of research into the window requirements of the construction industry and the shopping practices and consumption preferences of the people.

The other side of that picture is that enterprises, once established, face no genuine equivalent of competition as it operates in most industries under the market mechanism. The aluminum plant has pre-assigned customers for all the products in its production plan; there are no other state-owned aluminum plants or producers of vinyl windows appealing to its customers with the claim of producing a better product. There are no aggressive new state food shops seeking to build up their business by attracting other shops' customers. Many characteristics of Communist economies derive from that fundamental feature of the planning environment, which its critics deride as "monopoly." It has indeed been the experience of virtually all modern economies, capitalist and socialist alike, that when there are no alternative sellers who are eager for a customer's business, the quality of the goods or services tends to deteriorate. Exceptions can be found at various times and places, but the tendency is omni-present, and a society that fails to anticipate it is due for some hard learning. Hence, the relatively poor quality of goods and services in Communist economies cannot be ascribed entirely to state ownership of the enterprises: much of it must be ascribed to the planning environment within which the enterprises operated.

Although there is no way of determining what proportion of the inefficiency of state socialism is due to its state-ownership form and what proportion to the planning mechanism, the qualitative evidence suggests that the influence of the planning mechanism is substantial. For example, such problems as the ratchet principle and the safety factor reflect the peculiar information-requirements of the planning mechanism rather than any intrinsic qualities of state-enterprise management. That is good news for those socialists who are devoted to state ownership but regard state socialism as practiced in the Communist countries to be too inefficient to qualify for their Good Society. It gives them reason to expect that state ownership would be much more satisfactory if it were unencumbered by the planning mechanism. If that is so, then a form of market socialism – combining state ownership with the market mechanism – might satisfy the efficiency requirements of a Good Society.

10   Market Socialism

If market socialism were no more than an idea, with no empirical evidence on how it would work in practice, one should be extremely wary about recommending it for one's society, regardless of how attractive it might seem. Fortunately, there is some historical experience that provides a basis for cautious inferences about how market socialism might work out in practice. One example is the case of Hungary under a policy called the New Economic Mechanism. The other is the experience of the state-owned enterprises that operate in most capitalist countries.

HUNGARY

In 1956 a massive uprising against Soviet domination erupted in Hungary. The rebellion was crushed by the force of Soviet arms, and a chastened Communist Party was restored to power on the implicit condition that they would accept the continued domination of their foreign affairs by the USSR. The Hungarian Party under Janos Kadar wrung one large economic concession from Moscow, however. The country would be free to depart from the standard Soviet form of state socialism and, within limits, to greatly modify their economic mechanism.

After a decade of the freest public debate the country had known for years, the government launched the New Economic Mechanism in 1968. State ownership was retained as the basic ownership form, and the enterprises continued to be supervised by the same ministries that had supervised them in the past. The Central Planning Board was abolished, however, and the enterprises were expected thereafter to do for themselves much of what had previously been done for them by the planners: decide what to produce, find their own customers for their products, and arrange for their own sources of supply. The prices at which goods were bought and sold were initially determined largely by the government, as were wage rates, but many of those controls were phased out gradually. The reform also encouraged the formation and expansion of small-scale private enterprises producing a wide variety of goods and services.

Most significantly, managers of the state-owned enterprises were to make their decisions with the objective of making as much profit as possible. The profit, to be sure, was socialized, in the sense that it belonged to the government. Some portion of it was left with the enterprises to be used for incentive payments to management and workers, and for investment in the enterprise, but the rest was recovered by the government in the form of taxes.

In broad terms, therefore, the system as designed qualifies as a form of market socialism – state ownership combined with the rudiments of a market mechanism. With the establishment of the market mechanism, and with the obligation of managers to use the productive property for the purpose of maximizing profit, the major requirements for economic efficiency were in place. State ownership in that market economy should have been no less efficient than private ownership in a market economy.

State ownership under the market mechanism is still state ownership, however, and it retains certain properties that are the same as under the planning mechanism. One of those invariant properties is that the ability of millions of citizens-as-owners to control the use made of their productive property is so diluted that the effective owner becomes the government – the embodiment of the state. Sovereignty over production slips out of the hands of individual citizens and returns to the government.

If the objective of the government were that each enterprise maximize its profit – as originally intended by the drafters of the New Economic Mechanism – the Hungarian manager would have been in much the same position as the manager of a capitalist enterprise. In fact, however, every government has a variety of objectives, of which economic efficiency is but one, and rarely the most important. Above all is the objective of retaining and strengthening its power. Beyond that, the government is normally also committed to certain values that represent its idea of a Good Society, such as law and order, national honor, security, equality, full employment, and so forth. As the effective owner of the property, the government would wish it to be used to further all these objectives in varying degree.

Accordingly, the Hungarian manager was under constant pressure from the ministry to use the enterprise's property for purposes that conflicted with the earning of profit. For example, if the government signed an agreement to export buses to the USSR in exchange for imports of Soviet oil, the ministry would exert strong pressure on its automotive enterprises to sell their buses to the USSR, even though a larger profit would be earned by selling them to Italy.

The major purpose of government pressure on the managers, however, was to alleviate unemployment. In regions of high unemployment the government's ministries pressured their managers to create jobs for unemployed workers, which raised their labor costs and cut into their profit. The greatest threat of unemployment arose, however, from the insolvency of inefficient enterprises, which were now operating in a market environment. Rather than confront the unemployment that would result from the liquidation of such enterprises, the government provided them with subsidies to keep them in operation. They also received appropriations for investment in new equipment that, it was hoped, would enable them to become profitable. The extensive subsidization evolved into the "soft budget constraint" analyzed by Janos Kornai; that is, expenditures on projects undertaken with the expectation that if the enterprise lost money on them, the government would bail them out with subsidies.[6]

In addition to the wasteful use of resources that it entailed, the expectation of automatic financial bail-out contributed to a permanent state of shortage in the economy. There was little to lose by building up one's inventory of supplies or buying an expensive piece of new equipment, for if you couldn't pay for it, the government would. Hence the enterprises' demand for goods permanently exceeded the economy's capacity to supply them, creating what Kornai called a "shortage economy." The extent of shortage was not as large as it had been under the central planning mechanism, but it was sufficient to interfere with the efficient operation of the market mechanism.

The lesson of Hungarian market socialism is that state ownership gives a government the power to intervene in the management of enterprise in order to promote its own various interests, at the expense of the profit orientation of the enterprise. The consequence is inefficiency in the use of the country's resources.

Proponents of market socialism should not feel defeated by the Hungarian experience. The economy still labored under the weight of a Communist government, albeit a relatively tolerant one; one might expect that a Hungarian type of market socialism would perform more efficiently in a political system in which the government was less powerful and more responsible to the population. Nevertheless, economic performance under the New Economic Mechanism was distinctly better than it had been under central planning, particularly with respect to the availability and quality of consumer goods and services. Later on, Hungarian industry's response to the collapse of the Communist system was also singularly successful. They attracted more foreign capital than any of their neighbors, suggesting that their experience under the New Economic Mechanism had endowed management with a much more market-oriented disposition than they had under central planning.

STATE OWNERSHIP UNDER CAPITALISM

For people whose Good Society requires a democratic polity, the Hungarian experience is flawed because of the authoritarian restraints under which it had to operate. The experience of state ownership in capitalist countries may provide a better idea of how market socialism would work under democratic conditions. That evidence is also flawed, however, because the state sector is a relatively small portion of the whole economy, and state ownership might perform differently if it were the dominant form under full market socialism.

Around 1960 from 12 to 16 percent of the non-agricultural labor force was employed in government-owned enterprises in West Germany, Japan, and the United States. In France, Sweden, and Great Britain the range was 22 to 26 percent.[7] Those numbers include two quite distinct forms of government ownership, which differ from each other in a way that is of some importance for the goodness of the society. Under one arrangement, the enterprise is operated as a branch of the government. In countries where the railroads are government-owned, the responsible official is usually a minister of transportation who is an important member of the prime minister's party and is expected to be responsive to the constituencies upon which the government draws its political support. The prototype in the United States is the Post Office Department as it operated from the founding of the republic until 1970. The department was run by the postmaster-general, who was appointed by the President and served as a member of his cabinet. The postmaster-general was usually appointed to the job as a reward for loyal political service, and it was expected that he would use his authority in ways that would strengthen his and the President's political power.

Under this form of ownership the top government official possesses the same authority over the enterprise as ministers in a Communist planned economy possess over their state enterprises. It is therefore properly described by the same term – "state ownership" – signifying that it is essentially the same form of ownership as that in the planned economy, transplanted to a market economy.

The use of government-owned enterprises for the political benefit of the party in power conflicts with most views of how a Good Society ought to manage its affairs – not only because of its apparent inefficiency but also out of ethical and political concerns. The second form of government ownership was designed expressly to take the politics out of the operation of those enterprises. It is usually referred to as "public ownership." Public ownership is the subject of the next chapter. The rest of this section deals with pure state ownership.

A government depends on its ministers to assure that the enterprises are operated in ways that strengthen its political base and contribute to its hold on power. That requires that the state enterprises provide a level of service that the population finds satisfactory. The ministers are also expected, however, to be responsive to the main constituencies upon whom their party's power rests, and the state enterprises offer a natural opportunity for such responses. There are many senior- and middle-level management jobs on a railroad to which politically influential people can be appointed; a rail line can be extended into a region where the minister has a large following; the railroad payroll can be increased in times of growing unemployment to provide jobs for grateful workers. Political considerations were traditionally involved in such post-office activities as the appointment of the hundreds of local postmasters, the location and scale of new post offices, and the awarding of contracts to build them.

The extent to which political considerations enter into management decisions varies greatly from country to country. One does not read of significant political involvement in the operation of the Norwegian state-owned company that operates its North Sea oil fields. The US Post Office, on the other hand, was always regarded as a legitimate subject of political influence. At the other extreme, state-owned railroads have been notorious around the world for extensive overstaffing and other forms of inefficiency, and heavy subsidies have been required to compensate for operating losses. In authoritarian societies in particular, state enterprises have also been a major source of the private fortunes that military dictators and corrupt officials have been able to amass and to funnel abroad.

Hence, the evidence regarding the political use of state ownership in capitalist economies is mixed. In a well-organized society of public-spirited citizens that opts for some degree of state ownership, the enterprises may operate without significant political interference. The balance of the evidence, however, is broadly consistent with that under Hungarian market socialism. A society that adopts state ownership should therefore expect, or at least be prepared to find, that its government officials will place a variety of obligations on the enterprises for their political and personal benefit.

Government interference in the operation of a state enterprise for narrow political purposes should have no place in a Good Society. However, it is not at all self-evident that government should turn the operation of its enterprises over entirely to professional management. There may be good economic reasons why a certain enterprise should operate at a loss, contrary to what good management practice might be. There may be good social reasons why a railroad line should be run out to a remote region even though a hard-nosed manager would reject it on commercial grounds. These and other questions arise under both state ownership and public ownership, and will be explored in the latter context in the next chapter.

11 Discussion

The separation of ownership and control was first identified as a problem in capitalist industrial organization, and analytic tools like agency theory were developed to deal with the privately owned corporation. It is ironic that a set of ideas designed to understand the behavior of private enterprises turns out to be even more fruitful for understanding the behavior of Communist industrial organization. I say "more fruitful" because the consequences of the agency problem are much more severe under state ownership than under private ownership, as I argue in the text.

Among the reasons is the difficulty of designing management compensation plans that align the managers' interests with those of the owners. Comparing the behavior of management under the two forms of ownership, the divergence of managerial interests from those of the owners seems to me to be far larger under state ownership than under private ownership. I believe that the explanations is that which I offer in the text – the fuzziness of the concept of ownership when the state is the owner, and the longer administrative distance between owners and managers under state ownership.

The literature amply documents the failure of the incentives arrangements to eliminate dysfunctional managerial behavior, but there is one important positive achievement that should not be overlooked. The incentive contracts based on monetary bonuses did succeed in generating a high level of managerial effort and in focussing it on whatever performance indicators were specified in the bonus regulations. That should be recognized as an accomplishment of great importance. Critics of socialism often proclaim that in the absence of private ownership, no incentives could be devised to motivate people to take on the burdens of disciplining a labor force and running an enterprise at a high rate of production. It would indeed have been disastrous if socialist managers had been so inert that they responded to none of the incentives offered to them. What the Communist experience shows is that under a regime of state ownership it is possible to devise incentive contracts to which managers are highly responsive – so responsive, indeed, that with every change in the provisions of the contract, they quickly alter their behavior in ways that are in their personal interest under the terms of the new contract. A critic might dismiss that accomplishment by noting that a troika of hard-charging horses is of little use if they cannot be made to charge in the direction you want them to go. In the end, that criticism is valid, but things might nevertheless have been worse if the horses could not even be persuaded to leave the stable.

The point is important because it means that private ownership is not essential, in principle, in order to elicit a high level of managerial effort. With appropriately designed incentive contracts, a professional manager can be motivated to work intensely at the job of running his enterprise, without knowing or caring whether the owners are private persons or the state.

What matters, then, is not the ownership form, but the provisions of the management incentive contract, and it is there that the economic mechanism plays the critical role. The crucial distinction set forth in the text is that under the market mechanism, efficiency requires that the manager's effort be focussed on profit-making, whereas under the planning mechanism efficiency requires that the manager do a great many things that cannot be summarized in a single magnitude like profit. That was the cause of the longstanding cat-and-mouse game in which the authorities plugged one hole in the bonus regulations only to find that the managers had found another.

Hence my conviction that what ailed the Communist economies most was the planning mechanism and not state ownership as such, which raises the interesting question of how state ownership would work out if it were not saddled with the burden of the planning mechanism.

Market socialism   The text sketched out the evidence on that question from the experience of Hungarian market socialism and of state-owned enterprises in capitalist countries. My own assessment is that any society that combines state ownership with the market mechanism should have no doubt that the government will use the enterprises to serve a variety of purposes other than producing profitably and efficiently. As to whether that is a good or a bad thing, my view is that it is bad for the society.

For one thing, in the best of democratic societies the state means the government, which means politicians, which means people who need to get elected and who have other personal interests to further. That is not to deny that there are many public-spirited citizens in government and politics who do have the public interest at heart, although they too must compromise on some issues to be effective on others. In the complex give-and-take of political life, however, people who have a great deal to gain by getting a bill passed or an administrative action taken very often manage to get their way. One can therefore never be sure that the new electronics plant will be located where it would contribute most to the country's production, rather than where the strongest political pressures are applied. Even in more benign cases, moreover, such as the relief of unemployment, the society suffers if that is done by requiring enterprises to hire more workers than they can efficiently employ, rather than by macroeconomic policies or by eliminating restrictions that make it unprofitable for business to hire more labor.

For these various reasons, in my judgment market socialism based on state ownership would be too inefficient to qualify for most versions of a Good Society. Its efficiency could be increased by incorporating a large sphere of small-scale private enterprise, as it would very likely do if its proponents studied the experience of socialist economies of the past. Even in that case, I doubt that state ownership would commend itself to many socialists, now or in the future. Most proponents of market socialism whom I meet these days are more attracted to public ownership or worker ownership than to state ownership.

State ownership of selected enterprises such as utilities and airlines was highly popular in the capitalist and in the developing countries in the decades following World War II. In the course of time the political winds underwent a remarkable shift, and the election of Margaret Thatcher's government in Britain launched a historic wave of privatization that spread throughout the world. I expect that the political pendulum will swing back some day, but I doubt that state ownership will be high on the agenda under that wave. State ownership came in with the USSR and went out with the USSR, and I doubt that the world will see much of it again.

Notes

1   The Director of a Soviet enterprise should not be confused with a member of the board of directors of a capitalist corporation, who is also called Director. Western businessmen are sometimes confused when a Soviet official called the Director turns out to be the person who runs the company.
2   The Soviet bonus structure was originally linked almost exclusively to plan fulfillment. In the course of time additional bonuses were introduced for specific tasks, such as meeting certain standards of world-quality output, successfully introducing an innovation, or reducing production cost. However, the plan-fulfillment bonus remained the most important, in the eyes of both managers and planners.
3   Berliner, *Factory and Manager in the USSR*, pp. 32–9.
4   A ratchet is a mechanical device that applies force in one direction but not in the reverse direction. A ratchet wrench, for example, tightens a bolt when force is applied clockwise, but does not loosen the bolt when turned counterclockwise. It enables the mechanic to tighten a bolt without having to remove the wrench and readjust it after each clockwise application of force. It is the source of common expression, "ratcheting up," or continuously tightening something. Berliner, *Factory and Manager in the USSR*, ch. 6.
5   Johnson and Brooks, *Prospects for Soviet Agriculture in the 1980s*, p. 6.
6   Kornai, *The Socialist System*, pp. 140–5.
7   Pryor, *Property and Industrial Organization in Communist and Capitalist Nations*, p. 14. Government-owned enterprises include all units in which the government ownership share was 50 percent or more.

Chapter 25

The Public as Owner

> The evils that capitalism brings differ
> in intensity in different countries,
> but ... the root cause is the private
> ownership of the means of life. The
> remedy is public ownership.
> — *Clement Attlee*

CONTENTS

If you hate government and detest private property, there are only two ownership forms that would qualify for your Good Society.[1] One is worker ownership, to be discussed in the next chapter. The other is public ownership.

Public ownership is an arrangement in which the productive property can be socially rather than privately owned, while denying the government a direct hand in its management. Like all ownership forms, it can be organized in a great many different ways. One form is the public holding company, the modern origins of which go back to Italy in the depression years of the 1930s. In order to stave off the threatening bankruptcy of a number of large investment banks, the government acquired their shares and those of their industrial affiliates, and founded a holding company to hold the shares as a public trust. A second form is the "public authority," which is widely used in the United States. A prominent early version is the Tennessee Valley Authority, which was established in 1933 and has long been regarded as well managed and highly successful. Public authorities are now widely used for public purposes that have a large commercial element, such as the Port Authority of New York, the Massachusetts Bay Transit Authority, and so forth.

The form that has commanded the most interest, however, is the public corporation, an organizational form that was adopted for public enterprises in a number of countries after World War II. An American variant is the United States Post Office which, after two centuries as a government agency, was reorganized in 1970 as a quasi-independent public corporation. It was in Great Britain, however, that public enterprise became a dominating political issue and where it has been most closely studied. The Labour Party had long campaigned on the platform of broad nationalization, and after their electoral victory in 1945 a variety of enterprises in such industries as rail transportation, electricity, gas, and coal, were transformed into public corporations. By 1975 nationalized industry was estimated to account for 8 percent of total employment, 11 percent of total output, and 19 percent of fixed investment.[2]

After the electoral victory of Margaret Thatcher's Conservative Party in 1979, the new government undertook to privatize almost all of the public corporations. There is little likelihood that public enterprise will be restored to any extent in the near future, for renationalization was conspicuously absent from the program on which the new Labour Party under Tony Blair campaigned successfully in 1997. Moreover, the spark that Thatcher lit caught fire throughout the world and privatization became the fashion in a great many other countries, at all levels of economic development. It was further promoted by the massive privatization programs in the former Communist countries.

A ballot cast for the Conservatives in 1979 was as clearly a vote against public ownership as a ballot cast for Labour in 1945 had been a vote for it. The British experience represents a radical change in the people's answer to the question of who should own the property in a Good Society.

I   The Public Corporation

Social ownership of the productive property was long the central objective of the British Labour Party; socialism *meant* social ownership. Less attention was given to the question of how the economic mechanism should be organized. After World War II, indeed, Great Britain, along with a number of non-Communist countries, established a national planning agency for the purpose of incorporating some elements of economic planning into the market mechanism.[3] Very few British socialists, however, cherished the vision of a full Soviet-type planning mechanism. Social ownership in Great Britain, as in most of the capitalist world, was designed to operate in a market economy.

A second issue was whether social ownership should encompass most of the country's enterprises or a relatively small number. Supporters of general nationalization saw it as a way to remedy the most egregious evils of capitalism, but most proponents of social ownership intended it to be employed only in special circumstances, such as those in which private ownership produces results that are socially undesirable. In any case, barring a revolution, the process of nationalization had to proceed gradually, starting with a limited number of enterprises. Had it been an unqualified success, it is conceivable that nationalization would have been continuously extended and the economy gradually transformed into full market socialism. By the time the process was sharply reversed under the Thatcher government, however, few people still felt that public ownership of everything was the answer to Britain's economic problems.

In Britain, then, as in most modern economies, public ownership has been confined to a portion of the economy, and that is likely to be the case long into the future. The extent of it may ebb and flow over time, but even committed protagonists of universal public ownership do not expect to see it in their lifetimes.

Organization   Various forms of public ownership had their advocates in the Labour Party, including municipal ownership, worker ownership, and others. After decades of debate, the concept of the public corporation emerged as the dominant view in the 1930s.

Under both state and public ownership, the people are the ultimate owners of the property, but the legal owner is the government, presumably acting as the agent of the people. Unlike state ownership, however, under public ownership the government cedes one of the major rights of ownership – the right to control the use of the property – almost entirely to the corporation. There are no government planners telling the enterprise what it must produce, how much coal it may use, and from whom the coal will be delivered. The manager of a public corporation therefore has the power to make the same broad range of decisions that the manager of a private enterprise makes, with certain exceptions; borrowing money by issuing bonds, for example, requires the approval of government. The public corporation is subject not to the administrative law that applies to agencies of government but to the same civil law that applies to private companies. It can be sued under commercial law, and its bonds are liabilities of the corporation and not of the government.

The government's chief responsibility is to appoint a board of public directors and its chairman, and to approve matters of high policy such as capital investments and bond financing. It also has the important power of issuing "general directives."[4] The board, however, is supposed to be "near sovereign" over the enterprise, and is not subject to the day-to-day intervention of Parliament or the ministers.[5] The board develops the specific policies of the corporation and bears responsibility for monitoring the performance of the corporation and its management.

The chairman of the board is usually the chief executive officer, as in many private corporations. Top management earns a respectable salary, and the chief executive of a large public corporation can become a very powerful figure, dominating the board of directors and running the company very much as if it were his private domain, though always subject to monitoring by his minister. In Italy in particular, the independent "barons" of the holding companies enjoy enormous political influence, and ministers' careers have sometimes been wrecked in collisions with strong heads of huge holding companies.[6] The flamboyant Enrico Mattei, long the head of the huge National Fuel Trust, was the prototype of the public entrepreneur, presiding over the expansion of his company to its massive size. In the general view, he ran the company pretty much as he wished, interpreting the public interest however he wished.

Labor   Labor is hired by management in much the same manner as in private and state enterprises. Management–labor relations are conducted in negotiations with the trade unions over wage rates, working conditions, and other standard features of labor contracts. The life of a worker in a public corporation does not differ greatly from that of one in a private corporation, except that political and social pressures may exert more influence on who gets a job and whether staff should be cut. Employees of public corporations do not see themselves as working "for the government" itself in the manner of a civil servant, in contrast to employees of state-owned enterprises, who do sometimes see themselves that way.

2   Principals and Agents Once More

The founders of the public corporations in Britain were idealists and expected that the managers would serve as "custodians of the public interest," in the words of Herbert Morrison, the chief architect of postwar nationalization.[7] They would decide which and how many workers to employ, or where a new railroad line was needed, on the basis of their professional expertise, under the general rules laid down by the government. The chief executive would say to the minister, in effect, "I will run this railroad as a good railroad should be run; fire me if you don't like my performance, but don't tell me how to do my job."

Yet they are salaried officials and, like the managers of private and state enterprises, are in a position to promote their personal interests at the expense of those of the owners. Arrangements must therefore be made to assure that it is in management's interest to run the company in ways that the owners wish it to be run. The techniques available for harmonizing the interests of managers and owners are the same as under the other forms of ownership: incentive contracts that are compatible with the owners' interests, and the monitoring of management's work.

INCENTIVE CONTRACTS

In order to attract managers who are as competent as those in equivalent private companies, the compensation package should be competitive with those offered in such companies. There are certain difficulties in achieving that, however. For one thing, many citizens would regard it as unseemly that people who run publicly owned enterprises should earn capitalist-size salaries that are so much larger than their own. The compensation package of one chairman, for example, consisted only of a salary, a company car, and the option of membership in a private health-insurance scheme. The salary was inadequate by comparison with executives in private industry, but "in comparison with the wages received by the vast majority of workers in nationalized industries his pay was ample."[8]

Moreover, the compensation package cannot include stock-ownership options since the property is publicly owned. Nor would profit-linked bonuses assure compatibility between the interests of managers and owners, for the owners – the public and their government – expect more of their corporations than the mere pursuit of profit in the manner of private enterprises. The public corporation is expected to pursue a variety of social objectives that a profit-making company does not, some of which may conflict with the earning of profit. For example, the government may hold the view that a public corporation should, among other things, provide more job security for its workers than the private sector provides. When objectives of that sort are added onto management's responsibilities, it becomes difficult for the government to identify inefficiency in the management of the enterprise; for if labor costs are running high and profits low, management can claim, perhaps rightly, to be honoring the commitment to job security. Pure inefficiency can be easily masked as the pursuit of social objectives.

The multiplicity of objectives and the difficulty of specifying them makes it difficult to write contracts that motivate the manager/agent to make decisions that are the right ones from the perspective of government/owner. The government must therefore rely on highly impressionistic standards for evaluating enterprise performance and deciding whether the managers merit an increase in salary and the award of a bonus.

MONITORING

Management of the public corporation is responsible to the same officers that monitor the state-owned enterprise – government ministers and civil servants. In a democratic society, the public and their elected officials regard themselves as having a say as well. In addition, like a private corporation, the managers are monitored by their own board of directors. The public corporation is, if anything, over-monitored.

Ministers   The fundamental principle of the public corporation – that the government should not "interfere" in its day-to-day operation – limits the capacity of the government to serve as a monitor. But the corporation is obliged to issue regular reports, and the minister may request special reports on matters about which there is some question. Moreover, the minister has certain independent sources of information about the corporation: irritated MPs, for example, or citizen's groups. It is therefore unlikely that any major aspect of performance will not come to the attention of the minister's staff. Conflicts between chairmen and ministers often occur, with increasing frequency over the years – usually over a major issue like building or closing down a power station.[9] Such conflicts reflect the central issue in the control of the corporation – the right of the government to require an action that management regards as politically motivated rather than in the public interest. However, they may also be taken to some extent as evidence of the success of government monitoring, in the sense that ministers know a great deal about how the company is being managed.

Directors   The board of directors have the right to look closely into the day-to-day operations of the company, and are therefore in the best position to monitor the activities of management. The board is somewhat constrained by the fact that the chief executive is normally its chairman, but that is not unlike many private companies. Unlike most directors of private companies, however, they are not themselves owners of the property and their own wealth is not at stake. They receive remuneration for their services, but it is not the source of their livelihood, and they take the job for such reasons as public service, power, and prestige. Since their motivations are different from those of directors of private companies, it is difficult to judge whether their monitoring is as diligent as when the personal wealth of the monitors is directly at stake. Voting against a chief executive is not something most people would do with relish; it is somewhat easier to do if it would increase your personal bank account.

The public   Managers of a private corporation are monitored not only by their own directors, but also by outsiders seeking opportunities to increase their wealth by acquiring underpriced companies. There is no equivalent disciplining arrangement under public ownership, except for potential managers waiting in the wings to take over the job of a manager who has been dismissed. There are other types of outsider groups with an interest in monitoring management, however, such as consumer organizations and public interest groups. These outsiders bring enthusiasm and expertise to their task, but they are not able or motivated to spend as much time and money in monitoring management as a prospective purchaser of a private company finds worthwhile.

The literature provides no major instances of abuse of power for personal gain by the managers of British public corporations. That may say as much about British society as about public ownership, for in some other countries publicly owned enterprises have been repeatedly rocked by scandals. It does suggest, however, that the incentives- and monitoring arrangements have served well in assuring that managers do not use their power to advance their narrow personal interests.

Multiple objectives   A good control system must not only restrain managers from doing what they shouldn't do. It should also motivate them to do what they should do, which in this case is to actively promote the interests of the owners. How well it has succeeded in that respect is more difficult to answer. The reason is that there has been no clear and consistent statement of what "the" owners want their corporations to do. Not only are there many groups who regard themselves as owners and therefore entitled to a say – the public, politicians, trade unions, consumer organizations – but these groups hold different views about what the corporation's objectives should be, and there are also competing views within the groups. Because of the multiplicity of objectives, the manager/agents do not have a clear notion of how best to advance the interests of the owners/principals, and it has been difficult for monitors like the directors to hold them to account.

The following sections consider some of the major objectives that have been put forward in the public debate.

3 Monopoly

The advocates of selective nationalization assumed that private ownership can be relied upon to manage the great mass of the country's run-of-the-mill production facilities in reasonable conformity to the values of a Good Society. There is one case, however, in which private ownership cannot be made to serve the public interest, even when suitably regulated by government. That is the case of "natural monopoly." From that minimalist perspective, the objective of public ownership is to make more efficient use of the country's resources than would be made by private ownership under conditions of natural monopoly.

Ordinary monopoly refers to a market in which there is one producer of a good but where there could be several or many. Such monopolies are sometimes broken up by government order into two or more smaller companies, which then compete for business with each other and still manage to remain reasonably profitable. There are some monopolies, however, which cannot be broken up into smaller companies all of which can still earn a profit. That is the case when production takes place under the condition known as "declining cost."

Declining cost Suppose the average cost of running a railroad is $10,000 per train, and the manager were asked how much would it cost to run one additional train – that is to say, what is the marginal cost of railroad service? If the answer is $12,000, the company is said to be operating under increasing cost: running one more train would drive up the average cost for everybody because the marginal cost of an additional train would be larger than the average cost of all the trains combined. If the answer is $8,000, however, the company is operating under declining cost; running an additional train would *reduce* the average cost for everybody because the marginal cost would be lower than the average cost. With declining cost, everybody gains, so to speak, when output is increased.

Public utilities like railroads and electric-power plants have traditionally employed technologies under which the typical enterprise operates at declining cost. A city of 1 million customers, for example, could be fully supplied by one power company at an average cost of – say – $0.10 per KWH. If five separate companies each served only 200,000 customers in the same city, the average cost for each company would be much higher – perhaps $0.30 per KWH. Hence, contrary to the usual case, with declining cost the society would be better off under monopoly than under competition. It is for that reason that monopoly is referred to as the "natural" arrangement in such industries.

Regulation or public ownership? Like every monopoly, privately owned natural monopoly is inefficient because the company finds it most profitable to charge a price that is higher than the average cost of production and to produce less than the socially optimal level of output (chapter 17). In an ordinary monopoly, that cause of inefficiency is often remedied by government regulation. The regulatory agency may require the company to follow the socially optimal pricing rule, "price equals marginal cost"; that is, to charge a price no larger than the marginal cost of production. Under that rule, if the marginal cost of producing additional electric power is $0.10 per KWH, the producer is forbidden to charge more than that. The regulator's pricing rule – price must be equal to marginal cost – transforms an inefficient rogue monopolist into an efficient pussycat of a producer, rather as in perfect competition.

When an ordinary monopoly is compelled to behave in that socially optimal way, it makes less profit than if it were unregulated, but it still makes a profit. The trouble with natural monopoly is that if the company were compelled by the regulatory agency to behave in the socially optimal way, it would suffer an actual loss. The reason is that if it costs an average $0.12 per KWH to produce electric power, the price has to be no less than $0.12 per KWH merely to cover the production cost. Under conditions of declining cost, however, marginal cost is smaller than average cost, so that a price that is only equal to marginal cost – say it were $0.10 per KWH – would result in an actual loss of $0.02 for every KWH sold. Hence, an ordinary monopoly that does the right thing can still earn a profit, though somewhat reduced; but a natural monopoly that does the right thing cannot even cover its costs. Since private owners would not remain in a business that loses money, it follows that when the property is privately owned, efficiency is impossible to achieve under conditions of natural monopoly, even with government regulation.

There are several things that could be done in this case. The government regulators could permit the company to charge a price high enough to cover its average cost and still earn a reasonable profit. That is the approach generally used in the United States, where regulation has been preferred to public ownership. A privately owned company could then stay in business, but it would be inefficient; the company would still not produce as much electric power as ought to be produced. A second possibility is to set the regulated price at the low optimal level – equal to the marginal cost of production – and then cover the loss by a government subsidy. But if an industry cannot operate efficiently without a subsidy, the case for public ownership is strengthened. The public would be more inclined to support a subsidy paid to their own public corporation than if it were paid to cover the losses of a group of private capitalists.

Analysis of these optimal-pricing rules and other issues of natural monopoly generated a great deal of scholarly interest and occupied a prominent place in the economics journals after World War II. For all its honored place in economics, however, that literature evoked little more than yawns from those engaged in the political economy of public ownership. The optimal-pricing literature did finally penetrate the British political world in a 1967 White Paper that endorsed the golden rule that, with some exceptions, prices should be equal to marginal cost.[10] For many reasons, however, including the difficulty of actually calculating marginal cost, that pricing principle was not widely adopted.

In the end it was not the theoretical concern over the inefficiency of natural monopoly but practical politics that shaped the course of nationalization. Most of the nationalized industries were not monopolies at all but were in fact quite competitive – such as iron and steel, air transportation, and British Leyland. Road transportation, coal mines, and docks and harbors were nationalized not because they were monopolies but because they were so run-down after the war that there was little opposition to their nationalization, even by conservatives.[11] Moreover, in the course of time technological progress eroded many former monopolies: road and air transportation became active competitors for some of the railroads' business, gas competed with electricity in space heating, and electronic telecommunications increasingly ate into the monopolies of the postal services, telephone, and telegraph.[12] The natural-monopoly argument for nationalization simply disappeared from the political agenda.

4 Social Objectives

Under both public and state ownership, it is "the people" in the abstract who are the ultimate owners of the property. Authoritarian political regimes maintain the fiction that the government fully represents the interests of the people so that they have no further ownership role to play. In democratic societies, however, the principle of ownership by "the people" ceases to be purely abstract and is actually taken seriously by many of the citizens. And as owners, they claim the right to require "their" enterprise to promote their interests, or at least take them seriously into account.

Different groups, however, have different interests, which sometimes collide. Hence there is no clear, single objective that can guide managers in making such major decisions as the quality of the goods and services to produce, the price at which to sell them, the number of workers to employ, and the wage- and working conditions to provide. Navigating among conflicting objectives becomes one of the main problems of management and of the ministers and directors who bear the responsibility for monitoring management's performance.

PROFIT

What was never been in dispute, however, is that profit maximization should *not* be an objective of the public corporation. It was unthinkable for a Good Society to permit the use of its resources to be governed by the "profit motive." Profit had always been sinful to socialists, and it was virtually an axiom that profit considerations should not govern the production decisions of public corporations.

The hostility to profit derives from two concerns – justice and efficiency. The more powerful of the two is the concern over the injustice of large incomes being collected for no apparent reason other than the mere ownership of profit-making property. The issue of efficiency pales in comparison to the passion generated by that concern with justice.

Public ownership solves the problem of justice: no individual derives an income from the ownership of the productive property. However, it leaves unresolved the question of what should replace profit-making as the objective that the corporation should pursue. The question was usually dealt with in very general terms, such as the pronouncement that it should have a "public purpose." One popular formulation is that a public enterprise should conduct its business as a "socially responsible corporation," a notion popularized by critics of private corporations. A variant of that critique is that even private corporations should acknowledge that they have obligations to their "stakeholders" as well as to their stockholders.[13] Stakeholders are people who do not own shares but whose lives are so keenly affected by the company's decisions that their interests should be taken into account in those decisions, along with the interest of the stockholders in the company's profit. A public corporation, of course, does not have shareholders, but it does have the same stakeholders as private companies, such as workers and consumers. The corporation should therefore provide better working conditions and sell at lower prices than a private corporation concerned only with its stockholders' profit.

Yet there must be some limit to the public corporation's benevolence in these respects, else its costs might so exceed its revenues that it would require large subsidies to cover its losses; and the public is surely not prepared to tax itself to pay such subsidies without limit. That limit was recognized in the founding legislation of the British public corporations, which stipulated that they were to "ensure that revenues are not less than sufficient to meet all outgoings chargeable to the revenue account, taking one year with another."[14] As experience accumulated and deficiencies in the management of the corporations came to light, however, the early cavalier attitude toward profit came under challenge, from supporters of public ownership as well as its opponents. In 1961 the Labour government sought to tighten financial discipline by requiring that public enterprises not merely cover costs but also earn profits that were in line with those in the private sector.[15] Some influential socialist "revisionists" went further, arguing that efficiency should be a major objective and that public enterprises should provide a "yardstick for efficiency."[16] The compromise that emerged was that management should provide a high level of service, keep prices down, provide reasonable wages and working conditions for the workers, and still make a profit, "though not an embarrassingly large one."[17]

Profit and efficiency That modestly formulated objective is not inconsistent with the requirements of efficiency. The public enterprises did not sell their goods or services in perfectly competitive markets, but in markets that were imperfectly competitive in varying degrees. In such markets, a Good Society does *not* want its enterprises to maximize profit, for it is only in perfect markets that profit maximization is conducive to efficiency. Efficiency in imperfect markets requires that the enterprises charge the price that is equal to the marginal cost of production, not the higher price that maximizes the enterprise's profit.

It happens, however, that public enterprises that follow the rough rule of making some profit but not too much would come close to the golden rule – "price equals marginal cost": their price would be lower, and their profit smaller, than that of a profit-maximizing enterprise. Hence, if all enterprises in imperfectly competitive markets followed that rule, the country's resources would be more efficiently employed than if they sought to maximize their profit.

Had it been possible to run the enterprises on the basis of that broadly formulated objective alone – some profit, but not too much – the task of management would have been relatively uncomplicated. What opened Pandora's box were the additional objectives designed to promote the interests of the citizens-as-workers as well as the citizens-as-consumers.

WORKERS

The British trade unions were strong supporters of nationalization in the belief that wages and working conditions would be much better under public ownership than under private ownership, which they regarded as nakedly exploitative. Most socialists and other advocates of public ownership shared that view. Just what rights the workers should have as stakeholders, however, was a matter of longstanding dispute.

In the early years of the century the trade unions were committed to a certain principle of industrial democracy referred to as "workers' control."[18] It derives from that socialist view which sees the fundamental clash of interests to be that between capitalists and workers, from which it follows that when the capitalists are gone, control over the productive property should fall to the workers. It seemed beyond dispute that in a Good Socialist Society each enterprise would be owned, or at least run, by the people who worked in it.

That view was heatedly contested by other groups within the pro-nationalization movement. The most active opponents were socialists like Sidney and Beatrice Webb, who were friends of but not part of the labor movement. They argued that if labor were given that power, the enterprises would end up serving the parochial interests of their own workers, at the expense of the workers of other enterprises and of the public at large. Powerful opposition to workers' control also came from the consumer organizations, which feared that workers' control would degenerate into collusion between labor and management at the expense of the consumer.

The controversy reflected a fundamental difference in view among socialists generally. It was the central issue in the bitter conflict between Marxists and anarcho-syndicalists, with the former insisting that the state should control the enterprises in socialist economies, and the latter, fearing the power of such a state, arguing that the enterprises should be controlled by those who work in them. It flared up after the Russian Revolution until Stalin put an end to it by crushing the labor unions that demanded worker control. In the British controversy, the worker-control movement was eventually defeated in the Labour Party, which decided that control over the public corporations would be lodged with boards of public directors.

It was nevertheless generally accepted that nationalization would improve the conditions of labor in the public corporations. Management would respect the workers' rights as stakeholders in the enterprise; they would actively solicit and take account of the workers' views, and the workers would develop a cooperative relationship with management, in contrast to the adversarial relationship of the past.

Labor did indeed make considerable gains in some of the nationalized enterprises in the postwar years, but many of the gains were due not to nationalization as such but to the strong position of the trade unions under the Labour government. The National Dock Labour Scheme, for example, gave the trade unions extensive control over employment, wages, and job security in the seaports, which led to large-scale overstaffing.[19] Despite the relatively relaxed conditions of work in many of the public corporations, however, in the course of time the workers came to the bitter conclusion that their conditions did not differ much from those in private industry.[20] In part, the reason was that management, while not expected to operate like a profit-maximizing enterprise, came under sufficient financial pressure that they could not provide whatever conditions of pay and working conditions the workers thought they merited. Labor relations became tense, and strikes broke out from time to time. Moreover, industrial conflicts in the nationalized sector have a particularly severe social effect because they are more politicized than conflicts in the strictly private sector. Labor's disenchantment with the effect of nationalization on their own welfare contributed to the weakness of the opposition to the growing movement for privatization.

CONSUMERS

Industrial consumers of steel, coal, electric power, and other producer goods pressed for lower prices than they would have paid if the producers were profit-making companies. Their argument took the usual national-interest turn: lower prices for their inputs would enable them to compete more successfully with foreign companies and thus to save British jobs.

The interests of personal consumers are not as vigorously promoted in public affairs because they are more widely dispersed than workers and industrial consumers. In the debate on nationalization, however, their interests were forcefully promoted, both by the National Consumer Council and by non-trade-union socialists. The consumer interest lay in lower prices and better service from the public enterprises: lower railroad fares and more frequent trains, for example. They were particularly concerned that the trade unions not become so powerful that management would be intimidated into collusion with them at the consumers' expense.

THE PUBLIC

Apart from their roles as workers and consumers, citizens have a stake in the activity of the enterprise as it affects their community and society. Citizen groups held that as a socially responsible corporation, the public enterprise should be particularly sensitive to the aesthetic and environmental consequences of its actions, and should use some of its resources to enhance the quality of social life in its community. An airline or railroad, for example, should not cease to service a town on strictly financial grounds if that would depress its economic and social life.

Of particular importance was the employment policy of a corporation that was a major employer in a town. A private enterprise might close down an unprofitable plant without regard to the devastating effect it might have on the community; the public expects its own enterprises to be more protective of a community's welfare in such cases. That sentiment sparked the massive public protest that compelled the British Conservative government to abandon its plan to close down a number of unprofitable coal mines (chapter 20).

SUBSIDIES

It is rare that the demands of a stakeholder entail an increase in the enterprise's revenue or a decrease in its production cost. The direction is always the other way – to reduce revenue or increase cost. The pressures generated by the obligation to meet the various social objectives therefore always tended to reduce profits or generate losses. The consequence was a large and growing volume of subsidies required to keep many of the enterprises afloat. In the mid-1970s the finances of the nationalized industries were "in chaos," requiring subsidies in excess of £1 billion.[21] Coal, railroads, and the airlines are the industries most often cited, but heavy subsidies were paid elsewhere as well: the Post Office loss of £304 billion in 1974 was described as the "world's biggest ever loss."[22] The total of all operating losses was larger than the size of the government subsidies alone, however, for many public corporations "cross-subsidized" those of their own plants that were operating at a loss. Loss-making collieries, for example, were kept in operation by means of heavy subsidies paid out of profits earned in other pits.[23]

Hence, the public corporations did go a long way toward meeting the claims of the citizens-as-consumers and the citizens-as-workers, but at a considerable cost to the citizens-as-taxpayers. The declining reputation of public enterprise was due not only to the subsidies as such, however, but to many of the purposes for which they were needed. Subsidizing a loss-making coal mine so that a town would not be obliterated was one thing; subsidizing the operation of a loss-making railroad station for the convenience of a small number of affluent suburbanites was another. It was the proliferating tales of the latter kind of subsidy that contributed to the growing disenchantment with public enterprise.

5   The Intrusion of Politics

Dictators love state ownership because it concentrates economic power in the hands of the government. For the same reason, democrats fear it. Democratic socialists are attracted to public ownership because it offers a way of socializing the productive property while limiting the government's ability to use it for such illegitimate ends as strengthening its hold on power.

The government must tread a fine line in its responsibilities under public ownership. As the lawful owner of the property, it has the responsibility for assuring that it is used in the public interest. However, its authority is supposed to be limited to such matters as appointing the public directors and specifying such broad objectives as whether the enterprise should earn a profit. Having done those things, it is expected to forswear interference with management's decisions.

Yet the government must also deal with the complaints and demands of individual citizens and interest groups, all of whom cannot be satisfied by all of the corporation's decisions. In the UK, ministers and MPs receive large mailbags of complaints from labor, consumers, and the general public, making claims upon public enterprises that they would not presume to press upon private corporations. Such pressures make it difficult for a government to honor its obligation to keep hands off the management of the public corporations. There are, in addition, the standard pressures upon elected governments in every society, even when all the enterprises are privately owned. The British government's requirement that the Electricity Board extend electric power to rural areas is not unlike the requirements that most governments place on privately owned regulated companies; and when the bankruptcy of Rolls Royce, an important defense contractor, threatened the jobs of 80,000 workers in the city of Derby, it was a Conservative government that acquired its aero-engine and turbine divisions.[24] Nor do any governments conduct their own affairs purely on the basis of efficiency concerns: political pressures are of dominating importance not only in defense procurement and the closing of redundant military bases but in the demands of economic actors generally.

It was therefore inevitable that the government's political concerns would intrude in the management of public corporations. And indeed, there was a steady regression to greater ministerial and parliamentary involvement in their business.[25] In 1974 the Labour government actually widened the ministers' authority over the public enterprises. And when the Conservative government ran an anti-inflationary policy in 1970, they pressured the public corporations to keep prices down, despite rising costs.[26] Such pressures contributed to the increase in loss-making operations that then had to be covered by government subsidies.

One might have predicted that, under these circumstances, the wall between government and public enterprises would soon have been demolished. As it turned out, the wall was often bent and breached, but by and large it held. Management often had to tangle with ministers to have their way and they sometimes lost, but they also sometimes won. Most of the pressures, indeed, came not from the government but from MPs who insisted on raising parliamentary questions regarding the conduct of the enterprises.[27] Moreover, many of the instances of government interference would have occurred if the enterprises had been private rather than public corporations, especially if they were under government regulation.

The British did not succeed in keeping politics out of the management of the public corporations in the way that their proponents had originally hoped. On the other hand, the corporations operated with much greater autonomy than if they had been fully state-owned. In that sense they partially vindicated the faith of those who saw the public corporation as a way of socializing the productive property without giving the government the dangerous power that comes with full state ownership. The British experience therefore suggests that a Good Society that prefers social ownership but fears the power of the state would do well to choose the public corporation as its ownership form.

In most modern economies, however, the realistic alternative to public ownership is not state ownership but private ownership. There is now an abundance of evidence on the relative efficiency of these two ownership forms.

6 Performance

Both critics and supporters of public ownership cite a variety of specific respects in which the performance of the public enterprises did not meet the original expectations of their supporters: prices rose more rapidly than the retail price index, output grew more slowly than overall production, labor relations did not improve, and so forth.[28]

Individual indicators, however, provide no basis for assessing overall performance, particularly with respect to efficiency. For that purpose more systematic studies are required, and they have been produced in great profusion. The privatization program of Margaret Thatcher provided a spurt of interest in comparative performance because it made it possible to compare the very same enterprises under both public and private ownership.

In preparation for their own analysis comparing the efficiency of public and private ownership, Martin and Parker examined 63 studies covering a variety of countries, industries, and time periods. The studies differed in the measures used to assess performance. Some studies, for example, measured profitability, which is a poor measure because public corporations are not supposed to focus on profit-making to the same extent as private corporations. To find, as most studies did, that public-corporation profits have been lower than those in the private sector therefore says no more than that they have been doing what they are supposed to do. In fact, if their profit rates did prove to be as high as in private industry, the managers should be fired for impersonating private-enterprise managers.

More revealing are studies that probe into the narrower aspects of efficiency that are least affected by the pursuit of the social objectives imposed by the government. The most commonly used measures are cost of production, labor productivity, such as tons of coal per worker-hour, and aggregate productivity, in which the input of capital as well as of labor is taken into account.

Martin and Parker's conclusion is similar to that of most analysts who have surveyed the literature: "What is evident is the degree of variation in the conclusions, with some studies clearly finding that private ownership leads to improved performance, while others show no statistically significant difference."[29] Enthusiasts of private ownership would find this conclusion disappointing, and perhaps not believable; they would expect that in a large set of studies of this sort, the superiority of private ownership would leap forth unambiguously and universally. Enthusiasts of public ownership would also be disappointed, but less so. They would prefer that public ownership be shown to be superior; but with the bad press that it has been getting in recent decades, they would be relieved that the margin of difference is so small, and that in some cases public enterprise turns out to outperform private.

Of particular importance is another finding that is now widely accepted. The more competitive the industry, the larger the margin of advantage of private over public ownership; but where competition is weak, or where private enterprises are subject to government regulation, the difference in efficiency between the two forms of ownership virtually disappears. Vickers and Yarrow conclude, for example, that "privatization worked best where private ownership works best" – in industries where competition is keenest, such as British Aerospace and Jaguar motors.[30] Where competition was weak or absent, or where there were strong environmental or natural monopoly effects, there were no efficiency gains from privatization, as in airports and water supply, for example. And in networking industries, where some portions are competitive (long-distance telecom) and others not (electric-power grids), it was in the competitive portions that privatization brought efficiency gains. The effect of competition was also evident in the case of British Gas, which was privatized at a time when it faced no active competition. The emergence of a competing supplier ten years later was followed quickly by price discounts of about 25 percent in the trial area.[31]

The extent of competition, however, depends not only on purely economic factors but on the stance of government as well. Under the postwar Labour governments, the unions were able to restrict the supply of labor in their industries and greatly improve wage and security conditions. Many of those restrictions, such as the National Dock Labour Scheme, were removed under the Thatcher government, which enabled privatized companies like Associated British Ports to slim down their labor force dramatically.[32] That improvement in labor productivity cannot therefore be ascribed to privatization directly: if the public corporation had been able to hire and fire workers under the same labor-market conditions as the privatized company, its labor productivity would no doubt have been much higher. The performance of the public corporations has also varied over time. A judicious and conservative analyst offered the conclusion that after 1970, when greater attention was paid to efficiency and managerial independence and less to social objectives, the public corporations became "indistinguishable, for many purposes, from the large corporations of the private sector."[33]

In summary, there is good reason to believe that much of the apparent inefficiency in the public enterprises is the consequence not of the ownership form itself but of the vague and multiple objectives imposed on them by political and social pressures. Hence, if public-corporation managers were instructed to operate on a commercial basis in the manner of private managers, profit and efficiency would be considerably higher. The performance of public ownership would rival that of private ownership in markets where private incentives are dulled by government regulation or by the absence of effective competition, but when markets are vigorously competitive, public ownership under the best of conditions is unlikely to match the performance of private ownership. The difference, however, would not be as large as one would expect from the more doleful accounts of the British experience.

7 Discussion

To find the subject of this chapter even remotely interesting, you must be willing to entertain two ideas. One is that there may be times and circumstances in which private ownership may be a good thing. The other is that there may be times and circumstances in which social ownership may be a good thing.

Both of those ideas have been known to cause fits of apoplexy. Socialists who see the world through the slogan "private gain versus public good" would regard the first idea as preposterous. Some apostles of capitalism would find the second to be unthinkable.

Fortunately most people are more discriminating. They are more kindly disposed to one form of ownership, but are prepared to consider the possibility that there may be circumstances in which the other form would have a place in their Good Society. They simply want to be shown.

The merit of public ownership, as its proponents see it, is that it achieves certain ends that conform to their criteria of a Good Society. Perhaps the major expectation is that it would make for a more just society, which will be discussed presently in chapter 27. Another expectation, however, is that it would lead to a high level of production for the people – that is to say, it would be efficient.

The quality of management Proponents of public ownership expect that the managers of public enterprises would be more competent, and surely more dedicated to the public interest, than those of private enterprises. The impression I get from the literature is that the chief executives of public corporations are indeed as aggressively managerial as their private-enterprise counterparts, and if they exchanged positions with each other, there might well be no detectable difference in the performance of their companies.

My guess, however, is that in the long run the balance is somewhat tilted toward private managers. For one thing, as reported above, the compensation packages offered to public managers tend to be smaller than those that private owners find it worth offering to their managers, for ordinary citizens look askance at government "bureaucrats" racking up incomes equivalent to those of the capitalist tycoons. And indeed, the earnings of top managers rose more rapidly than average earnings after public corporations were privatized.[34] Moreover, public enterprises cannot offer their managers the equivalent of stock options and other such incentives for successful performance.

Some idealistic and highly talented managers would no doubt accept lower compensation for the privilege of public service; as a career, serving the public does have a nobler ring than making money. That might be the case, for example, in such public service as environmental protection or foreign policy. But most of the work of running a public railroad or coal mine is not all that different from running a private enterprise in the same industry, and it pays a lot less. I would therefore expect that, on balance, the best potential managers would enroll in schools of business administration rather than public administration, and that the best Masters of Business Administration would opt for private-sector jobs rather than public.

Monopoly The statistical evidence as reported above is too ambiguous to support a strong conclusion on the relative efficiency of public and private enterprises. It can be said in support of public enterprise that it has not been found to be dramatically less efficient than private ownership when its social obligations are taken into account. I have seen no claims, on the other hand, that it has been more efficient. Insofar as a Good Society is concerned with efficiency, the case for public ownership seems to me to be weaker than that for private ownership.

The argument for public ownership is stronger in markets where competition is weak. A solid body of economic theory demonstrating that the market mechanism is inefficient when markets are monopolistic supports the case against the "free" market when monopoly is present. A case *against* something, however, is not automatically a case *for* anything else.

For one thing, there are other ways of dealing with monopoly than public ownership. One is to give support to those forces that weaken monopoly power – for example, new technology that makes it possible and profitable for new firms to enter a previously monopolized market, or tough laws that penalize collusive control over markets. Another is government regulation. In the United States most natural monopolies are regulated by agencies of government, which limit the prices they may charge or impose other conditions on their operations. A government that has the wisdom to know what the optimal price should be could require a monopolistic enterprise to charge no more than that price; the efficiency gain would then be exactly the same if the enterprise were privately owned as if it were publicly owned.

Government regulation, to be sure, suffers from deficiencies of its own that have been extensively studied. Among other things, if a limit is placed on the profit that can be earned, there is no incentive to keeps costs down. Revenues that would break that profit barrier are spent instead on increasing managerial salaries and perks, or on smoothing labor relations by higher wages and overstaffing, or on expanding the size of the business. It is also well established that over time the industry tends to "capture" the regulators, who begin to see things more and more through the eyes of the people they are supposed to be regulating in the public interest. It is for such reasons that regulated private enterprises have not in general been found to be more efficient than equivalent public enterprises.

A certain political consideration enters into my own assessment of the two forms of ownership. Government has more important things to do for the welfare of a society than assuming responsibility for the production of its goods and services. The economy would be more efficient and the society better off materially if production were left to private owners, with a smaller and more effective government concentrating on guarding against abuses: by the promotion of competition, by the regulation of monopolies, by attending to the conditions of the disadvantaged, by public-safety and health protection, and so forth. Moreover, it is unwise to subject government to the continuous temptation that public enterprise offers to politicians to use it for strictly political purposes. The British have managed remarkably well, in my opinion, in insulating their public corporations from political interference, but I doubt that many countries could do as well over long periods. It is true that federal public enterprises in the United States like the TVA and the Post Office have an admirable record of administrative autonomy, but lower-level public authorities are not known to be reticent about using public property for political and personal benefit.

Social objectives   Most of the proponents of public ownership have favored it not primarily because of its efficiency but because it can serve a variety of other objectives that make for a better society, some examples of which are given in the text.

I share the view that I believe most economists hold, that most social objectives are best achieved directly through the action of government, rather than indirectly through the production system. Take airline service, for example. It is not possible to service every city with as many flights as the people would like to have. Under any arrangement, most cities will receive no service at all; many citizens will have to drive or take the bus to the nearest large city that has an air terminal; and many smaller cities will have fewer scheduled flights than their residents would wish. On what basis should a public airline decide which cities to service and which not, and how many flights to schedule in each?

The instruction that the airline should make a profit that is not "embarrassingly large" is a sensible one. It means that service will be provided to every city where the additional cost of providing it is no larger than the additional revenue that would be collected. The excluded cities are those in which the demand for service is not sufficient to produce enough revenue to cover the additional cost of providing it. Airline services are thus distributed efficiently, following the same principle that applies to housing, shoes, automobiles, and all other goods: given the distribution of income, the goods and services go to those cities that are willing and able to pay at least as much as it costs the society to produce them. The only cities excluded from consuming some good or service are those that are unable or unwilling to pay that much.

Under this arrangement, ticket prices are lower, more cities receive service, and profits are smaller, than they would be under a privately owned airline. Some people urge, however, that a socially responsible public corporation should go further than that. In their view, profit, no matter who earns it, comes out of the hides of the people. Therefore, if the public airline earns $1 million in profit, it should use that profit to cover the loss of extending the service to other cities – like Elmtown, shall we say – where the revenues would be less than the cost of providing the service. It should extend service to as many cities like Elmtown as it can until it ends up with no profit at all.

That proposal, which is often advanced in debates on the Good Society, reflects either a misunderstanding of what efficiency means, or a rejection of efficiency as a proper criterion of goodness in this matter. The proposal amounts to using the $1 million profit earned by the airline to "cross-subsidize" the cost of providing airline service to cities like Elmtown that cannot pay their way. The alternative is to eliminate service to the Elmtowns and to turn the $1 million profit over to the public treasury where it can be used for many meritorious purposes: children's day-care, income supplements for the poor, stipends for artists, and so forth. Looked at in those terms, providing service to Elmtown, commendable though it may be, is surely not the *optimal* use of the society's resources.

One might respond by arguing that it is not a matter of efficiency but of justice. The people of Elmtown may need airline service no less than those in larger cities, but they are, perhaps, poorer than people elsewhere. A public airline in a Good Society should provide its service not only to the rich but to the poor as well. The point is well taken, in the sense that efficiency should not be the only standard for assessing the goodness with which the society's resources are used. However, if the society decided that airline service for the poor citizens of Elmtown were more meritorious than other uses that might be made of the airline's profit, it would be better to respond to that need directly, by an income transfer to the poor, rather than indirectly by changing the airline's management rules. The treasury might give cash or vouchers – perhaps to the amount of $1/2 million – to the poor citizens of Elmtown to enable them to buy airline tickets along with everyone else. The airline might then find that the revenues produced by service to Elmtown would cover the cost of providing it, and it would provide that service on normal commercial grounds. The advantage of that direct method of providing the service would be that the benefit goes only to the poor. If the airline were obliged to provide the service by cross-subsidizing it out of its profit on other routes, the benefit would go to the rich citizens of Elmtown as well as to the poor. It often works out, indeed, that programs justified on the basis of the needs of the poor end up benefitting the well-off more than the poor.

The illustrative example applies to the consumers of a public enterprise's products, but it applies equally to its workers. Public enterprises should indeed be model employers, but there is no reason that workers in a public airline, for example, should be better paid and enjoy higher benefits than workers who hold equivalent jobs in private companies. British consumers were no different from those elsewhere in declining to pay more for the cost of labor in their public enterprises than they pay in private enterprises. The profits earned by an efficiently managed public enterprise should belong to all the people, and should not be divided up between that enterprise's consumers and workers.

Stakeholding involves not only sharing in the benefits of the enterprise's success, but also sharing in its failures. For the workers, that means the possibility that some may lose their jobs, or all of them may in the worst case. When unemployment rises, pressure builds up on the public enterprises to relieve the distress by taking on workers they do not need. As in the case of airline services, however, it is an inefficient solution. There are other social policies for dealing with unemployment that do not undermine the enterprises' ability to operate efficiently (chapter 19). Under the best of policies, however, a certain number of workers, mostly older ones, face the grim prospect of permanent unemployment. The least-costly solution that I know of is a lifetime pension, the burden of which is borne by the whole population in the form of taxes. It is more efficient than subsidizing obsolete public enterprises so that they remain in operation, or imposing bloated payrolls on otherwise well-managed public enterprises. Each such compromise with efficiency decreases the ability of the society to cope with its other social problems.

Whether that solution is not only more efficient but also more humane is a separate question. It is no doubt a crushing experience to realize that you are never likely to hold a regular job again, even a job well beneath the one you held you held at your peak. If selective overstaffing of public enterprises could diminish that pain, it is surely a policy worth entertaining, even at some loss of efficiency. The general experience, however, is that the presence on the shop floor of too many people clearly not working is bad for the morale of the work force, and in the long run leads to a serious erosion of effort.

In my own Good Society, all I require is that all known methods of providing efficiently for full employment should be put in place. If I, as an older worker, nevertheless end up with no prospect of another job again in my lifetime, I would regard it as a piece of bad luck but not an indictment of the social arrangements, since I can propose no better one. I would still be satisfied – I think – to live in a society that at least provides a modest pension for the small number of people with my bad fortune.

Would I prefer to be given a made-up job in some public enterprise where I was clearly not needed? Perhaps I would, at first, hoping that it might turn into a real job. But if it did not, I think I might eventually find it more humiliating than being retired on the pension. What I would prefer, I believe, is to be offered a made-up public-works job that had some social value, such as millions of workers held during the Great Depression.

Market socialism Most people who favor public enterprise intend it to be used only in limited circumstances such as natural monopolies. Others favor it not merely for reasons of efficiency but out of a variety of other social concerns. They have in mind a much broader extent of public ownership, including the possibility that it may dominate the economy. Private and other forms of ownership might be permitted to operate, but only in specified sectors, such as small-scale enterprises and high-tech entrepreneurial companies. Their version of a Good Society is market socialism, in which social ownership takes the form of public enterprise rather than state enterprise.

In assessing the evidence on how such a system might work, it is important to note that most of our experience with public enterprise is to be found in capitalist countries, where the public corporations swim in a sea of private enterprises. It is very likely that the private-enterprise environment exerts a considerable influence on the behavior of the management of the public enterprises. First, managerial skills and standards of performance are developed in the private sector, and are learned by the public managers, who often come out of the same schools, and even the same enterprises. Second, the private sector sets certain standards of performance that public enterprises must more or less live up to.

One cannot therefore infer from the experience of public ownership in Britain and elsewhere what the economic world would look like in an economy dominated by public enterprises. My own guess is that on matters of internal enterprise efficiency it would perform quite well relative to capitalist economies. The economy would be less efficient overall, however, because politics is likely to exert an even greater influence over the economy than it does in capitalist countries. Even if the public enterprises could escape politics in the narrow sense of interference in managerial decisions, they are likely to be subjected to political influence in the form of the requirement that they pursue a variety of social objectives rather than concentrate on efficiency. Judging from the British and Hungarian experiences, it is difficult to imagine that public enterprises would not succumb to the pressures to keep prices down in the interest of the citizens-as-consumers, and to maintain a larger work force than they need in the interest of the citizens-as-workers. In the course of a generation the efficiency of the economy would gradually decline.

The activity in which market socialism is least likely to match the performance of the capitalist countries, however, is not allocative efficiency but the invention and innovation of new products and new technology. But the discussion of that large topic must be deferred to the end of Part V.

Notes

1 Most of the hostility to "government" is directed not against government in general but against the national government. People who share that sentiment are often remarkably friendly to lower levels of government, on the view that they are closer to the people. When American conservatives and populists call for power to be returned to the people, for example, they often mean to state governments. Among socialists, some supporters of public ownership would have municipal governments, rather than the national state, own the productive property. In the United States municipalities still own many public services, primarily waterworks but also electric-power companies. The discussion in the text, however, deals primarily with national governments.
2 Redwood, *Public Enterprise in Crisis*, p. 17.
3 In Europe, the most extensive of those efforts was made in France, which developed an elaborate system of what was called "indicative planning." With the active participation of business and labor, the government produced a national plan specifying the directions of development that were thought to be most beneficial to the country. Business was induced to carry out the investments and other measures by such devices as subsidized loans from the Ministry of Finance. When the economy recovered from the effects of the war and business was again able to finance its own investments, the influence of the Ministry of Finance declined and indicative planning was eventually given up. Carre et al., *French Economic Growth*.
4 Sloman, *Socialising Public Ownership*, p. 27.
5 Redwood, *Public Enterprise in Crisis*, p. 24.
6 Posner, "Nationalization."
7 Martin and Parker, *The Impact of Privatization*, p. 16.
8 Sloman, *Socialising Public Ownership*, p. 100.
9 Sloman, *Socialising Public Ownership*, p. 99.
10 Redwood and Hatch, *Controlling Public Industries*, p. 65.
11 Martin and Parker, *The Impact of Privatization*, p. 65.
12 Posner, "Nationalization."
13 Sloman, *Socialising Public Ownership*, p. 133.
14 Martin and Parker, *The Impact of Privatization*, p. 50.
15 Shepherd, *Economic Performance under Public Ownership*, p. 27.
16 Tomlinson, *The Unequal Struggle*, p. 144.
17 Sloman, *Socialising Public Ownership*, p. 25.
18 Sloman, *Socialising Public Ownership*, ch. 3.
19 Martin and Parker, *The Impact of Privatization*, p. 187.
20 Sloman, *Socialising Public Ownership*, p. 43.
21 Pryke, *The Nationalized Industries*, p. 261.
22 Sloman, *Socialising Public Ownership*, p. 37.
23 Pryke, *The Nationalized Industries*, p. 254.
24 Sloman, *Socialising Public Ownership*, p. 70.
25 Redwood, *Public Enterprise in Crisis*, pp. 24–5.
26 Sloman, *Socialising Public Ownership*, p. 30.

27 Sloman, *Socialising Public Ownership*, p. 28.
28 Redwood, *Public Enterprise in Crisis*, pp. 2–5.
29 Martin and Parker, *The Impact of Privatization*, p. 67.
30 Vickers and Yarrow, *Privatization*, p. 428.
31 Martin and Parker, *The Impact of Privatization*, p. 218.
32 Martin and Parker, *The Impact of Privatization*, p. 187.
33 Posner, "Nationalization," p. 596.
34 Martin and Parker, *The Impact of Privatization*, p. 167.

Chapter 26

Workers as Owners

Let a hundred flowers blossom and a
hundred schools of thought contend.
– Mao Zedong

CONTENTS

Private, state, and public ownership all share a certain property – the workers are merely hired hands. They are paid to do what their employers tell them to do, and they are dismissed when their labor is no longer needed.

In some versions of the Good Society the very idea of citizens "employing" other citizens betokens a society of unacceptable class divisions – between those who come cap in hand seeking jobs, and those who dole the jobs out. From the perspective of that value, none of those three forms of ownership has a claim to goodness.

Things look rather different from a conservative perspective. The relation of employer to worker is a contract, and it is through contracts willingly entered into for mutual benefit that free people conduct their economic lives. Workers are not forced to take any particular jobs; they take those that they regard as the best of the alternatives available to them. It is no different from the contract between a homeowner and a self-employed plumber: the plumber does what the homeowner wants in return for a contracted payment.

That argument does not satisfy the critics of the employment relation. The plumber works "for himself," as it were, not for a boss. Plumbers can do that because, unlike workers who bring nothing but their labor to the job, they own their own productive property – tools, truck, fittings, and the rest. It is because they own their productive property that the home-owner with whom they contract is not their "boss." It follows that worker ownership of the productive property is the only ownership form that can liberate labor from subservience. In one formulation, in a Good Society labor should hire capital instead of capital hiring labor. Under that arrangement all the citizens are coequal workers, and none are dominant bosses.

Attitudes toward worker ownership follow no neat political pattern. Most people think of it as a broadly socialist idea, but it is not so easily pigeonholed. There are socialists and labor unionists who ridicule the idea of a "person who is neither worker nor capitalist," and view that organizational form as destructive of working-class solidarity.[1] On the other hand, certain limited forms of worker ownership appeal to groups of people who do not regard themselves as socialists of any stripe. The public cheered when the workers of Weirton Steel, which was about to shut down, saved their jobs by buying the company and turning it into a profitable enterprise.[2] Many ardent supporters of capitalism are also enthusiastic about the ownership by workers of shares of their company's stock.

It is in the socialist world, however, that worker ownership finds its most enthusiastic supporters – but also, ironically, its most implacable enemies. Marxian socialists and some others insisted that the property should be owned collectively by all the people and admin-istered by the people's state; Soviet state ownership embodied that view. On the other hand, socialists who feared the power of the state, notably anarchists and syndicalists, urged that the productive property of each enterprise be owned collectively by its own workers, who would run it with no interference from the state. Bitter, and sometimes bloody, conflicts have erupted over two visions of socialized property ownership, each holding that the other would lead to the corruption or destruction of a socialist society.

Those passions inflamed people who were fighting for the very soul of socialism. Most of the supporters of worker ownership today, however, see it in a more modest role – not as the predominant ownership form in socialist economies but as a progressive alternative to private ownership in some sectors of the capitalist economies. That is how it will be considered in this chapter, although some attention will be given to the prospect of market socialism based on worker ownership.

Worker ownership appeals particularly to people who place a high value on social and eco-nomic equality, but its supporters also contend that it is a more efficient arrangement than private ownership – at least under some production conditions. This chapter is concerned primarily with the question of efficiency; equity and other values are the subject of the next chapter.

I Forms of Worker Ownership

Like all forms of ownership, worker ownership comes in many shapes and sizes. Three that command most interest are employee stock ownership, partnerships, and producer cooperatives.

EMPLOYEE STOCK OWNERSHIP

Some executives believe that when workers hold shares of stock in their own company, they develop a genuine sense of ownership; they feel a certain loyalty to the company, and their morale and productivity are higher. It is therefore worth the company's while to enable their employees to buy shares of stock under privileged terms, to compensate them for the risk of having so many of their earnings-eggs in one company basket.

Presented as a form of "people's capitalism," employee stock ownership appeals to many non-socialists – populists, conservatives, and liberals – who view it as a means of strengthening working people's stake in the capitalist system. Sectors of American business and government have offered strong support for the arrangement, and tax incentives are offered to encourage firms to adopt Employee Stock Ownerships Plans, or ESOPs. The 1,000 corporations with the largest employee ownership now include almost a third of Fortune Magazine's 500 leading industrial corporations.[3]

Employee stock ownership, however, contributes very little to the social goals that most supporters of worker ownership have in mind. For one thing, their impact is still quite small: only 0.81 percent of all corporate stock was owned by ESOPs in 1983.[4] More important, however, is that stock ownership as such rarely gives workers any more right to participate in the control of their companies than they would have as ordinary shareholders. There are very few ESOPs in which workers hold a majority of the voting rights, most of which are held by the executives.[5] Management sometimes succeeds in creating an atmosphere in which workers feel that their views on matters of production are valued, but this form of worker participation is a corporate policy rather than the workers' right.

Since under employee stock ownership there are still workers and bosses, much as under the other three forms of ownership, it does not meet the goal of social equality sought by the more ardent advocates of worker ownership. It is an interesting footnote to the subject of worker ownership, but not part of the main text.

PARTNERSHIPS

In the celebrated law firm of Dewey, Cheatham, and Howe, as in most partnerships, the partners own the company, work in it full-time, manage it themselves, and share equally in the profits. None is the boss of the others. Partnerships may therefore be regarded as a form of worker ownership.

Yet they do not spark the interest of people seeking the best ownership form for their Good Society. The reason is that the decision to form a partnership is strictly business, with no higher social purpose. Lawyers or restaurant partners would just as soon operate as a corporation or an individual proprietorship if those ownership forms were more profitable. Partners do not insist that their incomes be equal or that they each have one vote, and they have no misgivings about hiring other lawyers and employees to work for them, sometimes in such large numbers that the partners' labor is a small proportion of the total.

Suppose, however, that the partners conceived an ideological aversion to hiring labor and voted to admit every employee into the partnership. Cleaners, clerks, receptionists, and law associates now enjoyed all the rights of partners, with one vote each. The partnership would then be transformed into a producer cooperative – the form of worker ownership that is most often advanced as the best candidate for the Good Society.

PRODUCER COOPERATIVES

Various forms of cooperative economic organization have found a place in market economies since the Industrial Revolution. They are often initiated by people who regard cooperative activity as having a social value in its own right, but also as having a strictly practical purpose. Thus, consumers have organized purchasing cooperatives to supply themselves with goods at lower prices by "eliminating the middleman." Agricultural marketing cooperatives have enabled farmers to get their products to market at a lower cost than if each marketed them himself. Producer cooperatives reflect the conviction that working people would enjoy both a higher real income and a more dignified life if they banded together than if they worked individually for private enterprises.

The conventional picture of producer cooperatives has been one of noble purpose but lamentable failure. The first scholarly investigation of the American record found a more mixed picture, however. Between the 1840s and the 1980s, 458 cooperatives operated in a variety of industries such as cooperage, foundries, and plywood. Only 39 survived more than 20 years. Of the 32 that were founded since 1921, however, 17 were still in operation in 1978 – a relatively low mortality rate compared to the experience of startup companies generally.[6]

In recent years there has been a remarkable surge in the number of new cooperatives and in their durability.[7] From 1976 to 1981, 6,700 new producer cooperatives were established in the European Community, bringing the total up to 14,000 by 1981 and accounting for about half a million jobs. That recent record of growth, however, has not yet established them as a significant presence. In Italy, which accounts for the largest number, producer cooperatives employ only about 2.5 percent of the non-agricultural labor force.

The authoritative review of the literature by Bonin, Jones, and Putterman identifies five rules that almost all producer cooperatives follow: (1) membership is strictly voluntary, (2) the members control the enterprise by participating in business decisions and in the appointment of management, (3) the capital is owned by the members, (4) each member has one vote, and (5) the profit is shared among the members. Those broad rules allow for a great deal of variation, however. The flavor of how they operate is best conveyed by an account of two cooperatives that are organized in somewhat different ways and have commanded a great deal of interest. They are the Mondragon complex and the American plywood cooperatives. The Yugoslav type of self-managed enterprise does not share all the characteristics of a producer cooperative, but it played so important a role in the evolution of the economic analysis of worker control that some attention will be given to it below.

2 The Mondragon Cooperatives

The Mondragon cooperative story[8] begins in 1941 with the arrival in that Basque town of a new young priest, Don José Maria Arzimendi. Concerned with the social as well as the spiritual welfare of his parishioners, he urged the business community to open the apprenticeship program to disadvantaged children who were not related to their employees. Rebuffed by the owners, he launched an initiative to establish an independent school for training boys in technical and crafts skills. With grass-roots monetary and social support, the school opened in 1943 with a class of 20 students. He later arranged for a Spanish university to provide the graduates with an opportunity to earn engineering degrees *in absentia*.

The school's graduates found good jobs in local industry, and some rose to minor supervisory positions. People from working-class families, however, understood that they could not advance into senior management. Five of them, inspired by the sermons and teachings of Don José Maria on the virtues of cooperation and equality, resolved to form a producer cooperative. They purchased a small bankrupt workshop that produced domestic cooking stoves, using their personal savings supplemented by loans and contributions from relatives, friends, and community supporters. In 1956 they founded Ulgor, the first worker cooperative in Mondragon.

After overcoming the usual hurdles of production startup, the cooperative began to cover its costs and production expanded. New members were taken in and other groups of workers, inspired and assisted by Ulgor, organized their own small production cooperatives. Within a few years the cooperatives took the major step of forming their own Cooperative Bank, which evolved into the central coordinating agency of the growing Mondragon complex. Along with banking operations, it offered the member cooperatives such services as market research, technical assistance, and project-feasibility analysis. It also spearheaded the formation of new cooperatives by searching out promising new production opportunities and offering initial assistance with financing. The Bank was the first of a number of supporting organizations that were established to serve various common needs of the member cooperatives, such as an Applied Industrial Research Cooperative, a Student Cooperative, and a Social Security Cooperative. The latter was established because members of cooperatives were classified by the government as "self-employed" and therefore did not qualify for state social insurance; the cooperatives established their own systems of financial support for retirement, unemployment, illness, and other social needs.

The Mondragon complex expanded rapidly in its first 15 years to encompass 70 cooperative factories with a work force of 15,000, accounting for 12.5 percent of the jobs in the province. There are now 300,000 depositors in the 93 branches of the Cooperative Bank. The typical manufacturing cooperative consisted of about 170 members, although a few were much larger. The range of their production included machine tools, refrigerators, furniture, bicycles, electrical products, and bus bodies.[9] The cooperatives are now the largest employer in the region and are a major financial presence. They have bought major shareholdings in a number of private firms and have established a holding company in which the cooperative group is the only shareholder.[10] Mondragon has become the principal showpiece of producer cooperation; a constant stream of foreign visitors comes to visit, either to study it or to find out whether it can be duplicated in their own countries.

RULES OF GOVERNANCE

All the cooperatives that form the Mondragon complex operate according to an established constitution. Some variation is allowed to take account of special circumstances, but there are certain fundamental rules to which all subscribe.

Self-management   Ultimate authority in each cooperative resides in its general assembly, in which each member has one vote.[11] The assembly elects a governing council that has overall responsibility for management policies and programs. The council elects the general manager, who is directly responsible not to the cooperative members but to the council – a provision designed to preserve their ability to control the work force.[12] Other governing committees include an audit committee, a management committee, and a social council, all staffed by members.

Membership   Each cooperative decides upon its own membership size. Applicants are screened for their social adaptability and community-mindedness, as well as their education and skill, and they work for a probationary period before they are admitted to full membership.[13] Discrimination on such grounds as religion or nationality is prohibited.

New members pay an entry fee that is about twice the average annual earnings in the co-operative. It is usually financed by a down-payment, with the balance paid off over a number of years. Entry fees are not pooled; the members' entry fees are allocated to their individual accounts, which are maintained in their names as long as they remain members.

It is a matter of high principle that the cooperatives do not hire non-member workers. The only exceptions are people with specialized knowledge and skills, who may be hired on fixed-period contracts, and they are limited to 10 percent of the number of members. As competition draws Mondragon into new lines of high-technology production, such contract employment is bound to increase, but the inclination is to keep it to the minimum.[14]

Wages   Each cooperative writes its own job-evaluation manual, in which jobs are rated by skill, responsibility, requirements for theoretical knowledge, and so forth. The wage of the lowest-rated job is set at an equal level to that paid for corresponding jobs in the private sector. The base wage for the highest-rated job – usually that of manager – is three times the lowest, in accordance with the cooperative ideal that the wage spread should be no more than 3 to 1. In practice, however, the ideal is breached by various additional payments for such features as dangerous work or above-average performance. Such supplements increase the actual range to 4.5:1 and higher in some of the cooperatives, but it is still much smaller than in Spanish industry generally.[15]

Profits and savings   Profits (net of payroll, interest, and depreciation) are allocated among three funds. About 20 percent is allocated to the Collective Fund, which is used for financing the capital requirements of the cooperative. Ten percent goes to a Social Fund that finances such non-production expenses as the cafeteria and other amenities. The remaining 70 percent is allocated as dividends to the Individual Account Fund, where they are distributed among the members' individual accounts in proportion to their wage earnings. Thus, the individual accounts grow over the years and provide a large sum of savings that become available to the members upon retirement.[16]

THE MISSION OF MONDRAGON

The rules of governance are designed to provide the members with a reasonable income and a fulfilling working life in an environment of social equality in which they collectively manage their own affairs. However, the mission extends beyond the welfare of the members alone. They have continued to pursue Don José Maria's goal of providing assistance to all citizens who wish to earn their livelihood in cooperative enterprise.[17] While not a national employment agency, Mondragon is committed to promoting the expansion of existing cooperatives by aiding other groups of workers to form new cooperatives.

3   The Pacific Northwest Plywood Cooperatives

The Olympic Veneer Company was founded as a producer cooperative in the state of Washington in 1921.[18] Its success led to a rapid proliferation of plywood cooperatives, and they have become the largest and most durable cooperatives in US manufacturing.

The plywood cooperatives have no supporting organizations: each one sets its own rules and stands on its own financial feet. Hence their organizational arrangements are more diverse than in Mondragon. The typical plywood cooperative is organized much like a privately owned joint-stock company, with the important difference that each stockholder owns only one share and casts only one vote for the board of directors. The board has the usual functions of appointing the chief executive officer and setting company policy. The stockholder-workers, however, participate actively in the formulation of policy; sometimes, indeed, to the annoyance of the managers. Members can leave the cooperative by selling their share to an outsider, but the purchaser must be accepted as a suitable member of the cooperative. Unlike Mondragon, most of the plywood cooperatives hire outside workers, some of whom may be among the top managers and may earn more than the members. The proportion of non-members has been growing and ranges from 0 to 62.5 percent; they are the first to be laid off when employment must be reduced.

Many of the plywood cooperatives were organized by workers for the purpose of saving their jobs. The companies for which they worked had failed or required extensive modernization to operate profitably, and the workers bought them out and reorganized them as cooperatives. The purchase of shares was financed out of their personal savings or with borrowed funds.

The plywood cooperators do not pay themselves wages, in the manner of Mondragon. Instead, rather like a small business, they regard the surplus of revenues over costs (including wages paid out to non-member workers) as their income. After setting some of the surplus aside for investment and other purposes, they treat the balance as their earnings. The worker-owners' earnings may therefore be thought of as the sum of their implicit wages as workers and their implicit dividends as owners. All members receive the same hourly earnings regardless of their jobs, unlike Mondragon where earnings are differentiated according to job. Job assignments vary and are sometimes rotated; the most attractive jobs are allocated on the basis of seniority or previous work performance.

Since the preservation of jobs was the main reason that many of the cooperatives were founded, one of their explicit objectives has been maintaining or increasing employment. Other than that, they have no missionary goals of the sort that inspire the Mondragon complex. The members may prefer the status of worker-owners to that of hired workers, much as lawyers may prefer being partners to working for a large law corporation, but they do not feel the call to promote the producer cooperative as a socially or morally superior ownership form. It merely suits their needs better than other ways of making a living at that point in their lives, much as a law partnership would cheerfully convert itself into a stockholding company if the partners thought it more useful for their purpose. The sale of a successful cooperative to a private company could provide the members with a larger retirement accumulation than they could have attained through the preservation of the cooperative; and indeed, three plywood cooperatives were sold to private companies within 30 years of their founding, for a substantial capital gain.[19]

4 Yugoslav Self-management

Like all the Communist countries after World War II, Yugoslavia adopted the Soviet version of Marxian socialism. After a few years, however, they rebelled against Stalin's efforts to subject them to Soviet political domination. Following the dramatic break with the USSR, the Yugoslavs undertook a searching inquiry into the question of how it came about that the abolition of private ownership and the introduction of socialism in the USSR culminated not in the free society envisioned by Marxists but in the monstrous political tyranny of Stalinism. The political leadership found their answer in the extreme centralization of power in the hands of the Soviet state, rediscovering, one might say, the forebodings of the anti-Marxian socialists a century earlier.

Out of these historical ruminations emerged a consensus for a different form of socialism in which the workers, rather than the state, manage the productive property of the enterprises.[20] The economic system was gradually transformed in two directions, both involving the extensive curtailment of state power. One was the transition from central planning toward the market mechanism, although government controls continued to prevail in varying degree over time. The other was the transformation of state ownership into "social ownership." That combination of markets and social ownership defines the economic system of market socialism, but only during the brief period 1965–73 was government intervention in the economy sufficiently relaxed that the economic system could be described as market socialist.[21]

Since the workers did not acquire full title to the ownership of the enterprises, the new arrangements do not qualify as worker ownership strictly speaking. The government, however, gradually transferred to the workers most of the rights of ownership, particularly the rights associated with the management of the enterprise's property. The practice of "self-management" – as it was called – merits attention here because at the time it evoked the prospect of a genuinely new form of socialism in which the workers are not hired hands but are collective managers of their own enterprises, even though they do not own the property.

Under the self-management regime, the workers served as the trustees of the society in managing the socially owned property. They enjoyed the right to control the use of the property and to appropriate the earnings derived from that use. Eventually they acquired the additional right to buy and sell capital goods and other productive property. An enterprise that bought a capital good, however, did not acquire full title to it; it had only the same rights of use that it had over its own enterprise's property. Enterprises were obliged to maintain the book value of the assets under their control by deducting an appropriate depreciation allowance from their revenues. The government also asserted its right of ownership by imposing an interest charge of about 4 to 6 percent on the value of the property.

Organization The workers elected a workers' council which in turn elected a management board of from three to eleven people who constituted the executive organ. The chief executive officer – called the director – was appointed through a nationwide competition by a joint commission consisting of members of both the workers' council and the local government. The director was therefore expected to represent not only the interests of the workers but also the interest of the society as represented formally by the local government and informally by the Party, newly renamed the League of Communists.

As in the plywood cooperatives, the members did not receive wages of the normal sort. The surplus of revenues over non-wage costs was distributed between a Business Fund that was used for investment and other purposes, and a Wage Fund; the proportions were determined by the workers' council. The Wage Fund was then distributed among the workers as their earnings. Earnings differentials were about 1:4 within enterprises, but since some enterprises were more profitable than others, inter-enterprise differentials for the same jobs were 1:3 or 1:4.[22]

In the quarter century after World War II, the average Yugoslav growth rate was about the same as in the centrally planned economies, but the economy was often in turmoil: rates of unemployment were high (10–20 percent), as were inflation rates (15–20 percent).[23] However, because of the operation of the market mechanism, limited though it was, the quality of people's lives as workers, consumers, and citizens became the source of covert envy in the rest of the socialist world. Had the Soviet-dominated regimes been free to choose a radically different economic model at that time, the Yugoslav way would have been a strong candidate as a better path to a socialist Good Society.

In the last decade of the country's existence, however, the economy went into a profound crisis. Per capita output and living standards dropped sharply, and strikes and other manifestations of social unrest escalated.[24] With the subsequent breakup of Yugoslavia, self-management disappeared almost without notice. The successor states reasserted their ownership of the productive assets and launched programs of privatization as soon as they came to power.[25] That the change in their formal status from self-managers to hired workers was accepted with no strong protest by the workers confirms the view that they never seriously regarded the property as their own.

Worker self-management was an imaginative invention in the search for a better form of socialism by the first country to break out of the mold of Soviet central planning. The system of social ownership and worker self-management that they developed has an important place in the repertory of economic arrangements of the past, but it is unlikely to find a place in future visions of the Good Society. However, since the Yugoslav self-management arrangement shares some of the properties of true worker-owned producer cooperatives, its experience contains certain lessons for the latter, some of which are reported below.

5 Issues of Efficiency

How efficient is worker ownership as an economic arrangement? The literature supplies an abundance of arguments on the question, some contending that it is more efficient than private ownership, and some that it is less.[26] On the positive side, cooperatives are expected to invest more in developing the members' skills; they should experience fewer work stoppages; members should be more willing to innovate and to share information; work effort should be better monitored. On the negative side, management decisions should be poorer because of the obligatory participation of members without appropriate skills; decision-making should be slow and cumbersome, member-workers should be averse to taking business risks because so much of their wealth is tied up in the cooperative; there should be more shirking if earnings are not tied closely to individual effort.

Since the full range of issues that have been explored is too large to be dealt with here, this section will address only three that are of particular interest for the Good Society.

Managerial salaries

Critics of producer cooperatives point out that under the other forms of ownership, the owners are free to hire the best managers they can attract and to pay whatever salaries that may require. Under worker ownership, however, the members select the managers from among themselves, and the managers' earnings cannot exceed the allowable limits of income differentiation. Because of those limitations, management will be less competent and efficiency lower than in privately owned enterprises. The criticism may be broadened to include technical expertise generally.

Most cooperatives have recognized the force of that argument and have departed from their normal rules in various ways in order to confront it. The Yugoslav self-managed enterprises were required to recruit their chief executives through nationwide competitions. The managers worked under compensation contracts that included profit-based bonuses that were designed to align the managers' personal interest with the workers' interest in profitability. The hiring of outside managers was an ideological transgression, for it conflicted with the ideal of self-management, but it was thought to be a small concession for the sake of the greater efficiency of the enterprise and the larger incomes of the members.

Pragmatic cooperatives like those in the plywood industry also hire outside managers when the members regard it as profitable to do so. Mondragon was more resistant, but it eventually became evident that the managerial and technical expertise required to meet the increasing competition could not always be found within their membership. Some of the cooperatives have therefore begun hiring non-members on four-year contracts as executives and as technical experts in such fields as marketing, and they have begun to compete among themselves for the best executives; the practice may remain exceptional, however, because the filling of top jobs by outsiders has generated some resentment among the more upwardly mobile members and among the members who do not have advanced degrees.

Self-imposed limits on the salaries that can paid to their own member-managers also continue to be a source of concern, however, for management earnings in Mondragon are 18–43 percent lower than in comparable Spanish companies. Turnover is therefore high, much of it to jobs in the private sector.[27] There is a similar pressure on the wages of high-level engineers. After an internal study reported that top engineers earned 30 percent less than comparable engineers in the private sector, proposals to increase the wage differential from the traditional 1:4.5 to 1:9 or 1:10 were brought before the General Assembly of the social security cooperative in 1991 and 1992. On both occasions the proposals were roundly defeated by the members.[28] The commitment to the 1:4.5 limit on wage inequality, which is particularly strong among rank-and-file workers, is likely to reduce the quality of managerial and top engineering personnel. The consequence is likely to be a lower level of cooperative productivity in the long run.

FREE-RIDERS

While worker-owners are spared the task of monitoring hired managers, they face a different monitoring problem to which analysts have paid a great deal of attention: they have to monitor each other. The reason derives from a certain feature of worker ownership that spawns the free-rider problem that has been encountered in other contexts above.

The commitment to equal sharing of the profit creates an incentive for the members to exert less time and effort on the job than they otherwise would. If I take long coffee breaks and lunches and frequent days off at the ball game while no one else does, the cooperative's profit falls by some small amount – say $5,000. Since the profits are shared equally, however, my personal loss is only a small proportion of that: in a 100-member cooperative I would lose only $50 in earnings. That is a very small price to pay for the large increase in leisure that I enjoy. It follows that the volume of effort and initiative put forth in a producer cooperative is likely to be less than under its private-enterprise twin, the owner of which has a powerful incentive to minimize shirking by labor.[29]

That proposition is the very opposite of the view held by friends of worker ownership, who believe the arrangement brings out the best in people. They find it perfectly reasonable that in the world of workers and bosses the workers will exert as little effort and initiative as they can get away with, within the terms of the labor contract. But in a participatory environment in which the workers are also the owners, one should expect far *more* effort and initiative, rather than less. Indeed, high morale and strong work incentive are among the principal reasons for expecting worker ownership to be more productive than private ownership.

That argument does not deny that the behavior of some members might conform to that of the free-rider calculus. As in all such matters, people range along a scale of susceptibility to temptations of that sort. At one end are the true cooperators – people for whom no personal gain would be large enough to tempt them into a free ride at the expense of their comrades. At the other extreme are the bad apples, who have no compunction against free-riding if it promised any personal gain at all. The proponents of worker ownership believe that very few people would behave like bad apples. Those who see the free-rider problem as of major significance believe that most people have some bad-apple inclination.

In practice, shirking has not proven to be a significant problem; it does not rank high among the things that cooperative members worry about.[30] The reason, however, is not that the free-rider model of behavior in a cooperative is wrong in its own terms, but that many of the features of cooperative organization tend to suppress it. Perhaps the first defense is that people who voluntarily join a cooperative are inclined by disposition to live by its spirit and rules; self-selection is the first protection against bad apples. The point is important because in involuntary cooperatives, like the Soviet collective farm and the Yugoslav self-managed enterprise, the membership is more representative of the population in general and is likely to contain a larger proportion of people inclined to be free-riders.

Moreover, of the self-selected applicant pool, some are weeded out by such devices as screening procedures and probationary periods, such as Mondragon and the plywood cooperatives employ. Mondragon managers and members are also constantly indoctrinated in the cooperative spirit precisely in order to counteract tendencies toward individualistic attitudes. Worker-owners also have both a personal and a social motivation to monitor the effort of their co-workers, for the cost of shirking is borne not by some remote boss but by the whole community, and informal monitoring takes very little effort, especially in a small cooperative.

For that reason the plywood cooperatives use many fewer supervisors per shift than similar private firms.[31] And as a last resort, there are usually procedures under which members charged with shirking are called to account and subjected to strong social pressures to mend their ways; penalties for infraction of work discipline in Mondragon include written warnings, temporary suspension, and expulsion in extreme cases.[32] For all these reasons, cooperatives, like college fraternities, tend to be relatively homogeneous in disposition, and share similar values on such matters as work effort and shirking. In general, it has been found that when groups are homogeneous in their interests, decisions tend to be more efficient.[33]

Hence, free-riding has turned out to be more interesting in theory than important in practice. It is a perpetual nuisance but of small dimension – smaller perhaps than cheating on college exams, or shirking by workers and managers in large private enterprises. It is rather like a dormant virus, lurking harmlessly when the organization protects itself but ready to leap into destructive action if the protections erode. Perhaps the most useful generalization is that free-riding is likely to be quite limited in small cooperatives, but it may become significant in large ones and could be of massive proportions in a cooperative that encompasses an entire society.

FOR MEMBERS ONLY

All enterprises set some limit on the number of people they employ. In a perfect market economy the enterprise employs the number of workers that is optimal in terms of its own profit, which happens also to be optimal for the economy. In a seminal article on the Yugoslav self-managed firm, however, Benjamin Ward demonstrated that producer cooperatives may limit their membership to a number that is not optimal for the economy.[34]

To capture the gist of the argument, imagine two restaurants that are identical in all respects except ownership form: one is a private firm owned by three sisters, and its twin is a cooperative owned by three friends. Each earns a total profit of $300,000 which is shared equally by the owners. Business is brisk and they estimate that by taking on another cook their total profit would increase by $60,000, which is to say that the marginal revenue product of labor is $60,000.

If the going wage for cooks is $40,000, the sisters would employ the cook because they would earn an additional profit of $20,000 by doing so; as in any private firm, it pays for them to increase employment whenever the marginal product of labor ($60,000) exceeds the wage ($40,000) (chapter 14). The cooperative, however, cannot simply hire the cook but must offer him a full membership in the club. But if they did so, the three members would suffer a decline in their earnings. Instead of $100,000 each ($300,000/3) they would earn only $90,000 each ($360,000/4). In general, a cooperative whose members seek to earn as much as they can would not take in new members unless the marginal product of additional labor were at least equal to the profit per member. In this illustration, the marginal product of labor in the cooperative remains at $60,000, while in the private-enterprise twin it would decline to less than that because of the increase in the work force.

The point is important because it implies that the marginal product of labor would be higher in cooperatives than in private enterprises. The society's output would therefore be larger if more workers were employed in cooperatives and fewer in private enterprises. Hence, for all their virtues, cooperatives make for an inefficient economy because of their members-only rule. If efficiency is one of the criteria of an economy's goodness, producer cooperatives are not a satisfactory ownership arrangement for a Good Society.

The Mondragon strike   The accounts of how cooperatives operate confirm that they are indeed concerned about how many members to admit. The primary source of the concern, however, does not appear to be the effect of increasing membership on their incomes. It springs rather from the social consequences of increasing size. The event that best captures the dangers that cooperatives see in excessive size is the Mondragon strike.

After an early history of rapid expansion, the largest cooperative, Ulgor, undertook a routine job reevaluation in which some jobs were downgraded and wage rates reduced. Instead of following normal channels of negotiation, 414 out of 3,250 members did the unthinkable – they went on strike. Tensions ran high, stormy meetings were held, and in the end some strikers were disciplined and some expelled. The incident led to extensive soul-searching about what had gone wrong, and the conclusion was that the cooperative had gotten so large that communication channels had broken down and many workers had become disaffected. The resolution was to limit the membership thereafter to a size in which all members could feel that their participation was genuine and their concerns were being addressed.

In the course of the next decade the size of the Ulgor cooperative was deliberately scaled back to fewer than 2,000; the released members were absorbed by other cooperatives.[35] The legacy of that traumatic experience is that it is the social consequences of membership size that dominates the Mondragon view of how large the individual cooperatives ought to be. Similar concerns about the social consequences of membership size have been expressed in some other producer cooperatives like the Israeli kibbutzim.

The optimal size At the other extreme, it was the large size of the typical Yugoslav enterprise – the legacy of the original Soviet-style of socialism – that made participatory self-management mere formalism for most of the workers. That, indeed, was the reason that late in the game a law was introduced breaking all enterprises down into a number of small so-called "basic units of labor," each of which operated as a quasi-autonomous unit of self-management with its own workers' council.[36] That arrangement of enterprises-within-enterprises proved to be a nightmare of managerial complexity and contributed to the economic crisis of the last years of the Yugoslav state.

The dominance of social concerns about size suggests that the optimal membership from the perspective of morale is usually smaller than the optimal membership from the perspective of income. Suppose a 600-member cooperative can increase its income by expanding until it reaches a membership of 1,000, beyond which income per member begins to decline. If they expect that morale would not be affected as long as they did not exceed 1,000 members, they would expand to that income optimum. If they believed that morale would begin to deteriorate well before they reached a size of 1,000, however, there would be serious debate about whether the additional income was worth the loss in the quality of participation and other social benefits of the cooperative life. The evidence that it is the social concerns that usually dominate the discussions about expansion suggests that most cooperatives are earning less income per capita than they could if they expanded. Hence the marginal product of labor in cooperatives should be even larger, relative to equivalent private enterprises, than would be the case if income concerns alone were at work.

Hiring labor Pragmatic cooperatives like the plywood companies do not feel bound by the members-only rule. If a good outside worker can bring in an additional revenue of $60,000 and can be hired at a fair wage of $40,000, the members can do two good things – give an unemployed worker a job, and increase the cooperative's profit by $20,000.

The additional income that could be earned by hiring outside labor is a perpetual entice-ment to relax the members-only rule, sometimes slightly, and sometimes a great deal. Even in the kibbutzim, which were second to none in their hostility to what they scorned as wage-slavery, the ideological barrier against hiring labor eventually cracked; as worker-owners themselves, the worker-part recoiled against hiring labor, but the owner-part saw the great benefit for themselves and their community. The Mondragon cooperatives also hire some labor, though usually for their specialized skills rather than for their low wage.

The practice of hiring non-member workers reduces the gap between the marginal product of labor in cooperatives and in private enterprises and therefore increases the efficiency with which the economy uses its labor resources. Comparisons of cooperatives and matched private enterprises, indeed, generally show no significant differences in the marginal product of labor in the two forms of ownership.[37] Differences may still exist, but they are not of such magnitude as to show up sharply in quantitative analysis. Hence a market economy in which producer cooperatives cohabit with private enterprises does not greatly suffer from inefficiency if the cooperatives are prepared to increase their incomes by hiring non-member workers.

6 Investment

This book has concentrated on the goodness of a society's arrangements for using its productive property to produce the goods and services that the people desire. To maintain that focus, little attention has been diverted to the process by which the size of productive property grows year to year – that is, to the process of investment in capital formation. In the case of the other ownership forms, that unexplored territory does not greatly affect the conclusions about the territory explored. In the case of worker ownership, however, there are certain problems in the investment process that are crucial in the assessment of its merits as an ownership form.

The concern that has been most often expressed is that a worker-owned enterprise will not invest in expansion at the same rate as its private-ownership twin. The workers will "eat up the seed corn" was the way it was put a century ago by the socialist critic of producer cooperatives, Beatrice Webb:[38] they will vote themselves the largest possible wages, leaving very little for investment. Hence, some of the country's investment resources that would produce a high yield in cooperative enterprises would be used instead in private enterprises where their yield is lower. Worker ownership is therefore an inefficient arrangement: the country's output would grow faster if some investment resources were reallocated from the private to the cooperative enterprises.

The issue came to the fore again with the adoption of worker self-management in the Yugoslav economy. The prediction of underinvestment carries particular force in that case because under self-management the workers do not fully own the property of their enterprises. They "rent" the property, as it were, from the society, and renters are notoriously uninterested in maintaining the property of their landlord, let alone paying for its expansion.

That particular critique does not apply to true producer cooperatives, where the workers are not mere renters but full owners of the productive property. However, there are other reasons for the concern about underinvestment that apply both to self-managed and to worker-owned enterprises, one of which is the "horizon problem."[39] Investment produces its benefits over time: $100,000 spent today to buy a new cost-saving machine may yield an increase in profits of perhaps $10,000 a year for the next 20 years. A privately owned or state-owned enterprise is likely to find that investment well worth making. In a worker-owned enterprise, however, the question must be put to the vote of the membership. The members would be asked, for example, whether they prefer receiving a $1,000-per-member dividend out of this year's profits, or allocating the profit to an investment which will yield $100 per member per year for 20 years. How that choice strikes a member like you depends on your time horizon – how long you expect to be working in the company. If you expect to retire in five years, for example, the investment would not be in your personal interest; you would forgo $1,000 in earnings this year, and collect only $500 over the next five years. The remaining 15 annual $100-payments would go to the members who work on after you. Hence, worker-owned enterprises may be expected to vote down some intrinsically profitable investments that their privately owned and state-owned twins would undertake.

Many cooperatives, however, have found ways of mitigating or eliminating the effect of differences in members' time horizons. In the plywood cooperatives, the members' ownership is represented by shares of stock, which may be sold to new members or to the cooperative when the member retires.[40] As with the market for corporation shares, the higher the profits expected from past investments, the higher the price of the cooperative's shares. Hence if you vote for a profitable investment to be made the year before you retire, you will not lose the benefit of the future profits that it will generate: you will capture it fully in the form of the higher price of your share when you sell it. You can therefore vote on an investment proposal entirely on its merits, without regard to your expected date of retirement.

The Mondragon cooperatives, which do not issue shares, escape the horizon problem in another way: by financing their investments not out of current profits but by loans from their Cooperative Bank. With external financing of that sort, cooperatives can invest without having to reduce the members' current consumption:[41] the financing comes not out of their current personal earnings but out of a long-term interest-bearing bank loan. The loan will be repaid in the future by the younger members who derive most of the future benefit of the investment. Yugoslavia accomplished the same result by channelling the savings of enterprises and citizens into investment banks which then made interest-bearing loans to the self-managed enterprises.

The quantitative evidence indicates that producer cooperatives do not necessarily suffer from a shortage of capital. The Mondragon cooperatives are in a stronger position to obtain capital than most private firms in Spain;[42] rather than eating up their seed corn, they invest about 36 percent of their gross value added, compared to about 8.4 percent in the province. By 1980 capital per worker had risen to the range of $30,000 to $40,000, compared to an average of about $40,000 in the United States at the time.[43] In Yugoslavia, the initial expectation of underinvestment turned into a concern about overinvestment, but the reason in that case lay not in enterprise organization but in the high rate of inflation: if the product that the enterprise sells for 1,000 dinars today is expected to fetch a price of 10,000 dinars in the future, there is a powerful incentive to borrow for investment today and repay the loan in depreciated dinars in the future.

In those two cases, however, the enterprises have substantial access to external sources of finance for their investments, which most cooperatives do not have. Privately owned banks are wary about lending to cooperatives for various reasons: they are unfamiliar, they appear to be more risky, arranging a secured loan is more time consuming, and so forth.[44] Nor can cooperatives tap into the vast market for corporate stocks, for large investors would be reluctant to buy stock in companies where the workers own most of the shares, where each shareholder has one vote regardless of the number of shares owned, and which are not as single-mindedly committed to profit maximization as the familiar capitalist firm. Hence, even if a cooperative's motivation to invest were no different from that of a private firm, it would be likely to invest less because of its more limited access to financing.

In their assessment of the empirical evidence, the reviewers of the literature conclude that the question of whether cooperatives tend to invest less than comparable private firms is not yet resolved.[45] Capital per worker has been found to be significantly lower in the American plywood cooperatives, in British footwear and clothing cooperatives, and elsewhere, than in matched private firms. By other measures, however, such as whether cooperatives invest enough to take advantage of economies of scale, the results are mixed. Access to credit and investment capital has nevertheless come to be widely regarded as the greatest problem that cooperatives confront.[46]

7 Performance

Underinvestment by producer cooperatives is a source of inefficiency in the economy because the country's investment resources are not optimally allocated between them and the private sector. That, however, does not preclude the efficient use by cooperatives of the resources that they do manage to secure.

Since efficiency is notoriously difficult to measure, most of the quantitative research approaches it indirectly through such measures as the productivity of labor. In Mondragon, which performs best by most measures, productivity is higher than in many of the private firms in the province that survive and prosper, and their net profit is roughly in the same range. The review of all recent research on the subject finds mixed results, however.[47] For example, a study of 500 French producer cooperatives found that those employing between 20 and 49 workers displayed higher labor productivity than private firms, but the opposite held with smaller firms. As in the underinvestment studies, the reviewers conclude that the empirical evidence regarding comparative productivity is inconclusive when data are available for both producer cooperatives and conventional firms.

That result would be surprising to people who expect decision-making to be impossibly cumbersome in organizations where everybody has the right to participate in management, and does so. They would expect that the higher labor productivity in conventional firms would show up boldly and unambiguously in the data. Enthusiasts of worker ownership, however, would not be dismayed by that result, for they see its virtue not in its materialistic but in its moral qualities: not, that is, in higher labor productivity but in the other values that they seek in a Good Society. From their perspective it is something of a bonus to learn that cooperatives may not be patently less productive than private firms.

High among those other values is job security. Virtually all studies that examine the response of producer cooperatives to changes in economic conditions find that they maintain a stabler employment level than private firms. In Mondragon, job security is almost guaranteed. In the plywood industry, when sales decline the cooperatives tend to sacrifice potential earnings in order to maintain employment, while private firms tend to reduce employment while maintaining earnings.[48] Both types of response are efficient in terms of the objectives of the owners: reducing employment in the face of declining sales is the proper policy when the objective is profit alone; maintaining employment at the cost of earnings is the proper policy when both job security and income are among the objectives.

Investigations of the quality of working life are generally more favorable to cooperatives. Absenteeism – one of the most reliable indicators of job satisfaction – is much lower in Mondragon than elsewhere. A survey of attitudes toward their enterprises shows that motivation and job satisfaction among the Mondragon cooperators was almost uniformly more favorable than among other workers in the province. For example, only 27 percent of Mondragon members would change their jobs for a 50-percent higher wage, but 54 percent of private-company workers would do so.[49] Another study found that 37 percent of Mondragon members reported that they participate in the organizational life of their enterprises, while only 7 percent of private-company workers participate.[50] Participation is important not only because it provides workers with a sense of control over their lives; most studies also find that it is usually associated with higher labor productivity.[51]

While Mondragon has created an exceptionally favorable work environment, the realities of market competition – both national and, increasingly, international – limit the extent to which work can be humanized and job mobility maintained. They cannot offer less monotonous and more interesting work without limit, and the inevitable pyramid of responsibility means that not everyone can expect promotion to top jobs, especially in view of the growing necessity of filling some top jobs with outsiders who have specialized expertise. To these technical limits to job satisfaction must be added the normal strains of social interaction. Dissenters grumble about cases of favoritism, jealousy, carelessness, and abuse of power. A critic of Mondragon reports that while managers state that "the cooperative belongs to 'everybody,' no worker ever referred to it as 'mine' or 'ours'."[52]

The differences between cooperatives and private firms in these studies are therefore not qualitative: they are matters of more-or-less, not of either-or. That 37 percent of Mondragon members participate in their enterprises' working life means that 63 percent do not. The proportion of non-participants is likely to be even larger in most producer cooperatives, for Mondragon is outstanding in its concern for the quality of life in the workplace. Hence producer cooperatives would be highly attractive to people who greatly value the opportunity for participation and its associated values, but many people would find the other ownership forms equally or more attractive.

8 Discussion

If you love the idea of worker ownership, you must first learn to love the market mechanism – or at least to make peace with it. For only the market mechanism can provide the space required for groups of workers to assume the responsibility, and take the corresponding risk, of managing their own production affairs. Worker ownership makes no sense under the central planning mechanism, the logic of which requires that the enterprises do what the planners tell them to do.

Popular attitudes toward worker ownership span the political spectrum. Some people regard it with the suspicion or hostility aroused by all things socialistic. Others are neutral: worker ownership may not be their cup of tea, but if other people choose that peculiar way of running their business, they see no threat to themselves or to the capitalist system. Yet others, perhaps most, are mildly positive. For example, a survey of popular attitudes reports that more people would prefer working in a company owned by its employees than in one run by outside investors or by the government.[53] Similar positive attitudes are expressed about jobs in which people are involved in the decisions related to their work. These generalized sentiments very likely apply not only to worker ownership in general but also to such specific forms as producer cooperatives.

In view of that broadly positive sentiment, friends of producer cooperatives often wonder why they do not occupy a significant place in any capitalist economies. One of the attractive features of capitalism, indeed, is that a great variety of organizational forms do manage to exist side-by-side; self-employment, individual proprietorships, partnerships, and corporations, both profit and non-profit. People dissatisfied with work conditions in hierarchical corporations can and do drop out to become self-employed or organize their own small proprietary companies or partnerships. One would think that producer cooperatives would flourish in that kind of environment. Yet they have nowhere caught on, at least not to the extent that enthusiasts expect.

A lot of thought has been given to the question of why cooperatives are underrepresented in the panoply of ownership forms.

Survival The popular picture of cooperatives is one of failure: they manage to come into existence and to operate for a time, but most are unable to survive for very long. That picture comes primarily from the experience of cooperatives whose ideology obliges them to regard all practices of privately owned enterprises as tainted by capitalism, such as wage differentiation, borrowing from banks, and so forth.[54] Most cooperatives, however, have been more flexible than that and more concerned with efficiency and profitability, particularly in recent years. Some, indeed, became so profitable that they disappeared because of their success rather than their failure: for example, the plywood cooperatives that were bought out by private owners under terms that involved a handsome capital gain for the members. Generally, however, the survival rates of cooperatives turn out to be about the same as or higher than private firms.[55] Since cooperatives once founded manage to survive reasonably well, the question is why few are founded and why their membership does not greatly expand.

Income and efficiency It is often thought that members of cooperatives willingly sacrifice some income for the sake of a more fulfilling work environment. The evidence reported above, however, indicates that membership in worker-owned enterprises does not, or at least need not, require a tradeoff of that sort. Since the earnings of cooperative members includes both their wage income as workers and their property income as owners, one must consider not their annual but their lifetime earnings, including retirement income and capital gains. There are no data on lifetime incomes, but the evidence suggests that they are at least as large and sometimes larger for cooperative members than for many equivalent workers in private industry.

That generalization does not extend to top managers and highly skilled workers, however, because their incomes are constrained by the aversion to inequality. The value of their labor – their marginal productivity – is higher than cooperatives are willing or able to pay. People with those qualities are therefore less likely to join cooperatives. That is not to deny that cooperatives attract many highly competent, and in some cases inspired, leaders and members. It means only that those who do join are likely on average to be less competent than those who take their chances in the higher-risk higher-income mainstream of private industry. Moreover, as the text reports, turnover is high, for some managers are lured away by private industry, for whom it is profitable to pay the full value of their labor. Those who remain with their cooperatives do indeed trade off income for quality of working conditions. Producer cooperatives may therefore be viewed as an arrangement in which the more productive people voluntarily subsidize the less productive. Yet it is not charity, for they do gain the non-pecuniary income of a more satisfying working life.

The ability of cooperatives to provide an income for most members that matches that of the private sector reflects the important finding that their efficiency is not notably different from that of private industry. Differences in income and efficiency therefore also do not count as reasons for the underrepresentation of producer cooperatives.

Participation and size My own candidate as the major reason for the underrepresentation of cooperatives is that the commitment to participation limits the number of people they admit as members. That theme appeared first in the case of the kibbutz (chapter 8) and reappeared more dramatically in the account of the Mondragon strike.

Imagine a newly founded producer cooperative that successfully overcomes the hurdles of startup. They can profitably sell everything they can produce, and as they gradually admit new members, earnings per member increase. As membership continues to expand, however, they cannot all participate in every decision as they did in the good old days. Power slips gradually into the hands of the elected managers, and the domain over which the members have real control shrinks. Elements of hierarchy appear that introduce new strains in relationships. Through quiet reflection or the shock of a strike, the members become aware that the quality of participation has been diluted, not unlike the dilution of ownership that occurs when the number of corporate shareholders increases. The rewards of ownership consist more and more of their share of the profits, and less and less of the satisfaction of participation.

At that point the cooperative confronts a momentous choice. One option is to cease growing. It then remains faithful to its participatory ideal but willingly sacrifices the additional earnings that continued expansion could bring. The Mondragon cooperatives chose that path.

They continue to assist actively in the creation of new cooperatives, but they limit membership in the established ones. Those that choose this path may be called pure cooperatives.

The second option is to continue expanding. That can be done by hiring outside workers, or by continuing to admit new members, or a combination of the two. However it is done, it leads to the degeneration – as purist critics call it – of a producer cooperative into a capitalist-type firm. The kibbutzim and the plywood cooperatives chose the path of augmenting the members' earnings by the hiring of labor. They may be called mixed cooperatives.

The commitment to limited membership greatly constricts the range of industries in which pure cooperatives can prosper. In particular, it excludes industries in which there are large economies of scale, where capitalist enterprises with thousands of employees can produce at a lower cost than the best-motivated cooperative of a few hundred members could attain. Pure cooperatives can satisfy the joint objectives of participation and earnings only in industries where small capitalist enterprises also flourish and with whom they can effectively compete.

Hence my conclusion that the commitment to genuine participation is the primary reason for the relatively small number of pure cooperatives in capitalist economies.

Investment   The underrepresentation of cooperatives is sometimes explained by the difficulties they face in securing credit and investment funds. That explanation has little force in the case of pure cooperatives, for by limiting their membership, they also limit their need for external financing. Most of the funds can be raised internally, through retained earnings or through the entrance fees of new members. Cooperatives that have access to supporting organizations like the Mondragon Cooperative Bank have access to more than enough funds to meet their investment needs.

Mixed cooperatives could conceivably operate in industries that require large quantities of capital. Having no inhibitions against expanding either their membership or their hired labor force, they could grow to the size that would be optimal for a privately owned enterprise in any industry. The capital required for an enterprise of that size, however, could not be raised by internal financing or bank credit alone. They would therefore have to tap the capital market. Perhaps if they gave up all trappings of their cooperative origin, they might find capitalists willing to buy their bonds or stock offerings on the same terms as they would buy those of conventional firms. If they remained recognizably cooperative, however, the disadvantage they face in raising capital would make them uncompetitive with large privately owned enterprises. Moreover, such incentive advantages as worker-owner participation confers on small cooperatives would be dissipated in large enterprises.

Hence, pure cooperatives do not need externally raised capital and mixed cooperatives cannot get it. Both therefore gravitate into industries in which the capital required for competitiveness is not so large as to be outside their reach. Inadequate access to investment financing is therefore not a major reason for the underrepresentation of pure cooperatives, but it is the reason that mixed cooperatives are confined to small-scale industries.

The appeal of cooperatives   One can understand why producer cooperatives are confined to industries in which small enterprises can operate successfully. Even within those industries, however, they are usually a small presence. What still needs to be explained is why they do not become the dominant ownership form in those industries.

The reason, I believe, is that the number of people who are attracted to the cooperative ideal is much smaller than the proponents of producer cooperatives think it is. It is useful to distinguish managers from workers in this respect.

The founding of successful companies of any type in market economies requires people of exceptional abilities. The five experienced young workers who founded and guided the first cooperative in Mondragon were such people. They could have formed their company as a partnership rather than a cooperative, and would very likely have become successful and perhaps wealthy. They chose to organize it as a cooperative because they were inspired by ideals of social and economic equality. If all people with entrepreneurial talent and drive were similarly motivated, the economy would abound with cooperatives.

While there will always be people with entrepreneurial talent who prefer working in a cooperative environment, most potential entrepreneurs in market economies are driven by other goals. They want the wealth, power, and esteem that comes of building an economic empire and being recognized as its founder. They have a strong compulsion to run their own show – to tell others what to do and not to have to persuade them. People who want to be boss are immune to the cooperative idea of an organization without bosses. As long as that is so, most new companies will be privately owned rather than worker owned. They will set the terms of the market competition for customers, for labor, and for supplies, that cooperatives will have to meet.

There would also be more cooperatives if workers had a strong preference for them. Queues would form for admission into them, and wage rates would have to rise in private firms in order to retain their labor force. That cooperatives do hold a certain appeal is shown by the fact that most of them are formed voluntarily, not, like the plywood cooperatives, as a last resort when jobs are at stake because of a business failure.[56] The strength of that appeal depends in some degree on historical and cultural conditions: it appears to be weaker in Great Britain than in France and Italy, which have strong cooperative traditions and supporting organizations. Nowhere, however, does the attraction to cooperatives appear to be very widespread. It is true that workers tend to light up at the idea of a company run by and for the workers themselves, rather than by and for a capitalist boss, but the attraction is often like that of the place you love to visit but wouldn't want to live in. The careful screening and probation practices of cooperatives testify to their awareness that cooperatives are not for everyone.

For all the satisfaction of participation and security that cooperatives offer, being a worker-owner also carries certain responsibilities that many people do not want to assume. It requires a certain amount of attendance at meetings and serving on committees, which may be a heady experience for the first year or two but can become increasingly distasteful on a permanent basis. And while cooperatives experience fewer of the normal social tensions of working organizations, such strains persist in one form or another. In a democratic workplace some members are repeatedly elected to the more responsible positions, and formal social equality coexists uncomfortably with informal social hierarchy. Accounts of the cooperative working life refer to excessive trivial discussion, confusion of responsibility and authority, jealousies and disappointments, and too many boring and repetitive jobs.[57]

The appeal of cooperatives to workers depends in part on the gap between working conditions there and the private sector. In times past that gap may well have been quite large, but a shrunken work week, longer vacations, higher real wages, stronger unions, and improved working conditions have greatly reduced the gap. A recent national poll reported that 54 percent of American working people declared themselves to be very satisfied with their jobs and another 36 percent were somewhat satisfied.[58]

With the narrowing of the gap in working conditions, the salience of job satisfaction in the overall quality of people's lives has also diminished. With the increase in leisure hours relative to working hours, and with the increase in income available for spending on leisure activities, today most workers' minds are occupied more with summer camping expeditions and backyard barbecues and less with the grievances of the workplace. Unless those trends are unexpectedly reversed, the time of producer cooperatives lies more in the past than in the future.

Market socialism   The failure of producer cooperatives to establish a strong presence in market economies lends itself readily to a Social Darwinist interpretation: institutions that do not survive in the capitalist market environment must be unfit. That interpretation assumes implicitly that the environment is good, so that anything that cannot flourish in it must be bad. An alternative view is that if good things do not flourish, it is the environment that may be bad.[59] Producer cooperatives may be seen as good things that fail to flourish because the capitalist market environment is bad for them, much as salmon will not thrive in polluted waters.

One implication of that view is that the goodness of a market-based society would be enhanced if measures were taken that were more supportive of producer cooperatives. Cooperatives might do some of that themselves by forming more and stronger organizations of mutual support, which are not uncommon in Europe. They might also petition government for tax relief and other privileges of the kind that are often extended to private enterprises that claim a special kind of goodness. Even with measures of that sort, however, producer cooperatives are unlikely to become the dominant ownership form. If market capitalism is to be transformed into market socialism, it would have to occur through political rather than economic processes.

Twice in recent years there have been efforts to enlist the power of government for that purpose. In Sweden and Denmark, whose citizens rank social equality particularly high among their criteria of a Good Society, labor leaders have advocated the gradual transfer of ownership and control of the productive property to the workers. The endorsement of that program by the Swedish Social Democrats, however, contributed to their defeat in 1976.[60] Moreover, the conservative tide and the collapse of Communism in the following decade have taken much of the heart out of such efforts in democratic countries, and may continue to do so for a long time in the future though probably not forever.

The second occasion followed the collapse of Communism. There were people in the former Communist countries who, while applauding the abolition of state ownership, hoped that the societies to come would escape the uglier features of capitalism by adopting some form of worker ownership. Their efforts roused little support: "No more experiments" was the slogan of a wearied population that wanted nothing more than to be a "normal" country at last. Nor was there any enthusiasm for replaying the self-management experience of Yugoslavia, the first country to have made the transition from central planning to markets decades earlier. Worker ownership was buried under the steamroller of privatization.

In both cases, however, worker ownership was rescued, in my opinion, by the failure of its friends to implant it through the power of government. Worker ownership works best when it grows out of the efforts of its founders and members, whether as plywood workers seeking to save their jobs or as Mondragon missionaries of social equality. It requires that the members be able to choose whom to admit, which means that they must have the power to exclude undesirables. Worker ownership implanted by government fiat in huge enterprises that were designed for very different purposes is likely to go the way of Yugoslav self-management, in which, despite the best efforts of its sponsors, participation remained a sham.

In the economy of my own Good Society, all ownership forms would contend for their place in the market. Each form would survive and expand in those activities in which it proved to be most successful, sometimes with public assistance if it were thought to serve a particular social purpose. Cooperatives would be regarded as but another of the many ownership arrangements to which capitalism is hospitable. They would compete in the market as buyers and sellers on the same terms as other companies; it is only their internal operations that would be a bit peculiar. Producer cooperatives would add to the social welfare by providing a workplace that some citizens regard as more satisfactory than that available under other ownership forms. They are likely always to remain a minor player in a market economy, however, because they can attain both their social ideals and a satisfactory income only in industries where small-scale production prevails.

Notes

1   Kasmir, *The Myth of Mondragon*, p. 10.
2   Marshall, *Unheard Voices*, pp. 189–90.
3   Blasi and Kruse, *The New Owners*, p. 242.
4   Blasi, *Employee Ownership*, p. 114.
5   Bonin, Jones, and Putterman, "Theoretical and empirical studies of producer cooperatives," p. 1292.
6   Jones, "U.S. producer cooperatives," p. 343.
7   Bonin, Jones, and Putterman, "Theoretical and empirical studies of producer cooperatives," p. 1290.
8   See Whyte and Whyte, *Making Mondragon*.
9   Bradley and Gelb, "Motivation and control in the Mondragon experiment," p. 213.
10 Kasmir, *The Myth of Mondragon*, pp. 29–30.
11 Whyte and Whyte, *Making Mondragon*.
12 Thomas and Logan, *Mondragon*, pp. 26–8.
13 Bradley and Gelb, "Motivation and control in the Mondragon experiment," p. 214.
14 Whyte and Whyte, *Making Mondragon*.
15 Bradley and Gelb, "Motivation and control in the Mondragon experiment," p. 214.
16 Members who resign before retirement may reclaim a negotiated portion – around 70 percent – from their individual accounts. Bradley and Gelb, "Motivation and control in the Mondragon experiment," p. 213.

The accumulation in the individual account represents the members' invested wealth. Since the members tie both their jobs and their investments to the fortunes of a single enterprise, they place themselves at greater risk than equivalent workers in private enterprises. The latter can spread the risk by investing their savings in other enterprises than the one for which they work; if their employer company goes bankrupt, they suffer the loss of their jobs but not of their wealth. Most worker-owners assume the same kind of risk, however; the proprietor of a small company risks the loss of both his implicit wage earnings and his invested wealth if his business fails. Worker-owners take that risk willingly in the anticipation of larger non-pecuniary rewards from owning and managing their own enterprises.

17 Whyte and Whyte, *Making Mondragon*, ch. 13.
18 Craig and Pencavel, "The behavior of worker cooperatives," p. 1084.
19 Jones, "U.S. producer cooperatives," p. 355.
20 Rusinow, *The Yugoslav Experiment, 1948–1974*, pp. 47–61.
21 Rusinow, "Yugoslavia," pp. 55–7.
22 Horvat, "Yugoslav economic policy in the post-war period," p. 117.
23 Milenkovitch, "Self management and thirty years of Yugoslav experience," p. 3.
24 Rusinow, "Yugoslavia," p. 53.
25 Bookman, "Former Yugoslavia," p. 648.
26 Estrin, Jones, and Svejnar, "The productivity effects of worker participation," pp. 42–5.
27 Whyte and Whyte, *Making Mondragon*, p. 204.
28 Kasmir, *The Myth of Mondragon*, pp. 35, 189.
29 Alchian and Demsetz, "Production, information costs, and economic organization," pp. 789–90.
30 Bonin, Jones, and Putterman, "Theoretical and empirical studies of producer cooperatives," pp. 1302–3.
31 Craig and Pencavel, "The behavior of worker cooperatives," pp. 1086–7.
32 Bradley and Gelb, "Motivation and control in the Mondragon experiment," p. 215.
33 Hansmann, *The Ownership of Enterprise*, pp. 288–90.
34 Ward, "The firm in Illyria."
35 Whyte and Whyte, *Making Mondragon*, p. 207.
36 Rusinow, "Yugoslavia," pp. 57–8.
37 Bonin, Jones, and Putterman, "Theoretical and empirical studies of producer cooperatives," p. 1305.

38   Coates, "Cooperatives," p. 665.
39   Jensen and Meckling, "Rights and production functions," pp. 480–3.
40   Craig and Pencavel, "The behavior of worker cooperatives," p. 1084.
41   Putterman, "On some recent explanations of why capital hires labor," pp. 181–2.
42   Whyte and Whyte, *Making Mondragon*, p. 98.
43   Thomas and Logan, *Mondragon*, p. 104.
44   Craig and Pencavel, "The behavior of worker cooperatives," pp. 1102–3.
45   Bonin, Jones, and Putterman, "Theoretical and empirical studies of producer cooperatives," p. 1311.
46   Thomas and Logan, *Mondragon*, p. 75.
47   Bonin, Jones, and Putterman, "Theoretical and empirical studies of producer cooperatives," pp. 1302–7.
48   Craig and Pencavel, "The behavior of worker cooperatives," p. 1103.
49   Bradley and Gelb, "Motivation and control in the Mondragon experiment," p. 220.
50   Whyte and Whyte, *Making Mondragon*, pp. 208–9.
51   Bonin, Jones, and Putterman, "Theoretical and empirical studies of producer cooperatives," p. 1304.
52   Kasmir, *The Myth of Mondragon*, p. 160.
53   Blasi, *Employee Ownership*, p. 5.
54   Putterman, "On some recent explanations of why capital hires labor," pp. 185–6.
55   Bonin, Jones, and Putterman, "Theoretical and empirical studies of producer cooperatives," p. 1314.
56   Bonin, Jones, and Putterman, "Theoretical and empirical studies of producer cooperatives," p. 1312.
57   Thomas and Logan, *Mondragon*, pp. 190–1.
58   *The New York Times*, October 27, 1997, p. A20.
59   Putterman, "On some recent explanations of why capital hires labor," pp. 185–6.
60   Marshall, *Unheard Voices*, pp. 185–6.

Chapter 27

████████████

Ownership and Justice

The law, in its majestic equality,
forbids the rich as well as the poor to
sleep under bridges, to beg in the
streets, and to steal bread.
            — *Anatole France*

Give us this day our daily interest.
            — *Molière*

CONTENTS

Judged by efficiency alone, private ownership would very likely be chosen by most people as the ownership form best suited to their Good Society. Like all economic arrangements, however, property ownership has implications not only for efficiency but also for other criteria of goodness. In the case of ownership, those other criteria – notably justice – loom particularly large in many people's assessment of what makes one society better than another.

To people for whom justice means equality, state ownership is the best arrangement: everybody presumably owns an equal share of the productive property. Under private ownership, in contrast, the distribution of property ownership is extremely unequal. In principle, it need not be. One can imagine a private-ownership arrangement in which everyone starts off with the same acre-and-a-mule, but if the property can be bought and sold, and if some owners are more able or more hardworking than others, the distribution will soon become unequal. Something of the sort indeed happened under the Homestead Law: each new settler was entitled to 160 acres of good prairie land as long as it lasted, but in the course of time that original equality vaporized as some settlers sold out to other people. A contemporary event of a similar nature is the privatization of state-owned property in the post-Communist countries: in most cases it started off with every citizen entitled in principle to one share of the country's productive property, but some people quickly bought up the shares of others and rapidly built up large concentrations of ownership.

Some of the issues of justice concern the extent of inequality of property ownership: for example, if inequality in ownership is too large it may undermine other institutions that the society values, such as equal justice under law. That matter will be discussed later on. A rather different set of concerns focusses on one of the most important rights that the law normally confers on property owners – the right to the income generated by the use of their property.

1   Property Income

No one questions the legitimacy of labor as a source of personal income. The issues of equity in wage earnings turn not on legitimacy but on distributive justice, as discussed in Part III – whether some workers should earn higher wages than others and how large the differences should be. The legitimacy of property ownership as a source of personal income, however, is perhaps the most hotly contested question in the economics of the Good Society. Many people regard labor not only as a legitimate source of income, but as the *only* legitimate source. From that perspective, income derived from property ownership is unjust, not only in the sense of distributive justice but also in the sense of elementary fairness. That is, the injustice is not only that property income increases income inequality, but also that people should derive any income at all from a source other than their own labor.

Although certain forms of property income are received under all forms of ownership, including state ownership, the heavy artillery of criticism is directed at private ownership, where they are largest. In the United States, for example, the national income generated in 1995 amounted to $5,814 billion. Labor accounted for 79 percent of that total, in the form of wages, salaries, and supplements such as employer contributions for social insurance. The remaining 21 percent may be regarded as property income - in such forms as corporate profits, income of proprietors and the self-employed, rental income, and interest.[1]

The view that property income is inequitable is the major reason that many people regard private ownership as entirely unacceptable in their Good Society. That view is held by virtually all socialists, but many supporters of capitalism are also squeamish about property income. The bloated capitalist clipping his bond coupons is the stock-in-trade of political cartoonists. The taint of illegitimacy is also reflected in many public policies, such as the practice in some states of levying higher tax rates on property income than on wages and salaries. Sentiment for rent control is fueled in part by the sense that it is unfair for anyone to earn an income from the mere ownership of a building.

The primary reason for the hostility to property income is that it is unfair because it is "unearned." Two rather different meanings are conveyed by that indictment. They can be delineated most sharply by concentrating on fixed capital – that portion of the country's productive property that takes the form of machinery, equipment, buildings, and so forth. One meaning is that *capital* does not earn income because *it* is unproductive. The other meaning is that *capitalists* – the owners of the productive property – do not merit an income because *they* are unproductive. The two meanings of unfairness are based on different lines of reasoning.

2 Does Capital Earn Income?

The assertion that capitalists do not earn their income is easy to comprehend and its significance is evident. There is something other-worldly, however, about a controversy on so abstract a question as whether *capital* earns income. It would never have attracted much attention, in fact, except for the powerful impact of a related proposition – that only labor is productive, in the sense that all the output and income produced in an economy is due to the use of labor and none of it to the use of capital.

The view that labor is the sole source of output and income was the general wisdom in the early nineteenth century; it was the doctrine of Adam Smith and the classical economists, as well as of Karl Marx. Marx, however, greatly elaborated upon the labor theory of value – as it was called – and it served as the foundation of his grand theory of capitalist exploitation.

Marx acknowledged that capital may *appear* to be productive because a worker with a machine obviously produces more than a worker with no machine. The apparent productivity of the machine, however, derives entirely from the labor that had been used to produce it sometime in the past. Capital is simply past labor that has been "embodied" in a product like machinery. The productivity of that embodied labor augments the productivity of current labor in the course of years as the machine gradually wears out. Hence the value of a blouse produced on a sewing machine, for example, is due entirely to the labor used to produce it – both the current labor of the seamstress, and a tiny part of the embodied labor of the forgotten machinists who had made the sewing machine.

The political-economic implication is clear: labor is entitled to all of the income produced in the country and not to the mere 79 percent they receive in the United States as wages and salaries. The 21 percent of so-called property income is really labor income that capitalism empowers the property owners to extract by the exploitation of the rightful recipients, the workers. Thus, the abstract proposition that labor alone is productive turns out to provide the justification of a revolutionary movement to give workers what is their due. It fuels the sentiment embodied in the thunderous pronouncement of the charismatic nineteenth-century anarchist, Pierre-Joseph Proudhon, "Property is Theft."

As in all fields of advancing scholarship, the labor theory of value had its day, but by the time Marx died it had passed from mainstream economics into history. It had been largely displaced by the new marginal-productivity theory, which led to a very different view of the relationship of labor income to property income (chapter 21). But it remained an article of faith among dogmatic Marxists who rejected any economic reasoning that was not rooted in the works of Marx.

In particular, Marx's labor theory of value dominated Soviet economic planning throughout the great industrialization drive of the 1930s and the postwar reconstruction years – with unfortunate consequences. The doctrine that labor was productive but capital was not misled the planners into the belief that minimizing the use of labor was important but minimizing the use of capital was not. It was as if labor had a real "price" that was equal to the wages that had to be paid to the workers, but since nothing had to be paid to the state for the use of the capital, the "price" of capital was in effect zero. Capital was treated as if it were available in unlimited amount, without having to pay an interest charge for its use.

That way of reasoning had a powerful influence on the design of new factories and plants. In designing a steel mill, for example, it is generally the case that the larger and more expensive a new mill, the lower the labor and other costs of producing a future ton of steel.[2] A small steel mill, for example, that may cost 1 million rubles to build, will produce sheet steel at 50 rubles of cost per ton. A large automated mill that may cost 1 billion rubles to build, however, will produce sheet steel at only 10 rubles of cost per ton. It seemed evident that the large mill is the better because the future costs of steel production will be much smaller. By that logic it made sense always to build the largest and most automated plant possible.

And so they did. The factories, power stations, and railroads built during those years were among the largest, and sometimes were the largest, in the world. Indeed, they were believed to demonstrate the advantage of socialism, because such large and expensive plants could not be built under a system where capitalists had to be paid huge sums of interest in order to finance them.

There were always some economists and engineers who sensed that there was something wrong about building ever-larger plants without regard to the huge quantities of capital tied up in them.[3] Some of them even got the attention of Stalin, who then criticized the practice of what he called "gigantomania" – the view that bigger is always better virtually without limit. Those who thought about it, however, recognized that it was a political hot potato and dropped it for safer research pursuits. The reason it was political dynamite is that one could not explain what was wrong with gigantomania without arguing that some of the capital that had been poured into a huge plant would have been more productive if it were used in a different plant. But that argument concedes that capital *is* productive and a price *should* be assigned to it, much as the wage rate is a price assigned to labor. To express that view, however, is to deny the validity of the venerable Marxian labor theory of value, and to employ the reasoning of bourgeois marginal-productivity economics instead. Everyone understood that that was the way to a prison labor camp or worse.

As it turned out, some design engineers, not fully understanding the subversive ideological implications of what they were writing about, began to propose ways of limiting the size of capital construction projects in the interest of efficiency. Some years after Stalin's death it gradually became safer to deal with these issues, and economists evolved a method of determining the optimal size of a construction project by including an additional charge in the estimated cost of the project: the larger the project, the larger the additional charge. That charge for capital served the same function as the interest rate serves under capitalism: the larger the capital charge, the smaller is the optimal size of the project under design. The capital charge looked like an interest rate and functioned as an interest rate, but was never called by that unpalatable name to the very end.

The matter can now be regarded as settled. Capital, along with labor, contributes to the production of socialist output as well as capitalist output. Therefore, both labor income and property income are earned under both systems. The national accounts of socialist countries in fact do provide implicitly for property income. In 1989, for example, the USSR produced 656.8 billion rubles of national income, roughly 73 percent of which consisted of wages plus supplements.[4] The remaining 27 percent may be thought of as property income. That estimate is not quite comparable to the 21 percent reported above for the United States because national accounting conventions differ in many ways. It is nevertheless clear that property income accounts for a large share of the income generated by production activity under state ownership.

No future socialist society is therefore likely to conduct its business in accordance with the archaic view that only labor is productive and the price of capital is zero – unless they have not read the story of the USSR.

3   Do Capitalists Earn Their Income?

The question of whether capital earns an income has important implications for the efficiency with which a society uses its capital. The issues are rather abstract, however, and do not get to the heart of what most people see as the question of justice. That question is not whether capital and other productive property earns an income, but whether the owners of the property have the right to receive that income.

State ownership   Under state ownership the property is owned by all the people and no one challenges their rightful claim to the income generated by the use of the property in production. In socialist economies that claim is exercised indirectly. The state collects the non-wage income and uses it to finance such public benefits as free educational and health services, subsidies for food, housing, and the arts, investment in the growth of the capital stock, and military defense. The citizens' personal income therefore consists of their wage earnings, plus a share of the property income in the form of the public benefits provided through the state.

The property income that the citizens-as-owners receive under state ownership is rarely regarded as "unearned." If there are issues of justice they lie in the political rather than the economic system: for example, if special groups like the Party or senior citizens or specific industries are able to appropriate benefits that are inequitably large. The property income that capitalists-as-owners receive under capitalism, however, is widely held to be "unearned." That charge is one of the most potent weapons in the socialist arsenal.

Private ownership   The controversy over the equity of private-property income mirrors that over labor income. The case for the equity of property income stands on the same ground as the case for wage differentiation – the contribution principle. The argument is that people who supply the capital and other property that contributes to production are entitled to the income produced by the property.

To some critics of private ownership, however, the equity of property income does not hinge on whether or not the property is productive. It depends rather on how the property was acquired in the first place. Income derived from inherited property, for example, is widely thought to be unearned. That standard of equity invites examination of the ways in which people acquire their property. The paths to property ownership are in fact quite diverse, and some of them are commonly regarded as sufficiently innocent to have found a legitimate place even in socialist societies.

A collection of property, like a collection of paintings, has a unique history. It is built up over a period of time out of a variety of sources, and it differs from other collections by the kinds of property of which it is composed and the date that each one entered the collection. All collections, however, derive from one or more of the same sources, the chief of which are savings out of current income, capital gains, and inheritance.

4   Savings

Under the planning mechanism, the planners decide how much of the country's resources should be devoted to consumption and how much to investment in the creation of new capital. Under the market mechanism no single organization has the power to make that momentous decision. The volume of consumption is determined in part by the way in which the millions of families spend their income. If they reduce consumption out of current income, thereby increasing their savings, more resources are released for investment and the economy can grow more rapidly from year to year. If they spend almost all of their earnings on consumption and save very little, fewer resources will be available for investment and the economy will grow more slowly.[5] Household savings are thus one of the critical determinants of the rate of economic growth. They are also the major source of the property that the citizens accumulate from year to year.

WAGES

The most elementary source of property ownership is savings out of wage income. Most of the unspent wages are used to purchase various forms of financial and other property that generate flows of income. The simplest type of income-earning financial property is a savings-bank deposit, which is rather like a loan to the bank for which it pays interest to the depositor. A bank is a "financial intermediary": it lends the money deposited with it to an enterprise that uses it as productive capital, to carry a larger inventory, for example, or to purchase a new machine. The loan enables the enterprise to make profits that more than cover the interest it pays to the bank for the loan. That interest is the source of the bank's revenues, out of which it pays interest to its depositors. A savings-bank deposit is therefore an indirect production loan to enterprises, or to other willing borrowers like home-buyers.

Since savings contribute to the growth of the society's output and consumption, property in the simple form of bank deposits should be regarded as fairly acquired, and all modern economies regard them as equitable. They are regarded in that way in all the socialist countries, where citizens could – and were urged to – open bank accounts that channelled savings indirectly to industry.

It is but a step from savings accounts to other ways of acquiring income-producing property out of savings. They may be used to buy interest-bearing government bonds, which are issued everywhere. The purchase of the government's bonds was regarded as a patriotic act in the socialist countries, and in the capitalist countries as well in times of national emergency. The range of possibilities is much wider under capitalism, however, because of the private ownership of most of the property. People who plan for the long run place part of their savings in pension funds or in life insurance policies that provide a flow of income in one's older years. Those organizations are also financial intermediaries, and they invest the savings left with them in industry or in government bonds. As an alternative, savers may eliminate the financial middleman and invest directly in industry by buying a corporation's bond, or by the somewhat riskier course of buying shares of a corporation's stock.

From the perspective of fairness, there is little difference between financial property in the form of a savings account, government bonds, shares of stock, or private pensions. If all property were acquired solely through savings out of wages, there would be no powerfully charged issue of equity. It would be regarded as inequitable only by those socialists who hold all private-property income to be categorically unearned because it is derived from the exploitation of labor.

By saving regularly out of each paycheck and reinvesting the income derived from those savings, a worker can build up a substantial amount of wealth in the course of a lifetime. A middle-class family that starts out owning no property at all and is reasonably prudent can retire with a pension fund, a house, and investment and other property worth several hundred thousand dollars. Their wealth will be larger than that of other families with the same wage income who saved less or not at all.

OTHER LABOR INCOME

Families whose income consists entirely of wages are usually at the lower end of the income scale. Families at higher income levels derive more of their income, and sometimes all of it, from other sources of income. One such source is self-employment: accountants, artisans, carpenters, and freelancers of all kinds work out of their homes and earn their income by providing services to individuals or companies. While most citizens of socialist countries were employed in state enterprises, certain kinds of self-employment were sanctioned: carpenters could build houses for other people, collective farmers could produce and sell the output of their private plots, and so forth. But the conditions were highly restrictive: the work had to be done on the person's own time because everyone was obliged to hold a state job, and the employment of other people's labor was forbidden. The population regarded income from those forms of self-employment as fairly earned.

The range of income-earning possibilities, however, is much wider in the capitalist countries. In addition to the foregoing it includes the so-called "proprietary income" earned by owners of shops and small companies, which can reach large proportions. There is also the income of partnerships, such as are common in law and accounting, which also reach very large amounts.

In all these cases, the recipients supply their capital as well as their labor to the business, and the owners are often notoriously hardworking. Their remuneration is sometimes challenged as unjustly large – the huge legal fees submitted in the tobacco company settlements, for example,[6] – but by and large incomes of those sorts are regarded as fairly earned.

Families that earn most of their income from these sources tend to be well-off, and generally save a larger proportion of their income. Each year's savings, plus the reinvestment of income earned on the productive property acquired in the past, provides the pot out of which they expand their collections of property each year.

EXECUTIVE COMPENSATION

In times past the remuneration of corporation executives consisted mainly of their salaries, sometimes supplemented by performance bonuses. They might have been considered merely high-wage workers who happened to have managerial responsibilities. If the wages of workers are regarded as justly earned, then the salaries of managers should have been regarded as no less justly earned.

With the explosive growth of executive compensation in recent decades (chapter 23), that judgment must be reassessed. The reason is not simply the size of executive incomes. A newly appointed chief executive officer may increase the value of a company's assets by so large an amount that she may be fully worth the large compensation package required to recruit her from her former job. It is similar to the huge salary-and-bonus packages that ball club owners offer to recruit top-level free-agent players.

There is a difference, however. The club owner is usually a single person or a small group. The offer presumably represents the owner's best guess about how much the player is worth and what it takes to sign him up. The owners of a corporation, however, consist of thousands or millions of persons, who must rely on their board of directors to represent their interests. The structure of corporate governance is such, however, that astute chief executive officers may exert such power over their boards that they can write their own compensation packages in varying degrees (chapter 23). In that case their earnings may greatly exceed their worth to the owners. The excess of their income over their worth may be regarded as unearned income, and the wealth accumulated by savings out of that income would be unearned wealth.

The excess incomes of corporate executives are significant not for their size, for they do not constitute a large proportion of the top incomes. They are significant rather because the corporate ladder has been transformed into a new way of acquiring and accumulating property. In the past a young person embarked on a managerial career knowing that very few made it to the top, but that those few could expect to earn many times more than an engineer or accountant. Now the managerial ladder offers not only large salaries, but also lawful ways of directly appropriating generous quantities of their company's stock and large chunks of the stockholders' wealth. In markets so imperfect, it is to be expected that some of the income will be unfairly earned, much as the income of monopolists is unfairly earned.

5   Capital Gains

Owners often have occasion to sell a piece of property. The reason may be personal: cash may be needed to finance a college education, or the family house is too large now that the children have gone. Another major reason is financial: some securities may be sold for cash in order to take advantage of an attractive investment opportunity, or recent events raise the prospect that the value of a certain company's stock may fall. Hence, a natural and inevitable consequence of private ownership is the rise of markets that specialize in the "exchange of assets" – the purchase and sale of property on behalf of customers.

The operations of property markets set the prices at which sales are likely to take place. The stock markets report the prices of the most recent sales of all securities, which gives potential sellers and buyers a good idea of the price at which they might sell or buy. A potential buyer of a house or a small business can learn from an agent the range of properties that are for sale and the prices at which they might be bought.

Because of the operations of the market, the value of property tends to vary from time to time. A home or a thousand shares of stock that were bought for $50,000 ten years ago may be salable today for $120,000. The difference is called a capital gain, or loss. In this case the gain is $70,000, or $35,000 in real value if the rate of inflation in the intervening period had been 50 percent.

While individual property values fluctuate widely, over the long run their average value has gained considerably – the historical average for stocks in the United States is 8 percent per year.[7] Hence a substantial portion of the wealth of older Americans today is the result of both the gradual accumulation of wealth out of current savings, and long-term capital gains on their property.

On the face of it, the case for the equity of long-term capital gains is not evident. Unlike savings that contribute to the expansion of production by releasing resources for investment, most capital gains make no contribution except to increase the wealth of passive property owners. There is one major respect, however, in which they make a huge contribution to the economy. They provide the incentive for entrepreneurs to take the risks involved in innovation.

INNOVATION

In the history of a family's collection of property, there are periods when it grows gradually, and others when it suddenly grows very rapidly. The spurts of growth are often the consequence of a large capital gain resulting from a successful innovation.

The stylized story is that of a scientist, engineer, tinkerer, or small businessman who has an idea for a new product that he believes to have enormous potential for sales and profits. Dipping into her own savings and tapping those of relatives and friends, she raises $100,000 with which to start a business for developing the idea. Unable to pay salaries high enough to attract the best co-workers, she offers them small salaries plus shares in the future profits of the business. If the young company can hold out long enough, they begin shipping output, which meets with extraordinary success. With the profits plowed back into the business and with loans from the local bank, output, sales, and profits continue to increase rapidly. After some years of a driving pace of work, they are earning $10 million in profits. A large corporation decides that the new product would be a valuable addition to their own product line, and offers to buy the company for $50 million. In accepting the offer the founders enjoy a capital gain of $49,900,000.

The Horatio Alger myth celebrates a society in which only ability and effort count, in contrast to a rigidly class-based society in which who you are is all that counts. It is often misinterpreted to mean that *every* American child can succeed in business. A more sensible interpretation is that *any* American child can succeed; to assert that anyone can make it is not at all to say that everyone can make it. Properly interpreted, there is some substance to the myth. The probability is vanishingly small for children from the most disadvantaged social backgrounds, but great new fortunes have been amassed by people of quite humble origins. Every generation produces its own crop of them. Ross Perot, for example, started out as an IBM salesman after graduating from the Naval Academy. Ten years later he borrowed $1,000 from his wife to start up a company he called Electronic Data Systems. Ten years after that, after selling shares in his company to the public, his net worth surpassed $1 billion. And one decade later he sold the company to General Motors for $2.55 billion.[8]

Most people would regard such capital gains as well earned, not only because of the contribution that new products make to the country's output but also because of the effort expended and the risk undertaken. Indeed it is innovations of that sort, in all fields ranging from fast-food shops to medical instruments, that have so radically changed the composition of the goods and services in the modern economy. And it is the prospect of such open-ended gains that serves as the major incentive for people to put in the effort and accept the financial risk inherent in innovation. About half of the great fortunes owned by Americans originated in capital gains earned over a short period of time in such fields as production, building construction, and finance. They are a much larger source of ownership than the patient acquisition of property out of current savings.[9]

That is not to say that if capital gains were eliminated or limited in some fashion, there would be no innovation at all. There are always people with the imagination and drive to build something new, without respect to material reward. The extent and rate of innovation, however, would have been vastly slower in the absence of the incentive of wealth accumulation.

The experience of the socialist countries supports that conclusion.[10] The Soviet Union was prideful of the fact that they had more engineers and scientists per capita than any country in the world. There were highly talented people among them, and they were at the top of the country's pay scale, as were the industrial managers. Innovation was highly encouraged, and special bonuses were paid to people responsible for successful innovations. But while the country's technology did indeed improve every year, no major technological or organizational innovation emerged in the USSR throughout its history. There were many reasons why that was so, particularly the difficulties that the planning bureaucracy placed in the way of people seeking to change things. But if the Soviet economy could have offered the prospect of capital gains equivalent to those in capitalist economies, many of their engineers and managers would have fought ferociously to overcome the obstacles created by planners and bureaucrats. From this perspective, an important advantage of private ownership is that it permits a society to offer much larger material rewards for innovation, in the form of capital gains, than is possible in a society committed to state ownership.

Chance

Inheritance aside, few people can accumulate great wealth without business acumen and other personal qualities. Pure chance, however – being in the right place at the right time – plays a role as well. For example, one business starts up but fails because general economic conditions worsen, while another succeeds because it happened to start up at the right time. That portion of accumulated wealth that reflects the effect of chance can be said to be unearned, but it is rarely regarded as unfair, any more than lottery winnings are regarded as unfair.

People like to dream, and for the material-minded a favorite dream is winning a lottery. One could make a case that lottery winnings are fairly earned, in the sense that they are a reward for risk-taking, but few people would require such a justification, or find the argument compelling. Only the stuffiest of moralists would insist that they are unearned and should find no place in a Good Society. Other critics would be people whose religious beliefs forbid all forms of gambling. The Communist societies were not conspicuously fun-loving, but they also found lotteries to be quite acceptable, and indeed made use of the eagerness of people to pay for their tickets in search of that dream. A good deal of government borrowing took the form of lottery bonds: if you bought such a bond, you received no interest but your name was entered in a lottery that paid huge sums to the winners.

Wealth acquired through chance, either in a pure lottery or in the lottery of business affairs, is somewhat different from that acquired through savings out of wages. Few people who would admit the former in their Good Society, however, would decline to admit the latter.

6 Inheritance

In societies in which the great majority of people own some property, there is little support for Proudhon's blanket condemnation of all property as theft: one's own property is certainly not theft. Most of the sources of property acquisition are regarded as at least acceptable and usually laudable on equity grounds, as long as they are not in violation of the law. There is one source of property acquisition, however, at which many people draw the line. That is property acquired through inheritance.

Hostility to inheritance has an ancient history. The notion that land and other worldly possessions are a gift of God and should be returned at death to His representatives on earth has a long history in Christian thought.[11] The vast church land-holdings at the dawn of the Industrial Revolution are in good part due to the bequests of the faithful over the centuries.

In modern societies the hostility to inheritance is rooted in secular values: it offends the sense of justice in both of its meanings, distributive justice as well as fairness. It increases the extent of inequality of income and consumption, thus compounding the inter-generational transmission of inequality. And it does so in a way that cannot be justified by any acceptable principle such as contribution to production.

Inheritance seems like the clearest possible case of something for nothing.[12] It is difficult to imagine any conception of a present-day Good Society that would enthusiastically embrace an arrangement in which two citizens, alike in all respects, enjoy different levels of income and wealth for no reason other than the accident of their parents' wealth.

If there were no more to it than that, inheritance would be banned from every version of a Good Society. There is, however, a great deal more to it than that.

The family   Inheritance has been a crucial element in family organization throughout history, from the smallest of clans to the largest of societies. When and to whom to pass the family wealth is the stuff of history and literature – not only in the lives of monarchs like King Lear and King George III, but in the lives of smallholders as well. The practical side of it is that elderly parents rely on their power to bequeath to assure that they will be taken care of in their infirmity. In that sense inheritance helps to cement the family and sustain the mutual obligations that provide much of the cement. These considerations build up to a reasonable case for the right to bequeath one's wealth to one's family.

Even in modern societies in which such values as equality and achievement are paramount, the legitimacy of the transfer of assets from parents to children has strong defenders. In Communist China, for example, state factory managers accept the obligation to hire the children of their workers,[13] much as the children of union members in capitalist countries sometimes have preference in admission to union membership when they come of age. The Soviet Union, which had abolished inheritance in the revolutionary purity of its early years, later reversed that ban, and its constitution listed inheritance as one of the rights of Soviet citizens.[14]

The heirs   Where doubts are expressed, they focus on the other side of the inheritance transaction – the heirs. One concern about the social consequence of inheritance was expressed by a towering giant of modern capitalism, Andrew Carnegie. A self-made millionaire himself, he worried about the "silver spoon" effect of inherited wealth on the personal character of heirs. The broader concern, however, is the inequality that inheritance promotes.

Attitudes toward inheritance reflect the clash between the two great values of freedom and equity. The freedom to dispose of one's property without restriction may be viewed as an essential right of the citizens of a free society. If you hold that view, then you would find nothing unacceptable in the inequality of ownership that is transmitted through inheritance. That view conflicts, however, with the value of equality of opportunity. A Good Society, in this latter view, can accept a distribution of ownership in which the rich hold more than the poor, but it cannot accept the legitimacy of the children of the rich inheriting more than the children of the poor.

INHERITANCE AND INEQUALITY

Inheritance is not the only source of inequality under private ownership. It turns out, moreover, that it is not even the major source. Since data on inheritance and gifts are hard to come by, the number of careful studies of the subject is small, but they all point in the same direction.

The most far-reaching study is that of Alan S. Blinder. Using the best data set then available, he developed a simulation model that made it possible to estimate how the income distribution would change if the subjects were equal in each of a variety of respects – same wage rates, same labor–leisure tastes, same time preferences, and same size of inheritances. The most powerful source of income inequality proved to be wage-rate inequality: when everyone was assumed to have the same wage rate, the standard measure of income inequality was reduced by 54 percent.[15] In contrast, when it was assumed that no one received any inheritance at all, the measure of inequality declined by only 2 percent. In another study of the records of people who had died in a certain period, John A. Brittain concluded that the wealth and bequests of the decedent parent showed much less influence on the economic status of heirs than the collective effect of such other parental characteristics as education and occupation. In fact, the removal of all property income, whether from inherited or otherwise-acquired property, reduced the standard measure of income inequality by only 15–20 percent.[16]

Sample studies are likely to understate the effect of inheritance because the samples would have to be extremely large to catch the small number of very large inherited fortunes. The results do nevertheless put the issue in a useful perspective. While the absence of inheritance would reduce the number of extremely rich by perhaps one-half,[17] the other half would still be there on the basis of the property they had assembled themselves. Nor would the elimination of inheritance make much of a dent in the inequality among the rest of the population. Therefore, people who are concerned primarily with justice as distributional equity should focus not on inheritance but on the major sources of inequality like differences in skills. But for people concerned mostly with justice as fairness, inheritance will remain an unacceptable feature of private ownership, however small its overall effect on inequality.

TAXATION

While the most committed egalitarians might wish to abolish inheritance completely, no society that employs private ownership has seriously considered that. All, however, employ some form of inheritance taxes, although nowhere do they account for a significant portion of government revenues. In the major capitalist countries they range from 0.1 percent of GDP in Germany to 0.3 percent in France.[18] Among the reasons are large exemptions, concessions for gift transfers to children and grandchildren, family trusts and foundations, and concern over the international mobility of financial wealth. Inheritance taxes serve more as a modestly useful revenue-raising device that provokes no mass opposition than as an instrument of egalitarian social policy.

Critics sometimes imagine that there is widespread smoldering indignation over inheritance and that a bold taxation proposal would enjoy vast support. It appears, however, that on the contrary, there is widespread support for the right to bequeath, even by people who have no expectation of inheritance. One small indication of that sentiment was uproar among blue-collar workers against the 1972 proposal by US Senator George McGovern to introduce much stiffer inheritance taxes. Sympathetic observers claim that the reason for the unexpected opposition was that the proposal was presented badly.[19] The protest did reveal, however, that large numbers of people regard their right to pass their property on to their children as something not to be easily surrendered.

Suppose an egalitarian fever gripped a private-ownership economy and inheritance taxes were sharply increased. Among the many ways in which property owners would very likely respond, two are of major significance.

One would be a decrease in savings, and therefore in growth and job creation. Older property owners would be increasingly disinclined to convert their current income into property that would shortly have to be surrendered to the government in taxes. More property would be sold for cash to increase current consumption: if $1 million in bonds would shrink to perhaps $1/2 million after inheritance taxes, it would pay to cash them in now and spend the money on grand family holidays and other forms of consumption. High estate taxation might discourage bequests and encourage expenditures that would increase the children's income-earning capabilities. That, perversely, would widen the extent of inequality because human capital is the major source of income inequality.[20] A second response would be an earlier withdrawal from entrepreneurship. A businessman who would otherwise work to accumulate wealth until age 70 might decide to throw in the towel at age 50. The economy would then lose the benefit of a significant volume of entrepreneurship.

Yet it is difficult to forecast how large those responses would be. They would be largest in the case of people who are primarily driven by the goal of founding a dynasty by leaving great wealth to their children. However, taxes often have opposing effects on effort, and it is difficult to foresee in advance which would dominate. An increase in inheritance taxes might lead not to a decrease but to an increase in entrepreneurial effort in order to make up for the wealth now taken away by the government. In the case of income taxes, there is evidence that even highly progressive tax rates do not seem to reduce work effort, and the same is likely to apply to inheritance.[21] When they reach the level of Swedish taxes, however, there appears to be a significant withdrawal of effort (chapter 21).

Family and dynasty, moreover, are not the only considerations that drive entrepreneurship. Much of the force comes from a variety of personal gratifications. Once a businessman has amassed a volume of wealth sufficient to support his consumption requirements for his lifetime, his motivation for continued acquisition of wealth often changes. Major reasons that older wealthy businessmen do not desist from the further accumulation of wealth are the continued drive for power, status, admiration of their peers, the sport of the game, and the pure pleasure of creating something of value. Those motives require only that a person be able to accumulate as much wealth as he can during his lifetime. They may not be greatly affected by what happens to the property after his death. Motivations like power may indeed be relatively more important in modern societies than in the past because family now plays a much smaller role in economic and social organization.

A society that adopts private ownership should therefore expect that it will not score high by the standard of economic justice because of the persistence of inheritance. Of all the factors that affect income inequality, however, property inheritance is not the main culprit. It is the unfairness of it than should rankle most, rather than the additional inequality that it spawns. Democratic societies that find it sufficiently galling could elect to increase the inheritance tax, but none have imposed confiscatory rates. Preservation of the ancient right of parents to transmit their possessions to their children, and a concern that a private-property economy might suffer if the right to bequeath were greatly restricted, have dominated whatever discomfort there may be with the unfairness of inheritance. Hence even strong egalitarians do not regard inheritance taxation as a promising route toward greater equality in a private-property economy.[22]

7　Inequality in Wealth

Suppose inheritance somehow evaporated and you concluded that all other sources of property acquisition are sufficiently fair to justify a place for private ownership in your Good Society. That disposes of the fairness aspect of equity, but the inequality aspect remains to be considered. For, while the individual paths to property accumulation may be acceptable, the overall distribution of ownership may exceed the bounds of acceptable inequality, much as each item in a family expenditure budget may be unimpeachable but the aggregate may be too large.

But how large is too large? A widely used measure of wealth inequality is the percentage of total wealth owned by the wealthiest 1 percent of households. If the top 1 percent of households owned 5 percent of all the wealth, would that be too large? Or 10 percent? Or 20 percent? Since that number is not one with which people have much experience, it is useful to consider the value of that number in various countries.

In the United States the share of the top 1 percent rose from 30 percent of total household wealth in 1983 to 37 percent in 1989, then declined back to 30 percent in 1992.[23] In France the share of the top 1 percent was 26 percent in 1983, and in the United Kingdom it has remained stable at about 20 percent since the mid-1970s. In Sweden the top 1 percent owned 17 percent of the wealth in 1975, but their share had risen to 21 percent in 1990.[24] The figures are not entirely comparable because methods and definitions vary among countries, but they provide a rough idea of the range of variation.

Judging from those numbers, a society that opts for private ownership and has a strong egalitarian tradition like Sweden can expect the wealthiest 1 percent of families to own around 20 percent of household wealth. For the purest of egalitarians, even that would be too high a price to pay for the efficiency and other benefits of private ownership; they should choose state ownership for their Good Society. Most citizens of modern societies, however, do not think of themselves as outdoing the Swedes in their devotion to equality, and would regard 20 percent as an acceptable degree of inequality. But in opting for private ownership they take a risk, for they may end up with an American-level of inequality where the wealthiest 1 percent own 30 percent or more of the wealth.

A great many factors contribute to changes in the degree of wealth inequality over time and among countries. In countries with a strong entrepreneurial tradition, for example, there are likely to be relatively more accumulations of great wealth. During periods of dynamic change in new technologies like electronics and biotechnology, or of rapid international trade expansion, large new fortunes are created that tend to increase the share of the top 1 percent. Large changes in the organization of financial markets can move in the same direction. The extent of inequality may be expected to increase most in countries like the United States where those changes have been occurring most rapidly.

Large forces of these sorts often overwhelm social and economic policy. For example, wealth inequality increased sharply in the United States during the Reagan years, but in the United Kingdom during the Thatcher years, where similar policies prevailed, the wealth distribution remained unchanged.[25] Nevertheless, a democratic society that accepts private ownership but holds inequality without limit to be unacceptable can contain it to some degree by acts of policy, notably taxation.

Twenty-two of the 24 OECD countries levy death and gift taxes of some sort, and 15 also tax capital gains. In addition, 11 levy an annual tax on wealth. However, with large exemptions and relatively low rates, wealth taxes, like inheritance taxes, account for a very small portion of total tax revenues. Wealth, death, and gift taxes together range from 0.01 percent in Australia to 3.06 percent in Switzerland. They account for 0.77 percent of total tax revenues in the United States, slightly above the OECD mean of 0.67 percent.[26] Nowhere have they been used to effect a significant reduction in wealth inequality.

Wealth inequality remains a matter of concern to people with strong egalitarian values, but nowhere is that concern sufficiently intense or extensive to have made a strong impact on the political agenda. The citizens of the capitalist countries seem to have become accustomed to the prevailing degree of wealth inequality and to find it politically acceptable. That does not signify, however, that they are prepared to accept inequality without limit. Large increases in wealth inequality, such as that in the United States between 1983 and 1989, generate a great deal of public attention and could stimulate efforts to restore the level to which the society had become accustomed.

8 Security

A society that assigns a large weight to job security as a criterion of goodness should look first not to its the ownership arrangements but to its economic mechanism, for planning, as we have seen, provides a degree of security that markets can never match (chapter 20). State ownership, with which planning must always be conjoined, usually contributes further to job security, for when the state is the owner, political considerations enter into all economic decisions and the interest of the citizens-as-workers in job security is everywhere a political force. Governments find it more difficult than private owners to dismiss workers, not only in democratic societies where their votes are important but in authoritarian societies as well.

A society that throws its lot in with the market mechanism should therefore expect a higher level of insecurity, but that level can still be influenced by the choice of ownership form. Worker ownership appears to dominate the other forms in that respect.

It has been found that when sales decline or other conditions change, producer cooperatives tend to maintain employment at the expense of profit, while equivalent private enterprises reduce employment in order to maintain profit (chapter 26). When output expands, cooperatives do not expand their labor force as readily as private companies, preferring to work overtime and weekends until that becomes too burdensome. Hence the larger the proportion of cooperatives in the economy, the greater the stability of employment in the face of fluctuations in economic activity.

The stability of employment in producer cooperatives reflects the social character of that form of ownership. It is more painful for cooperative members to vote to lay off some of their own than for a boss – even a compassionate one – to dismiss a worker. Cooperators would rather accept a cut in their income than do that. In cooperatives that hire outside workers, that sentiment spills over to them to some degree, but the hired workers are the first to be let go when retrenchment is no longer avoidable.

Employment in state-owned enterprises and public corporations is also likely to be more stable over time than in privately owned enterprises. Wages are likely to be maintained, however, so that the cost of job security is borne by the citizens generally and not by the workers; unlike cooperatives, where the members pay for their job security in the form of fluctuations in their income.

The tradeoff of income for security is not unknown in private enterprises. The Japanese experience with lifetime employment for a large segment of the labor force is based on precisely that tradeoff. There it takes the form of fluctuations in the annual bonuses, which makes it possible for the companies to reduce the cost of labor during periods of contraction without having to dismiss their workers. There is nothing to preclude the widespread use in capitalist economies of labor contracts that involve profit-and-loss sharing in such forms as profit-based bonuses. The workers in such a private-ownership "share economy" would enjoy considerably more job security than under the standard fixed-wage contracts.[27]

9 Discussion

Of all the property arrangements employed in modern societies, the one that strikes me as utterly indefensible on equity grounds is inheritance. It is not a unique feature of capitalism, of course. It has also been an acceptable practice in socialist societies, but since the magnitude of privately owned wealth is so small there, it is only a minor blemish. Under capitalism, however, where most of the wealth is privately owned, the amount of inheritable wealth is of very large proportions. Private ownership would seem to be totally inadmissible in a Good Society unless it is cleansed somehow of the inequity of inheritance.

Supporters of inheritance appear to identify with property owners who are approaching the end of their lives. From that perspective, there is some merit in the argument that the desire to pass one's wealth on to one's children helps to strengthen the family and therefore deserves social support. There is also merit in the argument is that inheritance is efficient: if wealth could not be transmitted to one's heirs, less of it would be accumulated and the growth rate would be lower. The right to bequeath is also a manifestation of economic freedom – the freedom to do what one wants with one's wealth.

However, it is on the other side – that of the heirs – that the equity damage is done. One can shrug one's shoulders about the unfairness of it and regard it as but one more of the unfortunate facts of life, but there is no ethical justification for tolerating it in a Good Society.

Someone may some day invent an arrangement under which parents would be free to bequeath their wealth to their children, but children would not be allowed to receive bequests from their parents. In the absence of a mystical solution of that sort, a society must weigh the benefits of permitting the older generation to bequeath against the costs of permitting the younger generation to inherit. Suppose a society judged the costs to be too high and imposed severe restrictions on inheritance. How would things work out?

The restrictions, we may imagine, would not amount to prohibition. Property owners, in anticipation of death, would be permitted to make gifts under limited conditions, as they may at present; but the rest of their wealth would have to be given up upon death, either to the government or to a non-profit purpose of their choice – church, library, university, theater, hospital, girl scouts, and so forth. A good deal of all wealth is indeed presently donated for such purposes; in this society all of it would be bequeathed in that manner.

It would be far from the ideal of equal opportunity, for family inequality in income, education, and other characteristics would still be transmitted to the children's generation. But that inequality would not be compounded by large bequests received on the death of rich parents and relatives. All large fortunes would belong to the people who amassed them during their lifetimes; none would have been derived by inheritance.

As I envision such a society, most of the population would experience few direct effects of the restrictions on inheritance, for the number of people who either possess or inherit large fortunes in present-day societies is very small. Parents and children would not love each other less if bequests amounted to only $1 million instead of $1 billion. Some older wealthy people would devote less effort to further accumulation of wealth, but most people whose lives have been spent in the contest for power, prestige, and deference, are unlikely to trade all that in for the golf course. The wealthy would become accustomed to thinking about how to arrange for the best social use of their wealth after their death, rather than how much to bequeath to which relations. Their relations would plan their lives, like ordinary people, knowing that their income and wealth will depend on their own effort and not on that of their parents.

I find that sketch an appealing one, and the restriction of inheritance is an item on my agenda for a Good Society. However, I do not assign it a high place on that agenda. For one thing, my main concern about inequality is not that some people have more than others but that some people have less than others. The elimination of poverty therefore tops my agenda, and the abolition of inheritance makes no contribution to that end. Second, the major source of income inequality, as reported in the text, is not the inheritance of wealth but the inheritance of social and personal characteristics like education, attitudes, aspiration, and so forth. Reducing that source of income inequality should have higher priority. Third, since no private-property society has restricted inheritance in that fashion, there is little empirical experience from which to assess all of its consequences, some of which might be very large. For example, the economy might suffer from a huge outflow of capital spirited abroad to escape the prohibition. Inheritance in an otherwise Good Society therefore seems to me more of an ethical irritant than a substantive malady. I wish it would go away, but it is not worth the effort to remove it.

I accept the argument in the text that non-inherited wealth – derived from such normal sources as savings out of wages, profits, and capital gains – should be regarded as having been fairly earned. Proprietors, professionals, and business executives contribute significantly to the production of goods and services, and their compensation is subject, in various degrees, to market controls. That is not to deny that if you reconstruct the history of any large fortune, you will find that some of the income streams that fed into it would not pass your test of fairness: for example, wealth derived from the exploitation of monopolistic markets, or from executive compensation under conditions of weak stockholder control, or from tax avoidance or evasion, or even from patently illegal activities. No tainted wealth would exist in an Ideal Society, but some of it is inevitable in a merely Good Society. It is therefore appropriate to regard wealth accumulated through the normal channels as innocent unless proven guilty.

Ownership and politics   There remains the issue of distributive justice. Even if all wealth were fairly acquired, one might still hold that its distribution is excessively unequal.

That sentiment may reflect no more than the envy of the rich by the poor. If that is the source of the sentiment, it is of no interest in the economics of the Good Society, because the person who holds it presumably identifies with the poor. The relevant question is why inequality might be regarded as excessive by people who judge it from behind a "veil of igno-rance" – that is, without knowing whether they would be among the rich or the poor. From that perspective, wealth inequality may not be objectionable in itself, but beyond a certain point it may be thought to have deleterious effects on the society generally. People who hold this view have diverse social effects in mind, but in my judgment the most momentous is the effect on the political institutions.

The democratic ideal is that the citizens enjoy equality in all aspects of political life. They have one vote each, they have equal access to their government, and they can expect equal justice under the law. That ideal could never be perfectly attained, even if wealth were equally distributed. The more unequal the distribution, however, the greater the departure from the ideal. Democratic capitalist societies have managed to live with imperfect versions of political equality for a long time, but in recent decades the use of wealth to gain political influence has accelerated in the United States and in other countries. Among the reasons is that the use of television, public-opinion polling, and other new techniques has greatly increased the cost of political campaigning, so that political actors are increasingly dependent on contributions from their wealthy supporters. Another reason is that as the power of government to influence the economic affairs of the citizens increases, there are greater benefits to be had by the direct or indirect bribery of government officials: when a vote for a particular subsidy can add billions to an industry's profits, it pays to contribute millions to make it happen.

A democratic society can tolerate a great deal of erosion of political equality by wealth inequality, but the further it proceeds, the greater the concern of people who place a high value on political equality. In the United States efforts to limit the influence of wealth on politics have been gaining momentum and may help to stem the tide to some extent. One way that can be done is by reducing the extent of wealth inequality, for example by taxing wealth as well as income. There are indeed voices calling for wealth taxes, but like inheritance taxes, they are proposed primarily for revenue-raising purposes.[28] There is no serious possibility of taxing wealth so heavily as to eliminate its power to influence politics.

The more promising approach is to reduce the influence of wealth inequality on critical areas of political life. The provision of public defenders for the poor, at public expense, is an important step in that direction. It is a far cry from equal treatment under law, but it responds to the society's value judgment that a certain minimal level of legal protection should be available to all citizens regardless of income. The central concern at present, however, is the escalating flow of private contributions to political campaigns. The concern may well lead to the imposition of new restrictions on the form and size of political contributions, but like the public-defender laws, they can restrict but not eliminate the influence of wealth on equality.

Hence, people who opt for private ownership in their Good Society should expect that wealth inequality will generate political inequality. In a democratic polity in which the public sentiment for equality is very strong, as in the Nordic countries perhaps, public policy can be enlisted in support of what James Tobin called "specific egalitarianism" – the insulation of specific areas of social and political life from the influence of wealth inequality.[29] Where hostility to government is relatively strong and public sentiment for political equality relatively weak, however, as in the United States, the power of the wealthy over social and political life will be larger. The best that political egalitarians can hope for is that there are enough like-minded citizens to enlist the power of government to set some limits on the power of wealth to influence social and political affairs.

State or private ownership? This chapter was devoted to the evaluation of the various ownership arrangements by criteria of goodness other than efficiency, such as justice and security. Most of the content, however, consists of a critical assessment of the performance of private ownership by those criteria. It might seem that people devoted to justice and other social values would do better to adopt state ownership than private ownership for their Good Society.

There is a sense in which that is correct. When individual citizens do not have the right to own productive property or to derive an income from its use, there can be no large accumulations of private wealth. Income inequality is limited to differences in wage earnings, and is not augmented by property incomes, all of which accrue to the state. The highest political officials and industrial executives earn substantially more than the average, especially when the perquisites of office are considered, but their wealth is still exceedingly small compared to that accumulated by their opposite numbers under private ownership. In these respects state ownership has a claim as a candidate for the Good Society on grounds of distributive justice.

With respect to other social criteria of goodness, however, state ownership comes off very badly. For one thing, the prohibition against private ownership of productive property closes off a large realm of individual choice – the right to earn an income by starting up and managing one's own business. People with strong egalitarian values may prefer a society that denies its citizens that choice, but people who place a high value on individual choice would shun that society.

In my view, however, the most ominous consequence of the prohibition against private ownership is that every citizen must earn her income by working for an enterprise owned by the state. The state has a monopoly, as it were, over the supply of jobs, which has the potential of completely undermining the institutions of political liberty.

It may be too strong to assert that state ownership is inherently incompatible with liberty. The only empirical evidence on the subject comes from the experience of the Communist countries, where the Party/State used its monopoly over jobs, among other means, to intimidate dissenters. The chief instrument of the suppression of dissent, however, was not the ownership form but the authoritarian political system. It therefore does not follow that a democratic government in a state-ownership economy – perhaps a form of market socialism – would use its monopoly over jobs in the same way. Since there is very little empirical experience with that sort of society, one can only speculate, but there is some indirect evidence on the relation of ownership form to political freedom.

In times of tension, democratic governments can be extremely harsh on dissenters. During the years that Senator Joseph McCarthy dominated national politics in the United States, the government was under great pressure to dismiss employees who had come under his anti-Communist fire. The fear of his wrath soon extended beyond government to private universities and businesses, some of which dismissed employees who were charged by the Senator or refused to cooperate with his committee. It was a time when many citizens were gripped by a fear for their livelihood and liberty in a manner eerily similar to that in the Communist world. That the country eventually recovered its political balance was due, among other things, to the courage of many private enterprises and universities who provided employment, openly or covertly, for people who had been fired from their jobs for political reasons. Had all enterprises been owned by the state, dissent might have been crushed and the democracy along with it.

The episode is consistent with the argument of a long stream of political thought starting with John Locke which holds that private property is the only guarantee, though an imperfect one, of political liberty. That view dominates my own assessment of the relative merits of state and private ownership. For all the inequity that comes from the adoption of private ownership, the protection that it affords for political liberty commends it for my own Good Society.

Notes

1 *Economic Report of the President*, February 1997, table B-26. The term "proprietors" refers to small businessmen, shopkeepers, farmers, and self-employed persons. Part of their income might be considered labor income – an imputed wage for their own labor used in the business – and rest income on their business property. The figure of 21 percent therefore overstates the size of pure property income by a few percentage points.

2 Labor cost here includes the cost of the past labor embodied in the capital, which is accounted for by including a depreciation charge in the calculation of cost of production.

3 Grossman, "Scarce capital and Soviet doctrine."

4 Goskomstat, *Narodnoe Khoziaistvo SSSR v 1989*, p. 12. The average annual wage was 2,885 rubles (p. 76) and total employment was 139.3 million (p. 47). Reported wages include incentive bonuses but not social insurance and other supplements. I arbitrarily added 20 percent to wages to make

the figure more comparable to that of the United States data, which include wage supplements in labor income.

5   In a capitalist economy, investment is financed not only out of the personal savings of households but out of other sources such as the retained earnings and depreciation allowances of corporations. In 1996 personal savings accounted for only about 21 percent of gross savings in the United States (US Bureau of the Census, *Statistical Abstract, 1997*, table 703).

6   *The New York Times*, February 11, 1998, p. A34.

7   *The New York Times*, February 11, 1998, p. D4.

8   *The New York Times*, February 22, 1998, Sec. 3, p. 1.

9   Thurow, *The Zero-Sum Society*, pp. 172–5.

10 Berliner, *The Innovation Decision in Soviet Industry*.

11 Goody, "Inheritance," p. 852.

12 Brittain, *The Inheritance of Economic Status*, p. 7.

13 Walder, *Communist Neo-traditionalism*, p. 58.

14 Goody, "Inheritance," p. 852.

15 Blinder, *Toward an Economic Theory of Income Distribution*, p. 122. Some of the subjects had received fairly large inheritances, but the sample was too small to capture any extremely large fortunes.

16 Brittain, *The Inheritance of Economic Status*, pp. 4–5.

17 Thurow, *The Zero-Sum Society*, p. 172.

18 Pechman, "Inheritance taxes," p. 857.

19 Brittain, *The Inheritance of Economic Status*, p. 30.

20 Brittain, *The Inheritance of Economic Status*, p. 7.

21 Thurow, *The Zero-Sum Society*, p. 168.

22 Putterman, Roemer, and Silvestre, "Does egalitarianism have a future?," p. 882.

23 *Economic Report of the President*, February 1997, p. 183.

24 Wolff, *Top Heavy*, p. 22.

25 Wolff, *Top Heavy*, p. 22.

26 Wolff, *Top Heavy*, p. 39.

27 Weitzman, *The Share Economy*.

28 Wolff, *Top Heavy*, ch. 9.

29 Tobin, "On limiting the domain of inequality," pp. 264–7.

Part VI

Conclusion

Chapter 28

The Best of
Economic Systems

Whoever cultivates the golden mean
avoids both the poverty of the hovel and
the envy of the palace.

— Horace

More than any other time in history,
mankind faces a crossroads. One path
leads to despair and utter hopelessness.
The other to total destruction. Let us
pray we have the wisdom to choose
correctly.

— Woody Allen

CONTENTS

We have come to a fork in the road. The sign on the right reads "Private Ownership, Mostly." The sign on the left reads "Social Ownership, Mostly." Both claim to be the road to the Good Society. On the journey travelled so far we have examined the various economic arrangements you are likely to encounter on the two roads ahead. Now it is time to choose. Should you take the capitalist road on the right, or the socialist road on the left?

This is a rare opportunity. Many people everywhere spend their lives grousing about the deficiencies of the economic system under which they live, but few are able to cut free and begin a new life under a system they believe to be better. The fork in the road provides the opportunity, in imagination if not in actuality, to quit grousing and commit yourself to what you believe to be the better economic system.

The citizens of most of the former Communist societies, who had been famous grousers, had that rare opportunity in actuality, and took it. Most are glad they did, but some are nostalgic for the security and the easy pace of working life under the system they abandoned. There are bound to be disappointments, as well as pleasant surprises, if one chooses an economic road knowing only that along one path the property is socially owned and along the other the property is privately owned.

The choice is not entirely blind, however, for the twentieth century has produced a rich store of knowledge on the experience of diverse societies that have been down those two roads before. The assessment of the arrangements employed in the two large families of economies has been the mission of this book. Whether you now judge the capitalist or the socialist family as your Good Society depends on your values. It is therefore appropriate to conclude with a review of the merits and demerits of the two grand systems, applying the same criteria as we have used in assessing the goodness of the economic arrangements of which they are composed.

I Efficiency

On the basis of the assessments presented in the text, one would expect the socialist combination of state ownership and central planning to be less efficient than the capitalist combination of markets and private ownership. Those assessments are based primarily on qualitative evidence, however. Before declaring one system to be better than the other, one needs to know how large the difference in efficiency is: a great deal rides on whether the difference is 5 percent or 50 percent.

A vast effort has been made to measure comparative efficiency. Quantitative studies of efficiency usually begin with some measure of total output, such as GDP. In the most influential of such studies, Professor Abram Bergson assembled a set of data on four socialist countries and seven capitalist countries in 1975.[1] GDP per capita in the socialist countries ranged from 41 percent (Yugoslavia) to 60 percent (USSR) of that in the United States. In all of the capitalist countries GDP per capita was higher than that, ranging from 62 percent (Spain) to 88 percent (West Germany) of that of the United States. All comparative studies confirm the finding that output per capita was smaller in the socialist countries.

That difference in GDP per capita, however, does not at all mean that socialism is less efficient than capitalism. Much or all of it may be due to the fact that the capitalist countries are better endowed with resources. For instance, the United States might be less efficient than the USSR but might nevertheless produce a larger GDP per capita because it has more capital per worker. The crucial question is, to what extent is the socialist output gap due to fewer and poorer resources, rather than to inefficiency in the use of the resources they do have?

To answer the question, Bergson developed a set of data on the inputs used in those economies – the quantities, and where possible the quality, of the labor, capital, and agricultural land used to produce the 1975 outputs. The data were then used to calculate "comparative productivity" – a measure that is designed to "hold resources constant." The technique asks, in effect, "If all the countries had used the same quantities and qualities of labor, capital, and land, which group would have produced the larger output?"

The major finding is that the socialist countries would have produced from 24 percent to 34 percent less output than the capitalist countries if all of them had the same resources. The wide range of the estimate reflects the many assumptions that had to be made at each stage of the research – the 24-percent figure emerges when all the assumptions are most favorable to socialism.

Data collected since the demise of the Communist states suggest that their 1975 levels of GDP were somewhat lower than were reported at the time, so that their comparative productivity was closer to the lower end of that range.[2] These results may be taken to mean that, judging from the experience of twentieth-century socialism, a country that adopts state ownership and central planning can expect to produce around one-third less output than if it adopts private ownership and markets. In some countries the margin of difference will be smaller and in some larger, but the order of magnitude is likely to be around one-third.

In gauging the significance of that number, it is important not to think of it as a *decline* in income. Since people become habituated to living at a certain level of income, a decline in income of that magnitude – say from $60,000 a year to $40,000 – would be a severe blow to one's sense of material well-being. It is rather a different matter if you and the people around you have become accustomed to living on $40,000 a year. You would not then experience directly the effect of the inefficiency of the economy. The only evidence of inefficiency would be indirect – that people in capitalist economies who are no smarter than you and work no harder than you enjoy a much higher living standard than you do. The observation of such differences would create a strong suspicion that most of the reason, though not all, is the inefficiency of the socialist economy.

MARKET SOCIALISM

The efficiency of an economy is the joint result of the efficiency of its economic mechanism and its ownership rules. I have argued above that the major source of the relative inefficiency of the Communist economies lies in the planning mechanism (chapter 24). If so, a market-based socialism should come considerably closer to the efficiency of capitalism. Instead of an efficiency gap of a third, it might be only one of 25 percent or less.

The smaller that gap, the stronger would be the attractiveness of socialism. Hence, if interest in a socialist alternative to capitalism should be rekindled in the future, market socialism is likely to be the strongest candidate. Its candidacy will be weakened, however, by the fact that it is untried. Just as Soviet socialism in practice proved to function differently than in its idealized version, market socialism is also likely to operate differently from its idealized version. The Soviet experience is likely to leave a permanent mark in the form of a more cautious approach to a commitment to socialism than that adopted by socialists of the past.

The case for market socialism is that a state-owned enterprise is essentially no different from the modern privately owned corporation: both are managed by salaried employees who are not themselves owners of the productive property. Therefore, the task of motivating management to work for the owners' interests, and of monitoring their work, is quite similar under the two ownership arrangements. There are reasons to expect, however, that social control over managers is likely to be weaker under market socialism (chapter 24). For one thing, capitalist boards of directors who personally own substantial shares of stock in their companies are likely to be more diligent monitors than boards of public directors who regard themselves as performing a public service, though they may be well paid for their service.

Secondly, there would be no outside investors searching for inefficient enterprises that can be profitably taken over and run more efficiently.

Soviet-style state ownership is only one form of social ownership. A future socialism that threw in its lot with market coordination rather than central-planning coordination might reject state ownership in favor of other forms of social ownership, such as worker owner-ship (chapter 26) or public ownership (chapter 25). That is all the more likely to occur if the society were to elect to operate under a democratic political system, for the rights of the citizens of a democratic polity would be threatened by the vast power that state ownership concentrates in the hands of the government.

My own view is that if you take the socialist road, you should be prepared to find that efficiency, and therefore the level of material welfare, will be around a third less than if you took the capitalist road, much as in the twentieth century. With different arrangements than those of the Communist past, such as market socialism, worker ownership, or public owner-ship, and possibly democratic politics, the gap might be narrowed to perhaps 20 percent. In any event, you should take the road on the left only if you expect that the socialist Good Society will perform better than the capitalist by other things that you value, which would compensate for the gap in efficiency. One of those other things of value is job security.

2   Security

That socialism would prove to be so much less efficient than capitalism is something the prophets of socialism never foresaw. That it would provide much greater job security than capitalism, however, was fully consistent with their image of a workers' state. Under no eco-nomic system, and certainly not under capitalism, are the workers likely to enjoy a greater degree of job security (chapter 20).

Inefficiency and job security are not unrelated, for the former is to some degree the con-sequence of the arrangements employed for maintaining job security. It has been found, for example, that investment in the USSR has been much less productive than in capitalist coun-tries.[3] Among the reasons is that when a new piece of capital is installed, if the enterprise is to make the best use of it the labor force must often be trimmed or expanded or otherwise redeployed. If labor cannot be redeployed, however, the society cannot make the best use of the new capital; it hardly pays to introduce labor-saving equipment if the labor released can-not be reallocated to other productive activities. Capitalism gains a great deal from its invest-ment because labor is readily dismissed or otherwise redeployed to take full advantage of the investment's productivity; the consequence is high productivity of investment but low job security. Socialism gains much less from its investment because labor is not easily dismissed or redeployed to accommodate to it; the consequence is low productivity of investment, but a high degree of job security.

The level of job security provided under both systems can be modified by acts of social and economic policy. The capitalist economies have been at this business for a long time, however, and it is unlikely, although always possible, that new policies will be invented that significantly increase job security. The range of twentieth-century experience, including Japanese lifetime employment, German social-market policies, and American labor-market flexibility, is likely to prevail into the next century. A future socialism, however, may well free itself from the rigidity of Soviet-type lifetime employment. As argued in the text (chap-ter 20), one can readily envision policies under which the workers would agree to change jobs, perhaps even several times during their working lives, under suitable income-maintenance and other social arrangements. The consequent reduction of job security would probably be regarded as a small thing if it were accompanied by such compensating arrangements. The result might be significant gains in the productivity of investment and the efficiency of the eco-nomy. The tradeoff of efficiency for security would then be rather more favorable to socialism.

Standing at the fork in the road, however, the path you should take depends on whether you assign the higher value to security or efficiency in your vision of the Good Society. The choice may be seen as that between the welfare of the citizens-as-consumers and of the same citizens-as-workers. Higher efficiency translates into higher income and more consumption. If you value your welfare as a consumer above your welfare as a worker, you should choose capitalism; but if you place the higher value on your welfare as a worker, you should choose socialism.

3 Justice

Everyone who thinks about the Good Society regards justice as one of the criteria of goodness. The two dimensions of economic justice considered in the text are the fairness of the rules that govern the people's income, and the equality with which that income is distributed.

WAGE INCOME

All capitalist economies and almost all socialist economies regard it as legitimate that workers who contribute more to production should be paid more. The two systems differ in the way that a worker's productivity is determined, but the principle of justice in both cases is that wages should differ according to contribution.

People who hold the value that pure equality is the only fair wage arrangement are therefore likely to be disappointed whichever road they take. However, the equality that they value might be found in small and homogeneous producer cooperatives or in communal settings like the Israeli kibbutz. Such communities, however, could not find a place under centrally planned socialism. Paradoxically, if you seek a society in which such equal-wage enterprises could find a home, you should choose the capitalist road, for markets are hospitable to any form of enterprise that can survive under its rules of the game. You might also find them down the socialist road if you are willing to take the chance that you may come upon a market-socialist economy somewhere along that road.

However, while wage equality may be maintained within such enterprises, some of them are likely to be more productive than others, and their members will therefore earn higher wages. Hence wage equality of that sort is strictly local: it prevails within those enterprises, but does not extend to the society as a whole.

In general, the larger and more heterogeneous the society the weaker the prospects for wage equality. The most determined effort to introduce that value in a large society was made in China under the leadership of Mao Zedong, but it was abandoned soon after his death. Prominent among the reasons was its corrosive effect on work incentives: workers in small cooperatives can manage to monitor each other's effort even though the wage is the same regardless of how hard one works. But when wage equality is maintained on a massive scale and administered by a bureaucracy, it has proven to be impossible to maintain work incentives in the long run.

Hence, since wages in all modern economies are likely to be differentiated according to some measure of contribution, people who hold that justice requires pure equality are likely to find the best of societies to be deficient in that respect.

PROPERTY INCOME

While few socialists still cling to the notion that wage inequality is unjust, virtually all still hold that the wage of labor is the only justly earned form of personal income. From that perspective it is unjust that anyone should receive an income derived from the ownership of productive property. Hence, social ownership of productive property is still the great common bond among people who think of themselves as socialists. Either form of socialism, centrally planned or market-based, would satisfy their sense of justice in this respect.

The competing value is that it is unjust for a society to deny its citizens the right to own productive property and to derive an income from its productive use. The prototype of justly earned property income is the thrifty worker who regularly saves some of her wage income and earns interest on her savings-bank account; the argument then extends to such other forms of property income as profits and stock dividends. While the socialist economies all made provision for some limited forms of property income such as interest on government bonds, capitalism, of course, is the better society by that criterion of justice.

INHERITANCE

The case for property income depends on the property having been fairly acquired (chapter 27). No such case can be made for property acquired by inheritance. Few people will regard it as fair that one citizen's income should be larger than another's by the sheer accident of having been born to richer parents. To people concerned with inequality as well as fairness, inheritance has the further disadvantage of contributing to the transmission of inequality from one generation to another.

On the other hand, most people regard it as eminently laudable that parents strive to leave their possessions to their children, and entirely fair that they be permitted to do so. Moreover, a society that accepts private property as its ownership arrangement implicitly gives the owners the right to dispose of their property in whatever way they wish, within certain limitations. Inheritance was also legal in the socialist countries, in accord with Soviet practice after Stalin came to regard the family as an ally rather than an enemy of socialism.

It appears that the pro-inheritance arguments have won the day in all countries. Among the reasons is that inheritance turns out not to be the major factor in explaining income inequality. It is much less important than "social inheritance," such as home environment and education. Hence, while taxes reduce the proportion of parental wealth that is transmitted to heirs – more in some countries than in others – nowhere are they close to confiscatory levels.

Hence, if you regard the practice of inheritance as a major blight on the goodness of a society, you will find few allies. Socialism would offend your sense of justice less than capitalism, but any society you choose as the best will offend you to some extent in that respect.

EQUALITY

On the basis of their coordination mechanisms and ownership arrangements, one would expect socialist income distribution to be more equal than capitalist. Socialist planners are likely to set the lowest wage high enough to satisfy the society's sense of justice, whereas the market-based wage earnings of the least skilled may be lower than the society holds to be decent. At the high end of the income distribution, the property income earned under capitalism should cause the incomes of the rich to be relatively higher than under socialism. The quantitative evidence, however, tells a more complex story.

In one of the most comprehensive analyses of comparative income inequality, Christian Morrison compiled data for four Communist countries and four capitalist countries during the 1970s.[4] The results are best captured in the data on the proportion of total income received by the poorest tenth of the population and the richest tenth. To interpret the data, start with the self-evident observation that if income were equally distributed, then every 10 percent of the population would receive exactly 10 percent of the total income. But if income were unequally distributed, the poorest tenth of the population would receive less than 10 percent of the total income and the richest tenth would receive more than 10 percent. The larger the deviation from 10 percent on both ends, the greater the inequality.

The countries in which the poorest 10 percent of the population received the smallest share of total income were the United States and Canada – 2.6 percent. The country in which they received the largest share of total income was Czechoslovakia – 5.2 percent. Hence, inequality at the low-income end was twice as large in the most unequal capitalist countries as it was in the most equal socialist country. That finding is consistent with the expectation that the poor would benefit most from the egalitarian thrust of socialism.

Contrary to expectation, however, in the most equal of the capitalist countries, the poorest tenth were relatively better off than in the most unequal of Communist countries: they received 4.3 to 4.4 percent in Sweden and Denmark compared to 3.4 percent in Poland and 3.6 percent in the USSR. Hence, the poor in a capitalist country that places a high value on equality may be better off relatively than the poor in a socialist country that places less value on equality.

At the highest-income end, the extremes conform to what one would expect. The richest tenth received the largest share in the United States – 25.5 percent; while the country in which they received the smallest share is Czechoslovakia – 17.7 percent. Within these extremes, however, there is no clear pattern. The richest tenth in the USSR and Poland received larger shares of the country's income – 23.2 and 22.3 percent – than in Sweden (20.5 percent) and the United Kingdom (22.9 percent).

These figures do not include the abundant supplementary benefits that the political and managerial elite received in the socialist countries. The benefits, which are not publicly acknowledged, include special "personal salaries," "thirteenth-month" bonuses, access to special shops, reserved hospitals and clinics, holiday resorts, and numerous other perks. When the estimated value of these benefits is included in the socialist income distribution, the differences in inequality between the two sets of countries shrinks. The difference is particularly pronounced at the high-income end. The countries in which the rich were the richest relatively were both socialist; the shares of the richest tenth in the USSR (27.2 percent) and in Poland (27.0 percent) were larger than in all four capitalist countries, including the United States (25.8 percent). The countries in which the richest tenth were the poorest relatively were both capitalist – they received 20.4 percent of the income in Sweden and 20.7 percent in the United Kingdom.

Small differences in these numbers should not carry great weight, for there are severe problems of comparability across countries. Moreover, income distribution may change over time: inequality has increased sharply in the capitalist countries since the 1970s, so that in the last years of the Communist regimes the difference in equality between the two systems may have been larger than in 1975.[5]

The broad picture, however, suggests two conclusions. One is that if a country is socialist, its income distribution is likely to be more equal than if it were capitalist. The other is that the overlap is very large, so that both capitalist and socialist countries may be found among those with the most equal distribution as well as the most unequal. The main reason for that muddy result is that in both systems governments play an important role in modifying the underlying income distribution.

While governments redistribute income in all countries, in the socialist countries the redistribution policy favors the elite and widens the gap between rich and poor, while in the capitalist countries redistribution favors the poor and greatly narrows the gap. The redistribution from rich to poor proceeded furthest in the European capitalist countries, but even in the United States, which remains the most unequal, inequality is much smaller than it would be in the absence of government action. The responsiveness of income distribution to popular attitudes in democratic countries underscores the point that the extent of inequality reveals more about the character of the people of the society than about who owns the property. In an international poll of popular attitudes, for example, only 29 percent of Americans thought that government has a responsibility to reduce income differentials, compared to 60–70 percent of Britons and Germans and over 80 percent of Italians and Austrians.[6] Those differences in values do not translate directly into relative degrees of income inequality, but they help to explain why the United States tops all lists of the most unequal of modern capitalist societies. European visitors regard the gap between rich and poor in the United States as "far wider than a civilized country should accept."[7]

What one makes of those results depends on the values one brings to the concept of justice. People whose only criterion of justice is that the rules must be fair can be attracted to either socialism or capitalism – if you believe that the only fair source of income is labor, you would regard socialism as the better economy and the socialist income distribution as the more just, but if you believe that property income is as fairly earned as labor income, you would regard capitalism as the better economy. You might support some government programs for assistance to the truly poor, but you would be opposed to the redistribution of income for the mere sake of greater equality.

If you hold that inequality beyond a certain degree is bad for the society, however, you should ask not whether the economic structure is capitalist or socialist, but what kind of redistributive policies the society is likely to adopt. The answer to that question is to be found not in the society's economic arrangements but in its historical and cultural traditions. To be sure, history and culture affect a system's performance by other criteria of goodness as well. Efficiency, for example, would very likely be higher in Germany than in Russia even if both were capitalist or both were socialist, but the weight of the evidence is that on the matter of efficiency, being capitalist or socialist makes more of a difference than being German or Russian. In the case of equality, however, history and culture appear to dominate: income would very likely be more unequal in a socialist country populated by Americans than in a capitalist country populated by Swedes.

Hence, the signs at the fork in the road provide very little guidance if you place a high value on equality. In seeking your Good Society you should ascertain whether the people share your values, rather than whether the property is owned socially or privately.

4 Digression on Economic Growth

An idealistic young person from a poor country might well say of this book: "It is fine for you people in rich countries to be so concerned about such things as security and equality. But in my country when we think about a good economic system we have only one criterion in mind – will it help to develop our economy and bring us out of poverty?"

The question of which economic arrangements are best suited to transform a poor agrarian economy into a rich industrial one occupies an important place on the economics agenda. The mission of this book, however, is to consider the best way to organize a modern economy, and I have therefore not looked into the process whereby an underdeveloped economy might transform itself into a modern one. However, the twentieth-century experience does have something important to say to my young idealist about the relative performance of the two systems in promoting economic growth.

The Soviet Union started out as an economic backwater of Europe in 1917 and emerged from the ruins of World War II as an industrial giant and a military superpower. No other country had transformed itself so rapidly during that period, and its socialist system and economic policy became the model for poor countries around the world that hoped to emulate Soviet economic-development performance. In the early postwar era, indeed, the growth record of the centrally planned economies merited that admiration. In the decade of the 1950s they grew on average at the rate of 5.7 percent a year, almost 15 percent faster than the growth rate of the major capitalist countries (5.0 percent).[8] It was widely believed during those years that it was only a matter of time before they would achieve what Stalin had earlier proclaimed as the principal Soviet economic objective – to overtake and surpass the leading capitalist countries.

In the next two decades, however, history took a different turn. Growth rates declined in the socialist planned economies to 4.3–4.4 percent, but in the capitalist world they increased to 5.5 percent – 25 percent higher than in the socialist economies. Thereafter the growth rate declined in both groups of countries, but by the late 1970s the capitalist rate (3.4) exceeded the socialist rate (2.6) by 30 percent.

A second development over that period which commanded attention in both groups of countries was the remarkable growth of the Japanese economy. In the 30 years between 1950 and 1980 its growth rate rose from 7.9 percent to the astonishing level of 12.2 percent. South Korea, Hong Kong, and other Asian countries also joined the club of rapidly growing economies. By the 1980s these countries largely surpassed the USSR in technological attainment and per capita output.

By the time the position of General Secretary of the Soviet Communist Party fell vacant in 1985, few people there or elsewhere still regarded Soviet socialism as the best system for a society that placed a high value on growth. Not only did the countries that embraced it fall increasingly behind the capitalist countries, but Japan and the Asian Tigers had demonstrated the high-growth capacity of capitalism under favorable conditions. The election of Mikhail Gorbachev by the Party leadership meant that they had finally come to the conclusion that the old system did not have the superior growth potential that it was once thought to have. It was not a decision to switch to the capitalist fork in the road, but it was a mandate to proceed with a more radical reform of the socialist system than had ever before been undertaken. As it happened, Gorbachev's effort to improve the socialist system so weakened the institutions of political and economic control which had made the old system work as well as it did that economic conditions deteriorated to the breaking point. The government lost its credibility as an economic manager and the proponents of capitalism were able to come to power and to start the economy down that new road.

5   Sovereignty: Citizen or Society?

Some people place a high value on living in a society in which they make their own decisions on the basis of what they regard as best for themselves. Others hold the Good Society to be one in which the citizens express their economic preferences in some societal fashion, on the basis of what they regard as best for the society rather than for themselves as individuals.

Where the sovereignty over production lies may not seem like something you need care much about in asking how good a society is. Yet it may exert an enormous influence over the kinds of goods and services that you and your children and your neighbors will consume. When the individual citizen-as-consumer is sovereign over production, for example, if enough people wish to buy pornographic books, they will be produced. When the society is sovereign, none might be produced, regardless of how many people would buy them if they were. And similarly for housing and automobiles and pet food.

If you value individual sovereignty, you declare that what other people consume is none of your business. All you wish from the economy is that it produce the things that you and others want to consume. Capitalism is then the better society for you. If you value societal sovereignty, on the other hand, you declare that there are certain things that should, or should not, be produced regardless of how much others, and perhaps even you, would like to consume them. Centrally planned socialism is ideally suited to the implementation of societal sovereignty, for it endows the planners with the power to decide what will and what will not be produced.

In practice, however, both principles of sovereignty have found their way into both systems. In the Communist economies the planners took their guidance from the Party, which used its power to implement its own values regarding what should be produced. Since the Party placed a very high value on machinery and other capital goods, for example, the volume of consumer goods produced was very likely smaller than it would have been if the citizens-as-consumers were sovereign over production. On the other hand, the Party also subsidized the production of goods like technical books as well as ballet and music conservatories – things that they wished people to consume in larger quantities. But the Party had little interest in the production of pots and pans, so most ordinary consumer goods were produced in quantities that largely reflected the consumption preferences of the people. Thus, consumer sovereignty was permitted to prevail over most such goods by default.

On this matter as elsewhere, the goodness of that economic system was tainted by the authoritarian political system with which it was conjoined in the Communist countries. Many people who would object to societal sovereignty when a Communist party is in power might find it acceptable in a democratic political context in which the people would have a voice in deciding where societal sovereignty should override individual preferences – whether in pornography or in the volume of consumer-goods production. Even in such a democratic context, however, the citizen risks the possibility that the society, through its political institutions, may prohibit the production of things that she as an individual may greatly wish to consume.

Like the socialist countries, capitalist countries also sometimes override their preferred principle of sovereignty – in this case by asserting societal sovereignty over individual sovereignty. Since such overrides often conflict with civil liberties and entrenched interests, it is difficult to enact legal prohibition against goods that most people want other people not to consume, such as gin, drugs, pornography, and tobacco. Government action usually operates in the opposite direction – getting people to consume more of some goods than they otherwise would, including "merit goods" like education and health services and recreation in public parks and beaches. If individual sovereignty were inviolable, capitalism would be much more troublesome for many people, for they would see it as opening the way to Sodom and Gomorrah. The possibility of introducing societal concerns into the economy through political action makes democratic capitalism more palatable to people with such concerns.

Hence, if it is important to you that the society collectively rather than the citizens individually decide what goods should be produced, socialism is the better road to your Good Society. But if you value individual sovereignty over production, capitalism is the better road. In a democratic society, however, either principle of sovereignty may be overridden in the case of certain special goods that enough people feel strongly about.

6 Choice: Citizen or Society?

Capitalism is the temple of individual choice because it makes the fullest use of the market mechanism. The extent of choice is always limited: low-income citizens are greatly restricted in the range of consumer goods they can acquire, and workers with few skills may have little choice but to take the first job that comes along. The choice is nevertheless free in the sense that no one has the power to tell the citizens what goods they may consume or what jobs they must take.

Socialists have long tended to see the Good Society as one in which citizens act in the public interest rather than in their self-interest. Acting on that value, the USSR flirted with the principle of societal choice in the first flush of the Russian Revolution, but they soon abandoned it, and for most of Soviet history the citizens-as-consumers chose the goods they wanted to buy, and the citizens-as-workers found the jobs they preferred and were free to quit them if they wished. Almost all the socialist countries followed the Soviet lead in those respects.

That abandonment of societal choice was viewed by some socialists as the ultimate betrayal of socialism, and at various times in the twentieth century some socialist societies committed themselves to its full implementation. In the Israeli kibbutz it flourished for half a century, during which the members' consumption consisted largely of goods and services that were issued to them by their community. That arrangement was gradually attenuated, however, as newer generations of members demanded increasing freedom to choose their own consumer goods (chapter 4). The most massive effort at societal choice was made in China, where young citizens were taught to "serve the people" – to accept the jobs and goods that were assigned to them by the society rather than to seek those that were best for themselves as individuals. Popular dissatisfaction with that arrangement was so great that it was replaced by individual choice of jobs and goods immediately after the death of its major champion, Mao Zedong (chapter 4).

Hence, if you value societal choice in consumer goods and jobs, in times past you would have found many socialists who shared your value. Today, however, only in some scattered romantic communes are there still people whose idea of a Good Society is that everyone eats the same food, wears the same clothes, and lives in similar houses. Individual choice is likely to prevail in all the economies down both the socialist and capitalist roads.

However, while individual choice has won the day, virtually all modern societies harbor islands of societal choice. Certain goods and services are thought to possess a special social quality: we would all be better off if people consumed more merit goods such as educational or health services than they would if they had to buy them on the market like ordinary goods. Hence, in all modern economies, market-based distribution is replaced or supplemented by government programs under which some of these kinds of services are supplied free or at low subsidized prices.

Judging from the economic experience of the last century, most people around the world value individual choice over societal choice in the case of ordinary goods, and both socialism and capitalism provided it. Many people also want the society to have a hand in the distribution of such services as education and health, which might incline them more to the socialist road. However, modern capitalist economies even the score in that respect by the widespread public provision of merit goods. Individual choice, supplemented by pockets of societal choice, thus predominates in all modern economies, socialist and capitalist. Some future socialist society may rise again to the ideal of societal choice, but the experience of the twentieth century suggests that the arrangement will not satisfy the generations that follow the founders.

7 What is the Good Society?

The moment of truth arrives when the surgeon concludes his account of the benefits and risks of proceeding – or not proceeding – with the operation. Which is the better course depends on your values – whether you place a higher value on a shorter but vigorous life or a longer but ailing life. So it is with the choice of the road to the Good Society. It depends on your values – how much you value security compared to justice and the other qualities you seek in your Good Society.

Values come in clusters. There are three large clusters that relate to the values associated with the goodness of an economy, which I shall call conservative, liberal, and socialist. Most people readily identify with one of those clusters. Some would demur, insisting on being a neo-this or a moderate-that, or on being too subtle to be pigeonholed like ordinary people. But if the price of admission were to wear one of the three tags, almost everyone could do so.

People don't ordinarily articulate the values that bring them to identify, if only under protest, with one of those clusters, but their values can be inferred from what they say, what they write, and what policies they support. I offer my own inferences about these three clusters as a convenient way of summarizing the values that should enter into the choice of the Good Society.

FOR CONSERVATIVES

No one doubts that if you think of yourself as a conservative, your values would direct you without hesitation down the capitalist road. The main reason, in my view, is that one value towers over all others in the conservative cluster – that the individual and not society must be the locus of sovereignty and choice.

Other values are of secondary importance. That capitalism is also the more efficient system adds to its goodness, but true conservatives would prefer it even if it turned out that socialism were the more efficient. Insecurity of jobs and income is an undesirable feature of capitalism, but some fluctuations in economic activity are inevitable when the citizens and not the government have the right to decide how much to save and invest, which job to choose, and what goods to produce. Some degree of insecurity also has the positive virtue of reinforcing the sense of individual responsibility, for it teaches people to insure themselves against certain risks and to save for a rainy day rather than rely on society to rescue them in times of need.

Economic justice means that the rules governing how people earn their incomes are fair, and since the capitalist rules are fair, there is no basis in equity for redistributing justly earned income from the rich to the poor. The rich do have a moral obligation to provide charity for the truly poor and disadvantaged, but society has no right to compel them to do so. Government social programs do little more than spawn "welfare queens."

That broad sketch leaves a great deal of room for variation in the values of people who think of themselves as conservatives and in the policies they support. The major source of variation is the extent to which societal concerns should be permitted to encroach on individual sovereignty and choice. At one end are libertarians who love not all markets but only "freemarkets," and resist all but the most minimal intervention of government. At the other end are moderate conservatives who concede that markets sometimes produce unacceptable outcomes and who support governmental action in some matters – monopoly, insecurity, extreme poverty, environment, education, and so forth. Social conservatives strongly affirm individual choice in economic matters, but insist on societal choice in family matters – sexual orientation and abortion are too important to allow each citizen to decide such matters for herself. But while conservatives joust among themselves on these issues, the values they share direct them without hesitation down the capitalist road to their Good Society.

FOR LIBERALS

The Good Society for liberals, and for their social-democratic cousins, is capitalism. And the reason is the same as in the case of conservatives – they wish the individual and not the society to be the locus of economic sovereignty and choice. They differ from conservatives in three respects, however.

First, conservatives do not merely cherish individualism but see societal solutions as fraught with evil. Liberals are pragmatic on that matter – they see nothing sinful in subordinating individual to societal decisions when they believe it would make for a better society. The second difference is that while individual sovereignty and choice loom much larger than other values in the conservative cluster, liberals regard them as broadly equal to other values in importance. Hence, a liberal Good Society contains many more restrictions on the market and on private ownership with the aim of improving the economy's performance with regard to the other criteria of goodness. That includes redressing income inequality and ameliorating poverty, reducing insecurity, protecting the environment, and other items on a long agenda of the unfinished business of liberal capitalism. Hence, the third difference: while liberals seek continuously to extend the domain of societal involvement in economic life, conservative energies are concentrated on contracting that domain by reducing taxes and bureaucratic interference in economic life.

Liberals spend so many of their waking hours deploring the deficiencies of capitalism and trying to fix them that some of them wonder from time to time whether socialism might be the better society after all. Were it not for the responsiveness of democratic capitalism to their efforts – partial though it is – many more of them would be tempted down the socialist road. In the last quarter-century, however, that temptation has all but vanished. One reason is that the rejection of socialism by almost all of the peoples who had lived under it undermined whatever silent attraction it had ever exercised over liberals abroad. The other is that liberals' confidence in the power of government to do more good than harm has diminished, and many now find more common ground with moderate conservatives.

FOR SOCIALISTS

What has united socialists of all stripes has been the conviction that it is only on the basis of social ownership that a Good Society can be built. They have differed widely, however, on the values they expected to flourish in that society. Over the years a number of the values held by many socialists in the past have been largely abandoned, so that the cluster is rather smaller and more homogeneous today.

A few decades ago much of the socialist world was fired up by the value of societal choice. Today, however, it is rare to find a socialist who shares the dreams of Mao Zedong or the original Israeli kibbutzim of a society in which consumer goods and jobs are distributed among the people by collective decision. Most socialists want a "normal" society in which the citizens choose their own consumer goods and jobs.

Societal sovereignty over production endured for a longer time. It was embodied in the central planning mechanism, which made it possible for the society to determine what goods were produced rather than relying on the decision of the citizens as individuals. With the gradual decline and eventual fall of the Communist economies, however, many socialists – perhaps most – now look to markets rather than central planning as the basic economic coordination mechanism in their socialist Good Society.

There was a time when socialists never doubted that by the criterion of efficiency, socialism would perform better than capitalism. The demise of centrally planned socialism put an end to that expectation. Market socialism is likely to surpass centrally planned socialism, but few expect it to rival or outperform capitalism.

Hence, on the crucial matters of who should decide what goods should be produced, how the goods and jobs should be distributed, and where the greater efficiency lies, there is now little to distinguish socialist values from those of liberals and conservatives. If there is any reason to choose the social-ownership road rather than the capitalist, it would be on account of the values of justice and security.

If economic justice is defined by the extent of equality in income distribution, one would expect socialist societies to be the more just. It turns out, however, that the redistribution of income through the political process has enabled capitalist societies populated by people with strong egalitarian values to attain greater equality than some of the socialist countries. Hence, social ownership no longer guarantees greater equality. A socialist with a deep commitment to equality would do better to search for a country in which most people share that commitment, rather than a country in which the property is socially owned.

Economic security is the feature of their socialist years that many people in the former Communist countries most regret having lost. It was the central-planning mechanism, along with state ownership, that made it possible, however, and the socialist economies of the future are likely to be based on the market mechanism. They will therefore be subject to many, if not all, of the forces that generate insecurity under capitalism. Because the enterprises will still be socially owned there might be more social supports for people who lose jobs, but they are not likely to differ greatly from similar supports in those capitalist countries that have done the most to reduce insecurity.

It is therefore no longer self-evident, as it was in the past, that socialism is the better society for people who hold socialist values. Social ownership offers no assurance that a society will better conform to the present-day socialist cluster of values than a capitalist society; it may in some respects, but may not in others. The paradox is that people who regard themselves as socialists today may find their Good Society not in socialism but in capitalism.

Notes

1 Bergson, "Comparative productivity: The USSR, Eastern Europe, and the West."
2 Bergson, "How big was the Soviet GDP?"
3 Weitzman, "Soviet post-war growth."
4 Morrison, "Income distribution in East European and Western countries," table 3. The Communist countries are Hungary, Poland, USSR, and Czechoslovakia, and the capitalist ones the United Kingdom, Sweden, Canada, and the United States. The figures refer to individual income, defined as per-capita family income.
5 A later study found that in 1985 the poorest tenth received a somewhat larger share of income in the USSR (3.9 percent) than in the United Kingdom (3.5 percent), and the richest tenth received more in the United Kingdom (23.5 percent) than in the USSR (20.6 percent) (Atkinson and Mickelwright, *Economic Transformation in Eastern Europe*, p. 112). Those numbers do not include the supplementary benefits of the elite in the USSR. If they were included, the degree of inequality in the two countries would be roughly the same.
6 *The Economist*, November 5, 1994, p. 20.
7 *The Economist*, June 12, 1997, p. 16.
8 Gregory and Stuart, *Comparative Economic Systems*, pp. 480–1. The averages are unweighted.

References

Alchian, Armand A. and Harold Demsetz, "Production, information costs, and economic organization," *American Economic Review*, 62 (5), December 1972, pp. 777–95.

Aoki, Masahiko, "Toward an economic model of the Japanese firm," *The Journal of Economic Literature*, 28 (1), March 1990, pp. 1–27.

Atkinson, Anthony B. and John Mickelwright, *Economic Transformation in Eastern Europe and the Distribution of Income* (Cambridge: Cambridge University Press, 1992).

Bajt, Alexander, "Investment cycles in European socialist economies: a review article," *Journal of Economic Literature*, 9 (1), March 1971, pp. 53–63.

Bardhan, Pranab and John E. Roemer, "Market socialism: a case for rejuvenation," *The Journal of Economic Perspectives*, 6 (3), Summer 1992, pp. 101–16.

Bardhan, Pranab B. and John E. Roemer (eds), *Market Socialism: The Current Debate* (New York: Oxford University Press, 1993).

Barkai, Haim, *Growth Patterns of the Kibbutz Economy* (New York: Elsevier North-Holland, 1977).

Barone, E. A., "The Ministry of Production in the collectivist state," reprinted in Hayek F. A. von (ed.), *Collectivist Economic Planning* (London: Routledge and Kegan Paul, 1935), pp. 245–90.

Baumol, William J. and Alan S. Blinder, *Economics: Principles and Policy*, 4th edn (San Diego: Harcourt Brace Jovanovich, 1988).

Ben Rafael, Eliezer, *Status, Power, and Conflict in the Kibbutz* (Aldershot: Gower, 1988).

Bergson, Abram, *The Economics of Soviet Planning* (New Haven: Yale University Press, 1964).

Bergson, Abram, "Comparative productivity: The USSR, Eastern Europe, and the West," *The American Economic Review*, 77 (3), June 1978, pp. 342–57.

Bergson, Abram, "How big was the Soviet GDP?", *Comparative Economic Studies*, 39 (1), Spring 1997, pp. 1–14.

Berle, A. A. and Gardiner C. Means, *The Modern Corporation and Private Property* (New York: Commerce Clearing House, 1932).

Berliner, Joseph S., *Factory and Manager in the USSR* (Cambridge, MA: Harvard University Press, 1957).

Berliner, Joseph S., *The Innovation Decision in Soviet Industry* (Cambridge, MA: MIT Press, 1976).

Bernardo, Robert M., *The Theory of Moral Incentives in Cuba* (University, AL: University of Alabama Press, 1971).

Blasi, Joseph, *The Communal Experience of the Kibbutz* (New Brunswick: Transaction Books, 1986).

Blasi, Joseph, *Employee Ownership: Revolution or Ripoff* (Cambridge, MA: Ballinger, 1988).

Blasi, Joseph and Douglas Kruse, *The New Owners* (New York: Harper, 1991).

Blinder, Alan S., *Toward an Economic Theory of Income Distribution* (Cambridge, MA: MIT Press, 1974).

Bonin, James P., Derek C. Jones, and Louis Putterman, "Theoretical and empirical studies of producer cooperatives: will they ever meet?," *Journal of Economic Literature* 31 (3), September 1993, pp. 1290–1320.

Bookman, Milica Z., "Former Yugoslavia: Serbia, Montenegro, Bosnia and Macedonia," in US Congress, Joint Economic Committee, *East-Central European Economies in Transition* (Washington, DC: GPO, 1994), pp. 639–62.

Bowers, Elain, "Gender stereotyping and gender division of labour in Russia," in Clarke (ed.), *Conflict and Change*, pp. 191–209.

Bradley, Keith and Gelb, Alan, "Motivation and control in the Mondragon experiment," *British Journal of Industrial Relations*, 19 (2), July 1981, pp. 211–31.

Brittain, John A., *The Inheritance of Economic Status* (Washington, DC: Brookings, 1977).

Card, David E. and Alan B. Krueger, *Myth and Measurement: The New Economics of the Minimum Wage* (Princeton, NJ: Princeton University Press, 1995).

Carre, Jean-Jacques, Paul Dubois, and Edmond Malinvaud, *French Economic Growth* (Stanford, CA: Stanford University Press, 1975).

Childs, Marquis W., *Sweden: The Middle Way* (New Haven: Yale University Press, 1936).

Clarke, Simon (ed.), *Conflict and Change in the Russian Industrial Enterprise* (Brookfield, VT: Edward Elgar, 1996).

Clinard, Marshall B., *The Black Market* (New York: Rinehart, 1952).

Coates, Ken, "Cooperatives," in Eatwell et al., (eds), *The New Palgrave*, vol. 1, pp. 664–6.

Comanor, William S. and Thomas A. Wilson, "The effect of advertising on competition: a survey," *Journal of Economic Literature*, 17 (2), June 1979, pp. 453–76.

Craig, Ben and John Pencavel, "The behavior of worker cooperatives: the plywood companies of the Pacific Northwest," *American Economic Review*, 82 (5), December 1992, pp. 1083–1105.

Dobb, Maurice, *Soviet Economic Development Since 1917* (London: Routledge & Kegan Paul, 1948).

Dodge, Norton T., *Women in the Soviet Union* (Baltimore: Johns Hopkins University Press, 1966).

Dominguez, Jorge T., *Cuba: Order and Revolution* (Cambridge, MA: Harvard University Press, 1978).

Eatwell, John, Murray Milgate, and Peter Newman (eds), *The New Palgrave: A Dictionary of Economics*, 4 vols (London: Macmillan, 1987).

Eckstein, Alexander, *China's Economic Revolution* (Cambridge: Cambridge University Press, 1977).

Economic Report of the President (Washington, DC, February 1997).

Estrin, Saul, Derek C. Jones, and Jan Svejnar, "The productivity effects of worker participation: producer cooperatives in Western economies," *Journal of Comparative Economics*, 11 (1), March 1987, pp. 40–61.

Farkas, Richard P., *Yugoslav Economic Development and Political Change* (New York: Praeger, 1975).

Freedman, Robert (ed.), *Marx on Economics* (New York: Harcourt, Brace, 1961).

Friedman, Milton, *Capitalism and Freedom* (Chicago: University of Chicago Press, 1963).

Fukuyama, Francis, *The End of History and the Last Man* (New York: Avon, 1992).

Galbraith, John Kenneth, *American Capitalism: The Concept of Countervailing Power* (New York: Houghton Mifflin, 1952).

Galbraith, John Kenneth, *The Affluent Society* (Boston: Houghton Mifflin, 1958).

Geiger, H. Kent, *The Family in Soviet Russia* (Cambridge, MA: Harvard University Press, 1968).

Goldman, Marshall I., *The Spoils of Progress: Environmental Pollution in the Soviet Union* (Cambridge, MA: MIT Press, 1972).

Goodman, Ann and Geoffrey Schleifer, "The Soviet labor market in the 1980s," in US Congress, Joint Economic Committee, *Soviet Economy in the 1980s: Problems and Prospects* (Washington, DC: GPO, 1982).

Goody, Jack, "Inheritance," in Eatwell et al. (eds), *The New Palgrave*, vol. 2, pp. 851–5.

Goskomstat, *Narodnoe Khoziaistvo SSSR v 1989* (USSR National Economy in 1989) (Moscow, 1990).

Granick, David, *Job Rights in the Soviet Union: Their Consequences* (Cambridge: Cambridge University Press, 1987).

Gray, Alexander, *The Socialist Tradition: Moses to Lenin* (London: Longmans, Green, 1947).

Gregory, Paul R. and Irwin L. Collier, Jr., "Unemployment in the Soviet Union: evidence from the Soviet Interview Project," *American Economic Review*, 68 (4), September 1988, pp. 613–32.

Gregory, Paul R. and Robert C. Stuart, *Comparative Economic Systems*, 2nd edn (Boston: Houghton Mifflin, 1985).

Gregory, Paul R. and Robert C. Stuart, *Soviet Economic Structure and Performance*, 3rd edn (New York: Harper & Row, 1990).

Grossman, Gregory, "Scarce capital and Soviet doctrine," *Quarterly Journal of Economics*, 67 (3), August 1953, pp. 311–43.

Grossman, Gregory, "Notes on the illegal economy and corruption." In US Congress, Joint Economic Committee, *Soviet Economy in a Time of Change* (Washington, DC: GPO, 1979), pp. 834–55.

Hansmann, Henry, *The Ownership of Enterprise* (Cambridge, MA: Harvard University Press, 1996).

Hart, Betty and Todd R. Risley, *Meaningful Differences in the Everyday Experience of Young American Children* (Baltimore: Brookes, 1995).

Hewett, Ed A., *Reforming the Soviet Economy: Equality versus Efficiency* (Washington, DC: Brookings, 1988).

Hoffman, Charles, *Work Incentive Practices and Policies in the People's Republic of China 1953–1965* (Albany: State University of New York Press, 1967).

Horvat, Branko, "Yugoslav economic policy in the post-war period: problems, ideas, institutional developments," *American Economic Review*, 51 (3), June 1971, pp. 71–169.

Huberman, Leo and Paul M. Sweezy, *Socialism in Cuba* (New York: Monthly Review Press, 1969).

Hughes, Gordon and Paul Hare, "The international competitiveness of industries in Bulgaria, Czechoslovakia, Hungary, and Poland," *Oxford Economic Papers*, 46, 1994, pp. 200–21.

Inkeles, Alex and Raymond A. Bauer, *The Soviet Citizen: Daily Life in a Totalitarian Society* (Cambridge, MA: Harvard University Press, 1959).

Ito, Takatoshi, *The Japanese Economy* (Cambridge, MA: MIT Press, 1992).

Jensen, Michael C. and William H. Meckling, "Rights and production functions: an application to labor-managed firms and codetermination," *Journal of Business*, 52 (4), October 1979, pp. 469–506.

Jimenez, Alexis C., "Worker incentives in Cuba," in Zimbalist (ed.), *Cuba's Socialist Economy*, pp. 129–39.

Johnson, D. Gale and Karen McConnell Brooks, *Prospects for Soviet Agriculture in the 1980s* (Bloomington: Indiana University Press, 1983).

Jones, Derek C., "U.S. producer cooperatives: the record to date," *Industrial Relations*, 18 (3), Fall 1979, pp. 342–57.

Kasmir, Sharryn, *The Myth of Mondragon: Cooperatives, Politics, and Working Class Life in a Basque Town* (Albany: State University of New York Press, 1996).

Kennan, John, "The elusive effects of minimum wages," *The Journal of Economic Literature*, 33 (4), December 1995, pp. 1949–65.

Keynes, John Maynard, *The General Theory of Employment, Interest, and Money* (New York: Harcourt, Brace and Co., 1936).

Kirsch, Leonard Joel, *Soviet Wages: Changes in Structure and Administration since 1956* (Cambridge, MA: MIT Press, 1972).

Kornai, Janos, *Economics of Shortage* (Amsterdam: North Holland Press, 1980).

Kornai, Janos, *The Socialist System: The Political Economy of Communism* (Princeton: Princeton University Press, 1992).

Lange, Oskar, "On the economic theory of socialism," *Review of Economic Studies*, 4 (1), October 1936, pp. 55–71; and 4 (2), February 1937, pp. 123–42.

Lapidus, Gail W., *Women in Soviet Society* (Berkeley: University of California Press, 1979).

Le Carre, John, *The Russia House* (New York: Knopf, 1989).

Leigh, J. Paul, *Causes of Death in the Workplace* (Westport, CT: Quorum Books, 1995).

Lindbeck, Assar, "The Swedish experiment," *Journal of Economic Literature*, 35 (3), September 1997, pp. 1273–1318.

Lindbeck, Assar and Dennis J. Snower, "Reorganization of firms and labor-market inequality," *American Economic Review*, 86 (2), May 1996, pp. 315–21.

Lindbeck, Assar, et al., *Turning Sweden Around* (Cambridge, MA: MIT Press, 1994).

Lundberg, Erik, "The rise and fall of the Swedish model," *Journal of Economic Literature*, 23 (1), March 1985, pp. 1–36.

Macfarquhar, Roderick, *The Origins of the Cultural Revolution: The Great Leap Forward 1958–1960*, vol. 2 (New York: Columbia University Press, 1983).

Marshall, Ray, *Unheard Voices: Labor and Economic Policy in a Competitive World* (New York: Basic Books, 1987).

Martin, Stephen and David Parker, *The Impact of Privatization: Ownership and Corporate Performance in the UK* (London: Routledge, 1997).

Marx, Karl, "Manifesto of the Communist Party," in Lewis S. Feuer (ed.), *Marx and Engels: Basic Writings on Politics and Philosophy* (Garden City: Doubleday, 1959), pp. 1–41.

Marx, Karl, "Critique of the Gotha Programme," in Robert Freedman (ed.), *Marx on Economics* (New York: Harcourt, Brace, 1961).

Matthews, Mervyn, *Poverty in the Soviet Union* (Cambridge: Cambridge University Press, 1986).

Milenkovitch, Deborah, "Self management and thirty years of Yugoslav experience," *ACES Bulletin*, 25 (3), Fall 1983, pp. 1–26.

Mitchell, B.R., *European Historical Statistics* (New York: Columbia University Press, 1975).

Monousova, Galina, "Gender differentiation in industrial relations," in Clarke (ed.), *Conflict and Change*, pp. 162–90.

Morrison, Christian, "Income distribution in East European and Western countries," *Journal of Comparative Economics*, 8 (2), June 1984, pp. 121–38.

Morton, Henry W., "The Soviet quest for better housing – an impossible dream," in US Congress, Joint Economic Committee, *Soviet Economy in a Time of Change* (Washington, DC: GPO, 1979), pp. 790–810.

Murrell, Peter, "Big Bang versus evolution: East European reforms in the light of recent economic history," *Plan Econ Report*, vi (26), June 29, 1990, pp. 1–11.

Myrdal, Gunnar, *An American Dilemma: The Negro Problem and Modern Democracy* (New York: Harper, 1944).

Near, Henry, *The Kibbutz Movement: A History*, vol. 1 (Oxford: Oxford University Press, 1992).

Nicholls, A. J., *Freedom with Social Responsibility: The Social Market Economy in Germany 1918–1963* (Oxford: Clarendon Press, 1994).

Nickell, Stephen, "Unemployment and labor market rigidities: Europe versus North America," *The Journal of Economic Perspectives* 11 (3), Summer 1997, pp. 55–74.

Nove, Alec, *An Economic History of the USSR* (London: Penguin, 1969).

Nozick, Robert, *Anarchy, State, and Utopia* (Oxford: Blackwell, 1974).

OECD, *Economic Surveys*: Germany 1996; Japan 1996; Sweden 1993–1994 (Paris).

Ofer, Gur and Aaron Vinocur, *The Soviet Household Under the Old Regime: Economic Conditions and Behavior in the 1970s* (Cambridge: Cambridge University Press, 1992).

Okun, Arthur, *Equality and Efficiency: The Big Tradeoff* (Washington, DC: Brookings, 1975).

Olsen, Gregg M., *The Struggle for Economic Democracy in Sweden* (Brookfield, VT: Aldershott, 1992).

Ozaki, Robert S., *Human Capitalism: The Japanese Enterprise System as World Model* (Tokyo: Kodasha, 1991).

Pechman, Joseph A., "Inheritance taxes," in Eatwell et al. (eds), *The New Palgrave*, vol. 2, pp. 855–7.

Perkins, Dwight, *Market Control and Planning in Communist China* (Cambridge, MA: Harvard University Press, 1966).

Phelps, Edmund S., "Low-wage employment subsidies versus the welfare state," *American Economic Review*, 84 (2), May 1994, pp. 54–8.

Posner, M. V., "Nationalization," in Eatwell et al. (eds), *The New Palgrave*, vol. 3, pp. 594–6.

Pryke, William, *The Nationalized Industries: Policies and Performance Since 1968* (Oxford: Martin Robertson, 1981).

Pryor, Frederick L., *Property and Industrial Organization in Communist and Capitalist Nations* (Bloomington: Indiana University Press, 1973).

Putterman, Louis, "On some recent explanations of why capital hires labor," *Economic Inquiry*, 22 (2), April 1994, pp. 171–87.

Putterman, Louis, John E. Roemer, and Joaquin Silvestre, "Does egalitarianism have a future?," *Journal of Economic Literature*, 36 (2), June 1998, pp. 861–902.

Quirk, Robert E., *Fidel Castro* (New York: Norton, 1993).

Radford, R. A., "The economic organization of a P.O.W. camp," *Economica*, New Series, XII (48), November 1945, pp. 189–201.

Rawls, John, *A Theory of Justice* (Cambridge, MA: Harvard University Press, 1971).

Redwood, John, *Public Enterprise in Crisis* (Oxford: Blackwell, 1980).

Redwood, John and John Hatch, *Controlling Public Industries* (Oxford: Blackwell, 1982).

Roemer, John E., *A Future for Socialism* (Cambridge, MA: Harvard University Press, 1994).

Rusinow, Dennison, *The Yugoslav Experiment, 1948–1974* (Berkeley: University of California Press, 1978).

Rusinow, Dennison, "Yugoslavia: enduring crisis and delayed reforms," in US Congress, Joint Economic Committee, *Pressures for Reforms in the East European Economies*, vol. II (Washington, DC: GPO, 1989), pp. 52–69.

Schmalensee, Richard, "Advertising," in Eatwell et al. (eds), *The New Palgrave*, vol. 1, pp. 34–5.

Schmalensee, Richard, *The Economics of Advertising* (Amsterdam: North Holland Publishing Co., 1972).

Sennett, Richard and Jonathan Cobb, *The Hidden Injuries of Class* (New York: Norton, 1993).

Shepher, Israel, *The Kibbutz: An Anthropological Study* (Norwood Editions, 1983).

Shepherd, William G., *Economic Performance under Public Ownership: British Fuel and Power* (New Haven: Yale University Press, 1965).

Sloman, Martyn, *Socialising Public Ownership* (London: Macmillan, 1978).

Smith, Adam, *An Inquiry Into the Nature and Causes of The Wealth of Nations* (Oxford: Clarendon Press, 1976).

Smyser, W. R., *The Economy of United Germany: Colossus at the Crossroads* (New York: St Martin's Press, 1992).

Spiro, Melford E., *Kibbutz: Venture in Utopia*, 2nd edn (New York: Schocken, 1970).

Stiglitz, Joseph E., *Whither Socialism?* (Cambridge, MA: MIT Press, 1994).

Strachey, John, "Tasks and achievements of British Labour," in R. S. Crossman (ed.), *New Fabian Essays* (London: Turnstile Press, 1953).

Sugden, Robert, "Welfare, resources, and capabilities: a review of *Inequality Reexamined*, by Amartya Sen," *Journal of Economic Literature*, 31 (4), December 1993, pp. 1947–62.

Sweezy, Paul M., *Socialism* (New York: McGraw-Hill, 1949).

Thernstrom, Stephan and Abigail Thernstrom, *America in Black and White: One Nation, Indivisible* (New York: Simon and Shuster, 1997).

Thomas, Henk and Chris Logan, *Mondragon: An Economic Analysis* (London: Allen & Unwin, 1982).

Thurow, Lester C., *Generating Inequality: Mechanisms of Distribution in the U.S. Economy* (New York: Basic Books, 1975).

Thurow, Lester C., *The Zero-Sum Society* (New York: Penguin, 1980).

Tobin, J., "On limiting the domain of inequality," *Journal of Law and Economics*, 13 (2), October 1970, pp. 263–7.

Tomlinson, Jim, *The Unequal Struggle: British Socialism and the Capitalist Enterprise* (London: Methuen, 1982).

US Bureau of the Census, *Statistical Abstract of the United States* (Washington, DC, various years).

US Congress, Joint Economic Committee, *USSR: Measures of Economic Growth and Development, 1950–1980* (Washington, DC: GPO, 1982).

US Directorate of Intelligence, *Handbook of Economic Statistics, 1990* (Washington, DC, 1990).

USSR Gosplan, *Metodicheskie ukazaniia k razrabotke planov razvitiia narodnogo khoziaistva SSSR* (Instructions for Preparing National Economic Plans) (Moscow, 1974).

Vickers, John and George Yarrow, *Privatization: An Economic Analysis* (Cambridge, MA: MIT Press, 1988).

Walder, Andrew G. *Communist Neo-traditionalism: Work and Authority in Chinese Industry* (Berkeley: University of California Press, 1986).

Ward, Benjamin, "The firm in Illyria: market syndicalism," *American Economic Review*, 48 (4), September 1968, pp. 566–89.

Weitzman, Martin, "Soviet post-war growth and capital-labor substitution," *American Economic Review*, 60 (4), September 1970, pp. 676–92.

Weitzman, Martin, *The Share Economy* (Cambridge, MA: Harvard University Press, 1984).

Welihozkiy, Toli, "Automobiles and the Soviet consumer," in US Congress, Joint Economic Committee, *Soviet Economy in a Time of Change* (Washington, DC: GPO, 1979), pp. 811–33.

Wheelwright, E. L. and Bruce McFarlane, *The Chinese Road to Socialism* (New York: Monthly Review Press, 1971).

Whyte, William F. and Kathleen K. Whyte, *Making Mondragon: The Growth and Dynamics of the Worker Cooperative Complex* (Ithaca, NY: Cornell University Press, 1988).

Widmayer, Ruth, "The evolution of Soviet education policy," *Harvard Education Review*, 24, 1954, pp. 159–75.

Wiles, P. J. D., *The Political Economy of Communism* (Cambridge, MA: Harvard University Press, 1962).

Wolff, Edward N., *Top Heavy: A Study of the Increasing Inequality of Wealth in America* (New York: Twentieth Century Fund, 1995).

Zaleski, Eugene, *Stalinist Planning for Economic Growth* (Chapel Hill: University of North Carolina Press, 1980).

Zimbalist, Andrew (ed.), *Cuba's Socialist Economy Towards the 1990s* (Boulder, CO: Lynne Riemer, 1987).

Zimbalist, Andrew and Susan Eckstein, "Patterns of Cuban development: the first twenty-five years," in Zimbalist (ed.), *Cuba's Socialist Economy*, pp. 7–24.

Index